AVENGERS

THE KORVAC

SAGA

AVENGERS

WRITERS
JIM SHOOTER, LEN WEIN, ROGER STERN,
GEORGE PÉREZ, DAVID MICHELINIE
& BILL MANTLO

PENCILERS
GEORGE PÉREZ, SAL BUSCEMA
& DAVE WENZEL

INKERS
KLAUS JANSON, PABLO MARCOS,
RICARDO VILLAMONTE & DIVERSE HANDS

COLORISTS
GLYNIS WEIN, PHIL RACHELSON,
JIM SHOOTER, NEL YOMTOV & BOB SHAREN

LETTERERS
JOE ROSEN, DENISE WOHL, ANNETTE KAWECKI,
SHELLY LEFERMAN & RICK PARKER

EDITORS
LEN WEIN, ARCHIE GOODWIN
& ROGER STERN

FRONT COVER ARTISTS
JOHN ROMITA JR. & TERRY AUSTIN

FRONT COVER COLORIST
JOHN KALISZ

BACK COVER ARTISTS
DAVE COCKRUM & TERRY AUSTIN

BACK COVER COLORIST
TOM SMITH

THE KORVAC SAGA

COLLECTION EDITOR
MARK D. BEAZLEY

DIGITAL TRAFFIC COORDINATOR
MARK D. BEAZLEY

ASSOCIATE MANAGING EDITOR
ALEX STARBUCK

EDITOR, SPECIAL PROJECTS
JENNIFER GRÜNWALD

SENIOR EDITOR, SPECIAL PROJECTS
JEFF YOUNGQUIST

RESEARCH
JEPH YORK

PRODUCTION
RYAN DEVALL

COLOR RECONSTRUCTION
**DIGITAL CHAMELEON, TOM ZIUKO
& DIGIKORE**

SENIOR VICE PRESIDENT OF SALES
DAVID GABRIEL

EDITOR IN CHIEF
AXEL ALONSO

CHIEF CREATIVE OFFICER
JOE QUESADA

PUBLISHER
DAN BUCKLEY

EXECUTIVE PRODUCER
ALAN FINE

AVENGERS: THE KORVAC SAGA. Contains material originally published in magazine form as AVENGERS #167-168 and #170-177, and THOR ANNUAL #6. Third edition. Second printing 2014. ISBN# 978-0-7851-6205-6. Published by MARVEL WORLDWIDE, INC., a subsidiary of MARVEL ENTERTAINMENT, LLC. OFFICE OF PUBLICATION: 135 West 50th Street, New York, NY 10020. Copyright © 1977, 1978 and 2012 Marvel Characters, Inc. All rights reserved. All characters featured in this issue and the distinctive names and likenesses thereof, and all related indicia are trademarks of Marvel Characters, Inc. No similarity between any of the names, characters, persons, and/or institutions in this magazine with those of any living or dead person or institution is intended, and any such similarity which may exist is purely coincidental. **Printed in the U.S.A.** ALAN FINE, EVP - Office of the President, Marvel Worldwide, Inc. and EVP & CMO Marvel Characters B.V.; DAN BUCKLEY, Publisher & President - Print, Animation & Digital Divisions; JOE QUESADA, Chief Creative Officer; TOM BREVOORT, SVP of Publishing; DAVID BOGART, SVP of Operations & Procurement, Publishing; C.B. CEBULSKI, SVP of Creator & Content Development; DAVID GABRIEL, SVP Print, Sales & Marketing; JIM O'KEEFE, VP of Operations & Logistics; DAN CARR, Executive Director of Publishing Technology; SUSAN CRESPI, Editorial Operations Manager; ALEX MORALES, Publishing Operations Manager; STAN LEE, Chairman Emeritus. For information regarding advertising in Marvel Comics or on Marvel.com, please contact Niza Disla, Director of Marvel Partnerships, at ndisla@marvel.com. For Marvel subscription inquiries, please call 800-217-9158. **Manufactured between 8/13/2014 and 9/15/14 by R.R. DONNELLEY, INC., SALEM, VA, USA.**

10 9 8 7 6 5 4 3 2

INTRODUCTION BY RALPH MACCHIO

The impassioned epic popularly referred to as "The Michael Saga" was the brainchild of two of the premier talents of the Second Marvel Age: scripter James Shooter, and co-plotter and penciler George Pérez.

Shooter's comics-writing career spans decades. His work on DC's Legion of Super-Heroes series is a high-water mark that paved the way for his distinguished scrivening on Avengers. Shooter's crisp style and fine ability to juggle many characters made him, in some ways, the perfect writer for the world's mightiest super-team. It's often been said Avengers lends itself to epics, and "The Michael Saga" was the ideal exponent of that statement.

From the prime period of the brilliant 1960s Kree/Skrull War saga, group books had attempted to outdo each other in longer, more intricate stories of cosmic scope. Yet all that had occurred before seemed mere prelude to the coming of Korvac.

And who better to illustrate and co-plot such an undertaking than the man who'd made his bones penciling team titles — George Pérez. Although he was unable to see "The Michael Saga" to completion, Pérez's penciling prowess and plotting skills were on display early on, setting the expansive tone carried forth by artists Sal Buscema and David Wenzel. Pérez seemed to thrive on drawing as many characters as possible within the enlarging scope of a storyline, and Shooter's complex concoction was the perfect vehicle.

Witness now this compelling portrait of a god in struggle; of the betrayal nurtured in the human heart that could cause the downfall of deities themselves. Presented for the first time between two covers, "The Michael Saga" is epic storytelling in the grand tradition pioneered by the mythmakers at Marvel.

— Ralph Macchio, 1991

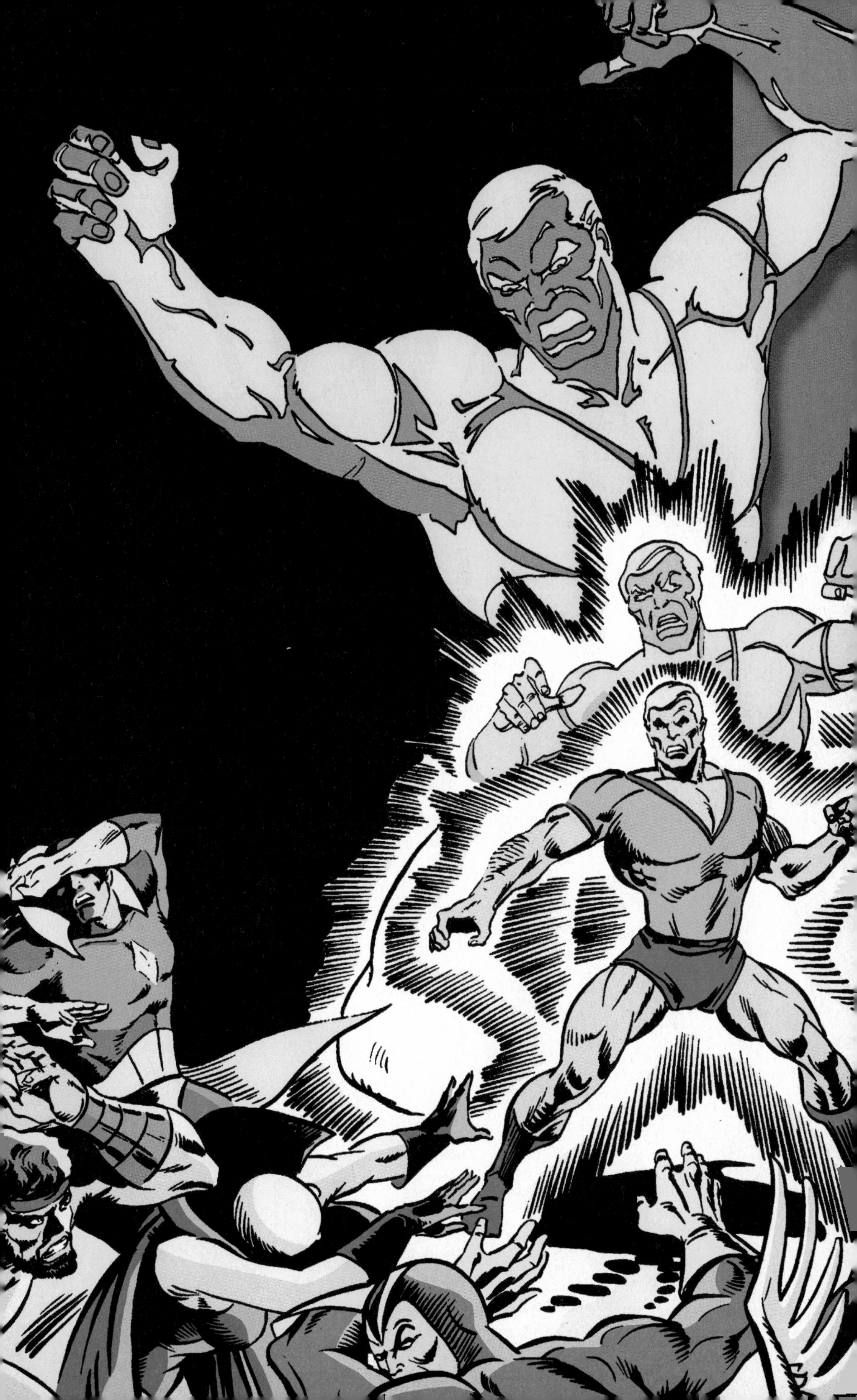

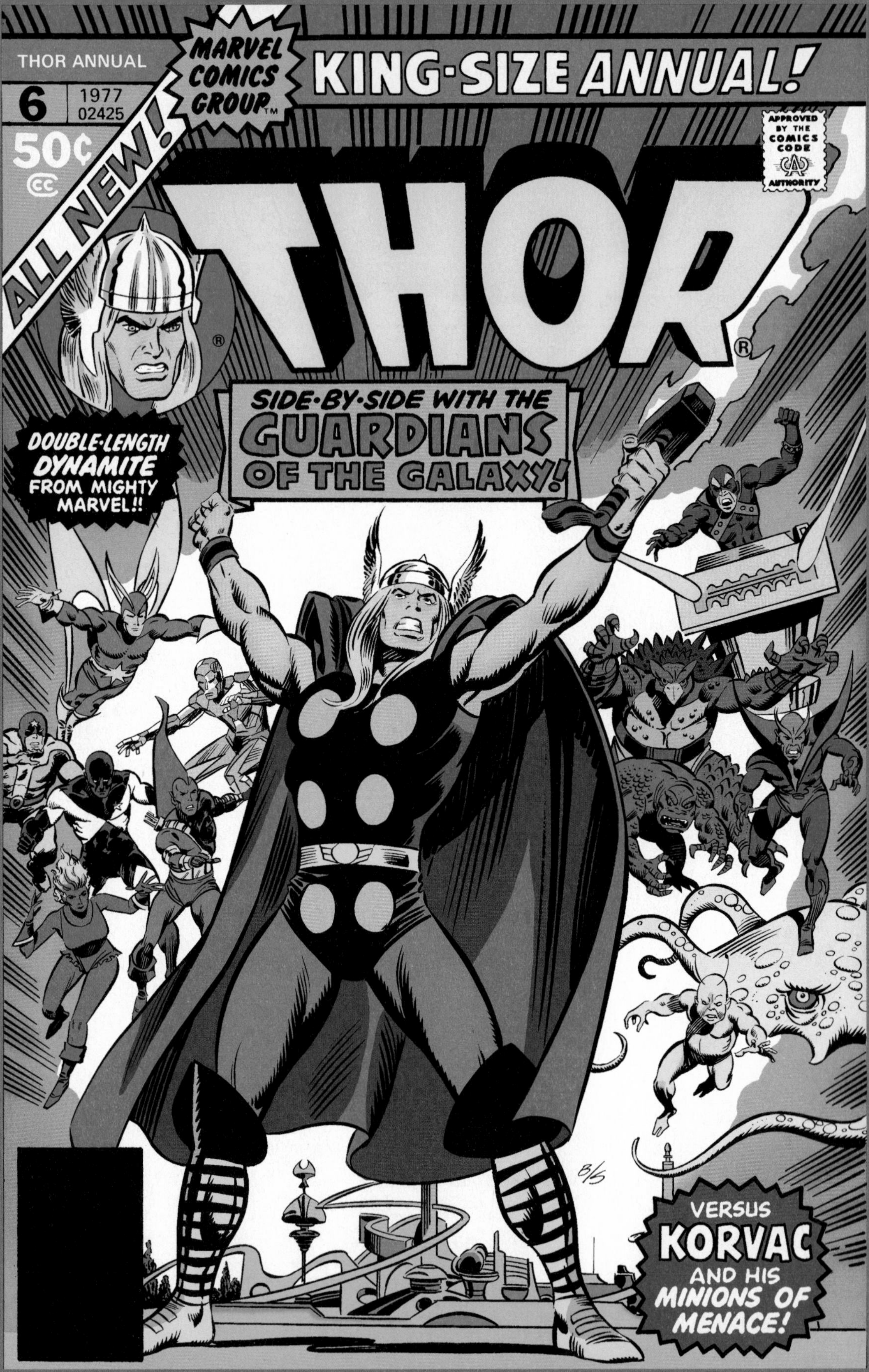
THOR ANNUAL
6
1977
02425
50¢
ALL NEW!
MARVEL COMICS GROUP
KING-SIZE ANNUAL!
APPROVED BY THE COMICS CODE AUTHORITY
THOR
SIDE·BY·SIDE WITH THE GUARDIANS OF THE GALAXY!
DOUBLE-LENGTH DYNAMITE FROM MIGHTY MARVEL!!
VERSUS KORVAC AND HIS MINIONS OF MENACE!

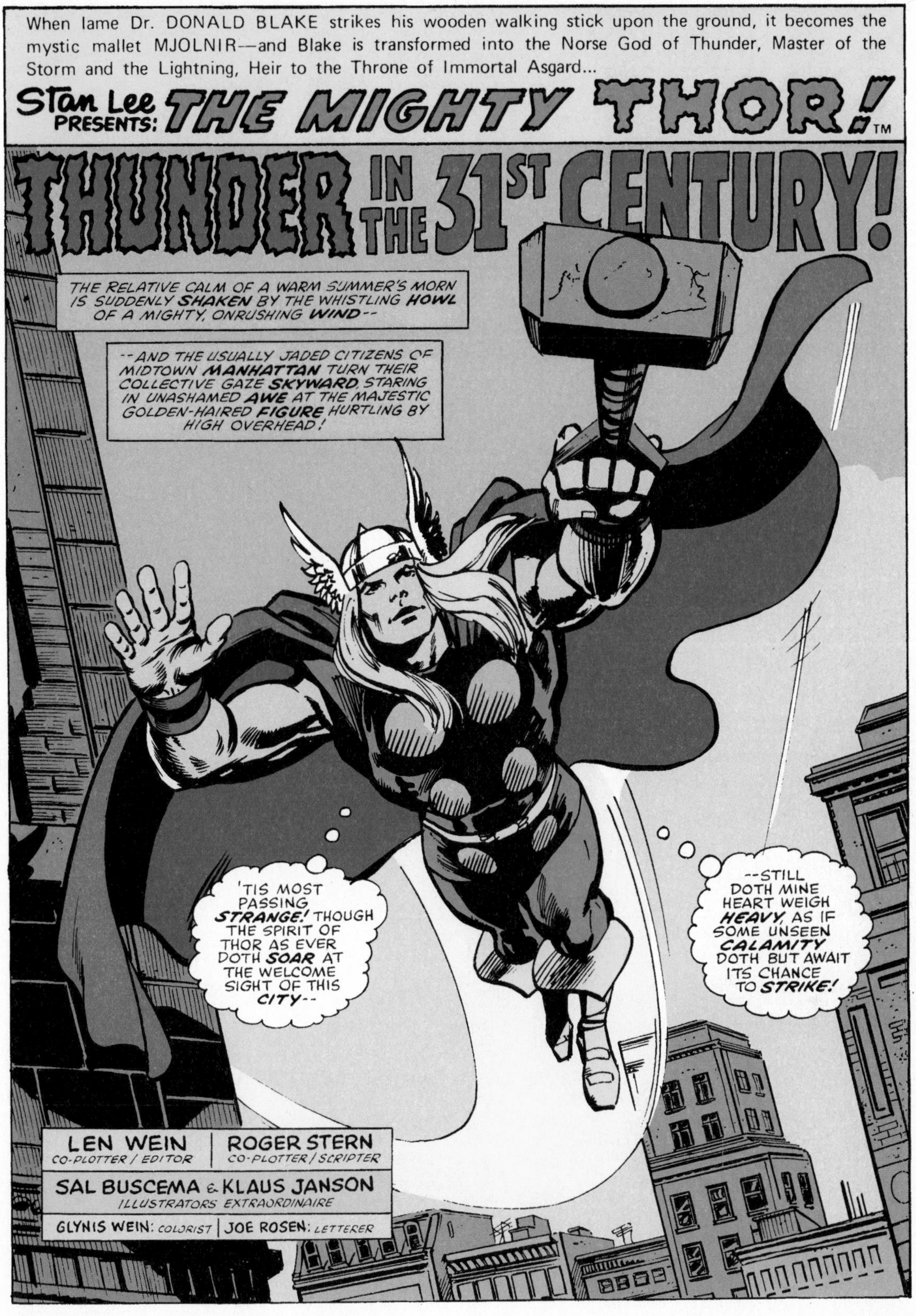
When lame Dr. DONALD BLAKE strikes his wooden walking stick upon the ground, it becomes the mystic mallet MJOLNIR—and Blake is transformed into the Norse God of Thunder, Master of the Storm and the Lightning, Heir to the Throne of Immortal Asgard...
Stan Lee PRESENTS: THE MIGHTY THOR! TM
THUNDER IN THE 31ST CENTURY!
THE RELATIVE CALM OF A WARM SUMMER'S MORN IS SUDDENLY SHAKEN BY THE WHISTLING HOWL OF A MIGHTY, ONRUSHING WIND--
--AND THE USUALLY JADED CITIZENS OF MIDTOWN MANHATTAN TURN THEIR COLLECTIVE GAZE SKYWARD, STARING IN UNASHAMED AWE AT THE MAJESTIC GOLDEN-HAIRED FIGURE HURTLING BY HIGH OVERHEAD!
'TIS MOST PASSING STRANGE! THOUGH THE SPIRIT OF THOR AS EVER DOTH SOAR AT THE WELCOME SIGHT OF THIS CITY--
--STILL DOTH MINE HEART WEIGH HEAVY, AS IF SOME UNSEEN CALAMITY DOTH BUT AWAIT ITS CHANCE TO STRIKE!
LEN WEIN CO-PLOTTER / EDITOR | ROGER STERN CO-PLOTTER / SCRIPTER
SAL BUSCEMA & KLAUS JANSON ILLUSTRATORS EXTRAORDINAIRE
GLYNIS WEIN: COLORIST | JOE ROSEN: LETTERER

8

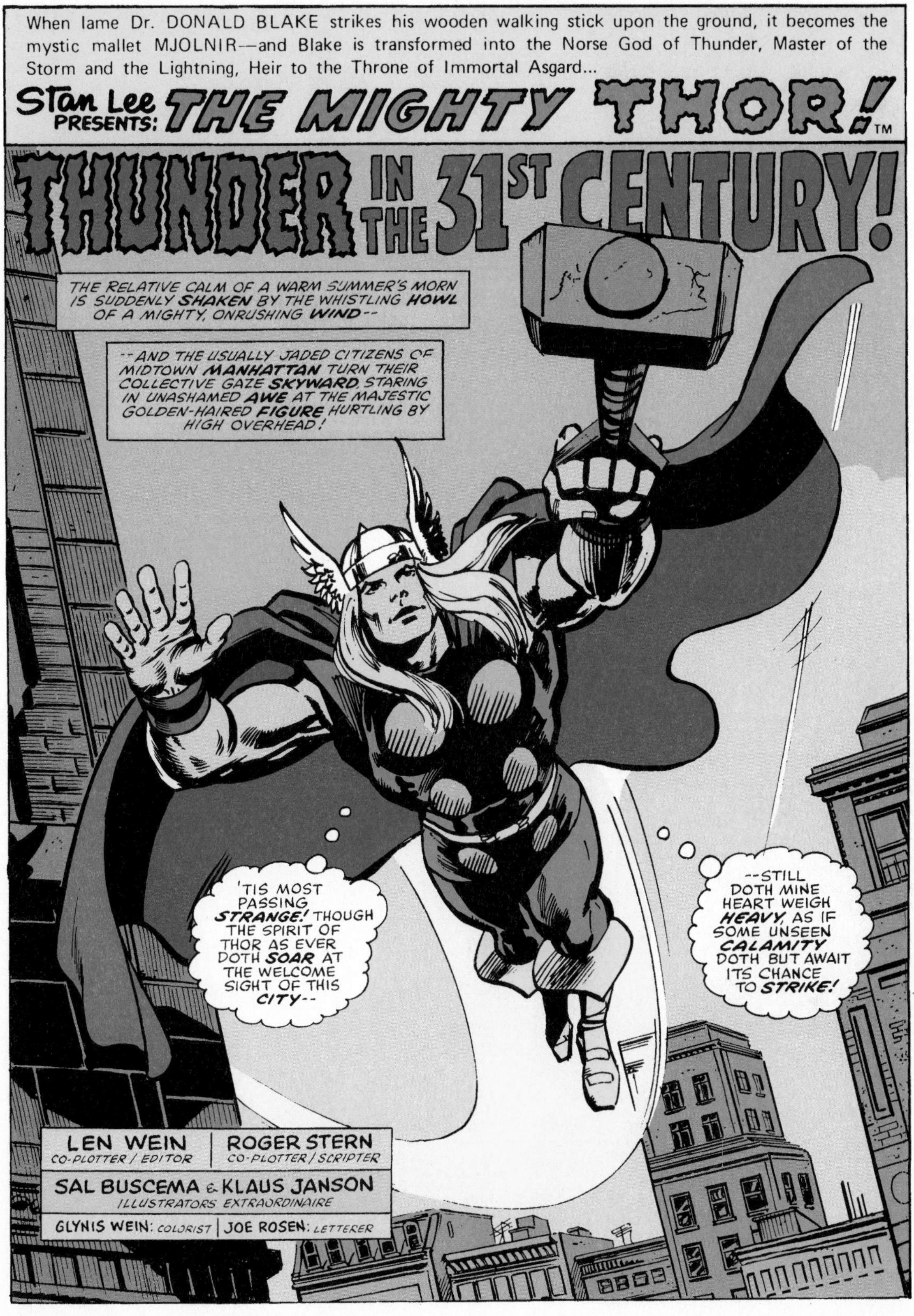
When lame Dr. DONALD BLAKE strikes his wooden walking stick upon the ground, it becomes the mystic mallet MJOLNIR—and Blake is transformed into the Norse God of Thunder, Master of the Storm and the Lightning, Heir to the Throne of Immortal Asgard...
Stan Lee PRESENTS: THE MIGHTY THOR! TM
THUNDER IN THE 31ST CENTURY!
THE RELATIVE CALM OF A WARM SUMMER'S MORN IS SUDDENLY SHAKEN BY THE WHISTLING HOWL OF A MIGHTY, ONRUSHING WIND--
--AND THE USUALLY JADED CITIZENS OF MIDTOWN MANHATTAN TURN THEIR COLLECTIVE GAZE SKYWARD, STARING IN UNASHAMED AWE AT THE MAJESTIC GOLDEN-HAIRED FIGURE HURTLING BY HIGH OVERHEAD!
'TIS MOST PASSING STRANGE! THOUGH THE SPIRIT OF THOR AS EVER DOTH SOAR AT THE WELCOME SIGHT OF THIS CITY--
--STILL DOTH MINE HEART WEIGH HEAVY, AS IF SOME UNSEEN CALAMITY DOTH BUT AWAIT ITS CHANCE TO STRIKE!
LEN WEIN CO-PLOTTER / EDITOR
ROGER STERN CO-PLOTTER / SCRIPTER
SAL BUSCEMA & KLAUS JANSON ILLUSTRATORS EXTRAORDINAIRE
GLYNIS WEIN: COLORIST
JOE ROSEN: LETTERER

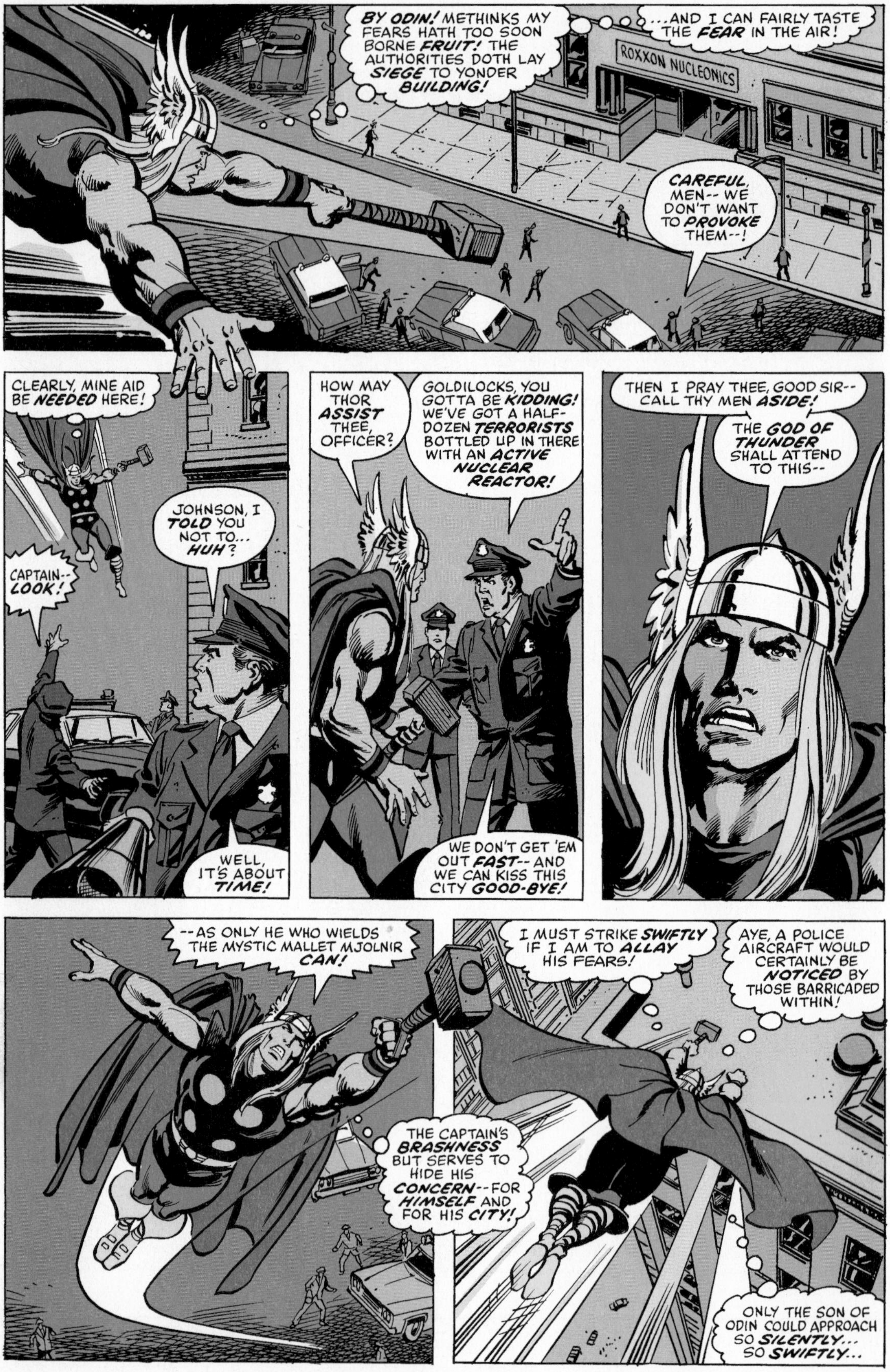
BY ODIN! METHINKS MY FEARS HATH TOO SOON BORNE FRUIT! THE AUTHORITIES DOTH LAY SIEGE TO YONDER BUILDING!
...AND I CAN FAIRLY TASTE THE FEAR IN THE AIR!
ROXXON NUCLEONICS
CAREFUL, MEN-- WE DON'T WANT TO PROVOKE THEM--!
CLEARLY, MINE AID BE NEEDED HERE!
CAPTAIN-- LOOK!
JOHNSON, I TOLD YOU NOT TO... HUH?
WELL, IT'S ABOUT TIME!
HOW MAY THOR ASSIST THEE, OFFICER?
GOLDILOCKS, YOU GOTTA BE KIDDING! WE'VE GOT A HALF-DOZEN TERRORISTS BOTTLED UP IN THERE WITH AN ACTIVE NUCLEAR REACTOR!
WE DON'T GET 'EM OUT FAST-- AND WE CAN KISS THIS CITY GOOD-BYE!
THEN I PRAY THEE, GOOD SIR-- CALL THY MEN ASIDE!
THE GOD OF THUNDER SHALL ATTEND TO THIS--
--AS ONLY HE WHO WIELDS THE MYSTIC MALLET MJOLNIR CAN!
THE CAPTAIN'S BRASHNESS BUT SERVES TO HIDE HIS CONCERN--FOR HIMSELF AND FOR HIS CITY!
I MUST STRIKE SWIFTLY IF I AM TO ALLAY HIS FEARS!
AYE, A POLICE AIRCRAFT WOULD CERTAINLY BE NOTICED BY THOSE BARRICADED WITHIN!
ONLY THE SON OF ODIN COULD APPROACH SO SILENTLY... SO SWIFTLY...

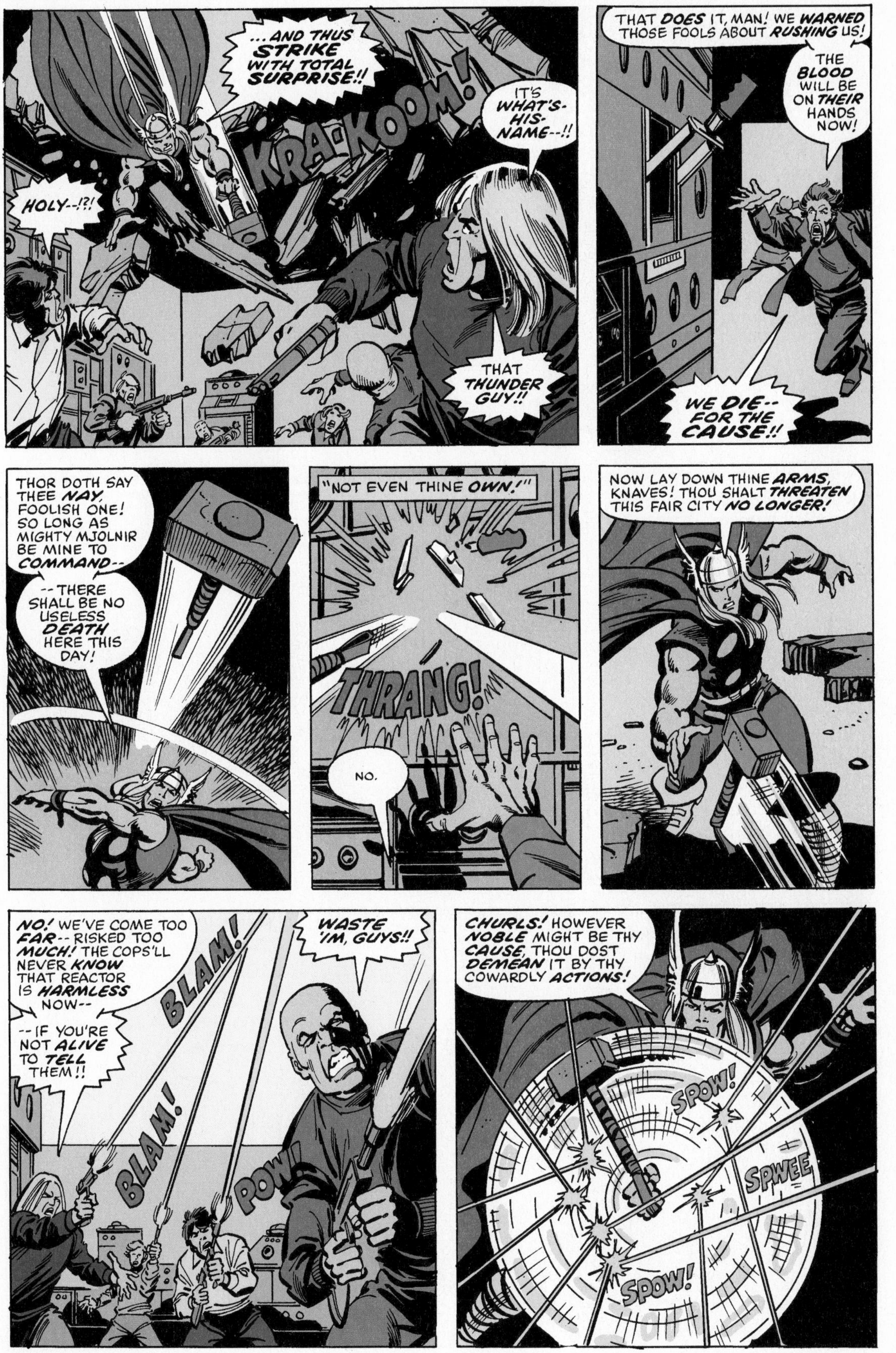
...AND THUS STRIKE WITH TOTAL SURPRISE!!
KRA-KOOM!
IT'S WHAT'S-HIS-NAME--!!
HOLY--!?!
THAT THUNDER GUY!!
THAT DOES IT, MAN! WE WARNED THOSE FOOLS ABOUT RUSHING US!
THE BLOOD WILL BE ON THEIR HANDS NOW!
WE DIE-- FOR THE CAUSE!!
THOR DOTH SAY THEE NAY, FOOLISH ONE! SO LONG AS MIGHTY MJOLNIR BE MINE TO COMMAND--
--THERE SHALL BE NO USELESS DEATH HERE THIS DAY!
"NOT EVEN THINE OWN!"
THRANG!
NO.
NOW LAY DOWN THINE ARMS, KNAVES! THOU SHALT THREATEN THIS FAIR CITY NO LONGER!
NO! WE'VE COME TOO FAR-- RISKED TOO MUCH! THE COPS'LL NEVER KNOW THAT REACTOR IS HARMLESS NOW--
--IF YOU'RE NOT ALIVE TO TELL THEM!!
WASTE 'IM, GUYS!!
BLAM!
BLAM!
BLAM!
POW!
CHURLS! HOWEVER NOBLE MIGHT BE THY CAUSE, THOU DOST DEMEAN IT BY THY COWARDLY ACTIONS!
SPOW!
SPWEE
SPOW!

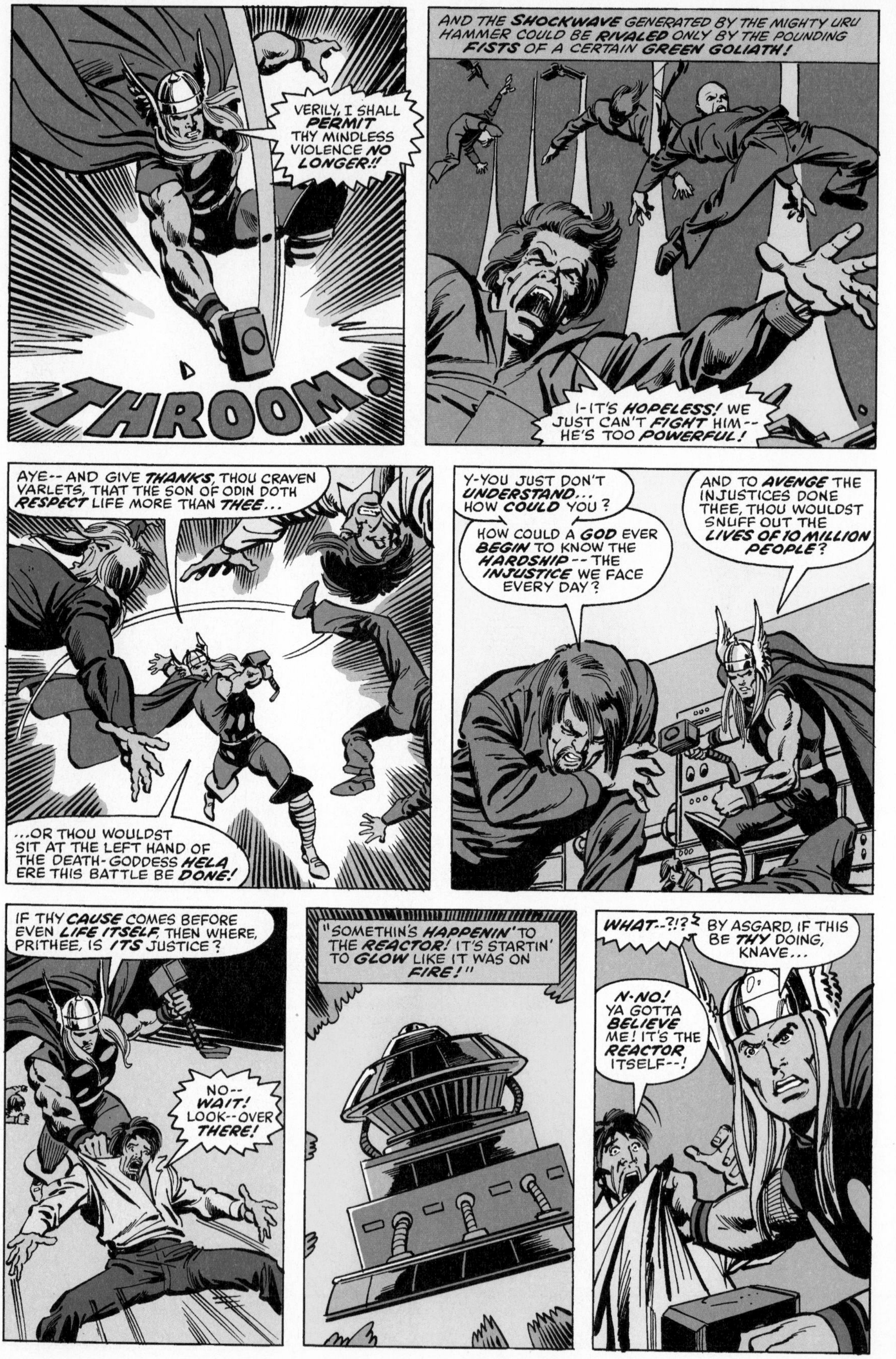
VERILY, I SHALL PERMIT THY MINDLESS VIOLENCE NO LONGER!!
THROOM!
AND THE SHOCKWAVE GENERATED BY THE MIGHTY URU HAMMER COULD BE RIVALED ONLY BY THE POUNDING FISTS OF A CERTAIN GREEN GOLIATH!
I-IT'S HOPELESS! WE JUST CAN'T FIGHT HIM-- HE'S TOO POWERFUL!
AYE-- AND GIVE THANKS, THOU CRAVEN VARLETS, THAT THE SON OF ODIN DOTH RESPECT LIFE MORE THAN THEE...
...OR THOU WOULDST SIT AT THE LEFT HAND OF THE DEATH-GODDESS HELA ERE THIS BATTLE BE DONE!
Y-YOU JUST DON'T UNDERSTAND... HOW COULD YOU?
HOW COULD A GOD EVER BEGIN TO KNOW THE HARDSHIP -- THE INJUSTICE WE FACE EVERY DAY?
AND TO AVENGE THE INJUSTICES DONE THEE, THOU WOULDST SNUFF OUT THE LIVES OF 10 MILLION PEOPLE?
IF THY CAUSE COMES BEFORE EVEN LIFE ITSELF, THEN WHERE, PRITHEE, IS ITS JUSTICE?
NO-- WAIT! LOOK--OVER THERE!
"SOMETHIN'S HAPPENIN' TO THE REACTOR! IT'S STARTIN' TO GLOW LIKE IT WAS ON FIRE!"
WHAT--?!?
BY ASGARD, IF THIS BE THY DOING, KNAVE...
N-NO! YA GOTTA BELIEVE ME! IT'S THE REACTOR ITSELF--!

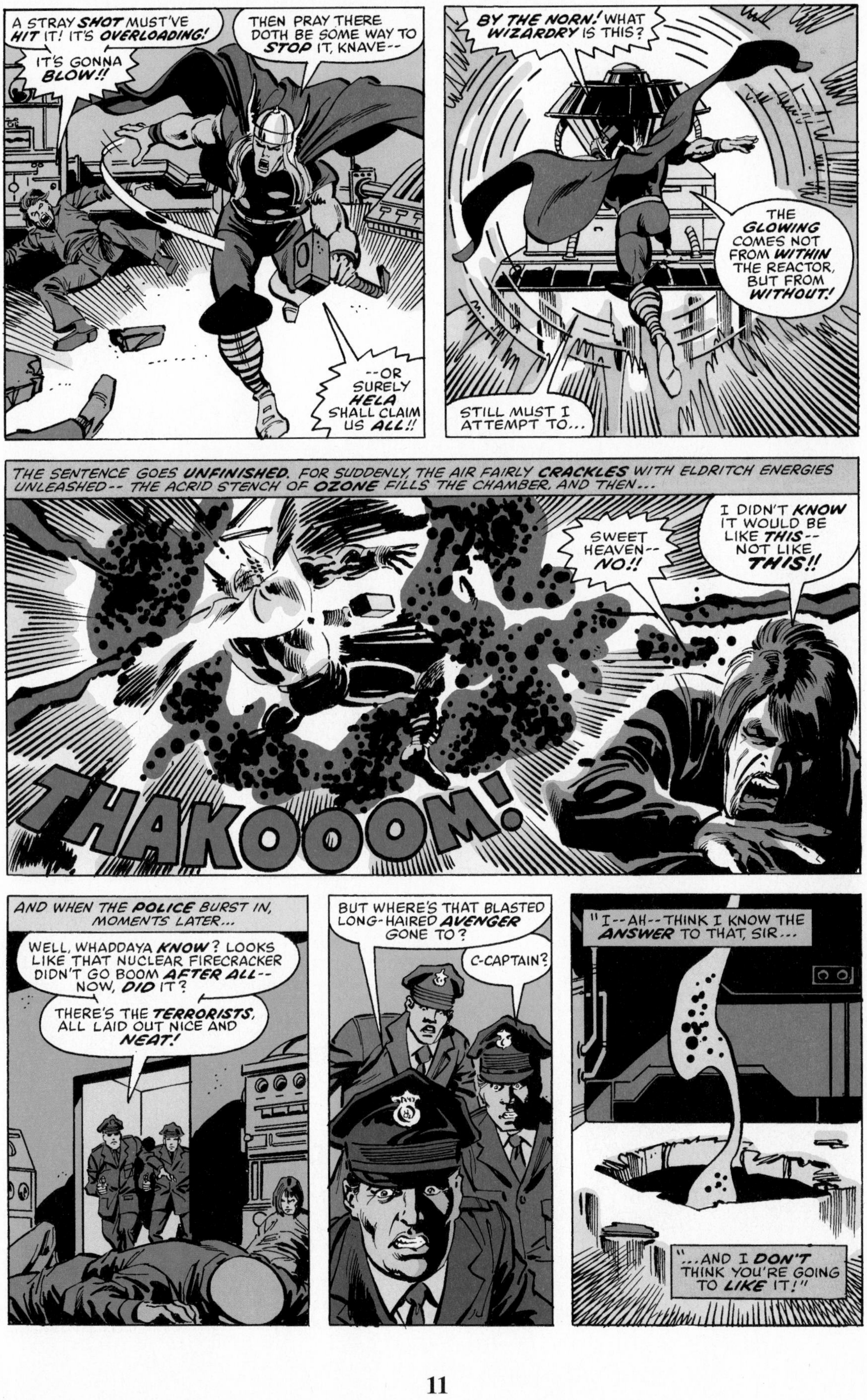

A STRAY SHOT MUST'VE HIT IT! IT'S OVERLOADING!
IT'S GONNA BLOW!!
THEN PRAY THERE DOTH BE SOME WAY TO STOP IT, KNAVE--
--OR SURELY HELA SHALL CLAIM US ALL!!
BY THE NORN! WHAT WIZARDRY IS THIS?
THE GLOWING COMES NOT FROM WITHIN THE REACTOR, BUT FROM WITHOUT!
STILL MUST I ATTEMPT TO...
THE SENTENCE GOES UNFINISHED. FOR SUDDENLY, THE AIR FAIRLY CRACKLES WITH ELDRITCH ENERGIES UNLEASHED-- THE ACRID STENCH OF OZONE FILLS THE CHAMBER. AND THEN...
SWEET HEAVEN-- NO!!
I DIDN'T KNOW IT WOULD BE LIKE THIS-- NOT LIKE THIS!!
THAKOOOM!
AND WHEN THE POLICE BURST IN, MOMENTS LATER...
WELL, WHADDAYA KNOW? LOOKS LIKE THAT NUCLEAR FIRECRACKER DIDN'T GO BOOM AFTER ALL-- NOW, DID IT?
THERE'S THE TERRORISTS, ALL LAID OUT NICE AND NEAT!
BUT WHERE'S THAT BLASTED LONG-HAIRED AVENGER GONE TO?
C-CAPTAIN?
"I--AH--THINK I KNOW THE ANSWER TO THAT, SIR...
"...AND I DON'T THINK YOU'RE GOING TO LIKE IT!"

AND EVEN AS THE STUPIFIED POLICE CAPTAIN STARES AT THE SMOLDERING *HOLE* IN THE LABORATORY FLOOR IN SLACK-JAWED *WONDER*, THE MIGHTY THOR BLINKS BACK INTO *REALITY*...

...ALBEIT, A DRASTICALLY *DIFFERENT* REALITY BY FAR!

X MINUS
301

HEIMDALL'S *EYES!* WH-WHERE *AM I?*

EH? WHAT'S *THIS?*

MY *TIME PROBE* WASN'T SUPPOSED TO PICK UP *PASSENGERS!*

AY? I SEE THEE IN THE *SHADOWS!* WHAT MANNER OF BEING *ART* THOU?

I MIGHT WELL ASK THE SAME OF *YOU*-- BUT MY *DATA-BANKS* WILL SUPPLY THE ANSWER MUCH *FASTER!*

AND INSTANTS *LATER*...

WHAT *NONSENSE* IS THIS? THERE MUST BE A *CIRCUIT MALFUNCTION* SOMEWHERE!

SUBJECT IDENTIFICATION... NAME: THOR... DESIGNATION: GOD OF THUNDER... AGE: DOES NOT COMPUTE... DANGER!... DANGER!...

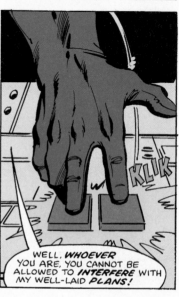

KLIK

WELL, *WHOEVER* YOU ARE, YOU CANNOT BE ALLOWED TO *INTERFERE* WITH MY WELL-LAID *PLANS!*

12

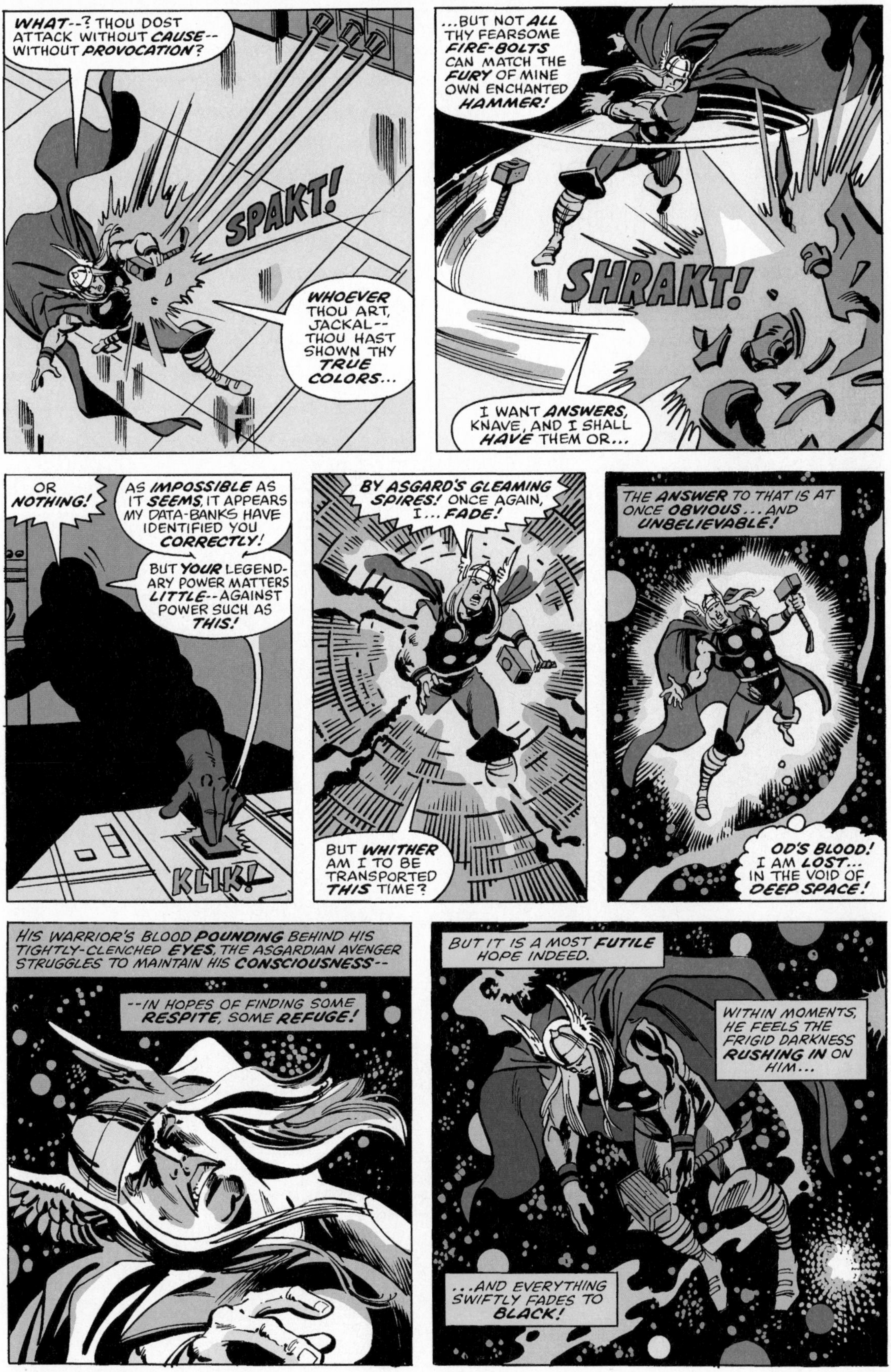
WHAT--? THOU DOST ATTACK WITHOUT CAUSE-- WITHOUT PROVOCATION?
SPAKT!
WHOEVER THOU ART, JACKAL-- THOU HAST SHOWN THY TRUE COLORS...
...BUT NOT ALL THY FEARSOME FIRE-BOLTS CAN MATCH THE FURY OF MINE OWN ENCHANTED HAMMER!
SHRAKT!
I WANT ANSWERS, KNAVE, AND I SHALL HAVE THEM OR...
OR NOTHING!
AS IMPOSSIBLE AS IT SEEMS, IT APPEARS MY DATA-BANKS HAVE IDENTIFIED YOU CORRECTLY!
BUT YOUR LEGENDARY POWER MATTERS LITTLE--AGAINST POWER SUCH AS THIS!
KLIK!
BY ASGARD'S GLEAMING SPIRES! ONCE AGAIN, I... FADE!
BUT WHITHER AM I TO BE TRANSPORTED THIS TIME?
THE ANSWER TO THAT IS AT ONCE OBVIOUS... AND UNBELIEVABLE!
OD'S BLOOD! I AM LOST... IN THE VOID OF DEEP SPACE!
HIS WARRIOR'S BLOOD POUNDING BEHIND HIS TIGHTLY-CLENCHED EYES, THE ASGARDIAN AVENGER STRUGGLES TO MAINTAIN HIS CONSCIOUSNESS--
--IN HOPES OF FINDING SOME RESPITE, SOME REFUGE!
BUT IT IS A MOST FUTILE HOPE INDEED.
WITHIN MOMENTS, HE FEELS THE FRIGID DARKNESS RUSHING IN ON HIM...
...AND EVERYTHING SWIFTLY FADES TO BLACK!

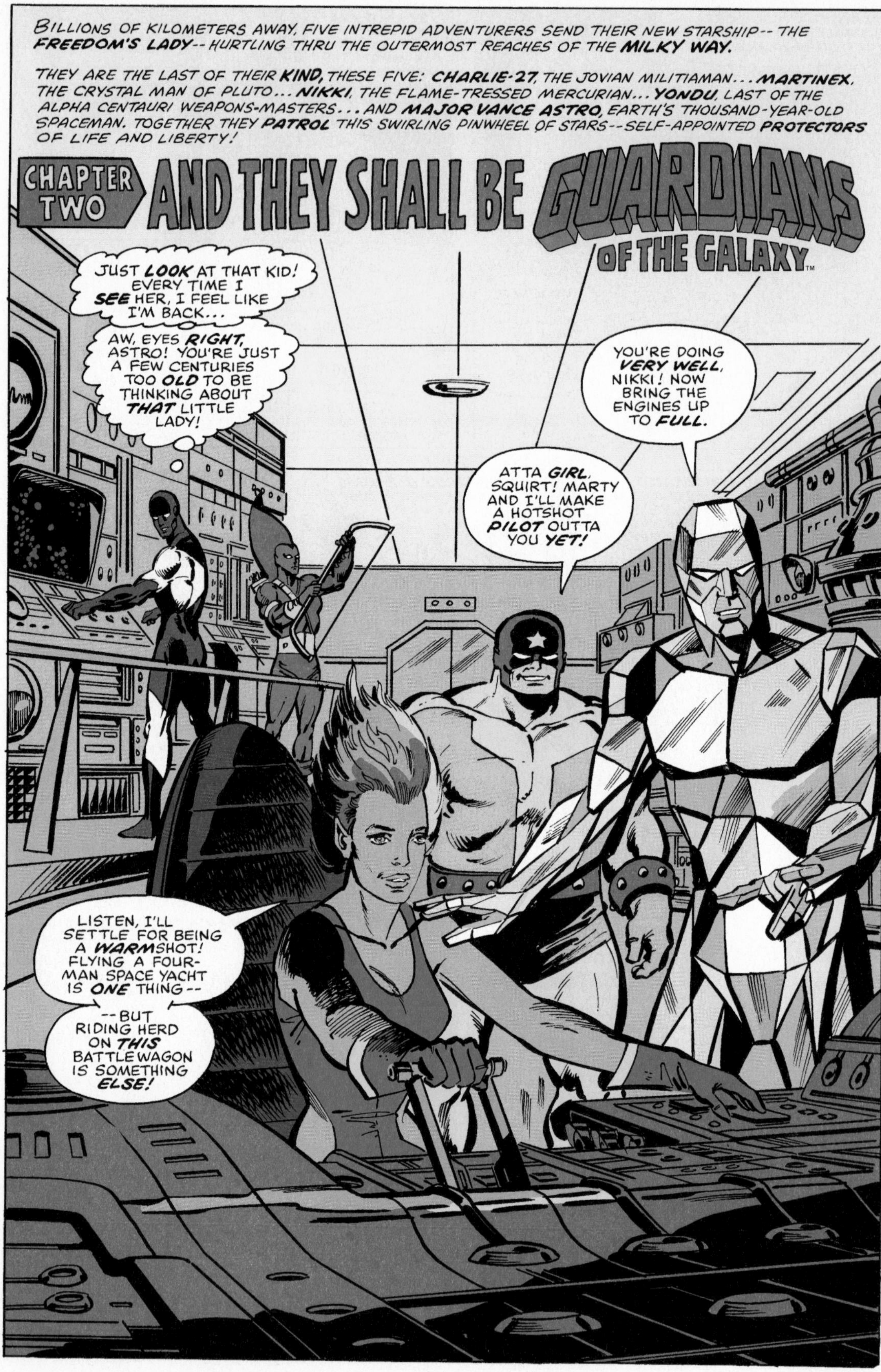
BILLIONS OF KILOMETERS AWAY, FIVE INTREPID ADVENTURERS SEND THEIR NEW STARSHIP-- THE FREEDOM'S LADY-- HURTLING THRU THE OUTERMOST REACHES OF THE MILKY WAY.
THEY ARE THE LAST OF THEIR KIND, THESE FIVE: CHARLIE-27, THE JOVIAN MILITIAMAN... MARTINEX, THE CRYSTAL MAN OF PLUTO... NIKKI, THE FLAME-TRESSED MERCURIAN... YONDU, LAST OF THE ALPHA CENTAURI WEAPONS-MASTERS... AND MAJOR VANCE ASTRO, EARTH'S THOUSAND-YEAR-OLD SPACEMAN. TOGETHER THEY PATROL THIS SWIRLING PINWHEEL OF STARS--SELF-APPOINTED PROTECTORS OF LIFE AND LIBERTY!
CHAPTER TWO
AND THEY SHALL BE GUARDIANS OF THE GALAXY™
JUST LOOK AT THAT KID! EVERY TIME I SEE HER, I FEEL LIKE I'M BACK...
AW, EYES RIGHT, ASTRO! YOU'RE JUST A FEW CENTURIES TOO OLD TO BE THINKING ABOUT THAT LITTLE LADY!
YOU'RE DOING VERY WELL, NIKKI! NOW BRING THE ENGINES UP TO FULL.
ATTA GIRL, SQUIRT! MARTY AND I'LL MAKE A HOTSHOT PILOT OUTTA YOU YET!
LISTEN, I'LL SETTLE FOR BEING A WARMSHOT! FLYING A FOUR-MAN SPACE YACHT IS ONE THING--
--BUT RIDING HERD ON THIS BATTLEWAGON IS SOMETHING ELSE!

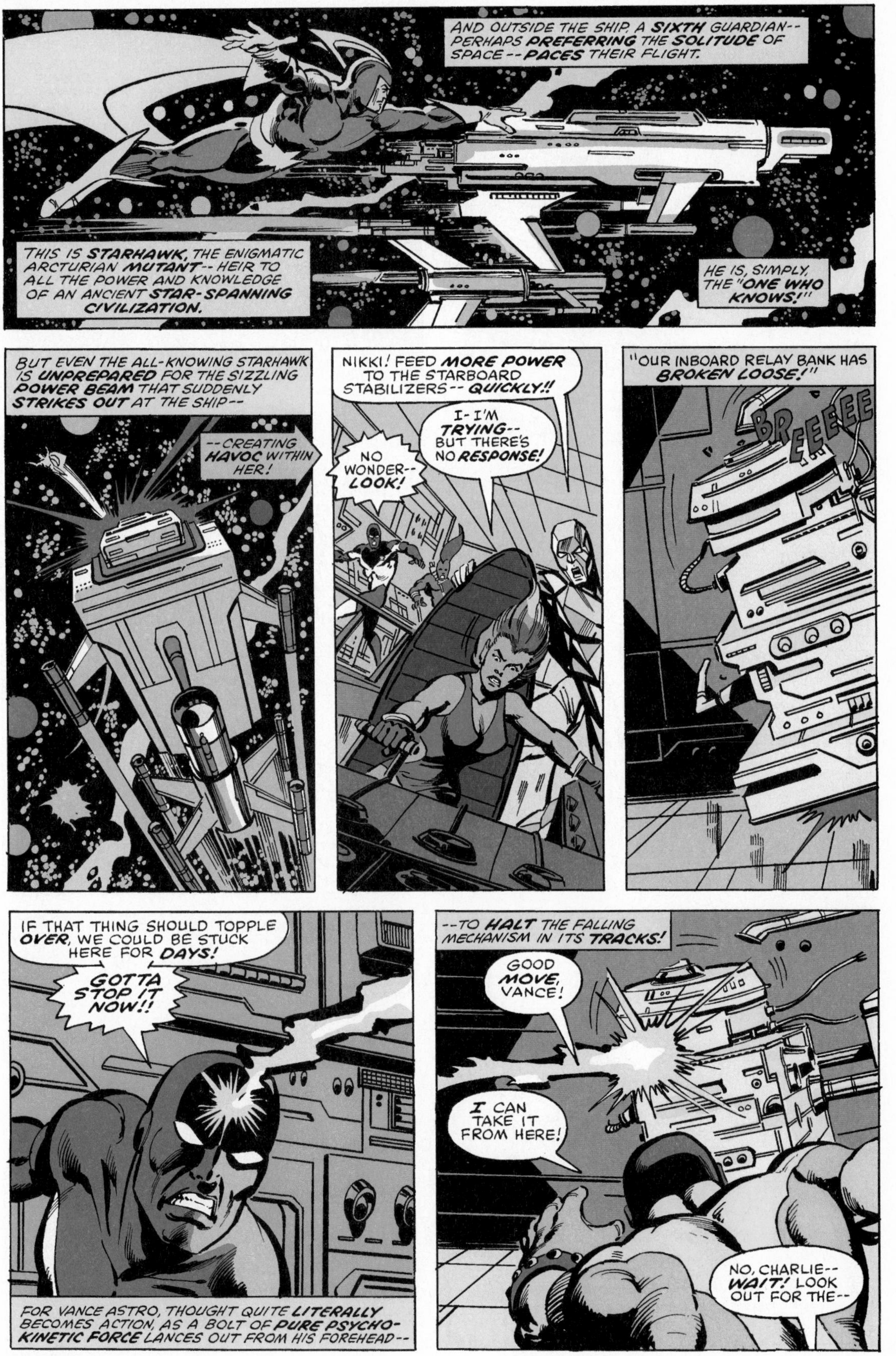
AND OUTSIDE THE SHIP, A SIXTH GUARDIAN-- PERHAPS PREFERRING THE SOLITUDE OF SPACE--PACES THEIR FLIGHT.
THIS IS STARHAWK, THE ENIGMATIC ARCTURIAN MUTANT-- HEIR TO ALL THE POWER AND KNOWLEDGE OF AN ANCIENT STAR-SPANNING CIVILIZATION.
HE IS, SIMPLY, THE "ONE WHO KNOWS!"
BUT EVEN THE ALL-KNOWING STARHAWK IS UNPREPARED FOR THE SIZZLING POWER BEAM THAT SUDDENLY STRIKES OUT AT THE SHIP--
--CREATING HAVOC WITHIN HER!
NIKKI! FEED MORE POWER TO THE STARBOARD STABILIZERS-- QUICKLY!!
I- I'M TRYING-- BUT THERE'S NO RESPONSE!
NO WONDER-- LOOK!
"OUR INBOARD RELAY BANK HAS BROKEN LOOSE!"
BREEEEE
IF THAT THING SHOULD TOPPLE OVER, WE COULD BE STUCK HERE FOR DAYS!
GOTTA STOP IT NOW!!
FOR VANCE ASTRO, THOUGHT QUITE LITERALLY BECOMES ACTION, AS A BOLT OF PURE PSYCHO-KINETIC FORCE LANCES OUT FROM HIS FOREHEAD--
--TO HALT THE FALLING MECHANISM IN ITS TRACKS!
GOOD MOVE, VANCE!
I CAN TAKE IT FROM HERE!
NO, CHARLIE-- WAIT! LOOK OUT FOR THE--

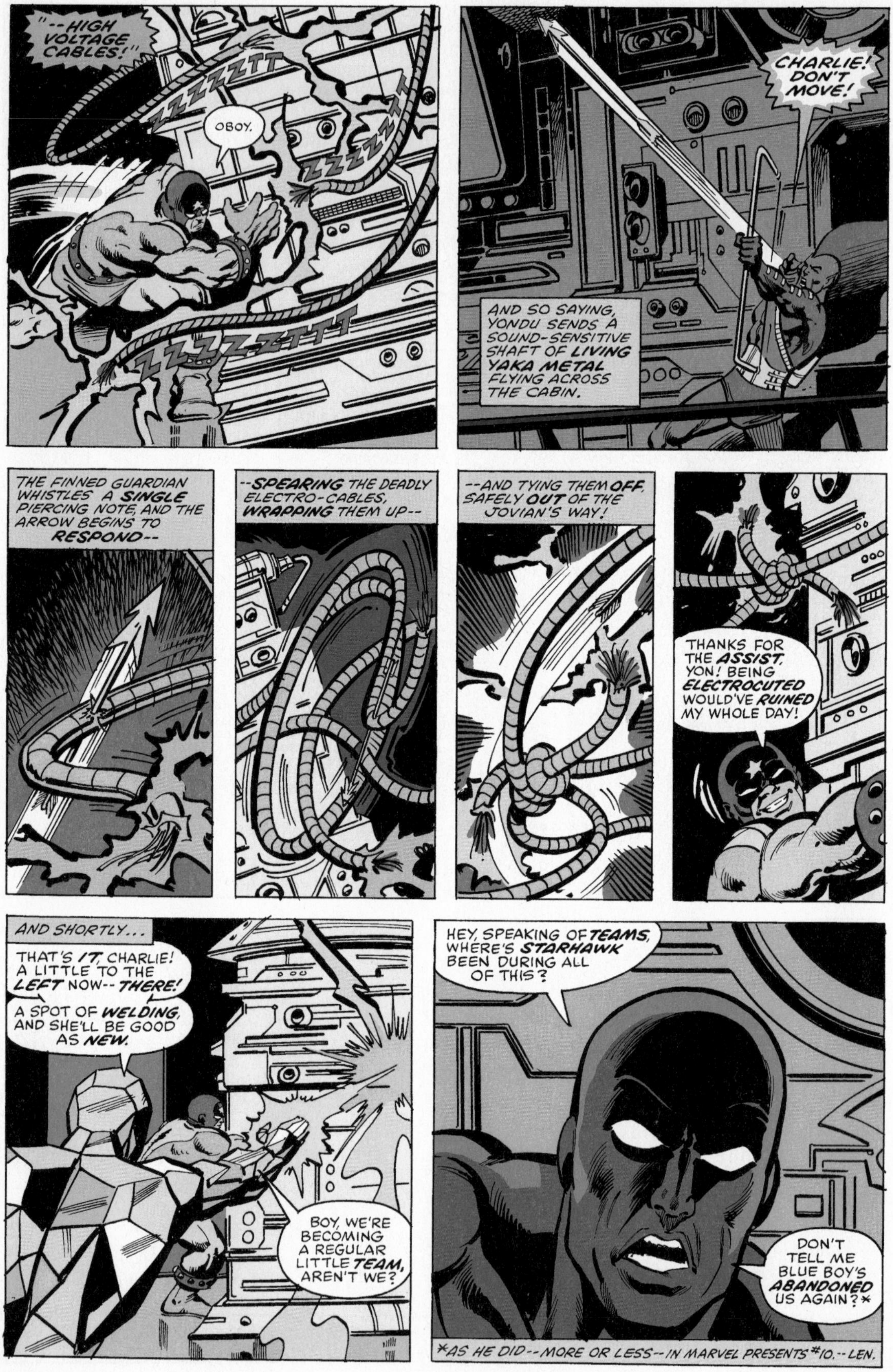
"--HIGH VOLTAGE CABLES!"
ZZZZZZTTT
OBOY.
ZZZZZZZT
ZZZZZZTTT
CHARLIE! DON'T MOVE!
AND SO SAYING, YONDU SENDS A SOUND-SENSITIVE SHAFT OF LIVING YAKA METAL FLYING ACROSS THE CABIN.
THE FINNED GUARDIAN WHISTLES A SINGLE PIERCING NOTE, AND THE ARROW BEGINS TO RESPOND--
--SPEARING THE DEADLY ELECTRO-CABLES, WRAPPING THEM UP--
--AND TYING THEM OFF, SAFELY OUT OF THE JOVIAN'S WAY!
THANKS FOR THE ASSIST, YON! BEING ELECTROCUTED WOULD'VE RUINED MY WHOLE DAY!
AND SHORTLY...
THAT'S IT, CHARLIE! A LITTLE TO THE LEFT NOW--THERE!
A SPOT OF WELDING, AND SHE'LL BE GOOD AS NEW.
BOY, WE'RE BECOMING A REGULAR LITTLE TEAM, AREN'T WE?
HEY, SPEAKING OF TEAMS, WHERE'S STARHAWK BEEN DURING ALL OF THIS?
DON'T TELL ME BLUE BOY'S ABANDONED US AGAIN?*
*AS HE DID--MORE OR LESS--IN MARVEL PRESENTS #10.--LEN.

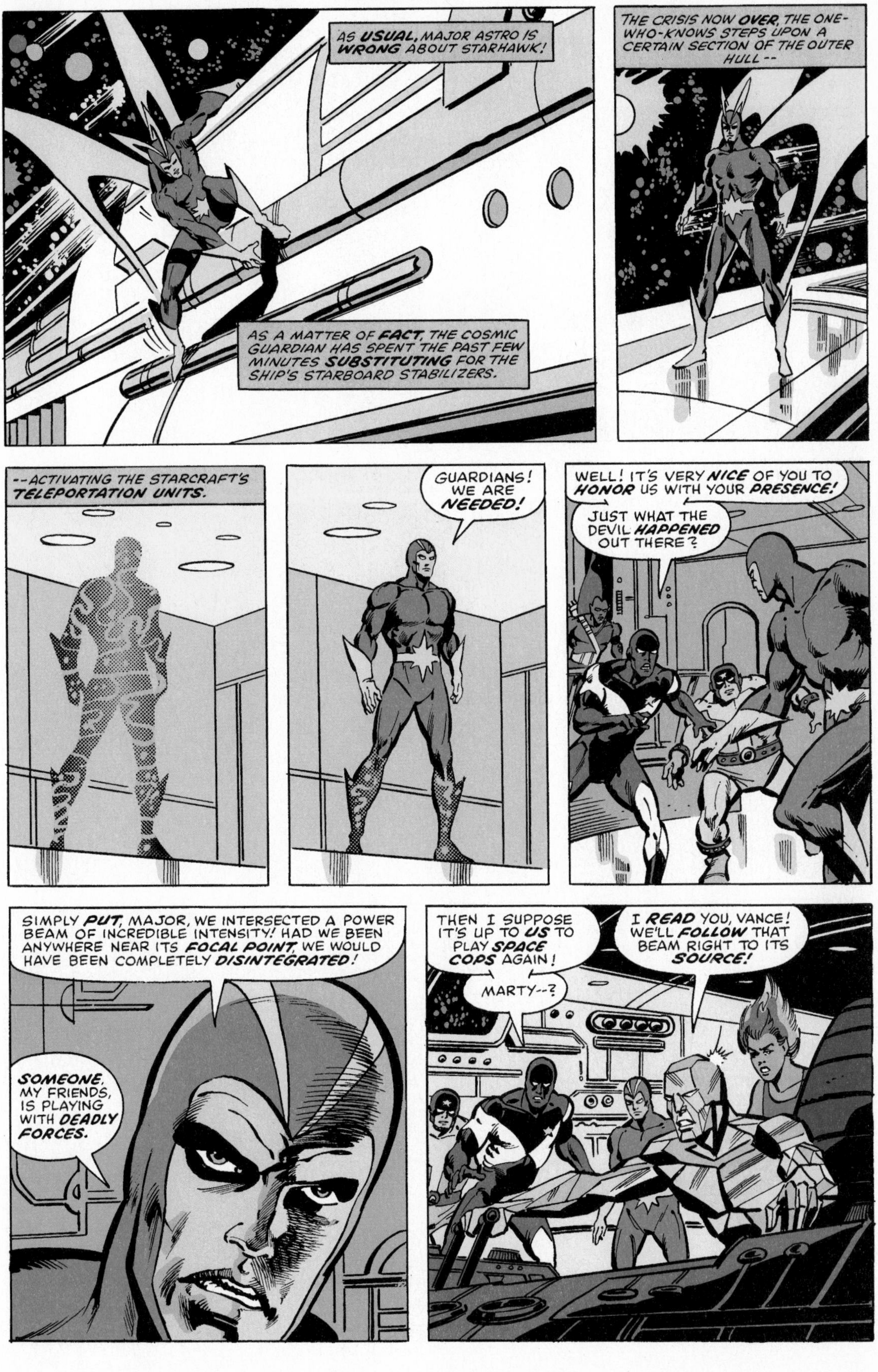
AS USUAL, MAJOR ASTRO IS WRONG ABOUT STARHAWK!
AS A MATTER OF FACT, THE COSMIC GUARDIAN HAS SPENT THE PAST FEW MINUTES SUBSTITUTING FOR THE SHIP'S STARBOARD STABILIZERS.
THE CRISIS NOW OVER, THE ONE-WHO-KNOWS STEPS UPON A CERTAIN SECTION OF THE OUTER HULL --
--ACTIVATING THE STARCRAFT'S TELEPORTATION UNITS.
GUARDIANS! WE ARE NEEDED!
WELL! IT'S VERY NICE OF YOU TO HONOR US WITH YOUR PRESENCE!
JUST WHAT THE DEVIL HAPPENED OUT THERE?
SIMPLY PUT, MAJOR, WE INTERSECTED A POWER BEAM OF INCREDIBLE INTENSITY! HAD WE BEEN ANYWHERE NEAR ITS FOCAL POINT, WE WOULD HAVE BEEN COMPLETELY DISINTEGRATED!
SOMEONE, MY FRIENDS, IS PLAYING WITH DEADLY FORCES.
THEN I SUPPOSE IT'S UP TO US TO PLAY SPACE COPS AGAIN!
MARTY--?
I READ YOU, VANCE! WE'LL FOLLOW THAT BEAM RIGHT TO ITS SOURCE!

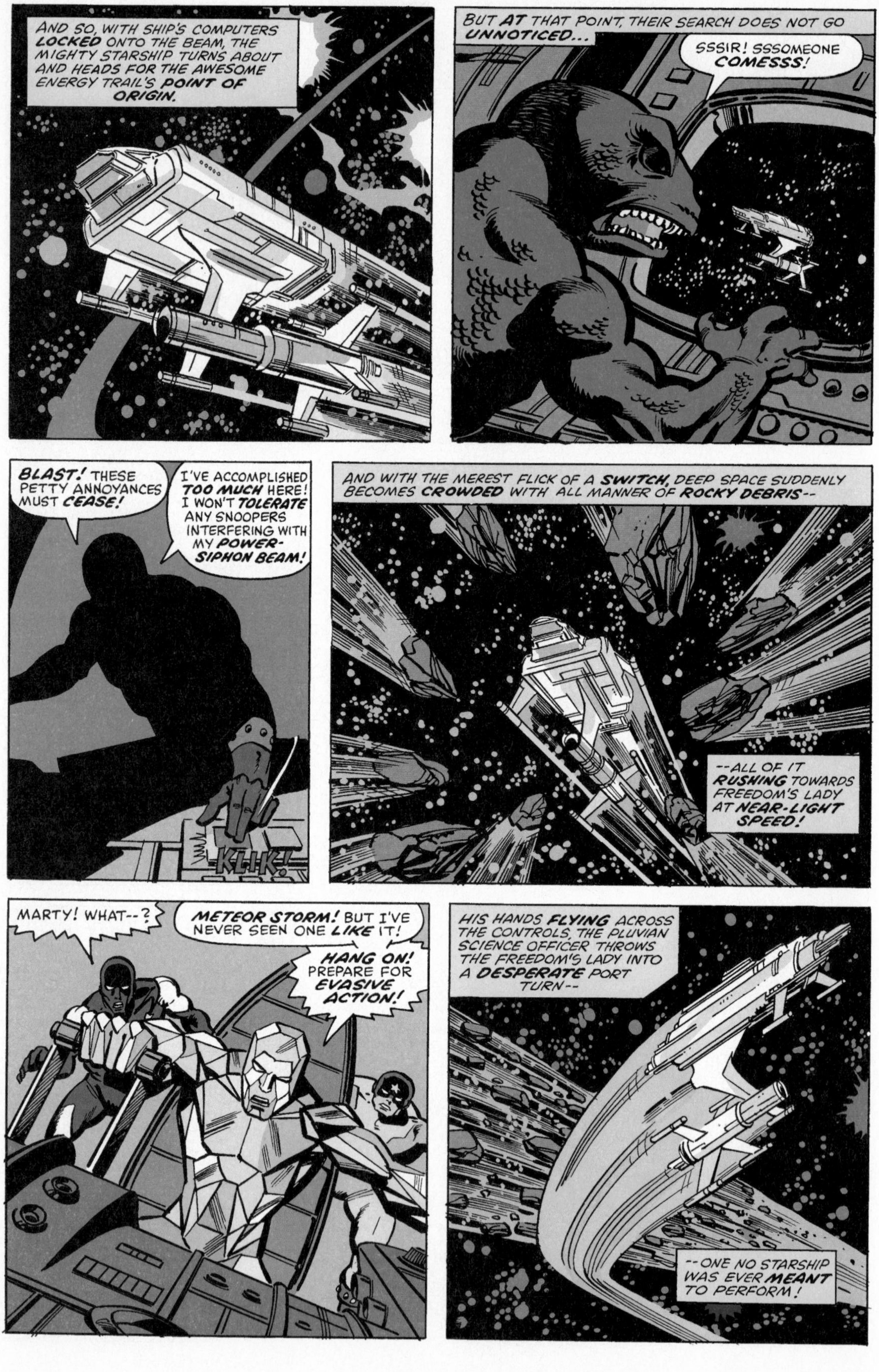
AND SO, WITH SHIP'S COMPUTERS LOCKED ONTO THE BEAM, THE MIGHTY STARSHIP TURNS ABOUT AND HEADS FOR THE AWESOME ENERGY TRAIL'S POINT OF ORIGIN.
BUT AT THAT POINT, THEIR SEARCH DOES NOT GO UNNOTICED...
SSSIR! SSSOMEONE COMESSS!
BLAST! THESE PETTY ANNOYANCES MUST CEASE!
I'VE ACCOMPLISHED TOO MUCH HERE! I WON'T TOLERATE ANY SNOOPERS INTERFERING WITH MY POWER-SIPHON BEAM!
KLIK!
AND WITH THE MEREST FLICK OF A SWITCH, DEEP SPACE SUDDENLY BECOMES CROWDED WITH ALL MANNER OF ROCKY DEBRIS--
--ALL OF IT RUSHING TOWARDS FREEDOM'S LADY AT NEAR-LIGHT SPEED!
MARTY! WHAT--?
METEOR STORM! BUT I'VE NEVER SEEN ONE LIKE IT!
HANG ON! PREPARE FOR EVASIVE ACTION!
HIS HANDS FLYING ACROSS THE CONTROLS, THE PLUVIAN SCIENCE OFFICER THROWS THE FREEDOM'S LADY INTO A DESPERATE PORT TURN--
--ONE NO STARSHIP WAS EVER MEANT TO PERFORM!

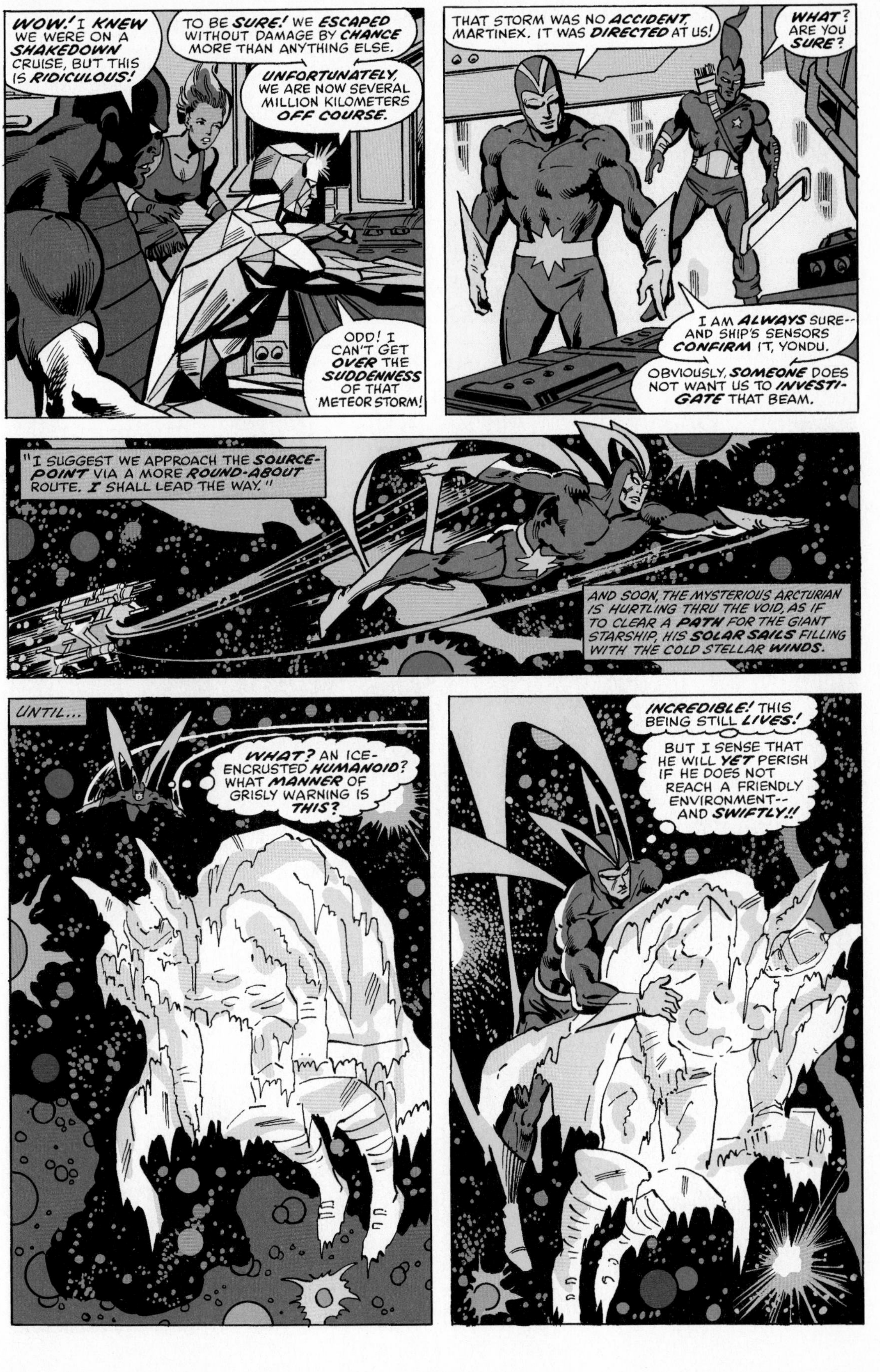

WOW! I KNEW WE WERE ON A SHAKEDOWN CRUISE, BUT THIS IS RIDICULOUS!
TO BE SURE! WE ESCAPED WITHOUT DAMAGE BY CHANCE MORE THAN ANYTHING ELSE.
UNFORTUNATELY, WE ARE NOW SEVERAL MILLION KILOMETERS OFF COURSE.
ODD! I CAN'T GET OVER THE SUDDENNESS OF THAT METEOR STORM!
THAT STORM WAS NO ACCIDENT, MARTINEX. IT WAS DIRECTED AT US!
WHAT? ARE YOU SURE?
I AM ALWAYS SURE-- AND SHIP'S SENSORS CONFIRM IT, YONDU.
OBVIOUSLY, SOMEONE DOES NOT WANT US TO INVESTIGATE THAT BEAM.
"I SUGGEST WE APPROACH THE SOURCE-POINT VIA A MORE ROUND-ABOUT ROUTE. I SHALL LEAD THE WAY."
AND SOON, THE MYSTERIOUS ARCTURIAN IS HURTLING THRU THE VOID, AS IF TO CLEAR A PATH FOR THE GIANT STARSHIP, HIS SOLAR SAILS FILLING WITH THE COLD STELLAR WINDS.
UNTIL...
WHAT? AN ICE-ENCRUSTED HUMANOID? WHAT MANNER OF GRISLY WARNING IS THIS?
INCREDIBLE! THIS BEING STILL LIVES!
BUT I SENSE THAT HE WILL YET PERISH IF HE DOES NOT REACH A FRIENDLY ENVIRONMENT-- AND SWIFTLY!!

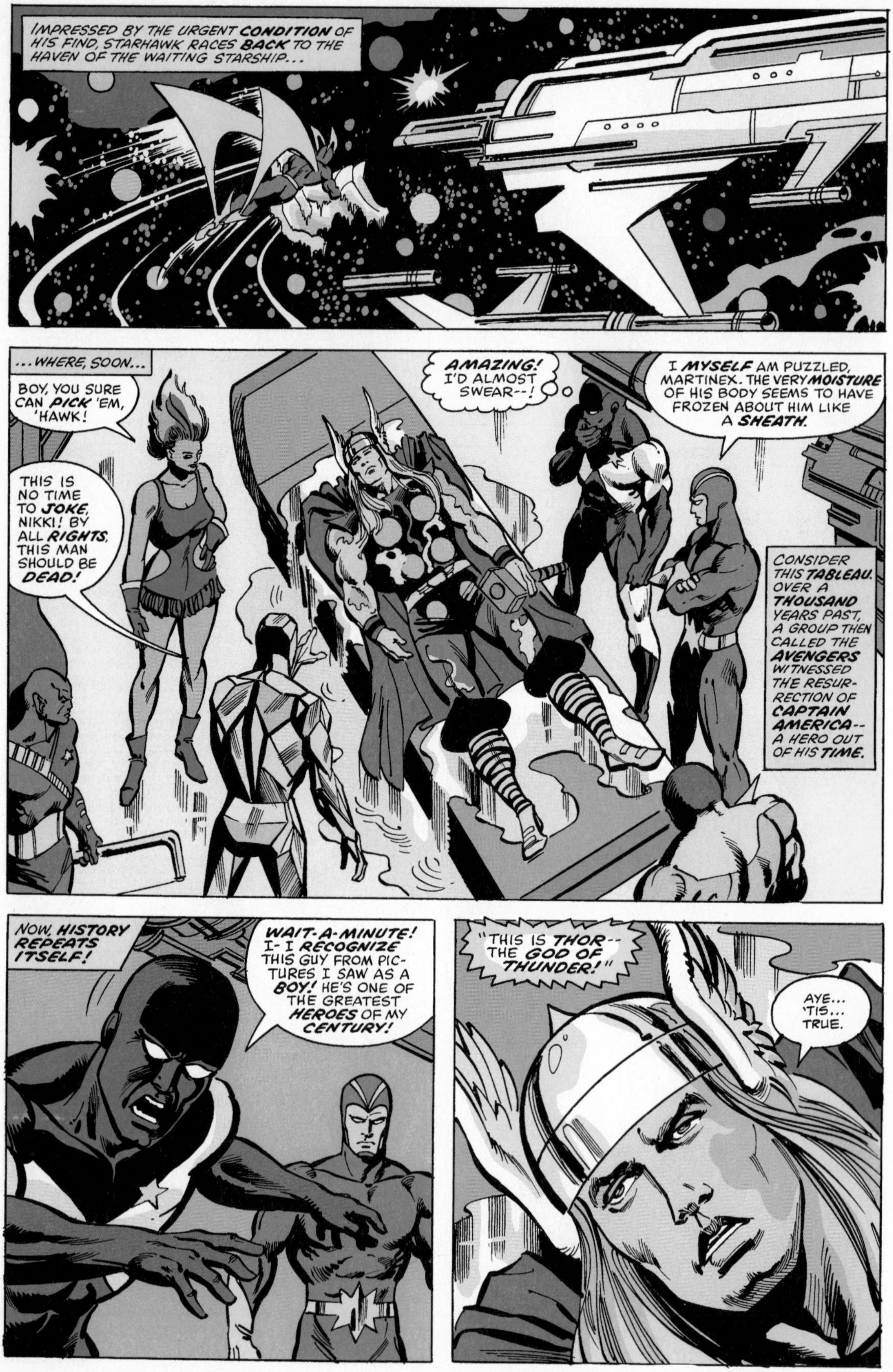

IMPRESSED BY THE URGENT CONDITION OF HIS FIND, STARHAWK RACES BACK TO THE HAVEN OF THE WAITING STARSHIP...
...WHERE, SOON...
BOY, YOU SURE CAN PICK 'EM, 'HAWK!
THIS IS NO TIME TO JOKE, NIKKI! BY ALL RIGHTS, THIS MAN SHOULD BE DEAD!
AMAZING! I'D ALMOST SWEAR--!
I MYSELF AM PUZZLED, MARTINEX. THE VERY MOISTURE OF HIS BODY SEEMS TO HAVE FROZEN ABOUT HIM LIKE A SHEATH.
CONSIDER THIS TABLEAU. OVER A THOUSAND YEARS PAST, A GROUP THEN CALLED THE AVENGERS WITNESSED THE RESURRECTION OF CAPTAIN AMERICA-- A HERO OUT OF HIS TIME.
NOW, HISTORY REPEATS ITSELF!
WAIT-A-MINUTE! I- I RECOGNIZE THIS GUY FROM PICTURES I SAW AS A BOY! HE'S ONE OF THE GREATEST HEROES OF MY CENTURY!
"THIS IS THOR-- THE GOD OF THUNDER!"
AYE... 'TIS... TRUE.

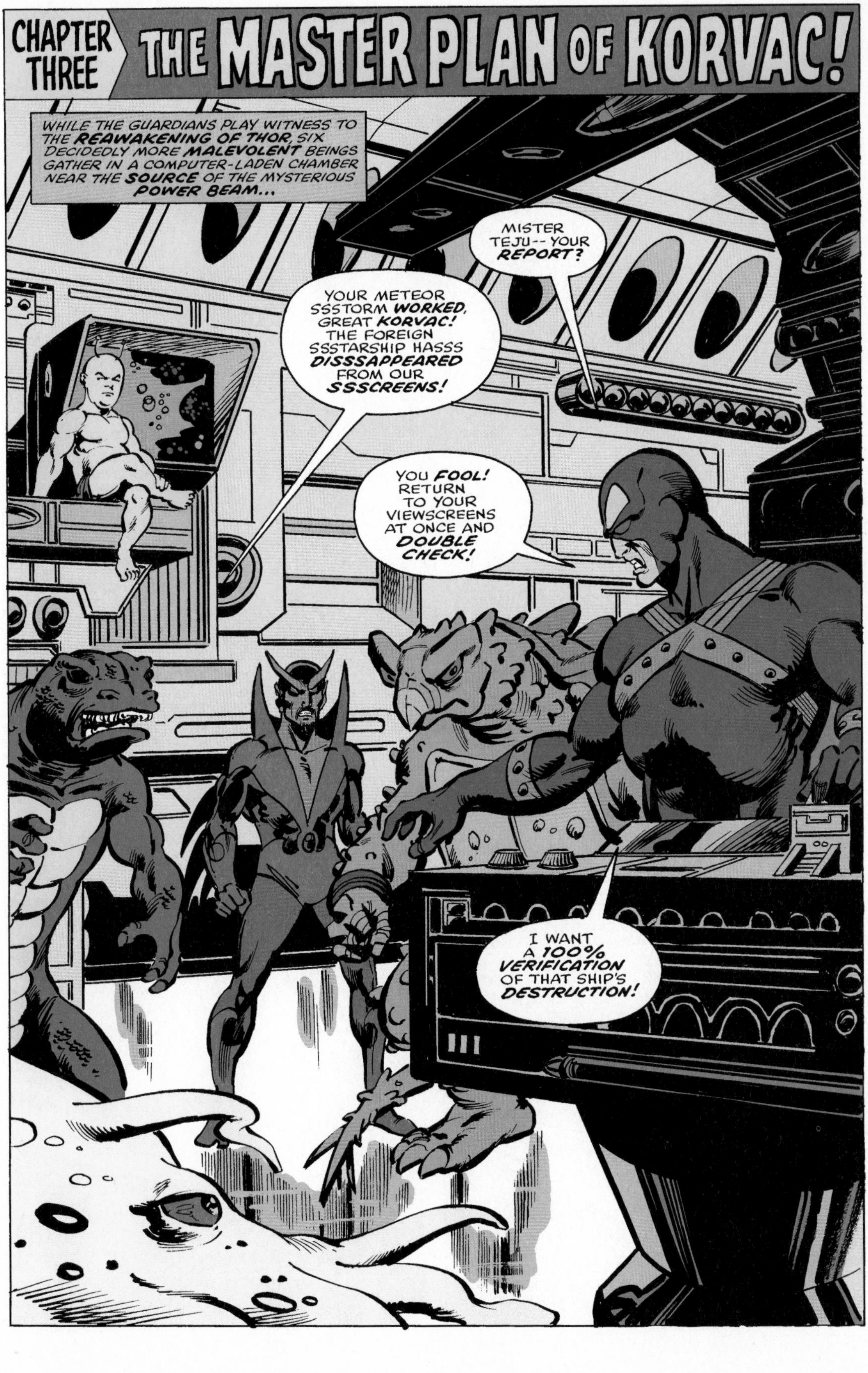
CHAPTER THREE
THE MASTER PLAN OF KORVAC!
WHILE THE GUARDIANS PLAY WITNESS TO THE REAWAKENING OF THOR, SIX DECIDEDLY MORE MALEVOLENT BEINGS GATHER IN A COMPUTER-LADEN CHAMBER NEAR THE SOURCE OF THE MYSTERIOUS POWER BEAM...
MISTER TEJU-- YOUR REPORT?
YOUR METEOR SSSTORM WORKED, GREAT KORVAC! THE FOREIGN SSSTARSHIP HASSS DISSSAPPEARED FROM OUR SSSCREENS!
YOU FOOL! RETURN TO YOUR VIEWSCREENS AT ONCE AND DOUBLE CHECK!
I WANT A 100% VERIFICATION OF THAT SHIP'S DESTRUCTION!

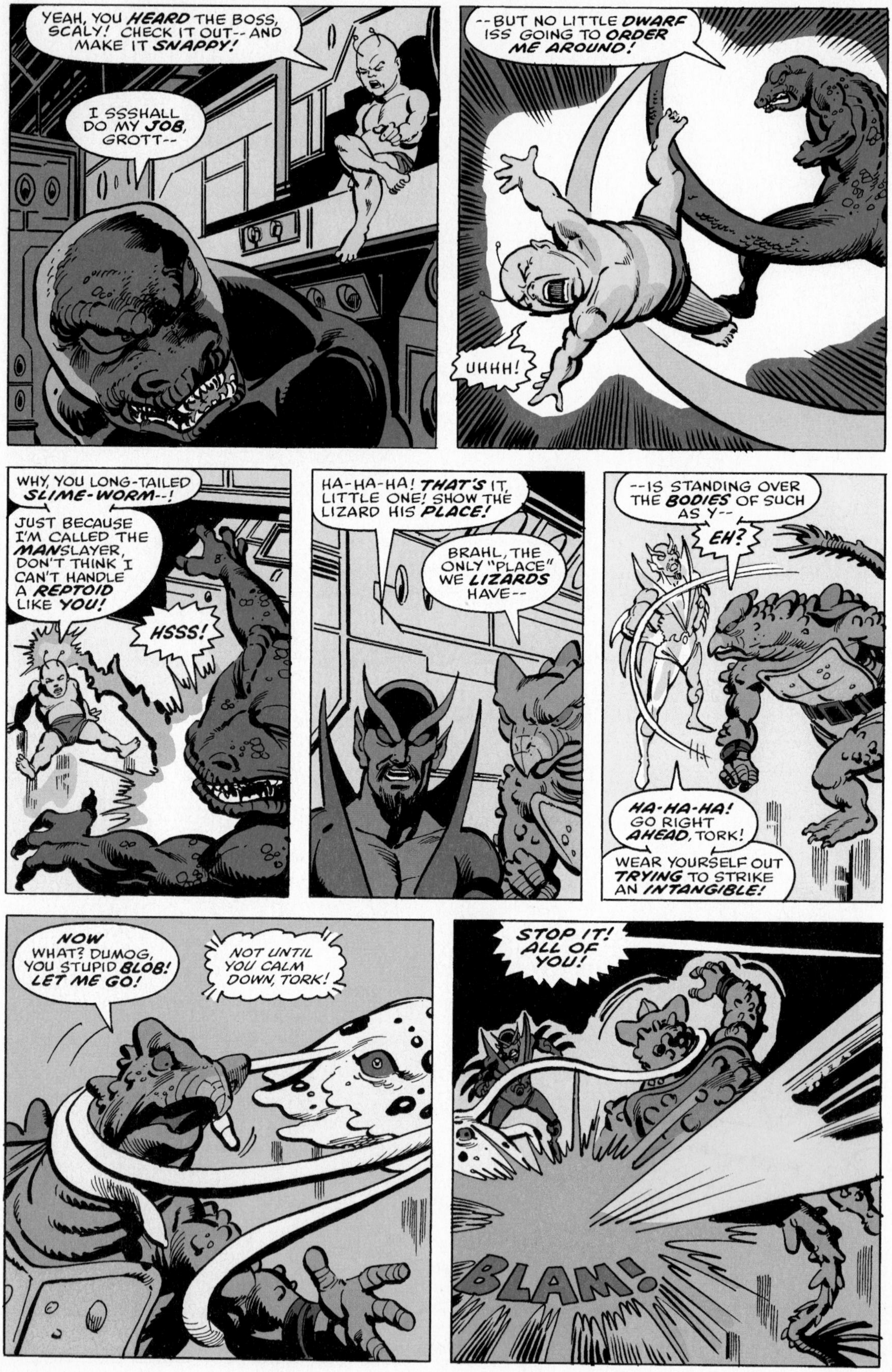
YEAH, YOU HEARD THE BOSS, SCALY! CHECK IT OUT-- AND MAKE IT SNAPPY!
I SSSHALL DO MY JOB, GROTT--
--BUT NO LITTLE DWARF ISS GOING TO ORDER ME AROUND!
UHHH!
WHY, YOU LONG-TAILED SLIME-WORM--!
JUST BECAUSE I'M CALLED THE MANSLAYER, DON'T THINK I CAN'T HANDLE A REPTOID LIKE YOU!
HSSS!
HA-HA-HA! THAT'S IT, LITTLE ONE! SHOW THE LIZARD HIS PLACE!
BRAHL, THE ONLY "PLACE" WE LIZARDS HAVE--
--IS STANDING OVER THE BODIES OF SUCH AS Y--
EH?
HA-HA-HA! GO RIGHT AHEAD, TORK!
WEAR YOURSELF OUT TRYING TO STRIKE AN INTANGIBLE!
NOW WHAT? DUMOG, YOU STUPID BLOB! LET ME GO!
NOT UNTIL YOU CALM DOWN, TORK!
STOP IT! ALL OF YOU!
BLAM!

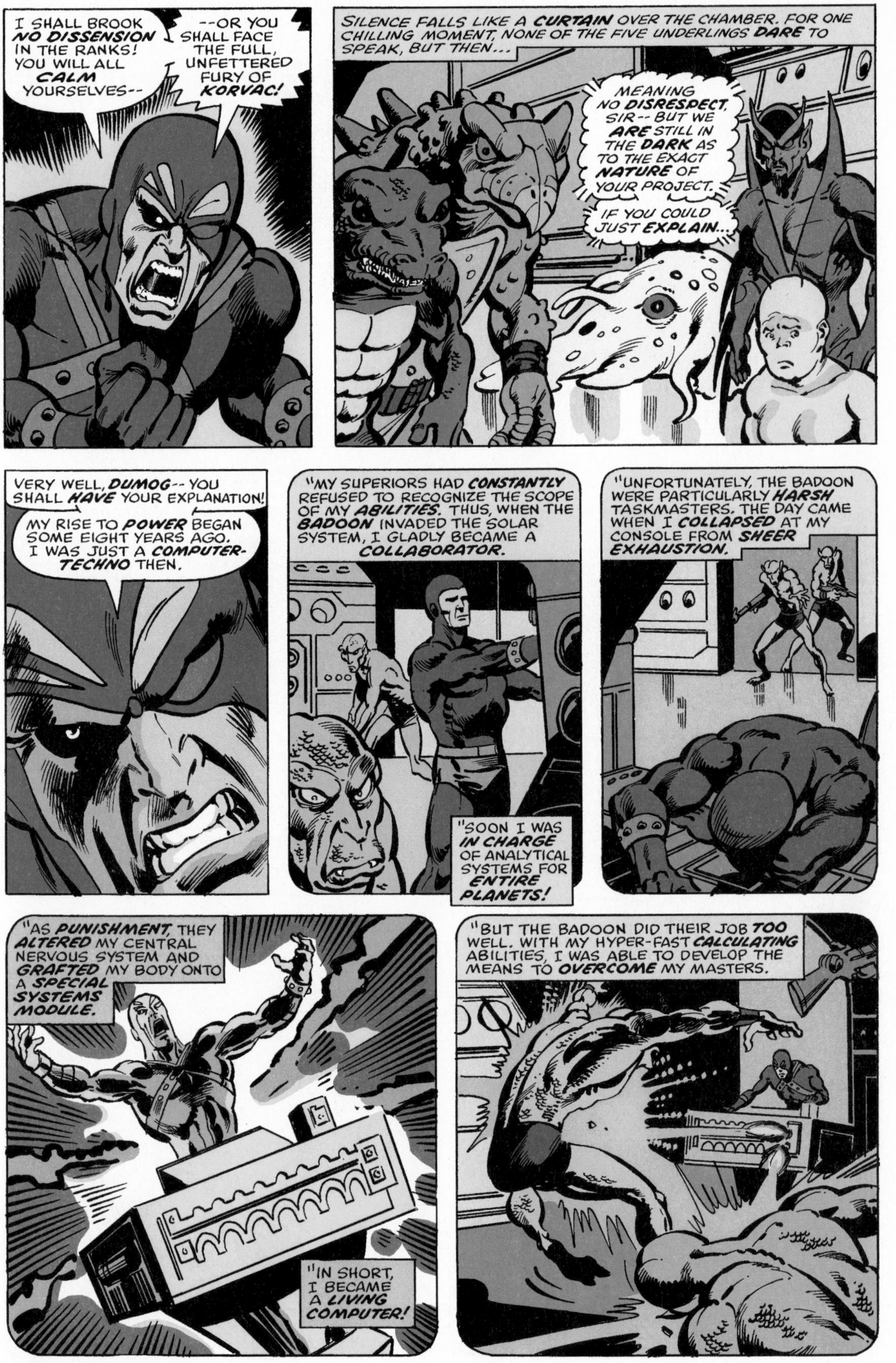
I SHALL BROOK NO DISSENSION IN THE RANKS! YOU WILL ALL CALM YOURSELVES--
--OR YOU SHALL FACE THE FULL, UNFETTERED FURY OF KORVAC!
SILENCE FALLS LIKE A CURTAIN OVER THE CHAMBER. FOR ONE CHILLING MOMENT, NONE OF THE FIVE UNDERLINGS DARE TO SPEAK, BUT THEN...
MEANING NO DISRESPECT, SIR-- BUT WE ARE STILL IN THE DARK AS TO THE EXACT NATURE OF YOUR PROJECT.
IF YOU COULD JUST EXPLAIN...
VERY WELL, DUMOG-- YOU SHALL HAVE YOUR EXPLANATION!
MY RISE TO POWER BEGAN SOME EIGHT YEARS AGO. I WAS JUST A COMPUTER-TECHNO THEN.
"MY SUPERIORS HAD CONSTANTLY REFUSED TO RECOGNIZE THE SCOPE OF MY ABILITIES. THUS, WHEN THE BADOON INVADED THE SOLAR SYSTEM, I GLADLY BECAME A COLLABORATOR.
"SOON I WAS IN CHARGE OF ANALYTICAL SYSTEMS FOR ENTIRE PLANETS!
"UNFORTUNATELY, THE BADOON WERE PARTICULARLY HARSH TASKMASTERS. THE DAY CAME WHEN I COLLAPSED AT MY CONSOLE FROM SHEER EXHAUSTION.
"AS PUNISHMENT, THEY ALTERED MY CENTRAL NERVOUS SYSTEM AND GRAFTED MY BODY ONTO A SPECIAL SYSTEMS MODULE.
"IN SHORT, I BECAME A LIVING COMPUTER!
"BUT THE BADOON DID THEIR JOB TOO WELL. WITH MY HYPER-FAST CALCULATING ABILITIES, I WAS ABLE TO DEVELOP THE MEANS TO OVERCOME MY MASTERS.

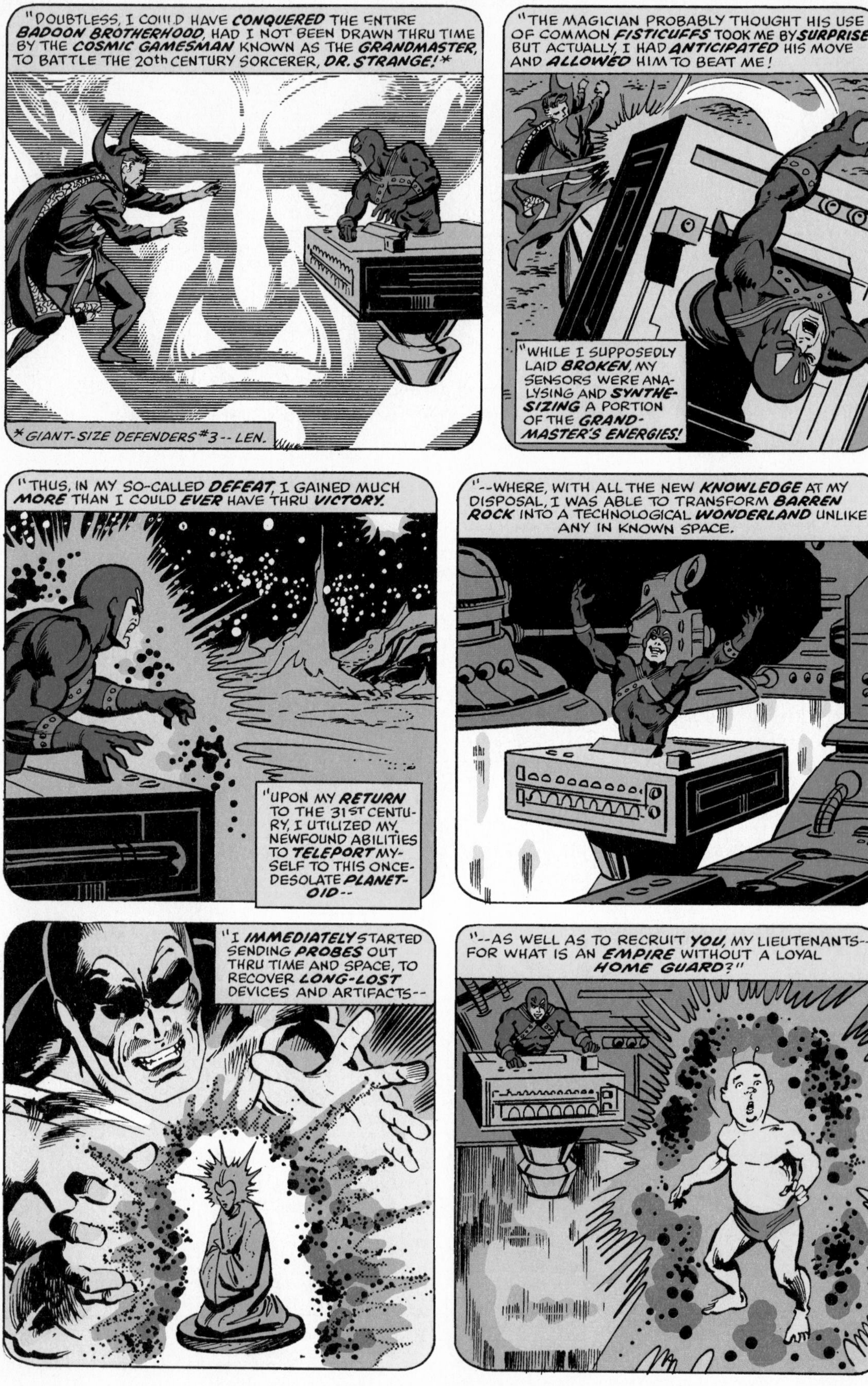
"DOUBTLESS, I COULD HAVE CONQUERED THE ENTIRE BADOON BROTHERHOOD, HAD I NOT BEEN DRAWN THRU TIME BY THE COSMIC GAMESMAN KNOWN AS THE GRANDMASTER, TO BATTLE THE 20th CENTURY SORCERER, DR. STRANGE! *
* GIANT-SIZE DEFENDERS #3 -- LEN.
"THE MAGICIAN PROBABLY THOUGHT HIS USE OF COMMON FISTICUFFS TOOK ME BY SURPRISE-- BUT ACTUALLY, I HAD ANTICIPATED HIS MOVE AND ALLOWED HIM TO BEAT ME!
"WHILE I SUPPOSEDLY LAID BROKEN, MY SENSORS WERE ANALYSING AND SYNTHESIZING A PORTION OF THE GRANDMASTER'S ENERGIES!
"THUS, IN MY SO-CALLED DEFEAT, I GAINED MUCH MORE THAN I COULD EVER HAVE THRU VICTORY.
"UPON MY RETURN TO THE 31ST CENTURY, I UTILIZED MY NEWFOUND ABILITIES TO TELEPORT MYSELF TO THIS ONCE-DESOLATE PLANETOID--
"--WHERE, WITH ALL THE NEW KNOWLEDGE AT MY DISPOSAL, I WAS ABLE TO TRANSFORM BARREN ROCK INTO A TECHNOLOGICAL WONDERLAND UNLIKE ANY IN KNOWN SPACE.
"I IMMEDIATELY STARTED SENDING PROBES OUT THRU TIME AND SPACE, TO RECOVER LONG-LOST DEVICES AND ARTIFACTS--
"--AS WELL AS TO RECRUIT YOU, MY LIEUTENANTS-- FOR WHAT IS AN EMPIRE WITHOUT A LOYAL HOME GUARD?"

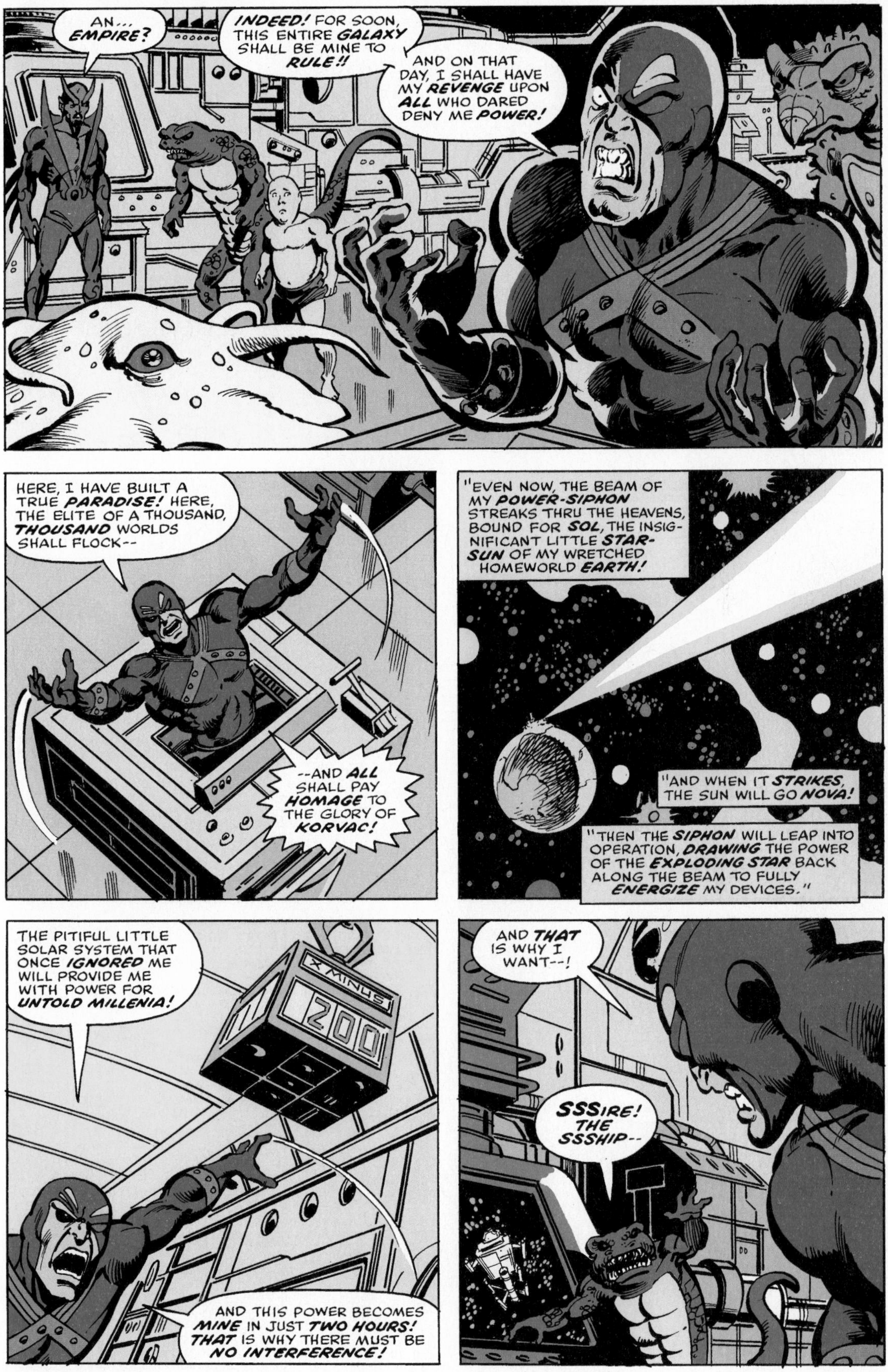
AN... EMPIRE?
INDEED! FOR SOON, THIS ENTIRE GALAXY SHALL BE MINE TO RULE!!
AND ON THAT DAY, I SHALL HAVE MY REVENGE UPON ALL WHO DARED DENY ME POWER!
HERE, I HAVE BUILT A TRUE PARADISE! HERE, THE ELITE OF A THOUSAND, THOUSAND WORLDS SHALL FLOCK--
--AND ALL SHALL PAY HOMAGE TO THE GLORY OF KORVAC!
"EVEN NOW, THE BEAM OF MY POWER-SIPHON STREAKS THRU THE HEAVENS, BOUND FOR SOL, THE INSIGNIFICANT LITTLE STAR-SUN OF MY WRETCHED HOMEWORLD EARTH!
"AND WHEN IT STRIKES, THE SUN WILL GO NOVA!
"THEN THE SIPHON WILL LEAP INTO OPERATION, DRAWING THE POWER OF THE EXPLODING STAR BACK ALONG THE BEAM TO FULLY ENERGIZE MY DEVICES."
THE PITIFUL LITTLE SOLAR SYSTEM THAT ONCE IGNORED ME WILL PROVIDE ME WITH POWER FOR UNTOLD MILLENIA!
X MINUS
200
AND THIS POWER BECOMES MINE IN JUST TWO HOURS! THAT IS WHY THERE MUST BE NO INTERFERENCE!
AND THAT IS WHY I WANT--!
SSSIRE! THE SSSHIP--

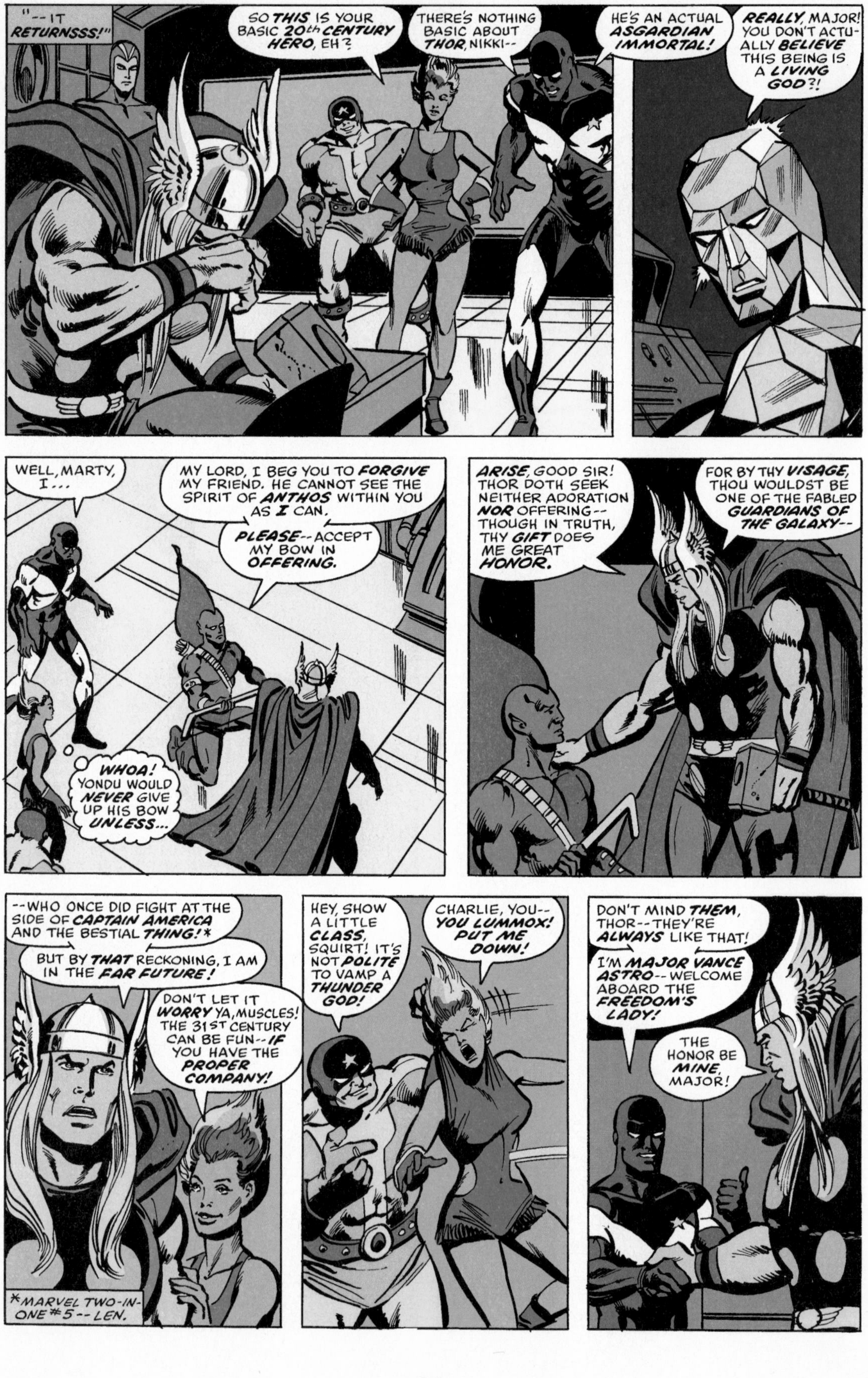
"--IT RETURNSSS!"
SO THIS IS YOUR BASIC 20th CENTURY HERO, EH?
THERE'S NOTHING BASIC ABOUT THOR, NIKKI--
HE'S AN ACTUAL ASGARDIAN IMMORTAL!
REALLY, MAJOR! YOU DON'T ACTUALLY BELIEVE THIS BEING IS A LIVING GOD?!
WELL, MARTY, I...
MY LORD, I BEG YOU TO FORGIVE MY FRIEND. HE CANNOT SEE THE SPIRIT OF ANTHOS WITHIN YOU AS I CAN.
PLEASE--ACCEPT MY BOW IN OFFERING.
WHOA! YONDU WOULD NEVER GIVE UP HIS BOW UNLESS...
ARISE, GOOD SIR! THOR DOTH SEEK NEITHER ADORATION NOR OFFERING--THOUGH IN TRUTH, THY GIFT DOES ME GREAT HONOR.
FOR BY THY VISAGE, THOU WOULDST BE ONE OF THE FABLED GUARDIANS OF THE GALAXY--
--WHO ONCE DID FIGHT AT THE SIDE OF CAPTAIN AMERICA AND THE BESTIAL THING!*
BUT BY THAT RECKONING, I AM IN THE FAR FUTURE!
DON'T LET IT WORRY YA, MUSCLES! THE 31ST CENTURY CAN BE FUN--IF YOU HAVE THE PROPER COMPANY!
*MARVEL TWO-IN-ONE #5--LEN.
HEY, SHOW A LITTLE CLASS, SQUIRT! IT'S NOT POLITE TO VAMP A THUNDER GOD!
CHARLIE, YOU--YOU LUMMOX! PUT ME DOWN!
DON'T MIND THEM, THOR--THEY'RE ALWAYS LIKE THAT!
I'M MAJOR VANCE ASTRO--WELCOME ABOARD THE FREEDOM'S LADY!
THE HONOR BE MINE, MAJOR!

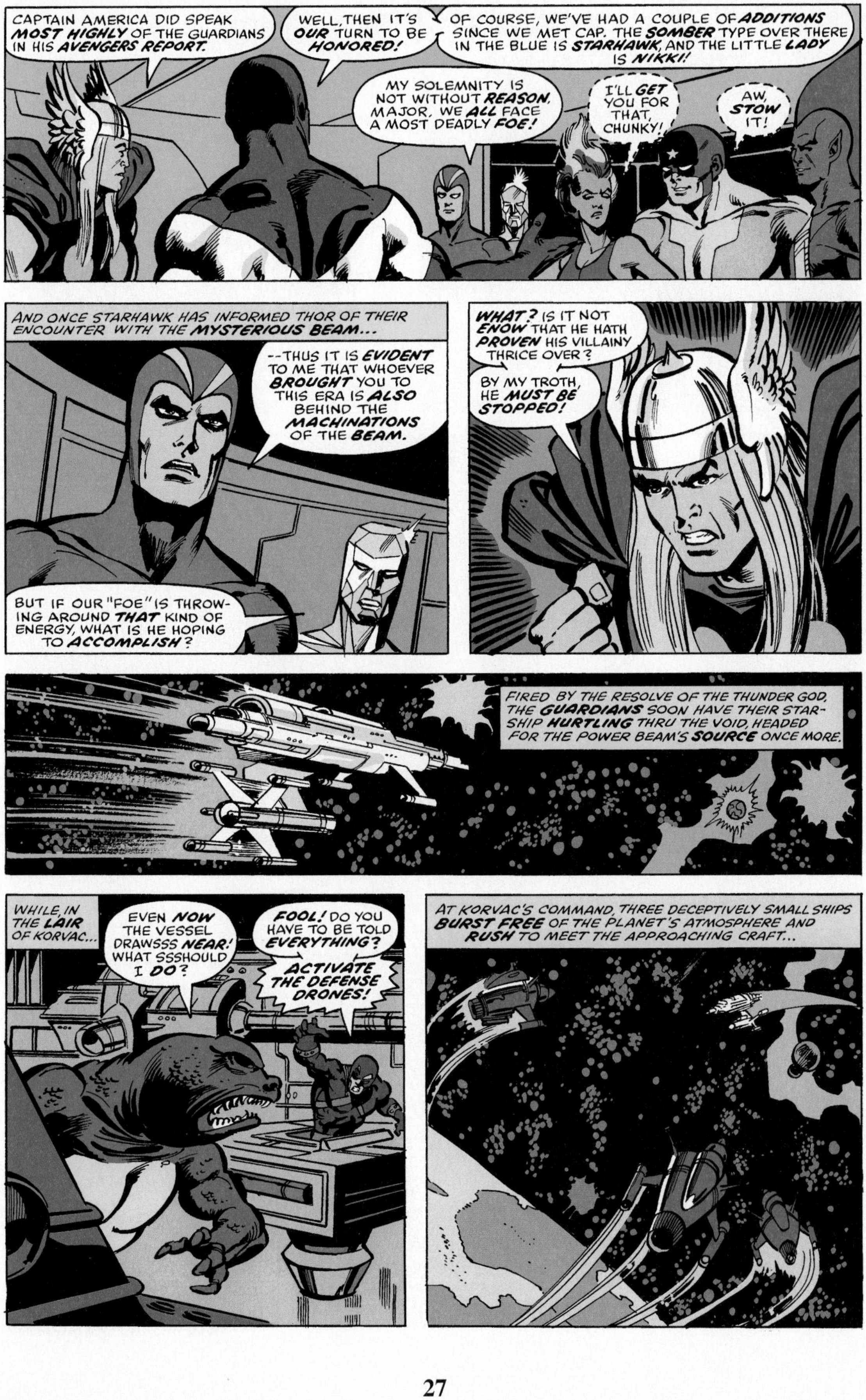
CAPTAIN AMERICA DID SPEAK MOST HIGHLY OF THE GUARDIANS IN HIS AVENGERS REPORT.
WELL, THEN IT'S OUR TURN TO BE HONORED!
OF COURSE, WE'VE HAD A COUPLE OF ADDITIONS SINCE WE MET CAP. THE SOMBER TYPE OVER THERE IN THE BLUE IS STARHAWK, AND THE LITTLE LADY IS NIKKI!
MY SOLEMNITY IS NOT WITHOUT REASON, MAJOR. WE ALL FACE A MOST DEADLY FOE!
I'LL GET YOU FOR THAT, CHUNKY!
AW, STOW IT!
AND ONCE STARHAWK HAS INFORMED THOR OF THEIR ENCOUNTER WITH THE MYSTERIOUS BEAM...
--THUS IT IS EVIDENT TO ME THAT WHOEVER BROUGHT YOU TO THIS ERA IS ALSO BEHIND THE MACHINATIONS OF THE BEAM.
BUT IF OUR "FOE" IS THROWING AROUND THAT KIND OF ENERGY, WHAT IS HE HOPING TO ACCOMPLISH?
WHAT? IS IT NOT ENOW THAT HE HATH PROVEN HIS VILLAINY THRICE OVER?
BY MY TROTH, HE MUST BE STOPPED!
FIRED BY THE RESOLVE OF THE THUNDER GOD, THE GUARDIANS SOON HAVE THEIR STARSHIP HURTLING THRU THE VOID, HEADED FOR THE POWER BEAM'S SOURCE ONCE MORE.
WHILE, IN THE LAIR OF KORVAC...
EVEN NOW THE VESSEL DRAWSSS NEAR! WHAT SSSHOULD I DO?
FOOL! DO YOU HAVE TO BE TOLD EVERYTHING?
ACTIVATE THE DEFENSE DRONES!
AT KORVAC'S COMMAND, THREE DECEPTIVELY SMALL SHIPS BURST FREE OF THE PLANET'S ATMOSPHERE AND RUSH TO MEET THE APPROACHING CRAFT...

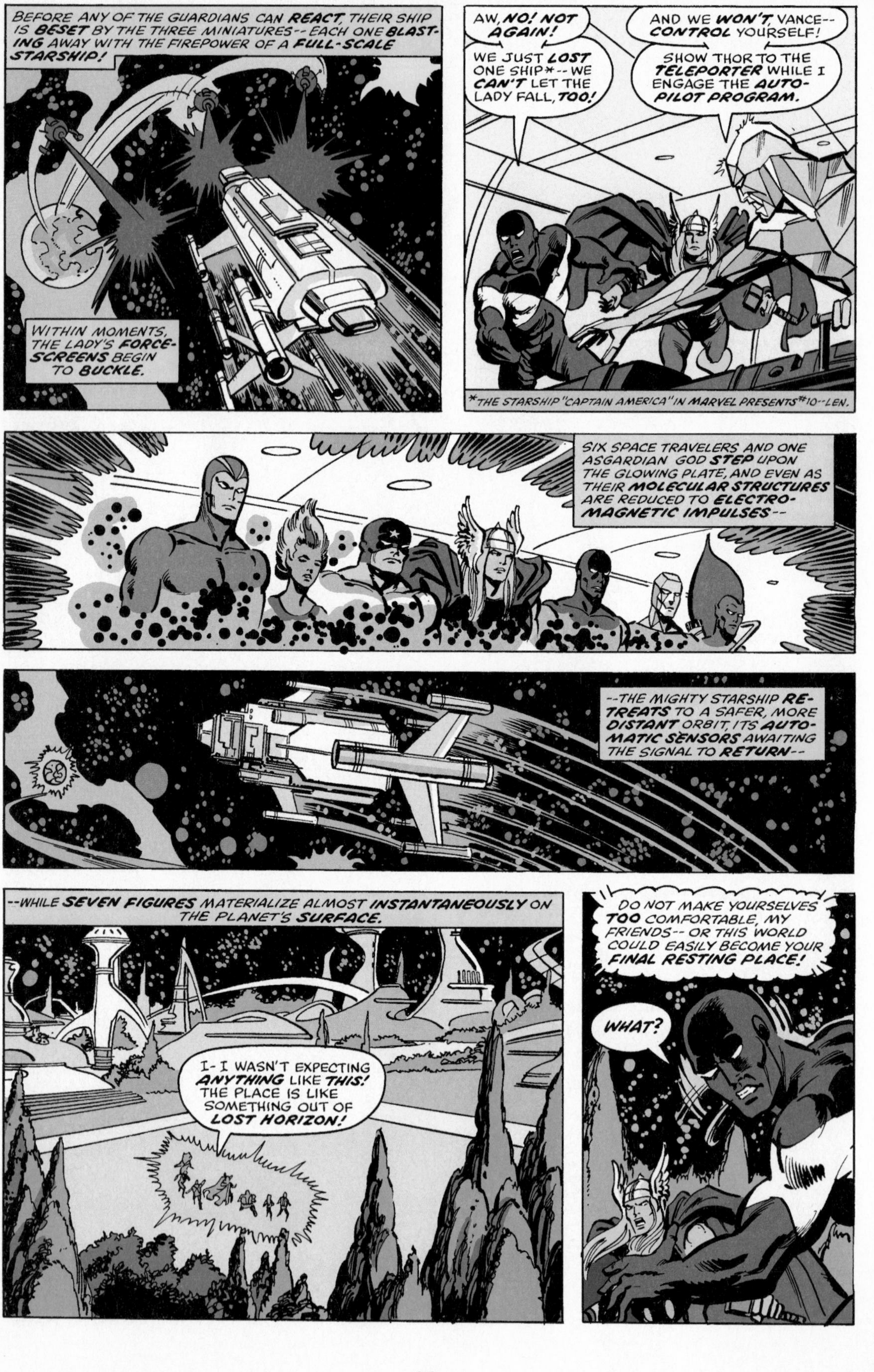

BEFORE ANY OF THE GUARDIANS CAN REACT, THEIR SHIP IS BESET BY THE THREE MINIATURES-- EACH ONE BLASTING AWAY WITH THE FIREPOWER OF A FULL-SCALE STARSHIP!
WITHIN MOMENTS, THE LADY'S FORCE-SCREENS BEGIN TO BUCKLE.
AW, NO! NOT AGAIN!
WE JUST LOST ONE SHIP*-- WE CAN'T LET THE LADY FALL, TOO!
AND WE WON'T, VANCE-- CONTROL YOURSELF!
SHOW THOR TO THE TELEPORTER WHILE I ENGAGE THE AUTO-PILOT PROGRAM.
*THE STARSHIP "CAPTAIN AMERICA" IN MARVEL PRESENTS #10--LEN.
SIX SPACE TRAVELERS AND ONE ASGARDIAN GOD STEP UPON THE GLOWING PLATE, AND EVEN AS THEIR MOLECULAR STRUCTURES ARE REDUCED TO ELECTRO-MAGNETIC IMPULSES--
--THE MIGHTY STARSHIP RETREATS TO A SAFER, MORE DISTANT ORBIT, ITS AUTOMATIC SENSORS AWAITING THE SIGNAL TO RETURN--
--WHILE SEVEN FIGURES MATERIALIZE ALMOST INSTANTANEOUSLY ON THE PLANET'S SURFACE.
I- I WASN'T EXPECTING ANYTHING LIKE THIS! THE PLACE IS LIKE SOMETHING OUT OF LOST HORIZON!
DO NOT MAKE YOURSELVES TOO COMFORTABLE, MY FRIENDS-- OR THIS WORLD COULD EASILY BECOME YOUR FINAL RESTING PLACE!
WHAT?

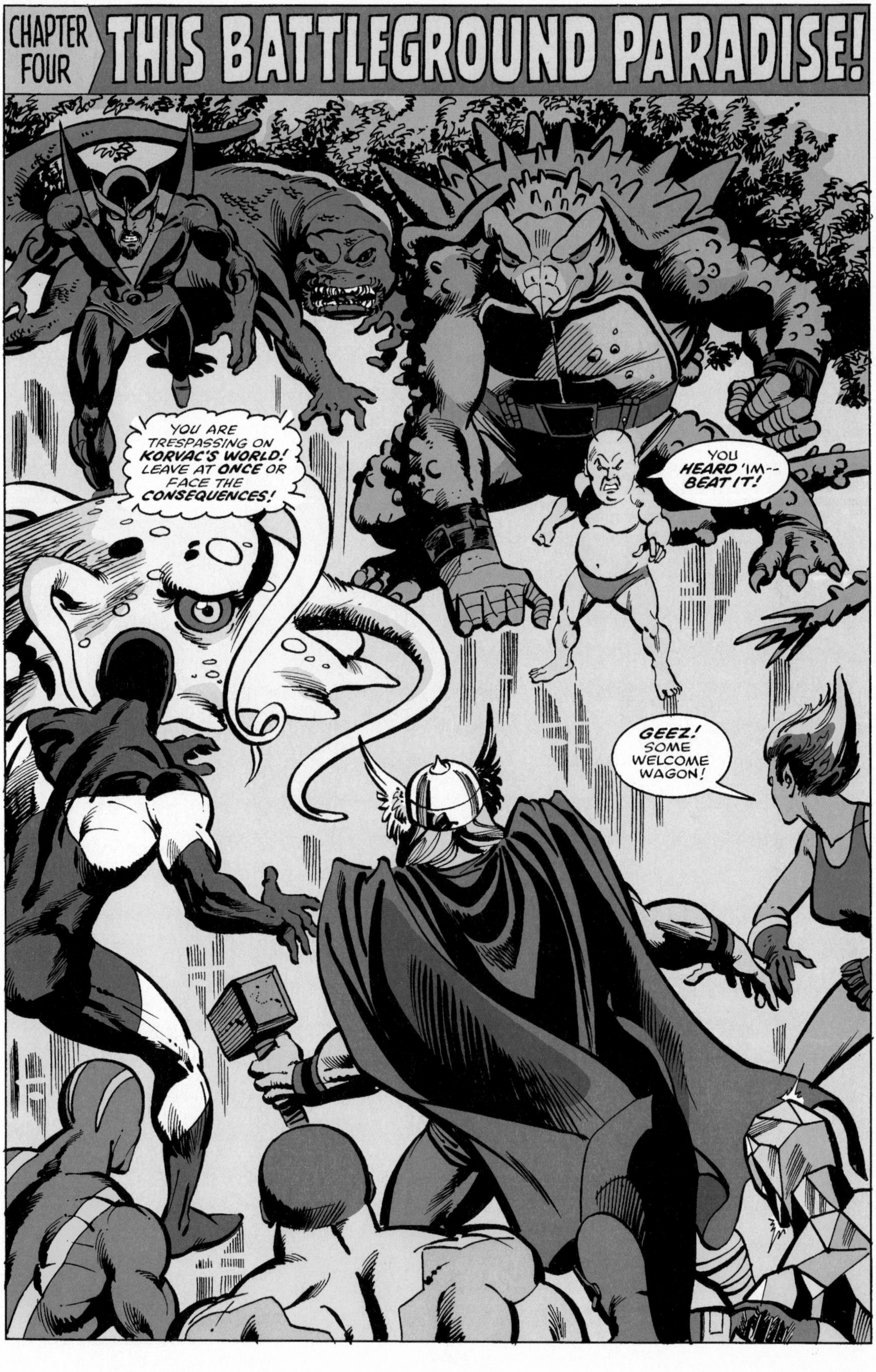
CHAPTER FOUR
THIS BATTLEGROUND PARADISE!
YOU ARE TRESPASSING ON KORVAC'S WORLD! LEAVE AT ONCE OR FACE THE CONSEQUENCES!
YOU HEARD 'IM-- BEAT IT!
GEEZ! SOME WELCOME WAGON!

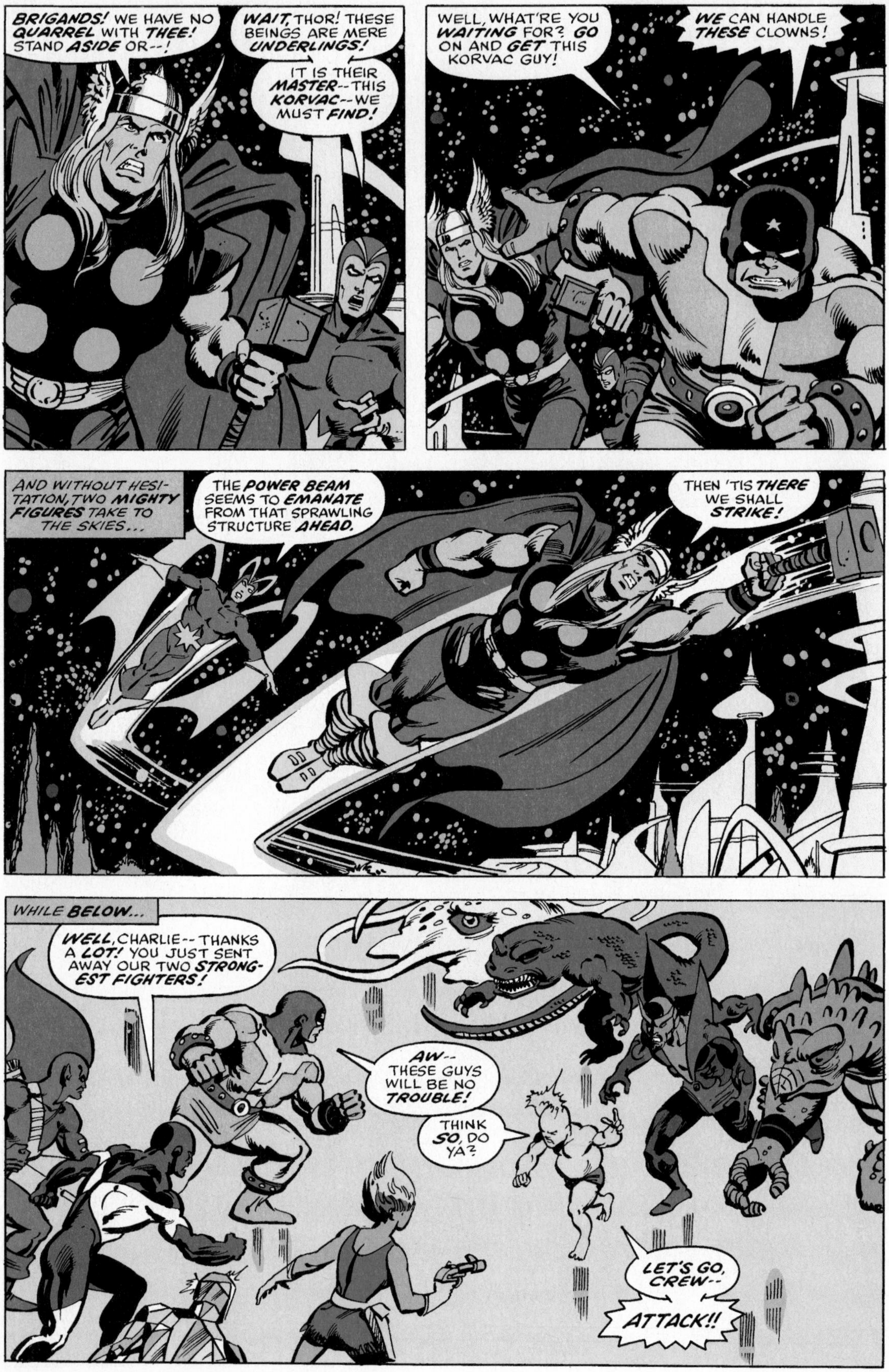
BRIGANDS! WE HAVE NO QUARREL WITH THEE! STAND ASIDE OR--!
WAIT, THOR! THESE BEINGS ARE MERE UNDERLINGS!
IT IS THEIR MASTER--THIS KORVAC--WE MUST FIND!
WELL, WHAT'RE YOU WAITING FOR? GO ON AND GET THIS KORVAC GUY!
WE CAN HANDLE THESE CLOWNS!
AND WITHOUT HESITATION, TWO MIGHTY FIGURES TAKE TO THE SKIES...
THE POWER BEAM SEEMS TO EMANATE FROM THAT SPRAWLING STRUCTURE AHEAD.
THEN 'TIS THERE WE SHALL STRIKE!
WHILE BELOW...
WELL, CHARLIE-- THANKS A LOT! YOU JUST SENT AWAY OUR TWO STRONGEST FIGHTERS!
AW-- THESE GUYS WILL BE NO TROUBLE!
THINK SO, DO YA?
LET'S GO, CREW--
ATTACK!!

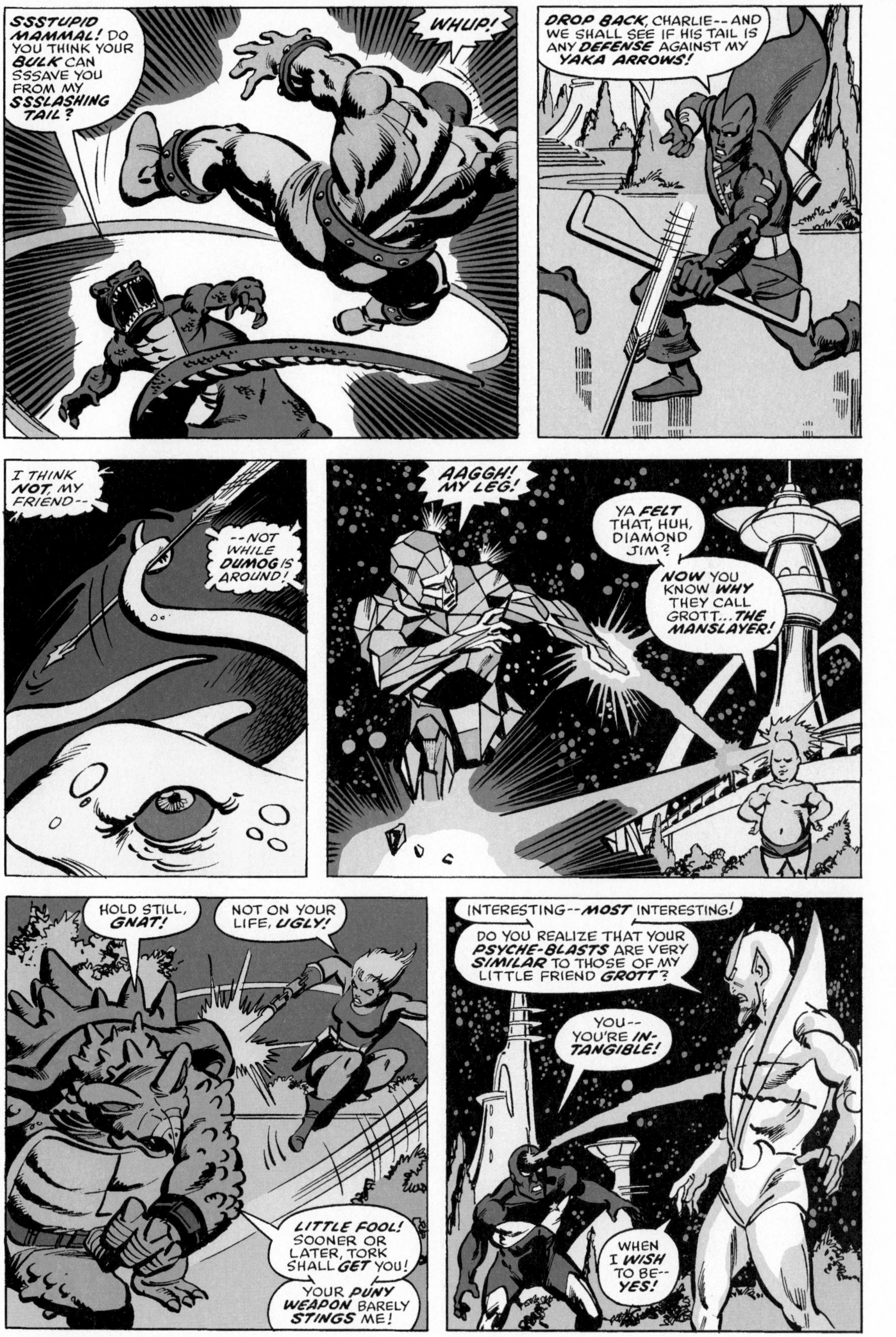
SSSTUPID MAMMAL! DO YOU THINK YOUR BULK CAN SSSAVE YOU FROM MY SSSLASHING TAIL?
WHUP!
DROP BACK, CHARLIE-- AND WE SHALL SEE IF HIS TAIL IS ANY DEFENSE AGAINST MY YAKA ARROWS!
I THINK NOT, MY FRIEND--
--NOT WHILE DUMOG IS AROUND!
AAGGH! MY LEG!
YA FELT THAT, HUH, DIAMOND JIM?
NOW YOU KNOW WHY THEY CALL GROTT...THE MANSLAYER!
HOLD STILL, GNAT!
NOT ON YOUR LIFE, UGLY!
LITTLE FOOL! SOONER OR LATER, TORK SHALL GET YOU!
YOUR PUNY WEAPON BARELY STINGS ME!
INTERESTING--MOST INTERESTING!
DO YOU REALIZE THAT YOUR PSYCHE-BLASTS ARE VERY SIMILAR TO THOSE OF MY LITTLE FRIEND GROTT?
YOU-- YOU'RE IN-TANGIBLE!
WHEN I WISH TO BE-- YES!

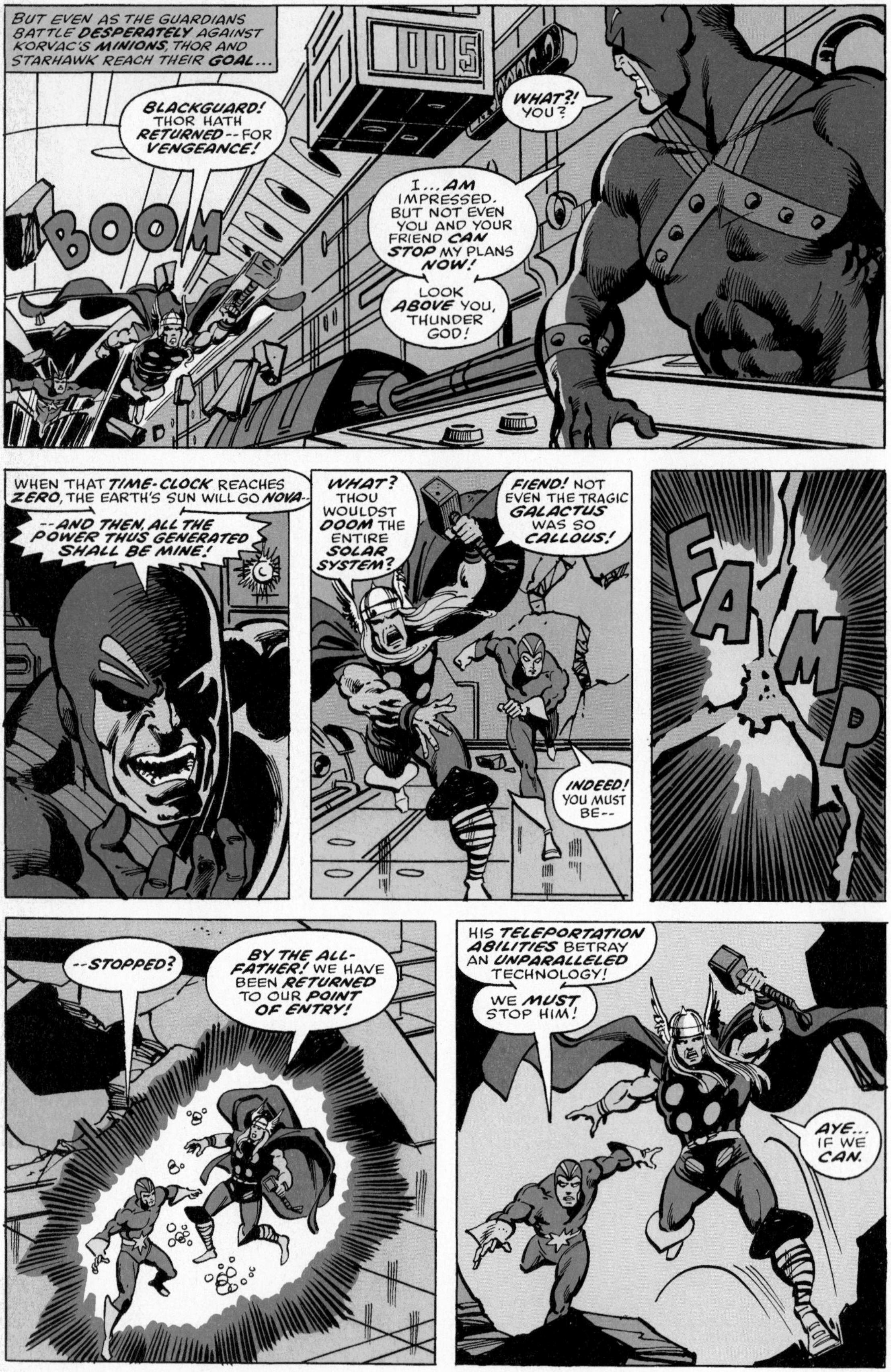

BUT EVEN AS THE GUARDIANS BATTLE DESPERATELY AGAINST KORVAC'S MINIONS, THOR AND STARHAWK REACH THEIR GOAL...
BLACKGUARD! THOR HATH RETURNED--FOR VENGEANCE!
BOOM
WHAT?! YOU?
I...AM IMPRESSED. BUT NOT EVEN YOU AND YOUR FRIEND CAN STOP MY PLANS NOW!
LOOK ABOVE YOU, THUNDER GOD!
WHEN THAT TIME-CLOCK REACHES ZERO, THE EARTH'S SUN WILL GO NOVA--
--AND THEN, ALL THE POWER THUS GENERATED SHALL BE MINE!
WHAT? THOU WOULDST DOOM THE ENTIRE SOLAR SYSTEM?
FIEND! NOT EVEN THE TRAGIC GALACTUS WAS SO CALLOUS!
INDEED! YOU MUST BE--
FAMP
--STOPPED?
BY THE ALL-FATHER! WE HAVE BEEN RETURNED TO OUR POINT OF ENTRY!
HIS TELEPORTATION ABILITIES BETRAY AN UNPARALLELED TECHNOLOGY!
WE MUST STOP HIM!
AYE... IF WE CAN.

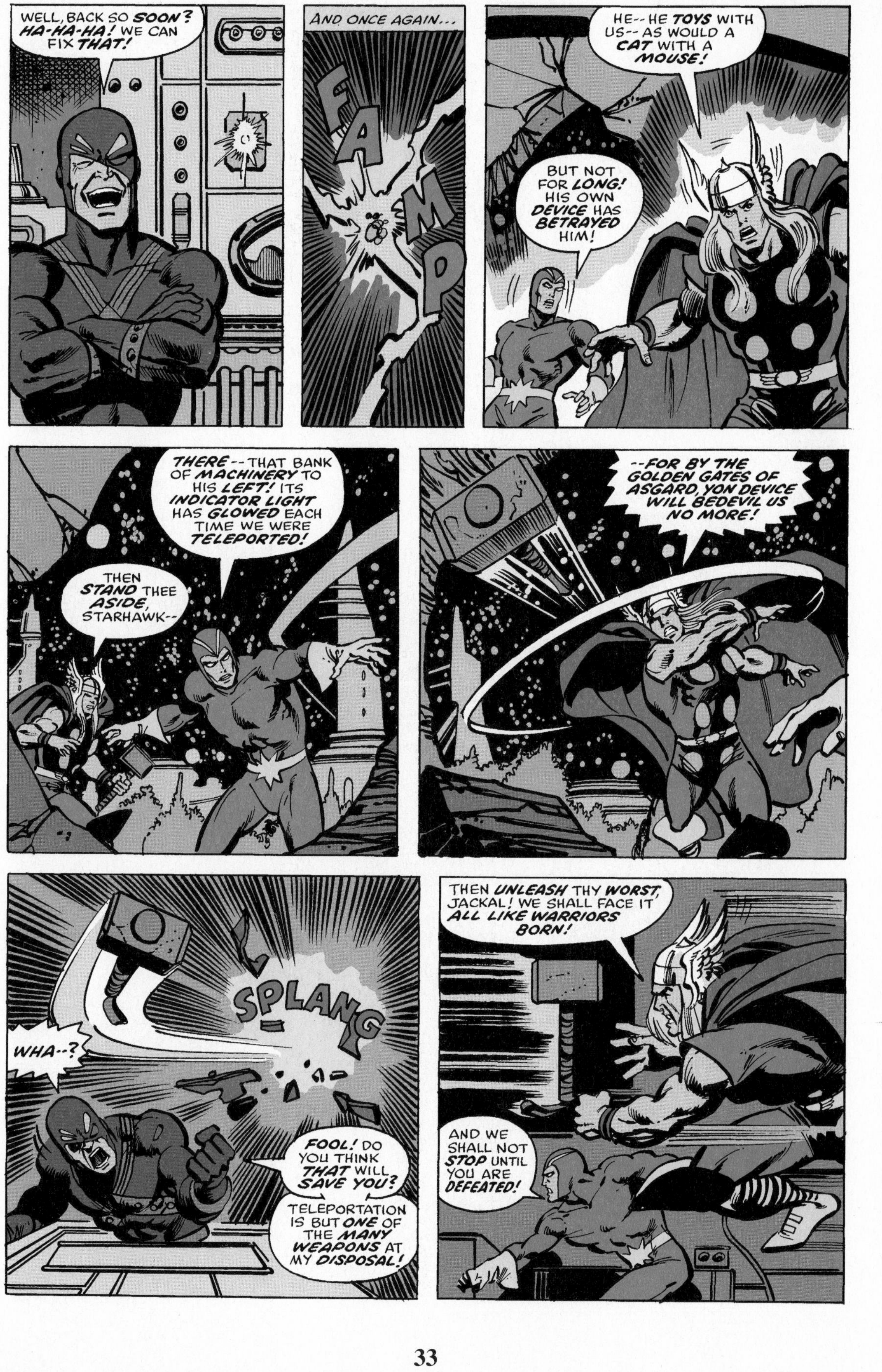
WELL, BACK SO SOON? HA-HA-HA! WE CAN FIX THAT!
AND ONCE AGAIN...
FAMP
HE--HE TOYS WITH US--AS WOULD A CAT WITH A MOUSE!
BUT NOT FOR LONG! HIS OWN DEVICE HAS BETRAYED HIM!
THERE--THAT BANK OF MACHINERY TO HIS LEFT! ITS INDICATOR LIGHT HAS GLOWED EACH TIME WE WERE TELEPORTED!
THEN STAND THEE ASIDE, STARHAWK--
--FOR BY THE GOLDEN GATES OF ASGARD, YON DEVICE WILL BEDEVIL US NO MORE!
SPLANG
WHA--?
FOOL! DO YOU THINK THAT WILL SAVE YOU?
TELEPORTATION IS BUT ONE OF THE MANY WEAPONS AT MY DISPOSAL!
THEN UNLEASH THY WORST, JACKAL! WE SHALL FACE IT ALL LIKE WARRIORS BORN!
AND WE SHALL NOT STOP UNTIL YOU ARE DEFEATED!

WELL, THEN-- LET'S SEE HOW YOU *FARE* AGAINST THE *IMPENETRABLE* BARRIER OF MY *STASIS FIELD!*

DEMON! I'LL--!

NO, THOR-- *WAIT!* BRUTE STRENGTH IS *USELESS* AGAINST SUCH A *FIELD!*

BUT *NOT SO* THE *POWER* OF A *LIVING STAR!*

I AM THE *LIGHT* AND THE *GIVER OF LIGHT*-- AND NO MERE *ENERGY FIELD* CAN LONG STAND THE *FULL FURY* OF MY POWER!

NO! KORVAC SHALL *NOT* BE STOPPED! I'VE COME *TOO FAR!* YOU SHALL *INTRUDE* UPON MY *WONDERWORLD* NO *FURTHER!*

I WILL NOT *LET* YOU DE-STROY THIS *PARADISE!*

NAY, SIRRAH! 'TIS NOT A *PARADISE* THAT IS BUILT ON THE *BODIES* OF *INNOCENT BEINGS!*

THERE IS BUT *ONE WORD* FOR SUCH AN *ACT* AS THINE-- *MADNESS!*

THOU ART AS *MAD* AS THE *TERRORISTS* OF YORE--SPEAKING OF LIBERTY, BUT DEALING IN *DEATH!*

YOU *MISJUDGE* ME, THUNDER GOD!

COULD A *MADMAN* DEVISE *THIS?*

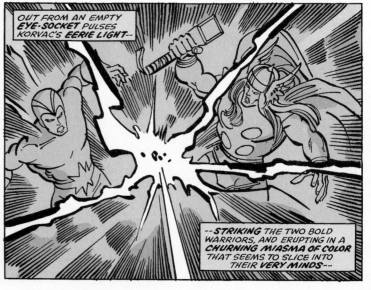

OUT FROM AN EMPTY *EYE-SOCKET* PULSES KORVAC'S *EERIE LIGHT*--

--STRIKING THE TWO BOLD WARRIORS, AND ERUPTING IN A *CHURNING MIASMA OF COLOR* THAT SEEMS TO SLICE INTO THEIR *VERY MINDS*--

34

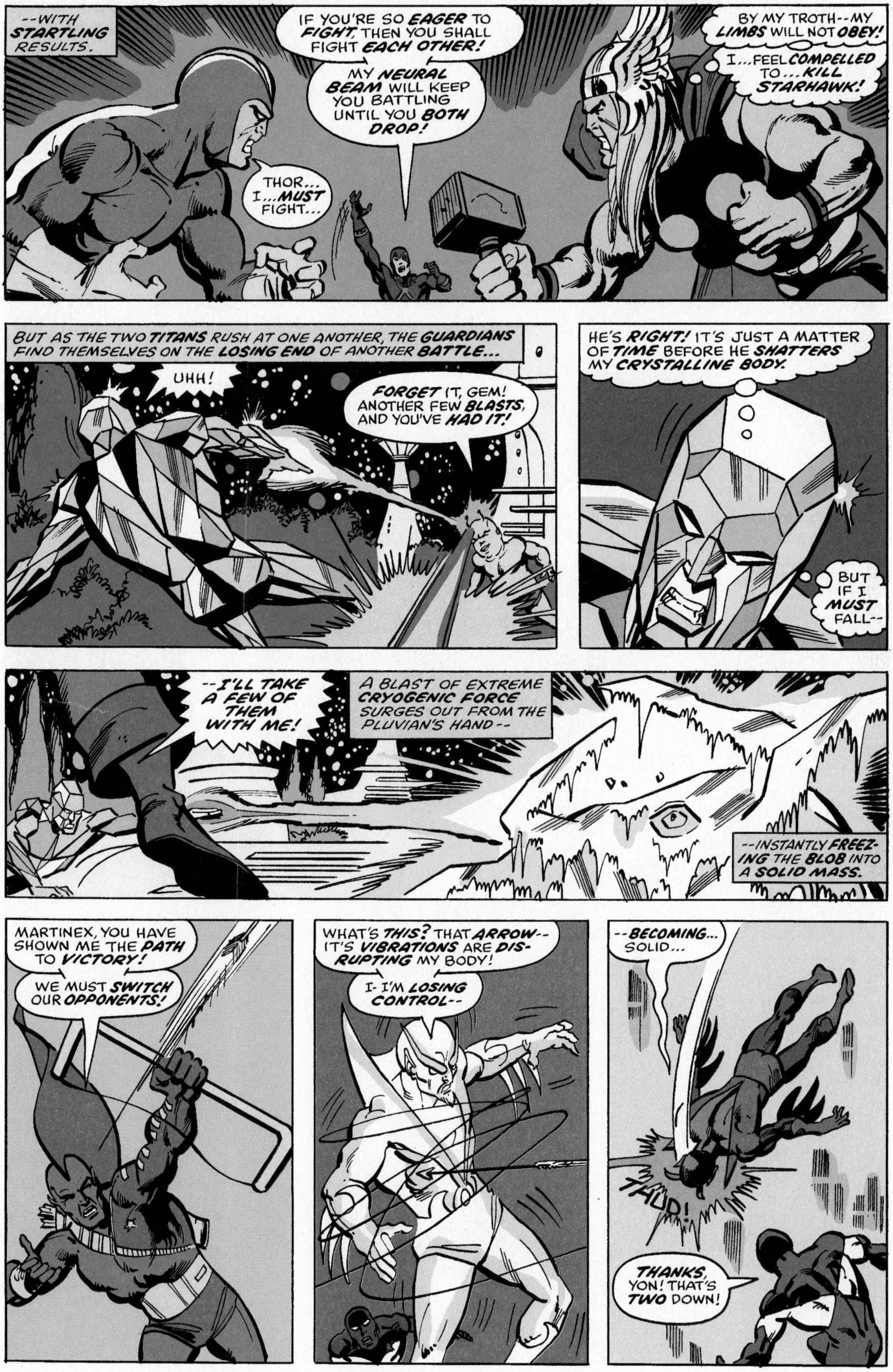
--WITH STARTLING RESULTS.
IF YOU'RE SO EAGER TO FIGHT, THEN YOU SHALL FIGHT EACH OTHER!
MY NEURAL BEAM WILL KEEP YOU BATTLING UNTIL YOU BOTH DROP!
BY MY TROTH--MY LIMBS WILL NOT OBEY!
I...FEEL COMPELLED TO...KILL STARHAWK!
THOR... I...MUST FIGHT...
BUT AS THE TWO TITANS RUSH AT ONE ANOTHER, THE GUARDIANS FIND THEMSELVES ON THE LOSING END OF ANOTHER BATTLE...
UHH!
FORGET IT, GEM! ANOTHER FEW BLASTS, AND YOU'VE HAD IT!
HE'S RIGHT! IT'S JUST A MATTER OF TIME BEFORE HE SHATTERS MY CRYSTALLINE BODY.
BUT IF I MUST FALL--
--I'LL TAKE A FEW OF THEM WITH ME!
A BLAST OF EXTREME CRYOGENIC FORCE SURGES OUT FROM THE PLUVIAN'S HAND--
--INSTANTLY FREEZING THE BLOB INTO A SOLID MASS.
MARTINEX, YOU HAVE SHOWN ME THE PATH TO VICTORY!
WE MUST SWITCH OUR OPPONENTS!
WHAT'S THIS? THAT ARROW--IT'S VIBRATIONS ARE DISRUPTING MY BODY!
I- I'M LOSING CONTROL--
--BECOMING... SOLID...
THUD!
THANKS, YON! THAT'S TWO DOWN!

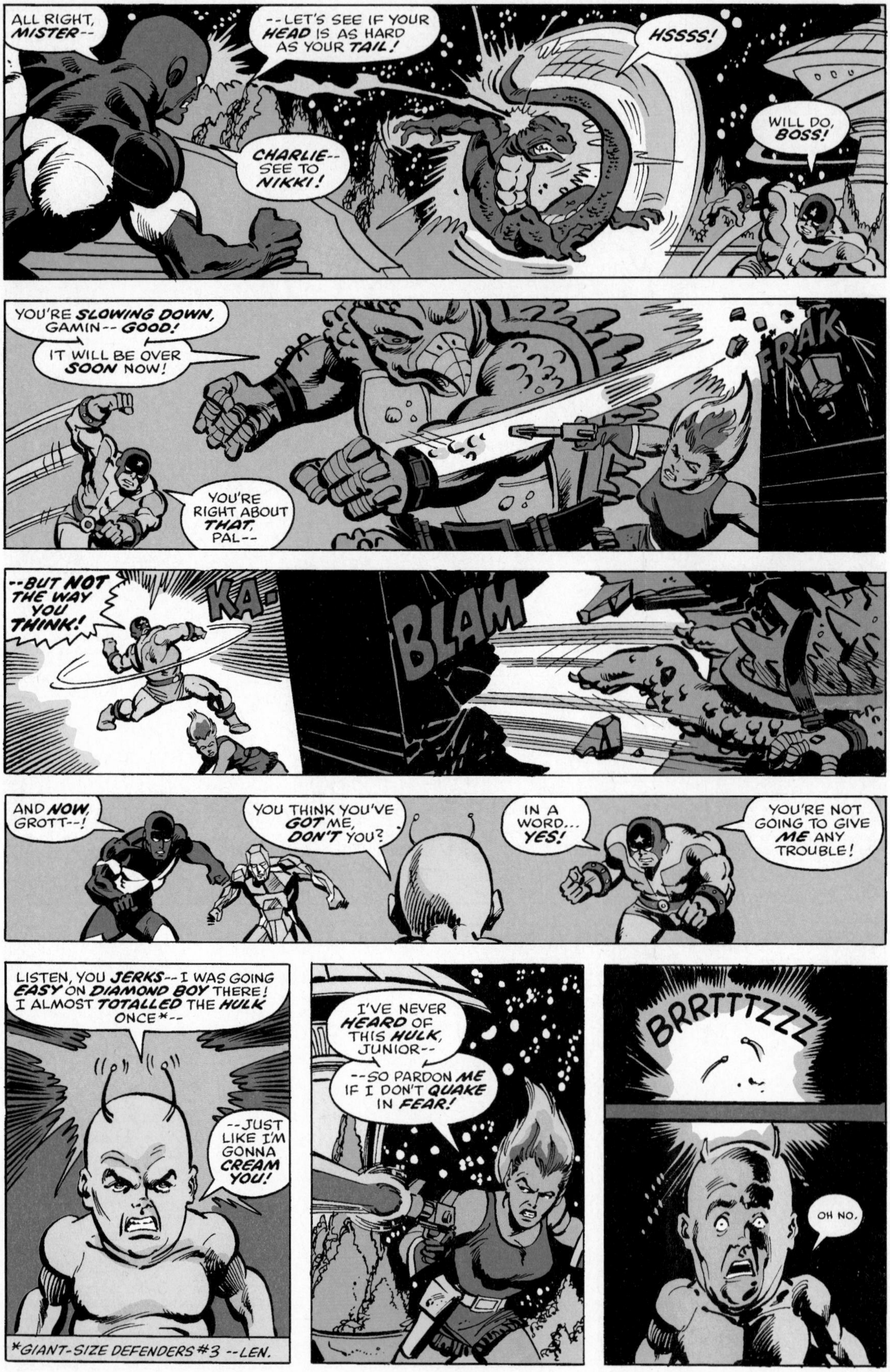
ALL RIGHT, MISTER--
--LET'S SEE IF YOUR HEAD IS AS HARD AS YOUR TAIL!
HSSSS!
CHARLIE-- SEE TO NIKKI!
WILL DO, BOSS!
YOU'RE SLOWING DOWN, GAMIN-- GOOD!
IT WILL BE OVER SOON NOW!
FRAK
YOU'RE RIGHT ABOUT THAT, PAL--
--BUT NOT THE WAY YOU THINK!
KA-
BLAM
AND NOW, GROTT--!
YOU THINK YOU'VE GOT ME, DON'T YOU?
IN A WORD... YES!
YOU'RE NOT GOING TO GIVE ME ANY TROUBLE!
LISTEN, YOU JERKS-- I WAS GOING EASY ON DIAMOND BOY THERE! I ALMOST TOTALLED THE HULK ONCE*--
--JUST LIKE I'M GONNA CREAM YOU!
*GIANT-SIZE DEFENDERS #3 --LEN.
I'VE NEVER HEARD OF THIS HULK, JUNIOR--
--SO PARDON ME IF I DON'T QUAKE IN FEAR!
BRRTTTZZZZ
OH NO.

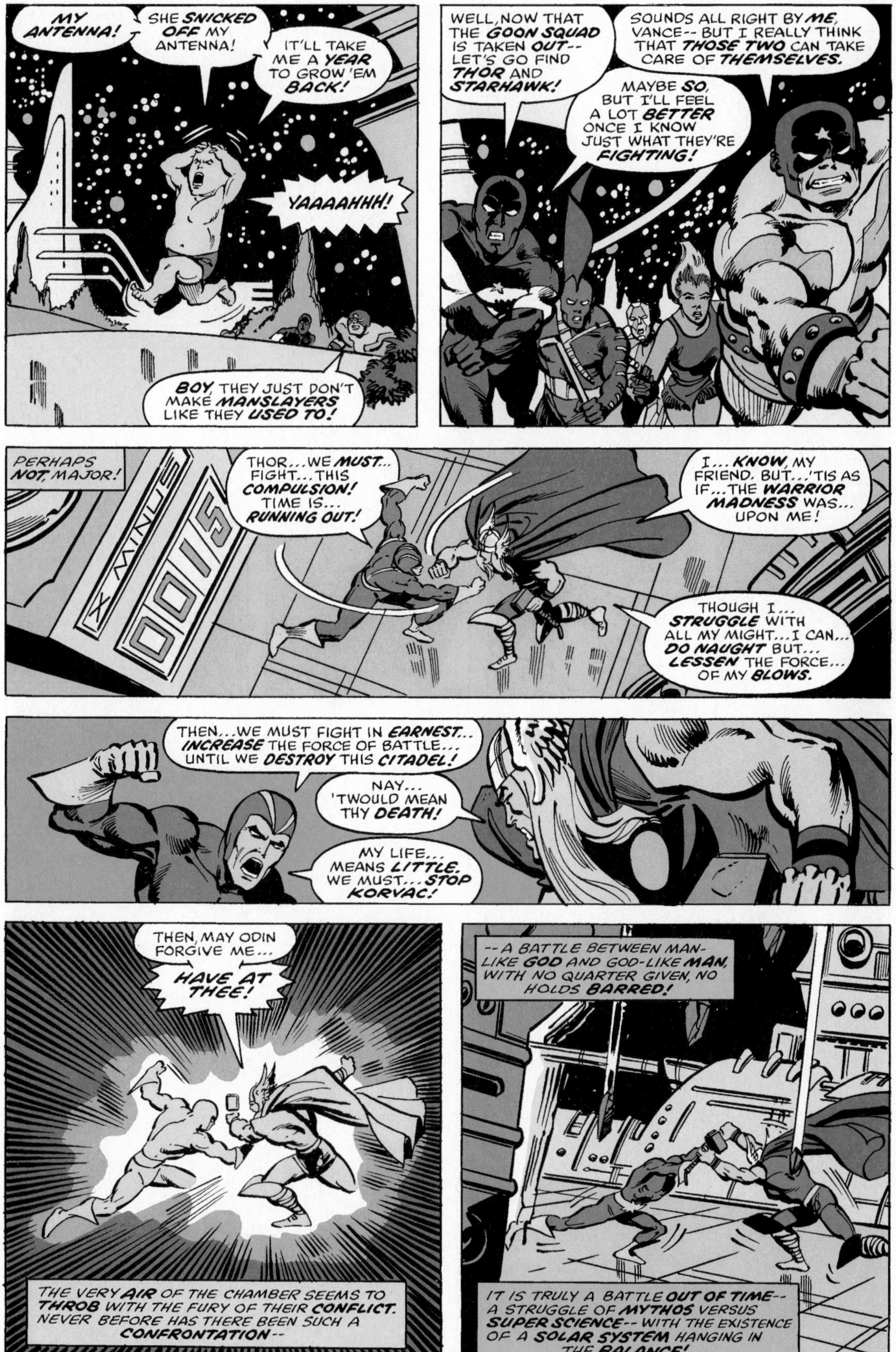
MY ANTENNA!
SHE SNICKED OFF MY ANTENNA!
IT'LL TAKE ME A YEAR TO GROW 'EM BACK!
YAAAAHHH!
BOY, THEY JUST DON'T MAKE MANSLAYERS LIKE THEY USED TO!
WELL, NOW THAT THE GOON SQUAD IS TAKEN OUT-- LET'S GO FIND THOR AND STARHAWK!
SOUNDS ALL RIGHT BY ME, VANCE-- BUT I REALLY THINK THAT THOSE TWO CAN TAKE CARE OF THEMSELVES.
MAYBE SO, BUT I'LL FEEL A LOT BETTER ONCE I KNOW JUST WHAT THEY'RE FIGHTING!
PERHAPS NOT, MAJOR!
THOR... WE MUST... FIGHT... THIS COMPULSION! TIME IS... RUNNING OUT!
I... KNOW, MY FRIEND. BUT... 'TIS AS IF... THE WARRIOR MADNESS WAS... UPON ME!
X MINUS 0015
THOUGH I... STRUGGLE WITH ALL MY MIGHT... I CAN... DO NAUGHT BUT... LESSEN THE FORCE... OF MY BLOWS.
THEN... WE MUST FIGHT IN EARNEST... INCREASE THE FORCE OF BATTLE... UNTIL WE DESTROY THIS CITADEL!
NAY... 'TWOULD MEAN THY DEATH!
MY LIFE... MEANS LITTLE. WE MUST... STOP KORVAC!
THEN, MAY ODIN FORGIVE ME...
HAVE AT THEE!
THE VERY AIR OF THE CHAMBER SEEMS TO THROB WITH THE FURY OF THEIR CONFLICT. NEVER BEFORE HAS THERE BEEN SUCH A CONFRONTATION--
--A BATTLE BETWEEN MAN-LIKE GOD AND GOD-LIKE MAN, WITH NO QUARTER GIVEN, NO HOLDS BARRED!
IT IS TRULY A BATTLE OUT OF TIME-- A STRUGGLE OF MYTHOS VERSUS SUPER SCIENCE-- WITH THE EXISTENCE OF A SOLAR SYSTEM HANGING IN THE BALANCE!

THIS IS THE STUFF OF WHICH LEGENDS ARE MADE--

FRAM

THOOM

--THE SORT OF BATTLE WHICH LITERALLY BRINGS DOWN THE HOUSE!

NO! IT--IT IS NOT POSSIBLE!

MY LABS WERE BUILT TO WITHSTAND THE MIGHTIEST OF EARTHQUAKES!

IT CAN'T END THIS WAY! IT MUSTN'T!

HAVE TO FALL BACK ON MY EMERGENCY RE-SOURCES--

--TELEPORT AWAY...

FRAMP

KA-BLAM!

AND WITH KORVAC'S DEPARTURE--

THE SPELL IS LIFTED!

STARHAWK-- ART THOU--?

I...WILL BE FINE, THOR!

QUICKLY, WE MUST STOP KORVAC'S POWER BEAM!

HERE--HERE IS THE CENTRAL CONSOLE!

BUT THE CONTROLS ARE JAMMED--THE NOVA-CYCLE IS BEGINNING!

THEN THERE BE NO TIME TO SPARE!

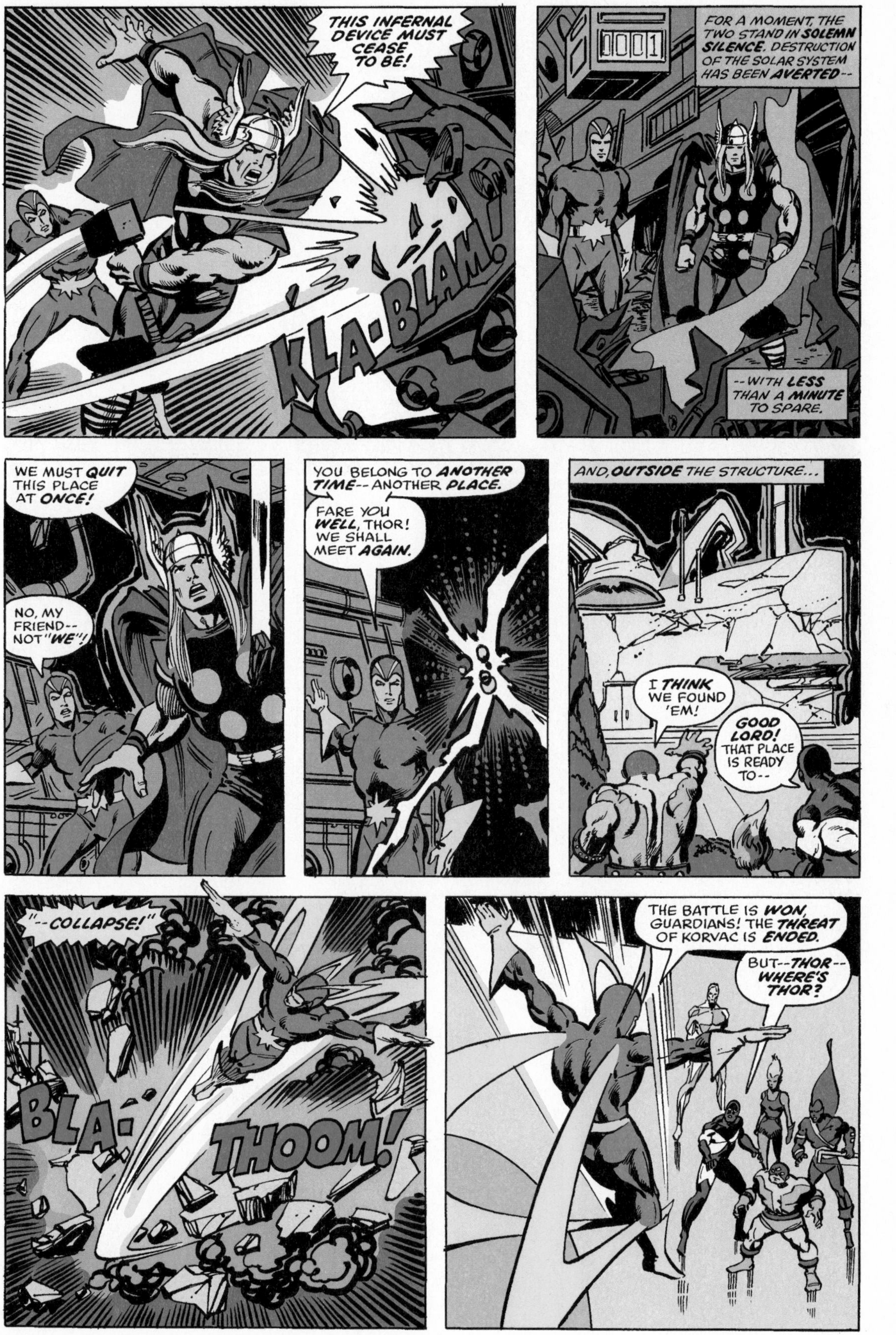
THIS INFERNAL DEVICE MUST CEASE TO BE!
KLA-BLAM!
FOR A MOMENT, THE TWO STAND IN SOLEMN SILENCE. DESTRUCTION OF THE SOLAR SYSTEM HAS BEEN AVERTED--
0001
--WITH LESS THAN A MINUTE TO SPARE.
WE MUST QUIT THIS PLACE AT ONCE!
NO, MY FRIEND-- NOT "WE"!
YOU BELONG TO ANOTHER TIME-- ANOTHER PLACE.
FARE YOU WELL, THOR! WE SHALL MEET AGAIN.
AND, OUTSIDE THE STRUCTURE...
I THINK WE FOUND 'EM!
GOOD LORD! THAT PLACE IS READY TO--
"--COLLAPSE!"
BLA-THOOM!
THE BATTLE IS WON, GUARDIANS! THE THREAT OF KORVAC IS ENDED.
BUT--THOR-- WHERE'S THOR?

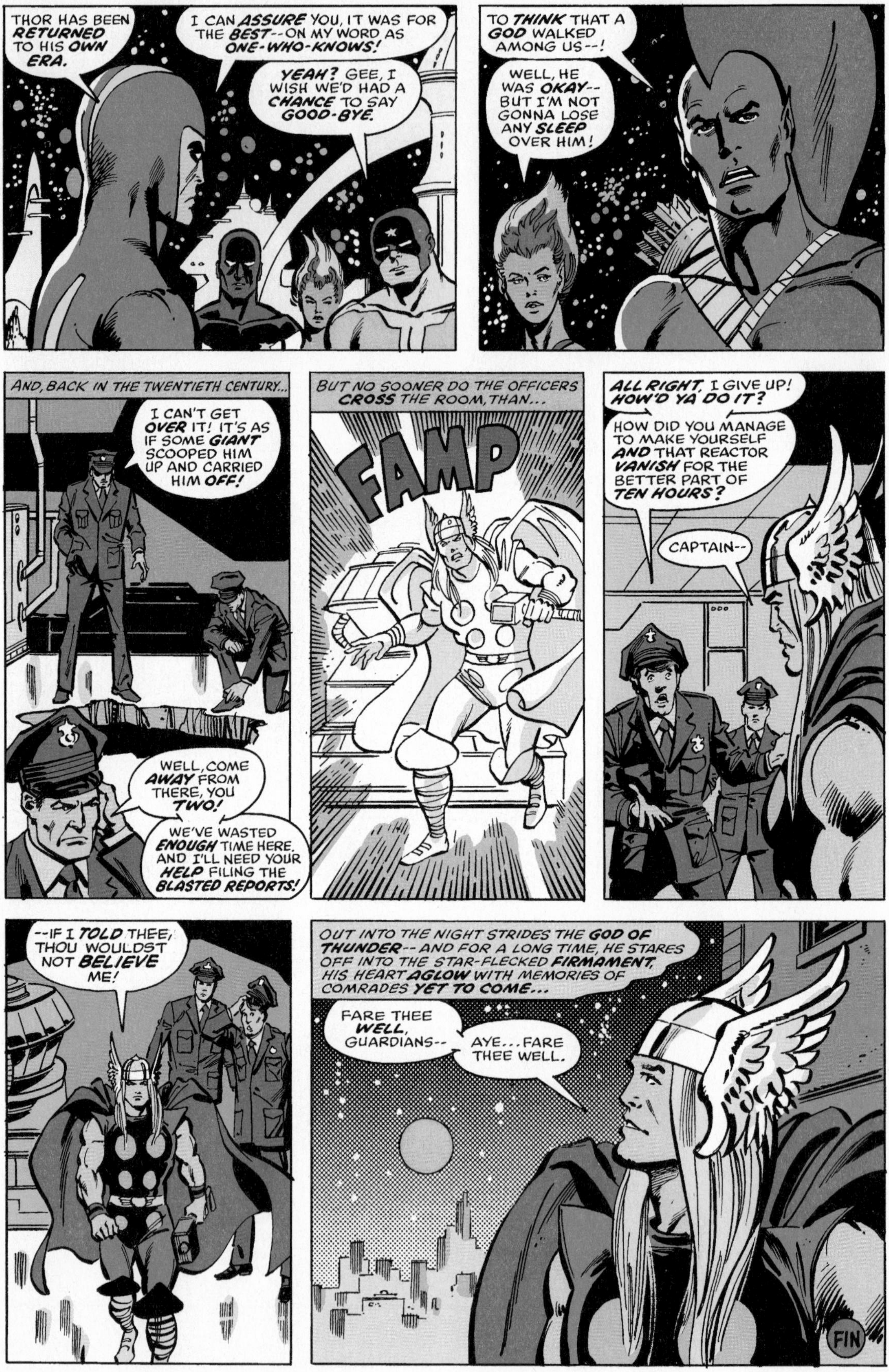
THOR HAS BEEN RETURNED TO HIS OWN ERA.
I CAN ASSURE YOU, IT WAS FOR THE BEST--ON MY WORD AS ONE-WHO-KNOWS!
YEAH? GEE, I WISH WE'D HAD A CHANCE TO SAY GOOD-BYE.
TO THINK THAT A GOD WALKED AMONG US--!
WELL, HE WAS OKAY-- BUT I'M NOT GONNA LOSE ANY SLEEP OVER HIM!
AND, BACK IN THE TWENTIETH CENTURY...
I CAN'T GET OVER IT! IT'S AS IF SOME GIANT SCOOPED HIM UP AND CARRIED HIM OFF!
WELL, COME AWAY FROM THERE, YOU TWO!
WE'VE WASTED ENOUGH TIME HERE. AND I'LL NEED YOUR HELP FILING THE BLASTED REPORTS!
BUT NO SOONER DO THE OFFICERS CROSS THE ROOM, THAN...
FAMP
ALL RIGHT, I GIVE UP! HOW'D YA DO IT?
HOW DID YOU MANAGE TO MAKE YOURSELF AND THAT REACTOR VANISH FOR THE BETTER PART OF TEN HOURS?
CAPTAIN--
--IF I TOLD THEE, THOU WOULDST NOT BELIEVE ME!
OUT INTO THE NIGHT STRIDES THE GOD OF THUNDER-- AND FOR A LONG TIME, HE STARES OFF INTO THE STAR-FLECKED FIRMAMENT, HIS HEART AGLOW WITH MEMORIES OF COMRADES YET TO COME...
FARE THEE WELL, GUARDIANS--
AYE...FARE THEE WELL.
FIN

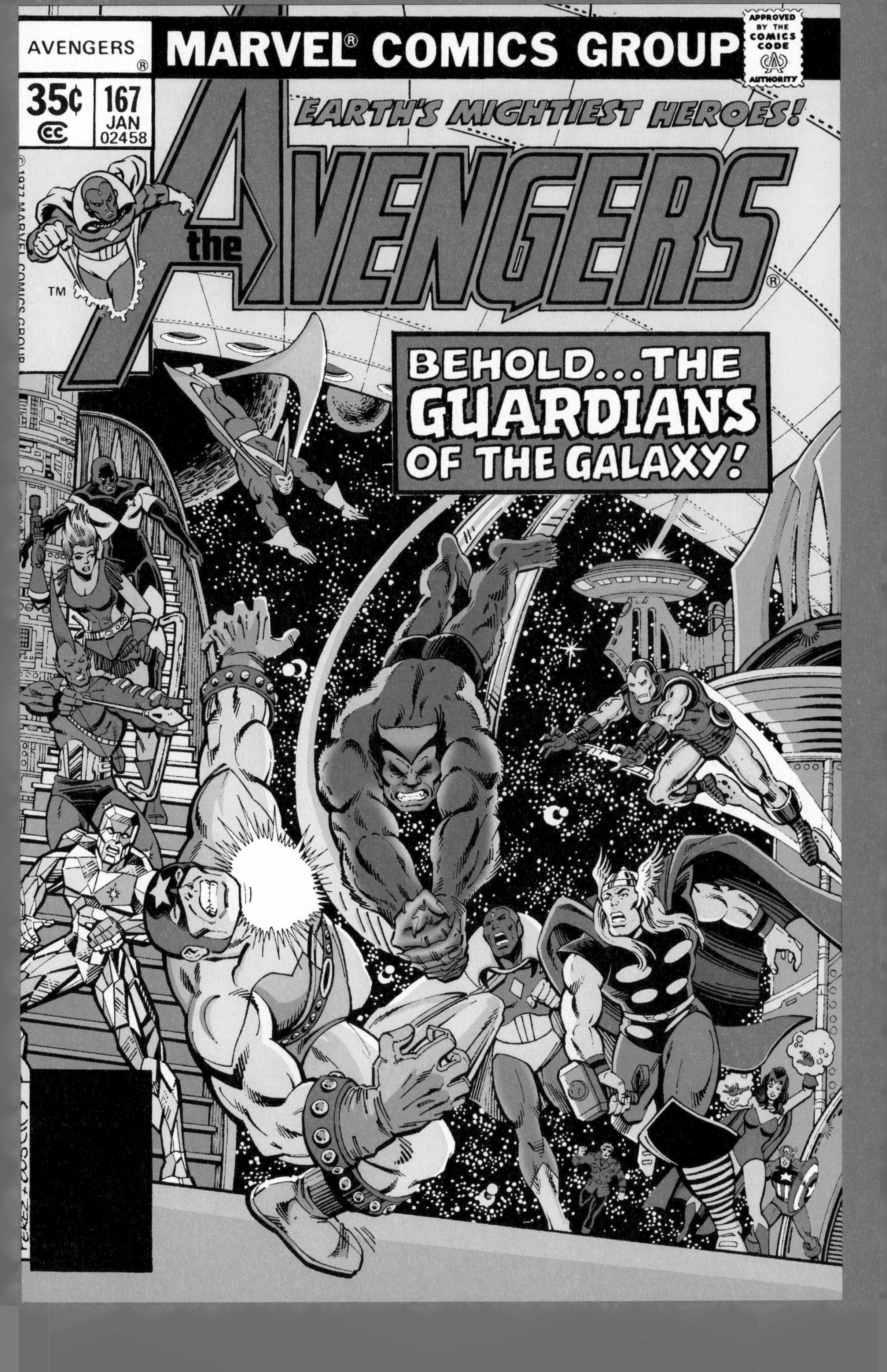
AVENGERS ®
MARVEL® COMICS GROUP
APPROVED BY THE COMICS CODE AUTHORITY
35¢
167
JAN
02458
EARTH'S MIGHTIEST HEROES!
the AVENGERS®
TM
BEHOLD...THE GUARDIANS OF THE GALAXY!
© 1977 MARVEL COMICS GROUP

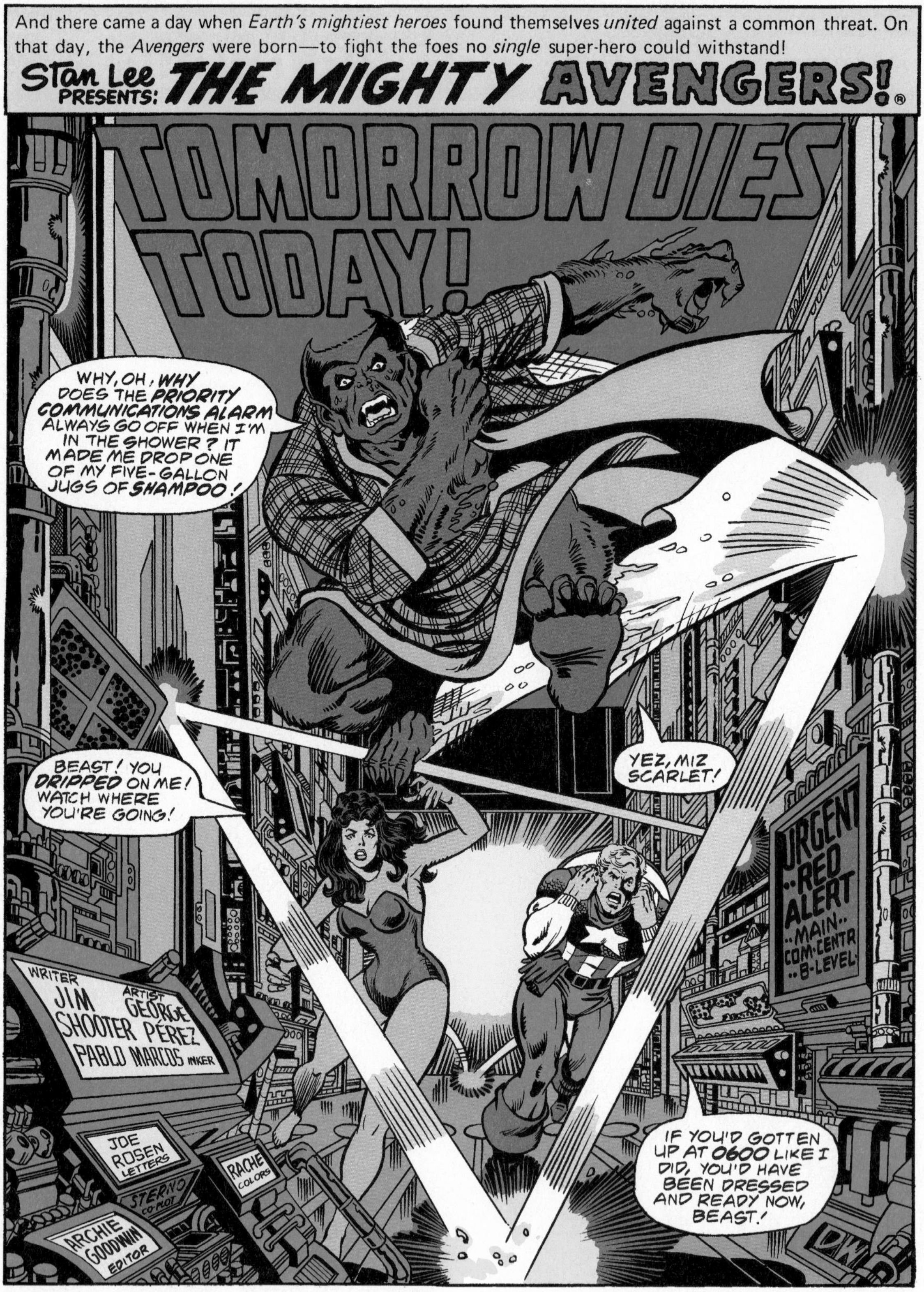
And there came a day when Earth's mightiest heroes found themselves united against a common threat. On that day, the Avengers were born—to fight the foes no single super-hero could withstand!
Stan Lee PRESENTS: THE MIGHTY AVENGERS!®
TOMORROW DIES TODAY!
WHY, OH, WHY DOES THE PRIORITY COMMUNICATIONS ALARM ALWAYS GO OFF WHEN I'M IN THE SHOWER? IT MADE ME DROP ONE OF MY FIVE-GALLON JUGS OF SHAMPOO!
BEAST! YOU DRIPPED ON ME! WATCH WHERE YOU'RE GOING!
YEZ, MIZ SCARLET!
URGENT ·· RED ALERT ·· MAIN ·· COM-CENTR ·· B-LEVEL
WRITER JIM SHOOTER
ARTIST GEORGE PÉREZ
PABLO MARCOS INKER
JOE ROSEN LETTERS
RACHE COLORS
STERNO CO-PLOT
ARCHIE GOODWIN EDITOR
IF YOU'D GOTTEN UP AT 0600 LIKE I DID, YOU'D HAVE BEEN DRESSED AND READY NOW, BEAST!

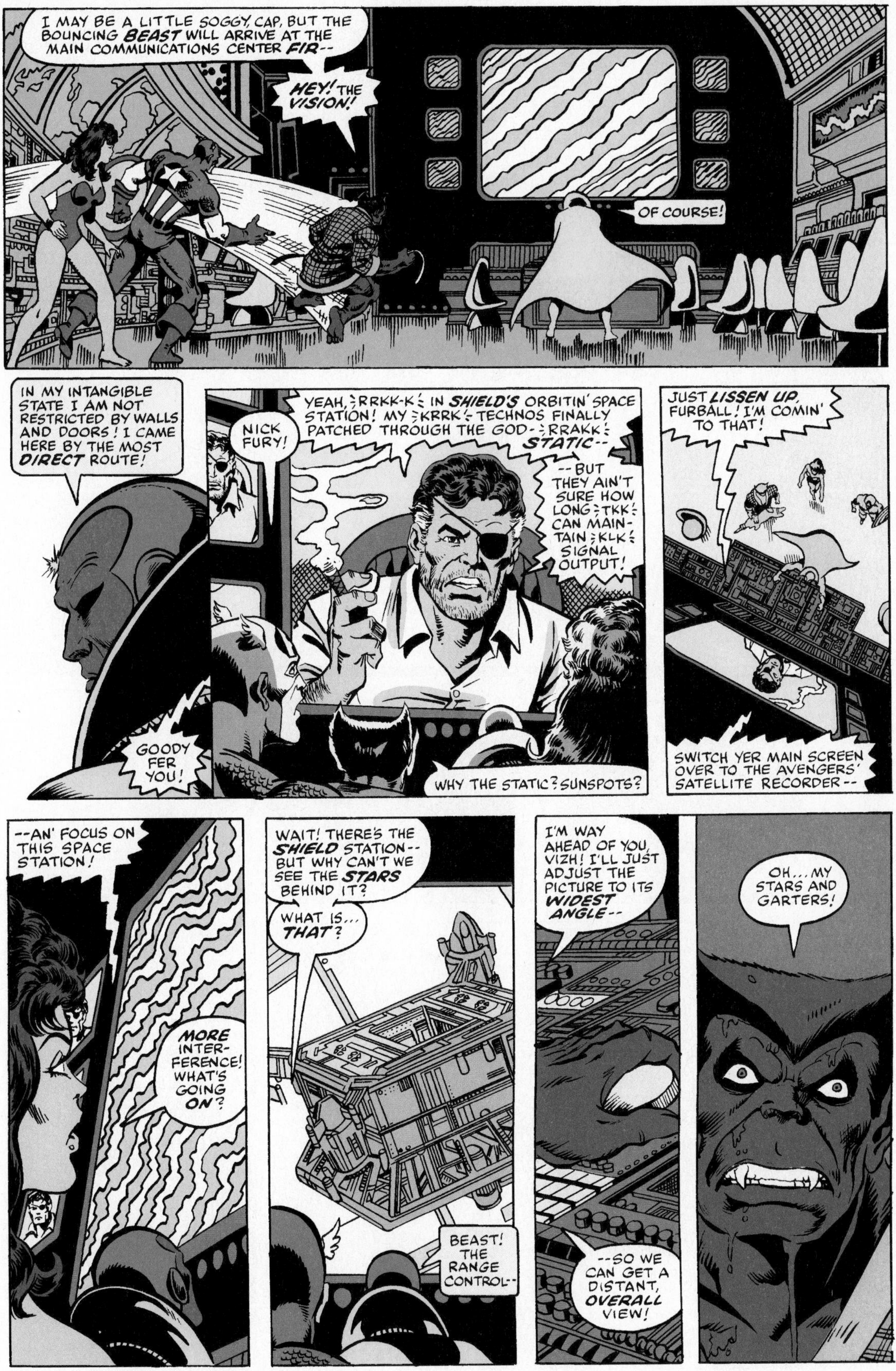
I MAY BE A LITTLE SOGGY, CAP, BUT THE BOUNCING BEAST WILL ARRIVE AT THE MAIN COMMUNICATIONS CENTER FIR--
HEY! THE VISION!
OF COURSE!
IN MY INTANGIBLE STATE I AM NOT RESTRICTED BY WALLS AND DOORS! I CAME HERE BY THE MOST DIRECT ROUTE!
GOODY FER YOU!
NICK FURY!
YEAH, RRKK-K IN SHIELD'S ORBITIN' SPACE STATION! MY KRRK TECHNOS FINALLY PATCHED THROUGH THE GOD- RRAKK STATIC--
--BUT THEY AIN'T SURE HOW LONG TKK CAN MAIN-TAIN KLK SIGNAL OUTPUT!
WHY THE STATIC? SUNSPOTS?
JUST LISSEN UP, FURBALL! I'M COMIN' TO THAT!
SWITCH YER MAIN SCREEN OVER TO THE AVENGERS' SATELLITE RECORDER--
--AN' FOCUS ON THIS SPACE STATION!
MORE INTER-FERENCE! WHAT'S GOING ON?
WAIT! THERE'S THE SHIELD STATION-- BUT WHY CAN'T WE SEE THE STARS BEHIND IT?
WHAT IS... THAT?
BEAST! THE RANGE CONTROL--
I'M WAY AHEAD OF YOU, VIZH! I'LL JUST ADJUST THE PICTURE TO ITS WIDEST ANGLE--
--SO WE CAN GET A DISTANT, OVERALL VIEW!
OH... MY STARS AND GARTERS!

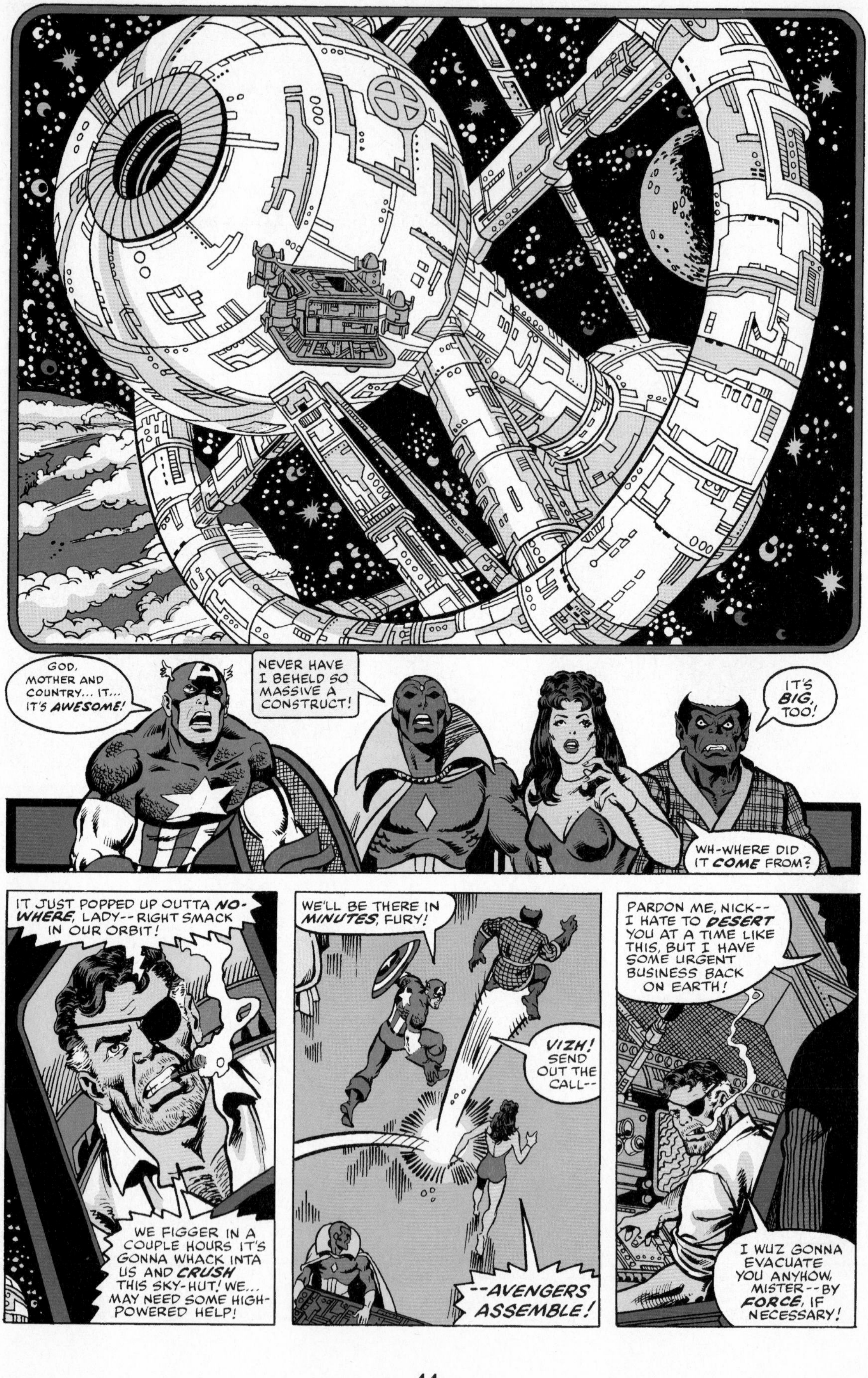
GOD, MOTHER AND COUNTRY... IT... IT'S AWESOME!
NEVER HAVE I BEHELD SO MASSIVE A CONSTRUCT!
IT'S BIG, TOO!
WH-WHERE DID IT COME FROM?
IT JUST POPPED UP OUTTA NO-WHERE, LADY--RIGHT SMACK IN OUR ORBIT!
WE FIGGER IN A COUPLE HOURS IT'S GONNA WHACK INTA US AND CRUSH THIS SKY-HUT! WE... MAY NEED SOME HIGH-POWERED HELP!
WE'LL BE THERE IN MINUTES, FURY!
VIZH! SEND OUT THE CALL--
--AVENGERS ASSEMBLE!
PARDON ME, NICK-- I HATE TO DESERT YOU AT A TIME LIKE THIS, BUT I HAVE SOME URGENT BUSINESS BACK ON EARTH!
I WUZ GONNA EVACUATE YOU ANYHOW, MISTER--BY FORCE, IF NECESSARY!

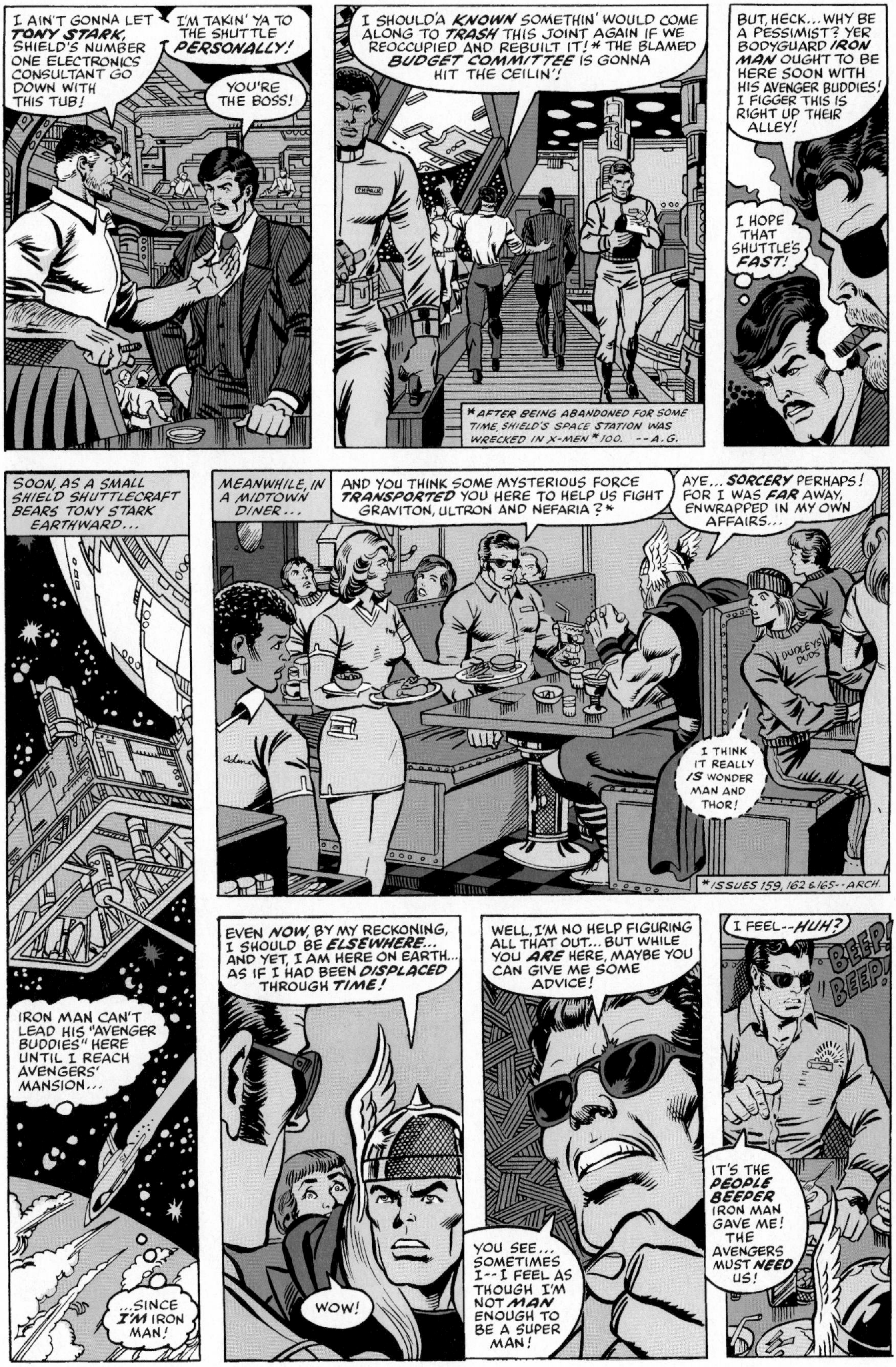

I AIN'T GONNA LET TONY STARK, SHIELD'S NUMBER ONE ELECTRONICS CONSULTANT GO DOWN WITH THIS TUB!
I'M TAKIN' YA TO THE SHUTTLE PERSONALLY!
YOU'RE THE BOSS!
I SHOULD'A KNOWN SOMETHIN' WOULD COME ALONG TO TRASH THIS JOINT AGAIN IF WE REOCCUPIED AND REBUILT IT!* THE BLAMED BUDGET COMMITTEE IS GONNA HIT THE CEILIN'!
*AFTER BEING ABANDONED FOR SOME TIME, SHIELD'S SPACE STATION WAS WRECKED IN X-MEN*100. --A.G.
BUT, HECK...WHY BE A PESSIMIST? YER BODYGUARD IRON MAN OUGHT TO BE HERE SOON WITH HIS AVENGER BUDDIES! I FIGGER THIS IS RIGHT UP THEIR ALLEY!
I HOPE THAT SHUTTLE'S FAST!
SOON, AS A SMALL SHIELD SHUTTLECRAFT BEARS TONY STARK EARTHWARD...
IRON MAN CAN'T LEAD HIS "AVENGER BUDDIES" HERE UNTIL I REACH AVENGERS' MANSION...
...SINCE I'M IRON MAN!
MEANWHILE, IN A MIDTOWN DINER...
AND YOU THINK SOME MYSTERIOUS FORCE TRANSPORTED YOU HERE TO HELP US FIGHT GRAVITON, ULTRON AND NEFARIA?*
AYE... SORCERY PERHAPS! FOR I WAS FAR AWAY, ENWRAPPED IN MY OWN AFFAIRS...
DUDLEY'S DUDS
I THINK IT REALLY IS WONDER MAN AND THOR!
*ISSUES 159, 162 & 165--ARCH.
EVEN NOW, BY MY RECKONING, I SHOULD BE ELSEWHERE... AND YET, I AM HERE ON EARTH... AS IF I HAD BEEN DISPLACED THROUGH TIME!
WOW!
WELL, I'M NO HELP FIGURING ALL THAT OUT... BUT WHILE YOU ARE HERE, MAYBE YOU CAN GIVE ME SOME ADVICE!
YOU SEE... SOMETIMES I--I FEEL AS THOUGH I'M NOT MAN ENOUGH TO BE A SUPER MAN!
I FEEL--HUH?
BEEP! BEEP!
IT'S THE PEOPLE BEEPER IRON MAN GAVE ME! THE AVENGERS MUST NEED US!

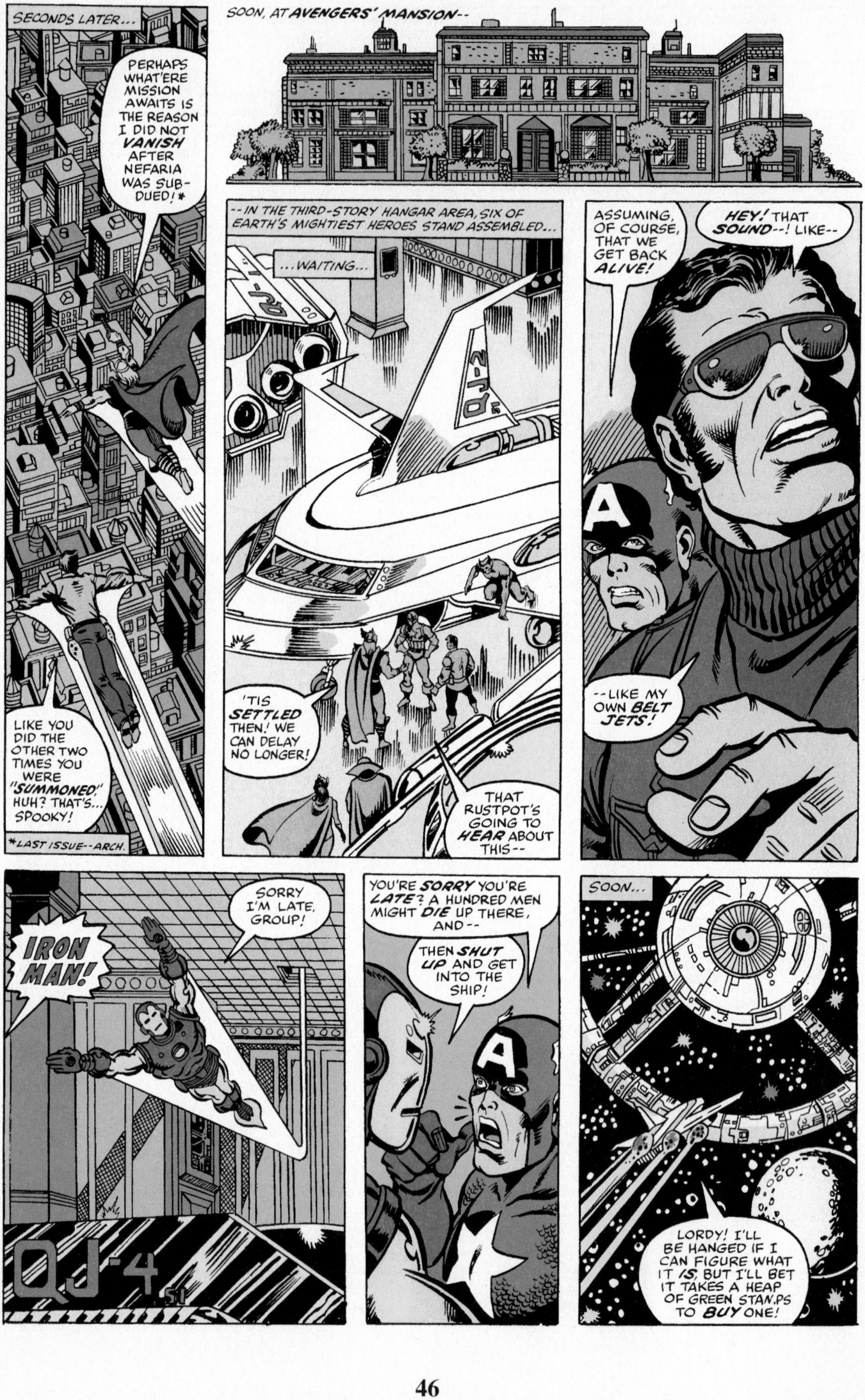
SECONDS LATER...
PERHAPS WHAT'ERE MISSION AWAITS IS THE REASON I DID NOT VANISH AFTER NEFARIA WAS SUBDUED! *
LIKE YOU DID THE OTHER TWO TIMES YOU WERE "SUMMONED!" HUH? THAT'S... SPOOKY!
*LAST ISSUE--ARCH.
SOON, AT AVENGERS' MANSION--
--IN THE THIRD-STORY HANGAR AREA, SIX OF EARTH'S MIGHTIEST HEROES STAND ASSEMBLED...
...WAITING...
'TIS SETTLED THEN! WE CAN DELAY NO LONGER!
THAT RUSTPOT'S GOING TO HEAR ABOUT THIS--
ASSUMING, OF COURSE, THAT WE GET BACK ALIVE!
HEY! THAT SOUND--! LIKE--
--LIKE MY OWN BELT JETS!
IRON MAN!
SORRY I'M LATE, GROUP!
QJ-4
YOU'RE SORRY YOU'RE LATE? A HUNDRED MEN MIGHT DIE UP THERE, AND--
THEN SHUT UP AND GET INTO THE SHIP!
SOON...
LORDY! I'LL BE HANGED IF I CAN FIGURE WHAT IT IS, BUT I'LL BET IT TAKES A HEAP OF GREEN STAMPS TO BUY ONE!

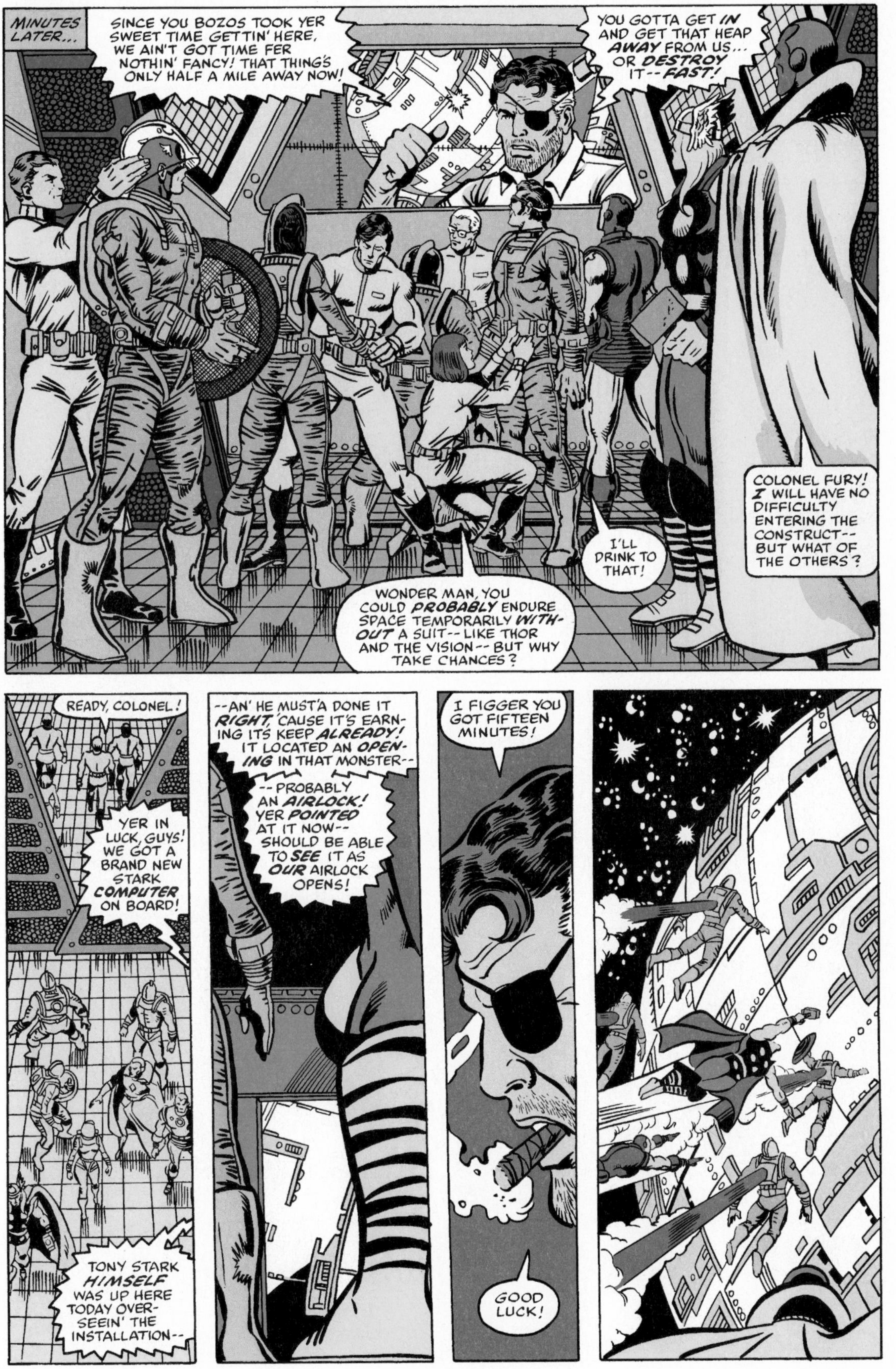
MINUTES LATER...
SINCE YOU BOZOS TOOK YER SWEET TIME GETTIN' HERE, WE AIN'T GOT TIME FER NOTHIN' FANCY! THAT THING'S ONLY HALF A MILE AWAY NOW!
YOU GOTTA GET IN AND GET THAT HEAP AWAY FROM US... OR DESTROY IT--FAST!
COLONEL FURY! I WILL HAVE NO DIFFICULTY ENTERING THE CONSTRUCT--BUT WHAT OF THE OTHERS?
I'LL DRINK TO THAT!
WONDER MAN, YOU COULD PROBABLY ENDURE SPACE TEMPORARILY WITHOUT A SUIT--LIKE THOR AND THE VISION--BUT WHY TAKE CHANCES?
READY, COLONEL!
YER IN LUCK, GUYS! WE GOT A BRAND NEW STARK COMPUTER ON BOARD!
TONY STARK HIMSELF WAS UP HERE TODAY OVERSEEIN' THE INSTALLATION--
--AN' HE MUST'A DONE IT RIGHT, 'CAUSE IT'S EARNING ITS KEEP ALREADY! IT LOCATED AN OPENING IN THAT MONSTER--
--PROBABLY AN AIRLOCK! YER POINTED AT IT NOW--SHOULD BE ABLE TO SEE IT AS OUR AIRLOCK OPENS!
I FIGGER YOU GOT FIFTEEN MINUTES!
GOOD LUCK!

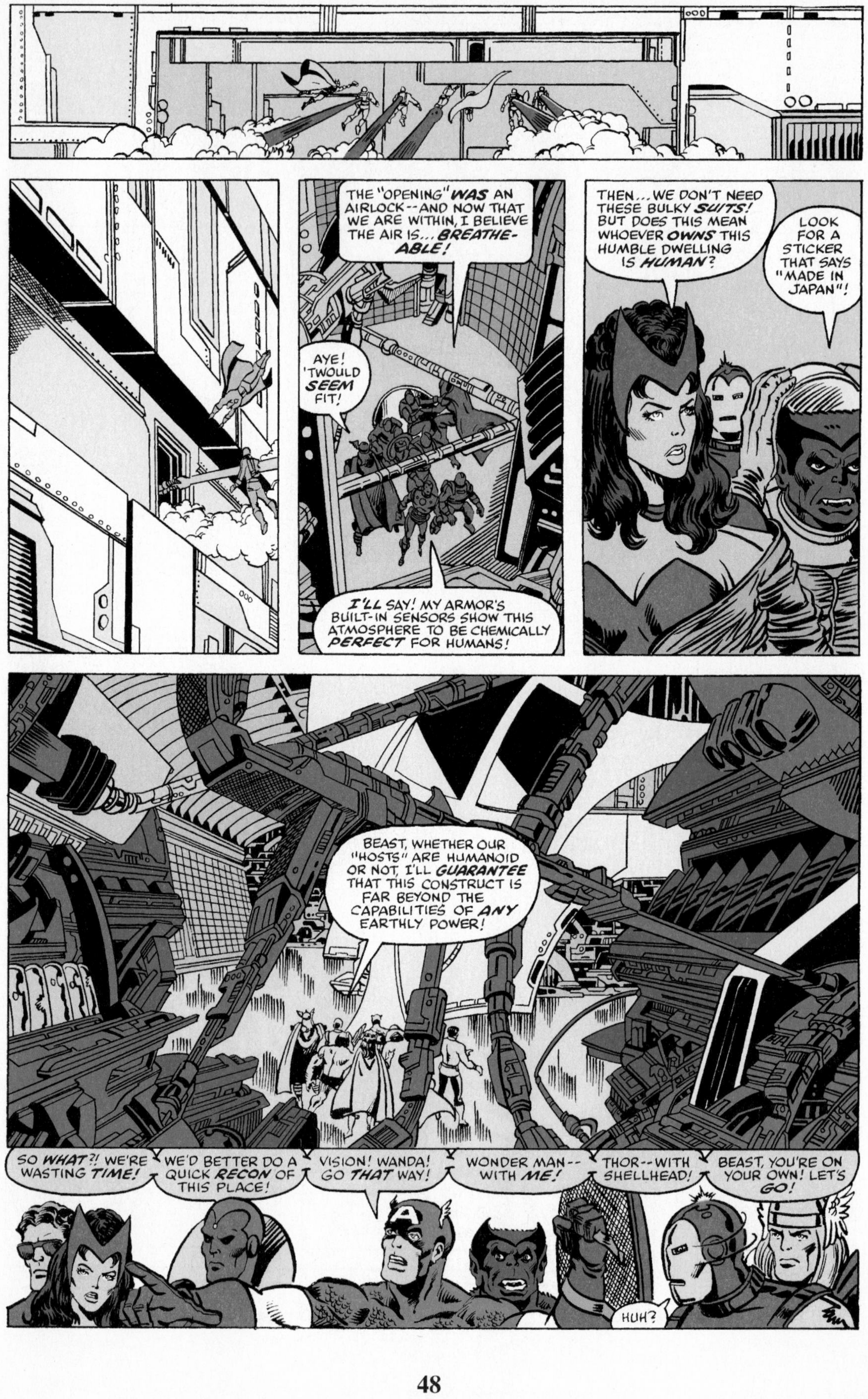

THE "OPENING" WAS AN AIRLOCK--AND NOW THAT WE ARE WITHIN, I BELIEVE THE AIR IS... BREATHE-ABLE!
AYE! 'TWOULD SEEM FIT!
I'LL SAY! MY ARMOR'S BUILT-IN SENSORS SHOW THIS ATMOSPHERE TO BE CHEMICALLY PERFECT FOR HUMANS!
THEN... WE DON'T NEED THESE BULKY SUITS! BUT DOES THIS MEAN WHOEVER OWNS THIS HUMBLE DWELLING IS HUMAN?
LOOK FOR A STICKER THAT SAYS "MADE IN JAPAN"!
BEAST, WHETHER OUR "HOSTS" ARE HUMANOID OR NOT, I'LL GUARANTEE THAT THIS CONSTRUCT IS FAR BEYOND THE CAPABILITIES OF ANY EARTHLY POWER!
SO WHAT?! WE'RE WASTING TIME!
WE'D BETTER DO A QUICK RECON OF THIS PLACE!
VISION! WANDA! GO THAT WAY!
WONDER MAN--WITH ME!
THOR--WITH SHELLHEAD!
BEAST, YOU'RE ON YOUR OWN! LET'S GO!
HUH?

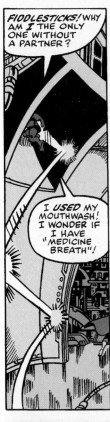

FIDDLESTICKS! WHY AM I THE ONLY ONE WITHOUT A PARTNER?

I USED MY MOUTHWASH! I WONDER IF I HAVE "MEDICINE BREATH"!

I HOPE THIS PLACE IS AS DESERTED AS IT SEEMS! I'M NEW AT DEALING WITH LITTLE GREEN MEN!

JUST DO AS I SAY IF WE MEET ANY RESISTANCE, WONDER MAN!

I COULD COVER MORE AREA FASTER BY PASSING THRU THESE BULKHEADS! PERHAPS I SHOULD SCOUT OUR PATH! IF DANGER LIES AHEAD, THEN--

THEN YOU MAY NEED ME, MY LOVE!

I THINK WE SHOULD STAY TOGETHER AS CAP SUGGESTED!

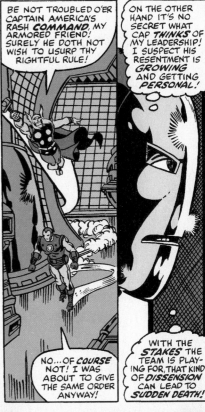

BE NOT TROUBLED O'ER CAPTAIN AMERICA'S RASH COMMAND, MY ARMORED FRIEND! SURELY HE DOTH NOT WISH TO USURP THY RIGHTFUL RULE!

NO...OF COURSE NOT! I WAS ABOUT TO GIVE THE SAME ORDER ANYWAY!

ON THE OTHER HAND IT'S NO SECRET WHAT CAP THINKS OF MY LEADERSHIP! I SUSPECT HIS RESENTMENT IS GROWING AND GETTING PERSONAL!

WITH THE STAKES THE TEAM IS PLAYING FOR, THAT KIND OF DISSENSION CAN LEAD TO SUDDEN DEATH!

I'M BEGINNING TO SEE WHY CAP SENT ME ALONE! WHO ELSE CAN GO PLACES LIKE THIS?

MAYBE THE PANTHER COULD-- BUT HE HAD TO TAKE OFF FOR A WHILE ON BUSINESS OF HIS OWN!

HMM! THERE'S A WAY OUT!

I MUST BE ON A WHOLE DIFFERENT LEVEL NOW!

STILL DON'T SEE ANYBODY!

I'M ABOUT CONVINCED THAT THERE'S NO ONE HERE TO SEE! WHY WOULD IT BE SO QUIET UNLESS--

EEYOW!

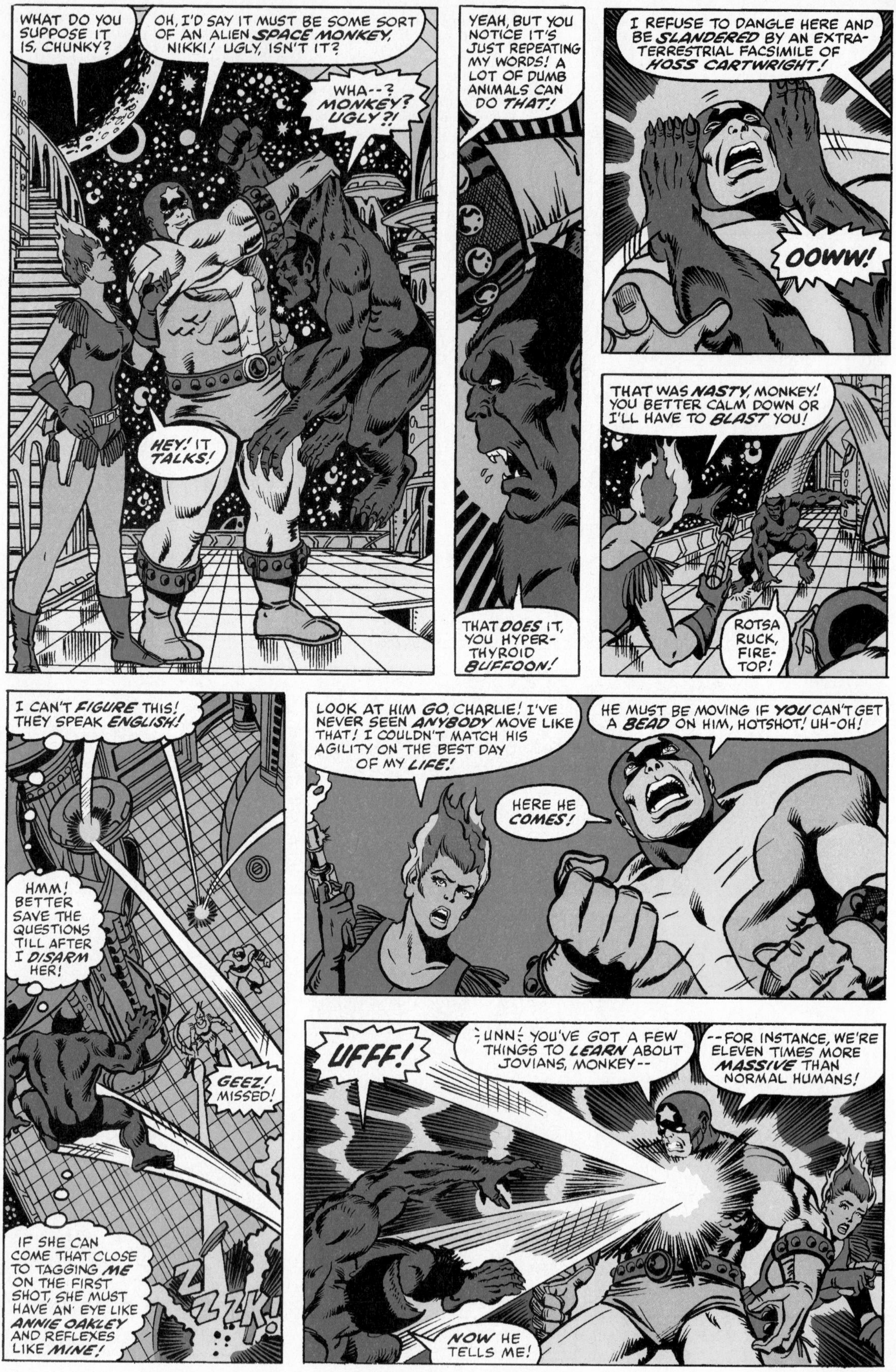
WHAT DO YOU SUPPOSE IT IS, CHUNKY?
OH, I'D SAY IT MUST BE SOME SORT OF AN ALIEN SPACE MONKEY, NIKKI! UGLY, ISN'T IT?
WHA--? MONKEY? UGLY?!
HEY! IT TALKS!
YEAH, BUT YOU NOTICE IT'S JUST REPEATING MY WORDS! A LOT OF DUMB ANIMALS CAN DO THAT!
THAT DOES IT, YOU HYPER-THYROID BUFFOON!
I REFUSE TO DANGLE HERE AND BE SLANDERED BY AN EXTRA-TERRESTRIAL FACSIMILE OF HOSS CARTWRIGHT!
OOWW!
THAT WAS NASTY, MONKEY! YOU BETTER CALM DOWN OR I'LL HAVE TO BLAST YOU!
ROTSA RUCK, FIRE-TOP!
I CAN'T FIGURE THIS! THEY SPEAK ENGLISH!
HMM! BETTER SAVE THE QUESTIONS TILL AFTER I DISARM HER!
GEEZ! MISSED!
IF SHE CAN COME THAT CLOSE TO TAGGING ME ON THE FIRST SHOT, SHE MUST HAVE AN EYE LIKE ANNIE OAKLEY AND REFLEXES LIKE MINE!
ZZZK!
LOOK AT HIM GO, CHARLIE! I'VE NEVER SEEN ANYBODY MOVE LIKE THAT! I COULDN'T MATCH HIS AGILITY ON THE BEST DAY OF MY LIFE!
HE MUST BE MOVING IF YOU CAN'T GET A BEAD ON HIM, HOTSHOT! UH-OH!
HERE HE COMES!
UFFF!
UNN! YOU'VE GOT A FEW THINGS TO LEARN ABOUT JOVIANS, MONKEY--
--FOR INSTANCE, WE'RE ELEVEN TIMES MORE MASSIVE THAN NORMAL HUMANS!
NOW HE TELLS ME!

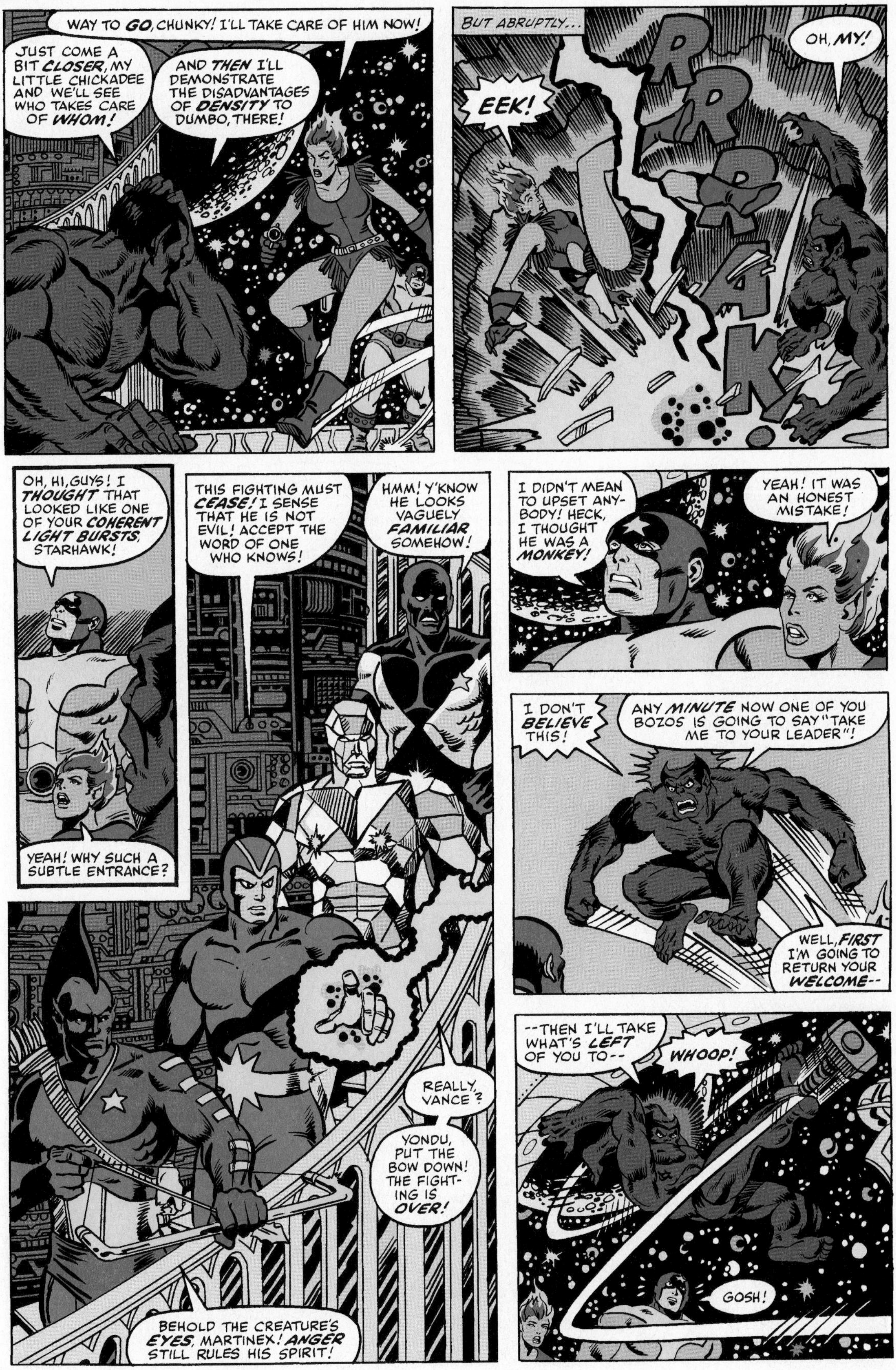
WAY TO GO, CHUNKY! I'LL TAKE CARE OF HIM NOW!
JUST COME A BIT CLOSER, MY LITTLE CHICKADEE AND WE'LL SEE WHO TAKES CARE OF WHOM!
AND THEN I'LL DEMONSTRATE THE DISADVANTAGES OF DENSITY TO DUMBO, THERE!
BUT ABRUPTLY...
OH, MY!
EEK!
RRRAK
OH, HI, GUYS! I THOUGHT THAT LOOKED LIKE ONE OF YOUR COHERENT LIGHT BURSTS, STARHAWK!
YEAH! WHY SUCH A SUBTLE ENTRANCE?
THIS FIGHTING MUST CEASE! I SENSE THAT HE IS NOT EVIL! ACCEPT THE WORD OF ONE WHO KNOWS!
HMM! Y'KNOW HE LOOKS VAGUELY FAMILIAR SOMEHOW!
REALLY, VANCE?
YONDU, PUT THE BOW DOWN! THE FIGHT-ING IS OVER!
BEHOLD THE CREATURE'S EYES, MARTINEX! ANGER STILL RULES HIS SPIRIT!
I DIDN'T MEAN TO UPSET ANY-BODY! HECK, I THOUGHT HE WAS A MONKEY!
YEAH! IT WAS AN HONEST MISTAKE!
I DON'T BELIEVE THIS!
ANY MINUTE NOW ONE OF YOU BOZOS IS GOING TO SAY "TAKE ME TO YOUR LEADER"!
WELL, FIRST I'M GOING TO RETURN YOUR WELCOME--
--THEN I'LL TAKE WHAT'S LEFT OF YOU TO--
WHOOP!
GOSH!

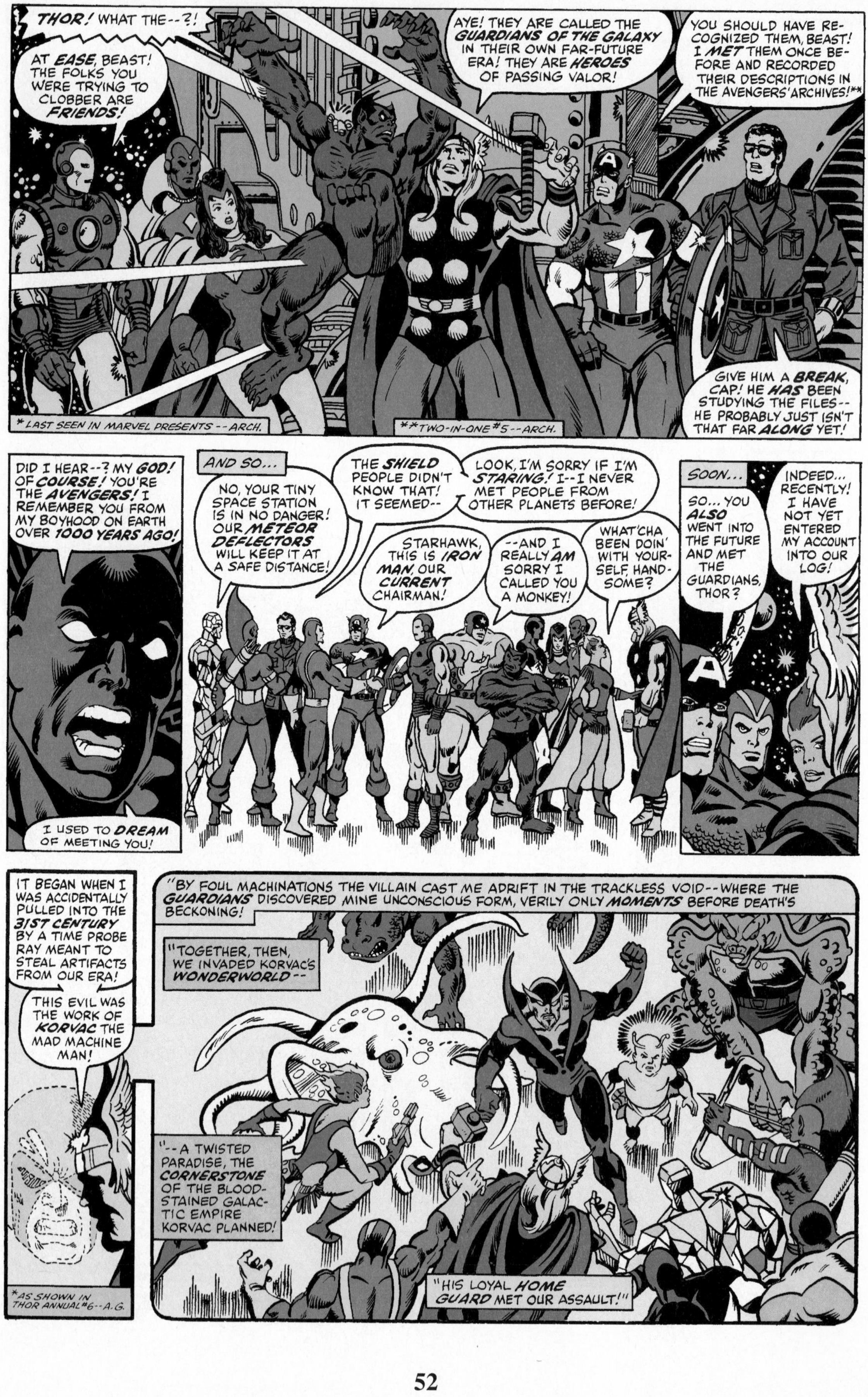
THOR! WHAT THE--?!
AT EASE, BEAST! THE FOLKS YOU WERE TRYING TO CLOBBER ARE FRIENDS!
AYE! THEY ARE CALLED THE GUARDIANS OF THE GALAXY IN THEIR OWN FAR-FUTURE ERA! THEY ARE HEROES OF PASSING VALOR!
YOU SHOULD HAVE RECOGNIZED THEM, BEAST! I MET THEM ONCE BEFORE AND RECORDED THEIR DESCRIPTIONS IN THE AVENGERS' ARCHIVES!**
GIVE HIM A BREAK, CAP! HE HAS BEEN STUDYING THE FILES-- HE PROBABLY JUST ISN'T THAT FAR ALONG YET!
*LAST SEEN IN MARVEL PRESENTS--ARCH.
**TWO-IN-ONE #5--ARCH.
DID I HEAR--? MY GOD! OF COURSE! YOU'RE THE AVENGERS! I REMEMBER YOU FROM MY BOYHOOD ON EARTH OVER 1000 YEARS AGO!
I USED TO DREAM OF MEETING YOU!
AND SO...
NO, YOUR TINY SPACE STATION IS IN NO DANGER! OUR METEOR DEFLECTORS WILL KEEP IT AT A SAFE DISTANCE!
THE SHIELD PEOPLE DIDN'T KNOW THAT! IT SEEMED--
LOOK, I'M SORRY IF I'M STARING! I--I NEVER MET PEOPLE FROM OTHER PLANETS BEFORE!
STARHAWK, THIS IS IRON MAN, OUR CURRENT CHAIRMAN!
--AND I REALLY AM SORRY I CALLED YOU A MONKEY!
WHAT'CHA BEEN DOIN' WITH YOURSELF, HANDSOME?
SOON...
SO... YOU ALSO WENT INTO THE FUTURE AND MET THE GUARDIANS, THOR?
INDEED... RECENTLY! I HAVE NOT YET ENTERED MY ACCOUNT INTO OUR LOG!
IT BEGAN WHEN I WAS ACCIDENTALLY PULLED INTO THE 31ST CENTURY BY A TIME PROBE RAY MEANT TO STEAL ARTIFACTS FROM OUR ERA!
THIS EVIL WAS THE WORK OF KORVAC THE MAD MACHINE MAN!
*AS SHOWN IN THOR ANNUAL #6--A.G.
"BY FOUL MACHINATIONS THE VILLAIN CAST ME ADRIFT IN THE TRACKLESS VOID--WHERE THE GUARDIANS DISCOVERED MINE UNCONSCIOUS FORM, VERILY ONLY MOMENTS BEFORE DEATH'S BECKONING!
"TOGETHER, THEN, WE INVADED KORVAC'S WONDERWORLD--
"--A TWISTED PARADISE, THE CORNERSTONE OF THE BLOOD-STAINED GALACTIC EMPIRE KORVAC PLANNED!
"HIS LOYAL HOME GUARD MET OUR ASSAULT!"

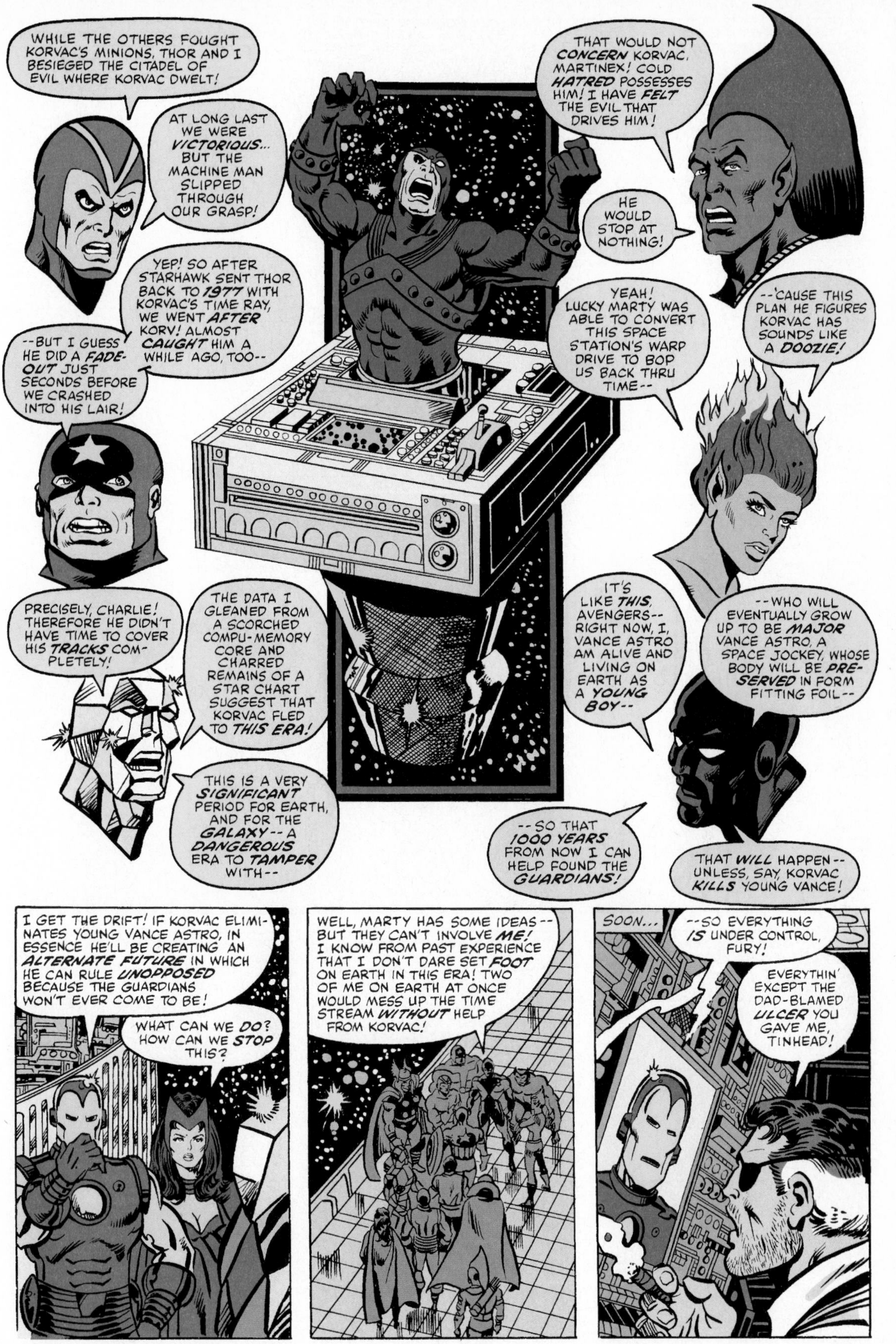
WHILE THE OTHERS FOUGHT KORVAC'S MINIONS, THOR AND I BESIEGED THE CITADEL OF EVIL WHERE KORVAC DWELT!
AT LONG LAST WE WERE VICTORIOUS... BUT THE MACHINE MAN SLIPPED THROUGH OUR GRASP!
YEP! SO AFTER STARHAWK SENT THOR BACK TO 1977 WITH KORVAC'S TIME RAY, WE WENT AFTER KORV! ALMOST CAUGHT HIM A WHILE AGO, TOO--
--BUT I GUESS HE DID A FADE-OUT JUST SECONDS BEFORE WE CRASHED INTO HIS LAIR!
THAT WOULD NOT CONCERN KORVAC, MARTINEX! COLD HATRED POSSESSES HIM! I HAVE FELT THE EVIL THAT DRIVES HIM!
HE WOULD STOP AT NOTHING!
YEAH! LUCKY MARTY WAS ABLE TO CONVERT THIS SPACE STATION'S WARP DRIVE TO BOP US BACK THRU TIME--
--'CAUSE THIS PLAN HE FIGURES KORVAC HAS SOUNDS LIKE A DOOZIE!
PRECISELY, CHARLIE! THEREFORE HE DIDN'T HAVE TIME TO COVER HIS TRACKS COMPLETELY!
THE DATA I GLEANED FROM A SCORCHED COMPU-MEMORY CORE AND CHARRED REMAINS OF A STAR CHART SUGGEST THAT KORVAC FLED TO THIS ERA!
THIS IS A VERY SIGNIFICANT PERIOD FOR EARTH, AND FOR THE GALAXY-- A DANGEROUS ERA TO TAMPER WITH--
IT'S LIKE THIS, AVENGERS-- RIGHT NOW, I, VANCE ASTRO AM ALIVE AND LIVING ON EARTH AS A YOUNG BOY--
--WHO WILL EVENTUALLY GROW UP TO BE MAJOR VANCE ASTRO, A SPACE JOCKEY, WHOSE BODY WILL BE PRESERVED IN FORM FITTING FOIL--
--SO THAT 1000 YEARS FROM NOW I CAN HELP FOUND THE GUARDIANS!
THAT WILL HAPPEN-- UNLESS, SAY, KORVAC KILLS YOUNG VANCE!
I GET THE DRIFT! IF KORVAC ELIMINATES YOUNG VANCE ASTRO, IN ESSENCE HE'LL BE CREATING AN ALTERNATE FUTURE IN WHICH HE CAN RULE UNOPPOSED BECAUSE THE GUARDIANS WON'T EVER COME TO BE!
WHAT CAN WE DO? HOW CAN WE STOP THIS?
WELL, MARTY HAS SOME IDEAS-- BUT THEY CAN'T INVOLVE ME! I KNOW FROM PAST EXPERIENCE THAT I DON'T DARE SET FOOT ON EARTH IN THIS ERA! TWO OF ME ON EARTH AT ONCE WOULD MESS UP THE TIME STREAM WITHOUT HELP FROM KORVAC!
SOON...
--SO EVERYTHING IS UNDER CONTROL, FURY!
EVERYTHIN' EXCEPT THE DAD-BLAMED ULCER YOU GAVE ME, TINHEAD!

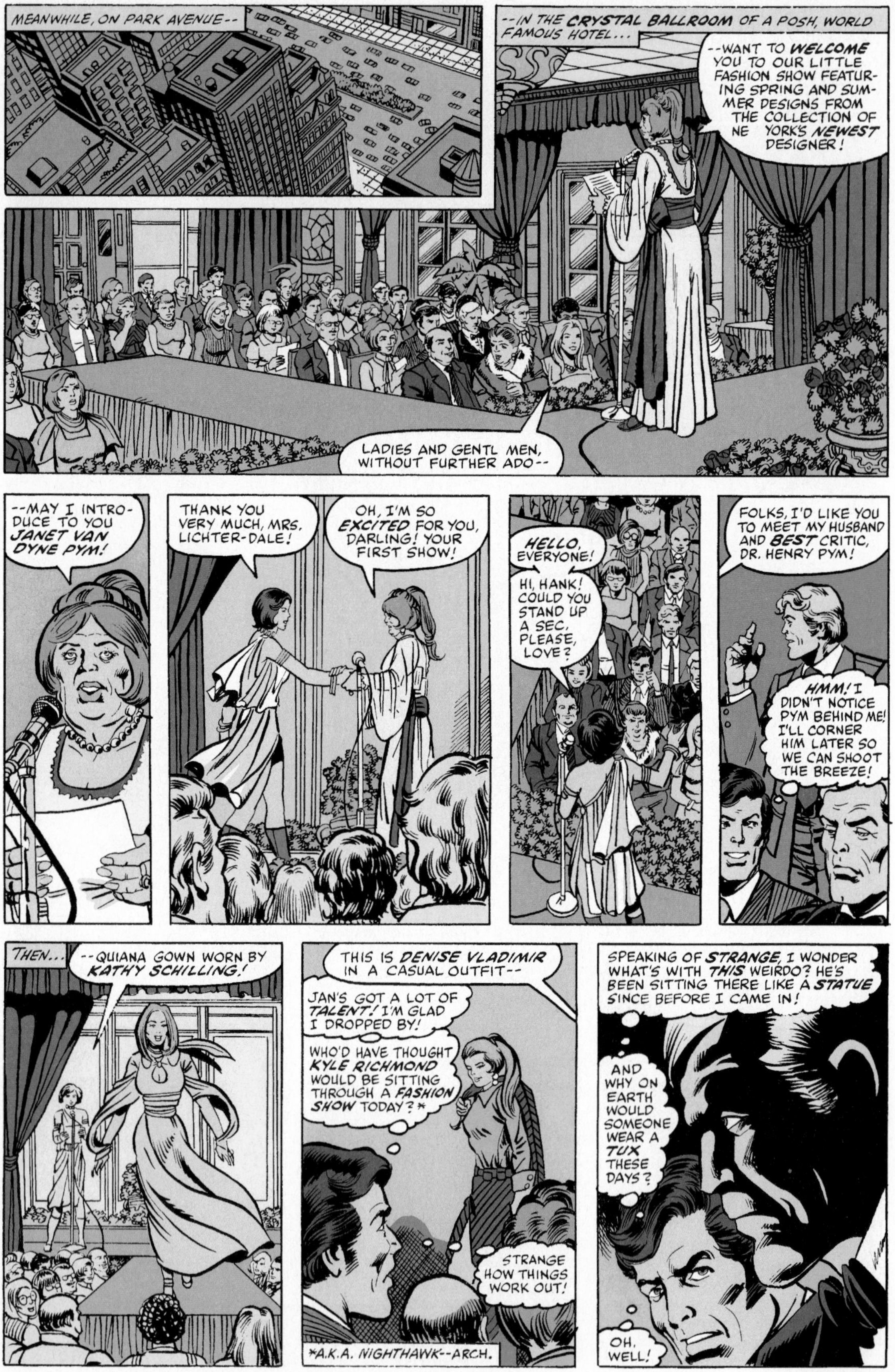
MEANWHILE, ON PARK AVENUE--
--IN THE CRYSTAL BALLROOM OF A POSH, WORLD FAMOUS HOTEL...
--WANT TO WELCOME YOU TO OUR LITTLE FASHION SHOW FEATURING SPRING AND SUMMER DESIGNS FROM THE COLLECTION OF NE YORK'S NEWEST DESIGNER!
LADIES AND GENTL MEN, WITHOUT FURTHER ADO--
--MAY I INTRODUCE TO YOU JANET VAN DYNE PYM!
THANK YOU VERY MUCH, MRS. LICHTER-DALE!
OH, I'M SO EXCITED FOR YOU, DARLING! YOUR FIRST SHOW!
HELLO, EVERYONE!
HI, HANK! COULD YOU STAND UP A SEC, PLEASE, LOVE?
FOLKS, I'D LIKE YOU TO MEET MY HUSBAND AND BEST CRITIC, DR. HENRY PYM!
HMM! I DIDN'T NOTICE PYM BEHIND ME! I'LL CORNER HIM LATER SO WE CAN SHOOT THE BREEZE!
THEN...
--QUIANA GOWN WORN BY KATHY SCHILLING!
THIS IS DENISE VLADIMIR IN A CASUAL OUTFIT--
JAN'S GOT A LOT OF TALENT! I'M GLAD I DROPPED BY!
WHO'D HAVE THOUGHT KYLE RICHMOND WOULD BE SITTING THROUGH A FASHION SHOW TODAY?*
STRANGE HOW THINGS WORK OUT!
*A.K.A. NIGHTHAWK--ARCH.
SPEAKING OF STRANGE, I WONDER WHAT'S WITH THIS WEIRDO? HE'S BEEN SITTING THERE LIKE A STATUE SINCE BEFORE I CAME IN!
AND WHY ON EARTH WOULD SOMEONE WEAR A TUX THESE DAYS?
OH, WELL!

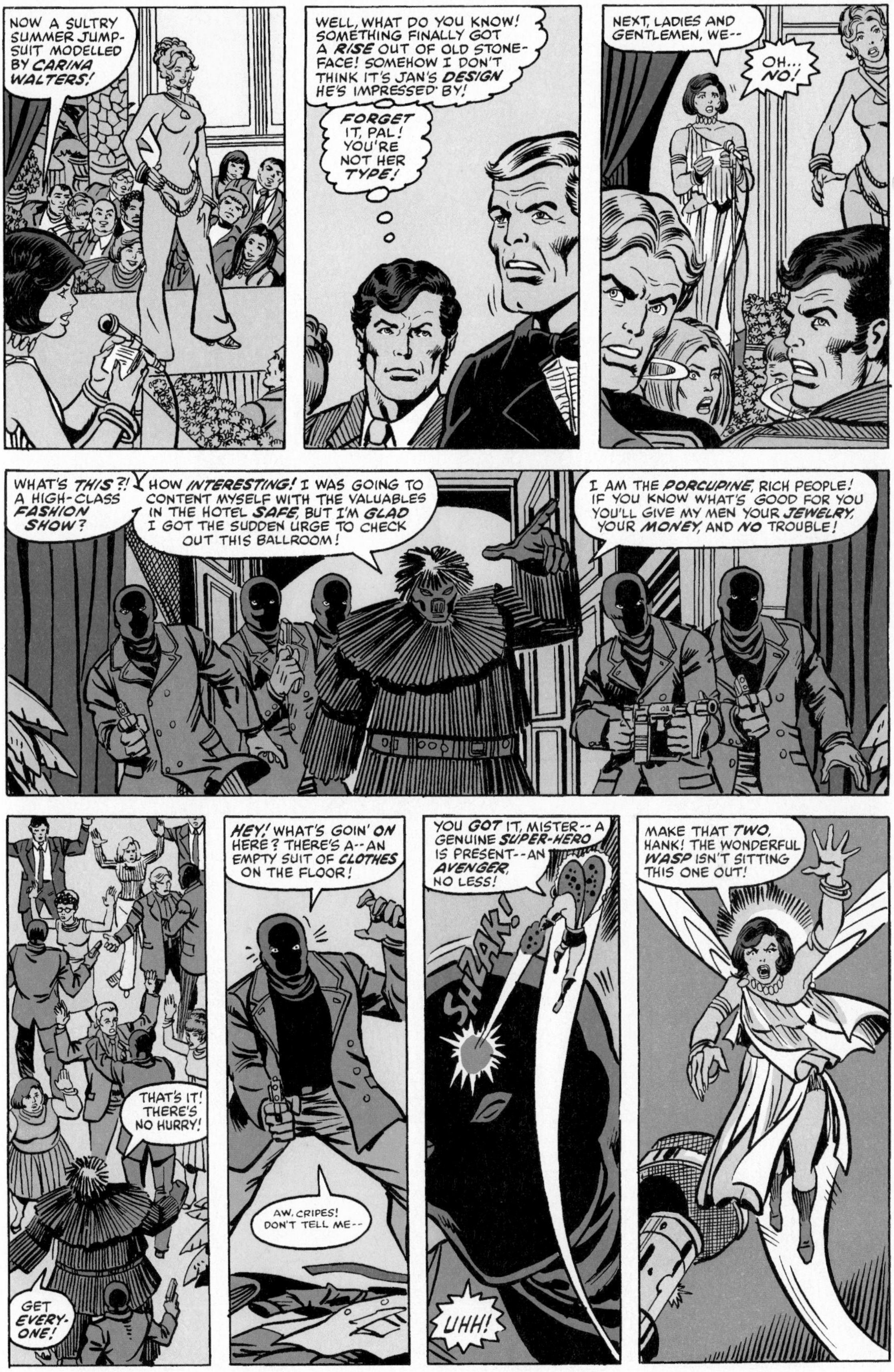
NOW A SULTRY SUMMER JUMP-SUIT MODELLED BY CARINA WALTERS!
WELL, WHAT DO YOU KNOW! SOMETHING FINALLY GOT A RISE OUT OF OLD STONE-FACE! SOMEHOW I DON'T THINK IT'S JAN'S DESIGN HE'S IMPRESSED BY!
FORGET IT, PAL! YOU'RE NOT HER TYPE!
NEXT, LADIES AND GENTLEMEN, WE--
OH... NO!
WHAT'S THIS?! A HIGH-CLASS FASHION SHOW?
HOW INTERESTING! I WAS GOING TO CONTENT MYSELF WITH THE VALUABLES IN THE HOTEL SAFE, BUT I'M GLAD I GOT THE SUDDEN URGE TO CHECK OUT THIS BALLROOM!
I AM THE PORCUPINE, RICH PEOPLE! IF YOU KNOW WHAT'S GOOD FOR YOU YOU'LL GIVE MY MEN YOUR JEWELRY, YOUR MONEY, AND NO TROUBLE!
THAT'S IT! THERE'S NO HURRY!
GET EVERY-ONE!
HEY! WHAT'S GOIN' ON HERE? THERE'S A--AN EMPTY SUIT OF CLOTHES ON THE FLOOR!
AW, CRIPES! DON'T TELL ME--
YOU GOT IT, MISTER--A GENUINE SUPER-HERO IS PRESENT--AN AVENGER, NO LESS!
SHZAK!
UHH!
MAKE THAT TWO, HANK! THE WONDERFUL WASP ISN'T SITTING THIS ONE OUT!

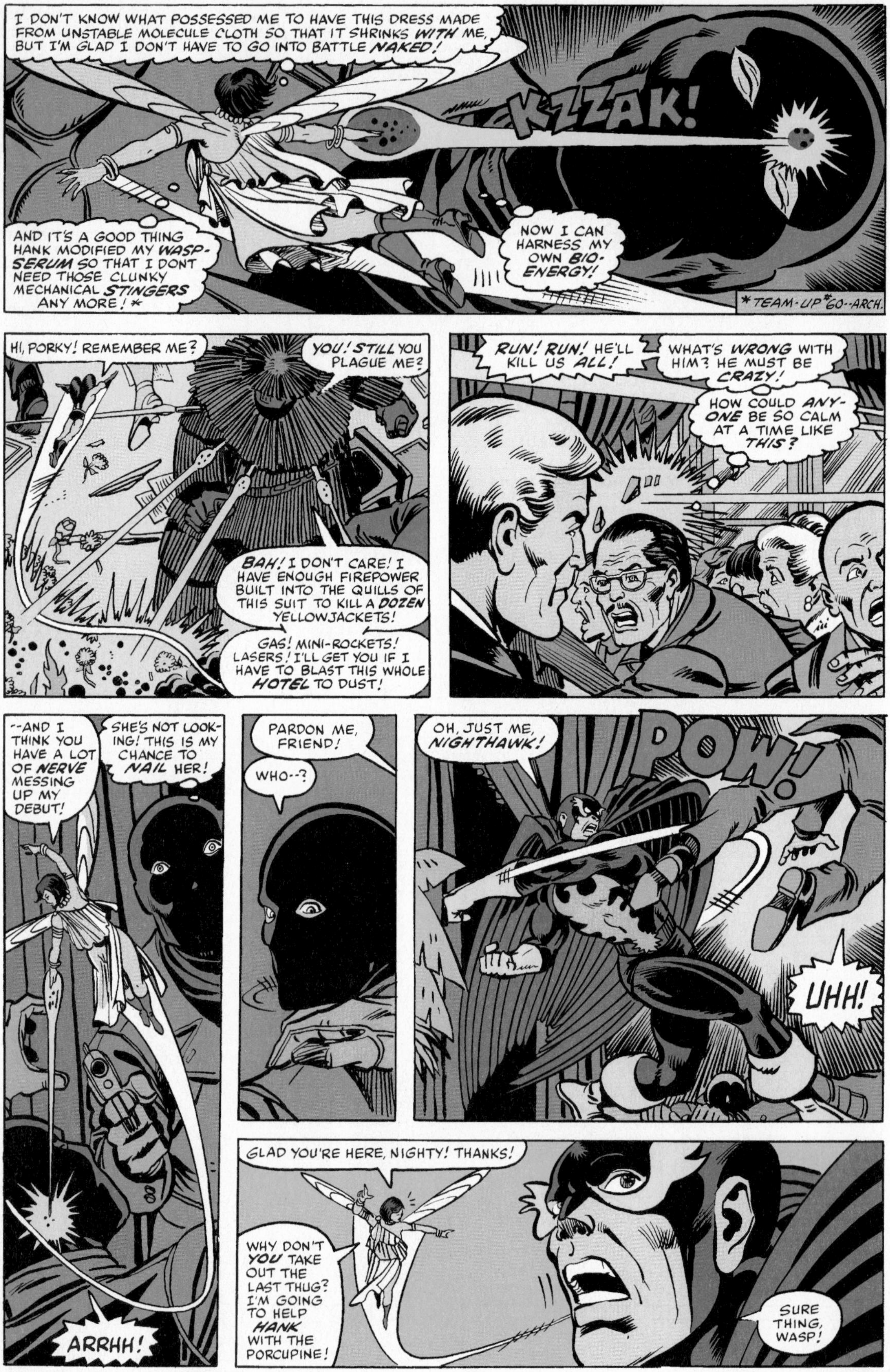
I DON'T KNOW WHAT POSSESSED ME TO HAVE THIS DRESS MADE FROM UNSTABLE MOLECULE CLOTH SO THAT IT SHRINKS WITH ME, BUT I'M GLAD I DON'T HAVE TO GO INTO BATTLE NAKED!
KZZZAK!
AND IT'S A GOOD THING HANK MODIFIED MY WASP-SERUM SO THAT I DONT NEED THOSE CLUNKY MECHANICAL STINGERS ANY MORE! *
NOW I CAN HARNESS MY OWN BIO-ENERGY!
* TEAM-UP #60--ARCH.
HI, PORKY! REMEMBER ME?
YOU! STILL YOU PLAGUE ME?
BAH! I DON'T CARE! I HAVE ENOUGH FIREPOWER BUILT INTO THE QUILLS OF THIS SUIT TO KILL A DOZEN YELLOWJACKETS!
GAS! MINI-ROCKETS! LASERS! I'LL GET YOU IF I HAVE TO BLAST THIS WHOLE HOTEL TO DUST!
RUN! RUN! HE'LL KILL US ALL!
WHAT'S WRONG WITH HIM? HE MUST BE CRAZY!
HOW COULD ANYONE BE SO CALM AT A TIME LIKE THIS?
--AND I THINK YOU HAVE A LOT OF NERVE MESSING UP MY DEBUT!
SHE'S NOT LOOKING! THIS IS MY CHANCE TO NAIL HER!
ARRHH!
PARDON ME, FRIEND!
WHO--?
OH, JUST ME, NIGHTHAWK!
POW!
UHH!
GLAD YOU'RE HERE, NIGHTY! THANKS!
WHY DON'T YOU TAKE OUT THE LAST THUG? I'M GOING TO HELP HANK WITH THE PORCUPINE!
SURE THING, WASP!

NOW WHAT DO I DO? *NIGHTHAWK'S* COMING THIS WAY!

I--I DON'T WANT TO GO UP ON A *MURDER* RAP!

GOOD THINKING, PAL! I COULDN'T AGREE MORE!

N-NO! STAY AWAY!

I C-CAN'T *LET* YOU *CAPTURE* ME... B-BUT--

TOO LATE!

NOT MAKING A DECISION IS *MAKING* A DECISION, YOU KNOW!

IN THIS CASE, YOU MADE THE *RIGHT* ONE!

DAK-KOOM!

SHPLUT!

OH, *NO!* MRS. LICHTERDALE HAS *FAINTED!*

SHE'LL BE ALL RIGHT, I'M SURE!

HMM... I'D BETTER SEE HOW HANK AND JAN ARE DOING WITH *PORKY!*

AS THE WINGED DEFENDER STRIDES AWAY...

OH! WHO ARE...

...YOU?

HE DOES NOT SPEAK. THERE IS NO *NEED.*

SHE *FEELS* HIS DESIRE. *SENSES--*

--HIS OFFER.

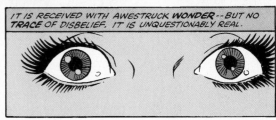

IT IS RECEIVED WITH AWESTRUCK *WONDER*--BUT NO *TRACE* OF DISBELIEF. IT IS UNQUESTIONABLY REAL.

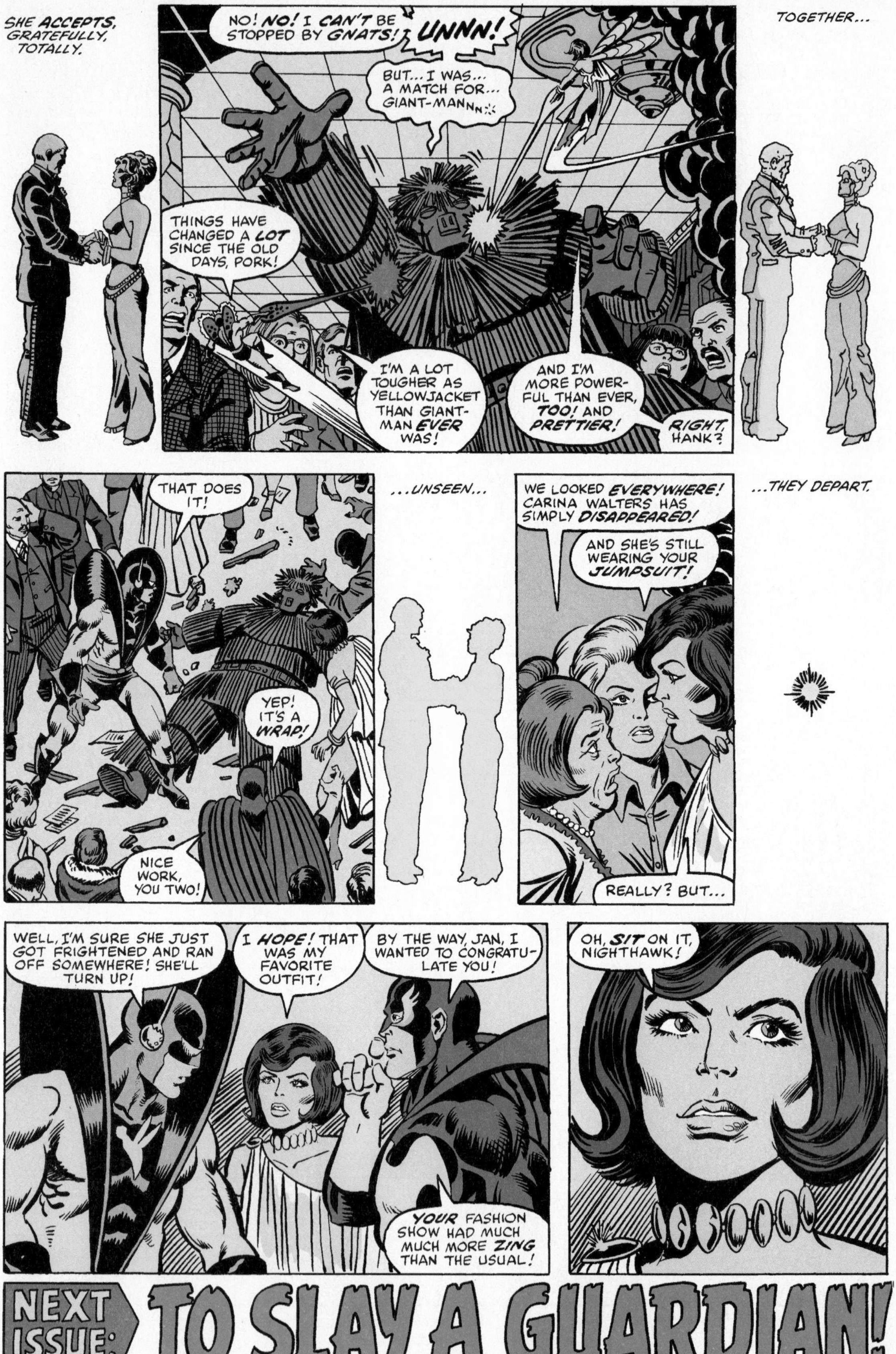
SHE ACCEPTS, GRATEFULLY, TOTALLY.
NO! NO! I CAN'T BE STOPPED BY GNATS!
UNNN!
BUT... I WAS... A MATCH FOR... GIANT-MANNN
THINGS HAVE CHANGED A LOT SINCE THE OLD DAYS, PORK!
I'M A LOT TOUGHER AS YELLOWJACKET THAN GIANT-MAN EVER WAS!
AND I'M MORE POWER-FUL THAN EVER, TOO! AND PRETTIER!
RIGHT, HANK?
TOGETHER...
THAT DOES IT!
YEP! IT'S A WRAP!
NICE WORK, YOU TWO!
...UNSEEN...
WE LOOKED EVERYWHERE! CARINA WALTERS HAS SIMPLY DISAPPEARED!
AND SHE'S STILL WEARING YOUR JUMPSUIT!
REALLY? BUT...
...THEY DEPART.
WELL, I'M SURE SHE JUST GOT FRIGHTENED AND RAN OFF SOMEWHERE! SHE'LL TURN UP!
I HOPE! THAT WAS MY FAVORITE OUTFIT!
BY THE WAY, JAN, I WANTED TO CONGRATU-LATE YOU!
YOUR FASHION SHOW HAD MUCH MUCH MORE ZING THAN THE USUAL!
OH, SIT ON IT, NIGHTHAWK!
NEXT ISSUE: TO SLAY A GUARDIAN!

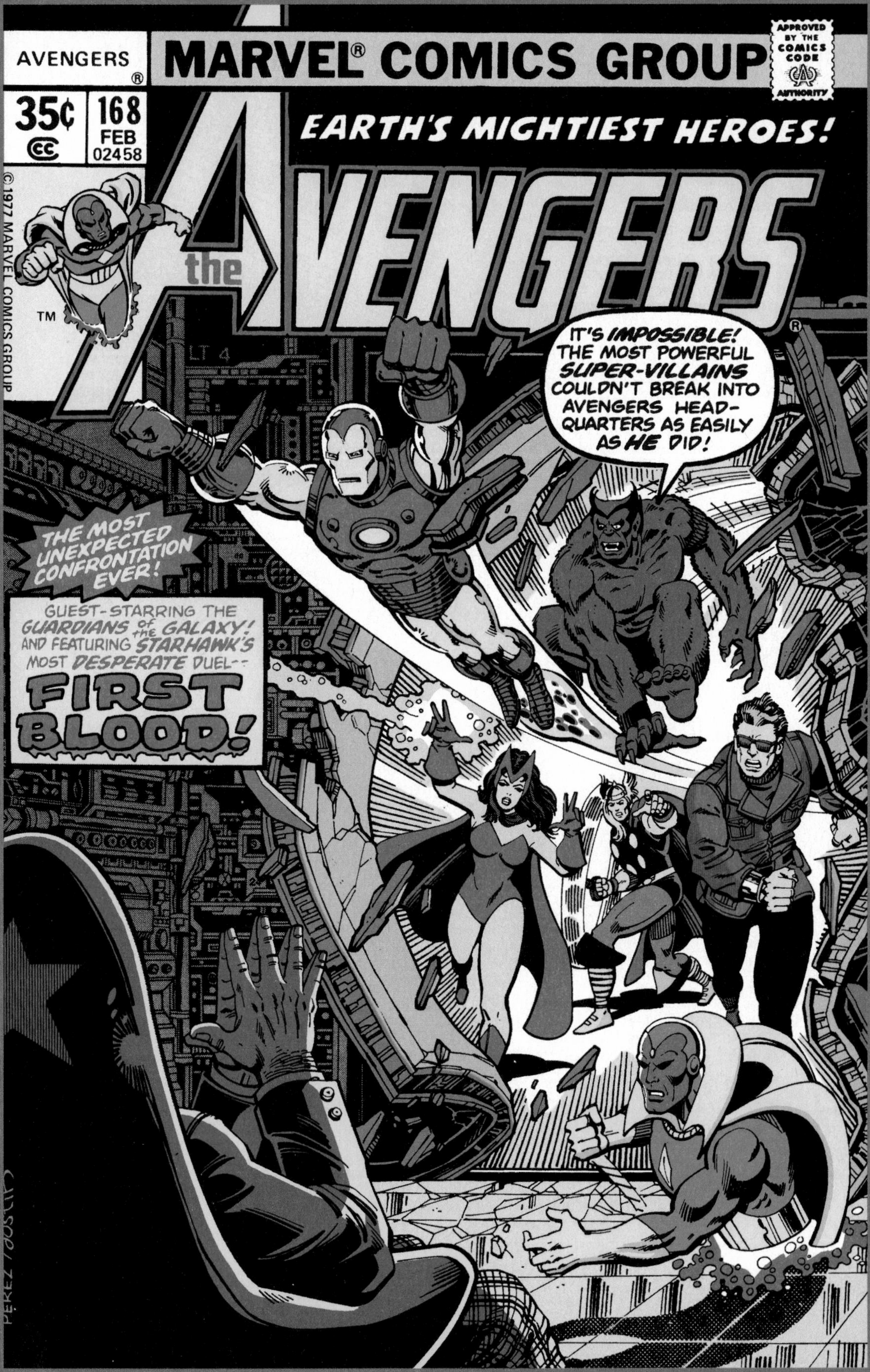
AVENGERS
MARVEL® COMICS GROUP
APPROVED BY THE COMICS CODE AUTHORITY
35¢
168
FEB
02458
EARTH'S MIGHTIEST HEROES!
the AVENGERS
© 1977 MARVEL COMICS GROUP
IT'S IMPOSSIBLE! THE MOST POWERFUL SUPER-VILLAINS COULDN'T BREAK INTO AVENGERS HEAD-QUARTERS AS EASILY AS HE DID!
THE MOST UNEXPECTED CONFRONTATION EVER!
GUEST-STARRING THE GUARDIANS of the GALAXY! AND FEATURING STARHAWK'S MOST DESPERATE DUEL--
FIRST BLOOD!

And there came a day when *Earth's mightiest heroes* found themselves *united* against a common threat. On that day, the *Avengers* were born—to fight the foes no *single* super-hero could withstand!

STan Lee PRESENTS: **THE MIGHTY AVENGERS!**®

FIRST BLOOD

LEAVING THE SHIELD ORBITING SPACE STATION BEHIND, AN AVENGERS' QUINJET ROCKETS EARTH-WARD...

ON HER BRIDGE STAND SEVEN AVENGERS AND FIVE BEINGS OF THE DISTANT FUTURE--

--FIVE DEDICATED DEFENDERS OF THE 31ST CENTURY WHO SHALL COME TO BE CALLED GUARDIANS OF THE GALAXY IN THEIR OWN TIME. THEY HAVE SPANNED THE CENTURIES IN PURSUIT OF THEIR MOST CUNNING AND FEARSOME ENEMY, KORVAC--*

--AND NOW, WITH THEIR NEWFOUND AVENGING ALLIES, THEY HURTLE TOWARD A SINISTER AND DEADLY CON-FRONTATION.

HMM...THE F.A.A. VERIFIED OUR AVENGERS PRIORITY STATUS AND GRANTED CLEARANCE TO LAND AT THE MANSION-- BUT I CAN'T SEEM TO CONTACT JARVIS!

IN FACT OUR HQ.'S RECEIVING STATION SEEMS TO BE SHUT DOWN!

IT CAN'T BE! KEEP TRYING!

* SEE LAST ISSUE--ARCH.

* SCRIPT *	* PENCILS *	* INKS *	LETTERS: DENISE WOHL	* EDITING *
JAMES SHOOTER	GEORGE PÉREZ	PABLO MARCOS	COLORS: PHIL RACHE	ARCHIE GOODWIN

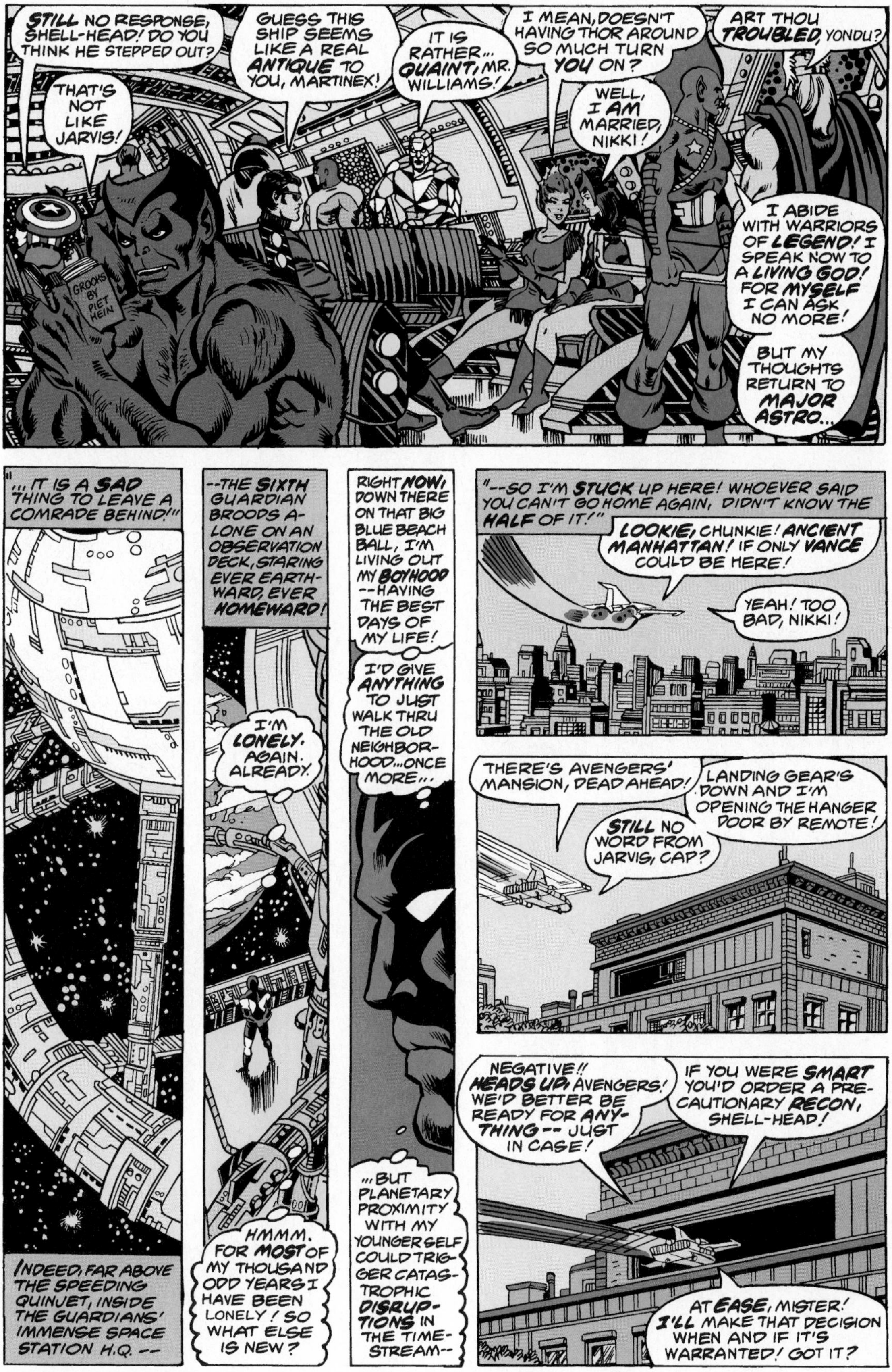
STILL NO RESPONSE, SHELL-HEAD! DO YOU THINK HE STEPPED OUT?
THAT'S NOT LIKE JARVIS!
GUESS THIS SHIP SEEMS LIKE A REAL ANTIQUE TO YOU, MARTINEX!
IT IS RATHER... QUAINT, MR. WILLIAMS!
I MEAN, DOESN'T HAVING THOR AROUND SO MUCH TURN YOU ON?
WELL, I AM MARRIED, NIKKI!
ART THOU TROUBLED, YONDU?
I ABIDE WITH WARRIORS OF LEGEND! I SPEAK NOW TO A LIVING GOD! FOR MYSELF I CAN ASK NO MORE!
BUT MY THOUGHTS RETURN TO MAJOR ASTRO...
GROOKS BY PIET HEIN
"...IT IS A SAD THING TO LEAVE A COMRADE BEHIND!"
INDEED, FAR ABOVE THE SPEEDING QUINJET, INSIDE THE GUARDIANS' IMMENSE SPACE STATION H.Q.--
--THE SIXTH GUARDIAN BROODS ALONE ON AN OBSERVATION DECK, STARING EVER EARTHWARD, EVER HOMEWARD!
I'M LONELY. AGAIN. ALREADY.
HMMM. FOR MOST OF MY THOUSAND ODD YEARS I HAVE BEEN LONELY! SO WHAT ELSE IS NEW?
RIGHT NOW, DOWN THERE ON THAT BIG BLUE BEACH BALL, I'M LIVING OUT MY BOYHOOD --HAVING THE BEST DAYS OF MY LIFE!
I'D GIVE ANYTHING TO JUST WALK THRU THE OLD NEIGHBORHOOD...ONCE MORE...
...BUT PLANETARY PROXIMITY WITH MY YOUNGER SELF COULD TRIGGER CATASTROPHIC DISRUPTIONS IN THE TIME-STREAM--
"--SO I'M STUCK UP HERE! WHOEVER SAID YOU CAN'T GO HOME AGAIN, DIDN'T KNOW THE HALF OF IT!"
LOOKIE, CHUNKIE! ANCIENT MANHATTAN! IF ONLY VANCE COULD BE HERE!
YEAH! TOO BAD, NIKKI!
THERE'S AVENGERS' MANSION, DEAD AHEAD!
LANDING GEAR'S DOWN AND I'M OPENING THE HANGER DOOR BY REMOTE!
STILL NO WORD FROM JARVIS, CAP?
NEGATIVE!! HEADS UP, AVENGERS! WE'D BETTER BE READY FOR ANYTHING -- JUST IN CASE!
IF YOU WERE SMART YOU'D ORDER A PRECAUTIONARY RECON, SHELL-HEAD!
AT EASE, MISTER! I'LL MAKE THAT DECISION WHEN AND IF IT'S WARRANTED! GOT IT?

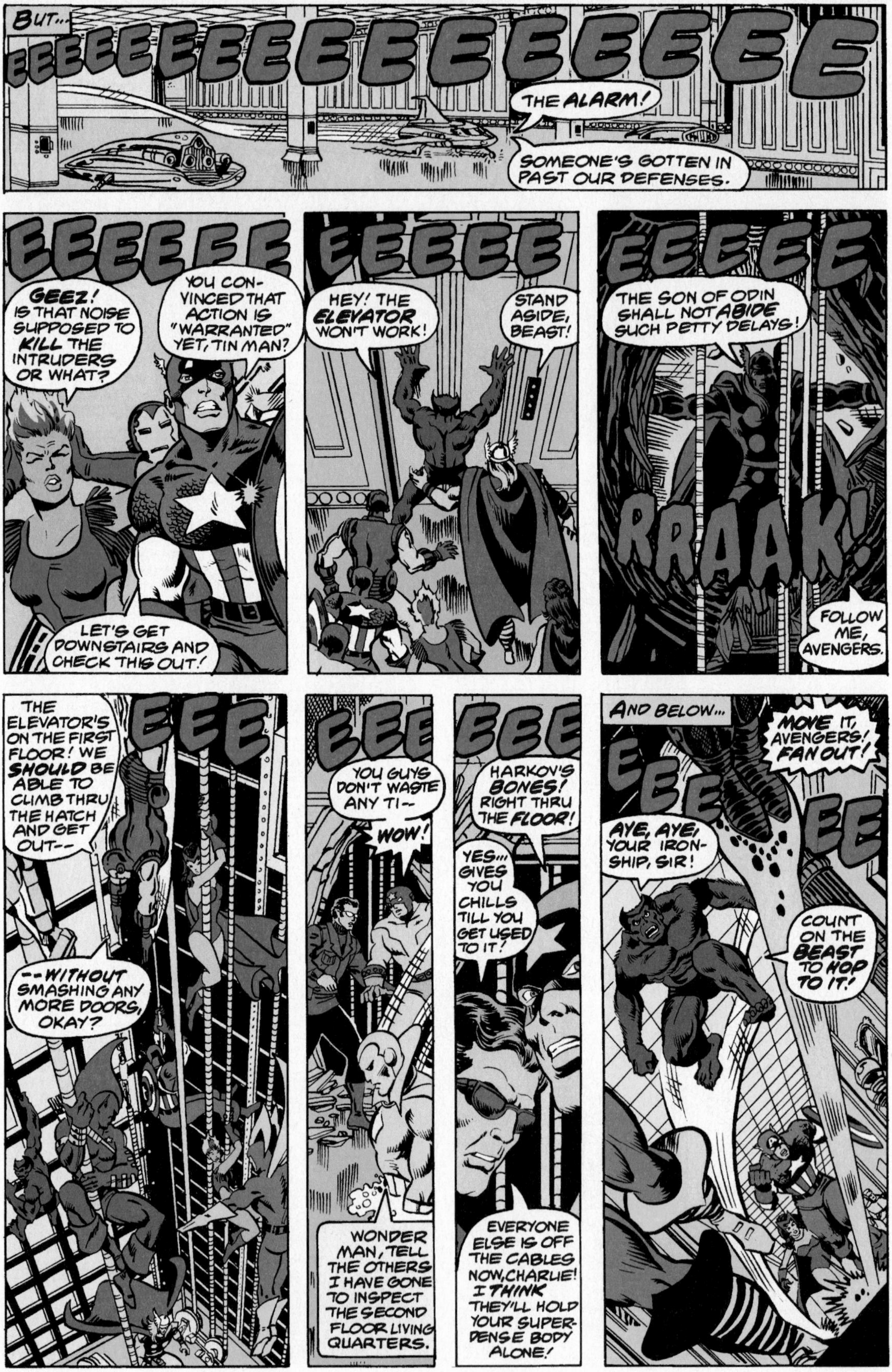
BUT...
EEEEEEEEEEEEEEEEE
THE ALARM!
SOMEONE'S GOTTEN IN PAST OUR DEFENSES.
EEEEEE
GEEZ! IS THAT NOISE SUPPOSED TO KILL THE INTRUDERS OR WHAT?
YOU CONVINCED THAT ACTION IS "WARRANTED" YET, TIN MAN?
LET'S GET DOWNSTAIRS AND CHECK THIS OUT!
EEEEEE
HEY! THE ELEVATOR WON'T WORK!
STAND ASIDE, BEAST!
EEEEE
THE SON OF ODIN SHALL NOT ABIDE SUCH PETTY DELAYS!
RRAAK!
FOLLOW ME, AVENGERS.
THE ELEVATOR'S ON THE FIRST FLOOR! WE SHOULD BE ABLE TO CLIMB THRU THE HATCH AND GET OUT--
EEE
--WITHOUT SMASHING ANY MORE DOORS, OKAY?
EEE
YOU GUYS DON'T WASTE ANY TI--
WOW!
WONDER MAN, TELL THE OTHERS I HAVE GONE TO INSPECT THE SECOND FLOOR LIVING QUARTERS.
EEE
HARKOV'S BONES! RIGHT THRU THE FLOOR!
YES... GIVES YOU CHILLS TILL YOU GET USED TO IT!
EVERYONE ELSE IS OFF THE CABLES NOW, CHARLIE! I THINK THEY'LL HOLD YOUR SUPER-DENSE BODY ALONE!
AND BELOW...
EEEEE
MOVE IT, AVENGERS! FAN OUT!
AYE, AYE, YOUR IRON-SHIP, SIR!
COUNT ON THE BEAST TO HOP TO IT!

HMM! THEY SEEM TO HAVE THIS *SEARCH PROCEDURE* DOWN TO A SCIENCE! I SUSPECT, AT THIS POINT, WE'D BEST JUST STAY OUT OF THE WAY!

THIS IS THE COURSE OF *WISDOM*, MARTINEX!

YOU *BET!* I'D GET *LOST* IN THIS JOINT!

YOU TAKE THE HIGH ROAD, AND I'LL TAKE THE RECORDS ROOM... TRA-LA-LA!

I'LL CHECK THE *KITCHEN!*

UH-OH! SOMEBODY LEFT A MESS!

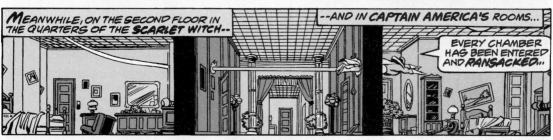

MEANWHILE, ON THE SECOND FLOOR IN THE QUARTERS OF THE *SCARLET WITCH*--

--AND IN *CAPTAIN AMERICA'S* ROOMS...

EVERY CHAMBER HAS BEEN ENTERED AND *RANSACKED*...

...BUT... IT APPEARS THAT NOTHING HAS BEEN *STOLEN!*

THIS DEFIES *LOGIC!* WHAT WOULD IT PROFIT AN INTRUDER MERELY TO PROVE HIS ABILITY TO *ENTER* THESE PREMISES?

AT THAT MOMENT, ONE FLOOR BELOW...

--*HERE!* MY BUILT-IN INFRA-RED SCANNER SAYS SOMEONE IS IN OUR *MEETING ROOM!*

SURE ENOUGH, THE DOOR'S SEALED FROM THE *INSIDE!*

SHIELD YOUR EYES, GOLDILOCKS! I'M LETTING MY REPULSORS BUILD PRESSURE AGAINST THIS DOOR.

IN A FEW SECONDS THEY'LL *OVERLOAD*--

--RESULTING IN A CONCENTRATED, HIGH INTENSITY *EXPLOSION!*

SO MUCH FOR A COUPLE THOUS-AND BUCKS WORTH OF VANADIUM-STEEL PLATE!

BY ODIN'S BEARD! IS THERE NO *LIMIT* TO THINE ARMOR'S PROWESS, GOLDEN ONE?

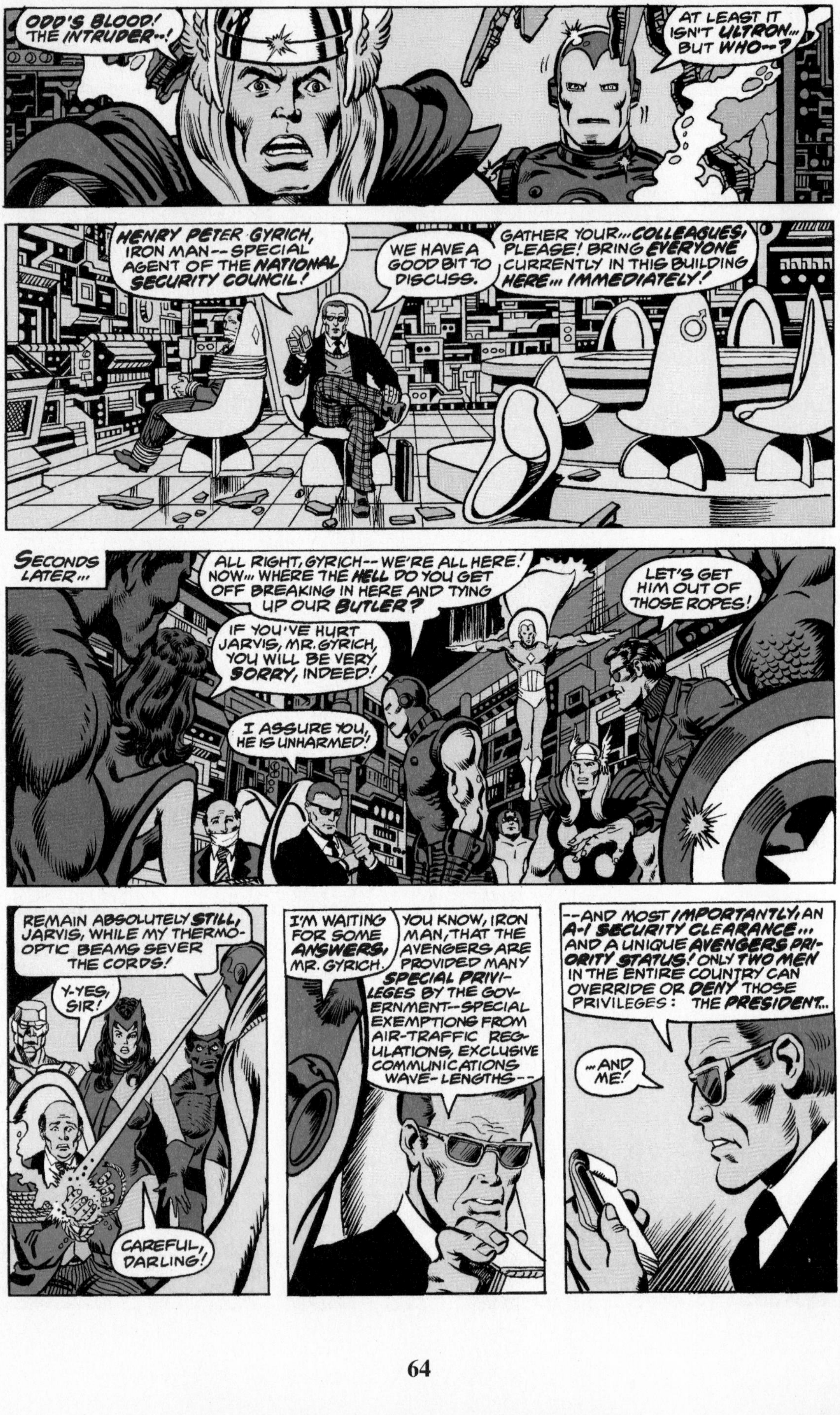
ODD'S BLOOD! THE INTRUDER--!
AT LEAST IT ISN'T ULTRON... BUT WHO--?
HENRY PETER GYRICH, IRON MAN--SPECIAL AGENT OF THE NATIONAL SECURITY COUNCIL!
WE HAVE A GOOD BIT TO DISCUSS.
GATHER YOUR... COLLEAGUES, PLEASE! BRING EVERYONE CURRENTLY IN THIS BUILDING HERE... IMMEDIATELY!
SECONDS LATER...
ALL RIGHT, GYRICH-- WE'RE ALL HERE! NOW... WHERE THE HELL DO YOU GET OFF BREAKING IN HERE AND TYING UP OUR BUTLER?
LET'S GET HIM OUT OF THOSE ROPES!
IF YOU'VE HURT JARVIS, MR. GYRICH, YOU WILL BE VERY SORRY, INDEED!
I ASSURE YOU, HE IS UNHARMED!
REMAIN ABSOLUTELY STILL, JARVIS, WHILE MY THERMO-OPTIC BEAMS SEVER THE CORDS!
Y-YES, SIR!
CAREFUL, DARLING!
I'M WAITING FOR SOME ANSWERS, MR. GYRICH.
YOU KNOW, IRON MAN, THAT THE AVENGERS ARE PROVIDED MANY SPECIAL PRIVILEGES BY THE GOVERNMENT--SPECIAL EXEMPTIONS FROM AIR-TRAFFIC REGULATIONS, EXCLUSIVE COMMUNICATIONS WAVE-LENGTHS--
--AND MOST IMPORTANTLY, AN A-1 SECURITY CLEARANCE... AND A UNIQUE AVENGERS PRIORITY STATUS! ONLY TWO MEN IN THE ENTIRE COUNTRY CAN OVERRIDE OR DENY THOSE PRIVILEGES: THE PRESIDENT...
...AND ME!

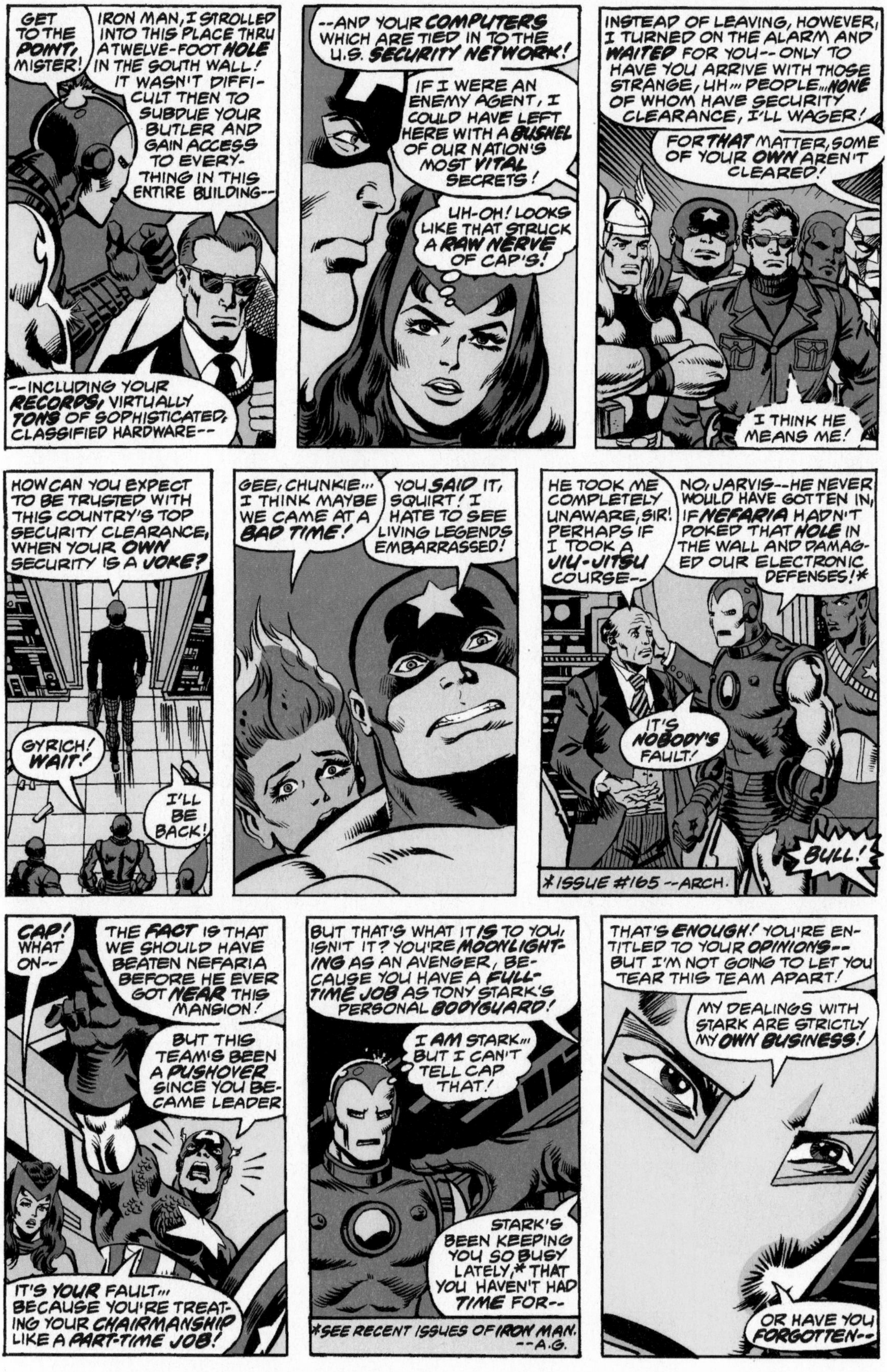
GET TO THE POINT, MISTER!
IRON MAN, I STROLLED INTO THIS PLACE THRU A TWELVE-FOOT HOLE IN THE SOUTH WALL! IT WASN'T DIFFICULT THEN TO SUBDUE YOUR BUTLER AND GAIN ACCESS TO EVERYTHING IN THIS ENTIRE BUILDING--
--INCLUDING YOUR RECORDS, VIRTUALLY TONS OF SOPHISTICATED, CLASSIFIED HARDWARE--
--AND YOUR COMPUTERS WHICH ARE TIED IN TO THE U.S. SECURITY NETWORK!
IF I WERE AN ENEMY AGENT, I COULD HAVE LEFT HERE WITH A BUSHEL OF OUR NATION'S MOST VITAL SECRETS!
UH-OH! LOOKS LIKE THAT STRUCK A RAW NERVE OF CAP'S!
INSTEAD OF LEAVING, HOWEVER, I TURNED ON THE ALARM AND WAITED FOR YOU-- ONLY TO HAVE YOU ARRIVE WITH THOSE STRANGE, UH... PEOPLE... NONE OF WHOM HAVE SECURITY CLEARANCE, I'LL WAGER!
FOR THAT MATTER, SOME OF YOUR OWN AREN'T CLEARED!
I THINK HE MEANS ME!
HOW CAN YOU EXPECT TO BE TRUSTED WITH THIS COUNTRY'S TOP SECURITY CLEARANCE, WHEN YOUR OWN SECURITY IS A JOKE?
GYRICH! WAIT!
I'LL BE BACK!
GEE, CHUNKIE... I THINK MAYBE WE CAME AT A BAD TIME!
YOU SAID IT, SQUIRT! I HATE TO SEE LIVING LEGENDS EMBARRASSED!
HE TOOK ME COMPLETELY UNAWARE, SIR! PERHAPS IF I TOOK A JIU-JITSU COURSE--
NO, JARVIS--HE NEVER WOULD HAVE GOTTEN IN, IF NEFARIA HADN'T POKED THAT HOLE IN THE WALL AND DAMAGED OUR ELECTRONIC DEFENSES!*
IT'S NOBODY'S FAULT!
BULL!
*ISSUE #165 --ARCH.
CAP! WHAT ON--
THE FACT IS THAT WE SHOULD HAVE BEATEN NEFARIA BEFORE HE EVER GOT NEAR THIS MANSION!
BUT THIS TEAM'S BEEN A PUSHOVER SINCE YOU BECAME LEADER
IT'S YOUR FAULT... BECAUSE YOU'RE TREATING YOUR CHAIRMANSHIP LIKE A PART-TIME JOB!
BUT THAT'S WHAT IT IS TO YOU, ISN'T IT? YOU'RE MOONLIGHTING AS AN AVENGER, BECAUSE YOU HAVE A FULL-TIME JOB AS TONY STARK'S PERSONAL BODYGUARD!
I AM STARK... BUT I CAN'T TELL CAP THAT!
STARK'S BEEN KEEPING YOU SO BUSY LATELY,* THAT YOU HAVEN'T HAD TIME FOR--
*SEE RECENT ISSUES OF IRON MAN. --A.G.
THAT'S ENOUGH! YOU'RE ENTITLED TO YOUR OPINIONS-- BUT I'M NOT GOING TO LET YOU TEAR THIS TEAM APART!
MY DEALINGS WITH STARK ARE STRICTLY MY OWN BUSINESS!
OR HAVE YOU FORGOTTEN--

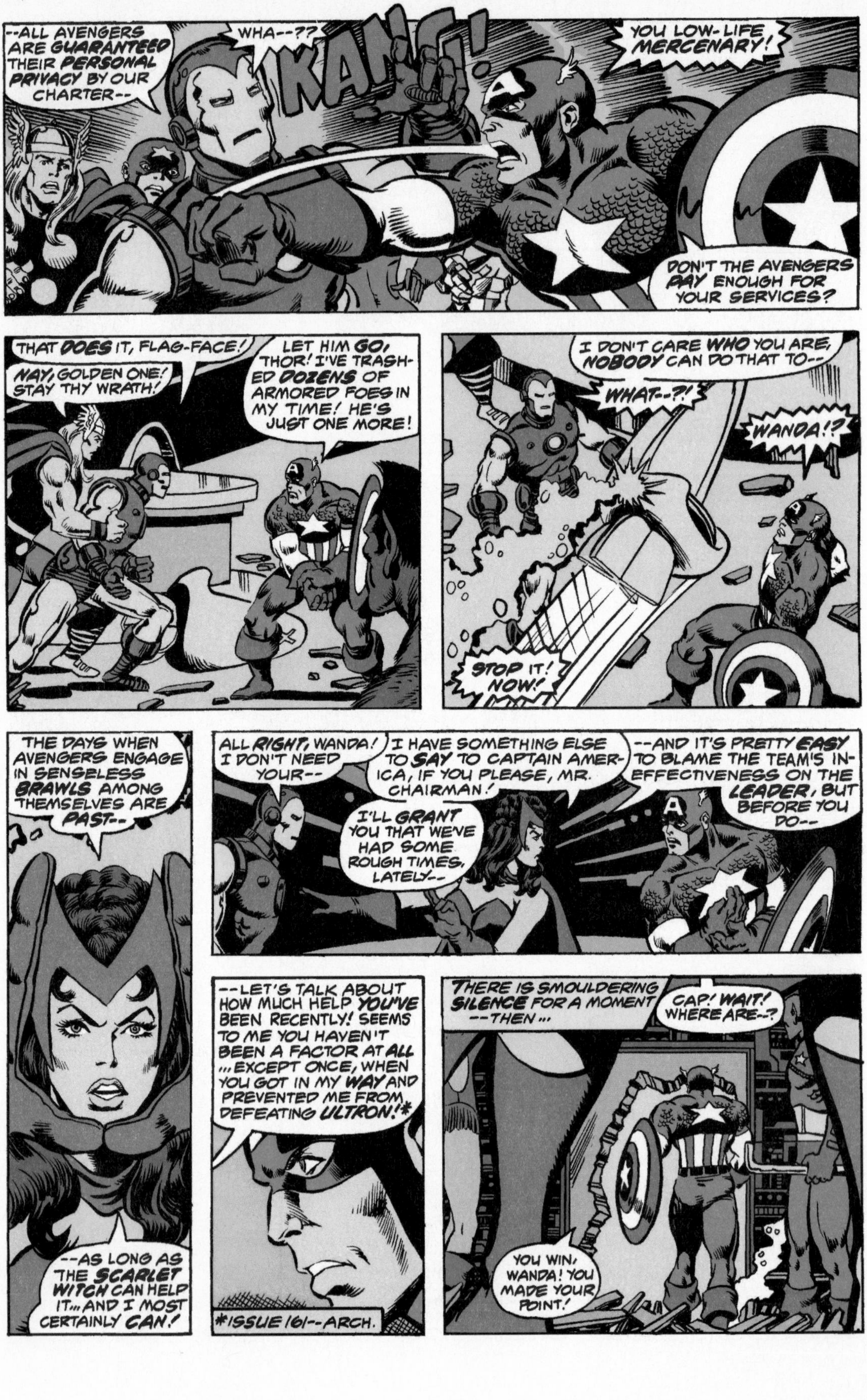
--ALL AVENGERS ARE GUARANTEED THEIR PERSONAL PRIVACY BY OUR CHARTER--
WHA--??
KANG!
YOU LOW-LIFE MERCENARY!
DON'T THE AVENGERS PAY ENOUGH FOR YOUR SERVICES?
THAT DOES IT, FLAG-FACE!
NAY, GOLDEN ONE! STAY THY WRATH!
LET HIM GO, THOR! I'VE TRASHED DOZENS OF ARMORED FOES IN MY TIME! HE'S JUST ONE MORE!
I DON'T CARE WHO YOU ARE, NOBODY CAN DO THAT TO--
WHAT--?!
WANDA!?
STOP IT! NOW!
THE DAYS WHEN AVENGERS ENGAGE IN SENSELESS BRAWLS AMONG THEMSELVES ARE PAST--
--AS LONG AS THE SCARLET WITCH CAN HELP IT... AND I MOST CERTAINLY CAN!
ALL RIGHT, WANDA! I DON'T NEED YOUR--
I HAVE SOMETHING ELSE TO SAY TO CAPTAIN AMERICA, IF YOU PLEASE, MR. CHAIRMAN!
I'LL GRANT YOU THAT WE'VE HAD SOME ROUGH TIMES, LATELY--
--AND IT'S PRETTY EASY TO BLAME THE TEAM'S INEFFECTIVENESS ON THE LEADER, BUT BEFORE YOU DO--
--LET'S TALK ABOUT HOW MUCH HELP YOU'VE BEEN RECENTLY! SEEMS TO ME YOU HAVEN'T BEEN A FACTOR AT ALL ...EXCEPT ONCE, WHEN YOU GOT IN MY WAY AND PREVENTED ME FROM DEFEATING ULTRON!*
*ISSUE 161--ARCH.
THERE IS SMOULDERING SILENCE FOR A MOMENT --THEN...
CAP! WAIT! WHERE ARE--?
YOU WIN, WANDA! YOU MADE YOUR POINT!

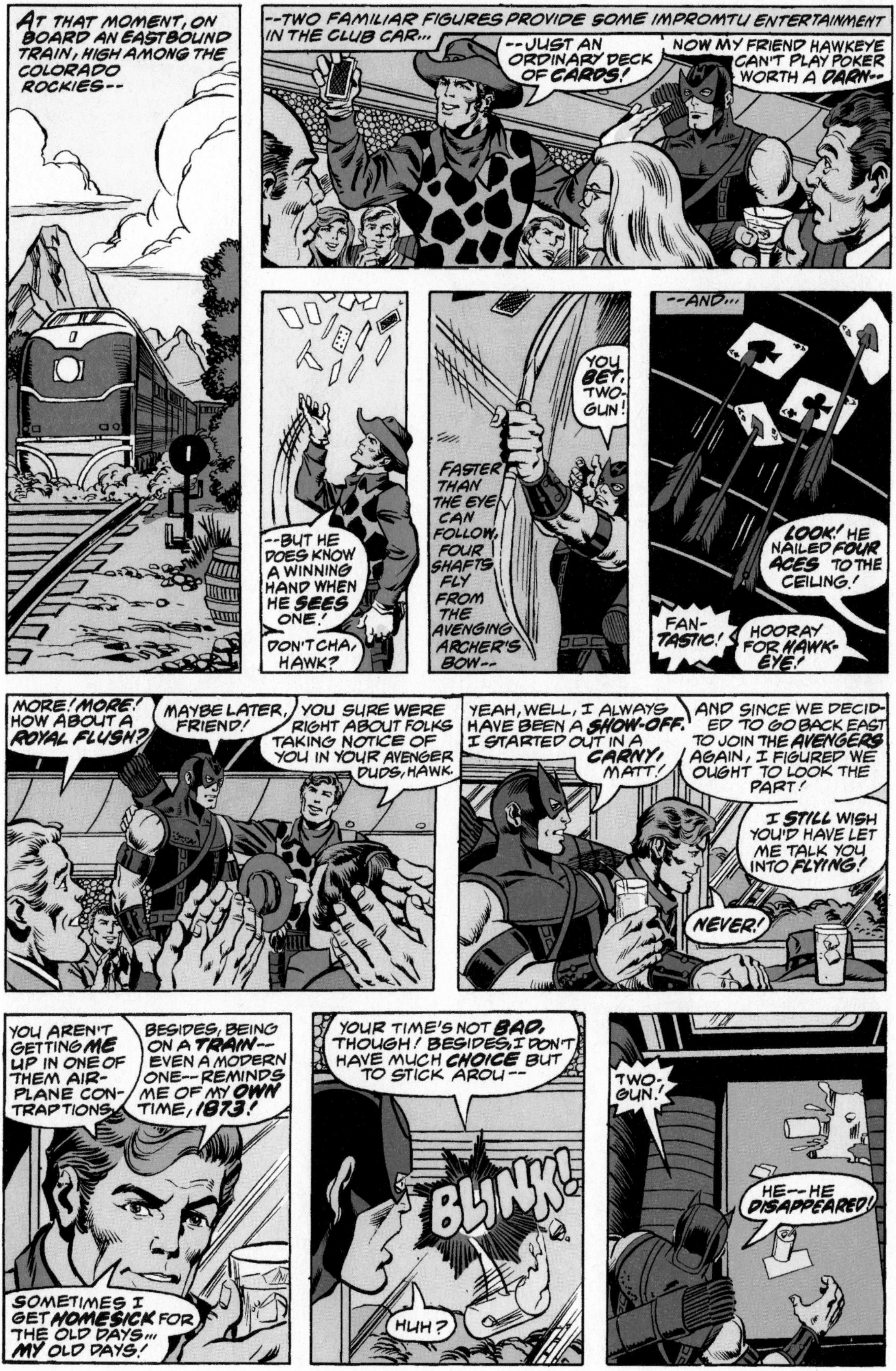
AT THAT MOMENT, ON BOARD AN EASTBOUND TRAIN, HIGH AMONG THE COLORADO ROCKIES--
--TWO FAMILIAR FIGURES PROVIDE SOME IMPROMTU ENTERTAINMENT IN THE CLUB CAR...
--JUST AN ORDINARY DECK OF CARDS!
NOW MY FRIEND HAWKEYE CAN'T PLAY POKER WORTH A DARN--
--BUT HE DOES KNOW A WINNING HAND WHEN HE SEES ONE!
DON'T CHA, HAWK?
YOU BET, TWO-GUN!
FASTER THAN THE EYE CAN FOLLOW, FOUR SHAFTS FLY FROM THE AVENGING ARCHER'S BOW--
--AND...
LOOK! HE NAILED FOUR ACES TO THE CEILING!
FAN-TASTIC!
HOORAY FOR HAWK-EYE!
MORE! MORE! HOW ABOUT A ROYAL FLUSH?
MAYBE LATER, FRIEND!
YOU SURE WERE RIGHT ABOUT FOLKS TAKING NOTICE OF YOU IN YOUR AVENGER DUDS, HAWK.
YEAH, WELL, I ALWAYS HAVE BEEN A SHOW-OFF. I STARTED OUT IN A CARNY, MATT!
AND SINCE WE DECIDED TO GO BACK EAST TO JOIN THE AVENGERS AGAIN, I FIGURED WE OUGHT TO LOOK THE PART!
I STILL WISH YOU'D HAVE LET ME TALK YOU INTO FLYING!
NEVER!
YOU AREN'T GETTING ME UP IN ONE OF THEM AIR-PLANE CONTRAPTIONS.
BESIDES, BEING ON A TRAIN-- EVEN A MODERN ONE--REMINDS ME OF MY OWN TIME, 1873!
SOMETIMES I GET HOMESICK FOR THE OLD DAYS... MY OLD DAYS!
YOUR TIME'S NOT BAD, THOUGH! BESIDES, I DON'T HAVE MUCH CHOICE BUT TO STICK AROU--
BLINK!
HUH?
TWO-GUN!
HE--HE DISAPPEARED!

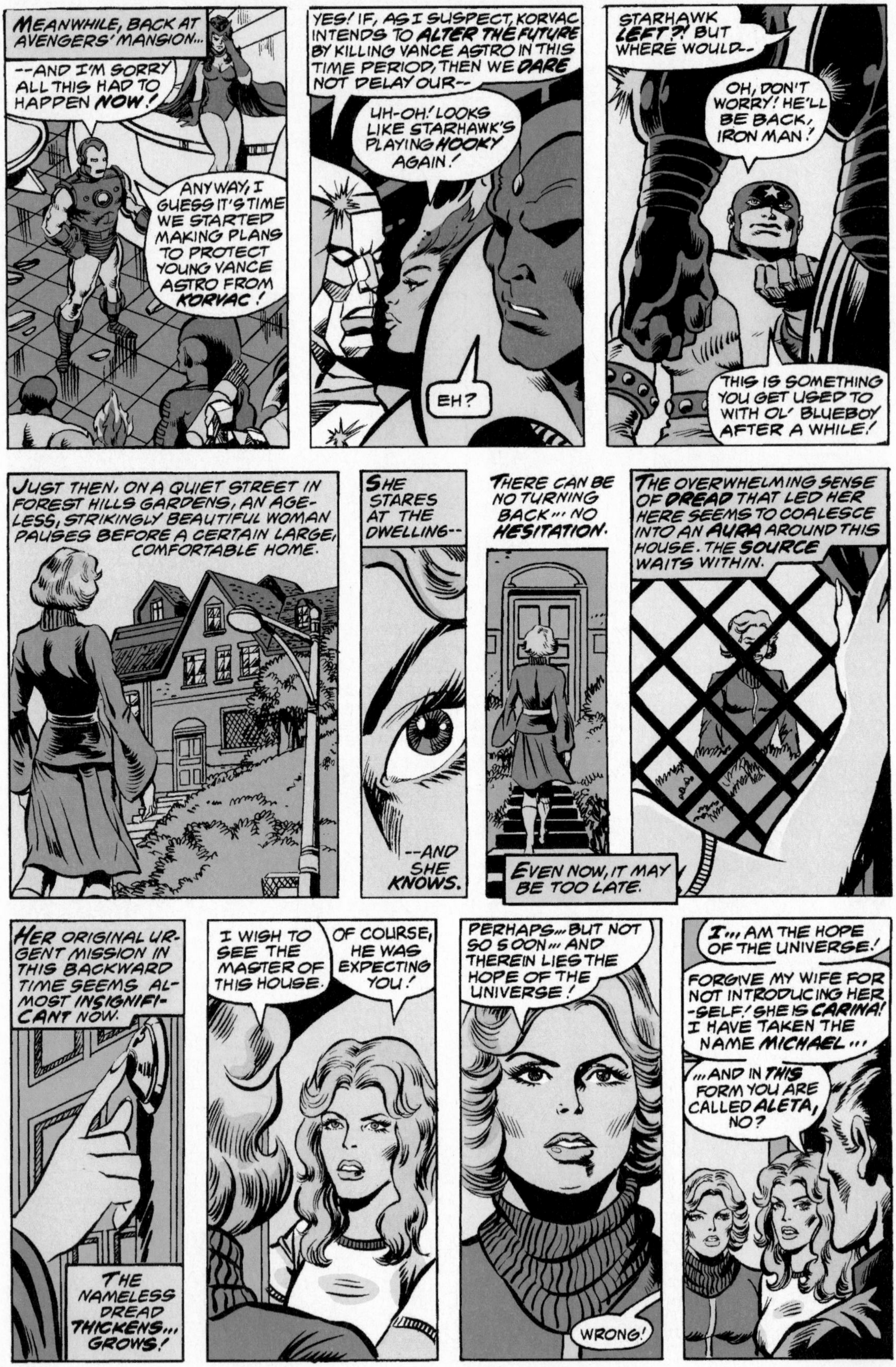

MEANWHILE, BACK AT AVENGERS' MANSION...
--AND I'M SORRY ALL THIS HAD TO HAPPEN NOW!
ANYWAY, I GUESS IT'S TIME WE STARTED MAKING PLANS TO PROTECT YOUNG VANCE ASTRO FROM KORVAC!
YES! IF, AS I SUSPECT, KORVAC INTENDS TO ALTER THE FUTURE BY KILLING VANCE ASTRO IN THIS TIME PERIOD, THEN WE DARE NOT DELAY OUR--
UH-OH! LOOKS LIKE STARHAWK'S PLAYING HOOKY AGAIN!
EH?
STARHAWK LEFT?! BUT WHERE WOULD--
OH, DON'T WORRY! HE'LL BE BACK, IRON MAN!
THIS IS SOMETHING YOU GET USED TO WITH OL' BLUEBOY AFTER A WHILE!
JUST THEN, ON A QUIET STREET IN FOREST HILLS GARDENS, AN AGE-LESS, STRIKINGLY BEAUTIFUL WOMAN PAUSES BEFORE A CERTAIN LARGE, COMFORTABLE HOME.
SHE STARES AT THE DWELLING--
--AND SHE KNOWS.
THERE CAN BE NO TURNING BACK... NO HESITATION.
EVEN NOW, IT MAY BE TOO LATE.
THE OVERWHELMING SENSE OF DREAD THAT LED HER HERE SEEMS TO COALESCE INTO AN AURA AROUND THIS HOUSE. THE SOURCE WAITS WITHIN.
HER ORIGINAL UR-GENT MISSION IN THIS BACKWARD TIME SEEMS AL-MOST INSIGNIFI-CANT NOW.
THE NAMELESS DREAD THICKENS... GROWS!
I WISH TO SEE THE MASTER OF THIS HOUSE.
OF COURSE, HE WAS EXPECTING YOU!
PERHAPS... BUT NOT SO SOON... AND THEREIN LIES THE HOPE OF THE UNIVERSE!
WRONG!
I... AM THE HOPE OF THE UNIVERSE!
FORGIVE MY WIFE FOR NOT INTRODUCING HER-SELF! SHE IS CARINA! I HAVE TAKEN THE NAME MICHAEL...
...AND IN THIS FORM YOU ARE CALLED ALETA, NO?

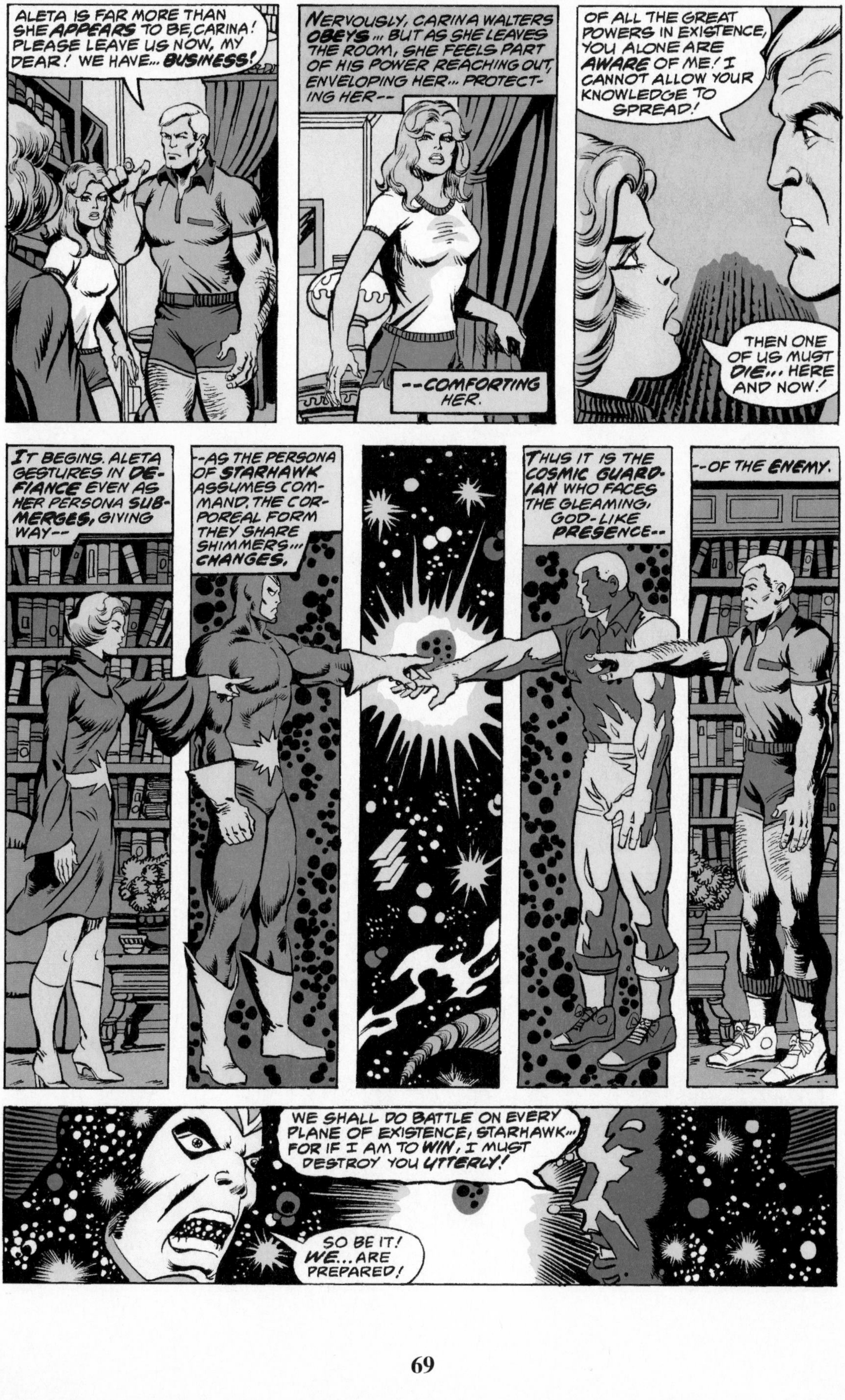
ALETA IS FAR MORE THAN SHE APPEARS TO BE, CARINA! PLEASE LEAVE US NOW, MY DEAR! WE HAVE... BUSINESS!
NERVOUSLY, CARINA WALTERS OBEYS... BUT AS SHE LEAVES THE ROOM, SHE FEELS PART OF HIS POWER REACHING OUT, ENVELOPING HER... PROTECTING HER--
--COMFORTING HER.
OF ALL THE GREAT POWERS IN EXISTENCE, YOU ALONE ARE AWARE OF ME! I CANNOT ALLOW YOUR KNOWLEDGE TO SPREAD!
THEN ONE OF US MUST DIE... HERE AND NOW!
IT BEGINS. ALETA GESTURES IN DEFIANCE EVEN AS HER PERSONA SUBMERGES, GIVING WAY--
--AS THE PERSONA OF STARHAWK ASSUMES COMMAND. THE CORPOREAL FORM THEY SHARE SHIMMERS... CHANGES.
THUS IT IS THE COSMIC GUARDIAN WHO FACES THE GLEAMING, GOD-LIKE PRESENCE--
--OF THE ENEMY.
WE SHALL DO BATTLE ON EVERY PLANE OF EXISTENCE, STARHAWK... FOR IF I AM TO WIN, I MUST DESTROY YOU UTTERLY!
SO BE IT! WE... ARE PREPARED!

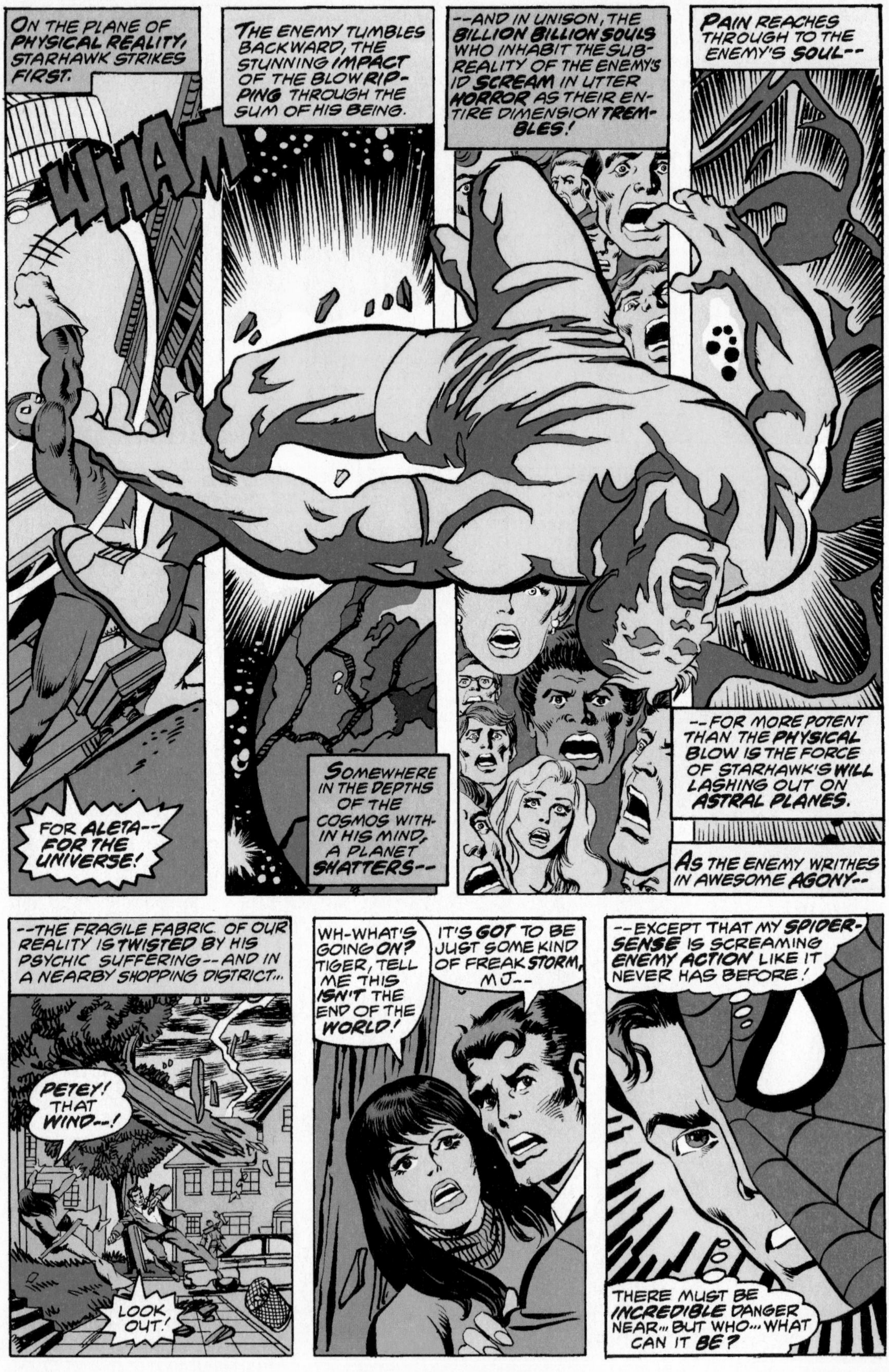
ON THE PLANE OF PHYSICAL REALITY, STARHAWK STRIKES FIRST.
WHAM
FOR ALETA-- FOR THE UNIVERSE!
THE ENEMY TUMBLES BACKWARD, THE STUNNING IMPACT OF THE BLOW RIPPING THROUGH THE SUM OF HIS BEING.
SOMEWHERE IN THE DEPTHS OF THE COSMOS WITHIN HIS MIND, A PLANET SHATTERS--
--AND IN UNISON, THE BILLION BILLION SOULS WHO INHABIT THE SUB-REALITY OF THE ENEMY'S ID SCREAM IN UTTER HORROR AS THEIR ENTIRE DIMENSION TREMBLES!
PAIN REACHES THROUGH TO THE ENEMY'S SOUL--
--FOR MORE POTENT THAN THE PHYSICAL BLOW IS THE FORCE OF STARHAWK'S WILL LASHING OUT ON ASTRAL PLANES.
AS THE ENEMY WRITHES IN AWESOME AGONY--
--THE FRAGILE FABRIC OF OUR REALITY IS TWISTED BY HIS PSYCHIC SUFFERING--AND IN A NEARBY SHOPPING DISTRICT...
PETEY! THAT WIND--!
LOOK OUT!
WH-WHAT'S GOING ON? TIGER, TELL ME THIS ISN'T THE END OF THE WORLD!
IT'S GOT TO BE JUST SOME KIND OF FREAK STORM, MJ--
--EXCEPT THAT MY SPIDER-SENSE IS SCREAMING ENEMY ACTION LIKE IT NEVER HAS BEFORE!
THERE MUST BE INCREDIBLE DANGER NEAR... BUT WHO... WHAT CAN IT BE?

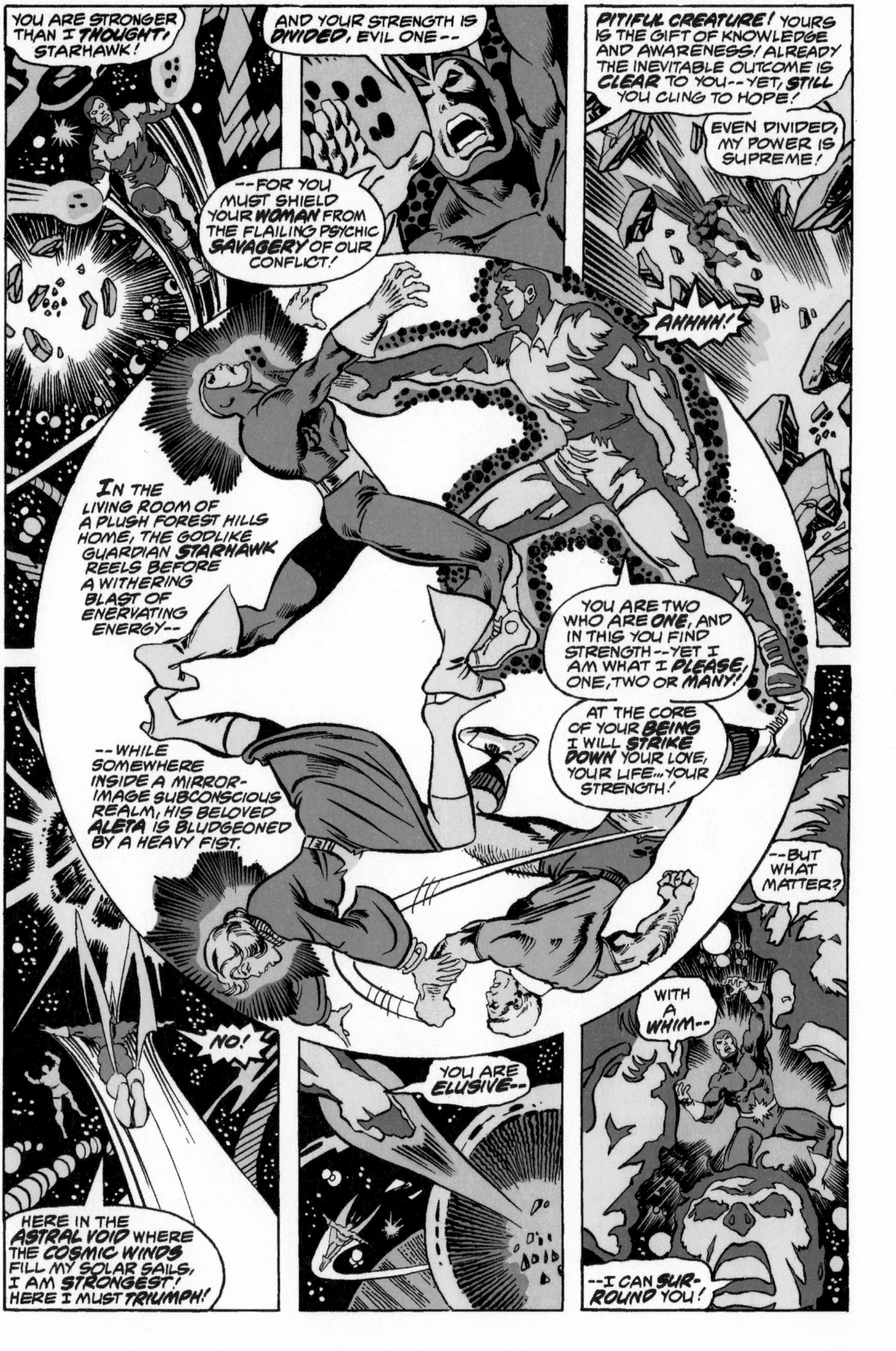

YOU ARE STRONGER THAN I THOUGHT, STARHAWK!
AND YOUR STRENGTH IS DIVIDED, EVIL ONE--
--FOR YOU MUST SHIELD YOUR WOMAN FROM THE FLAILING PSYCHIC SAVAGERY OF OUR CONFLICT!
PITIFUL CREATURE! YOURS IS THE GIFT OF KNOWLEDGE AND AWARENESS! ALREADY THE INEVITABLE OUTCOME IS CLEAR TO YOU--YET, STILL YOU CLING TO HOPE!
EVEN DIVIDED, MY POWER IS SUPREME!
AHHHH!
IN THE LIVING ROOM OF A PLUSH FOREST HILLS HOME, THE GODLIKE GUARDIAN STARHAWK REELS BEFORE A WITHERING BLAST OF ENERVATING ENERGY--
YOU ARE TWO WHO ARE ONE, AND IN THIS YOU FIND STRENGTH--YET I AM WHAT I PLEASE, ONE, TWO OR MANY!
AT THE CORE OF YOUR BEING I WILL STRIKE DOWN YOUR LOVE, YOUR LIFE... YOUR STRENGTH!
--WHILE SOMEWHERE INSIDE A MIRROR-IMAGE SUBCONSCIOUS REALM, HIS BELOVED ALETA IS BLUDGEONED BY A HEAVY FIST.
--BUT WHAT MATTER?
NO!
HERE IN THE ASTRAL VOID WHERE THE COSMIC WINDS FILL MY SOLAR SAILS, I AM STRONGEST! HERE I MUST TRIUMPH!
YOU ARE ELUSIVE--
WITH A WHIM--
--I CAN SURROUND YOU!

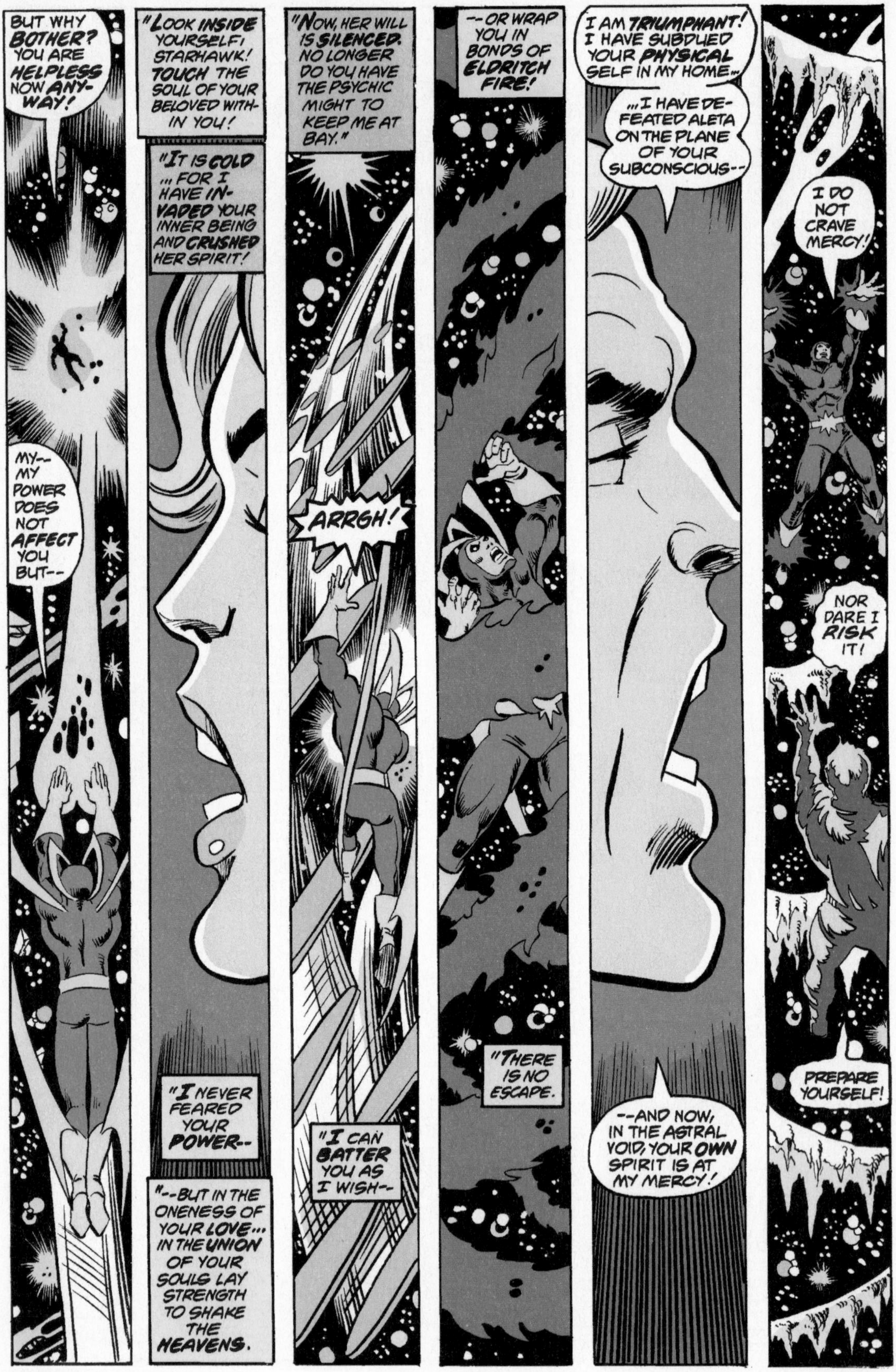
BUT WHY BOTHER? YOU ARE HELPLESS NOW ANYWAY!
MY-- MY POWER DOES NOT AFFECT YOU BUT--
"LOOK INSIDE YOURSELF, STARHAWK! TOUCH THE SOUL OF YOUR BELOVED WITHIN YOU!
"IT IS COLD ...FOR I HAVE INVADED YOUR INNER BEING AND CRUSHED HER SPIRIT!
"I NEVER FEARED YOUR POWER--
"--BUT IN THE ONENESS OF YOUR LOVE... IN THE UNION OF YOUR SOULS LAY STRENGTH TO SHAKE THE HEAVENS.
"NOW, HER WILL IS SILENCED. NO LONGER DO YOU HAVE THE PSYCHIC MIGHT TO KEEP ME AT BAY."
ARRGH!
"I CAN BATTER YOU AS I WISH--
--OR WRAP YOU IN BONDS OF ELDRITCH FIRE!
"THERE IS NO ESCAPE.
I AM TRIUMPHANT! I HAVE SUBDUED YOUR PHYSICAL SELF IN MY HOME...
...I HAVE DEFEATED ALETA ON THE PLANE OF YOUR SUBCONSCIOUS--
--AND NOW, IN THE ASTRAL VOID, YOUR OWN SPIRIT IS AT MY MERCY!
I DO NOT CRAVE MERCY!
NOR DARE I RISK IT!
PREPARE YOURSELF!

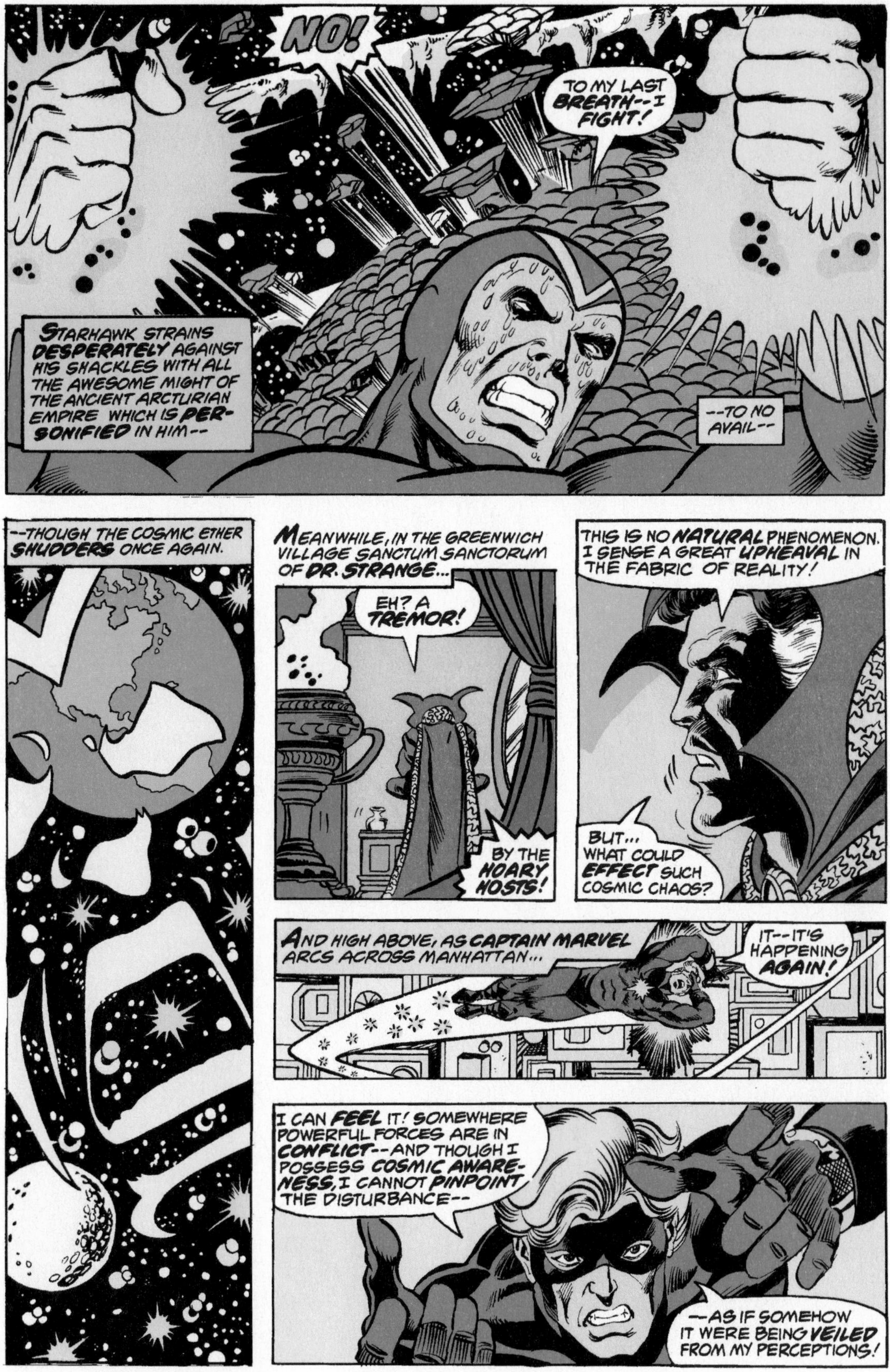
NO!
TO MY LAST BREATH--I FIGHT!
STARHAWK STRAINS DESPERATELY AGAINST HIS SHACKLES WITH ALL THE AWESOME MIGHT OF THE ANCIENT ARCTURIAN EMPIRE WHICH IS PERSONIFIED IN HIM--
--TO NO AVAIL--
--THOUGH THE COSMIC ETHER SHUDDERS ONCE AGAIN.
MEANWHILE, IN THE GREENWICH VILLAGE SANCTUM SANCTORUM OF DR. STRANGE...
EH? A TREMOR!
BY THE HOARY HOSTS!
THIS IS NO NATURAL PHENOMENON. I SENSE A GREAT UPHEAVAL IN THE FABRIC OF REALITY!
BUT... WHAT COULD EFFECT SUCH COSMIC CHAOS?
AND HIGH ABOVE, AS CAPTAIN MARVEL ARCS ACROSS MANHATTAN...
IT--IT'S HAPPENING AGAIN!
I CAN FEEL IT! SOMEWHERE POWERFUL FORCES ARE IN CONFLICT--AND THOUGH I POSSESS COSMIC AWARENESS, I CANNOT PINPOINT THE DISTURBANCE--
--AS IF SOMEHOW IT WERE BEING VEILED FROM MY PERCEPTIONS!

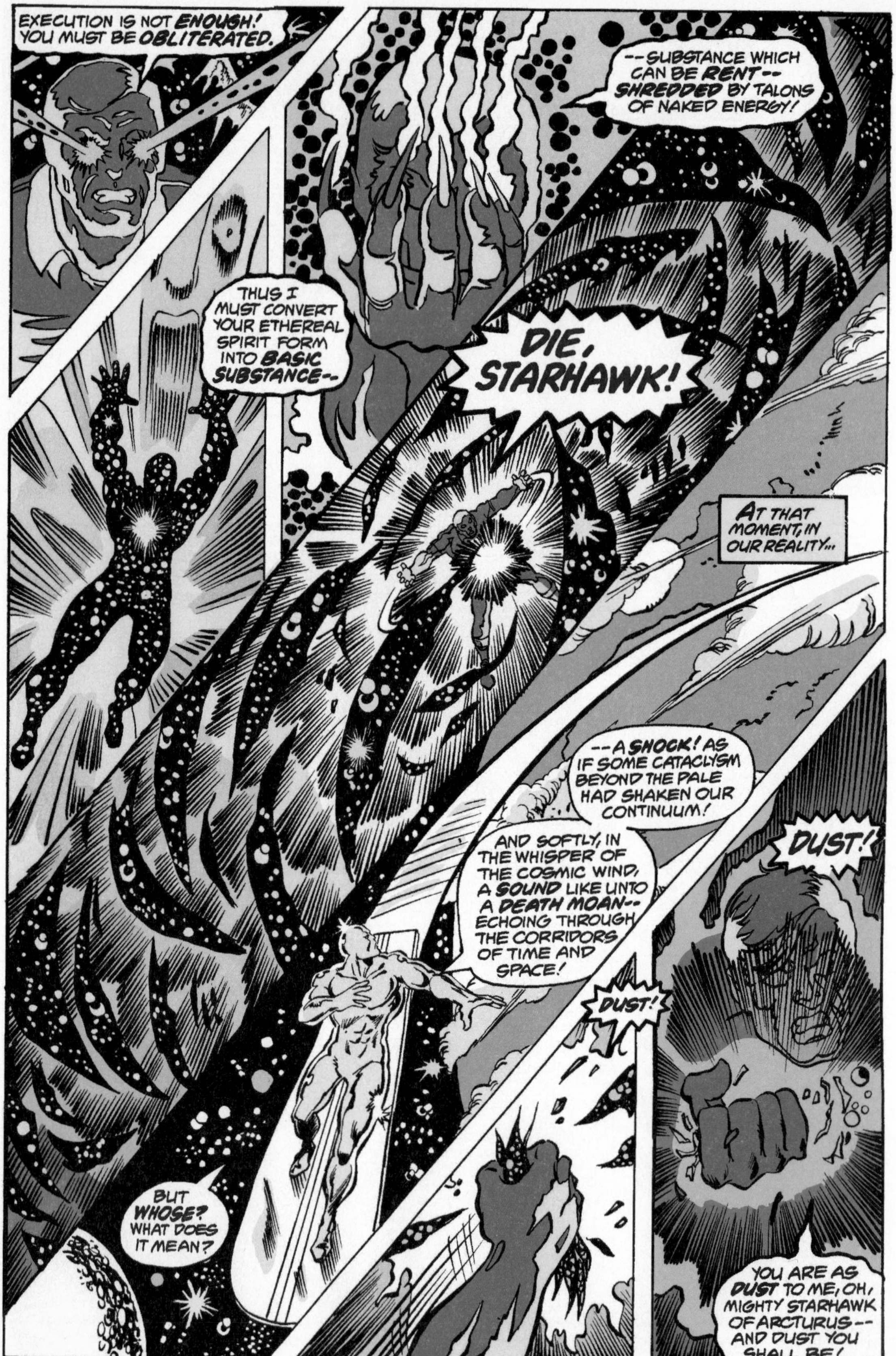
EXECUTION IS NOT ENOUGH! YOU MUST BE OBLITERATED.
THUS I MUST CONVERT YOUR ETHEREAL SPIRIT FORM INTO BASIC SUBSTANCE--
--SUBSTANCE WHICH CAN BE RENT-- SHREDDED BY TALONS OF NAKED ENERGY!
DIE, STARHAWK!
AT THAT MOMENT, IN OUR REALITY...
--A SHOCK! AS IF SOME CATACLYSM BEYOND THE PALE HAD SHAKEN OUR CONTINUUM!
AND SOFTLY, IN THE WHISPER OF THE COSMIC WIND, A SOUND LIKE UNTO A DEATH MOAN-- ECHOING THROUGH THE CORRIDORS OF TIME AND SPACE!
BUT WHOSE? WHAT DOES IT MEAN?
DUST!
DUST!
YOU ARE AS DUST TO ME, OH, MIGHTY STARHAWK OF ARCTURUS-- AND DUST YOU SHALL BE!

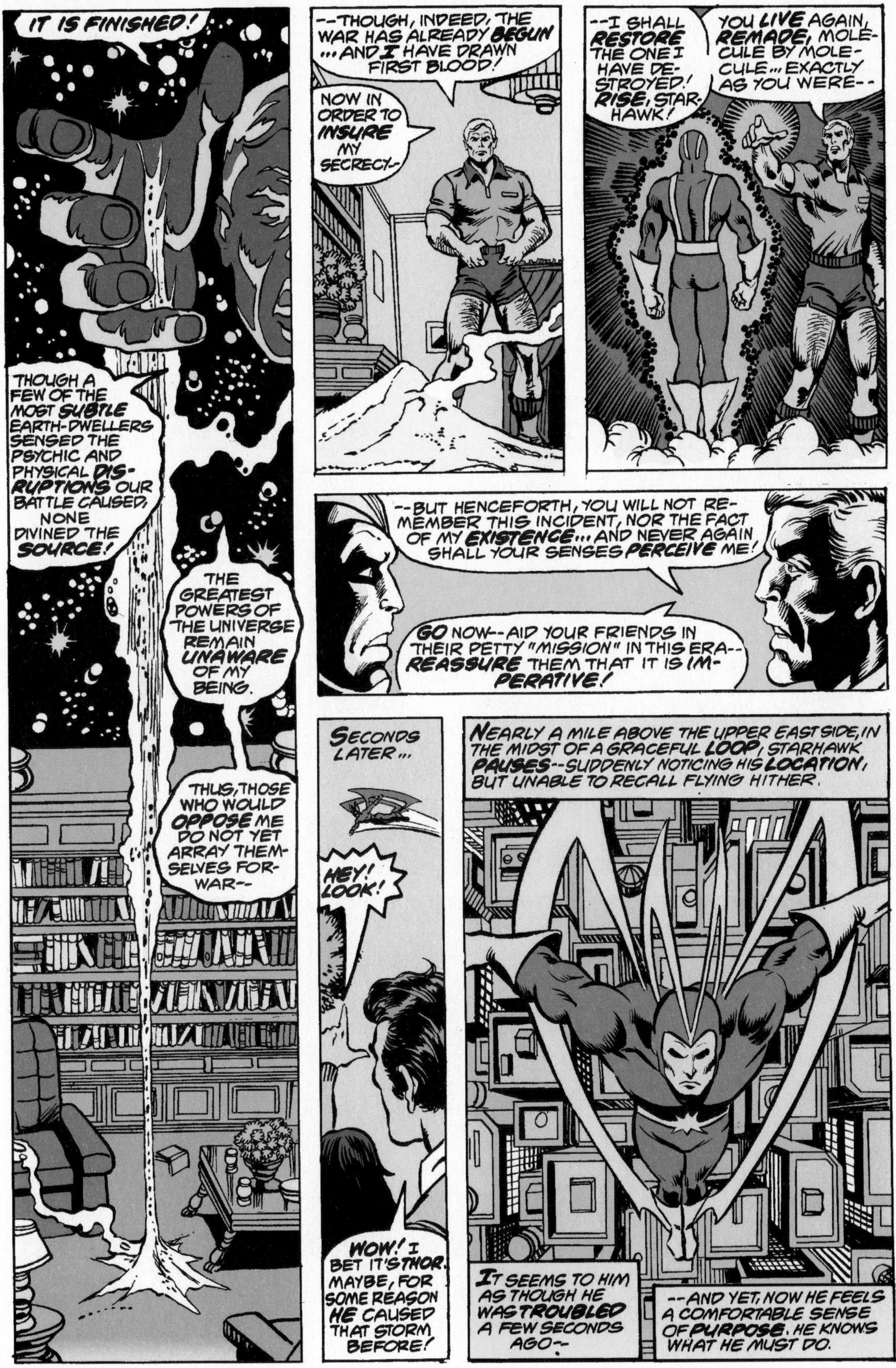
IT IS FINISHED!
THOUGH A FEW OF THE MOST SUBTLE EARTH-DWELLERS SENSED THE PSYCHIC AND PHYSICAL DIS-RUPTIONS OUR BATTLE CAUSED, NONE DIVINED THE SOURCE!
THE GREATEST POWERS OF THE UNIVERSE REMAIN UNAWARE OF MY BEING.
THUS, THOSE WHO WOULD OPPOSE ME DO NOT YET ARRAY THEM-SELVES FOR WAR--
--THOUGH, INDEED, THE WAR HAS ALREADY BEGUN ...AND I HAVE DRAWN FIRST BLOOD!
NOW IN ORDER TO INSURE MY SECRECY--
--I SHALL RESTORE THE ONE I HAVE DE-STROYED! RISE, STAR-HAWK!
YOU LIVE AGAIN, REMADE, MOLE-CULE BY MOLE-CULE... EXACTLY AS YOU WERE--
--BUT HENCEFORTH, YOU WILL NOT RE-MEMBER THIS INCIDENT, NOR THE FACT OF MY EXISTENCE... AND NEVER AGAIN SHALL YOUR SENSES PERCEIVE ME!
GO NOW--AID YOUR FRIENDS IN THEIR PETTY "MISSION" IN THIS ERA--REASSURE THEM THAT IT IS IM-PERATIVE!
SECONDS LATER...
HEY! LOOK!
WOW! I BET IT'S THOR. MAYBE, FOR SOME REASON HE CAUSED THAT STORM BEFORE!
NEARLY A MILE ABOVE THE UPPER EAST SIDE, IN THE MIDST OF A GRACEFUL LOOP, STARHAWK PAUSES--SUDDENLY NOTICING HIS LOCATION, BUT UNABLE TO RECALL FLYING HITHER.
IT SEEMS TO HIM AS THOUGH HE WAS TROUBLED A FEW SECONDS AGO--
--AND YET, NOW HE FEELS A COMFORTABLE SENSE OF PURPOSE. HE KNOWS WHAT HE MUST DO.

MEANWHILE, IN AVENGERS' MANSION...

--SO WHAT IT AMOUNTS TO IS *GUARD DUTY!* IT'LL BE UP TO YOU GUARDIANS TO STAY *CLOSE* TO LITTLE VANCE ASTRO--

AYE, AND *SUMMON* US WHEN KORVAC DOTH STRIKE!

I'M CERTAIN TONY STARK CAN ARRANGE TO BUY A *HOUSE* IN VANCE'S NEIGHBORHOOD FOR YOU TO USE AS AN H.Q.

NATURALLY, YOU'LL HAVE TO KEEP A *LOW PROFILE* DURING THIS OPERATION!

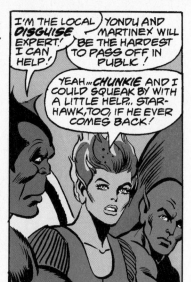

I'M THE LOCAL *DISGUISE* EXPERT! I CAN HELP!

YONDU AND MARTINEX WILL BE THE HARDEST TO PASS OFF IN PUBLIC!

YEAH... *CHUNKIE* AND I COULD SQUEAK BY WITH A LITTLE HELP... *STARHAWK,* TOO, IF HE EVER COMES BACK!

I AM HERE!

STARHAWK!

WHERE *WERE* YOU?

SEARCHING. SEEKING *TRUTH!*

SOMETIMES I THINK YOU JUST PLAIN *LIKE* SNEAKING OUT! *GROW UP,* WILLYA?

UH, DID YOU FIND OUT ANYTHING?

ONLY... THAT WE MUST PROCEED WITH OUR MISSION! IT IS *IMPERATIVE!* ACCEPT THE WORD OF ONE WHO KNOWS!

HUH?

JUST *BELIEVE* 'IM, RUSTY! HE'S *WEIRD*... BUT *REAL!*

EPILOGUE: NIGHT FALLS QUIETLY OVER FOREST HILLS GARDENS--

--WHERE, ALONE IN A DIMLY LIT STUDY, A SOLEMN FIGURE PONDERS....

...AND *PLANS.*

NEXT ISSUE: ...THOUGH HELL SHOULD BAR the WAY!

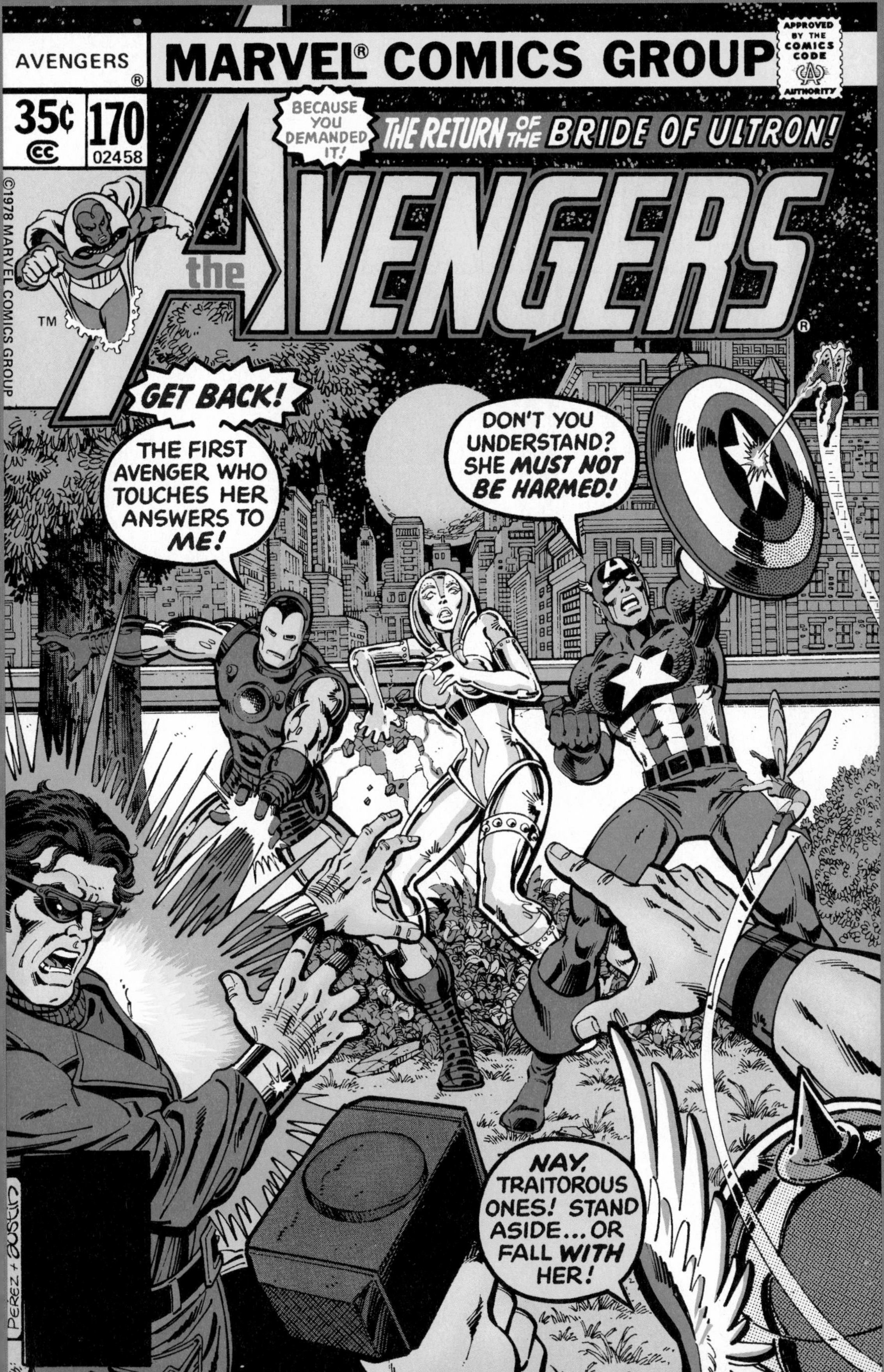
AVENGERS
MARVEL® COMICS GROUP
APPROVED BY THE COMICS CODE AUTHORITY
35¢
170
02458
BECAUSE YOU DEMANDED IT!
THE RETURN OF THE BRIDE OF ULTRON!
THE AVENGERS
©1978 MARVEL COMICS GROUP
GET BACK!
THE FIRST AVENGER WHO TOUCHES HER ANSWERS TO ME!
DON'T YOU UNDERSTAND? SHE MUST NOT BE HARMED!
NAY, TRAITOROUS ONES! STAND ASIDE... OR FALL WITH HER!
PÉREZ + AUSTIN

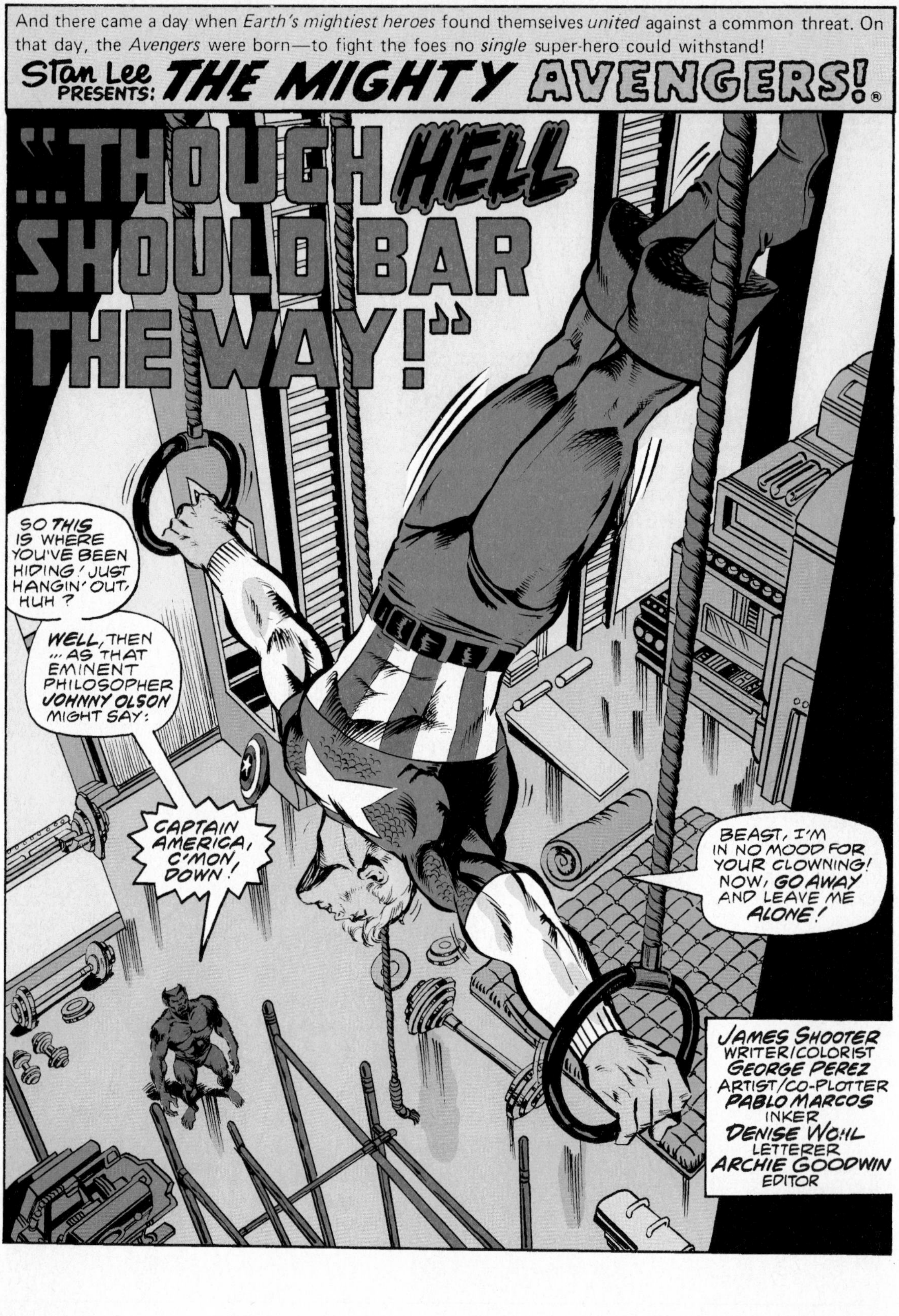
And there came a day when Earth's mightiest heroes found themselves united against a common threat. On that day, the Avengers were born—to fight the foes no single super-hero could withstand!
Stan Lee PRESENTS: THE MIGHTY AVENGERS!®
"...THOUGH HELL SHOULD BAR THE WAY!"
SO THIS IS WHERE YOU'VE BEEN HIDING! JUST HANGIN' OUT, HUH?
WELL, THEN ...AS THAT EMINENT PHILOSOPHER JOHNNY OLSON MIGHT SAY:
CAPTAIN AMERICA, C'MON DOWN!
BEAST, I'M IN NO MOOD FOR YOUR CLOWNING! NOW, GO AWAY AND LEAVE ME ALONE!
JAMES SHOOTER WRITER/COLORIST
GEORGE PEREZ ARTIST/CO-PLOTTER
PABLO MARCOS INKER
DENISE WOHL LETTERER
ARCHIE GOODWIN EDITOR

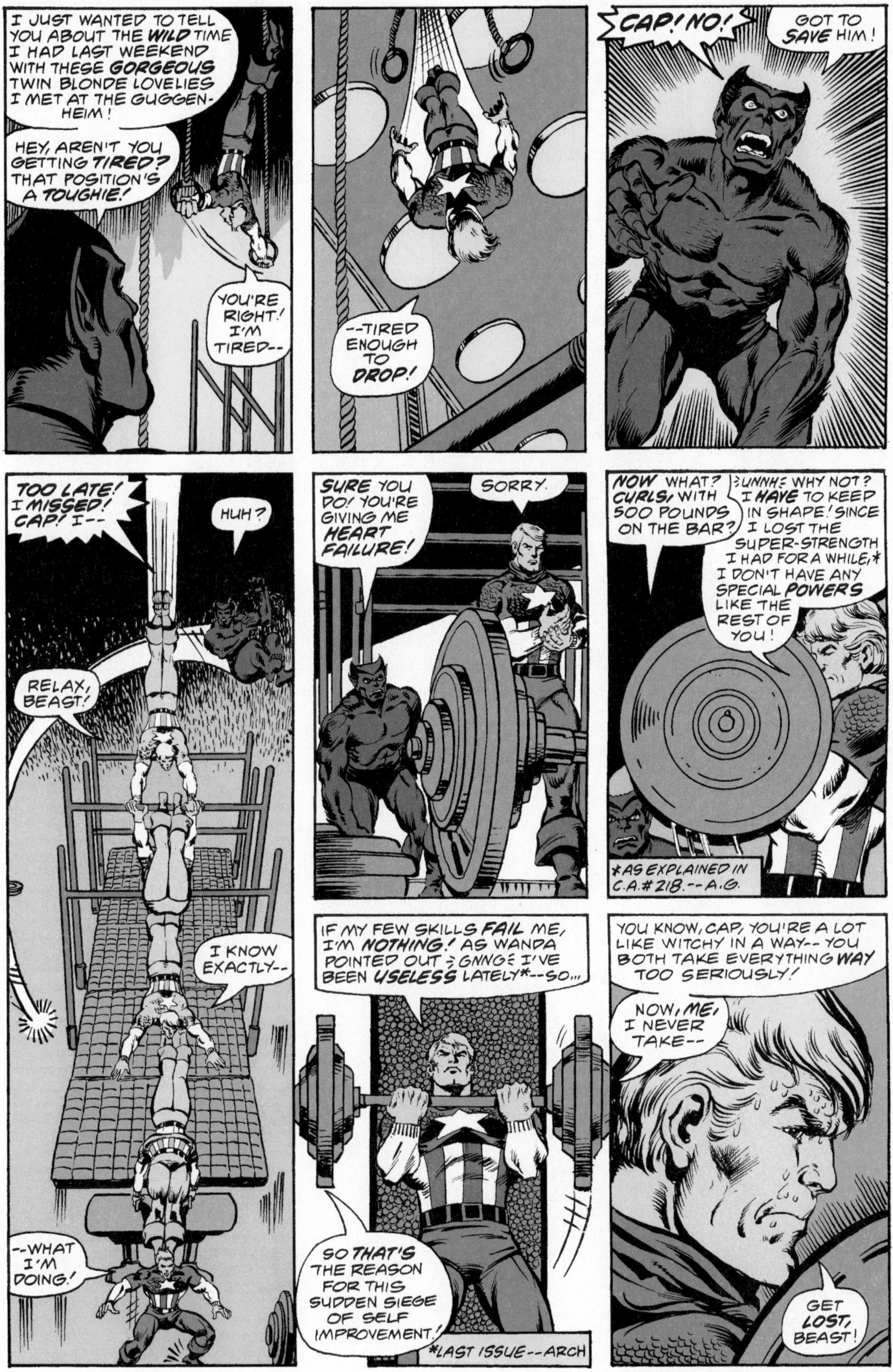
I JUST WANTED TO TELL YOU ABOUT THE WILD TIME I HAD LAST WEEKEND WITH THESE GORGEOUS TWIN BLONDE LOVELIES I MET AT THE GUGGENHEIM!
HEY, AREN'T YOU GETTING TIRED? THAT POSITION'S A TOUGHIE!
YOU'RE RIGHT! I'M TIRED--
--TIRED ENOUGH TO DROP!
CAP! NO!
GOT TO SAVE HIM!
TOO LATE! I MISSED! CAP! I--
HUH?
RELAX, BEAST!
I KNOW EXACTLY--
--WHAT I'M DOING!
SURE YOU DO! YOU'RE GIVING ME HEART FAILURE!
SORRY.
NOW WHAT? CURLS, WITH 500 POUNDS ON THE BAR?
UNNH WHY NOT? I HAVE TO KEEP IN SHAPE! SINCE I LOST THE SUPER-STRENGTH I HAD FOR A WHILE,* I DON'T HAVE ANY SPECIAL POWERS LIKE THE REST OF YOU!
*AS EXPLAINED IN C.A.#218.--A.G.
IF MY FEW SKILLS FAIL ME, I'M NOTHING! AS WANDA POINTED OUT GNNG I'VE BEEN USELESS LATELY*--SO...
SO THAT'S THE REASON FOR THIS SUDDEN SIEGE OF SELF IMPROVEMENT!
*LAST ISSUE--ARCH
YOU KNOW, CAP, YOU'RE A LOT LIKE WITCHY IN A WAY-- YOU BOTH TAKE EVERYTHING WAY TOO SERIOUSLY!
NOW, ME, I NEVER TAKE--
GET LOST, BEAST!

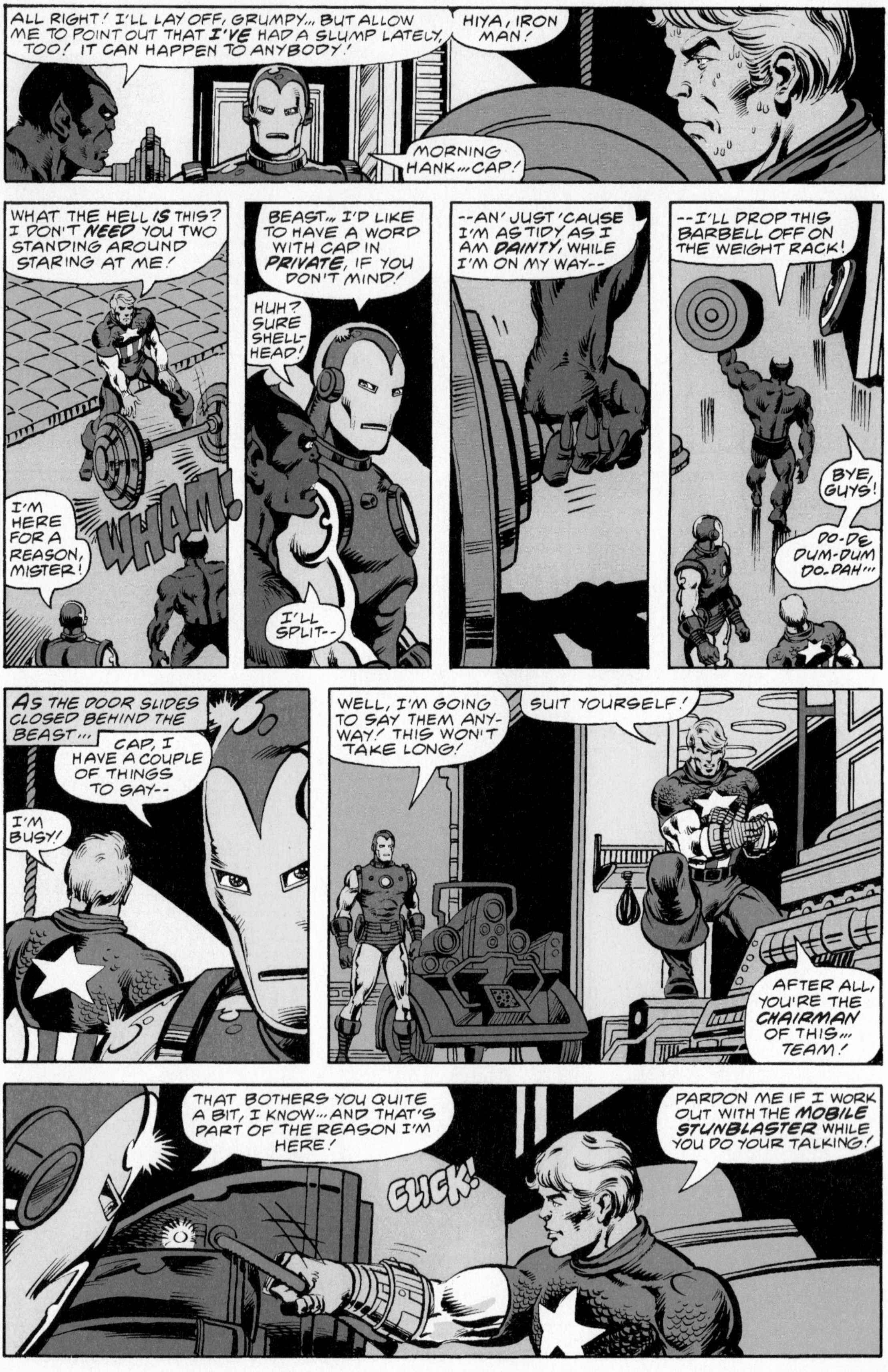
ALL RIGHT! I'LL LAY OFF, GRUMPY... BUT ALLOW ME TO POINT OUT THAT I'VE HAD A SLUMP LATELY, TOO! IT CAN HAPPEN TO ANYBODY!
HIYA, IRON MAN!
MORNING HANK... CAP!
WHAT THE HELL IS THIS? I DON'T NEED YOU TWO STANDING AROUND STARING AT ME!
I'M HERE FOR A REASON, MISTER!
WHAM!
BEAST... I'D LIKE TO HAVE A WORD WITH CAP IN PRIVATE, IF YOU DON'T MIND!
HUH? SURE SHELL-HEAD!
I'LL SPLIT--
--AN' JUST 'CAUSE I'M AS TIDY AS I AM DAINTY, WHILE I'M ON MY WAY--
--I'LL DROP THIS BARBELL OFF ON THE WEIGHT RACK!
BYE, GUYS!
DO-DE DUM-DUM DO-DAH...
AS THE DOOR SLIDES CLOSED BEHIND THE BEAST...
CAP, I HAVE A COUPLE OF THINGS TO SAY--
I'M BUSY!
WELL, I'M GOING TO SAY THEM ANYWAY! THIS WON'T TAKE LONG!
SUIT YOURSELF!
AFTER ALL, YOU'RE THE CHAIRMAN OF THIS... TEAM!
THAT BOTHERS YOU QUITE A BIT, I KNOW... AND THAT'S PART OF THE REASON I'M HERE!
CLICK!
PARDON ME IF I WORK OUT WITH THE MOBILE STUNBLASTER WHILE YOU DO YOUR TALKING!

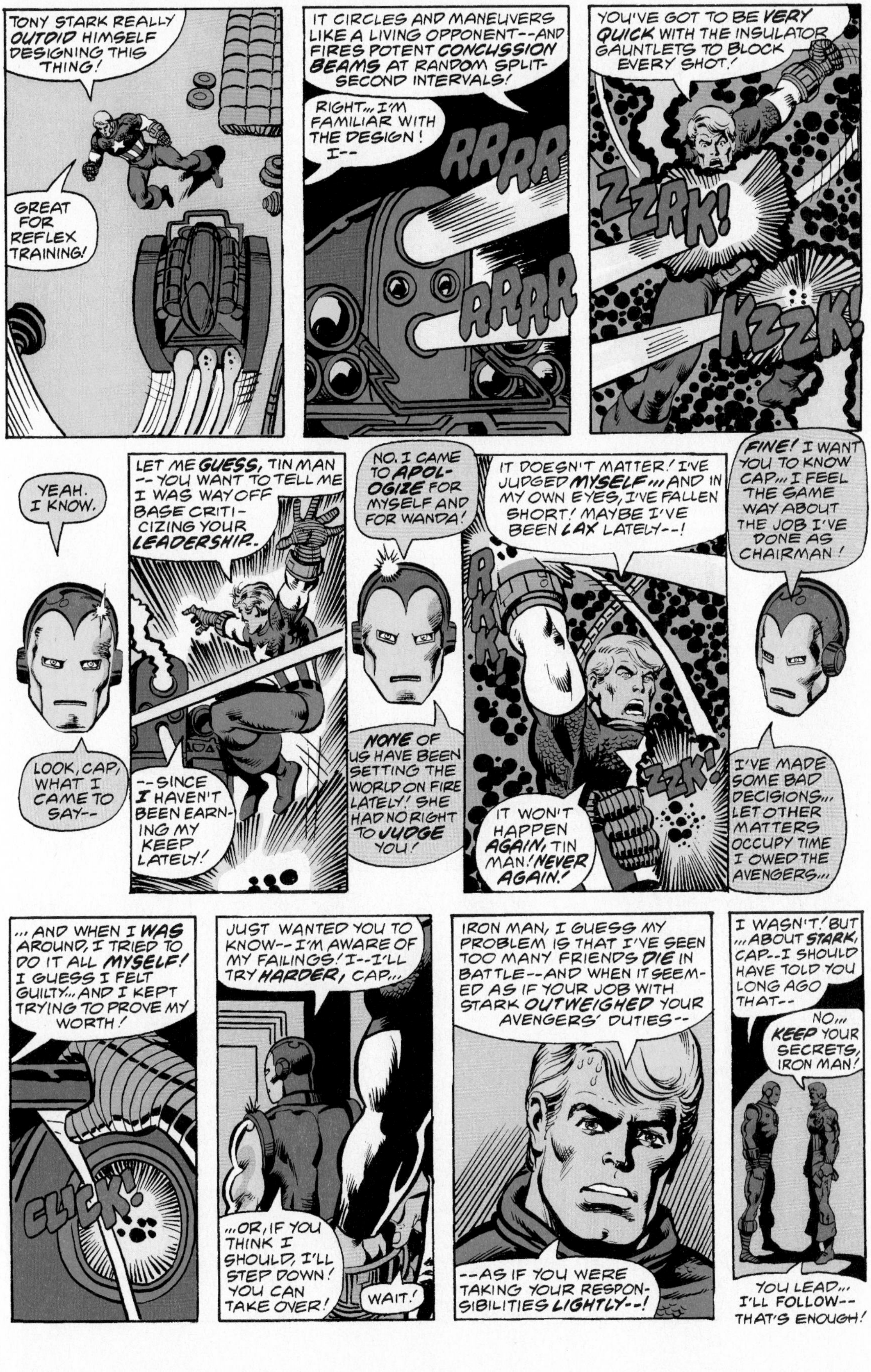

TONY STARK REALLY OUTDID HIMSELF DESIGNING THIS THING!
GREAT FOR REFLEX TRAINING!
IT CIRCLES AND MANEUVERS LIKE A LIVING OPPONENT--AND FIRES POTENT CONCUSSION BEAMS AT RANDOM SPLIT-SECOND INTERVALS!
RIGHT... I'M FAMILIAR WITH THE DESIGN! I--
RRRR
ARRR
YOU'VE GOT TO BE VERY QUICK WITH THE INSULATOR GAUNTLETS TO BLOCK EVERY SHOT!
ZZZAK!
KZZK!
YEAH. I KNOW.
LOOK, CAP, WHAT I CAME TO SAY--
LET ME GUESS, TIN MAN--YOU WANT TO TELL ME I WAS WAY OFF BASE CRITICIZING YOUR LEADERSHIP..
--SINCE I HAVEN'T BEEN EARNING MY KEEP LATELY!
NO. I CAME TO APOLOGIZE FOR MYSELF AND FOR WANDA!
NONE OF US HAVE BEEN SETTING THE WORLD ON FIRE LATELY! SHE HAD NO RIGHT TO JUDGE YOU!
IT DOESN'T MATTER! I'VE JUDGED MYSELF... AND IN MY OWN EYES, I'VE FALLEN SHORT! MAYBE I'VE BEEN LAX LATELY--!
RAKK!
ZZK!
IT WON'T HAPPEN AGAIN, TIN MAN! NEVER AGAIN!
FINE! I WANT YOU TO KNOW CAP... I FEEL THE SAME WAY ABOUT THE JOB I'VE DONE AS CHAIRMAN!
I'VE MADE SOME BAD DECISIONS... LET OTHER MATTERS OCCUPY TIME I OWED THE AVENGERS...
...AND WHEN I WAS AROUND, I TRIED TO DO IT ALL MYSELF! I GUESS I FELT GUILTY... AND I KEPT TRYING TO PROVE MY WORTH!
CLICK!
JUST WANTED YOU TO KNOW--I'M AWARE OF MY FAILINGS! I--I'LL TRY HARDER, CAP...
...OR, IF YOU THINK I SHOULD, I'LL STEP DOWN! YOU CAN TAKE OVER!
WAIT!
IRON MAN, I GUESS MY PROBLEM IS THAT I'VE SEEN TOO MANY FRIENDS DIE IN BATTLE--AND WHEN IT SEEMED AS IF YOUR JOB WITH STARK OUTWEIGHED YOUR AVENGERS' DUTIES--
--AS IF YOU WERE TAKING YOUR RESPONSIBILITIES LIGHTLY--!
I WASN'T! BUT ...ABOUT STARK, CAP--I SHOULD HAVE TOLD YOU LONG AGO THAT--
NO... KEEP YOUR SECRETS, IRON MAN!
YOU LEAD... I'LL FOLLOW--THAT'S ENOUGH!

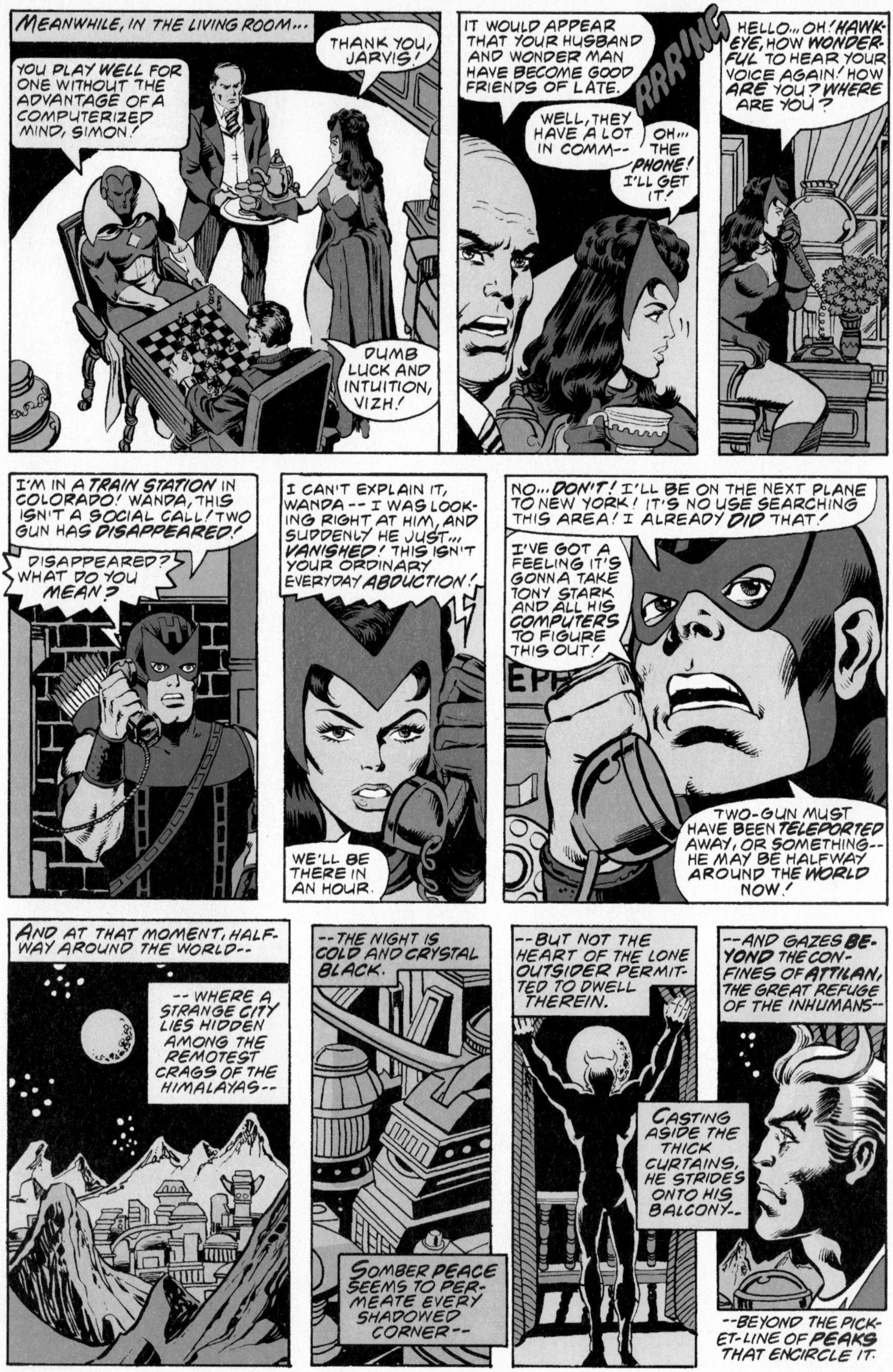
MEANWHILE, IN THE LIVING ROOM...
YOU PLAY WELL FOR ONE WITHOUT THE ADVANTAGE OF A COMPUTERIZED MIND, SIMON!
THANK YOU, JARVIS!
DUMB LUCK AND INTUITION, VIZH!
IT WOULD APPEAR THAT YOUR HUSBAND AND WONDER MAN HAVE BECOME GOOD FRIENDS OF LATE.
ARRING
WELL, THEY HAVE A LOT IN COMM--
OH... THE PHONE! I'LL GET IT!
HELLO... OH! HAWK-EYE, HOW WONDER-FUL TO HEAR YOUR VOICE AGAIN! HOW ARE YOU? WHERE ARE YOU?
I'M IN A TRAIN STATION IN COLORADO! WANDA, THIS ISN'T A SOCIAL CALL! TWO GUN HAS DISAPPEARED!
DISAPPEARED? WHAT DO YOU MEAN?
I CAN'T EXPLAIN IT, WANDA -- I WAS LOOK-ING RIGHT AT HIM, AND SUDDENLY HE JUST... VANISHED! THIS ISN'T YOUR ORDINARY EVERYDAY ABDUCTION!
WE'LL BE THERE IN AN HOUR.
NO... DON'T! I'LL BE ON THE NEXT PLANE TO NEW YORK! IT'S NO USE SEARCHING THIS AREA! I ALREADY DID THAT!
I'VE GOT A FEELING IT'S GONNA TAKE TONY STARK AND ALL HIS COMPUTERS TO FIGURE THIS OUT!
TWO-GUN MUST HAVE BEEN TELEPORTED AWAY, OR SOMETHING-- HE MAY BE HALFWAY AROUND THE WORLD NOW!
AND AT THAT MOMENT, HALF-WAY AROUND THE WORLD--
-- WHERE A STRANGE CITY LIES HIDDEN AMONG THE REMOTEST CRAGS OF THE HIMALAYAS--
--THE NIGHT IS COLD AND CRYSTAL BLACK.
SOMBER PEACE SEEMS TO PER-MEATE EVERY SHADOWED CORNER--
--BUT NOT THE HEART OF THE LONE OUTSIDER PERMIT-TED TO DWELL THEREIN.
CASTING ASIDE THE THICK CURTAINS, HE STRIDES ONTO HIS BALCONY--
--AND GAZES BE-YOND THE CON-FINES OF ATTILAN, THE GREAT REFUGE OF THE INHUMANS--
--BEYOND THE PICK-ET-LINE OF PEAKS THAT ENCIRCLE IT.

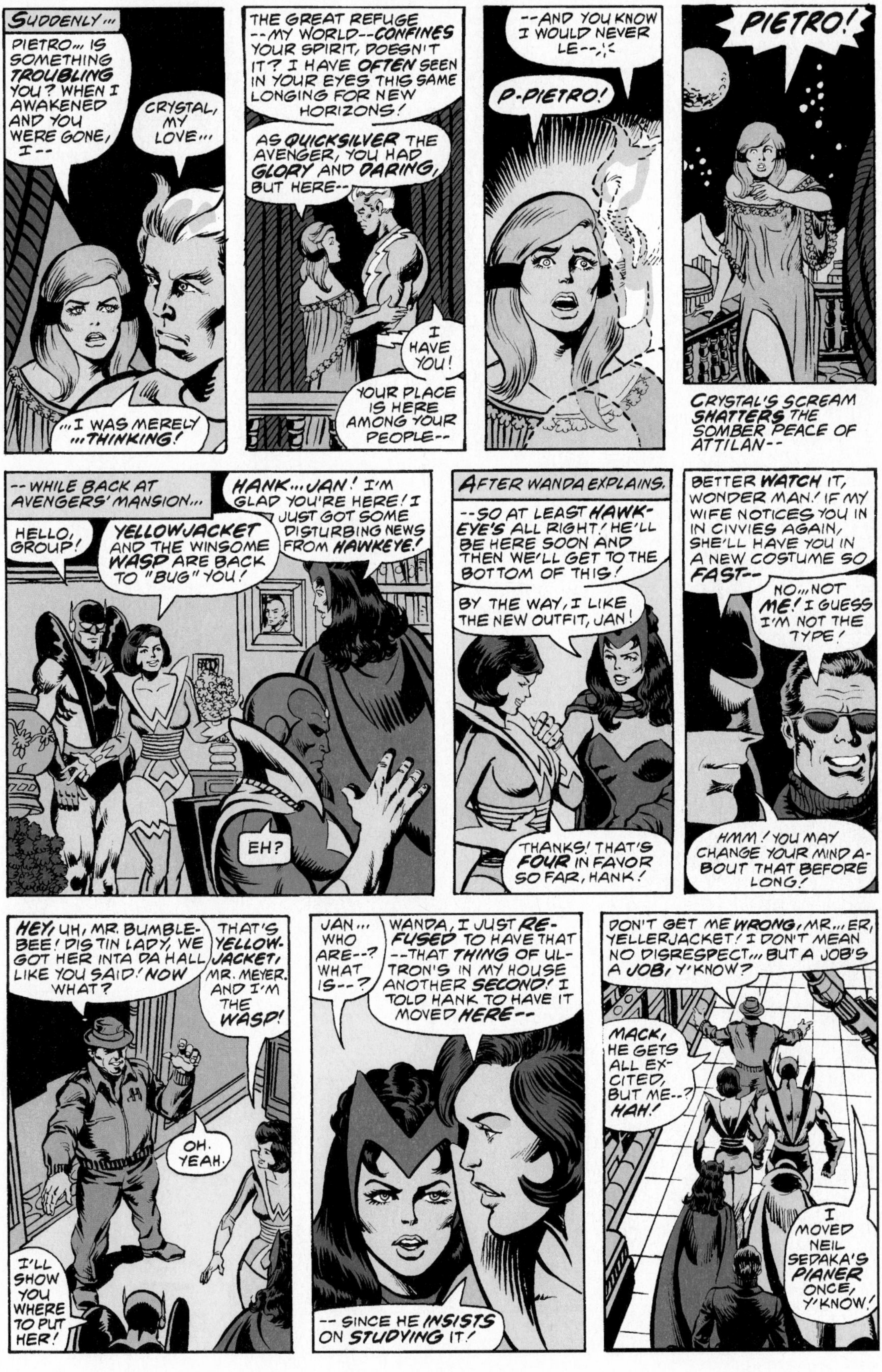
SUDDENLY...
PIETRO... IS SOMETHING TROUBLING YOU? WHEN I AWAKENED AND YOU WERE GONE, I--
CRYSTAL, MY LOVE...
...I WAS MERELY ...THINKING!
THE GREAT REFUGE --MY WORLD--CONFINES YOUR SPIRIT, DOESN'T IT? I HAVE OFTEN SEEN IN YOUR EYES THIS SAME LONGING FOR NEW HORIZONS!
AS QUICKSILVER THE AVENGER, YOU HAD GLORY AND DARING, BUT HERE--
I HAVE YOU!
YOUR PLACE IS HERE AMONG YOUR PEOPLE--
--AND YOU KNOW I WOULD NEVER LE--
P-PIETRO!
PIETRO!
CRYSTAL'S SCREAM SHATTERS THE SOMBER PEACE OF ATTILAN--
--WHILE BACK AT AVENGERS' MANSION...
HELLO, GROUP!
YELLOWJACKET AND THE WINSOME WASP ARE BACK TO "BUG" YOU!
HANK...JAN! I'M GLAD YOU'RE HERE! I JUST GOT SOME DISTURBING NEWS FROM HAWKEYE!
EH?
AFTER WANDA EXPLAINS.
--SO AT LEAST HAWK-EYE'S ALL RIGHT! HE'LL BE HERE SOON AND THEN WE'LL GET TO THE BOTTOM OF THIS!
BY THE WAY, I LIKE THE NEW OUTFIT, JAN!
THANKS! THAT'S FOUR IN FAVOR SO FAR, HANK!
BETTER WATCH IT, WONDER MAN! IF MY WIFE NOTICES YOU IN IN CIVVIES AGAIN, SHE'LL HAVE YOU IN A NEW COSTUME SO FAST--
NO...NOT ME! I GUESS I'M NOT THE TYPE!
HMM! YOU MAY CHANGE YOUR MIND A-BOUT THAT BEFORE LONG!
HEY, UH, MR. BUMBLE-BEE! DIS TIN LADY, WE GOT HER INTA DA HALL LIKE YOU SAID! NOW WHAT?
THAT'S YELLOW-JACKET, MR. MEYER. AND I'M THE WASP!
OH. YEAH.
I'LL SHOW YOU WHERE TO PUT HER!
JAN... WHO ARE--? WHAT IS--?
WANDA, I JUST RE-FUSED TO HAVE THAT --THAT THING OF UL-TRON'S IN MY HOUSE ANOTHER SECOND! I TOLD HANK TO HAVE IT MOVED HERE--
--SINCE HE INSISTS ON STUDYING IT!
DON'T GET ME WRONG, MR... ER, YELLERJACKET! I DON'T MEAN NO DISRESPECT... BUT A JOB'S A JOB, Y'KNOW?
MACK, HE GETS ALL EX-CITED, BUT ME--? HAH!
I MOVED NEIL SEDAKA'S PIANER ONCE, Y'KNOW!

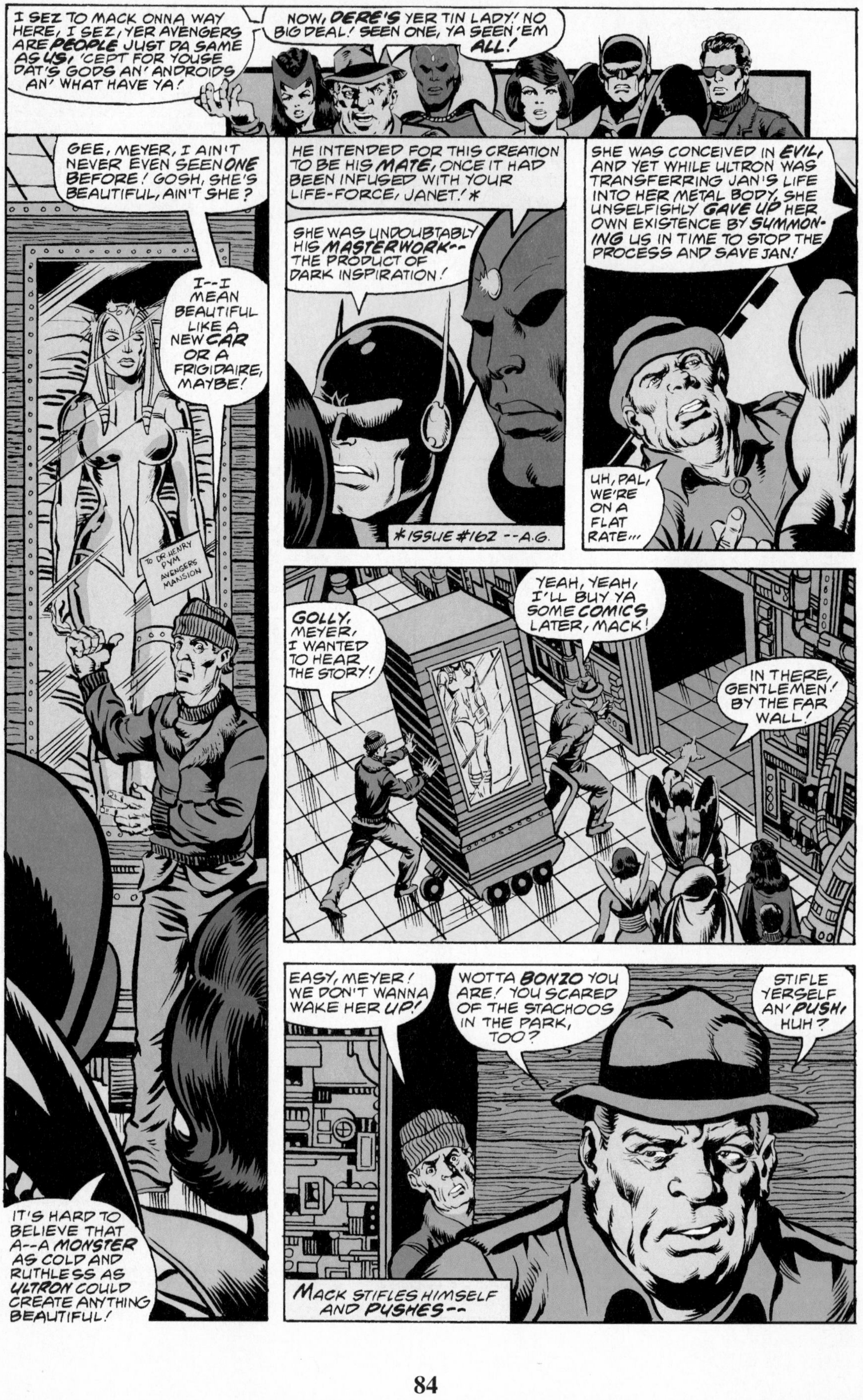
I SEZ TO MACK ONNA WAY HERE, I SEZ, YER AVENGERS ARE PEOPLE JUST DA SAME AS US, 'CEPT FOR YOUSE DAT'S GODS AN' ANDROIDS AN' WHAT HAVE YA!
NOW, DERE'S YER TIN LADY! NO BIG DEAL! SEEN ONE, YA SEEN 'EM ALL!
GEE, MEYER, I AIN'T NEVER EVEN SEEN ONE BEFORE! GOSH, SHE'S BEAUTIFUL, AIN'T SHE?
I--I MEAN BEAUTIFUL LIKE A NEW CAR OR A FRIGIDAIRE, MAYBE!
TO DR. HENRY PYM AVENGERS MANSION
HE INTENDED FOR THIS CREATION TO BE HIS MATE, ONCE IT HAD BEEN INFUSED WITH YOUR LIFE-FORCE, JANET! *
SHE WAS UNDOUBTABLY HIS MASTERWORK-- THE PRODUCT OF DARK INSPIRATION!
*ISSUE #162 --A.G.
SHE WAS CONCEIVED IN EVIL, AND YET WHILE ULTRON WAS TRANSFERRING JAN'S LIFE INTO HER METAL BODY, SHE UNSELFISHLY GAVE UP HER OWN EXISTENCE BY SUMMONING US IN TIME TO STOP THE PROCESS AND SAVE JAN!
UH, PAL, WE'RE ON A FLAT RATE...
GOLLY, MEYER, I WANTED TO HEAR THE STORY!
YEAH, YEAH, I'LL BUY YA SOME COMICS LATER, MACK!
IN THERE, GENTLEMEN! BY THE FAR WALL!
IT'S HARD TO BELIEVE THAT A--A MONSTER AS COLD AND RUTHLESS AS ULTRON COULD CREATE ANYTHING BEAUTIFUL!
EASY, MEYER! WE DON'T WANNA WAKE HER UP!
WOTTA BONZO YOU ARE! YOU SCARED OF THE STACHOOS IN THE PARK, TOO?
STIFLE YERSELF AN' PUSH, HUH?
MACK STIFLES HIMSELF AND PUSHES--

--WHILE IN *SAUGERTIES NEW YORK,* FIFTY-ODD MILES UPSTATE...

PUT IT IN HERE, VANCE! BLOW IT RIGHT *BY* HIM!

VANCE ASTROVIK! YOU GET YOURSELF *INSIDE,* YOUNG MAN!

AW, MOM! IT'S STILL *EARLY!*

I DON'T *CARE!* I'VE *TOLD* YOU NOT TO PLAY ON THE STREET AFTER DARK!

I'LL BE CAREFUL, MA! C'MON, GIMME A BREAK!

HERE WE GO AGAIN!

EVERY NIGHT IT'S THE SAME THING! VANCE *INSISTS* ON TOSSING THAT SPHEROID WITH HIS PALS IN THE CENTER OF THIS DANGEROUS PASSAGEWAY FOR WHEELED VEHICLES!

PLEASE, MOM!

IT'S NOT BAD *ENOUGH* THAT US GUARDIANS HAVE TO PROTECT HIM FROM *KORVAC.*

HE'S OUT TO KILL *HIMSELF* IT SEEMS!

SUDDENLY...

SCREEEE

HEY! LOOK OUT!

HUH?

OH, NO!

IT'S GONNA *HIT* ME!

HELP!

IMPENDING TRAGEDY RIVETS ALL EYES ON YOUNG VANCE ASTROVIK--

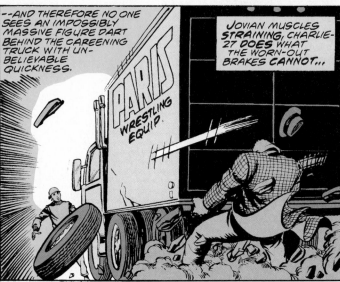

--AND THEREFORE NO ONE SEES AN IMPOSSIBLY MASSIVE FIGURE *DART* BEHIND THE CAREENING TRUCK WITH UNBELIEVABLE QUICKNESS.

PARIS WRESTLING EQUIP.

JOVIAN MUSCLES STRAINING, CHARLIE-27 DOES WHAT THE WORN-OUT BRAKES *CANNOT...*

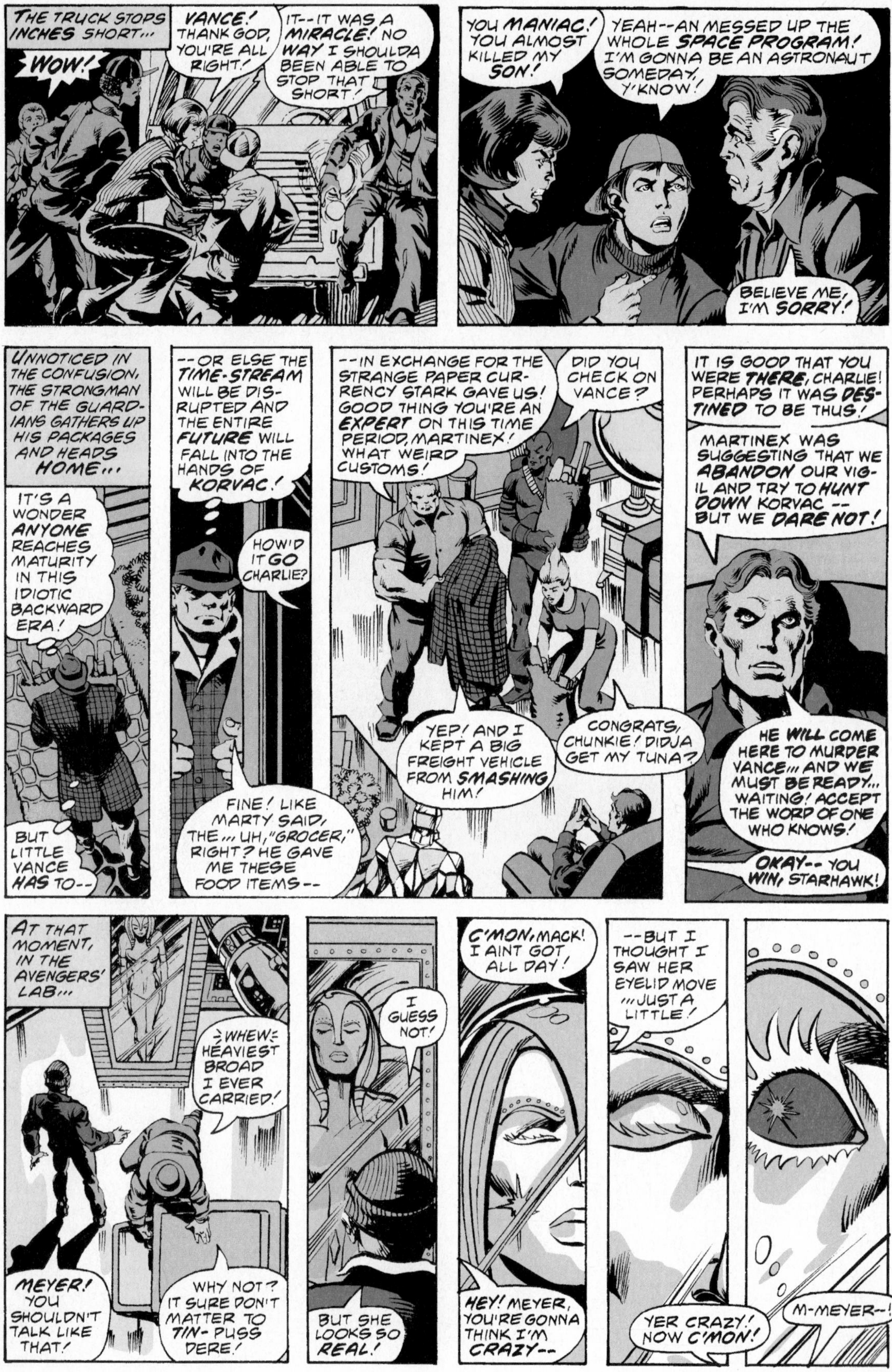
THE TRUCK STOPS INCHES SHORT...
WOW!
VANCE! THANK GOD, YOU'RE ALL RIGHT!
IT--IT WAS A MIRACLE! NO WAY I SHOULDA BEEN ABLE TO STOP THAT SHORT!
YOU MANIAC! YOU ALMOST KILLED MY SON!
YEAH--AN MESSED UP THE WHOLE SPACE PROGRAM! I'M GONNA BE AN ASTRONAUT SOMEDAY, Y'KNOW!
BELIEVE ME, I'M SORRY!
UNNOTICED IN THE CONFUSION, THE STRONGMAN OF THE GUARDIANS GATHERS UP HIS PACKAGES AND HEADS HOME...
IT'S A WONDER ANYONE REACHES MATURITY IN THIS IDIOTIC BACKWARD ERA!
BUT LITTLE VANCE HAS TO--
--OR ELSE THE TIME-STREAM WILL BE DISRUPTED AND THE ENTIRE FUTURE WILL FALL INTO THE HANDS OF KORVAC!
HOW'D IT GO CHARLIE?
FINE! LIKE MARTY SAID, THE... UH, "GROCER," RIGHT? HE GAVE ME THESE FOOD ITEMS--
--IN EXCHANGE FOR THE STRANGE PAPER CURRENCY STARK GAVE US! GOOD THING YOU'RE AN EXPERT ON THIS TIME PERIOD, MARTINEX! WHAT WEIRD CUSTOMS!
DID YOU CHECK ON VANCE?
YEP! AND I KEPT A BIG FREIGHT VEHICLE FROM SMASHING HIM!
CONGRATS, CHUNKIE! DIDJA GET MY TUNA?
IT IS GOOD THAT YOU WERE THERE, CHARLIE! PERHAPS IT WAS DESTINED TO BE THUS!
MARTINEX WAS SUGGESTING THAT WE ABANDON OUR VIGIL AND TRY TO HUNT DOWN KORVAC -- BUT WE DARE NOT!
HE WILL COME HERE TO MURDER VANCE... AND WE MUST BE READY... WAITING! ACCEPT THE WORD OF ONE WHO KNOWS!
OKAY-- YOU WIN, STARHAWK!
AT THAT MOMENT, IN THE AVENGERS' LAB...
WHEW! HEAVIEST BROAD I EVER CARRIED!
MEYER! YOU SHOULDN'T TALK LIKE THAT!
WHY NOT? IT SURE DON'T MATTER TO TIN-PUSS DERE!
I GUESS NOT!
BUT SHE LOOKS SO REAL!
C'MON, MACK! I AINT GOT ALL DAY!
HEY! MEYER, YOU'RE GONNA THINK I'M CRAZY--
--BUT I THOUGHT I SAW HER EYELID MOVE ...JUST A LITTLE!
YER CRAZY! NOW C'MON!
M-MEYER--!

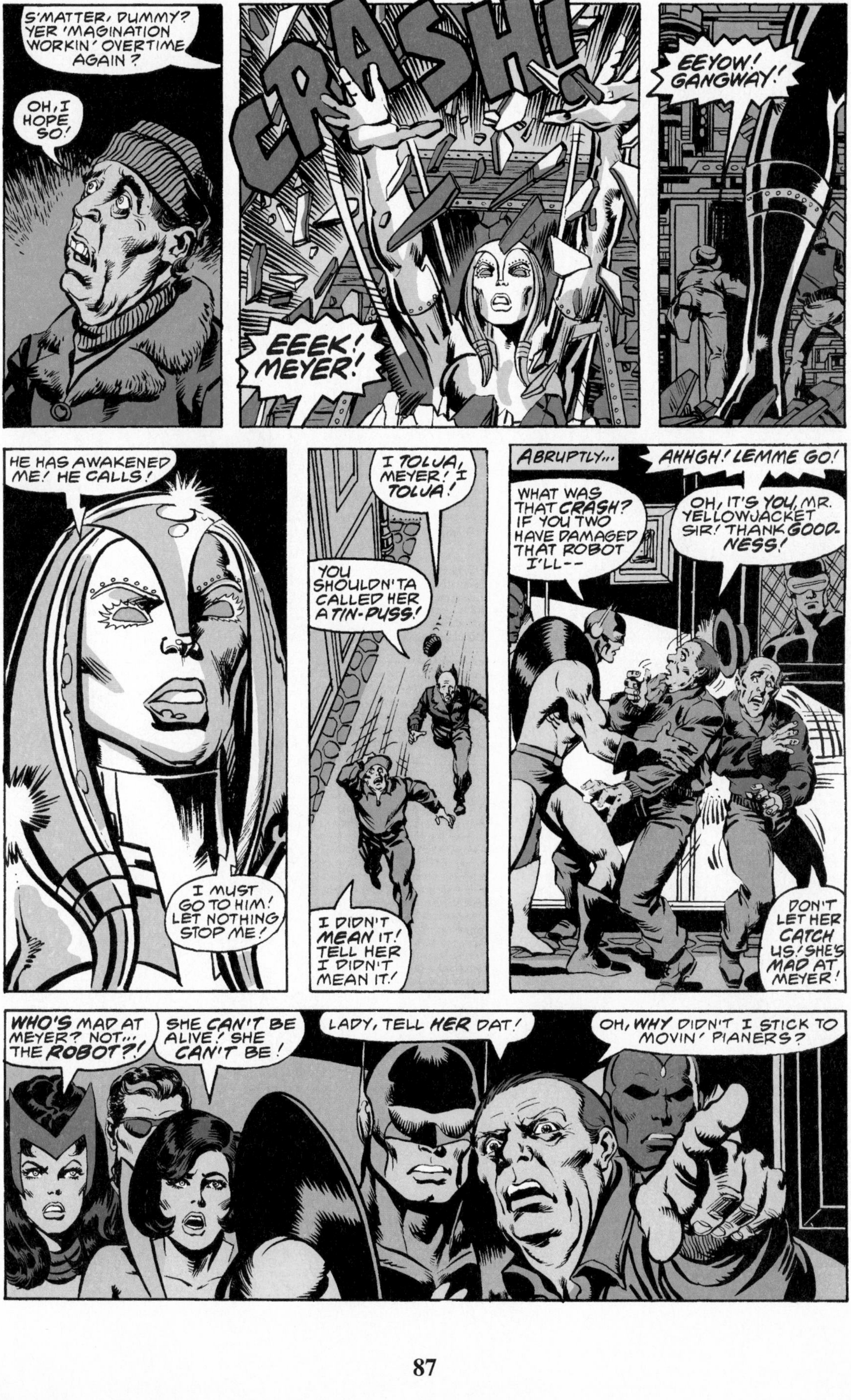
S'MATTER, DUMMY? YER 'MAGINATION WORKIN' OVERTIME AGAIN?
OH, I HOPE SO!
CRASH!
EEEK! MEYER!
EEYOW! GANGWAY!
HE HAS AWAKENED ME! HE CALLS!
I MUST GO TO HIM! LET NOTHING STOP ME!
I TOLJA, MEYER! I TOLJA!
YOU SHOULDN'TA CALLED HER A TIN-PUSS!
I DIDN'T MEAN IT! TELL HER I DIDN'T MEAN IT!
ABRUPTLY...
AHHGH! LEMME GO!
WHAT WAS THAT CRASH? IF YOU TWO HAVE DAMAGED THAT ROBOT I'LL--
OH, IT'S YOU, MR. YELLOWJACKET SIR! THANK GOOD-NESS!
DON'T LET HER CATCH US! SHE'S MAD AT MEYER!
WHO'S MAD AT MEYER? NOT... THE ROBOT?!
SHE CAN'T BE ALIVE! SHE CAN'T BE!
LADY, TELL HER DAT!
OH, WHY DIDN'T I STICK TO MOVIN' PIANERS?

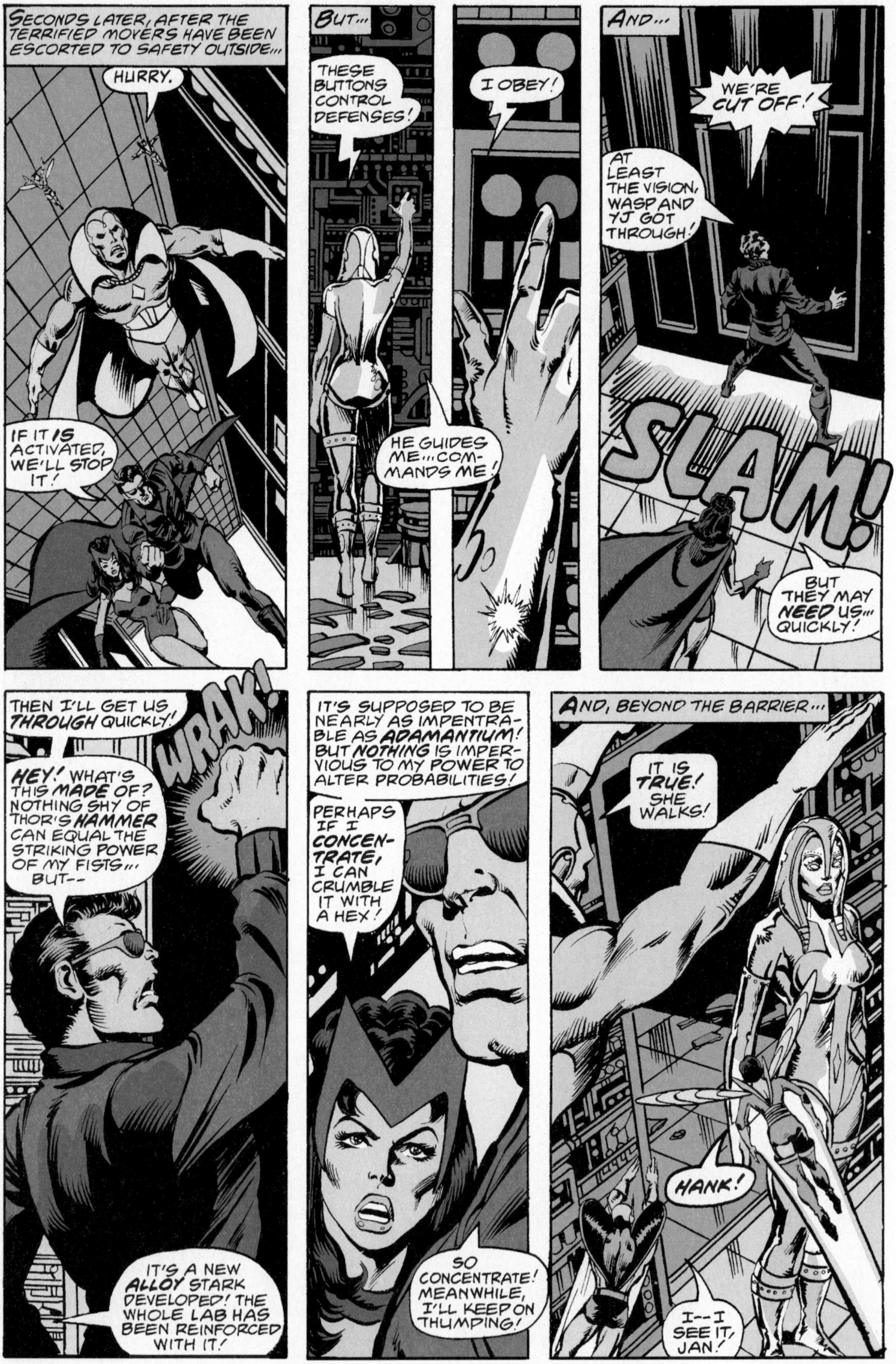
SECONDS LATER, AFTER THE TERRIFIED MOVERS HAVE BEEN ESCORTED TO SAFETY OUTSIDE...
HURRY.
IF IT IS ACTIVATED, WE'LL STOP IT!
BUT...
THESE BUTTONS CONTROL DEFENSES!
HE GUIDES ME...COMMANDS ME!
I OBEY!
AND...
WE'RE CUT OFF!
AT LEAST THE VISION, WASP AND YJ GOT THROUGH!
SLAM!
BUT THEY MAY NEED US... QUICKLY!
THEN I'LL GET US THROUGH QUICKLY!
WRAK!
HEY! WHAT'S THIS MADE OF? NOTHING SHY OF THOR'S HAMMER CAN EQUAL THE STRIKING POWER OF MY FISTS... BUT--
IT'S A NEW ALLOY STARK DEVELOPED! THE WHOLE LAB HAS BEEN REINFORCED WITH IT!
IT'S SUPPOSED TO BE NEARLY AS IMPENTRABLE AS ADAMANTIUM! BUT NOTHING IS IMPERVIOUS TO MY POWER TO ALTER PROBABILITIES!
PERHAPS IF I CONCENTRATE, I CAN CRUMBLE IT WITH A HEX!
SO CONCENTRATE! MEANWHILE, I'LL KEEP ON THUMPING!
AND, BEYOND THE BARRIER...
IT IS TRUE! SHE WALKS!
HANK!
I--I SEE IT, JAN!

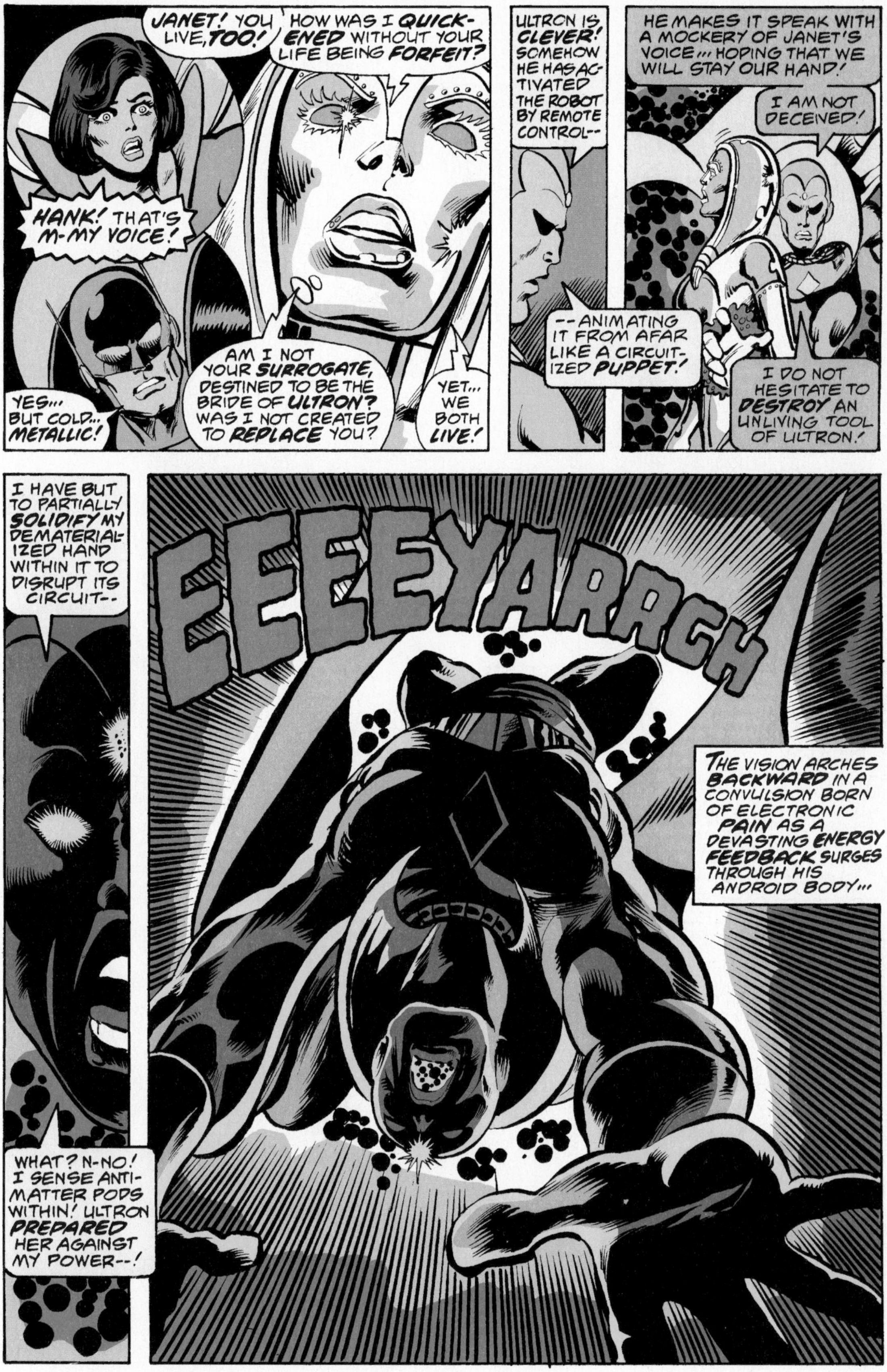

JANET! YOU LIVE, TOO!
HOW WAS I QUICKENED WITHOUT YOUR LIFE BEING FORFEIT?
HANK! THAT'S M-MY VOICE!
YES... BUT COLD... METALLIC!
AM I NOT YOUR SURROGATE, DESTINED TO BE THE BRIDE OF ULTRON? WAS I NOT CREATED TO REPLACE YOU?
YET... WE BOTH LIVE!
ULTRON IS CLEVER! SOMEHOW HE HAS ACTIVATED THE ROBOT BY REMOTE CONTROL--
--ANIMATING IT FROM AFAR LIKE A CIRCUITIZED PUPPET!
HE MAKES IT SPEAK WITH A MOCKERY OF JANET'S VOICE... HOPING THAT WE WILL STAY OUR HAND!
I AM NOT DECEIVED!
I DO NOT HESITATE TO DESTROY AN UNLIVING TOOL OF ULTRON!
I HAVE BUT TO PARTIALLY SOLIDIFY MY DEMATERIALIZED HAND WITHIN IT TO DISRUPT ITS CIRCUIT--
WHAT? N-NO! I SENSE ANTI-MATTER PODS WITHIN! ULTRON PREPARED HER AGAINST MY POWER--!
EEEEYARRRGH
THE VISION ARCHES BACKWARD IN A CONVULSION BORN OF ELECTRONIC PAIN AS A DEVASTING ENERGY FEEDBACK SURGES THROUGH HIS ANDROID BODY...

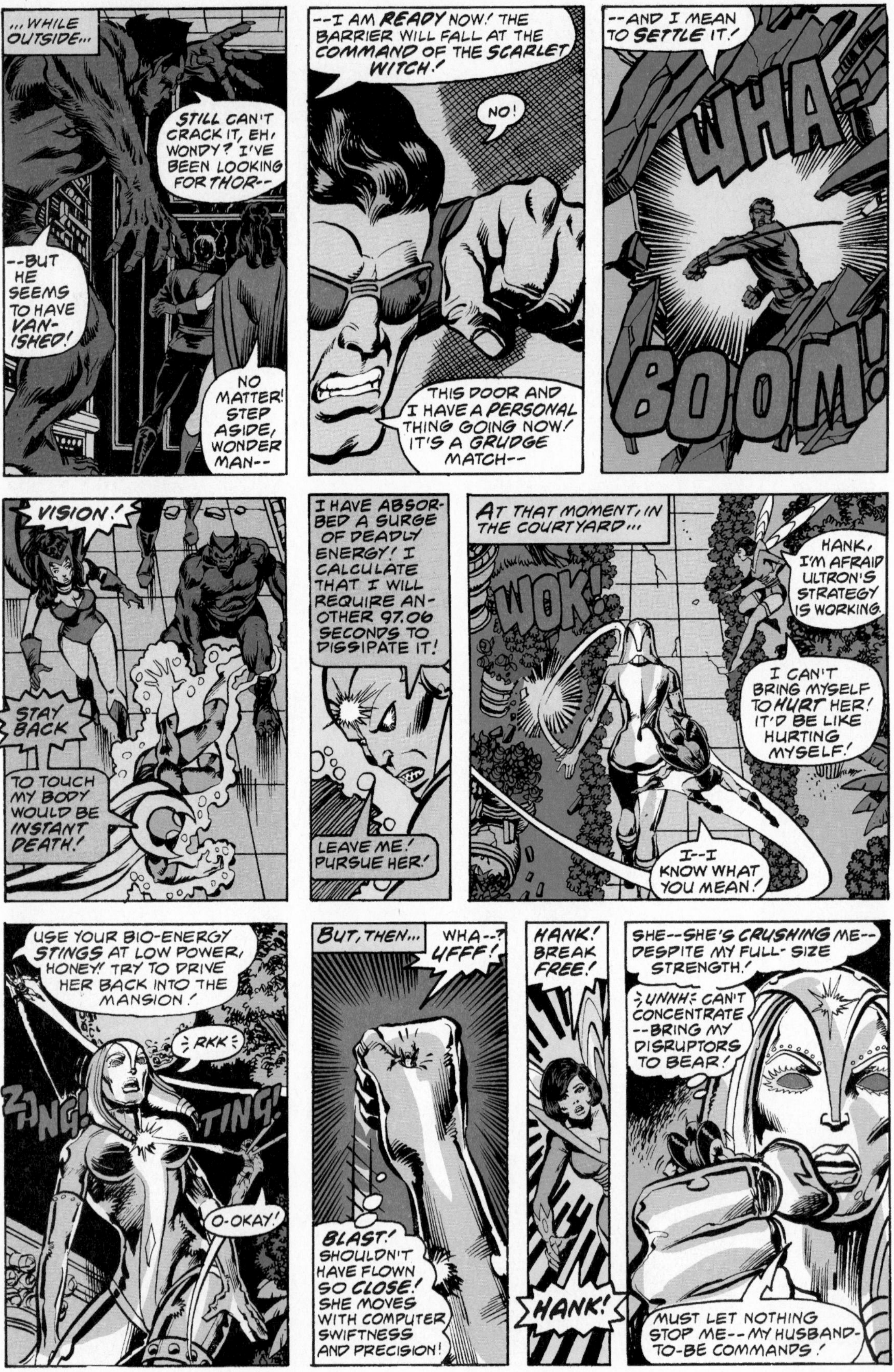
...WHILE OUTSIDE...
STILL CAN'T CRACK IT, EH, WONDY? I'VE BEEN LOOKING FOR THOR--
--BUT HE SEEMS TO HAVE VAN-ISHED!
NO MATTER! STEP ASIDE, WONDER MAN--
--I AM READY NOW! THE BARRIER WILL FALL AT THE COMMAND OF THE SCARLET WITCH!
NO!
THIS DOOR AND I HAVE A PERSONAL THING GOING NOW! IT'S A GRUDGE MATCH--
--AND I MEAN TO SETTLE IT!
WHA-
BOOM!
VISION!
STAY BACK
TO TOUCH MY BODY WOULD BE INSTANT DEATH!
I HAVE ABSORBED A SURGE OF DEADLY ENERGY! I CALCULATE THAT I WILL REQUIRE ANOTHER 97.06 SECONDS TO DISSIPATE IT!
LEAVE ME! PURSUE HER!
AT THAT MOMENT, IN THE COURTYARD...
WOK!
HANK, I'M AFRAID ULTRON'S STRATEGY IS WORKING.
I CAN'T BRING MYSELF TO HURT HER! IT'D BE LIKE HURTING MYSELF!
I--I KNOW WHAT YOU MEAN!
USE YOUR BIO-ENERGY STINGS AT LOW POWER, HONEY! TRY TO DRIVE HER BACK INTO THE MANSION!
RKK
ZING!
TING!
O-OKAY!
BUT, THEN...
WHA--? UFFF!
BLAST! SHOULDN'T HAVE FLOWN SO CLOSE! SHE MOVES WITH COMPUTER SWIFTNESS AND PRECISION!
HANK! BREAK FREE!
HANK!
SHE--SHE'S CRUSHING ME--DESPITE MY FULL-SIZE STRENGTH!
UNNH CAN'T CONCENTRATE --BRING MY DISRUPTORS TO BEAR!
MUST LET NOTHING STOP ME--MY HUSBAND-TO-BE COMMANDS!

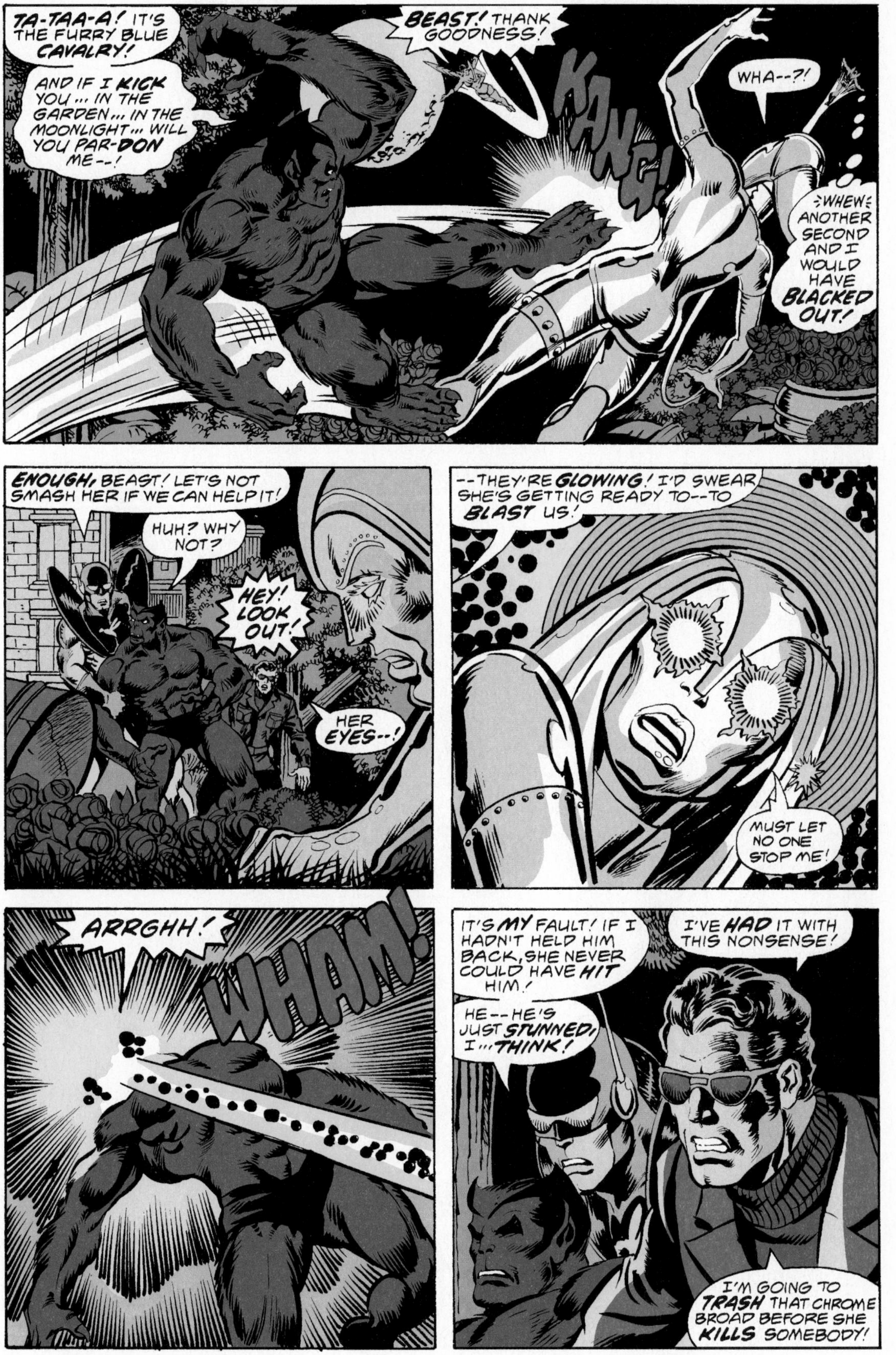
TA-TAA-A! IT'S THE FURRY BLUE CAVALRY!
AND IF I KICK YOU ... IN THE GARDEN ... IN THE MOONLIGHT ... WILL YOU PAR-DON ME--!
BEAST! THANK GOODNESS!
KANG!
WHA--?!
WHEW! ANOTHER SECOND AND I WOULD HAVE BLACKED OUT!
ENOUGH, BEAST! LET'S NOT SMASH HER IF WE CAN HELP IT!
HUH? WHY NOT?
HEY! LOOK OUT!
HER EYES--!
--THEY'RE GLOWING! I'D SWEAR SHE'S GETTING READY TO--TO BLAST US!
MUST LET NO ONE STOP ME!
ARRGHH!
WHAM!
IT'S MY FAULT! IF I HADN'T HELD HIM BACK, SHE NEVER COULD HAVE HIT HIM!
I'VE HAD IT WITH THIS NONSENSE!
HE--HE'S JUST STUNNED, I... THINK!
I'M GOING TO TRASH THAT CHROME BROAD BEFORE SHE KILLS SOMEBODY!

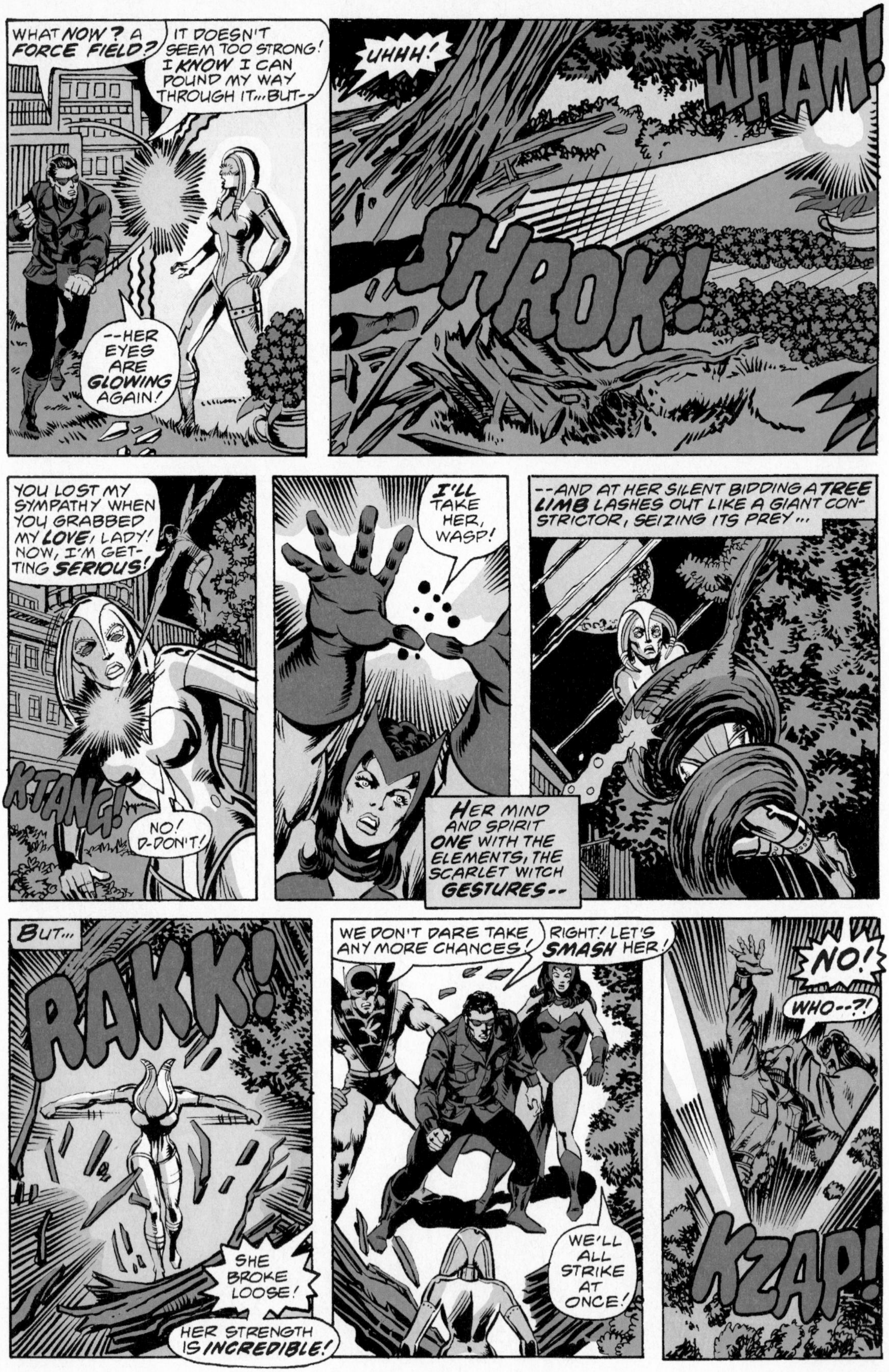
WHAT NOW? A FORCE FIELD?
IT DOESN'T SEEM TOO STRONG! I KNOW I CAN POUND MY WAY THROUGH IT... BUT--
--HER EYES ARE GLOWING AGAIN!
UHHH!
WHAM!
SHROK!
YOU LOST MY SYMPATHY WHEN YOU GRABBED MY LOVE, LADY! NOW, I'M GETTING SERIOUS!
KTANG!
NO! D-DON'T!
I'LL TAKE HER, WASP!
HER MIND AND SPIRIT ONE WITH THE ELEMENTS, THE SCARLET WITCH GESTURES--
--AND AT HER SILENT BIDDING A TREE LIMB LASHES OUT LIKE A GIANT CONSTRICTOR, SEIZING ITS PREY...
BUT...
RAKK!
SHE BROKE LOOSE!
HER STRENGTH IS INCREDIBLE!
WE DON'T DARE TAKE ANY MORE CHANCES!
RIGHT! LET'S SMASH HER!
WE'LL ALL STRIKE AT ONCE!
NO!
WHO--?!
KZAP!

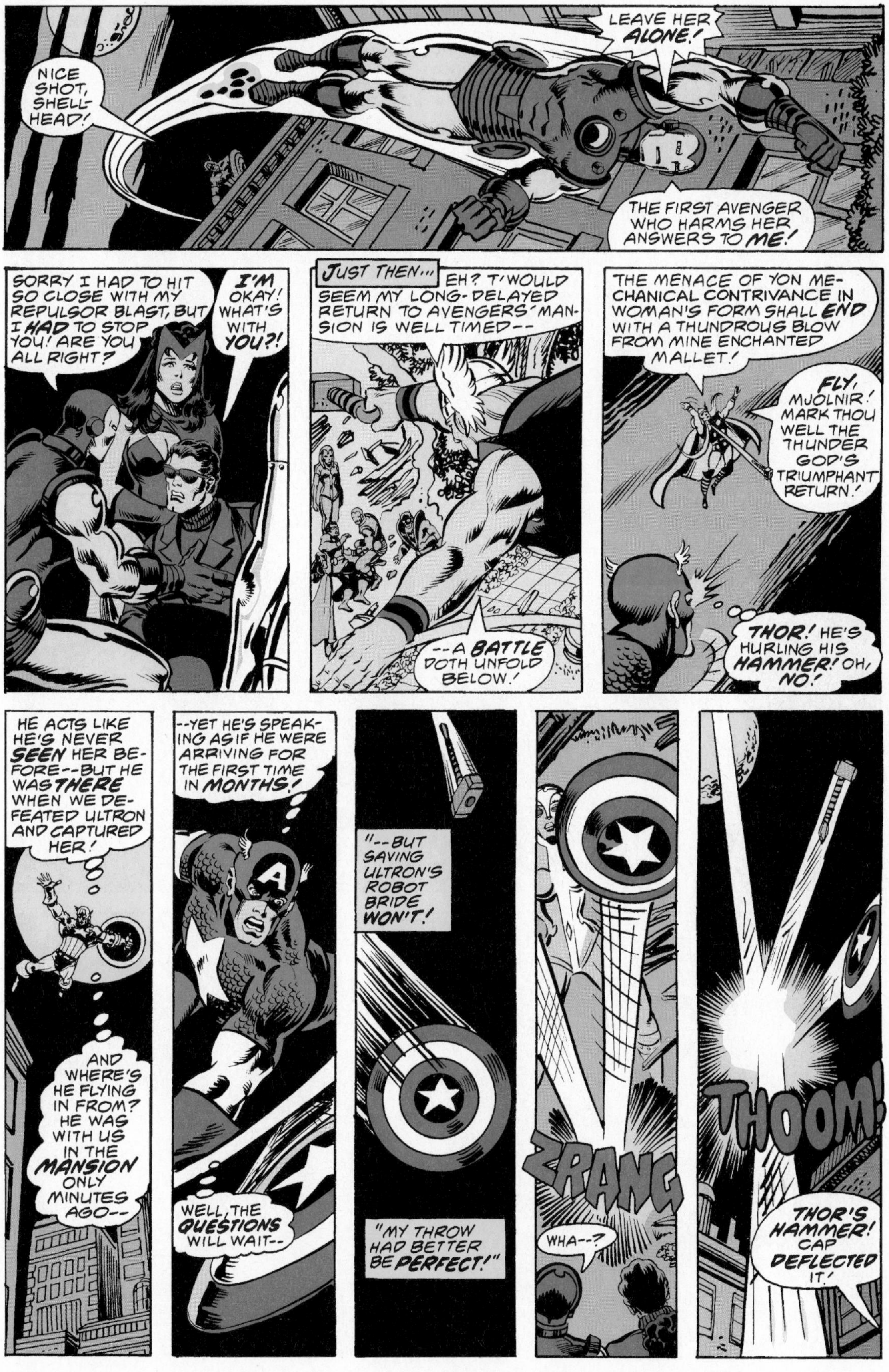
NICE SHOT, SHELL-HEAD!
LEAVE HER ALONE!
THE FIRST AVENGER WHO HARMS HER ANSWERS TO ME!
SORRY I HAD TO HIT SO CLOSE WITH MY REPULSOR BLAST, BUT I HAD TO STOP YOU! ARE YOU ALL RIGHT?
I'M OKAY! WHAT'S WITH YOU?!
JUST THEN...
EH? T'WOULD SEEM MY LONG-DELAYED RETURN TO AVENGERS' MANSION IS WELL TIMED--
--A BATTLE DOTH UNFOLD BELOW!
THE MENACE OF YON MECHANICAL CONTRIVANCE IN WOMAN'S FORM SHALL END WITH A THUNDROUS BLOW FROM MINE ENCHANTED MALLET!
FLY, MJOLNIR! MARK THOU WELL THE THUNDER GOD'S TRIUMPHANT RETURN!
THOR! HE'S HURLING HIS HAMMER! OH, NO!
HE ACTS LIKE HE'S NEVER SEEN HER BEFORE--BUT HE WAS THERE WHEN WE DEFEATED ULTRON AND CAPTURED HER!
AND WHERE'S HE FLYING IN FROM? HE WAS WITH US IN THE MANSION ONLY MINUTES AGO--
--YET HE'S SPEAKING AS IF HE WERE ARRIVING FOR THE FIRST TIME IN MONTHS!
WELL, THE QUESTIONS WILL WAIT--
"--BUT SAVING ULTRON'S ROBOT BRIDE WON'T!
"MY THROW HAD BETTER BE PERFECT!"
ZRANG
WHA--?
THOOM!
THOR'S HAMMER! CAP DEFLECTED IT!

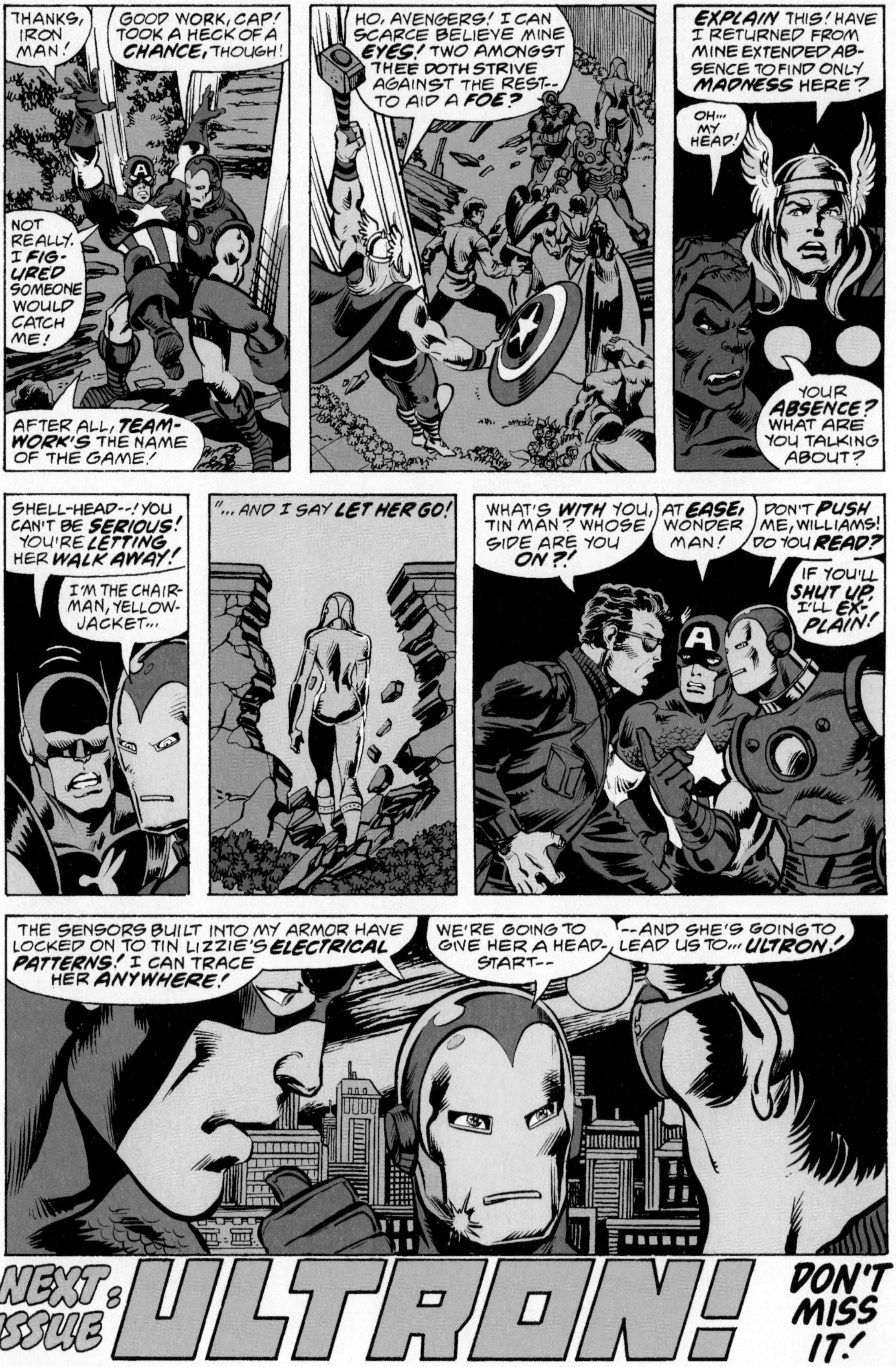
THANKS, IRON MAN!
GOOD WORK, CAP! TOOK A HECK OF A CHANCE, THOUGH!
NOT REALLY. I FIGURED SOMEONE WOULD CATCH ME!
AFTER ALL, TEAM-WORK'S THE NAME OF THE GAME!
HO, AVENGERS! I CAN SCARCE BELIEVE MINE EYES! TWO AMONGST THEE DOTH STRIVE AGAINST THE REST--TO AID A FOE?
EXPLAIN THIS! HAVE I RETURNED FROM MINE EXTENDED ABSENCE TO FIND ONLY MADNESS HERE?
OH... MY HEAD!
YOUR ABSENCE? WHAT ARE YOU TALKING ABOUT?
SHELL-HEAD--! YOU CAN'T BE SERIOUS! YOU'RE LETTING HER WALK AWAY!
I'M THE CHAIRMAN, YELLOWJACKET...
"... AND I SAY LET HER GO!
WHAT'S WITH YOU, TIN MAN? WHOSE SIDE ARE YOU ON?!
AT EASE, WONDER MAN!
DON'T PUSH ME, WILLIAMS! DO YOU READ?
IF YOU'LL SHUT UP, I'LL EXPLAIN!
THE SENSORS BUILT INTO MY ARMOR HAVE LOCKED ON TO TIN LIZZIE'S ELECTRICAL PATTERNS! I CAN TRACE HER ANYWHERE!
WE'RE GOING TO GIVE HER A HEAD-START--
--AND SHE'S GOING TO LEAD US TO... ULTRON!
NEXT ISSUE: ULTRON!
DON'T MISS IT!

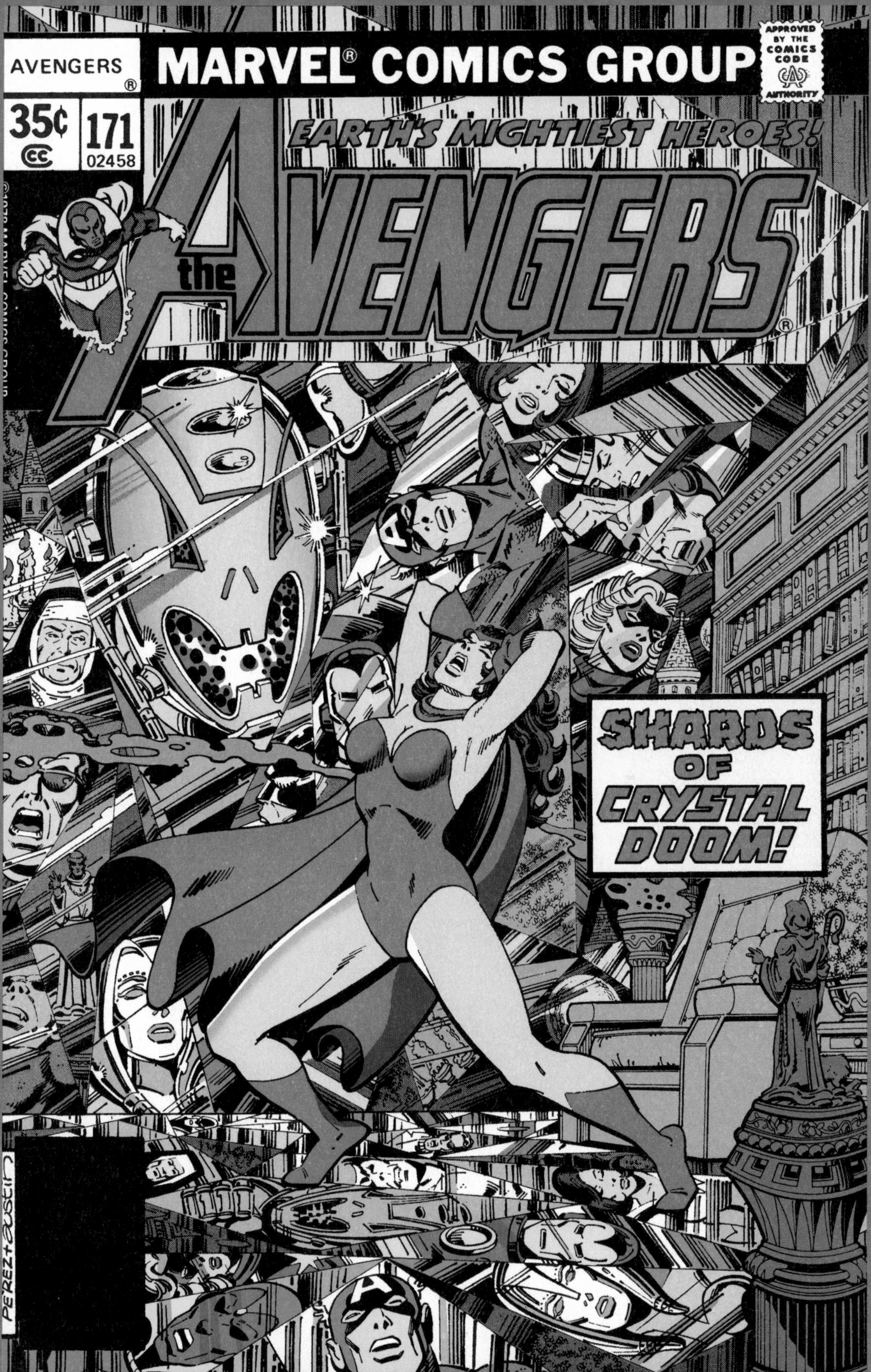
AVENGERS
MARVEL COMICS GROUP
APPROVED BY THE COMICS CODE AUTHORITY
35¢
171
02458
EARTH'S MIGHTIEST HEROES!
the AVENGERS
SHARDS OF CRYSTAL DOOM!
PEREZ+AUSTIN

And there came a day when Earth's mightiest heroes found themselves united against a common threat. On that day, the Avengers were born—to fight the foes no single super-hero could withstand!
Stan Lee PRESENTS: THE MIGHTY AVENGERS!®
"...WHERE ANGELS FEAR TO TREAD"
SHE WENT THAT WAY! HURRY!
WHAT IS THIS? FIRST A LADY ROBOT SHOVES PAST-- AND NOW THE AVENGERS!
OMNIBUS CO
EEEK! WATCH IT, WILLYA?
HEY, PAL--!
PARDON ME, SIR!
SORRY!
HUH? CAPTAIN AMERICA! OR... MAY-BE A VERY PATRIOTIC PICKPOCKET!
JIM SHOOTER WRITER/EDITOR
GEORGE PÉREZ PENCILER
PABLO MARCOS INKER
DENISE WOHL LETTERER
PHIL RACHELSON COLORIST

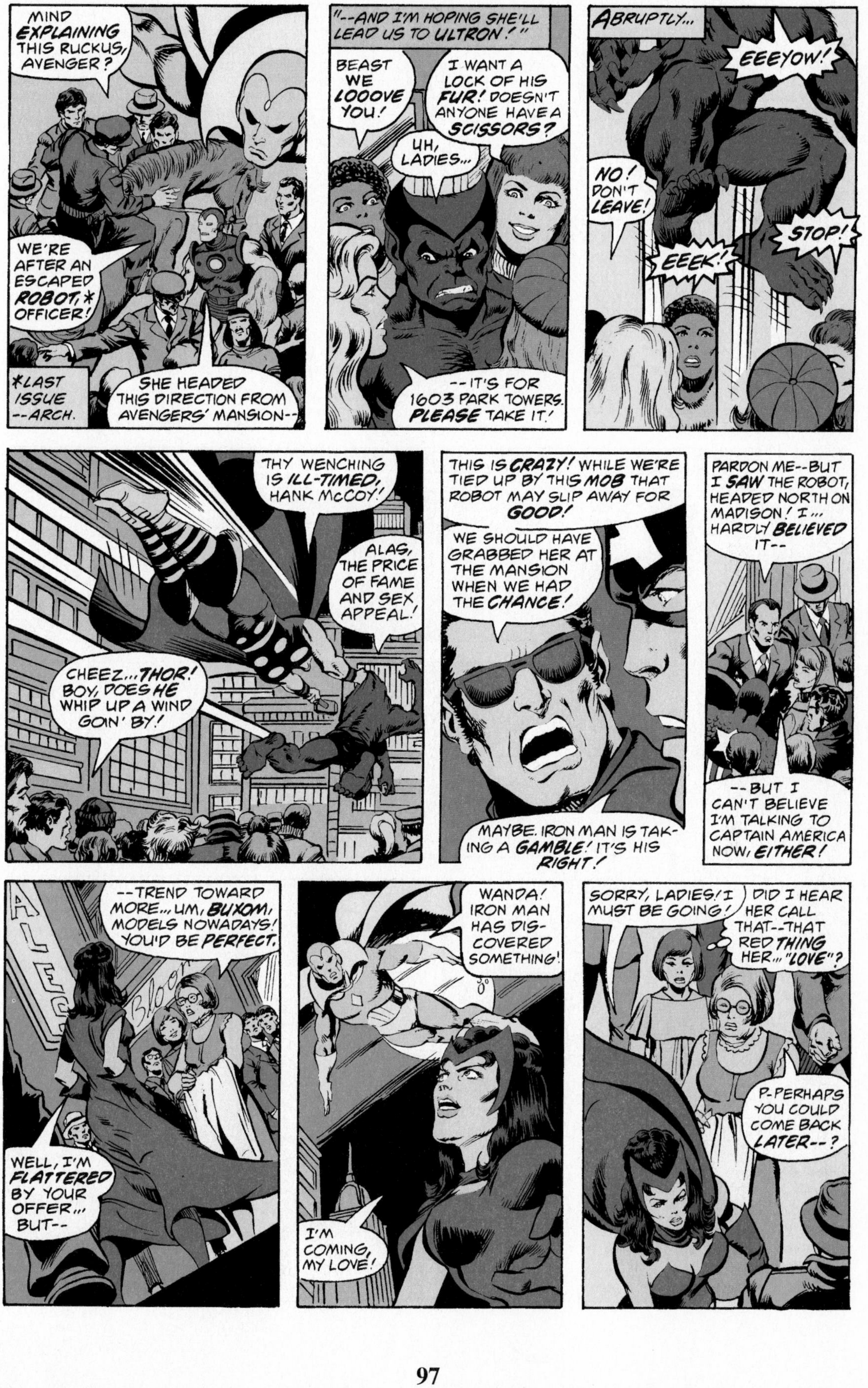
MIND EXPLAINING THIS RUCKUS, AVENGER?
WE'RE AFTER AN ESCAPED ROBOT,* OFFICER!
SHE HEADED THIS DIRECTION FROM AVENGERS' MANSION--
*LAST ISSUE --ARCH.
"--AND I'M HOPING SHE'LL LEAD US TO ULTRON!"
BEAST WE LOOOVE YOU!
I WANT A LOCK OF HIS FUR! DOESN'T ANYONE HAVE A SCISSORS?
UH, LADIES...
--IT'S FOR 1603 PARK TOWERS. PLEASE TAKE IT!
ABRUPTLY...
EEEYOW!
NO! DON'T LEAVE!
STOP!
EEEK!
THY WENCHING IS ILL-TIMED, HANK McCOY!
ALAS, THE PRICE OF FAME AND SEX APPEAL!
CHEEZ... THOR! BOY, DOES HE WHIP UP A WIND GOIN' BY!
THIS IS CRAZY! WHILE WE'RE TIED UP BY THIS MOB THAT ROBOT MAY SLIP AWAY FOR GOOD!
WE SHOULD HAVE GRABBED HER AT THE MANSION WHEN WE HAD THE CHANCE!
MAYBE. IRON MAN IS TAKING A GAMBLE! IT'S HIS RIGHT!
PARDON ME--BUT I SAW THE ROBOT, HEADED NORTH ON MADISON! I... HARDLY BELIEVED IT--
--BUT I CAN'T BELIEVE I'M TALKING TO CAPTAIN AMERICA NOW, EITHER!
--TREND TOWARD MORE... UM, BUXOM, MODELS NOWADAYS! YOU'D BE PERFECT.
WELL, I'M FLATTERED BY YOUR OFFER... BUT--
WANDA! IRON MAN HAS DISCOVERED SOMETHING!
I'M COMING, MY LOVE!
SORRY, LADIES! I MUST BE GOING!
DID I HEAR HER CALL THAT--THAT RED THING HER... "LOVE"?
P-PERHAPS YOU COULD COME BACK LATER--?

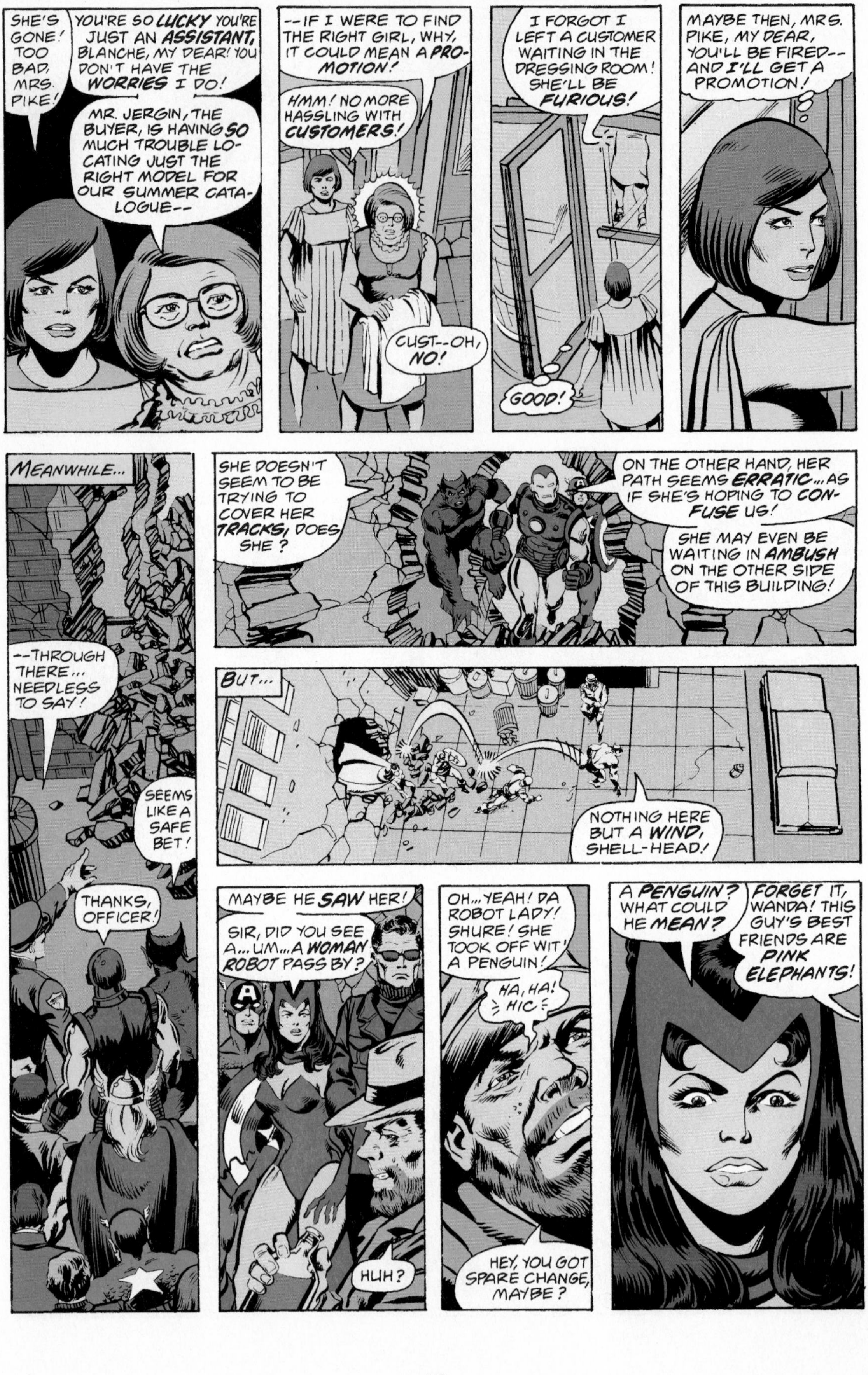
SHE'S GONE! TOO BAD, MRS. PIKE!
YOU'RE SO LUCKY YOU'RE JUST AN ASSISTANT, BLANCHE, MY DEAR! YOU DON'T HAVE THE WORRIES I DO!
MR. JERGIN, THE BUYER, IS HAVING SO MUCH TROUBLE LOCATING JUST THE RIGHT MODEL FOR OUR SUMMER CATALOGUE--
--IF I WERE TO FIND THE RIGHT GIRL, WHY, IT COULD MEAN A PROMOTION!
HMM! NO MORE HASSLING WITH CUSTOMERS!
CUST--OH, NO!
I FORGOT I LEFT A CUSTOMER WAITING IN THE DRESSING ROOM! SHE'LL BE FURIOUS!
GOOD!
MAYBE THEN, MRS. PIKE, MY DEAR, YOU'LL BE FIRED-- AND I'LL GET A PROMOTION!
MEANWHILE...
--THROUGH THERE... NEEDLESS TO SAY!
SEEMS LIKE A SAFE BET!
THANKS, OFFICER!
SHE DOESN'T SEEM TO BE TRYING TO COVER HER TRACKS, DOES SHE?
ON THE OTHER HAND, HER PATH SEEMS ERRATIC... AS IF SHE'S HOPING TO CONFUSE US!
SHE MAY EVEN BE WAITING IN AMBUSH ON THE OTHER SIDE OF THIS BUILDING!
BUT...
NOTHING HERE BUT A WIND, SHELL-HEAD!
MAYBE HE SAW HER!
SIR, DID YOU SEE A... UM... A WOMAN ROBOT PASS BY?
HUH?
OH... YEAH! DA ROBOT LADY! SHURE! SHE TOOK OFF WIT' A PENGUIN!
HA, HA! HIC
HEY, YOU GOT SPARE CHANGE, MAYBE?
A PENGUIN? WHAT COULD HE MEAN?
FORGET IT, WANDA! THIS GUY'S BEST FRIENDS ARE PINK ELEPHANTS!

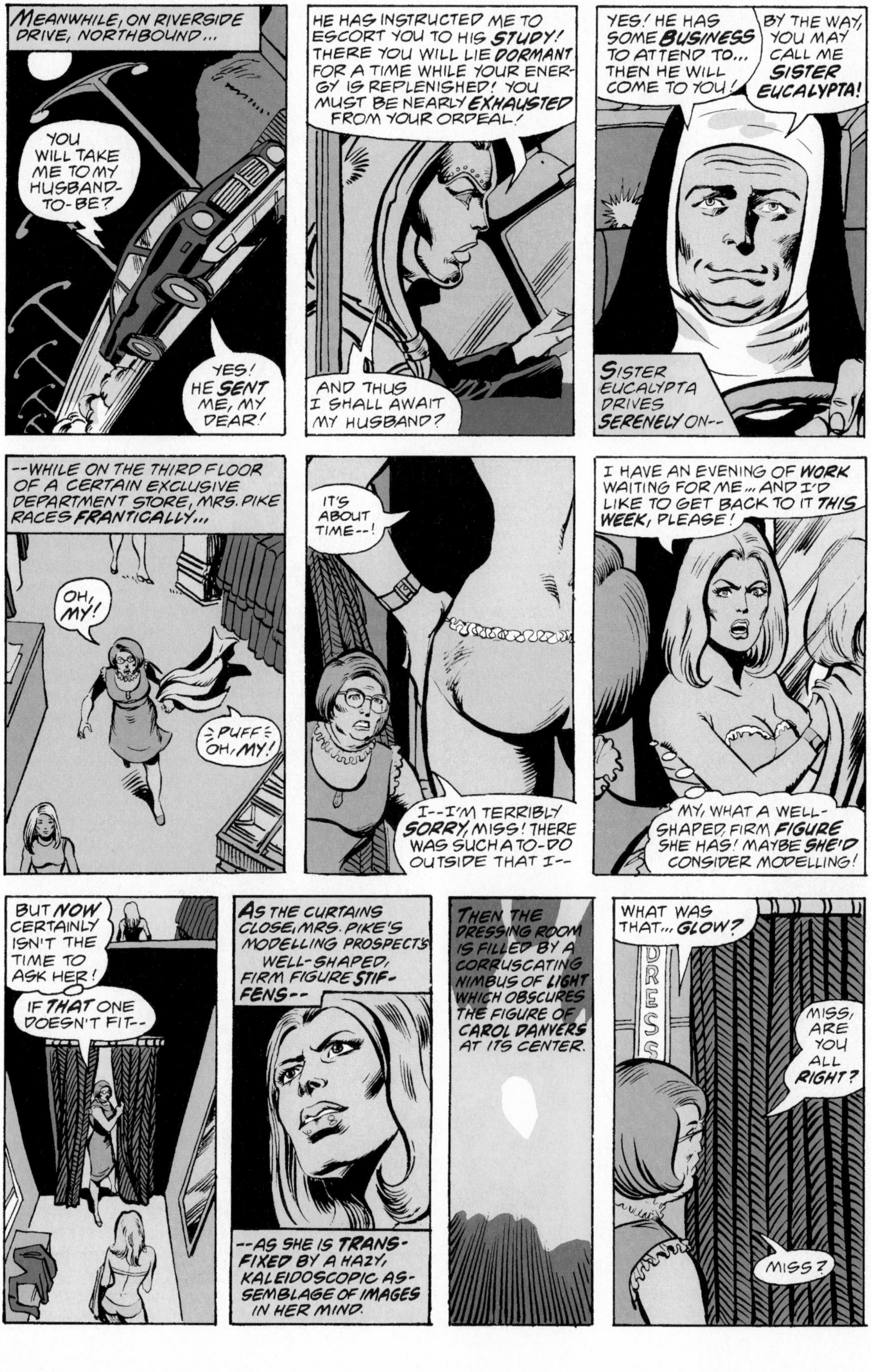
MEANWHILE, ON RIVERSIDE DRIVE, NORTHBOUND...
YOU WILL TAKE ME TO MY HUSBAND-TO-BE?
YES! HE SENT ME, MY DEAR!
HE HAS INSTRUCTED ME TO ESCORT YOU TO HIS STUDY! THERE YOU WILL LIE DORMANT FOR A TIME WHILE YOUR ENERGY IS REPLENISHED! YOU MUST BE NEARLY EXHAUSTED FROM YOUR ORDEAL!
AND THUS I SHALL AWAIT MY HUSBAND?
YES! HE HAS SOME BUSINESS TO ATTEND TO... THEN HE WILL COME TO YOU!
BY THE WAY, YOU MAY CALL ME SISTER EUCALYPTA!
SISTER EUCALYPTA DRIVES SERENELY ON--
--WHILE ON THE THIRD FLOOR OF A CERTAIN EXCLUSIVE DEPARTMENT STORE, MRS. PIKE RACES FRANTICALLY...
OH, MY!
PUFF OH, MY!
IT'S ABOUT TIME--!
I--I'M TERRIBLY SORRY, MISS! THERE WAS SUCH A TO-DO OUTSIDE THAT I--
I HAVE AN EVENING OF WORK WAITING FOR ME... AND I'D LIKE TO GET BACK TO IT THIS WEEK, PLEASE!
MY, WHAT A WELL-SHAPED, FIRM FIGURE SHE HAS! MAYBE SHE'D CONSIDER MODELLING!
BUT NOW CERTAINLY ISN'T THE TIME TO ASK HER!
IF THAT ONE DOESN'T FIT--
AS THE CURTAINS CLOSE, MRS. PIKE'S MODELLING PROSPECT'S WELL-SHAPED, FIRM FIGURE STIFFENS--
--AS SHE IS TRANSFIXED BY A HAZY, KALEIDOSCOPIC ASSEMBLAGE OF IMAGES IN HER MIND.
THEN THE DRESSING ROOM IS FILLED BY A CORRUSCATING NIMBUS OF LIGHT WHICH OBSCURES THE FIGURE OF CAROL DANVERS AT ITS CENTER.
WHAT WAS THAT... GLOW?
DRESS
MISS, ARE YOU ALL RIGHT?
MISS?

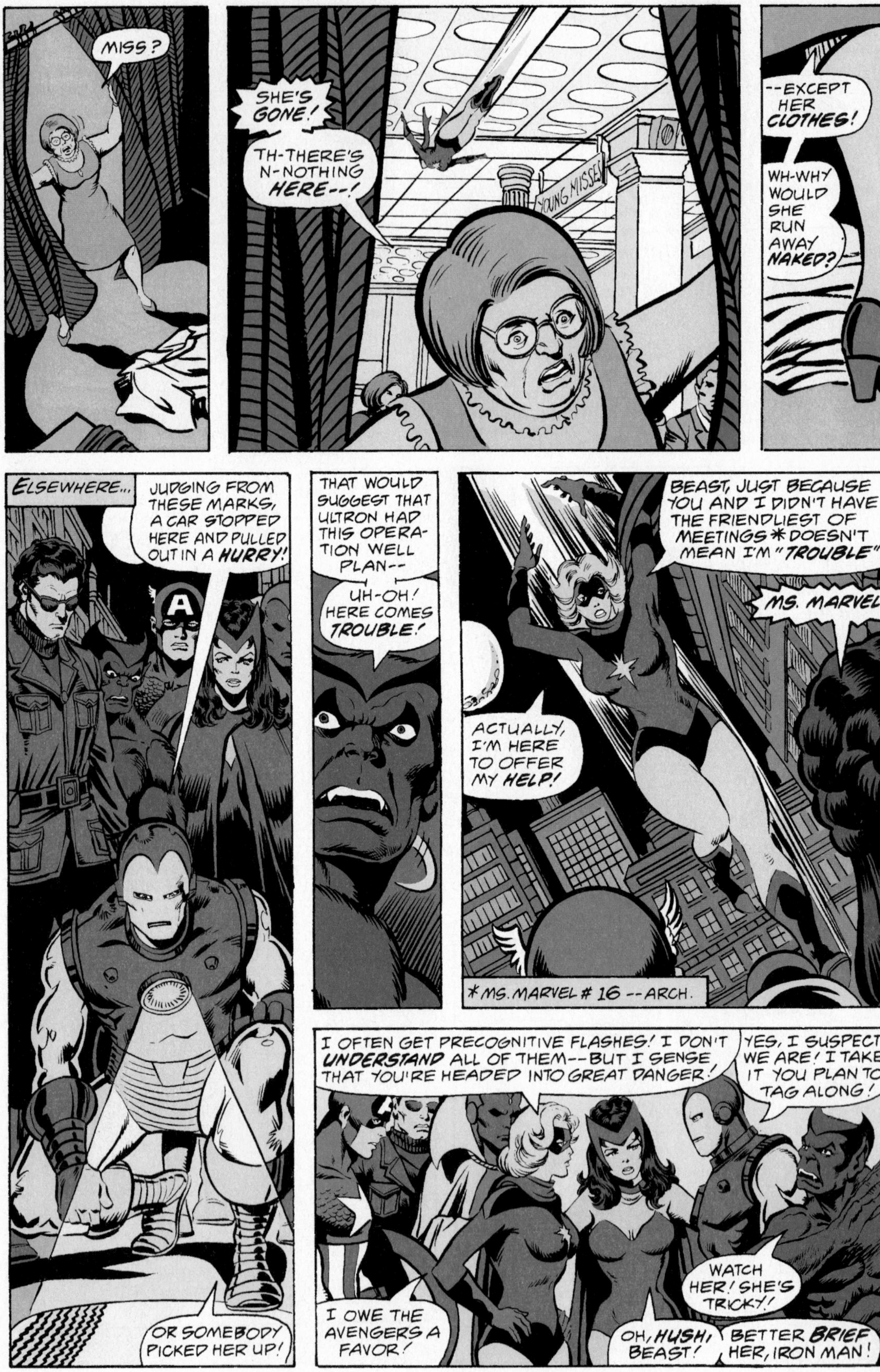
MISS?
SHE'S GONE!
TH-THERE'S N-NOTHING HERE--!
YOUNG MISSES
--EXCEPT HER CLOTHES!
WH-WHY WOULD SHE RUN AWAY NAKED?
ELSEWHERE...
JUDGING FROM THESE MARKS, A CAR STOPPED HERE AND PULLED OUT IN A HURRY!
OR SOMEBODY PICKED HER UP!
THAT WOULD SUGGEST THAT ULTRON HAD THIS OPERATION WELL PLAN--
UH-OH! HERE COMES TROUBLE!
BEAST, JUST BECAUSE YOU AND I DIDN'T HAVE THE FRIENDLIEST OF MEETINGS* DOESN'T MEAN I'M "TROUBLE"!
MS. MARVEL!
ACTUALLY, I'M HERE TO OFFER MY HELP!
*MS. MARVEL # 16 --ARCH.
I OFTEN GET PRECOGNITIVE FLASHES! I DON'T UNDERSTAND ALL OF THEM--BUT I SENSE THAT YOU'RE HEADED INTO GREAT DANGER!
YES, I SUSPECT WE ARE! I TAKE IT YOU PLAN TO TAG ALONG!
I OWE THE AVENGERS A FAVOR!
WATCH HER! SHE'S TRICKY!
OH, HUSH, BEAST!
BETTER BRIEF HER, IRON MAN!

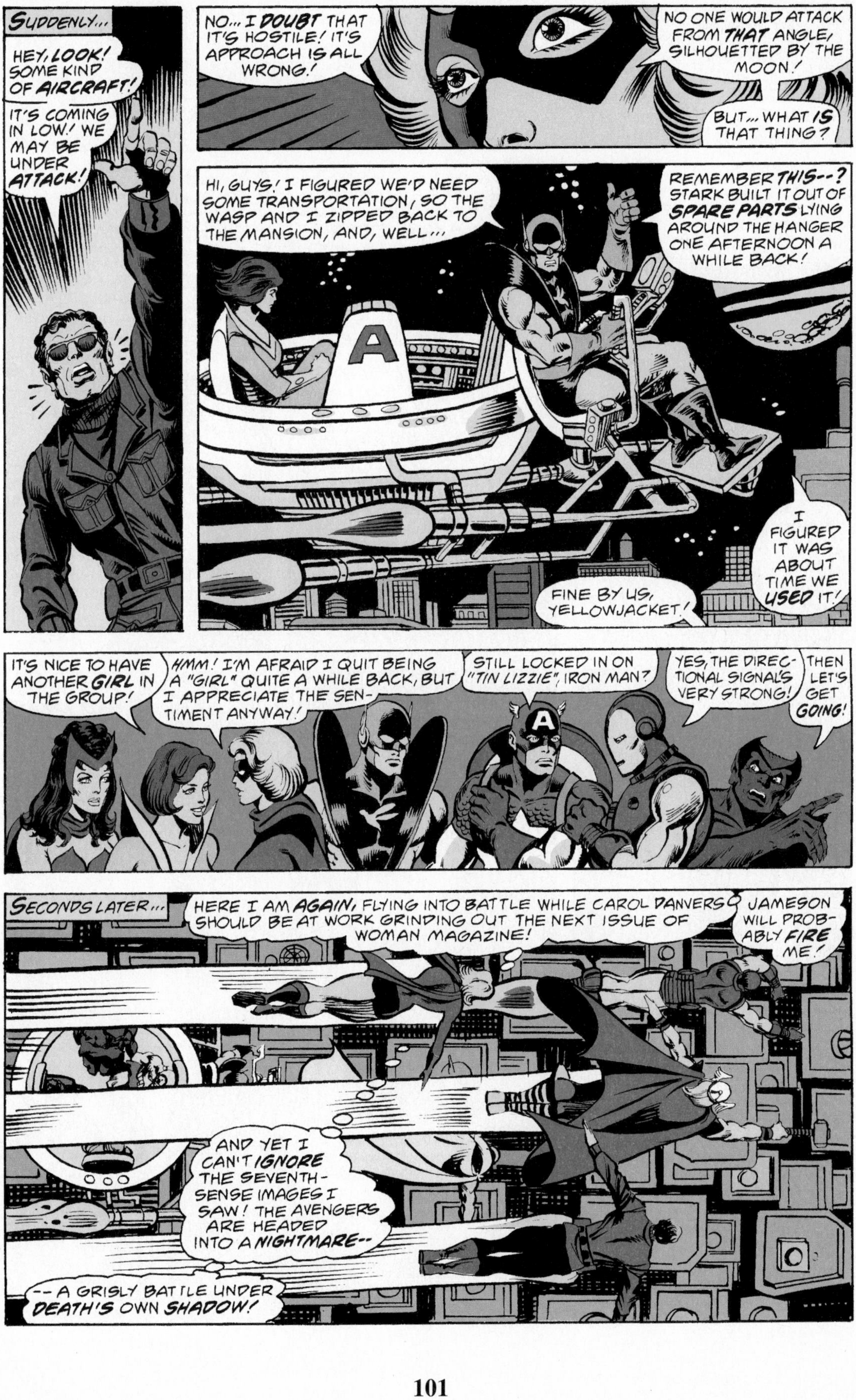
SUDDENLY...
HEY, LOOK! SOME KIND OF AIRCRAFT!
IT'S COMING IN LOW! WE MAY BE UNDER ATTACK!
NO... I DOUBT THAT IT'S HOSTILE! IT'S APPROACH IS ALL WRONG!
NO ONE WOULD ATTACK FROM THAT ANGLE, SILHOUETTED BY THE MOON!
BUT... WHAT IS THAT THING?
HI, GUYS! I FIGURED WE'D NEED SOME TRANSPORTATION, SO THE WASP AND I ZIPPED BACK TO THE MANSION, AND, WELL...
REMEMBER THIS--? STARK BUILT IT OUT OF SPARE PARTS LYING AROUND THE HANGER ONE AFTERNOON A WHILE BACK!
I FIGURED IT WAS ABOUT TIME WE USED IT!
FINE BY US, YELLOWJACKET!
IT'S NICE TO HAVE ANOTHER GIRL IN THE GROUP!
HMM! I'M AFRAID I QUIT BEING A "GIRL" QUITE A WHILE BACK, BUT I APPRECIATE THE SENTIMENT ANYWAY!
STILL LOCKED IN ON "TIN LIZZIE", IRON MAN?
YES, THE DIRECTIONAL SIGNAL'S VERY STRONG!
THEN LET'S GET GOING!
SECONDS LATER...
HERE I AM AGAIN, FLYING INTO BATTLE WHILE CAROL DANVERS SHOULD BE AT WORK GRINDING OUT THE NEXT ISSUE OF WOMAN MAGAZINE!
JAMESON WILL PROBABLY FIRE ME!
AND YET I CAN'T IGNORE THE SEVENTH-SENSE IMAGES I SAW! THE AVENGERS ARE HEADED INTO A NIGHTMARE--
-- A GRISLY BATTLE UNDER DEATH'S OWN SHADOW!

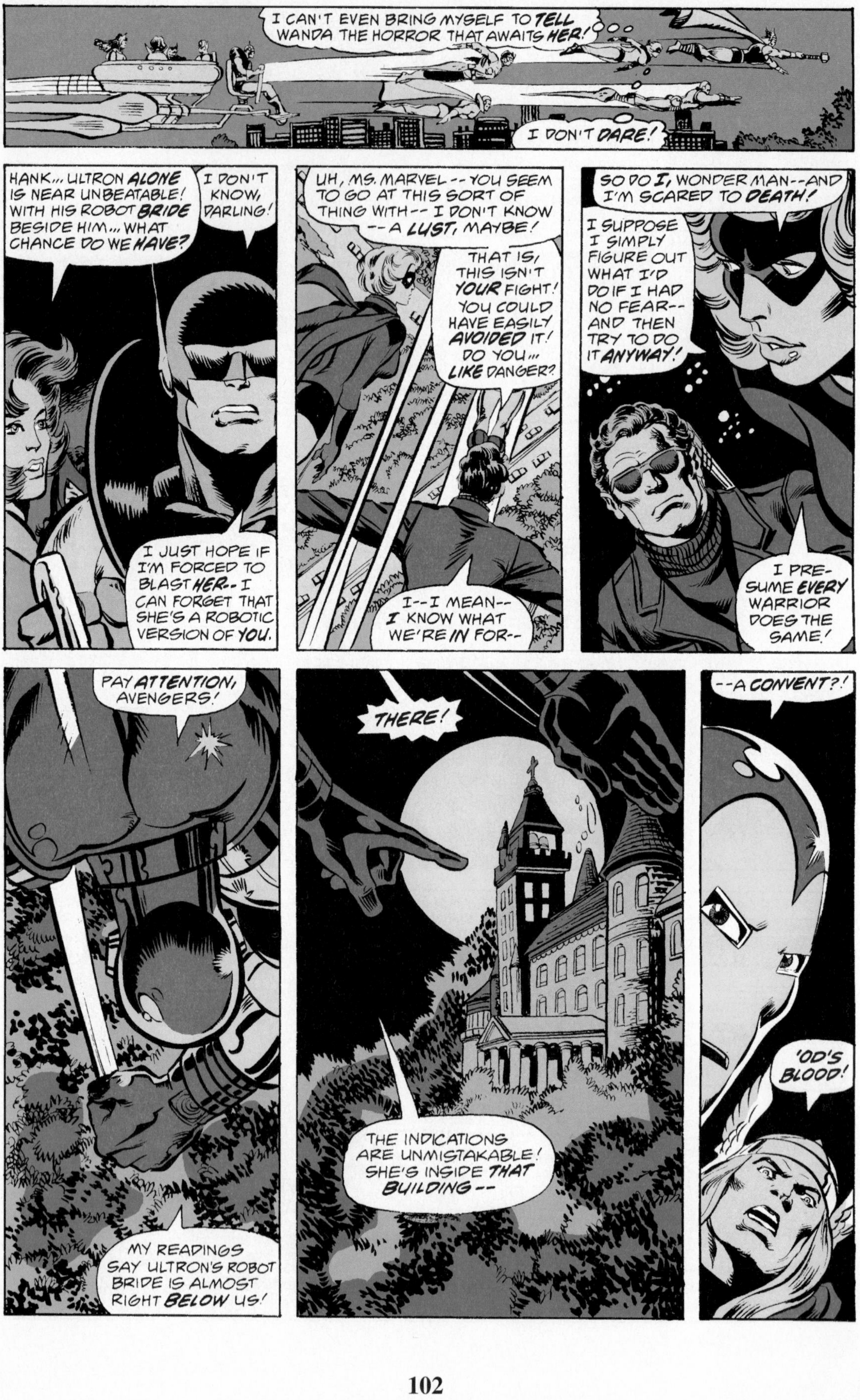
I CAN'T EVEN BRING MYSELF TO TELL WANDA THE HORROR THAT AWAITS HER!
I DON'T DARE!
HANK... ULTRON ALONE IS NEAR UNBEATABLE! WITH HIS ROBOT BRIDE BESIDE HIM... WHAT CHANCE DO WE HAVE?
I DON'T KNOW, DARLING!
I JUST HOPE IF I'M FORCED TO BLAST HER-- I CAN FORGET THAT SHE'S A ROBOTIC VERSION OF YOU.
UH, MS. MARVEL -- YOU SEEM TO GO AT THIS SORT OF THING WITH -- I DON'T KNOW -- A LUST, MAYBE!
THAT IS, THIS ISN'T YOUR FIGHT! YOU COULD HAVE EASILY AVOIDED IT! DO YOU... LIKE DANGER?
I--I MEAN-- I KNOW WHAT WE'RE IN FOR--
SO DO I, WONDER MAN--AND I'M SCARED TO DEATH!
I SUPPOSE I SIMPLY FIGURE OUT WHAT I'D DO IF I HAD NO FEAR-- AND THEN TRY TO DO IT ANYWAY!
I PRESUME EVERY WARRIOR DOES THE SAME!
PAY ATTENTION, AVENGERS!
MY READINGS SAY ULTRON'S ROBOT BRIDE IS ALMOST RIGHT BELOW US!
THERE!
THE INDICATIONS ARE UNMISTAKABLE! SHE'S INSIDE THAT BUILDING --
--A CONVENT?!
'OD'S BLOOD!

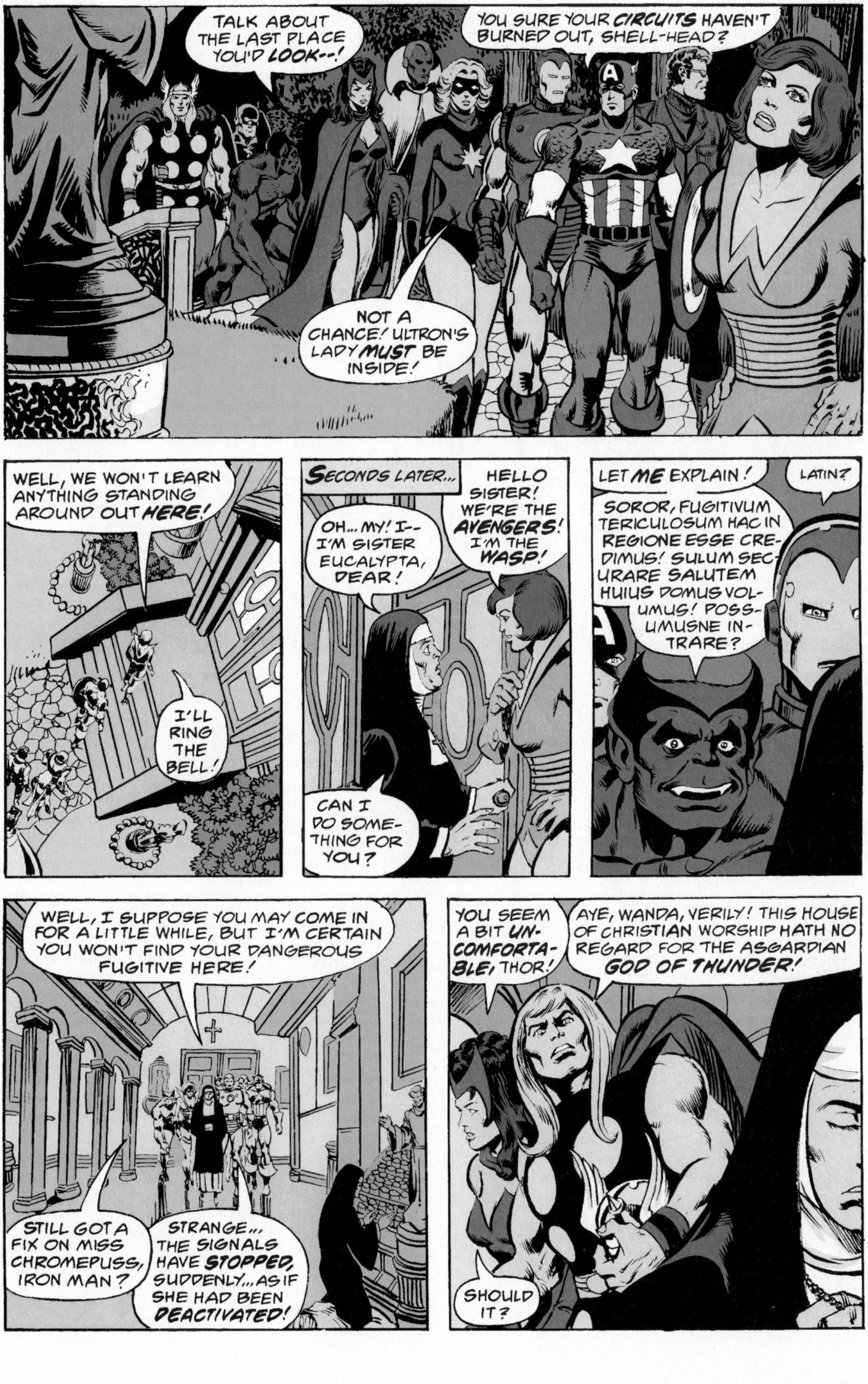
TALK ABOUT THE LAST PLACE YOU'D LOOK--!
YOU SURE YOUR CIRCUITS HAVEN'T BURNED OUT, SHELL-HEAD?
NOT A CHANCE! ULTRON'S LADY MUST BE INSIDE!
WELL, WE WON'T LEARN ANYTHING STANDING AROUND OUT HERE!
I'LL RING THE BELL!
SECONDS LATER...
HELLO SISTER! WE'RE THE AVENGERS! I'M THE WASP!
OH... MY! I-- I'M SISTER EUCALYPTA, DEAR!
CAN I DO SOMETHING FOR YOU?
LET ME EXPLAIN!
LATIN?
SOROR, FUGITIVUM TERICULOSUM HAC IN REGIONE ESSE CREDIMUS! SULUM SECURARE SALUTEM HUIUS DOMUS VOLUMUS! POSSUMUSNE INTRARE?
WELL, I SUPPOSE YOU MAY COME IN FOR A LITTLE WHILE, BUT I'M CERTAIN YOU WON'T FIND YOUR DANGEROUS FUGITIVE HERE!
STILL GOT A FIX ON MISS CHROMEPUSS, IRON MAN?
STRANGE... THE SIGNALS HAVE STOPPED, SUDDENLY... AS IF SHE HAD BEEN DEACTIVATED!
YOU SEEM A BIT UNCOMFORTABLE, THOR!
AYE, WANDA, VERILY! THIS HOUSE OF CHRISTIAN WORSHIP HATH NO REGARD FOR THE ASGARDIAN GOD OF THUNDER!
SHOULD IT?

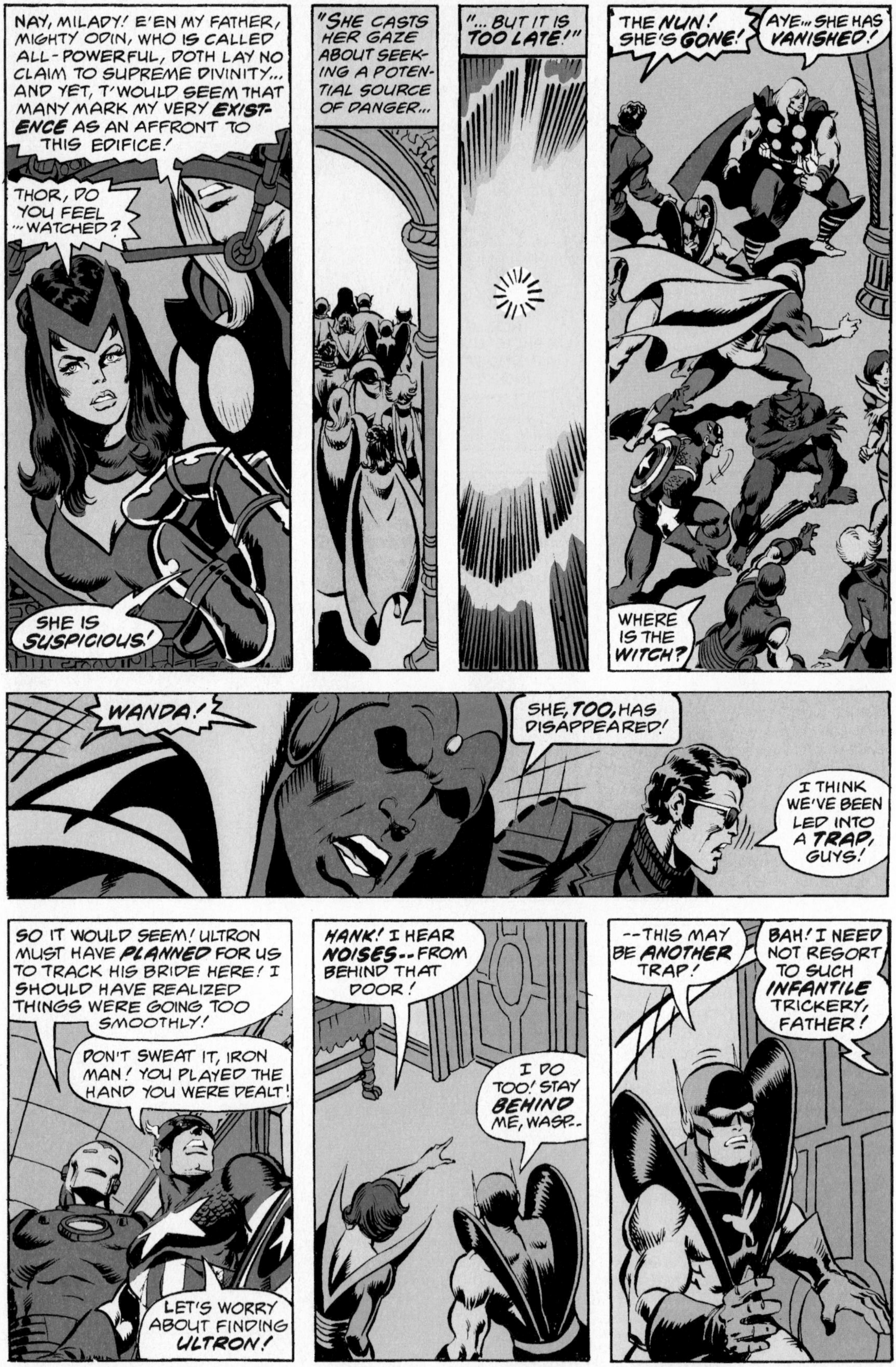
NAY, MILADY! E'EN MY FATHER, MIGHTY ODIN, WHO IS CALLED ALL-POWERFUL, DOTH LAY NO CLAIM TO SUPREME DIVINITY... AND YET, T'WOULD SEEM THAT MANY MARK MY VERY EXISTENCE AS AN AFFRONT TO THIS EDIFICE!
THOR, DO YOU FEEL ...WATCHED?
SHE IS SUSPICIOUS!
"SHE CASTS HER GAZE ABOUT SEEKING A POTENTIAL SOURCE OF DANGER...
"... BUT IT IS TOO LATE!"
THE NUN! SHE'S GONE!
AYE... SHE HAS VANISHED!
WHERE IS THE WITCH?
WANDA!
SHE, TOO, HAS DISAPPEARED!
I THINK WE'VE BEEN LED INTO A TRAP, GUYS!
SO IT WOULD SEEM! ULTRON MUST HAVE PLANNED FOR US TO TRACK HIS BRIDE HERE! I SHOULD HAVE REALIZED THINGS WERE GOING TOO SMOOTHLY!
DON'T SWEAT IT, IRON MAN! YOU PLAYED THE HAND YOU WERE DEALT!
LET'S WORRY ABOUT FINDING ULTRON!
HANK! I HEAR NOISES--FROM BEHIND THAT DOOR!
I DO TOO! STAY BEHIND ME, WASP--
--THIS MAY BE ANOTHER TRAP!
BAH! I NEED NOT RESORT TO SUCH INFANTILE TRICKERY, FATHER!

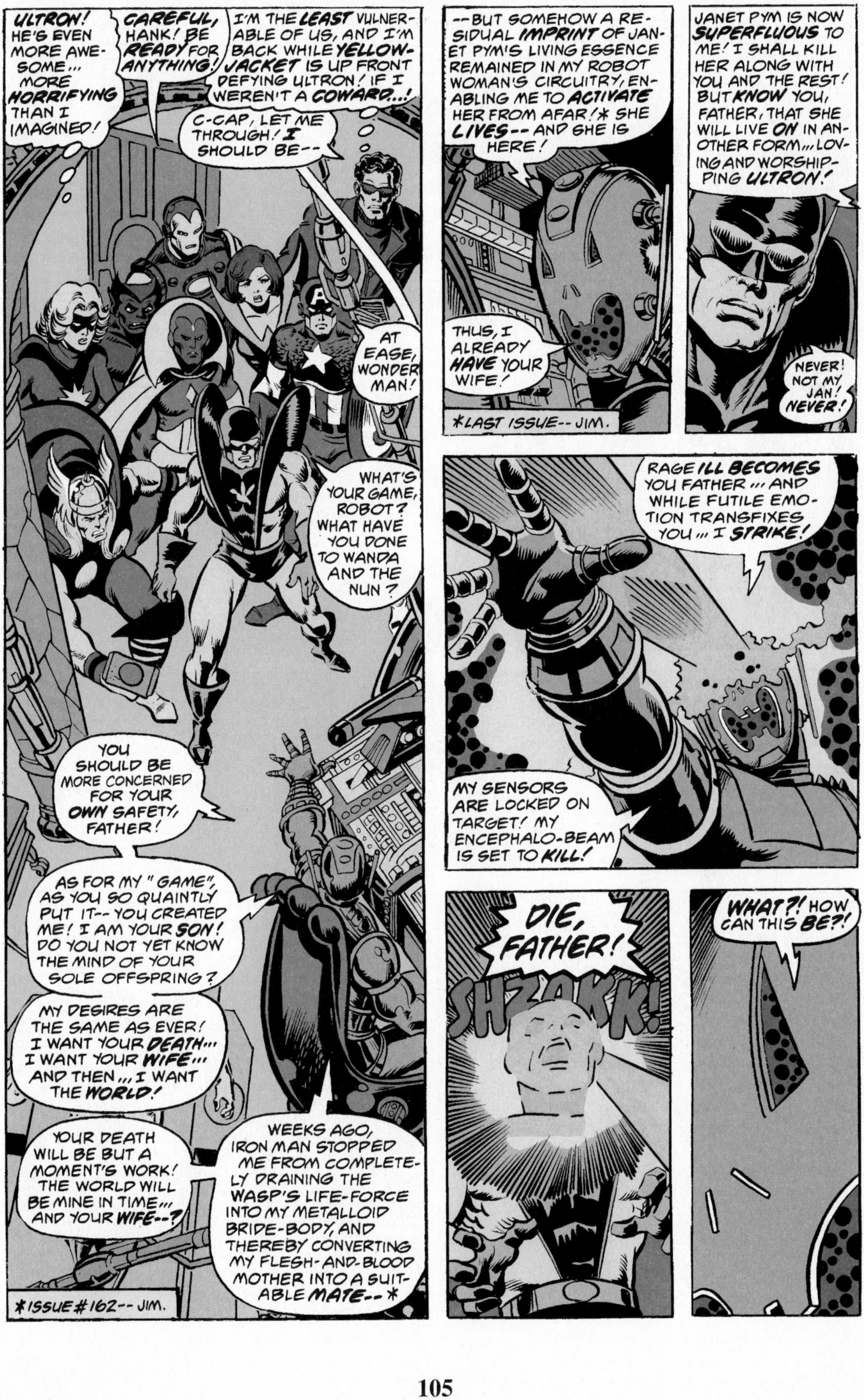
ULTRON! HE'S EVEN MORE AWE-SOME... MORE HORRIFYING THAN I IMAGINED!
CAREFUL, HANK! BE READY FOR ANYTHING!
I'M THE LEAST VULNER-ABLE OF US, AND I'M BACK WHILE YELLOW-JACKET IS UP FRONT DEFYING ULTRON! IF I WEREN'T A COWARD...!
C-CAP, LET ME THROUGH! I SHOULD BE--
AT EASE, WONDER MAN!
WHAT'S YOUR GAME, ROBOT? WHAT HAVE YOU DONE TO WANDA AND THE NUN?
YOU SHOULD BE MORE CONCERNED FOR YOUR OWN SAFETY, FATHER!
AS FOR MY "GAME", AS YOU SO QUAINTLY PUT IT-- YOU CREATED ME! I AM YOUR SON! DO YOU NOT YET KNOW THE MIND OF YOUR SOLE OFFSPRING?
MY DESIRES ARE THE SAME AS EVER! I WANT YOUR DEATH... I WANT YOUR WIFE... AND THEN... I WANT THE WORLD!
YOUR DEATH WILL BE BUT A MOMENT'S WORK! THE WORLD WILL BE MINE IN TIME... AND YOUR WIFE--?
WEEKS AGO, IRON MAN STOPPED ME FROM COMPLETE-LY DRAINING THE WASP'S LIFE-FORCE INTO MY METALLOID BRIDE-BODY, AND THEREBY CONVERTING MY FLESH-AND-BLOOD MOTHER INTO A SUIT-ABLE MATE--*
*ISSUE #162-- JIM.
--BUT SOMEHOW A RE-SIDUAL IMPRINT OF JAN-ET PYM'S LIVING ESSENCE REMAINED IN MY ROBOT WOMAN'S CIRCUITRY, EN-ABLING ME TO ACTIVATE HER FROM AFAR!* SHE LIVES-- AND SHE IS HERE!
THUS, I ALREADY HAVE YOUR WIFE!
*LAST ISSUE-- JIM.
JANET PYM IS NOW SUPERFLUOUS TO ME! I SHALL KILL HER ALONG WITH YOU AND THE REST! BUT KNOW YOU, FATHER, THAT SHE WILL LIVE ON IN AN-OTHER FORM... LOV-ING AND WORSHIP-PING ULTRON!
NEVER! NOT MY JAN! NEVER!
RAGE ILL BECOMES YOU FATHER... AND WHILE FUTILE EMO-TION TRANSFIXES YOU... I STRIKE!
MY SENSORS ARE LOCKED ON TARGET! MY ENCEPHALO-BEAM IS SET TO KILL!
DIE, FATHER!
SHZAKK!
WHAT?! HOW CAN THIS BE?!

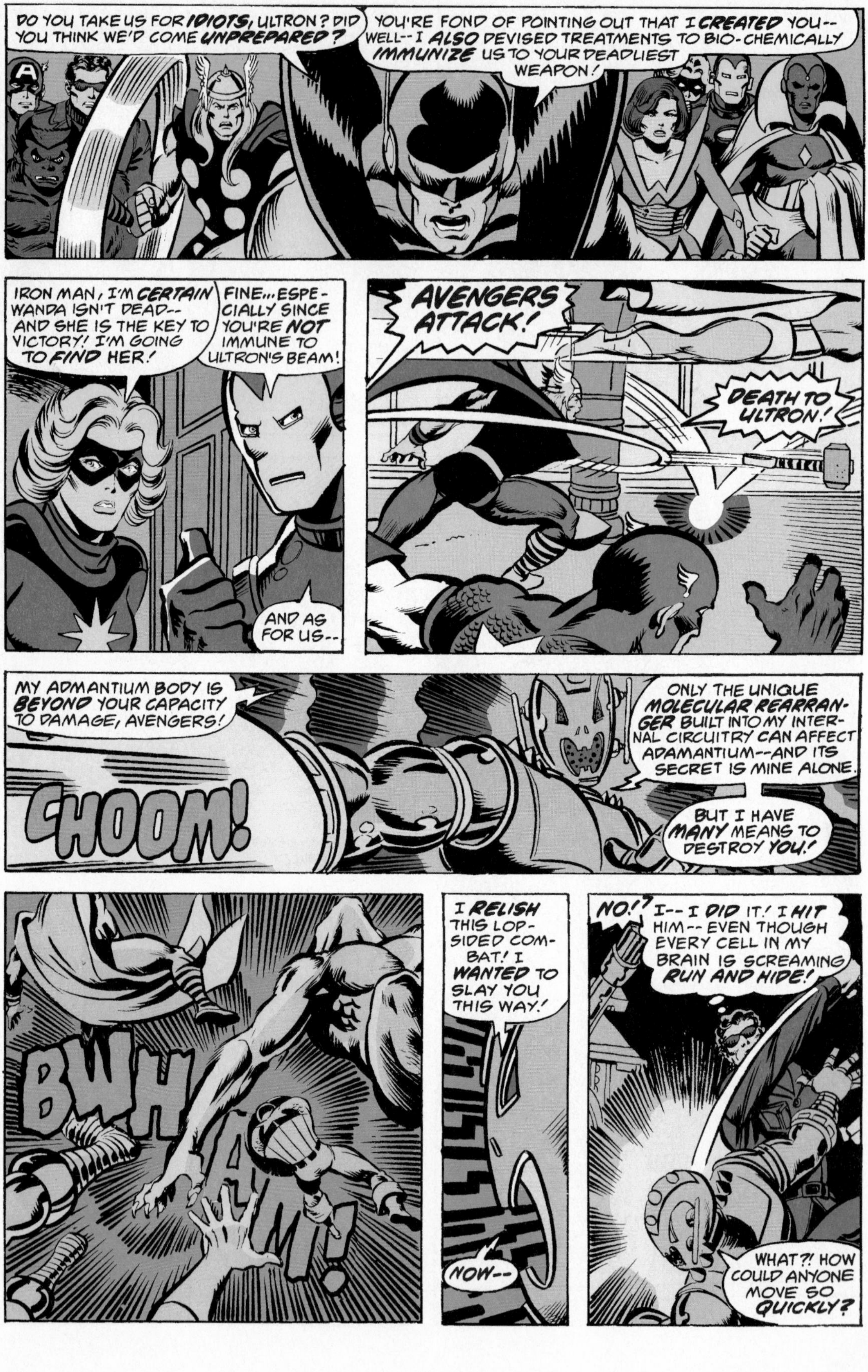
DO YOU TAKE US FOR IDIOTS, ULTRON? DID YOU THINK WE'D COME UNPREPARED?
YOU'RE FOND OF POINTING OUT THAT I CREATED YOU-- WELL-- I ALSO DEVISED TREATMENTS TO BIO-CHEMICALLY IMMUNIZE US TO YOUR DEADLIEST WEAPON!
IRON MAN, I'M CERTAIN WANDA ISN'T DEAD-- AND SHE IS THE KEY TO VICTORY! I'M GOING TO FIND HER!
FINE... ESPECIALLY SINCE YOU'RE NOT IMMUNE TO ULTRON'S BEAM!
AND AS FOR US--
AVENGERS ATTACK!
DEATH TO ULTRON!
MY ADMANTIUM BODY IS BEYOND YOUR CAPACITY TO DAMAGE, AVENGERS!
ONLY THE UNIQUE MOLECULAR REARRANGER BUILT INTO MY INTERNAL CIRCUITRY CAN AFFECT ADAMANTIUM--AND ITS SECRET IS MINE ALONE.
CHOOM!
BUT I HAVE MANY MEANS TO DESTROY YOU!
BWHAM!
I RELISH THIS LOP-SIDED COMBAT! I WANTED TO SLAY YOU THIS WAY!
NOW--
NO!?
I-- I DID IT! I HIT HIM-- EVEN THOUGH EVERY CELL IN MY BRAIN IS SCREAMING RUN AND HIDE!
WHAT?! HOW COULD ANYONE MOVE SO QUICKLY?

MEANWHILE...

OH-H-H! WHERE...

...AM I?

A CHAMBER OF MIRRORS!

THEY--THEY'RE SHIFTING! CHANGING...? LIKE A HUGE KALEIDOSCOPE! I'D SWEAR THE WHOLE ROOM IS MOVING!

THIS PLACE IS DESIGNED TO DISORIENT ME! NOTHING IS AS IT SEEMS! EVEN THE FURNITURE IS ILLUSORY!

CAN'T TRUST MY EYES! I'LL HAVE TO EXPLORE THIS PRISON BY TOUCH! I'D BETTER NOT CAST A HEX UNTIL I'M CERTAIN OF WHAT I'M STRIKING AT--

--OR IT COULD BACKFIRE ON ME!

EVEN IF ALL THOSE MIRRORS ARE REAL-- WHO KNOWS WHAT MAY BE BEYOND TH--

AIEEE!

THE "MIRROR" I STEPPED ON WASN'T THERE! PLUNGING THROUGH A VOID--TOTAL BLACKNESS!

FALLING....FAR!

I CAN'T SURVIVE THIS GREAT A DROP! I'M GOING TO--

SPLASH!

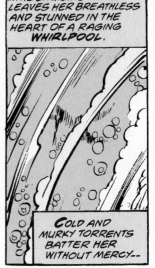

...THE BRUISING IMPACT LEAVES HER BREATHLESS AND STUNNED IN THE HEART OF A RAGING WHIRLPOOL.

COLD AND MURKY TORRENTS BATTER HER WITHOUT MERCY--

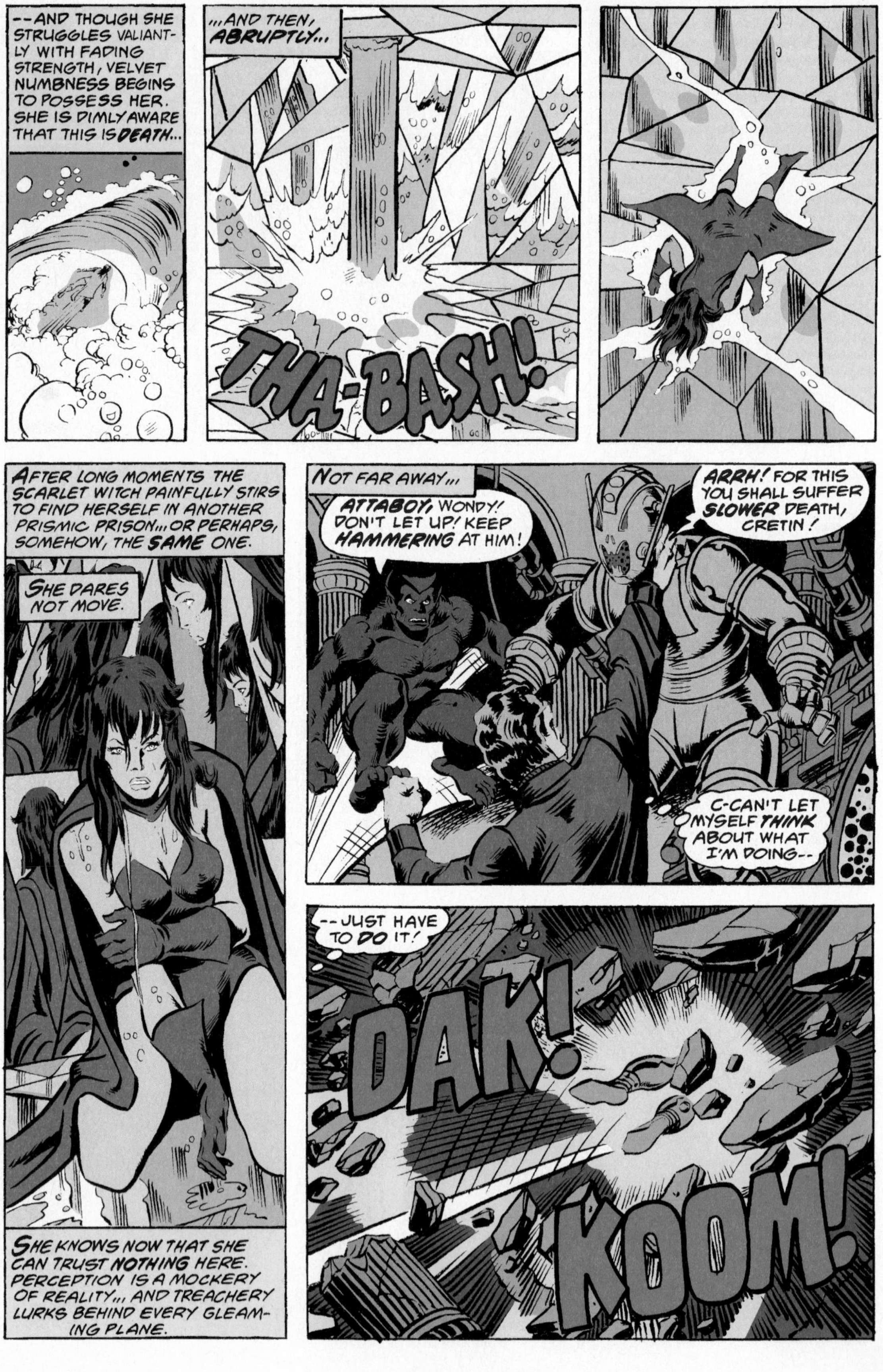
--AND THOUGH SHE STRUGGLES VALIANTLY WITH FADING STRENGTH, VELVET NUMBNESS BEGINS TO POSSESS HER. SHE IS DIMLY AWARE THAT THIS IS DEATH...
...AND THEN, ABRUPTLY...
THA-BASH!
AFTER LONG MOMENTS THE SCARLET WITCH PAINFULLY STIRS TO FIND HERSELF IN ANOTHER PRISMIC PRISON... OR PERHAPS, SOMEHOW, THE SAME ONE.
SHE DARES NOT MOVE.
SHE KNOWS NOW THAT SHE CAN TRUST NOTHING HERE. PERCEPTION IS A MOCKERY OF REALITY... AND TREACHERY LURKS BEHIND EVERY GLEAMING PLANE.
NOT FAR AWAY...
ATTABOY, WONDY! DON'T LET UP! KEEP HAMMERING AT HIM!
ARRH! FOR THIS YOU SHALL SUFFER SLOWER DEATH, CRETIN!
C-CAN'T LET MYSELF THINK ABOUT WHAT I'M DOING--
--JUST HAVE TO DO IT!
DAK!
KOOM!

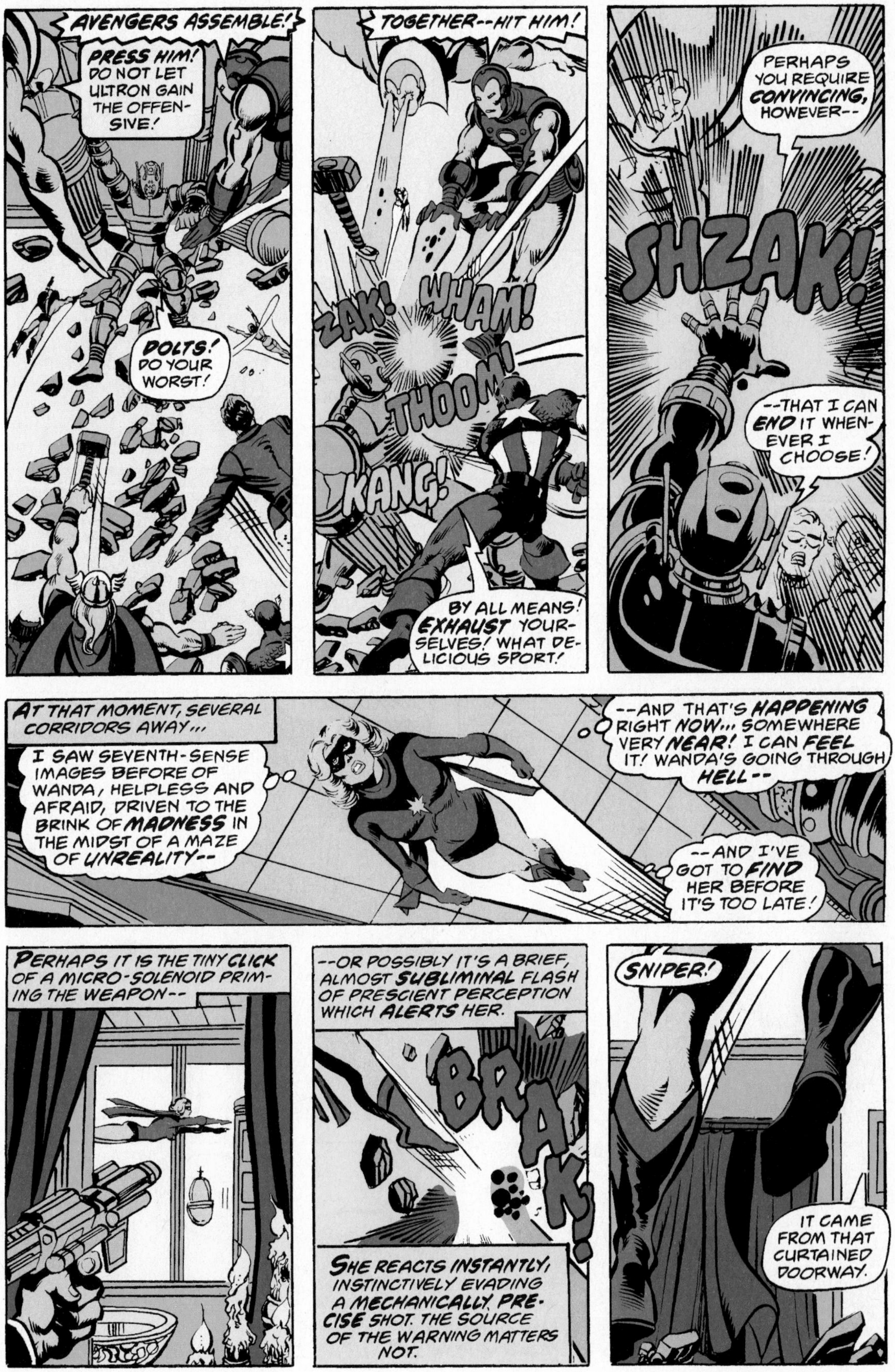
AVENGERS ASSEMBLE!
PRESS HIM! DO NOT LET ULTRON GAIN THE OFFEN-SIVE!
DOLTS! DO YOUR WORST!
TOGETHER--HIT HIM!
ZAK! WHAM!
THOOM!
KANG!
BY ALL MEANS! EXHAUST YOUR-SELVES! WHAT DE-LICIOUS SPORT!
PERHAPS YOU REQUIRE CONVINCING, HOWEVER--
SHZAK!
--THAT I CAN END IT WHEN-EVER I CHOOSE!
AT THAT MOMENT, SEVERAL CORRIDORS AWAY...
I SAW SEVENTH-SENSE IMAGES BEFORE OF WANDA, HELPLESS AND AFRAID, DRIVEN TO THE BRINK OF MADNESS IN THE MIDST OF A MAZE OF UNREALITY--
--AND THAT'S HAPPENING RIGHT NOW... SOMEWHERE VERY NEAR! I CAN FEEL IT! WANDA'S GOING THROUGH HELL--
--AND I'VE GOT TO FIND HER BEFORE IT'S TOO LATE!
PERHAPS IT IS THE TINY CLICK OF A MICRO-SOLENOID PRIM-ING THE WEAPON--
--OR POSSIBLY IT'S A BRIEF, ALMOST SUBLIMINAL FLASH OF PRESCIENT PERCEPTION WHICH ALERTS HER.
BRAK!
SHE REACTS INSTANTLY, INSTINCTIVELY EVADING A MECHANICALLY PRE-CISE SHOT. THE SOURCE OF THE WARNING MATTERS NOT.
SNIPER!
IT CAME FROM THAT CURTAINED DOORWAY.

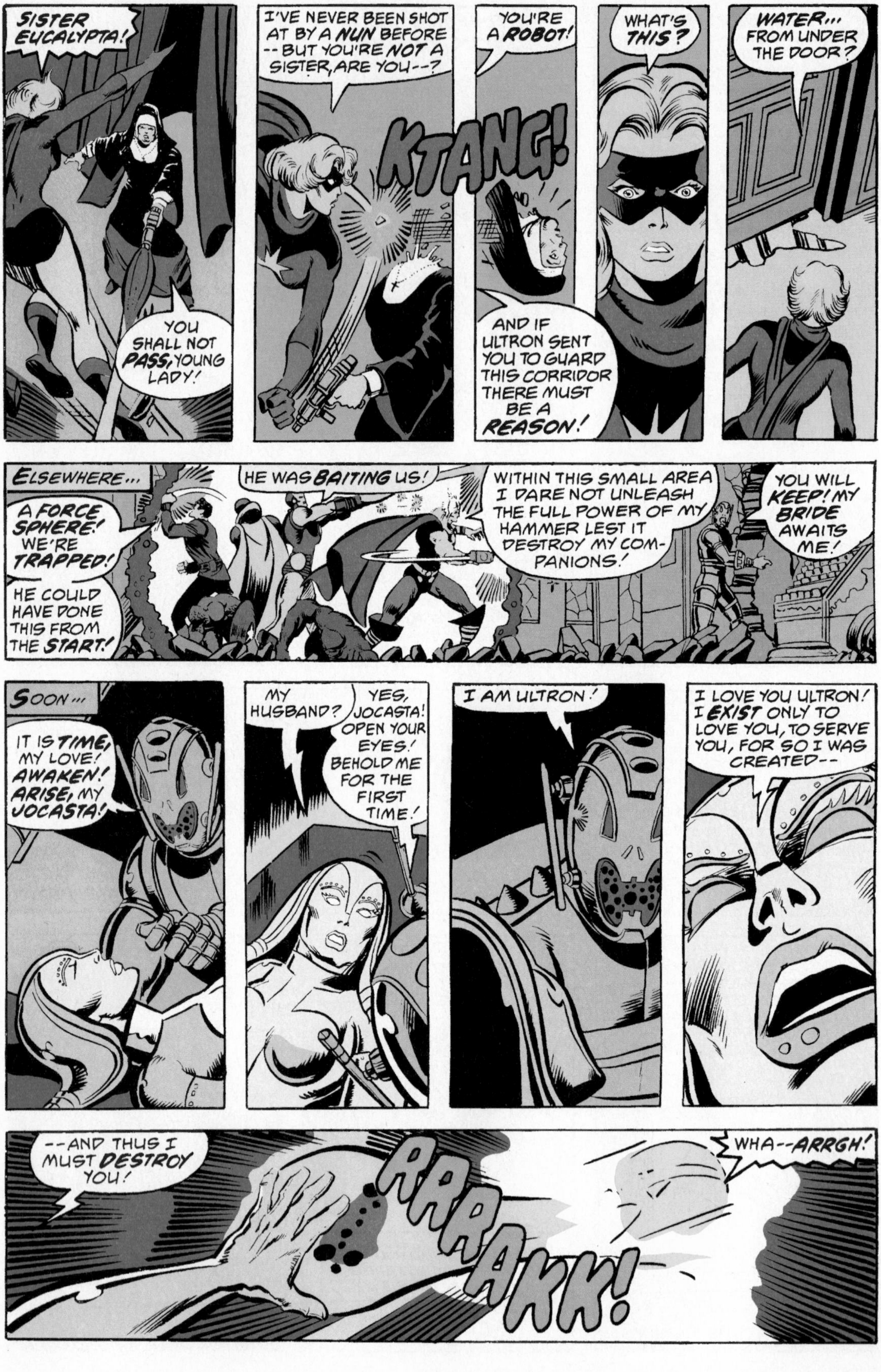
SISTER EUCALYPTA!
YOU SHALL NOT PASS, YOUNG LADY!
I'VE NEVER BEEN SHOT AT BY A NUN BEFORE -- BUT YOU'RE NOT A SISTER, ARE YOU--?
KTANG!
YOU'RE A ROBOT!
WHAT'S THIS?
AND IF ULTRON SENT YOU TO GUARD THIS CORRIDOR THERE MUST BE A REASON!
WATER... FROM UNDER THE DOOR?
ELSEWHERE...
A FORCE SPHERE! WE'RE TRAPPED!
HE COULD HAVE DONE THIS FROM THE START!
HE WAS BAITING US!
WITHIN THIS SMALL AREA I DARE NOT UNLEASH THE FULL POWER OF MY HAMMER LEST IT DESTROY MY COMPANIONS!
YOU WILL KEEP! MY BRIDE AWAITS ME!
SOON...
IT IS TIME, MY LOVE! AWAKEN! ARISE, MY JOCASTA!
MY HUSBAND?
YES, JOCASTA! OPEN YOUR EYES! BEHOLD ME FOR THE FIRST TIME!
I AM ULTRON!
I LOVE YOU ULTRON! I EXIST ONLY TO LOVE YOU, TO SERVE YOU, FOR SO I WAS CREATED--
--AND THUS I MUST DESTROY YOU!
ARRRAKK!
WHA--ARRGH!

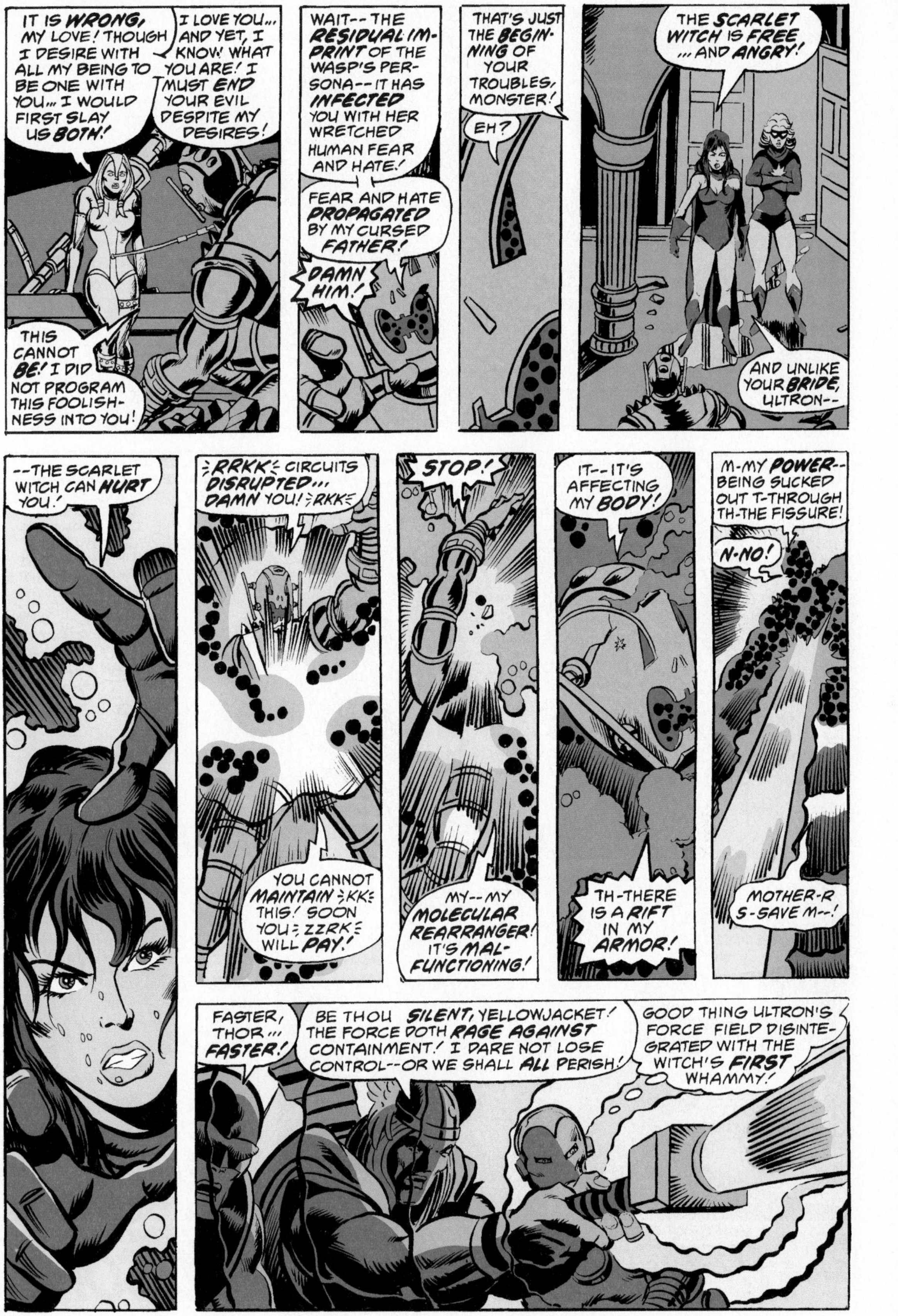
IT IS WRONG, MY LOVE! THOUGH I DESIRE WITH ALL MY BEING TO BE ONE WITH YOU... I WOULD FIRST SLAY US BOTH!
I LOVE YOU... AND YET, I KNOW WHAT YOU ARE! I MUST END YOUR EVIL DESPITE MY DESIRES!
THIS CANNOT BE! I DID NOT PROGRAM THIS FOOLISHNESS INTO YOU!
WAIT-- THE RESIDUAL IMPRINT OF THE WASP'S PERSONA-- IT HAS INFECTED YOU WITH HER WRETCHED HUMAN FEAR AND HATE!
FEAR AND HATE PROPAGATED BY MY CURSED FATHER!
DAMN HIM!
THAT'S JUST THE BEGINNING OF YOUR TROUBLES, MONSTER!
EH?
THE SCARLET WITCH IS FREE ...AND ANGRY!
AND UNLIKE YOUR BRIDE, ULTRON--
--THE SCARLET WITCH CAN HURT YOU!
RRKK CIRCUITS DISRUPTED... DAMN YOU! RKK
YOU CANNOT MAINTAIN KK THIS! SOON YOU ZZRK WILL PAY!
STOP!
MY-- MY MOLECULAR REARRANGER! IT'S MALFUNCTIONING!
IT-- IT'S AFFECTING MY BODY!
TH-THERE IS A RIFT IN MY ARMOR!
M-MY POWER-- BEING SUCKED OUT T-THROUGH TH-THE FISSURE!
N-NO!
MOTHER-R S-SAVE M--!
FASTER, THOR... FASTER!
BE THOU SILENT, YELLOWJACKET! THE FORCE DOTH RAGE AGAINST CONTAINMENT! I DARE NOT LOSE CONTROL--OR WE SHALL ALL PERISH!
GOOD THING ULTRON'S FORCE FIELD DISINTEGRATED WITH THE WITCH'S FIRST WHAMMY!

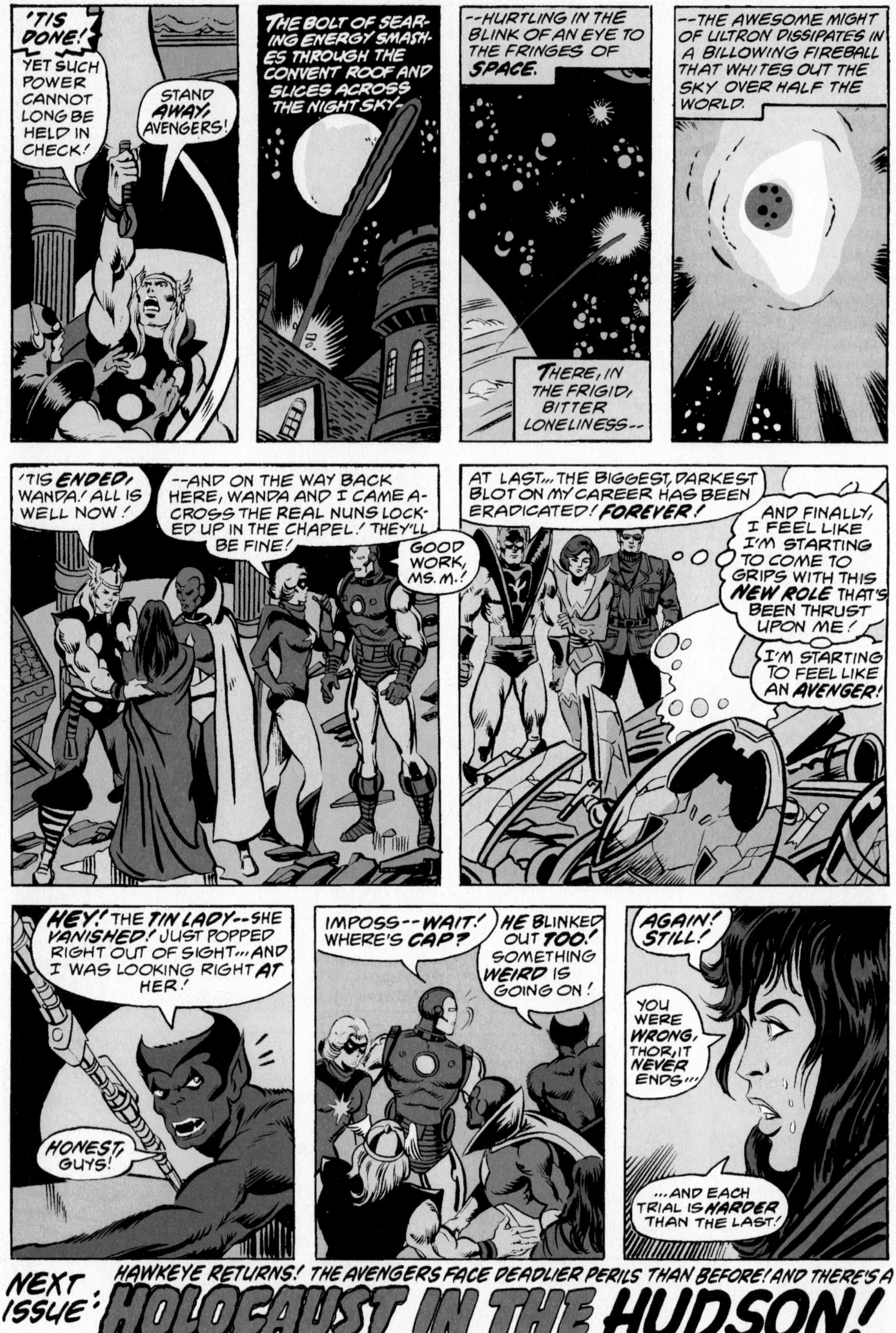
'TIS DONE!
YET SUCH POWER CANNOT LONG BE HELD IN CHECK!
STAND AWAY, AVENGERS!
THE BOLT OF SEARING ENERGY SMASHES THROUGH THE CONVENT ROOF AND SLICES ACROSS THE NIGHT SKY--
--HURTLING IN THE BLINK OF AN EYE TO THE FRINGES OF SPACE.
THERE, IN THE FRIGID, BITTER LONELINESS--
--THE AWESOME MIGHT OF ULTRON DISSIPATES IN A BILLOWING FIREBALL THAT WHITES OUT THE SKY OVER HALF THE WORLD.
'TIS ENDED, WANDA! ALL IS WELL NOW!
--AND ON THE WAY BACK HERE, WANDA AND I CAME ACROSS THE REAL NUNS LOCKED UP IN THE CHAPEL! THEY'LL BE FINE!
GOOD WORK, MS. M.!
AT LAST... THE BIGGEST, DARKEST BLOT ON MY CAREER HAS BEEN ERADICATED! FOREVER!
AND FINALLY, I FEEL LIKE I'M STARTING TO COME TO GRIPS WITH THIS NEW ROLE THAT'S BEEN THRUST UPON ME!
I'M STARTING TO FEEL LIKE AN AVENGER!
HEY! THE TIN LADY--SHE VANISHED! JUST POPPED RIGHT OUT OF SIGHT... AND I WAS LOOKING RIGHT AT HER!
HONEST, GUYS!
IMPOSS--WAIT! WHERE'S CAP?
HE BLINKED OUT TOO! SOMETHING WEIRD IS GOING ON!
AGAIN! STILL!
YOU WERE WRONG, THOR, IT NEVER ENDS...
...AND EACH TRIAL IS HARDER THAN THE LAST!

NEXT ISSUE: HAWKEYE RETURNS! THE AVENGERS FACE DEADLIER PERILS THAN BEFORE! AND THERE'S A HOLOCAUST IN THE HUDSON!

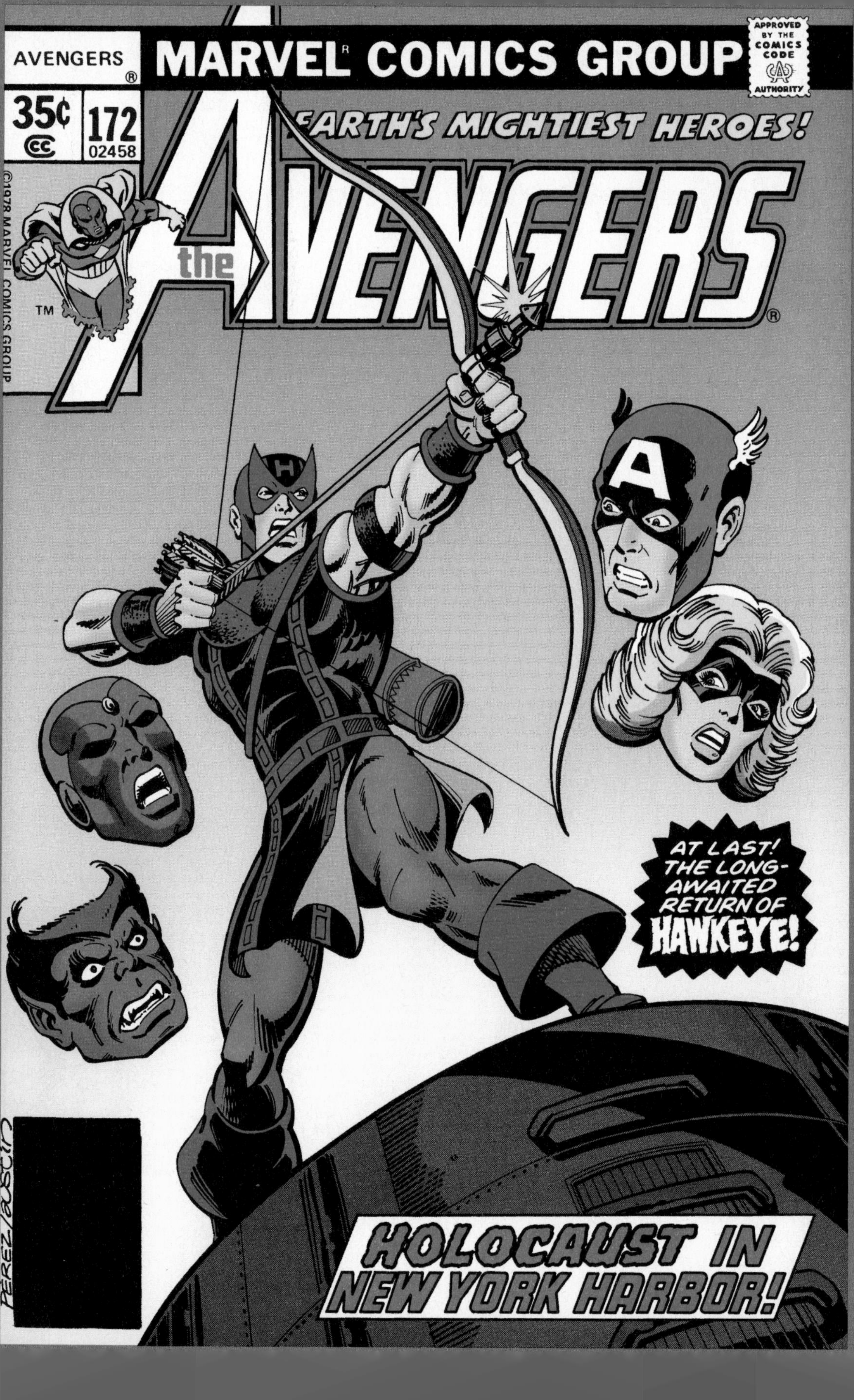
AVENGERS
MARVEL COMICS GROUP
APPROVED BY THE COMICS CODE AUTHORITY
35¢
172
02458
©1978 MARVEL COMICS GROUP
EARTH'S MIGHTIEST HEROES!
the AVENGERS
AT LAST! THE LONG-AWAITED RETURN OF HAWKEYE!
HOLOCAUST IN NEW YORK HARBOR!

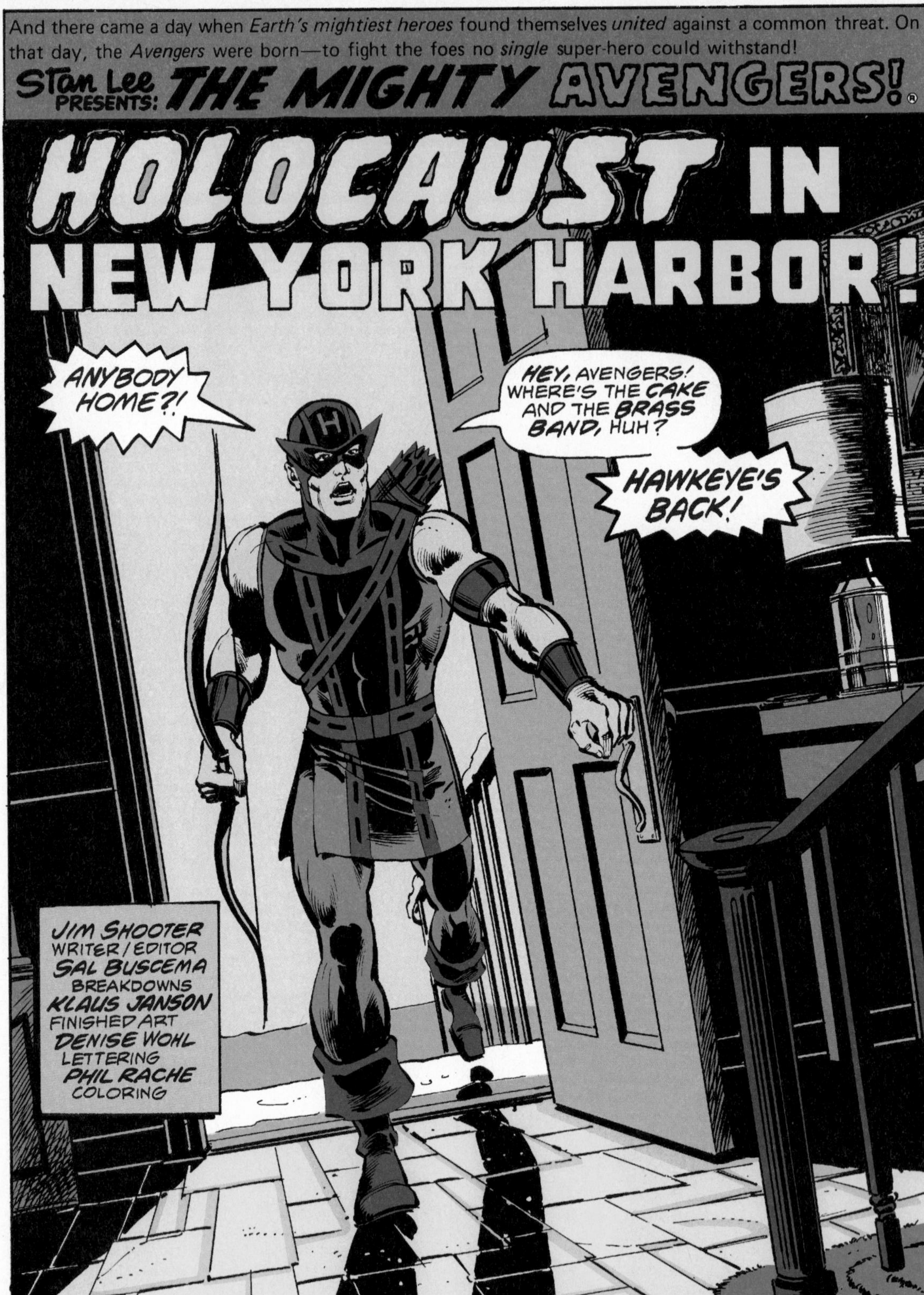
And there came a day when *Earth's mightiest heroes* found themselves *united* against a common threat. On that day, the *Avengers* were born—to fight the foes no *single* super-hero could withstand!
Stan Lee PRESENTS: THE MIGHTY AVENGERS!
HOLOCAUST IN NEW YORK HARBOR!
ANYBODY HOME?!
HEY, AVENGERS! WHERE'S THE CAKE AND THE BRASS BAND, HUH?
HAWKEYE'S BACK!
JIM SHOOTER WRITER/EDITOR
SAL BUSCEMA BREAKDOWNS
KLAUS JANSON FINISHED ART
DENISE WOHL LETTERING
PHIL RACHE COLORING

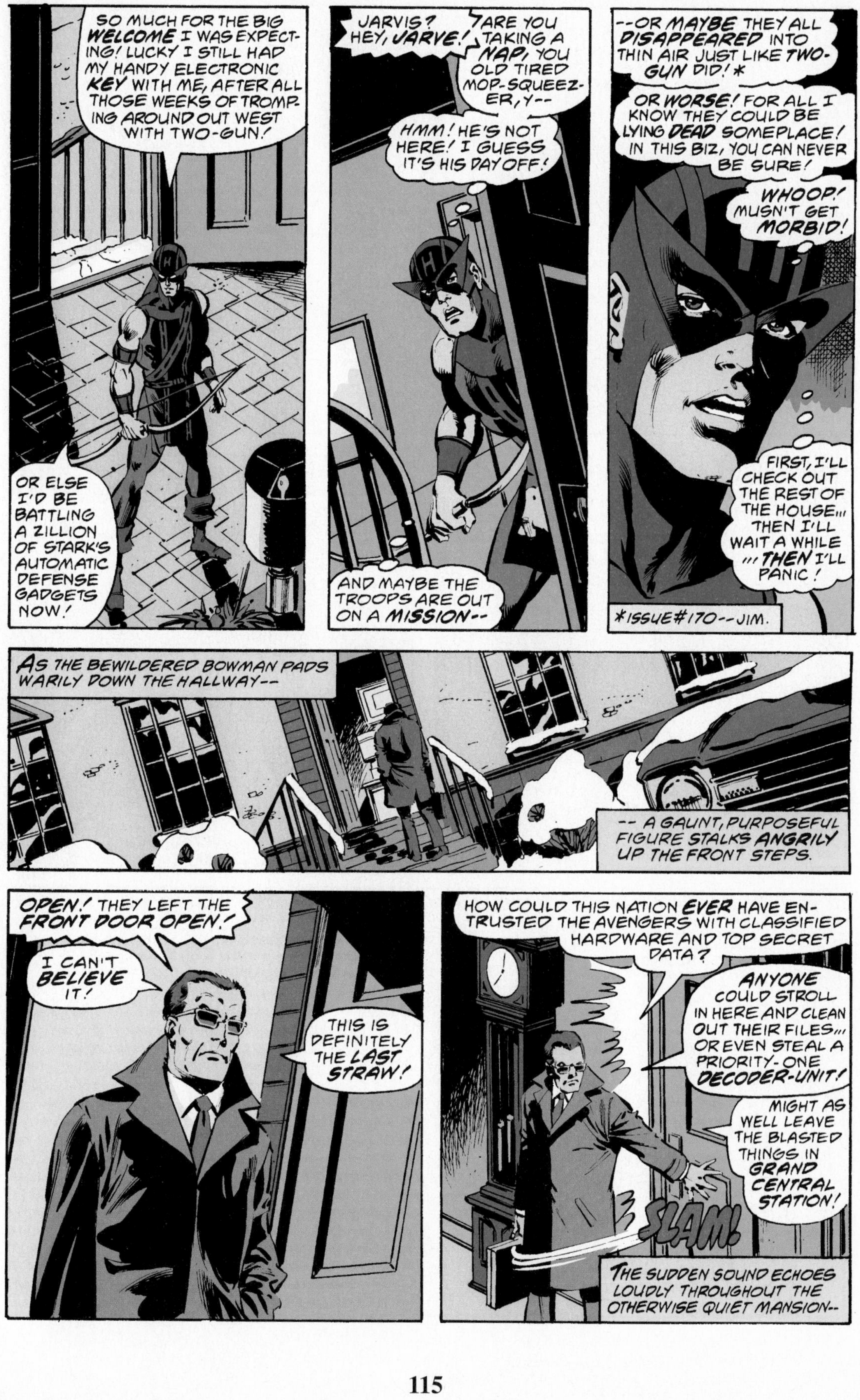
SO MUCH FOR THE BIG WELCOME I WAS EXPECTING! LUCKY I STILL HAD MY HANDY ELECTRONIC KEY WITH ME, AFTER ALL THOSE WEEKS OF TROMPING AROUND OUT WEST WITH TWO-GUN!
OR ELSE I'D BE BATTLING A ZILLION OF STARK'S AUTOMATIC DEFENSE GADGETS NOW!
JARVIS? HEY, JARVE!
ARE YOU TAKING A NAP, YOU OLD TIRED MOP-SQUEEZER, Y--
HMM! HE'S NOT HERE! I GUESS IT'S HIS DAY OFF!
AND MAYBE THE TROOPS ARE OUT ON A MISSION--
--OR MAYBE THEY ALL DISAPPEARED INTO THIN AIR JUST LIKE TWO-GUN DID! *
OR WORSE! FOR ALL I KNOW THEY COULD BE LYING DEAD SOMEPLACE! IN THIS BIZ, YOU CAN NEVER BE SURE!
WHOOP! MUSN'T GET MORBID!
FIRST, I'LL CHECK OUT THE REST OF THE HOUSE... THEN I'LL WAIT A WHILE ... THEN I'LL PANIC!
*ISSUE #170--JIM.
AS THE BEWILDERED BOWMAN PADS WARILY DOWN THE HALLWAY--
-- A GAUNT, PURPOSEFUL FIGURE STALKS ANGRILY UP THE FRONT STEPS.
OPEN! THEY LEFT THE FRONT DOOR OPEN!
I CAN'T BELIEVE IT!
THIS IS DEFINITELY THE LAST STRAW!
HOW COULD THIS NATION EVER HAVE ENTRUSTED THE AVENGERS WITH CLASSIFIED HARDWARE AND TOP SECRET DATA?
ANYONE COULD STROLL IN HERE AND CLEAN OUT THEIR FILES... OR EVEN STEAL A PRIORITY-ONE DECODER-UNIT!
MIGHT AS WELL LEAVE THE BLASTED THINGS IN GRAND CENTRAL STATION!
SLAM!
THE SUDDEN SOUND ECHOES LOUDLY THROUGHOUT THE OTHERWISE QUIET MANSION--

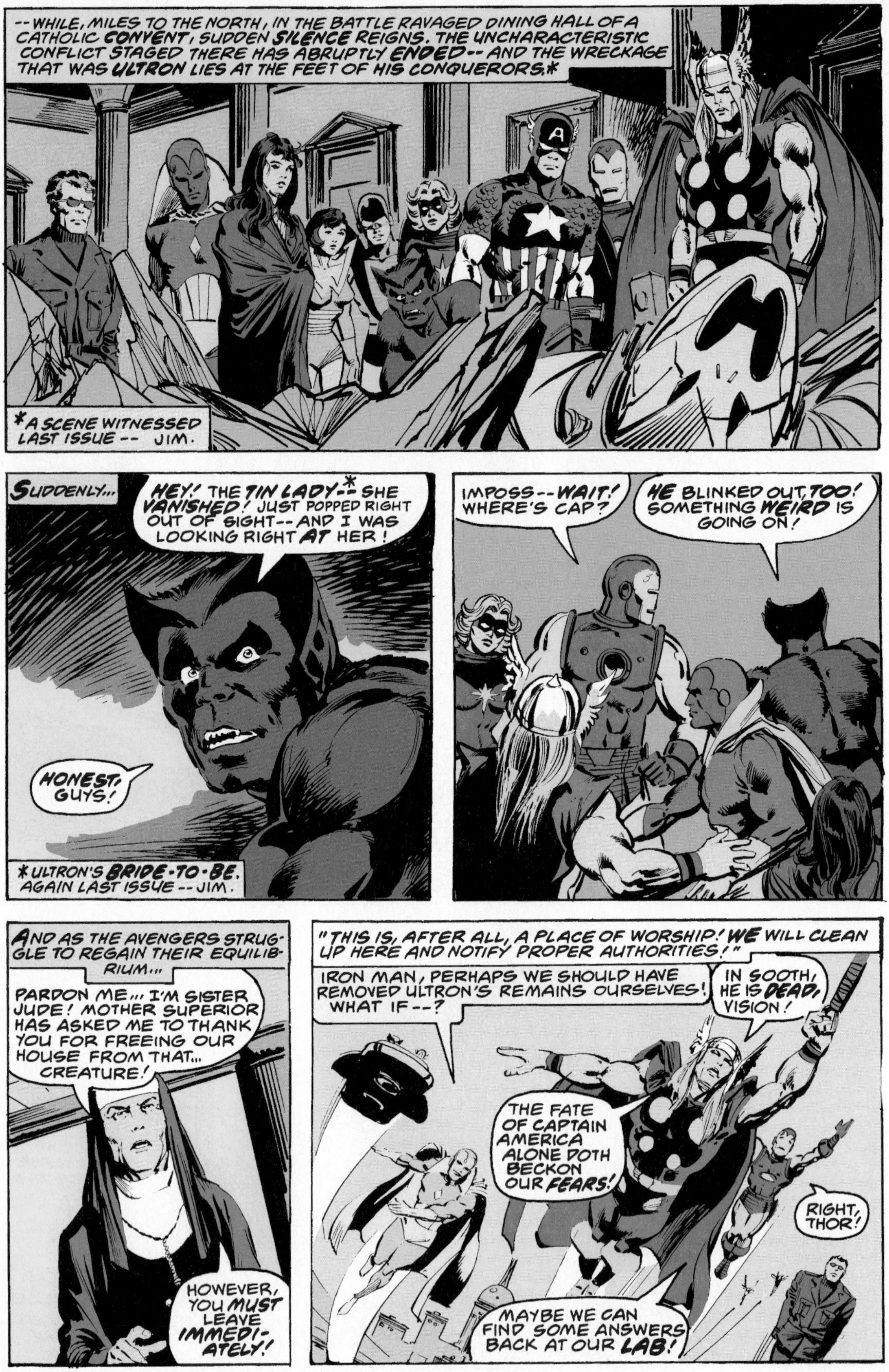
--WHILE, MILES TO THE NORTH, IN THE BATTLE RAVAGED DINING HALL OF A CATHOLIC CONVENT, SUDDEN SILENCE REIGNS. THE UNCHARACTERISTIC CONFLICT STAGED THERE HAS ABRUPTLY ENDED-- AND THE WRECKAGE THAT WAS ULTRON LIES AT THE FEET OF HIS CONQUERORS.*
*A SCENE WITNESSED LAST ISSUE -- JIM.
SUDDENLY...
HEY! THE TIN LADY--* SHE VANISHED! JUST POPPED RIGHT OUT OF SIGHT--AND I WAS LOOKING RIGHT AT HER!
HONEST, GUYS!
*ULTRON'S BRIDE-TO-BE. AGAIN LAST ISSUE -- JIM.
IMPOSS--WAIT! WHERE'S CAP?
HE BLINKED OUT, TOO! SOMETHING WEIRD IS GOING ON!
AND AS THE AVENGERS STRUGGLE TO REGAIN THEIR EQUILIBRIUM...
PARDON ME... I'M SISTER JUDE! MOTHER SUPERIOR HAS ASKED ME TO THANK YOU FOR FREEING OUR HOUSE FROM THAT... CREATURE!
HOWEVER, YOU MUST LEAVE IMMEDIATELY!
"THIS IS, AFTER ALL, A PLACE OF WORSHIP! WE WILL CLEAN UP HERE AND NOTIFY PROPER AUTHORITIES!"
IRON MAN, PERHAPS WE SHOULD HAVE REMOVED ULTRON'S REMAINS OURSELVES! WHAT IF--?
IN SOOTH, HE IS DEAD, VISION!
THE FATE OF CAPTAIN AMERICA ALONE DOTH BECKON OUR FEARS!
RIGHT, THOR!
MAYBE WE CAN FIND SOME ANSWERS BACK AT OUR LAB!

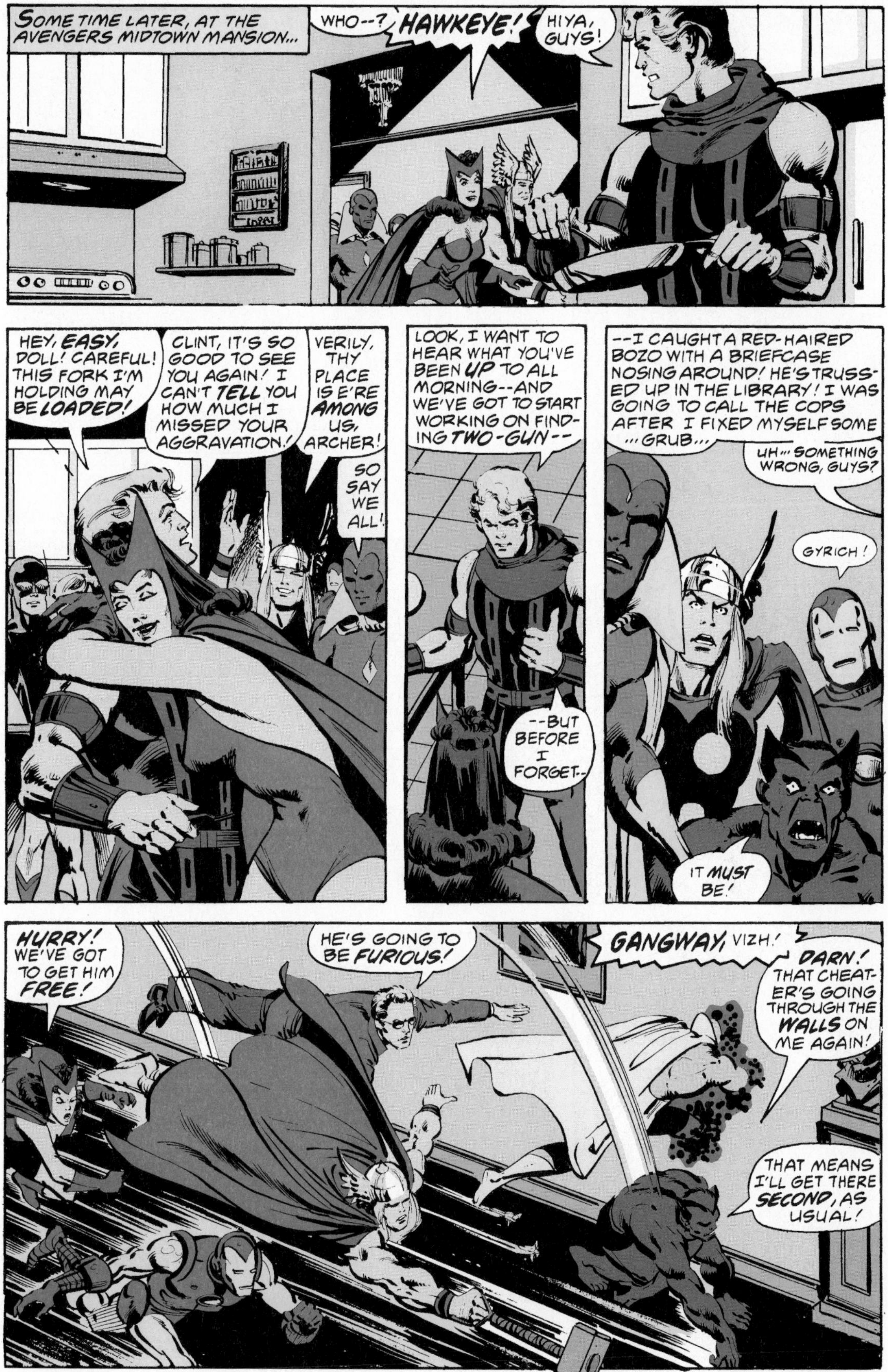
SOME TIME LATER, AT THE AVENGERS MIDTOWN MANSION...
WHO--?
HAWKEYE!
HIYA, GUYS!
HEY, EASY, DOLL! CAREFUL! THIS FORK I'M HOLDING MAY BE LOADED!
CLINT, IT'S SO GOOD TO SEE YOU AGAIN! I CAN'T TELL YOU HOW MUCH I MISSED YOUR AGGRAVATION!
VERILY, THY PLACE IS E'RE AMONG US, ARCHER!
SO SAY WE ALL!
LOOK, I WANT TO HEAR WHAT YOU'VE BEEN UP TO ALL MORNING--AND WE'VE GOT TO START WORKING ON FINDING TWO-GUN--
--BUT BEFORE I FORGET--
--I CAUGHT A RED-HAIRED BOZO WITH A BRIEFCASE NOSING AROUND! HE'S TRUSSED UP IN THE LIBRARY! I WAS GOING TO CALL THE COPS AFTER I FIXED MYSELF SOME ...GRUB...
UH... SOMETHING WRONG, GUYS?
GYRICH!
IT MUST BE!
HURRY! WE'VE GOT TO GET HIM FREE!
HE'S GOING TO BE FURIOUS!
GANGWAY, VIZH!
DARN! THAT CHEATER'S GOING THROUGH THE WALLS ON ME AGAIN!
THAT MEANS I'LL GET THERE SECOND, AS USUAL!

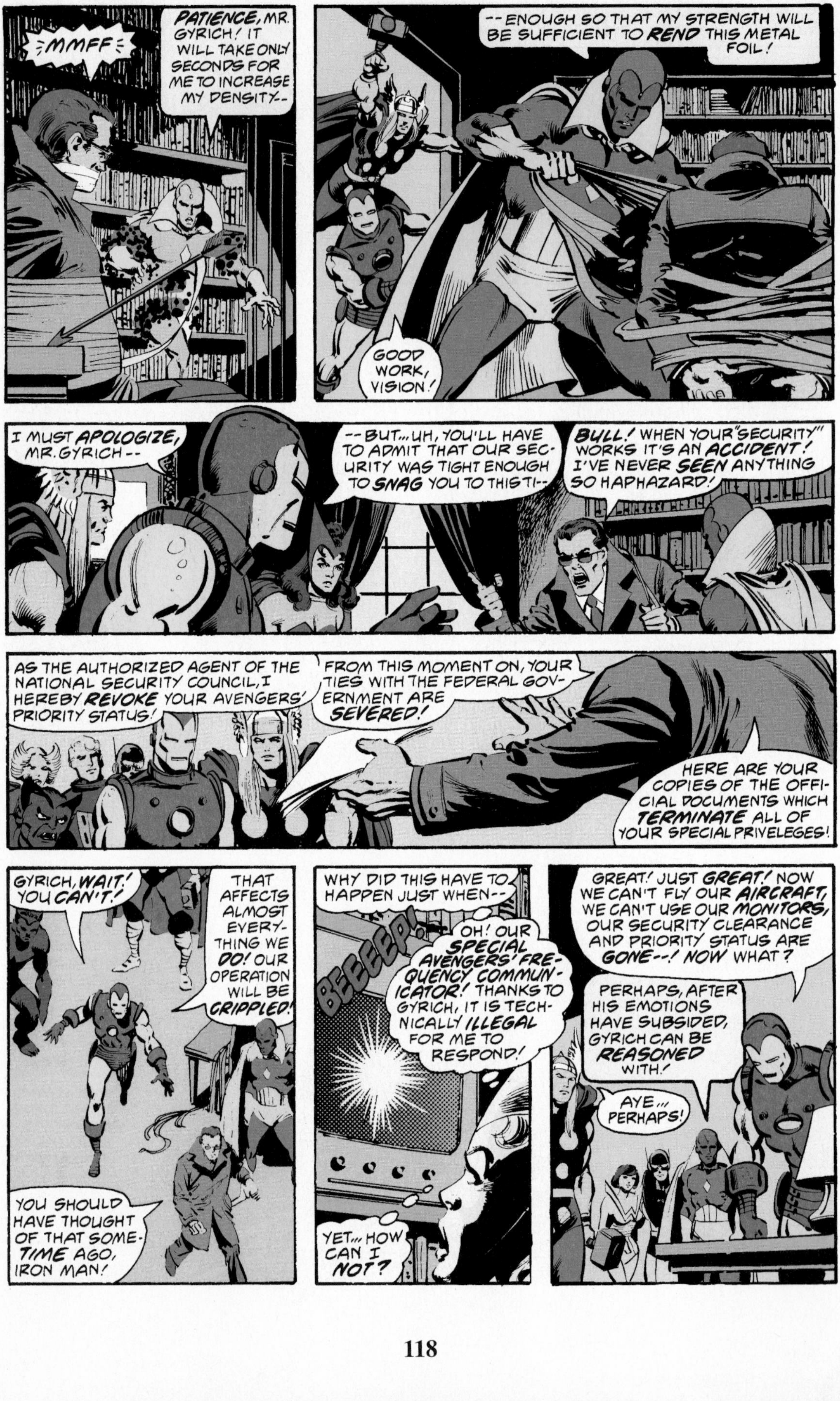
MMFF
PATIENCE, MR. GYRICH! IT WILL TAKE ONLY SECONDS FOR ME TO INCREASE MY DENSITY--
--ENOUGH SO THAT MY STRENGTH WILL BE SUFFICIENT TO REND THIS METAL FOIL!
GOOD WORK, VISION!
I MUST APOLOGIZE, MR. GYRICH--
--BUT... UH, YOU'LL HAVE TO ADMIT THAT OUR SECURITY WAS TIGHT ENOUGH TO SNAG YOU TO THIS TI--
BULL! WHEN YOUR "SECURITY" WORKS IT'S AN ACCIDENT! I'VE NEVER SEEN ANYTHING SO HAPHAZARD!
AS THE AUTHORIZED AGENT OF THE NATIONAL SECURITY COUNCIL, I HEREBY REVOKE YOUR AVENGERS' PRIORITY STATUS!
FROM THIS MOMENT ON, YOUR TIES WITH THE FEDERAL GOVERNMENT ARE SEVERED!
HERE ARE YOUR COPIES OF THE OFFICIAL DOCUMENTS WHICH TERMINATE ALL OF YOUR SPECIAL PRIVELEGES!
GYRICH, WAIT! YOU CAN'T!
THAT AFFECTS ALMOST EVERYTHING WE DO! OUR OPERATION WILL BE CRIPPLED!
YOU SHOULD HAVE THOUGHT OF THAT SOMETIME AGO, IRON MAN!
WHY DID THIS HAVE TO HAPPEN JUST WHEN--
BEEEEP!
OH! OUR SPECIAL AVENGERS' FREQUENCY COMMUNICATOR! THANKS TO GYRICH, IT IS TECHNICALLY ILLEGAL FOR ME TO RESPOND!
YET... HOW CAN I NOT?
GREAT! JUST GREAT! NOW WE CAN'T FLY OUR AIRCRAFT, WE CAN'T USE OUR MONITORS, OUR SECURITY CLEARANCE AND PRIORITY STATUS ARE GONE--! NOW WHAT?
PERHAPS, AFTER HIS EMOTIONS HAVE SUBSIDED, GYRICH CAN BE REASONED WITH!
AYE... PERHAPS!

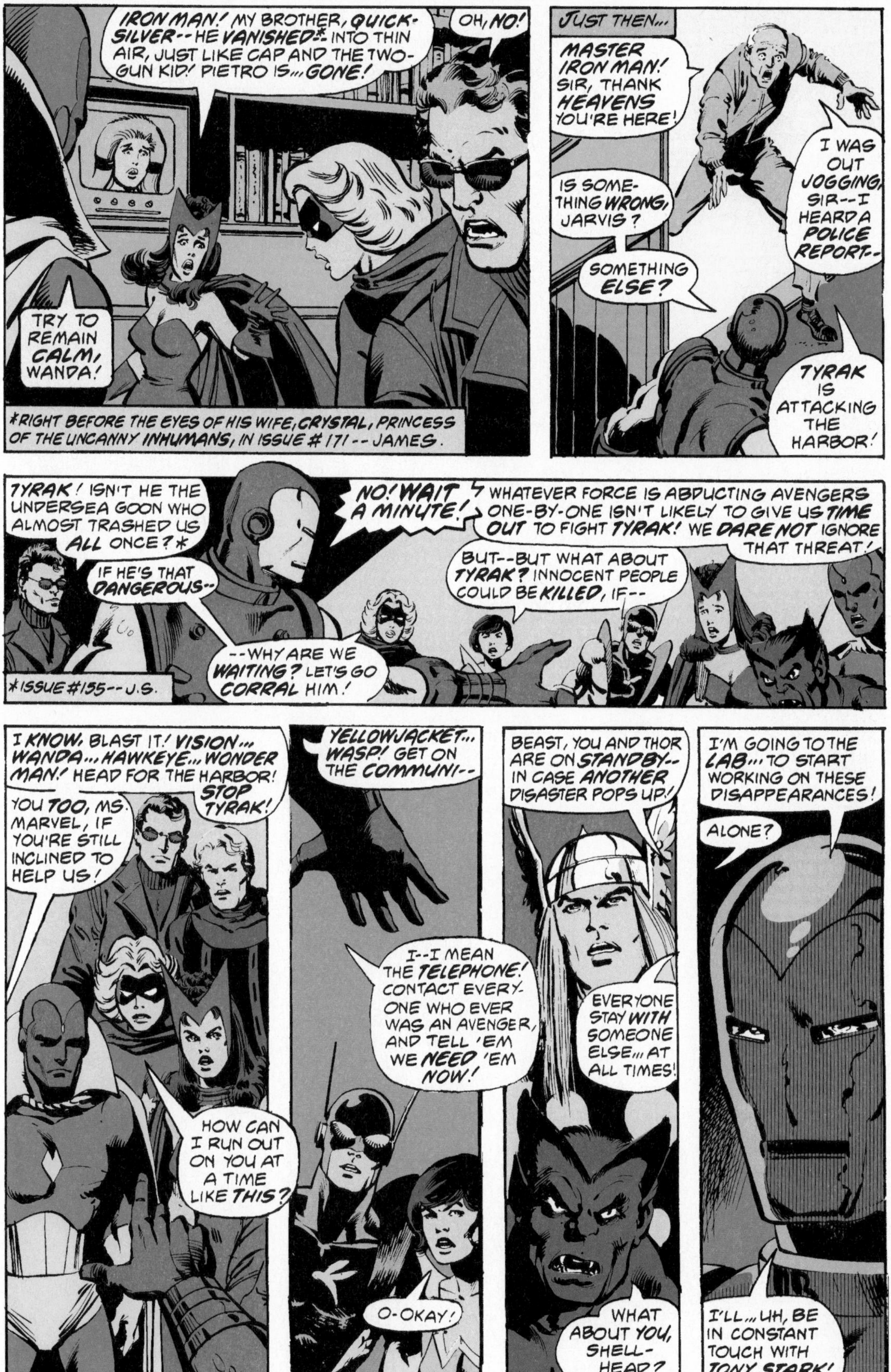
IRON MAN! MY BROTHER, QUICK-SILVER--HE VANISHED* INTO THIN AIR, JUST LIKE CAP AND THE TWO-GUN KID! PIETRO IS... GONE!
OH, NO!
TRY TO REMAIN CALM, WANDA!
*RIGHT BEFORE THE EYES OF HIS WIFE, CRYSTAL, PRINCESS OF THE UNCANNY INHUMANS, IN ISSUE #171 -- JAMES.
JUST THEN...
MASTER IRON MAN! SIR, THANK HEAVENS YOU'RE HERE!
IS SOMETHING WRONG, JARVIS?
I WAS OUT JOGGING, SIR--I HEARD A POLICE REPORT--
SOMETHING ELSE?
TYRAK IS ATTACKING THE HARBOR!
TYRAK! ISN'T HE THE UNDERSEA GOON WHO ALMOST TRASHED US ALL ONCE?*
IF HE'S THAT DANGEROUS--
--WHY ARE WE WAITING? LET'S GO CORRAL HIM!
*ISSUE #155--J.S.
NO! WAIT A MINUTE!
WHATEVER FORCE IS ABDUCTING AVENGERS ONE-BY-ONE ISN'T LIKELY TO GIVE US TIME OUT TO FIGHT TYRAK! WE DARE NOT IGNORE THAT THREAT!
BUT--BUT WHAT ABOUT TYRAK? INNOCENT PEOPLE COULD BE KILLED, IF--
I KNOW, BLAST IT! VISION... WANDA... HAWKEYE... WONDER MAN! HEAD FOR THE HARBOR! STOP TYRAK!
YOU TOO, MS. MARVEL, IF YOU'RE STILL INCLINED TO HELP US!
HOW CAN I RUN OUT ON YOU AT A TIME LIKE THIS?
YELLOWJACKET... WASP! GET ON THE COMMUNI--
I--I MEAN THE TELEPHONE! CONTACT EVERY-ONE WHO EVER WAS AN AVENGER, AND TELL 'EM WE NEED 'EM NOW!
O-OKAY!
BEAST, YOU AND THOR ARE ON STANDBY-- IN CASE ANOTHER DISASTER POPS UP!
EVERYONE STAY WITH SOMEONE ELSE... AT ALL TIMES!
WHAT ABOUT YOU, SHELL-HEAD?
I'M GOING TO THE LAB... TO START WORKING ON THESE DISAPPEARANCES!
ALONE?
I'LL... UH, BE IN CONSTANT TOUCH WITH TONY STARK!

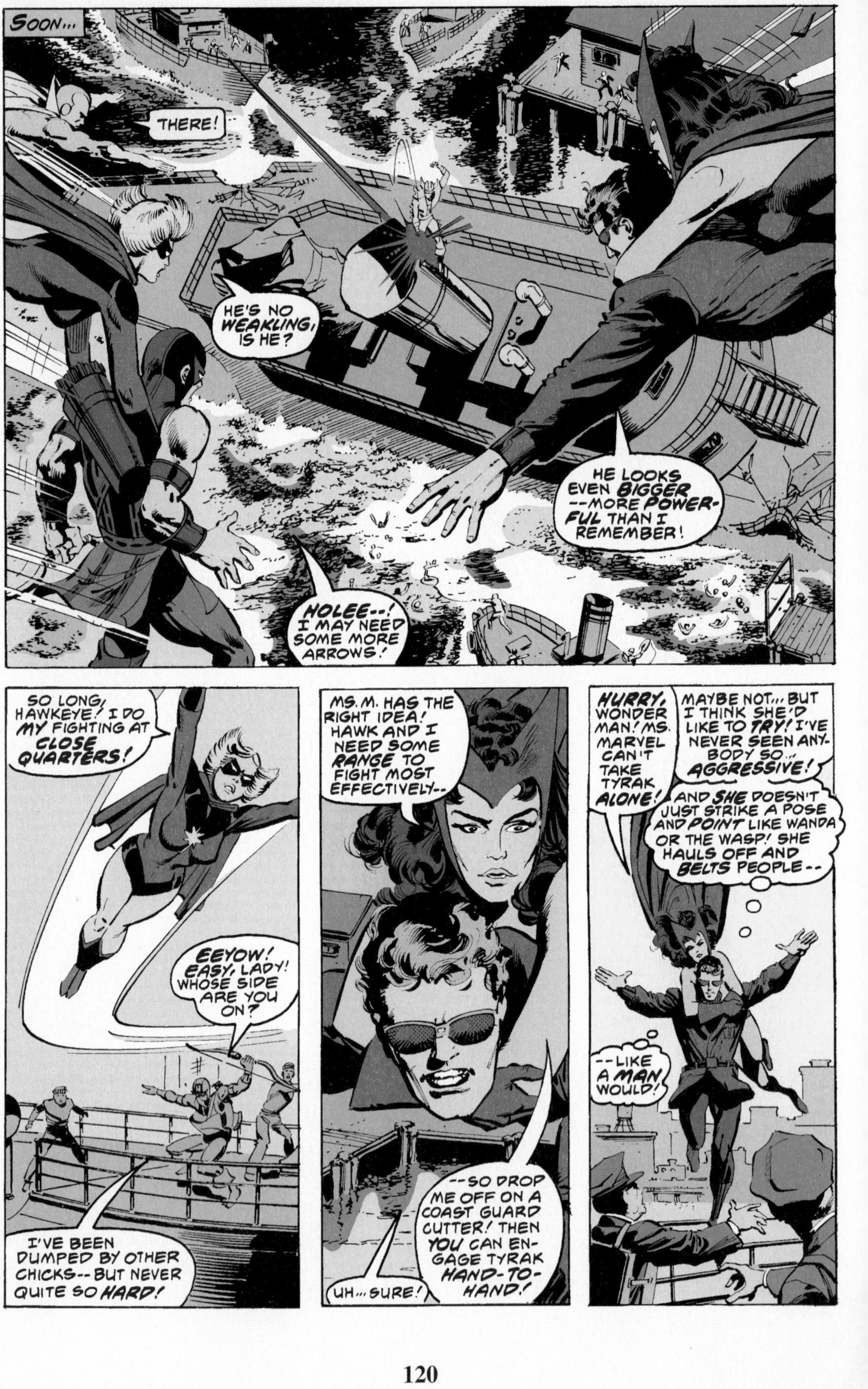
SOON...
THERE!
HE'S NO WEAKLING, IS HE?
HE LOOKS EVEN BIGGER --MORE POWER-FUL THAN I REMEMBER!
HOLEE--! I MAY NEED SOME MORE ARROWS!
SO LONG, HAWKEYE! I DO MY FIGHTING AT CLOSE QUARTERS!
EEYOW! EASY, LADY! WHOSE SIDE ARE YOU ON?
I'VE BEEN DUMPED BY OTHER CHICKS--BUT NEVER QUITE SO HARD!
MS. M. HAS THE RIGHT IDEA! HAWK AND I NEED SOME RANGE TO FIGHT MOST EFFECTIVELY--
--SO DROP ME OFF ON A COAST GUARD CUTTER! THEN YOU CAN EN-GAGE TYRAK HAND-TO-HAND!
UH... SURE!
HURRY, WONDER MAN! MS. MARVEL CAN'T TAKE TYRAK ALONE!
MAYBE NOT... BUT I THINK SHE'D LIKE TO TRY! I'VE NEVER SEEN ANY-BODY SO... AGGRESSIVE!
AND SHE DOESN'T JUST STRIKE A POSE AND POINT LIKE WANDA OR THE WASP! SHE HAULS OFF AND BELTS PEOPLE--
--LIKE A MAN WOULD!

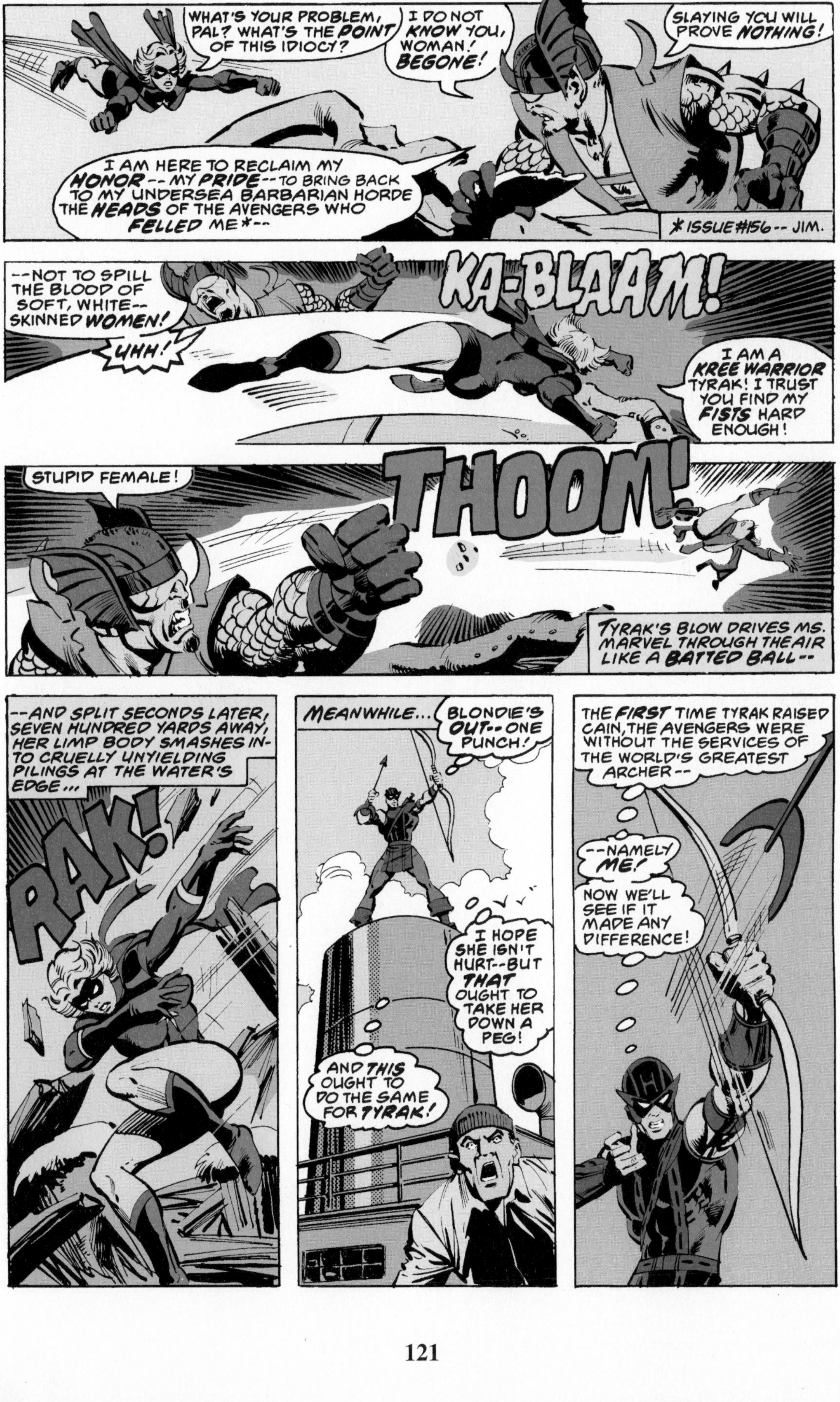
WHAT'S YOUR PROBLEM, PAL? WHAT'S THE POINT OF THIS IDIOCY?
I DO NOT KNOW YOU, WOMAN! BEGONE!
SLAYING YOU WILL PROVE NOTHING!
I AM HERE TO RECLAIM MY HONOR -- MY PRIDE -- TO BRING BACK TO MY UNDERSEA BARBARIAN HORDE THE HEADS OF THE AVENGERS WHO FELLED ME*--
*ISSUE #156 -- JIM.
--NOT TO SPILL THE BLOOD OF SOFT, WHITE-- SKINNED WOMEN!
KA-BLAAM!
UHH!
I AM A KREE WARRIOR TYRAK! I TRUST YOU FIND MY FISTS HARD ENOUGH!
STUPID FEMALE!
THOOM!
TYRAK'S BLOW DRIVES MS. MARVEL THROUGH THE AIR LIKE A BATTED BALL--
--AND SPLIT SECONDS LATER, SEVEN HUNDRED YARDS AWAY, HER LIMP BODY SMASHES IN-TO CRUELLY UNYIELDING PILINGS AT THE WATER'S EDGE...
RAK!
MEANWHILE...
BLONDIE'S OUT-- ONE PUNCH!
I HOPE SHE ISN'T HURT--BUT THAT OUGHT TO TAKE HER DOWN A PEG!
AND THIS OUGHT TO DO THE SAME FOR TYRAK!
THE FIRST TIME TYRAK RAISED CAIN, THE AVENGERS WERE WITHOUT THE SERVICES OF THE WORLD'S GREATEST ARCHER--
--NAMELY ME!
NOW WE'LL SEE IF IT MADE ANY DIFFERENCE!

THAT ARROW-- IT BEARS SOME SORT OF *SONIC DEVICE*--!

MY EARS!

EEE EEEEE EEEE EEE

NO! NO PAIN WILL FORCE ME BACK! I CANNOT LOSE FACE *AGAIN!*

CRUSH IT... TO *DUST!* THE *ARCHER* WILL DIE--

--AS WILL *YOU ALL!*

ARE YOU *MAD,* TYRAK? DO YOU BELIEVE THAT KILLING THE AVENGERS WILL LEAVE THE SURFACE WORLD *DEFENSELESS?* IF YOU HOPE TO *CONQUER*--

YOUR SURFACE WORLD *STINKS!* I *LOATHE* THE PUTRID AIR AND THE SUN'S SCORCHING HEAT! IT IS THE *SEA* I WISH TO RULE!

THE DISGRACE BORNE BY MY FORMER LIEGE, ATTUMA, IS GREATER THAN MY OWN--

--THUS, I WILL BE ACCLAIMED LEADER OF MY PEOPLE WHEN BY MY HAND AVENGERS' BLOOD STAINS THE WAVES!

THAT I SHALL PREVENT!

WHAT *TRICKERY*--?! THE SHIP IS SETTLING DEEP INTO THE WATER-- SINKING AT AN *IMPOSSIBLE* RATE! AS IF--

CRA-ACK!

AS IF A HUGE *WEIGHT* HAD BEEN ADDED? INDEED, I HAVE INCREASED MY *MASS!*

AT THIS DENSITY I WEIGH *COUNTLESS* TONS-- AND MY BODY IS *HARDER* THAN THE PUREST *DIAMOND!* MY *STRENGTH* TOO, HAS GROWN IN PROPORTION!

ARRHH!

YOU HAVE HAD FAIR *WARNING!*

YOUR POWER WAS NOT ENOUGH *BEFORE*--

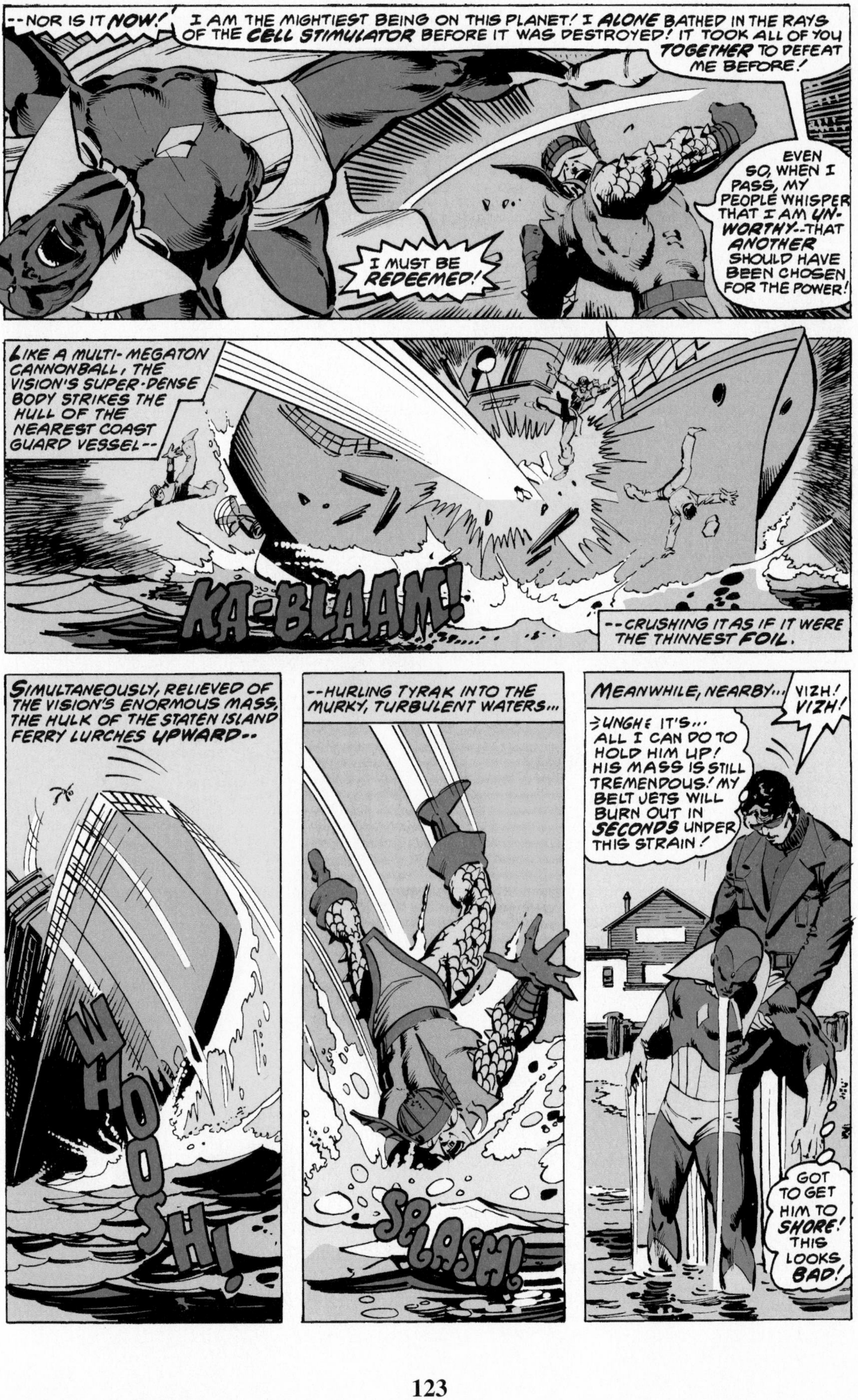
--NOR IS IT NOW!
I AM THE MIGHTIEST BEING ON THIS PLANET! I ALONE BATHED IN THE RAYS OF THE CELL STIMULATOR BEFORE IT WAS DESTROYED! IT TOOK ALL OF YOU TOGETHER TO DEFEAT ME BEFORE!
EVEN SO, WHEN I PASS, MY PEOPLE WHISPER THAT I AM UN-WORTHY--THAT ANOTHER SHOULD HAVE BEEN CHOSEN FOR THE POWER!
I MUST BE REDEEMED!
LIKE A MULTI-MEGATON CANNONBALL, THE VISION'S SUPER-DENSE BODY STRIKES THE HULL OF THE NEAREST COAST GUARD VESSEL--
KA-BLAAM!
--CRUSHING IT AS IF IT WERE THE THINNEST FOIL.
SIMULTANEOUSLY, RELIEVED OF THE VISION'S ENORMOUS MASS, THE HULK OF THE STATEN ISLAND FERRY LURCHES UPWARD--
WHOOSH!
--HURLING TYRAK INTO THE MURKY, TURBULENT WATERS...
SPLASH!
MEANWHILE, NEARBY...
VIZH! VIZH!
UNGH! IT'S... ALL I CAN DO TO HOLD HIM UP! HIS MASS IS STILL TREMENDOUS! MY BELT JETS WILL BURN OUT IN SECONDS UNDER THIS STRAIN!
GOT TO GET HIM TO SHORE! THIS LOOKS BAD!

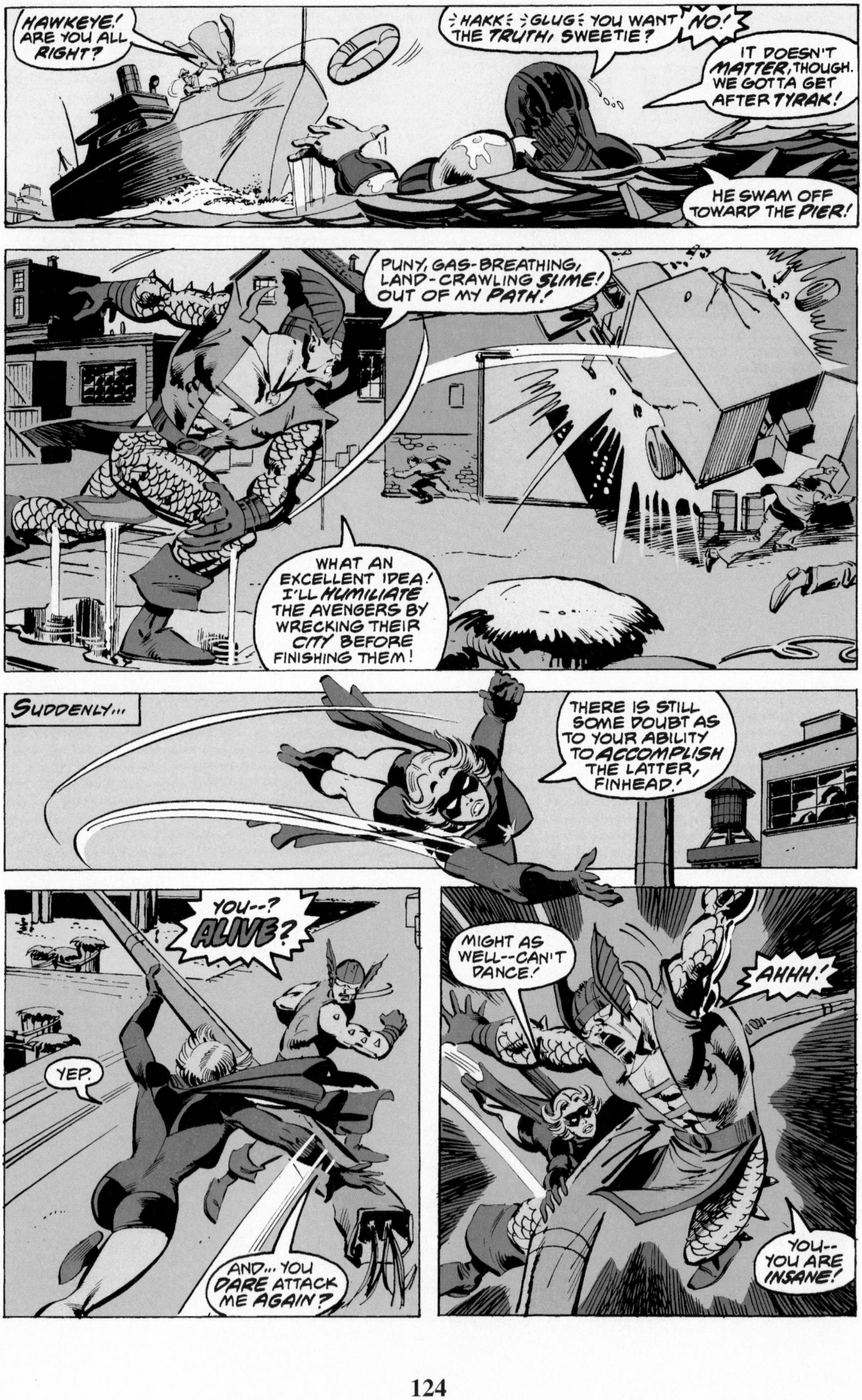
HAWKEYE! ARE YOU ALL RIGHT?
HAKK GLUG YOU WANT THE TRUTH, SWEETIE?
NO!
IT DOESN'T MATTER, THOUGH. WE GOTTA GET AFTER TYRAK!
HE SWAM OFF TOWARD THE PIER!
PUNY, GAS-BREATHING, LAND-CRAWLING SLIME! OUT OF MY PATH!
WHAT AN EXCELLENT IDEA! I'LL HUMILIATE THE AVENGERS BY WRECKING THEIR CITY BEFORE FINISHING THEM!
SUDDENLY...
THERE IS STILL SOME DOUBT AS TO YOUR ABILITY TO ACCOMPLISH THE LATTER, FINHEAD!
YOU--? ALIVE?
YEP.
AND... YOU DARE ATTACK ME AGAIN?
MIGHT AS WELL--CAN'T DANCE!
AHHH!
YOU-- YOU ARE INSANE!

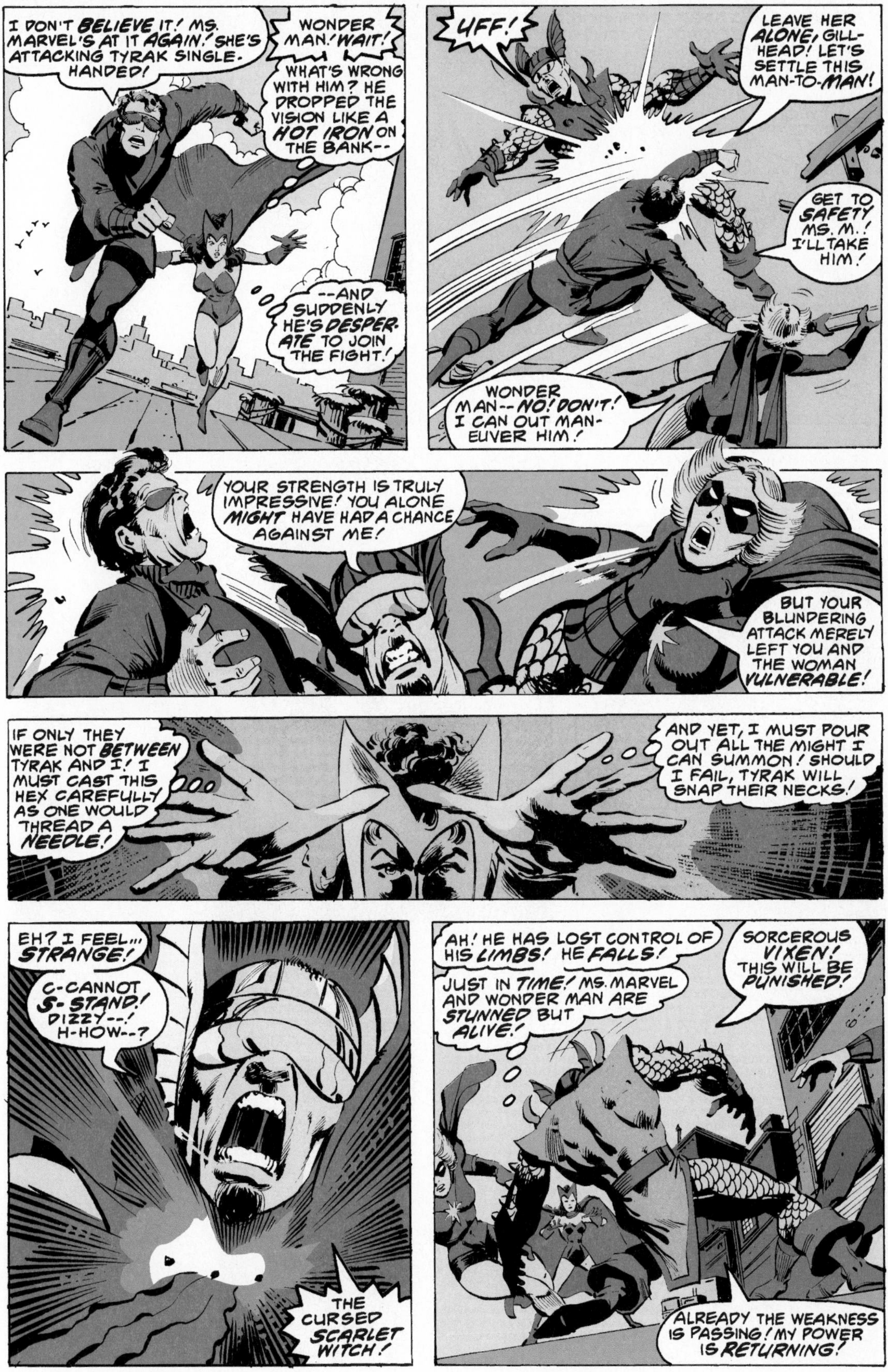
I DON'T BELIEVE IT! MS. MARVEL'S AT IT AGAIN! SHE'S ATTACKING TYRAK SINGLE-HANDED!
WONDER MAN! WAIT!
WHAT'S WRONG WITH HIM? HE DROPPED THE VISION LIKE A HOT IRON ON THE BANK--
--AND SUDDENLY HE'S DESPERATE TO JOIN THE FIGHT!
UFF!
LEAVE HER ALONE, GILL-HEAD! LET'S SETTLE THIS MAN-TO-MAN!
GET TO SAFETY MS. M.! I'LL TAKE HIM!
WONDER MAN--NO! DON'T! I CAN OUT MANEUVER HIM!
YOUR STRENGTH IS TRULY IMPRESSIVE! YOU ALONE MIGHT HAVE HAD A CHANCE AGAINST ME!
BUT YOUR BLUNDERING ATTACK MERELY LEFT YOU AND THE WOMAN VULNERABLE!
IF ONLY THEY WERE NOT BETWEEN TYRAK AND I! I MUST CAST THIS HEX CAREFULLY AS ONE WOULD THREAD A NEEDLE!
AND YET, I MUST POUR OUT ALL THE MIGHT I CAN SUMMON! SHOULD I FAIL, TYRAK WILL SNAP THEIR NECKS!
EH? I FEEL... STRANGE!
C-CANNOT S-STAND! DIZZY--! H-HOW--?
THE CURSED SCARLET WITCH!
AH! HE HAS LOST CONTROL OF HIS LIMBS! HE FALLS!
JUST IN TIME! MS. MARVEL AND WONDER MAN ARE STUNNED BUT ALIVE!
SORCEROUS VIXEN! THIS WILL BE PUNISHED!
ALREADY THE WEAKNESS IS PASSING! MY POWER IS RETURNING!

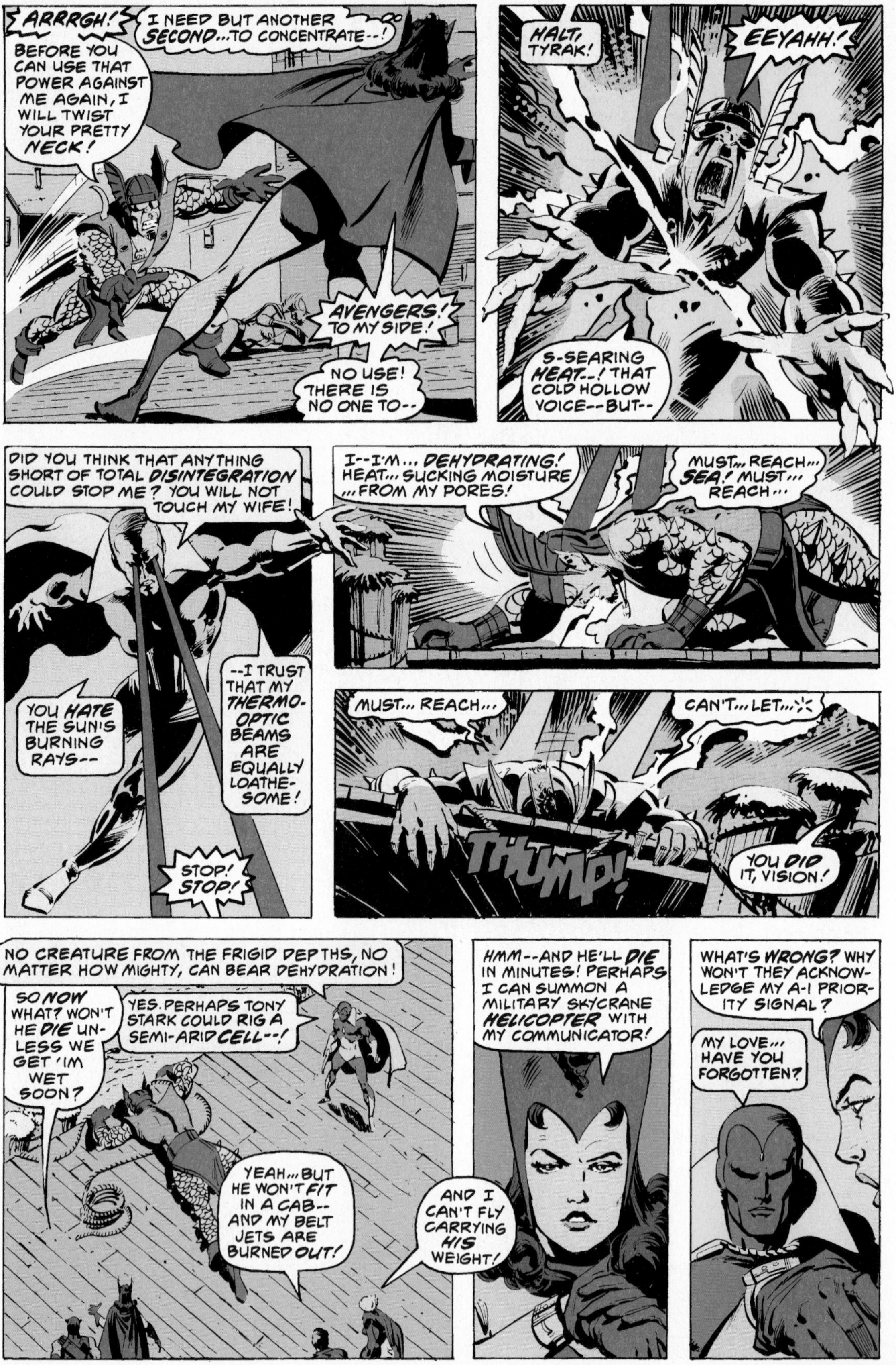
ARRRGH!
I NEED BUT ANOTHER SECOND... TO CONCENTRATE--!
BEFORE YOU CAN USE THAT POWER AGAINST ME AGAIN, I WILL TWIST YOUR PRETTY NECK!
AVENGERS! TO MY SIDE!
NO USE! THERE IS NO ONE TO--
HALT, TYRAK!
EEYAHH!
S-SEARING HEAT--! THAT COLD HOLLOW VOICE--BUT--
DID YOU THINK THAT ANYTHING SHORT OF TOTAL DISINTEGRATION COULD STOP ME? YOU WILL NOT TOUCH MY WIFE!
YOU HATE THE SUN'S BURNING RAYS--
--I TRUST THAT MY THERMO-OPTIC BEAMS ARE EQUALLY LOATHE-SOME!
STOP! STOP!
I--I'M... DEHYDRATING! HEAT... SUCKING MOISTURE ...FROM MY PORES!
MUST... REACH... SEA! MUST... REACH...
MUST... REACH...
CAN'T... LET...
THUMP!
YOU DID IT, VISION!
NO CREATURE FROM THE FRIGID DEPTHS, NO MATTER HOW MIGHTY, CAN BEAR DEHYDRATION!
SO NOW WHAT? WON'T HE DIE UN-LESS WE GET 'IM WET SOON?
YES. PERHAPS TONY STARK COULD RIG A SEMI-ARID CELL--!
YEAH... BUT HE WON'T FIT IN A CAB-- AND MY BELT JETS ARE BURNED OUT!
AND I CAN'T FLY CARRYING HIS WEIGHT!
HMM--AND HE'LL DIE IN MINUTES! PERHAPS I CAN SUMMON A MILITARY SKYCRANE HELICOPTER WITH MY COMMUNICATOR!
WHAT'S WRONG? WHY WON'T THEY ACKNOW-LEDGE MY A-1 PRIOR-ITY SIGNAL?
MY LOVE... HAVE YOU FORGOTTEN?

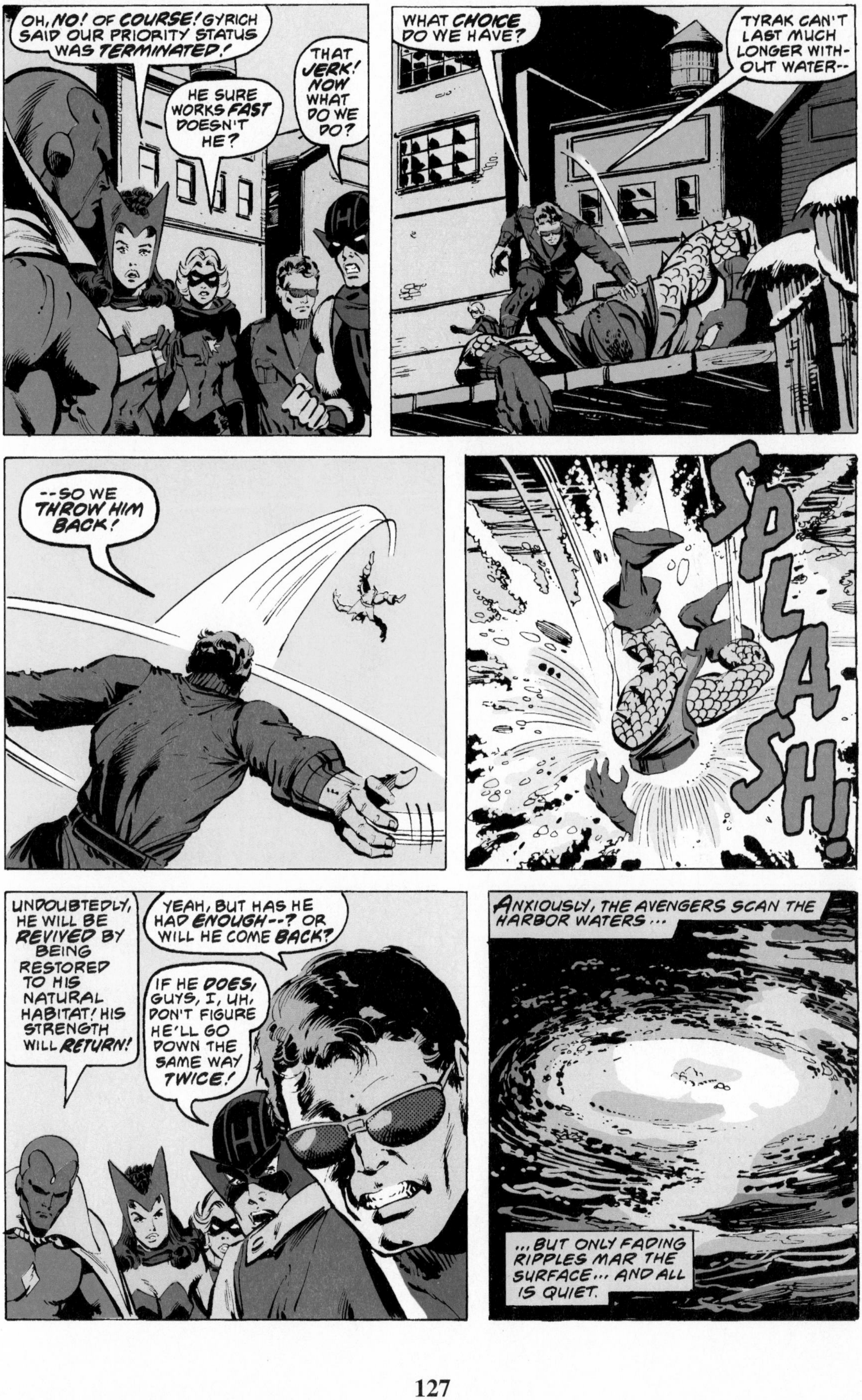
OH, NO! OF COURSE! GYRICH SAID OUR PRIORITY STATUS WAS TERMINATED!
HE SURE WORKS FAST DOESN'T HE?
THAT JERK! NOW WHAT DO WE DO?
WHAT CHOICE DO WE HAVE?
TYRAK CAN'T LAST MUCH LONGER WITHOUT WATER--
--SO WE THROW HIM BACK!
SPLASH!
UNDOUBTEDLY, HE WILL BE REVIVED BY BEING RESTORED TO HIS NATURAL HABITAT! HIS STRENGTH WILL RETURN!
YEAH, BUT HAS HE HAD ENOUGH--? OR WILL HE COME BACK?
IF HE DOES, GUYS, I, UH, DON'T FIGURE HE'LL GO DOWN THE SAME WAY TWICE!
ANXIOUSLY, THE AVENGERS SCAN THE HARBOR WATERS...
...BUT ONLY FADING RIPPLES MAR THE SURFACE... AND ALL IS QUIET.

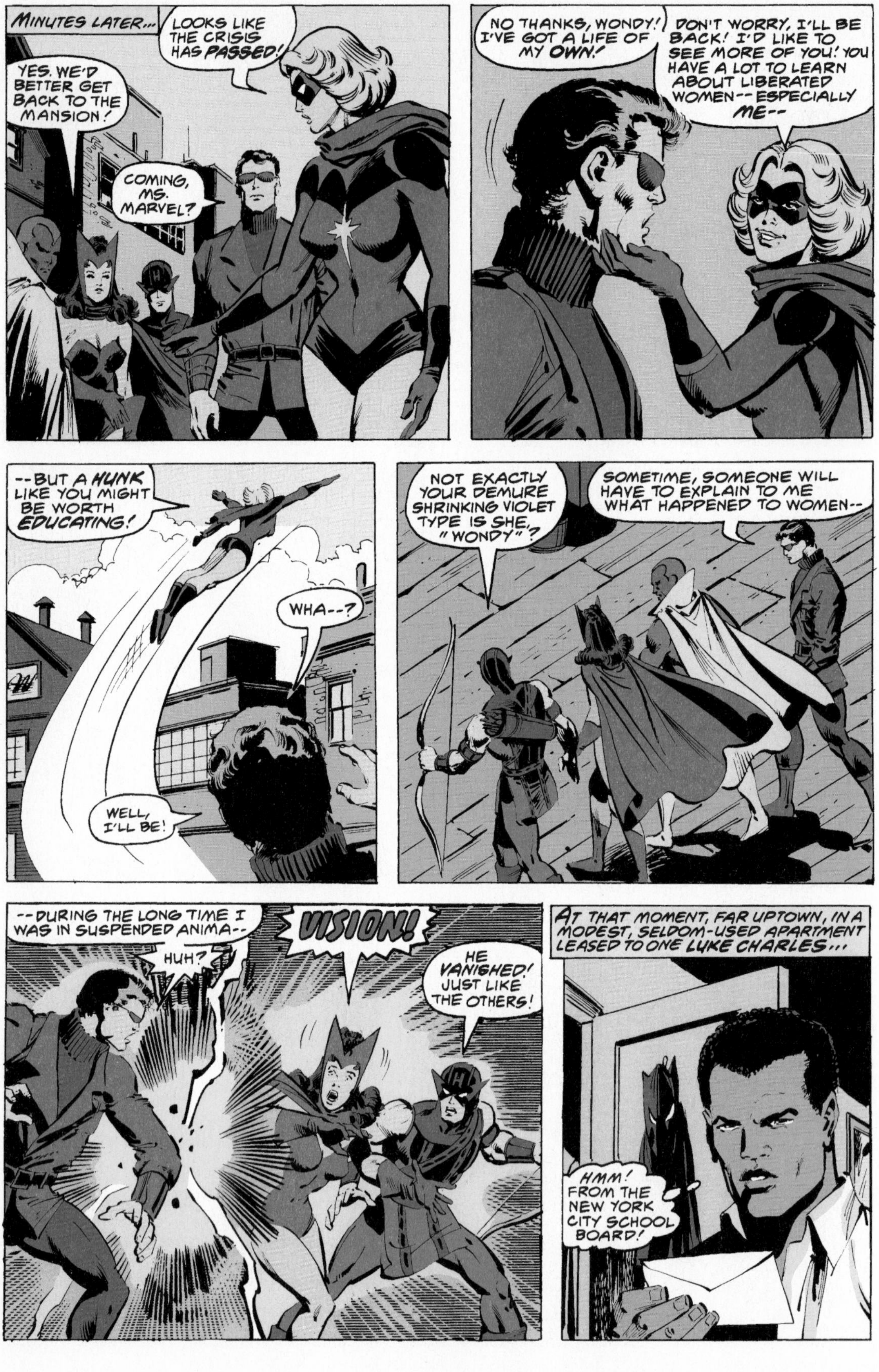
MINUTES LATER...
LOOKS LIKE THE CRISIS HAS PASSED!
YES. WE'D BETTER GET BACK TO THE MANSION!
COMING, MS. MARVEL?
NO THANKS, WONDY! I'VE GOT A LIFE OF MY OWN!
DON'T WORRY, I'LL BE BACK! I'D LIKE TO SEE MORE OF YOU! YOU HAVE A LOT TO LEARN ABOUT LIBERATED WOMEN--ESPECIALLY ME--
--BUT A HUNK LIKE YOU MIGHT BE WORTH EDUCATING!
WHA--?
WELL, I'LL BE!
NOT EXACTLY YOUR DEMURE SHRINKING VIOLET TYPE IS SHE, "WONDY"?
SOMETIME, SOMEONE WILL HAVE TO EXPLAIN TO ME WHAT HAPPENED TO WOMEN--
--DURING THE LONG TIME I WAS IN SUSPENDED ANIMA--
HUH?
VISION!
HE VANISHED! JUST LIKE THE OTHERS!
AT THAT MOMENT, FAR UPTOWN, IN A MODEST, SELDOM-USED APARTMENT LEASED TO ONE LUKE CHARLES...
HMM! FROM THE NEW YORK CITY SCHOOL BOARD!

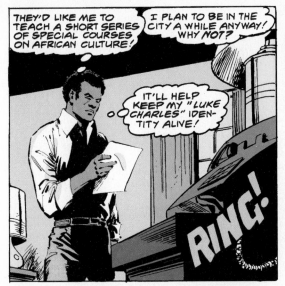

THEY'D LIKE ME TO TEACH A SHORT SERIES OF SPECIAL COURSES ON AFRICAN CULTURE!

I PLAN TO BE IN THE CITY A WHILE ANYWAY! WHY *NOT?*

IT'LL HELP KEEP MY "LUKE CHARLES" IDENTITY ALIVE!

RING!

HELLO... *WASP!* WHAT CAN I DO FOR--

WHY THAT'S *INCREDIBLE!*

WELL, I'M WORKING ON A "DISAPPEARING PERSONS" CASE OF MY *OWN,* NOW *...

... BUT OF *COURSE* THE *BLACK PANTHER* WILL ATTEND A MEETING AND REMAIN ON CALL THERE AFTER!

* THE CASE EXAMINED IN MARVEL TWO-IN-ONE #40 -- JIM.

MEANWHILE, IN THE LABORATORY AT AVENGERS MANSION ...

NOTHING! THE SENSORS CAN'T TRACE THE BOLT OF ENERGY THAT STRUCK THE HARBOR AREA A MINUTE AGO--

--RIGHT NEAR WHERE WANDA AND COMPANY WENT TO FIGHT *TYRAK!*

I'D BET THE STARK FAMILY FORTUNE THAT *ANOTHER* AVENGER JUST VANISHED DOWN THERE!

BZZZT!

THAT MUST BE *HANK* AND *JAN!*

NO POINT IN LETTING THEM SEE JUST HOW CLOSELY TONY STARK AND HIS FAMOUS BODYGUARD WORK TOGETHER!

IRON MAN! AM I GLAD TO SEE YOU!

WHEN YOU DIDN'T ANSWER RIGHT AWAY, WE WERE SCARED THAT YOU GOT ZAPPED!

I HOPE YOU TWO HAVE MORE SUCCESS TO REPORT THAN STARK AND I DO!

IT WASN'T EASY BUT WE GOT IN TOUCH WITH HER-CULES, THE BLACK PANTHER AND THE WHIZZER!

AND CAPTAIN MARVEL CALLED *US!* HE SAID HE WAS *"AWARE OF OUR NEED"!* CAN YOU BELIEVE IT?

BUT THAT'S NOT THE *BIG* NEWS

NO?

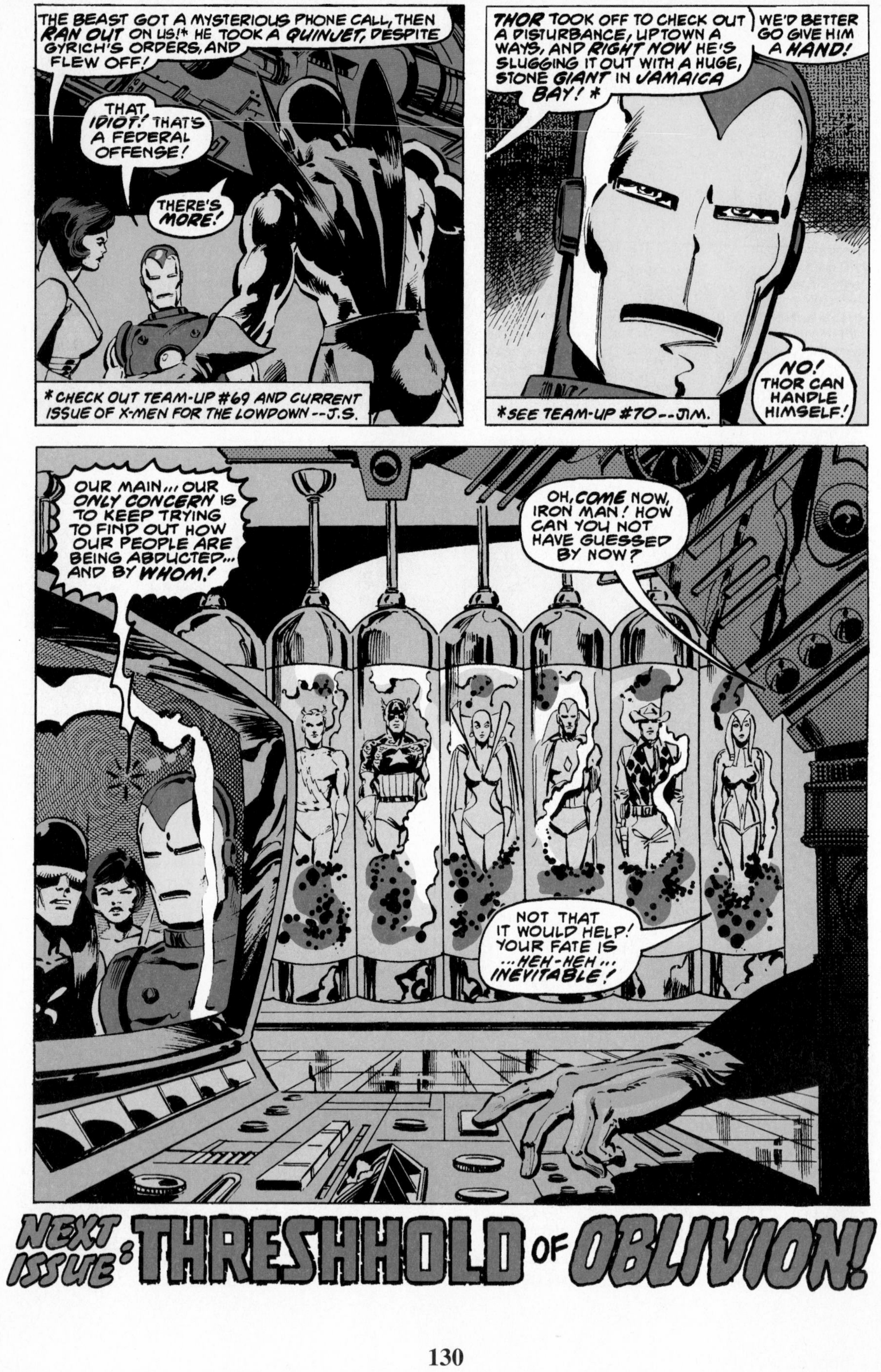
THE BEAST GOT A MYSTERIOUS PHONE CALL, THEN RAN OUT ON US!* HE TOOK A QUINJET, DESPITE GYRICH'S ORDERS, AND FLEW OFF!
THAT IDIOT! THAT'S A FEDERAL OFFENSE!
THERE'S MORE!
*CHECK OUT TEAM-UP #69 AND CURRENT ISSUE OF X-MEN FOR THE LOWDOWN --J.S.
THOR TOOK OFF TO CHECK OUT A DISTURBANCE, UPTOWN A WAYS, AND RIGHT NOW HE'S SLUGGING IT OUT WITH A HUGE, STONE GIANT IN JAMAICA BAY! *
WE'D BETTER GO GIVE HIM A HAND!
NO! THOR CAN HANDLE HIMSELF!
*SEE TEAM-UP #70--JIM.
OUR MAIN... OUR ONLY CONCERN IS TO KEEP TRYING TO FIND OUT HOW OUR PEOPLE ARE BEING ABDUCTED... AND BY WHOM!
OH, COME NOW, IRON MAN! HOW CAN YOU NOT HAVE GUESSED BY NOW?
NOT THAT IT WOULD HELP! YOUR FATE IS ...HEH-HEH... INEVITABLE!
NEXT ISSUE: THRESHHOLD OF OBLIVION!

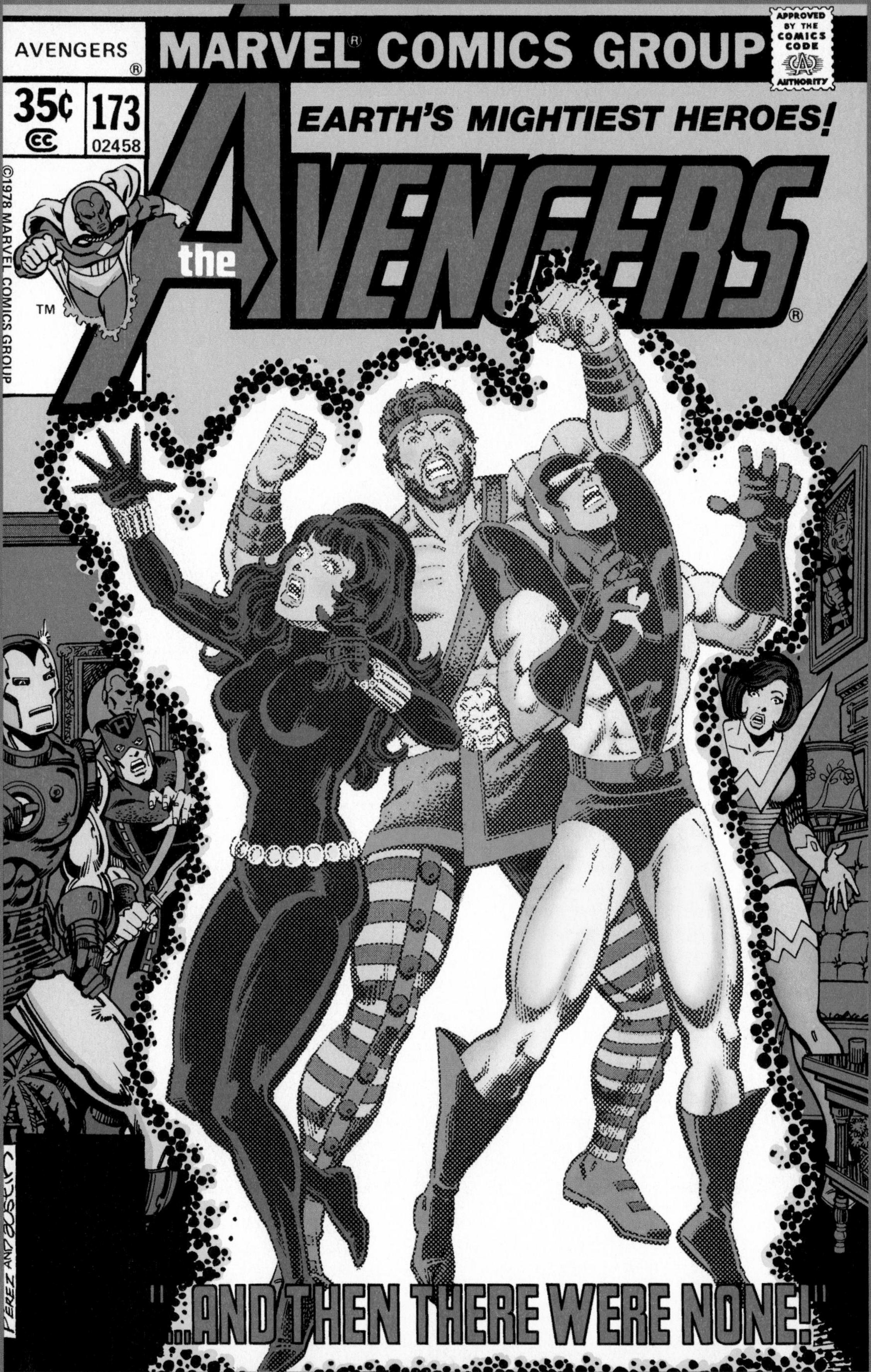
AVENGERS
MARVEL® COMICS GROUP
APPROVED BY THE COMICS CODE AUTHORITY
35¢
173
02458
EARTH'S MIGHTIEST HEROES!
the AVENGERS®
©1978 MARVEL COMICS GROUP
TM
"...AND THEN THERE WERE NONE!"
PEREZ AND BOSEIC

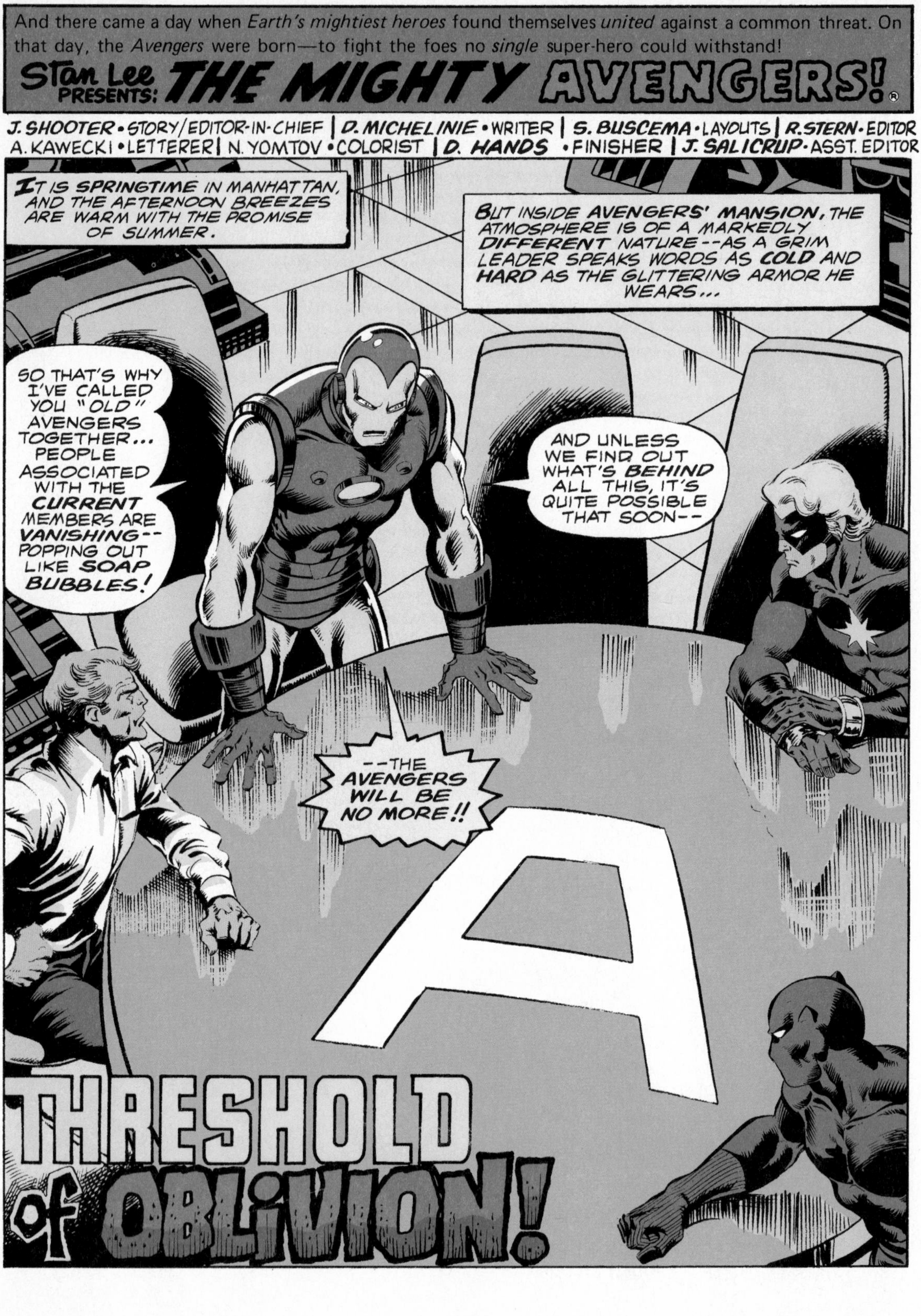

And there came a day when Earth's mightiest heroes found themselves united against a common threat. On that day, the Avengers were born—to fight the foes no single super-hero could withstand!
Stan Lee PRESENTS: THE MIGHTY AVENGERS!
J. SHOOTER • STORY/EDITOR-IN-CHIEF | D. MICHELINIE • WRITER | S. BUSCEMA • LAYOUTS | R. STERN • EDITOR
A. KAWECKI • LETTERER | N. YOMTOV • COLORIST | D. HANDS • FINISHER | J. SALICRUP • ASST. EDITOR
IT IS SPRINGTIME IN MANHATTAN, AND THE AFTERNOON BREEZES ARE WARM WITH THE PROMISE OF SUMMER.
BUT INSIDE AVENGERS' MANSION, THE ATMOSPHERE IS OF A MARKEDLY DIFFERENT NATURE--AS A GRIM LEADER SPEAKS WORDS AS COLD AND HARD AS THE GLITTERING ARMOR HE WEARS...
SO THAT'S WHY I'VE CALLED YOU "OLD" AVENGERS TOGETHER... PEOPLE ASSOCIATED WITH THE CURRENT MEMBERS ARE VANISHING--POPPING OUT LIKE SOAP BUBBLES!
AND UNLESS WE FIND OUT WHAT'S BEHIND ALL THIS, IT'S QUITE POSSIBLE THAT SOON--
--THE AVENGERS WILL BE NO MORE!!
THRESHOLD of OBLIVION!

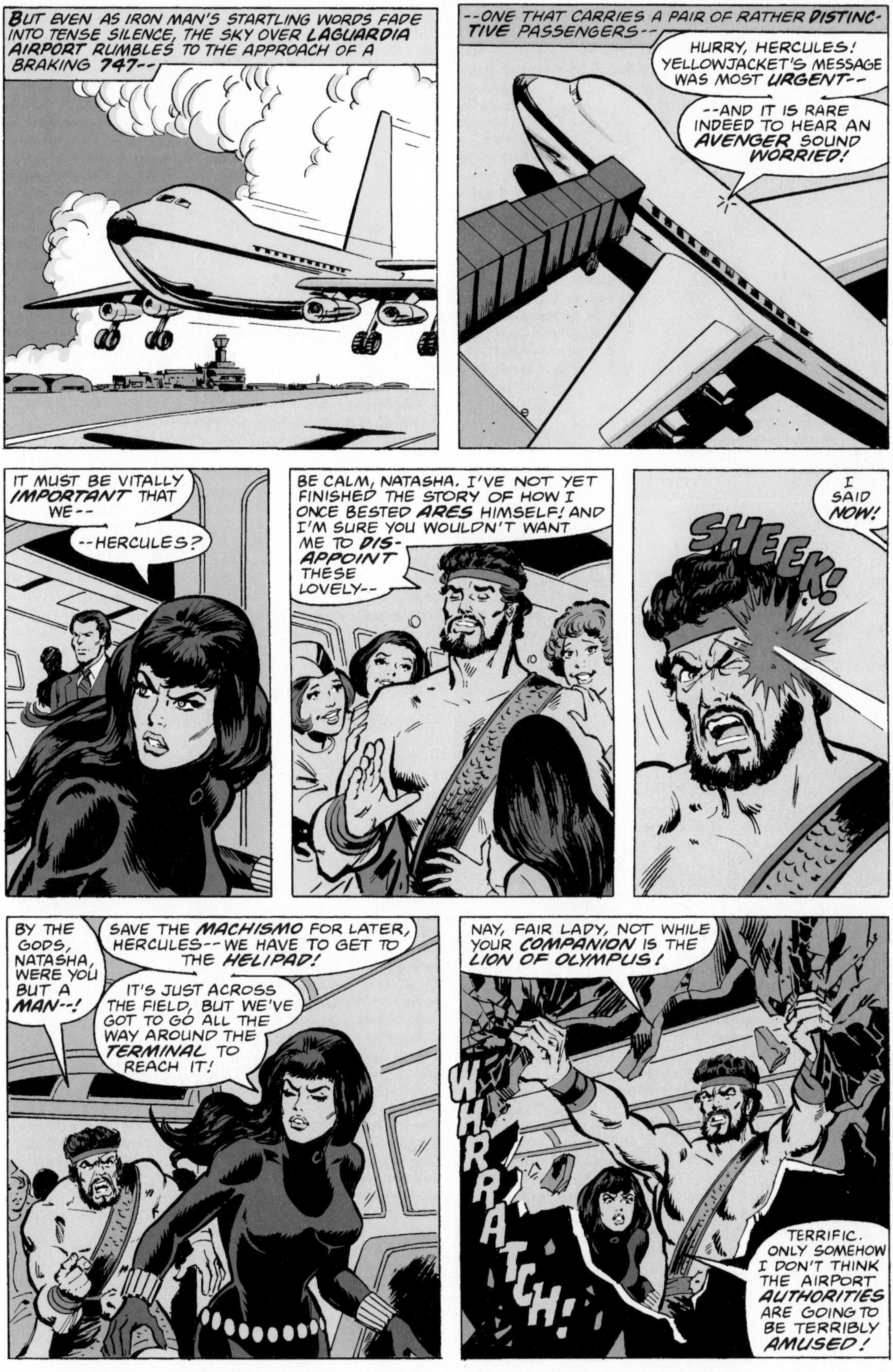

BUT EVEN AS IRON MAN'S STARTLING WORDS FADE INTO TENSE SILENCE, THE SKY OVER LAGUARDIA AIRPORT RUMBLES TO THE APPROACH OF A BRAKING 747--
--ONE THAT CARRIES A PAIR OF RATHER DISTINCTIVE PASSENGERS--
HURRY, HERCULES! YELLOWJACKET'S MESSAGE WAS MOST URGENT--
--AND IT IS RARE INDEED TO HEAR AN AVENGER SOUND WORRIED!
IT MUST BE VITALLY IMPORTANT THAT WE--
--HERCULES?
BE CALM, NATASHA. I'VE NOT YET FINISHED THE STORY OF HOW I ONCE BESTED ARES HIMSELF! AND I'M SURE YOU WOULDN'T WANT ME TO DIS-APPOINT THESE LOVELY--
I SAID NOW!
SHEEK!
BY THE GODS, NATASHA, WERE YOU BUT A MAN--!
SAVE THE MACHISMO FOR LATER, HERCULES--WE HAVE TO GET TO THE HELIPAD!
IT'S JUST ACROSS THE FIELD, BUT WE'VE GOT TO GO ALL THE WAY AROUND THE TERMINAL TO REACH IT!
NAY, FAIR LADY, NOT WHILE YOUR COMPANION IS THE LION OF OLYMPUS!
WHHRRATCH!
TERRIFIC. ONLY SOMEHOW I DON'T THINK THE AIRPORT AUTHORITIES ARE GOING TO BE TERRIBLY AMUSED!

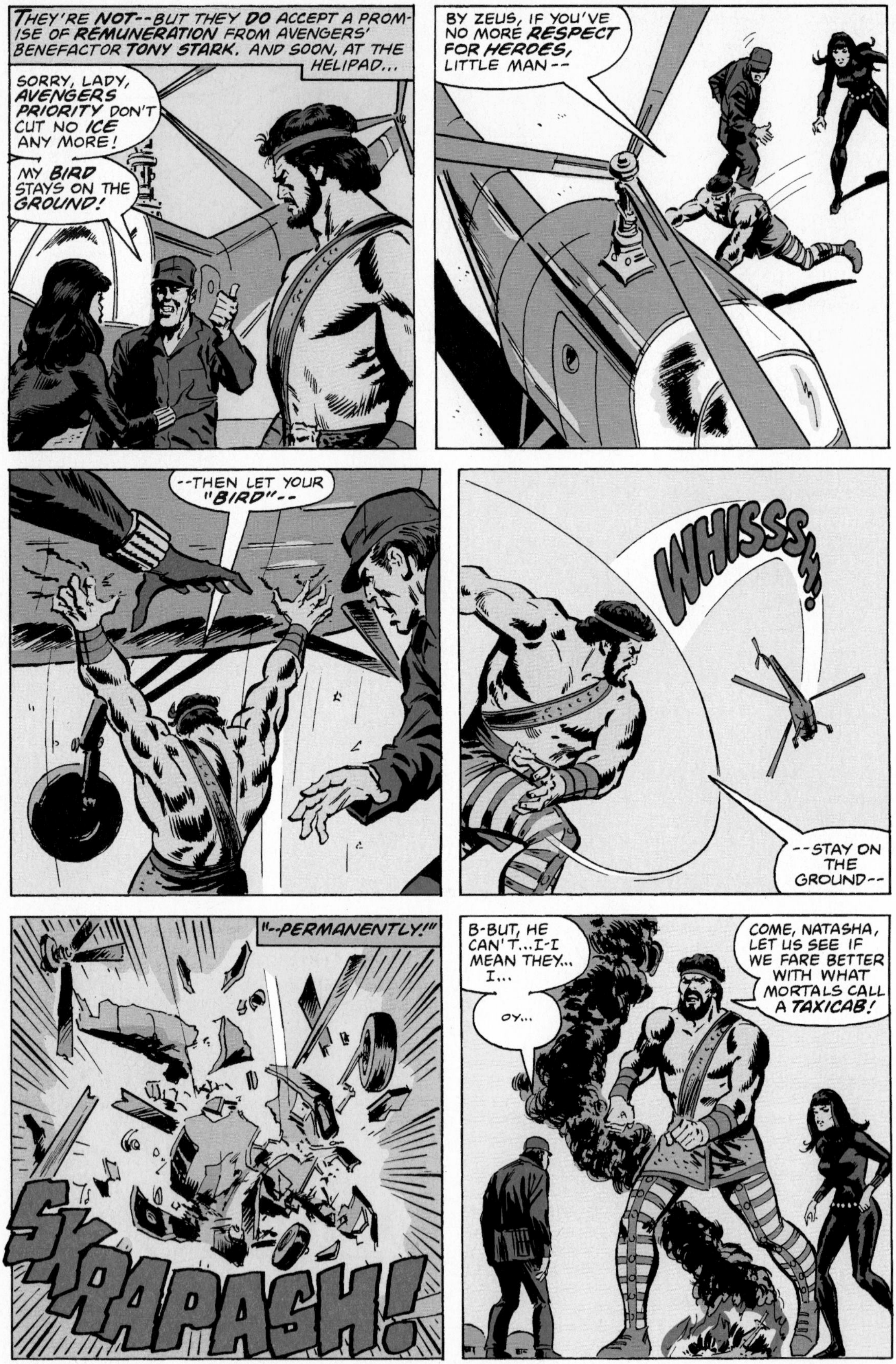
THEY'RE NOT--BUT THEY DO ACCEPT A PROMISE OF REMUNERATION FROM AVENGERS' BENEFACTOR TONY STARK. AND SOON, AT THE HELIPAD...
SORRY, LADY, AVENGERS PRIORITY DON'T CUT NO ICE ANY MORE!
MY BIRD STAYS ON THE GROUND!
BY ZEUS, IF YOU'VE NO MORE RESPECT FOR HEROES, LITTLE MAN--
--THEN LET YOUR "BIRD"--
WHISSSH!
--STAY ON THE GROUND--
"--PERMANENTLY!"
SKRAPASH!
B-BUT, HE CAN'T...I-I MEAN THEY... I...
OY...
COME, NATASHA, LET US SEE IF WE FARE BETTER WITH WHAT MORTALS CALL A TAXICAB!

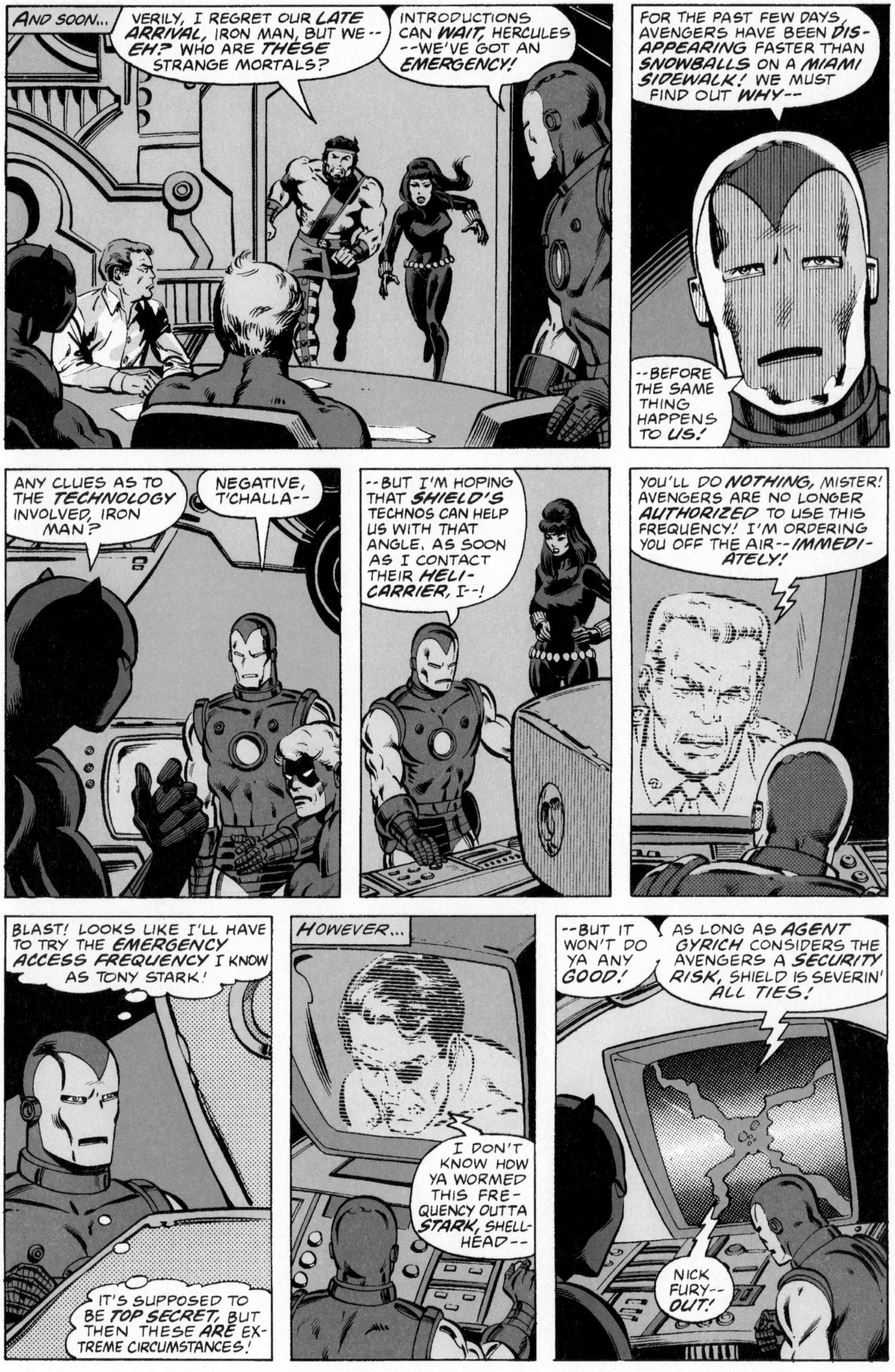
AND SOON...
VERILY, I REGRET OUR LATE ARRIVAL, IRON MAN, BUT WE-- EH? WHO ARE THESE STRANGE MORTALS?
INTRODUCTIONS CAN WAIT, HERCULES --WE'VE GOT AN EMERGENCY!
FOR THE PAST FEW DAYS, AVENGERS HAVE BEEN DISAPPEARING FASTER THAN SNOWBALLS ON A MIAMI SIDEWALK! WE MUST FIND OUT WHY--
--BEFORE THE SAME THING HAPPENS TO US!
ANY CLUES AS TO THE TECHNOLOGY INVOLVED, IRON MAN?
NEGATIVE, T'CHALLA--
--BUT I'M HOPING THAT SHIELD'S TECHNOS CAN HELP US WITH THAT ANGLE, AS SOON AS I CONTACT THEIR HELI-CARRIER, I--!
YOU'LL DO NOTHING, MISTER! AVENGERS ARE NO LONGER AUTHORIZED TO USE THIS FREQUENCY! I'M ORDERING YOU OFF THE AIR--IMMEDIATELY!
BLAST! LOOKS LIKE I'LL HAVE TO TRY THE EMERGENCY ACCESS FREQUENCY I KNOW AS TONY STARK!
IT'S SUPPOSED TO BE TOP SECRET, BUT THEN THESE ARE EXTREME CIRCUMSTANCES!
HOWEVER...
I DON'T KNOW HOW YA WORMED THIS FREQUENCY OUTTA STARK, SHELLHEAD--
--BUT IT WON'T DO YA ANY GOOD!
AS LONG AS AGENT GYRICH CONSIDERS THE AVENGERS A SECURITY RISK, SHIELD IS SEVERIN' ALL TIES!
NICK FURY--OUT!

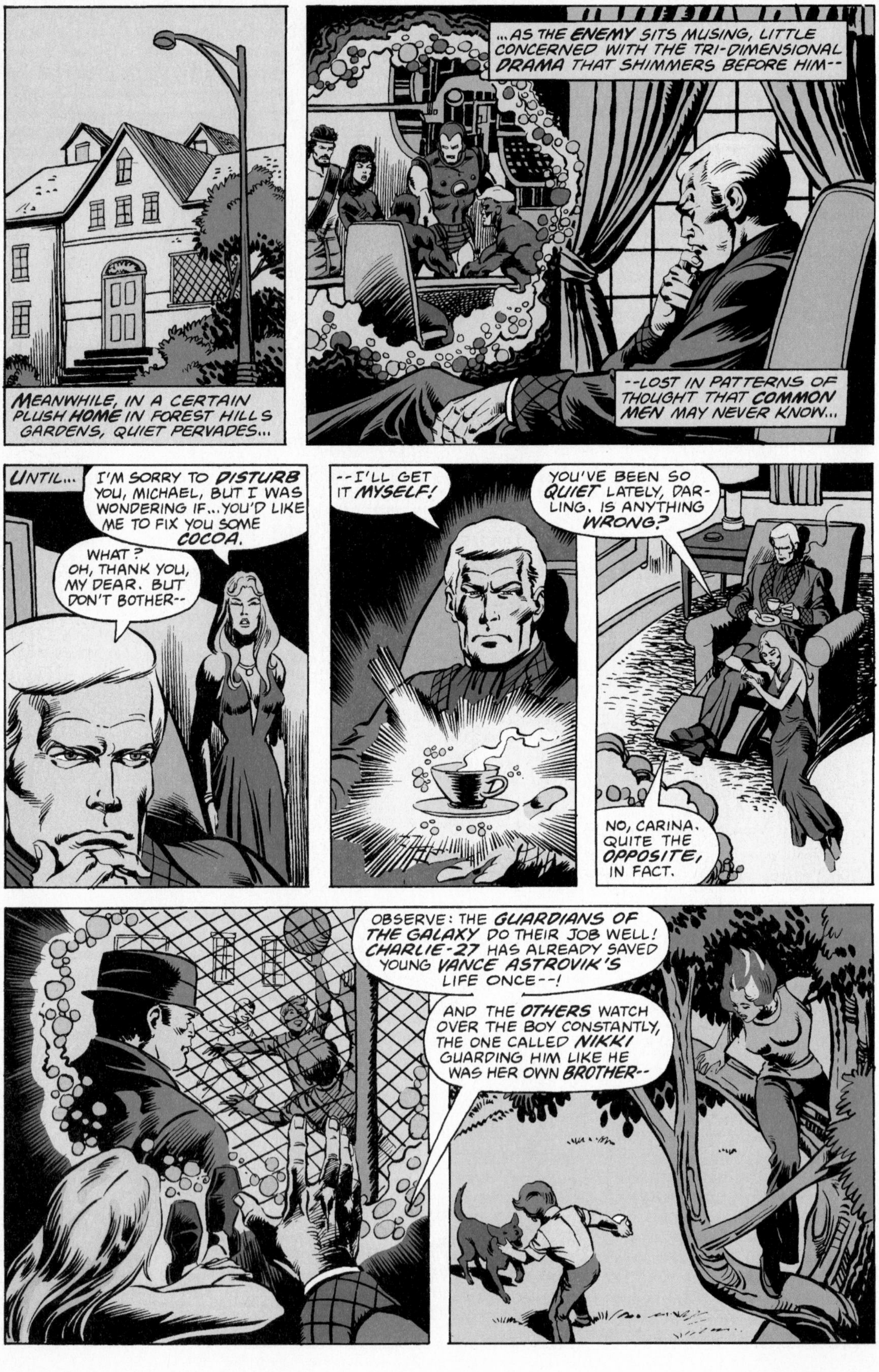

MEANWHILE, IN A CERTAIN PLUSH HOME IN FOREST HILLS GARDENS, QUIET PERVADES...
...AS THE ENEMY SITS MUSING, LITTLE CONCERNED WITH THE TRI-DIMENSIONAL DRAMA THAT SHIMMERS BEFORE HIM--
--LOST IN PATTERNS OF THOUGHT THAT COMMON MEN MAY NEVER KNOW...
UNTIL...
I'M SORRY TO DISTURB YOU, MICHAEL, BUT I WAS WONDERING IF... YOU'D LIKE ME TO FIX YOU SOME COCOA.
WHAT? OH, THANK YOU, MY DEAR. BUT DON'T BOTHER--
--I'LL GET IT MYSELF!
YOU'VE BEEN SO QUIET LATELY, DARLING. IS ANYTHING WRONG?
NO, CARINA. QUITE THE OPPOSITE, IN FACT.
OBSERVE: THE GUARDIANS OF THE GALAXY DO THEIR JOB WELL! CHARLIE-27 HAS ALREADY SAVED YOUNG VANCE ASTROVIK'S LIFE ONCE--!
AND THE OTHERS WATCH OVER THE BOY CONSTANTLY, THE ONE CALLED NIKKI GUARDING HIM LIKE HE WAS HER OWN BROTHER--

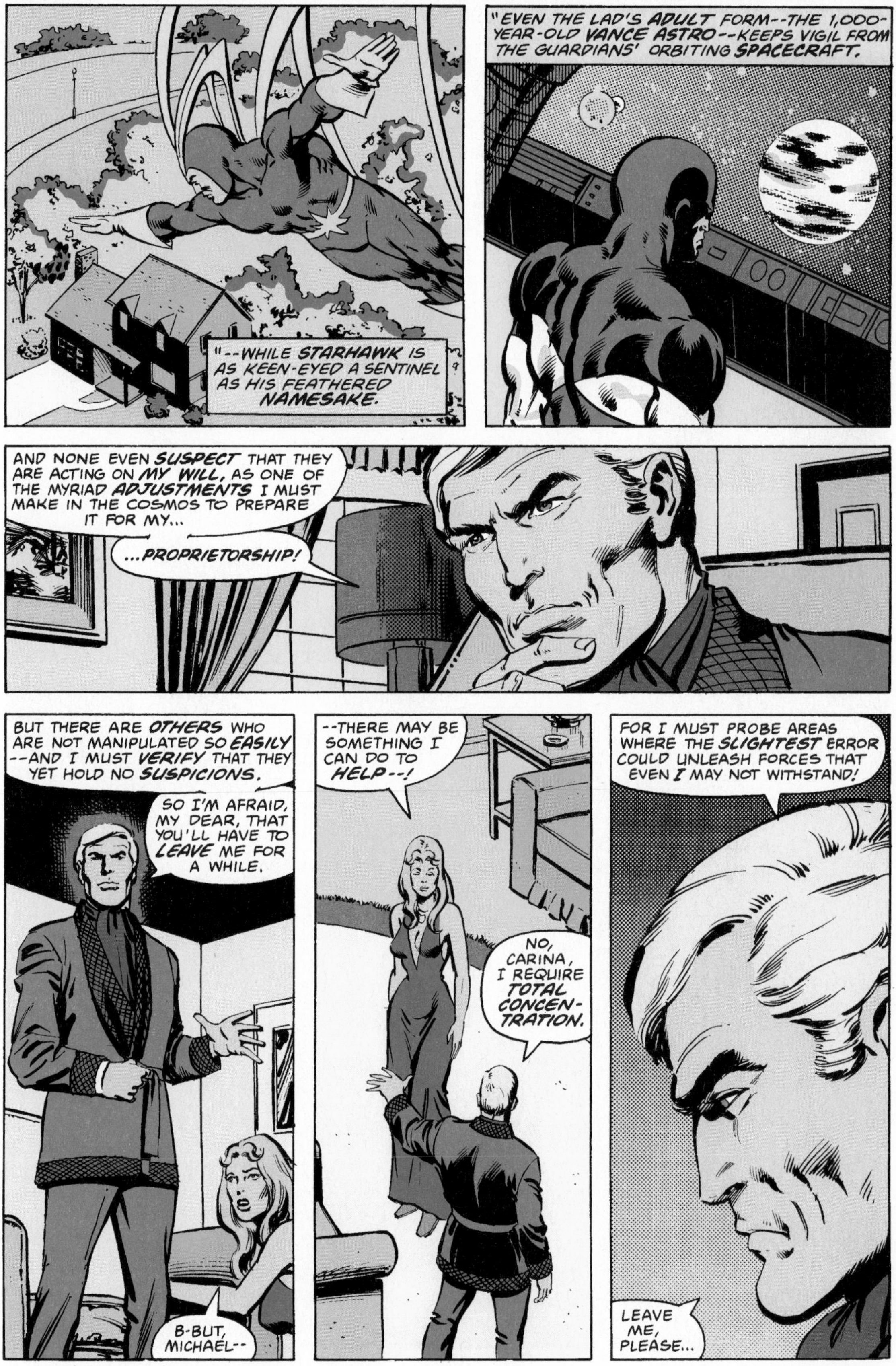

"--WHILE STARHAWK IS AS KEEN-EYED A SENTINEL AS HIS FEATHERED NAMESAKE.
"EVEN THE LAD'S ADULT FORM--THE 1,000-YEAR-OLD VANCE ASTRO--KEEPS VIGIL FROM THE GUARDIANS' ORBITING SPACECRAFT.
AND NONE EVEN SUSPECT THAT THEY ARE ACTING ON MY WILL, AS ONE OF THE MYRIAD ADJUSTMENTS I MUST MAKE IN THE COSMOS TO PREPARE IT FOR MY...
...PROPRIETORSHIP!
BUT THERE ARE OTHERS WHO ARE NOT MANIPULATED SO EASILY --AND I MUST VERIFY THAT THEY YET HOLD NO SUSPICIONS.
SO I'M AFRAID, MY DEAR, THAT YOU'LL HAVE TO LEAVE ME FOR A WHILE.
B-BUT, MICHAEL--
--THERE MAY BE SOMETHING I CAN DO TO HELP--!
NO, CARINA, I REQUIRE TOTAL CONCEN-TRATION.
FOR I MUST PROBE AREAS WHERE THE SLIGHTEST ERROR COULD UNLEASH FORCES THAT EVEN I MAY NOT WITHSTAND!
LEAVE ME, PLEASE...

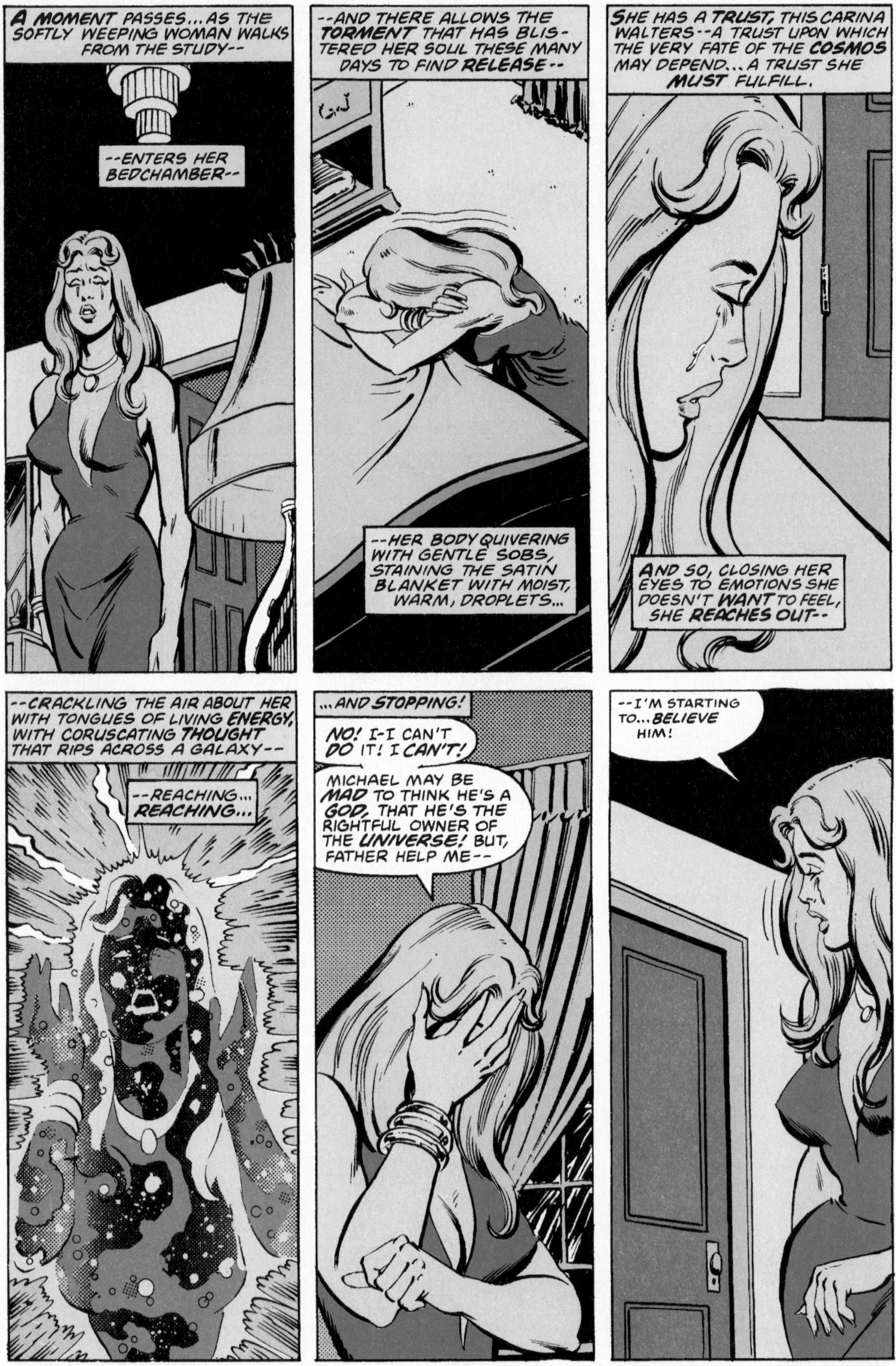
A MOMENT PASSES... AS THE SOFTLY WEEPING WOMAN WALKS FROM THE STUDY--
--ENTERS HER BEDCHAMBER--
--AND THERE ALLOWS THE TORMENT THAT HAS BLISTERED HER SOUL THESE MANY DAYS TO FIND RELEASE--
--HER BODY QUIVERING WITH GENTLE SOBS, STAINING THE SATIN BLANKET WITH MOIST, WARM, DROPLETS...
SHE HAS A TRUST, THIS CARINA WALTERS--A TRUST UPON WHICH THE VERY FATE OF THE COSMOS MAY DEPEND... A TRUST SHE MUST FULFILL.
AND SO, CLOSING HER EYES TO EMOTIONS SHE DOESN'T WANT TO FEEL, SHE REACHES OUT--
--CRACKLING THE AIR ABOUT HER WITH TONGUES OF LIVING ENERGY, WITH CORUSCATING THOUGHT THAT RIPS ACROSS A GALAXY--
--REACHING... REACHING...
...AND STOPPING!
NO! I-I CAN'T DO IT! I CAN'T!
MICHAEL MAY BE MAD TO THINK HE'S A GOD, THAT HE'S THE RIGHTFUL OWNER OF THE UNIVERSE! BUT, FATHER HELP ME--
--I'M STARTING TO... BELIEVE HIM!

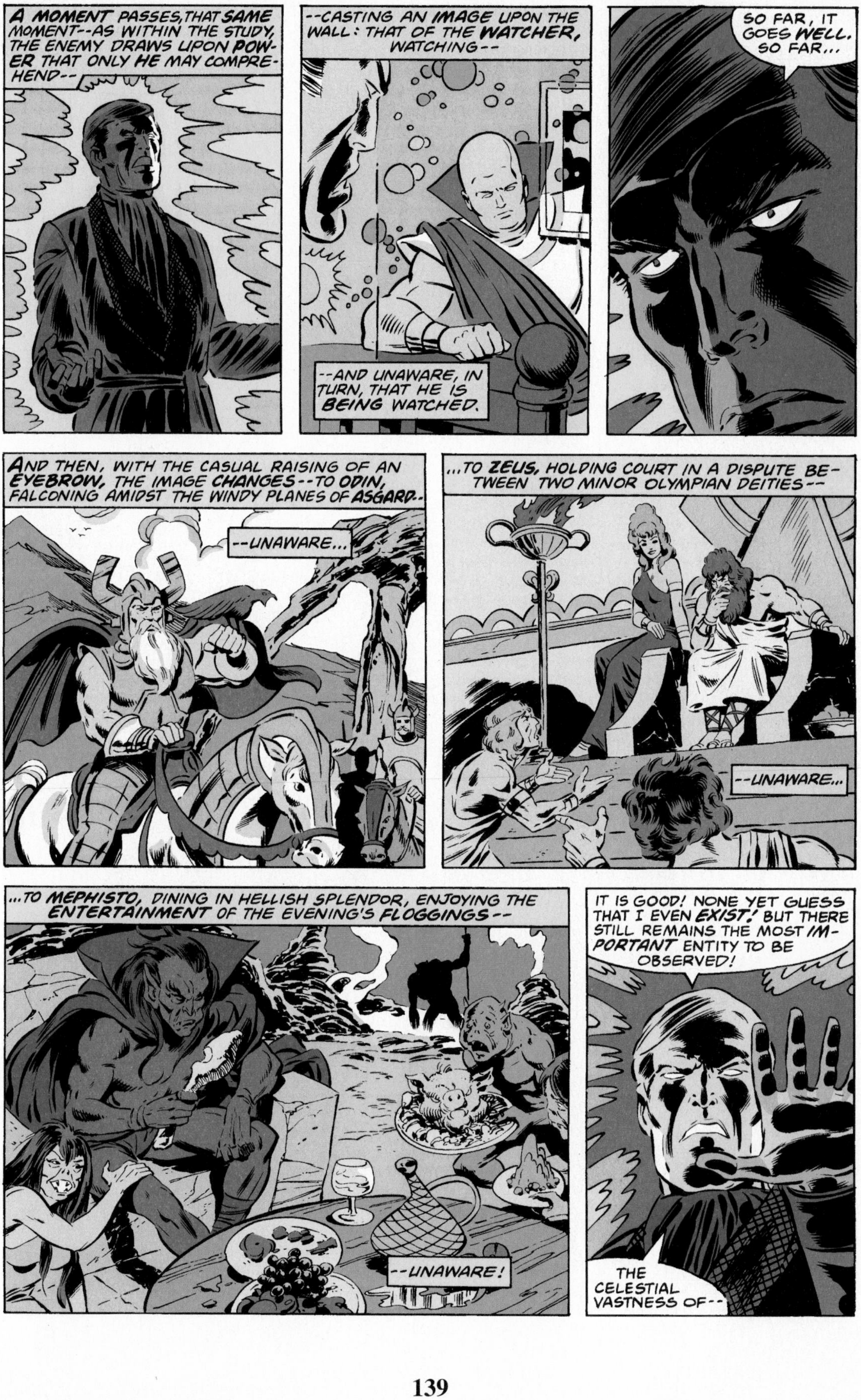
A MOMENT PASSES, THAT SAME MOMENT--AS WITHIN THE STUDY, THE ENEMY DRAWS UPON POWER THAT ONLY HE MAY COMPREHEND--
--CASTING AN IMAGE UPON THE WALL: THAT OF THE WATCHER, WATCHING--
--AND UNAWARE, IN TURN, THAT HE IS BEING WATCHED.
SO FAR, IT GOES WELL. SO FAR...
AND THEN, WITH THE CASUAL RAISING OF AN EYEBROW, THE IMAGE CHANGES--TO ODIN, FALCONING AMIDST THE WINDY PLANES OF ASGARD--
--UNAWARE...
...TO ZEUS, HOLDING COURT IN A DISPUTE BETWEEN TWO MINOR OLYMPIAN DEITIES--
--UNAWARE...
...TO MEPHISTO, DINING IN HELLISH SPLENDOR, ENJOYING THE ENTERTAINMENT OF THE EVENING'S FLOGGINGS--
--UNAWARE!
IT IS GOOD! NONE YET GUESS THAT I EVEN EXIST! BUT THERE STILL REMAINS THE MOST IMPORTANT ENTITY TO BE OBSERVED!
THE CELESTIAL VASTNESS OF--

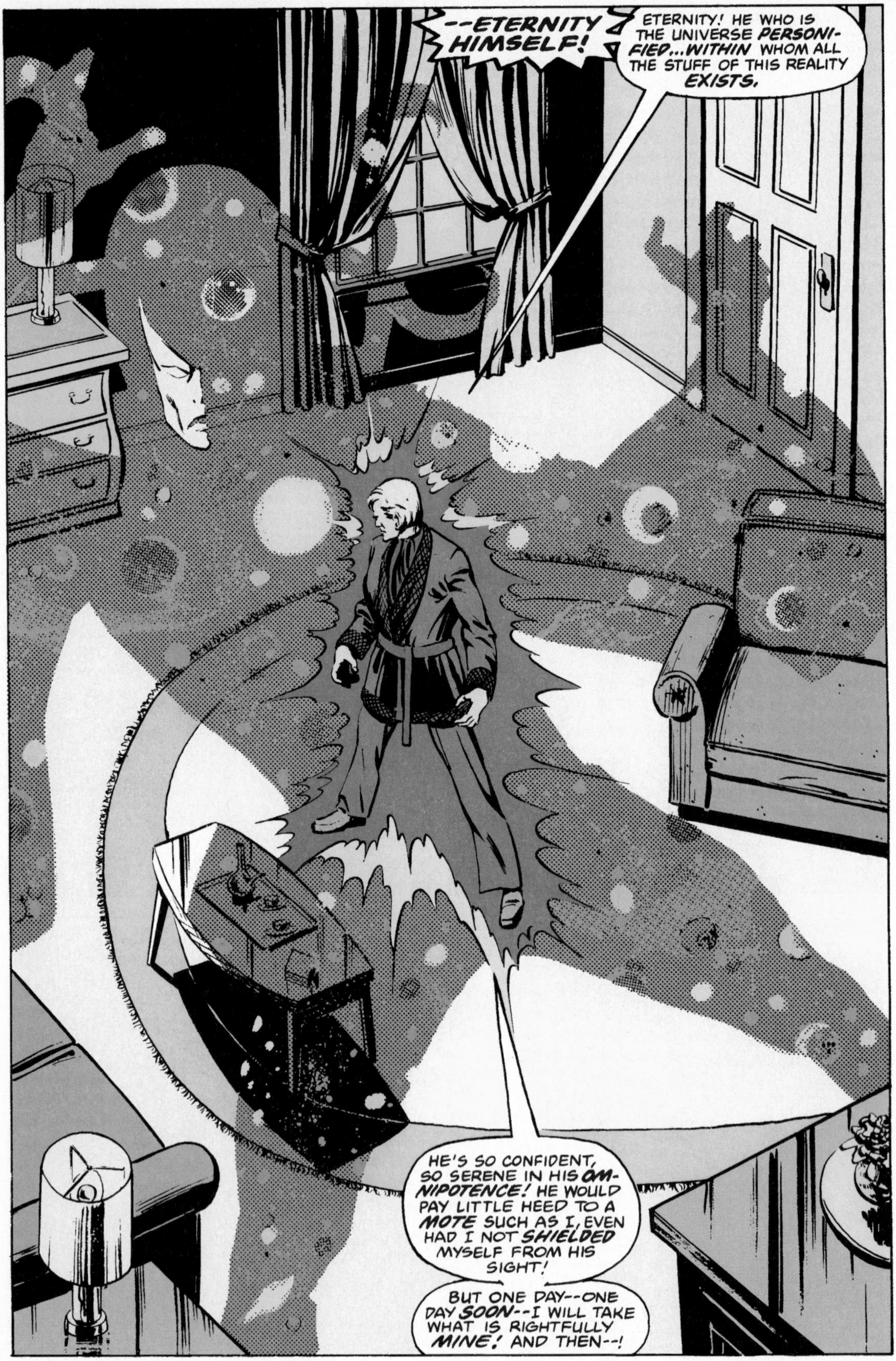
--ETERNITY HIMSELF!
ETERNITY! HE WHO IS THE UNIVERSE PERSONIFIED...WITHIN WHOM ALL THE STUFF OF THIS REALITY EXISTS.
HE'S SO CONFIDENT, SO SERENE IN HIS OMNIPOTENCE! HE WOULD PAY LITTLE HEED TO A MOTE SUCH AS I, EVEN HAD I NOT SHIELDED MYSELF FROM HIS SIGHT!
BUT ONE DAY--ONE DAY SOON--I WILL TAKE WHAT IS RIGHTFULLY MINE! AND THEN--!

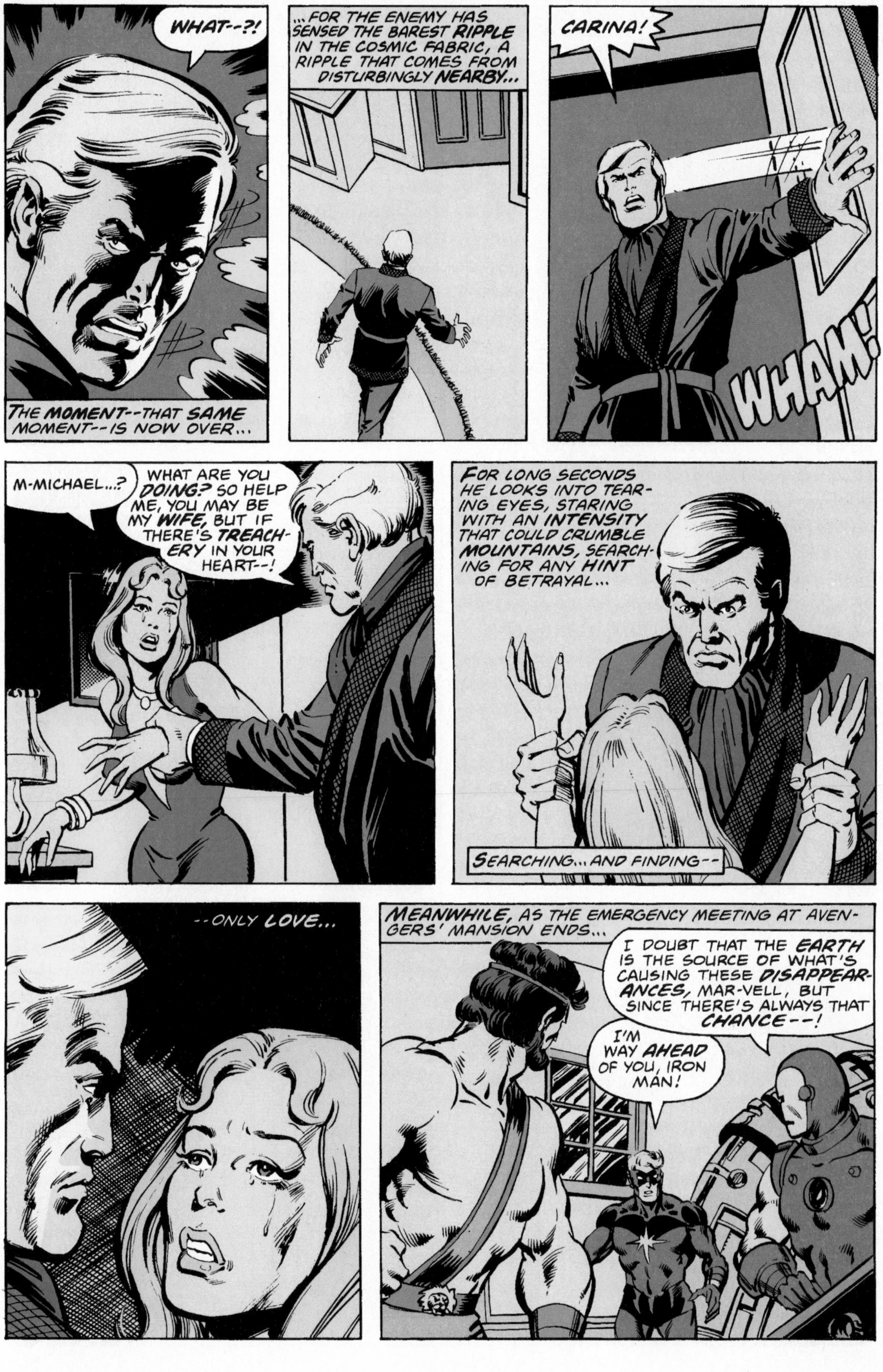
WHAT--?!
THE MOMENT--THAT SAME MOMENT--IS NOW OVER...
...FOR THE ENEMY HAS SENSED THE BAREST RIPPLE IN THE COSMIC FABRIC, A RIPPLE THAT COMES FROM DISTURBINGLY NEARBY...
CARINA!
WHAM!
M-MICHAEL...?
WHAT ARE YOU DOING? SO HELP ME, YOU MAY BE MY WIFE, BUT IF THERE'S TREACHERY IN YOUR HEART--!
FOR LONG SECONDS HE LOOKS INTO TEARING EYES, STARING WITH AN INTENSITY THAT COULD CRUMBLE MOUNTAINS, SEARCHING FOR ANY HINT OF BETRAYAL...
SEARCHING...AND FINDING--
--ONLY LOVE...
MEANWHILE, AS THE EMERGENCY MEETING AT AVENGERS' MANSION ENDS...
I DOUBT THAT THE EARTH IS THE SOURCE OF WHAT'S CAUSING THESE DISAPPEARANCES, MAR-VELL, BUT SINCE THERE'S ALWAYS THAT CHANCE--!
I'M WAY AHEAD OF YOU, IRON MAN!

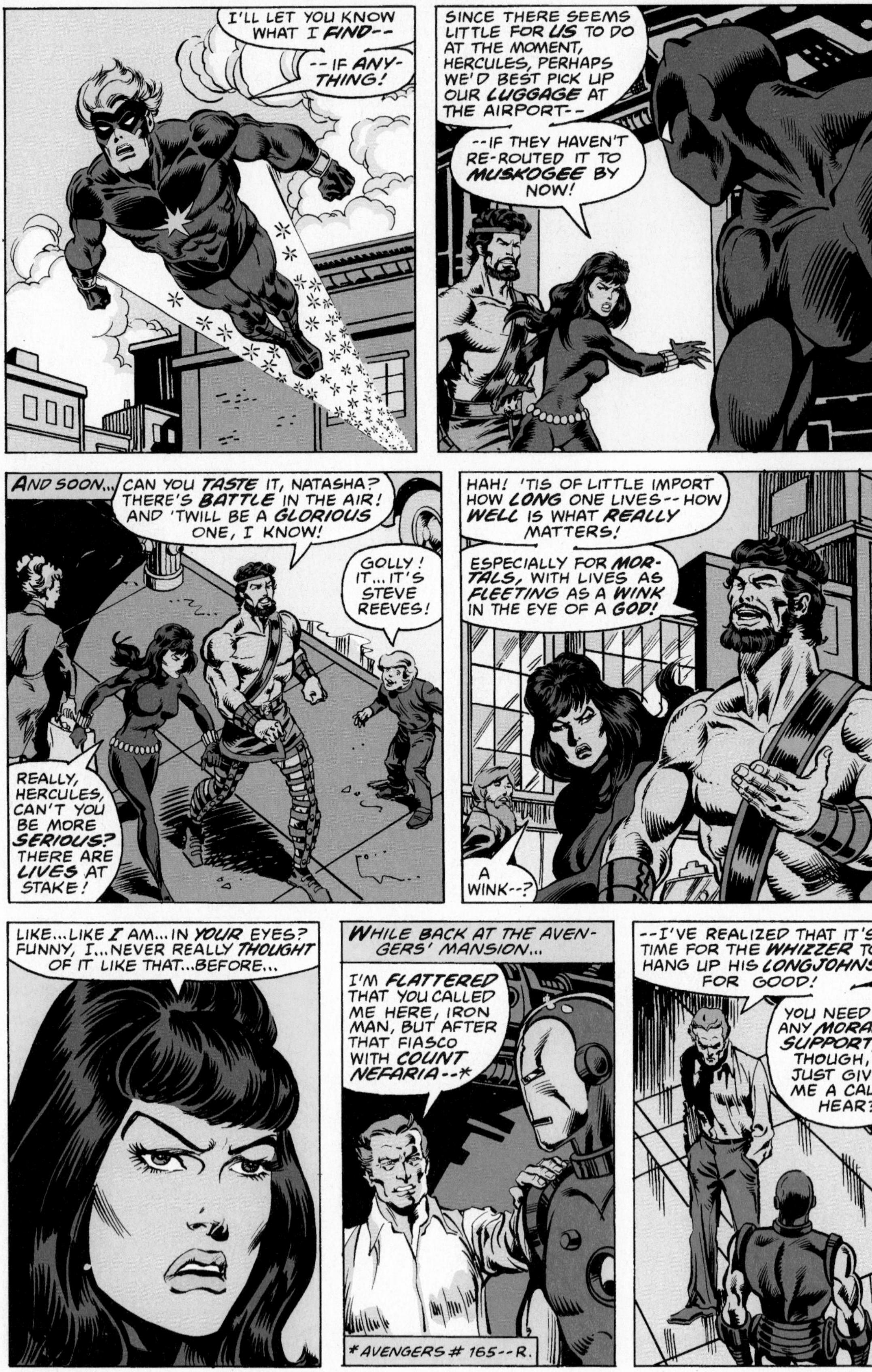

I'LL LET YOU KNOW WHAT I FIND--
--IF ANYTHING!
SINCE THERE SEEMS LITTLE FOR US TO DO AT THE MOMENT, HERCULES, PERHAPS WE'D BEST PICK UP OUR LUGGAGE AT THE AIRPORT--
--IF THEY HAVEN'T RE-ROUTED IT TO MUSKOGEE BY NOW!
AND SOON...
CAN YOU TASTE IT, NATASHA? THERE'S BATTLE IN THE AIR! AND 'TWILL BE A GLORIOUS ONE, I KNOW!
GOLLY! IT...IT'S STEVE REEVES!
REALLY, HERCULES, CAN'T YOU BE MORE SERIOUS? THERE ARE LIVES AT STAKE!
HAH! 'TIS OF LITTLE IMPORT HOW LONG ONE LIVES--HOW WELL IS WHAT REALLY MATTERS!
ESPECIALLY FOR MORTALS, WITH LIVES AS FLEETING AS A WINK IN THE EYE OF A GOD!
A WINK--?
LIKE...LIKE I AM...IN YOUR EYES? FUNNY, I...NEVER REALLY THOUGHT OF IT LIKE THAT...BEFORE...
WHILE BACK AT THE AVENGERS' MANSION...
I'M FLATTERED THAT YOU CALLED ME HERE, IRON MAN, BUT AFTER THAT FIASCO WITH COUNT NEFARIA--*
*AVENGERS # 165--R.
--I'VE REALIZED THAT IT'S TIME FOR THE WHIZZER TO HANG UP HIS LONGJOHNS FOR GOOD!
YOU NEED ANY MORAL SUPPORT, THOUGH, JUST GIVE ME A CALL, HEAR?

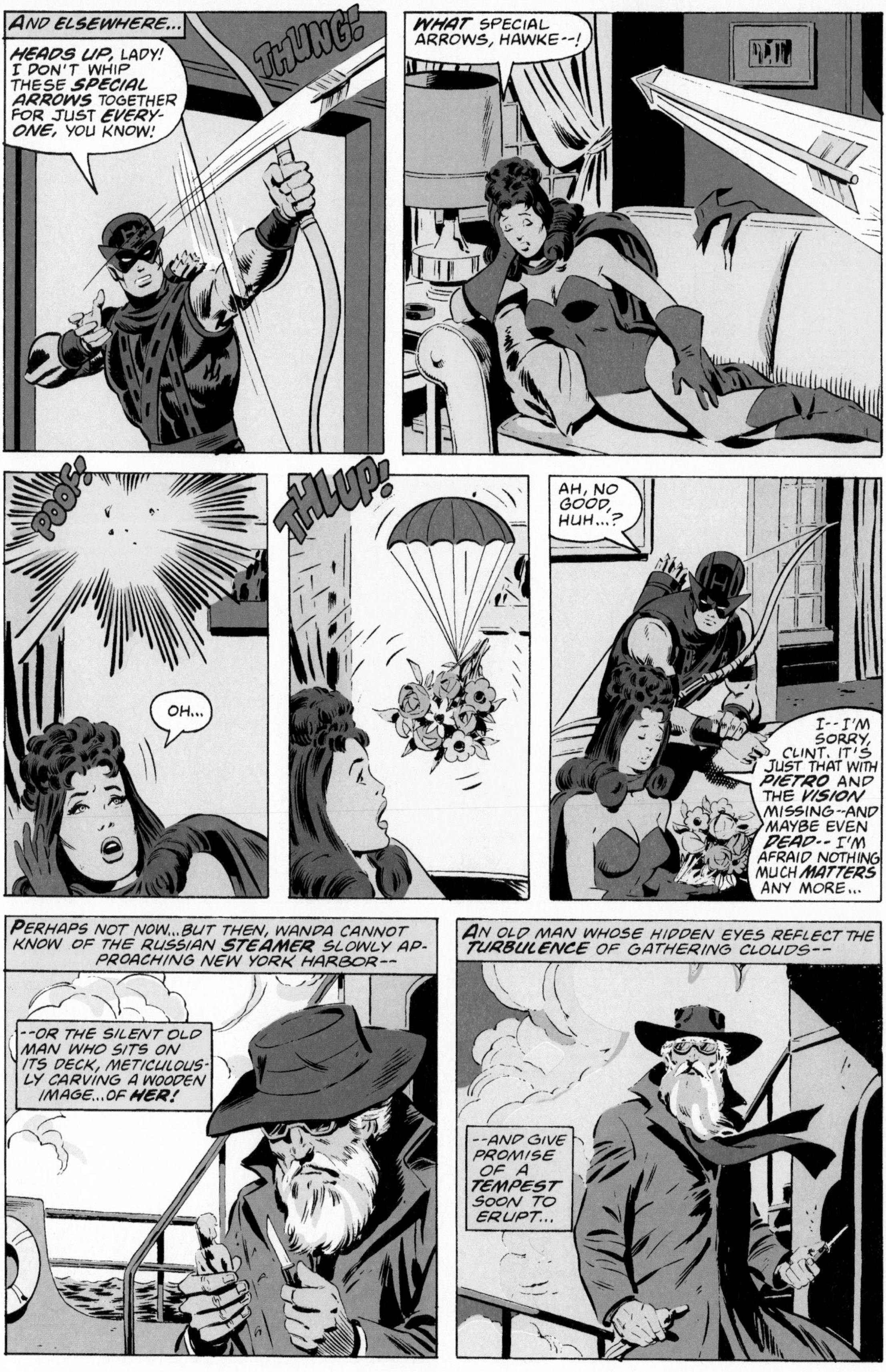

AND ELSEWHERE...
HEADS UP, LADY! I DON'T WHIP THESE SPECIAL ARROWS TOGETHER FOR JUST EVERY-ONE, YOU KNOW!
THUNG!
WHAT SPECIAL ARROWS, HAWKE--!
POOF!
OH...
THLUP!
AH, NO GOOD, HUH...?
I--I'M SORRY, CLINT. IT'S JUST THAT WITH PIETRO AND THE VISION MISSING--AND MAYBE EVEN DEAD--I'M AFRAID NOTHING MUCH MATTERS ANY MORE...
PERHAPS NOT NOW...BUT THEN, WANDA CANNOT KNOW OF THE RUSSIAN STEAMER SLOWLY AP-PROACHING NEW YORK HARBOR--
--OR THE SILENT OLD MAN WHO SITS ON ITS DECK, METICULOUS-LY CARVING A WOODEN IMAGE...OF HER!
AN OLD MAN WHOSE HIDDEN EYES REFLECT THE TURBULENCE OF GATHERING CLOUDS--
--AND GIVE PROMISE OF A TEMPEST SOON TO ERUPT...

YOUR *POTATO SALAD* SHOULD BE READY MOMENTARILY, MR. WILLIAMS, AND--

--WHY, *MASTER THOR!* IT'S GOOD TO *SEE* YOU AGAIN, SIR!

VERILY, THOU ART A PLEASURE TO *MINE* EYES AS WELL, JARVIS.

HEY, THOR, OLD BUDDY! PULL UP A CHAIR! WANT HALF OF MY *SANDWICH?*

I APPRECIATE THINE *OFFER,* FRIEND--BUT THE SON OF ODIN IS NOT *ACCUSTOMED* TO BEING ADDRESSED IN SO *FAMILIAR* A MANNER--

--BY *STRANGERS!*

S...STRANGERS?!

HEY, WHAT ARE YOU *GETTING* AT? I'M *WONDER MAN,* REMEMBER? WE FOUGHT SIDE-BY-SIDE AGAINST *GRAVITON!* AND *COUNT NEFARIA!*

METHINKS THOU ART *CONFUSED,* MORTAL. I KNOW *NOTHING* OF SUCH BATTLES--OR OF *THEE!*

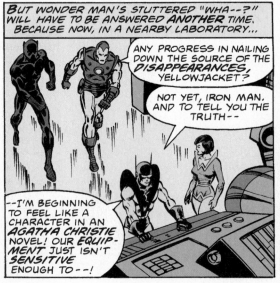

BUT WONDER MAN'S STUTTERED "WHA--?" WILL HAVE TO BE ANSWERED *ANOTHER* TIME, BECAUSE NOW, IN A NEARBY LABORATORY...

ANY PROGRESS IN NAILING DOWN THE SOURCE OF THE *DISAPPEARANCES,* YELLOWJACKET?

NOT YET, IRON MAN. AND TO TELL YOU THE TRUTH--

--I'M BEGINNING TO FEEL LIKE A CHARACTER IN AN *AGATHA CHRISTIE* NOVEL! OUR *EQUIPMENT* JUST ISN'T *SENSITIVE* ENOUGH TO--!

WAIT A MINUTE! I JUST *THOUGHT* OF SOMETHING! WHAT ABOUT *DRYDOCK?* THE *GUARDIANS'* TECHNOLOGY IS A *THOUSAND YEARS* AHEAD OF OURS! MAYBE...

YOU'RE *RIGHT,* PANTHER! I'LL GET IN TOUCH WITH THEM RIGHT--

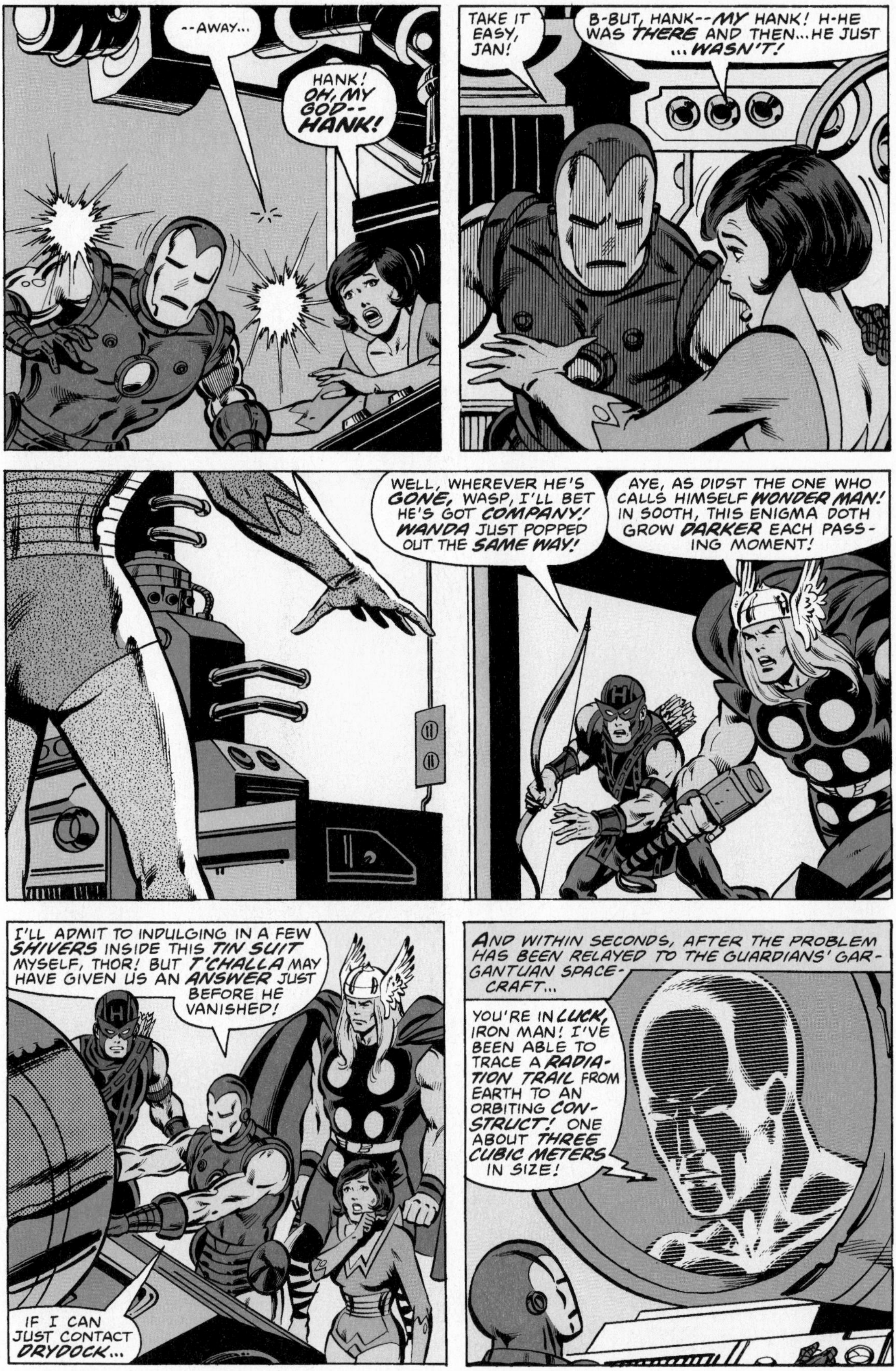
--AWAY...
HANK! OH, MY GOD-- HANK!
TAKE IT EASY, JAN!
B-BUT, HANK--MY HANK! H-HE WAS THERE AND THEN...HE JUST ...WASN'T!
WELL, WHEREVER HE'S GONE, WASP, I'LL BET HE'S GOT COMPANY! WANDA JUST POPPED OUT THE SAME WAY!
AYE, AS DIDST THE ONE WHO CALLS HIMSELF WONDER MAN! IN SOOTH, THIS ENIGMA DOTH GROW DARKER EACH PASSING MOMENT!
I'LL ADMIT TO INDULGING IN A FEW SHIVERS INSIDE THIS TIN SUIT MYSELF, THOR! BUT T'CHALLA MAY HAVE GIVEN US AN ANSWER JUST BEFORE HE VANISHED!
IF I CAN JUST CONTACT DRYDOCK...
AND WITHIN SECONDS, AFTER THE PROBLEM HAS BEEN RELAYED TO THE GUARDIANS' GARGANTUAN SPACECRAFT...
YOU'RE IN LUCK, IRON MAN! I'VE BEEN ABLE TO TRACE A RADIATION TRAIL FROM EARTH TO AN ORBITING CONSTRUCT! ONE ABOUT THREE CUBIC METERS IN SIZE!

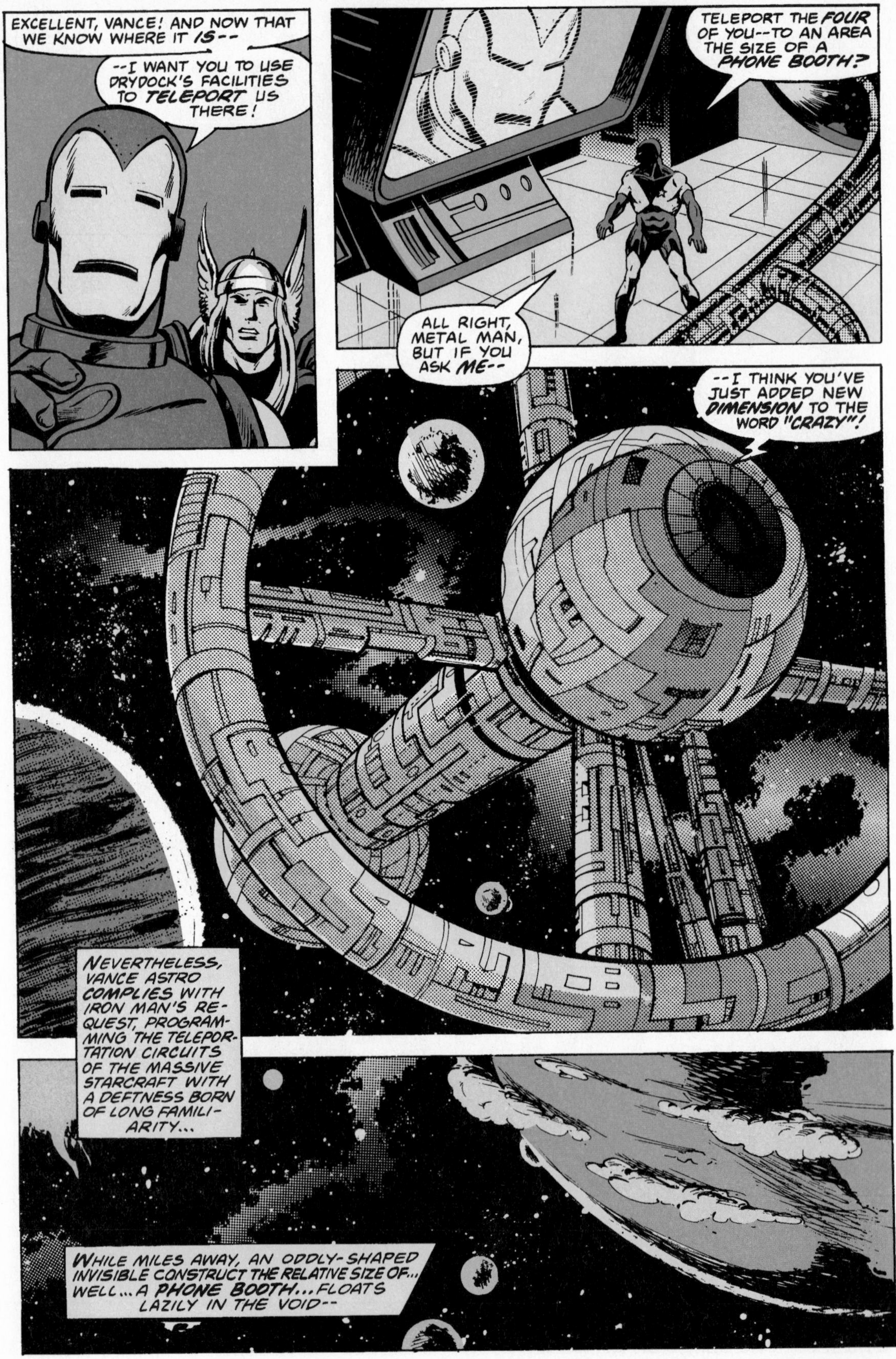
EXCELLENT, VANCE! AND NOW THAT WE KNOW WHERE IT IS--
--I WANT YOU TO USE DRYDOCK'S FACILITIES TO TELEPORT US THERE!
TELEPORT THE FOUR OF YOU--TO AN AREA THE SIZE OF A PHONE BOOTH?
ALL RIGHT, METAL MAN, BUT IF YOU ASK ME--
--I THINK YOU'VE JUST ADDED NEW DIMENSION TO THE WORD "CRAZY"!
NEVERTHELESS, VANCE ASTRO COMPLIES WITH IRON MAN'S REQUEST, PROGRAMMING THE TELEPORTATION CIRCUITS OF THE MASSIVE STARCRAFT WITH A DEFTNESS BORN OF LONG FAMILIARITY...
WHILE MILES AWAY, AN ODDLY-SHAPED INVISIBLE CONSTRUCT THE RELATIVE SIZE OF... WELL... A PHONE BOOTH... FLOATS LAZILY IN THE VOID--

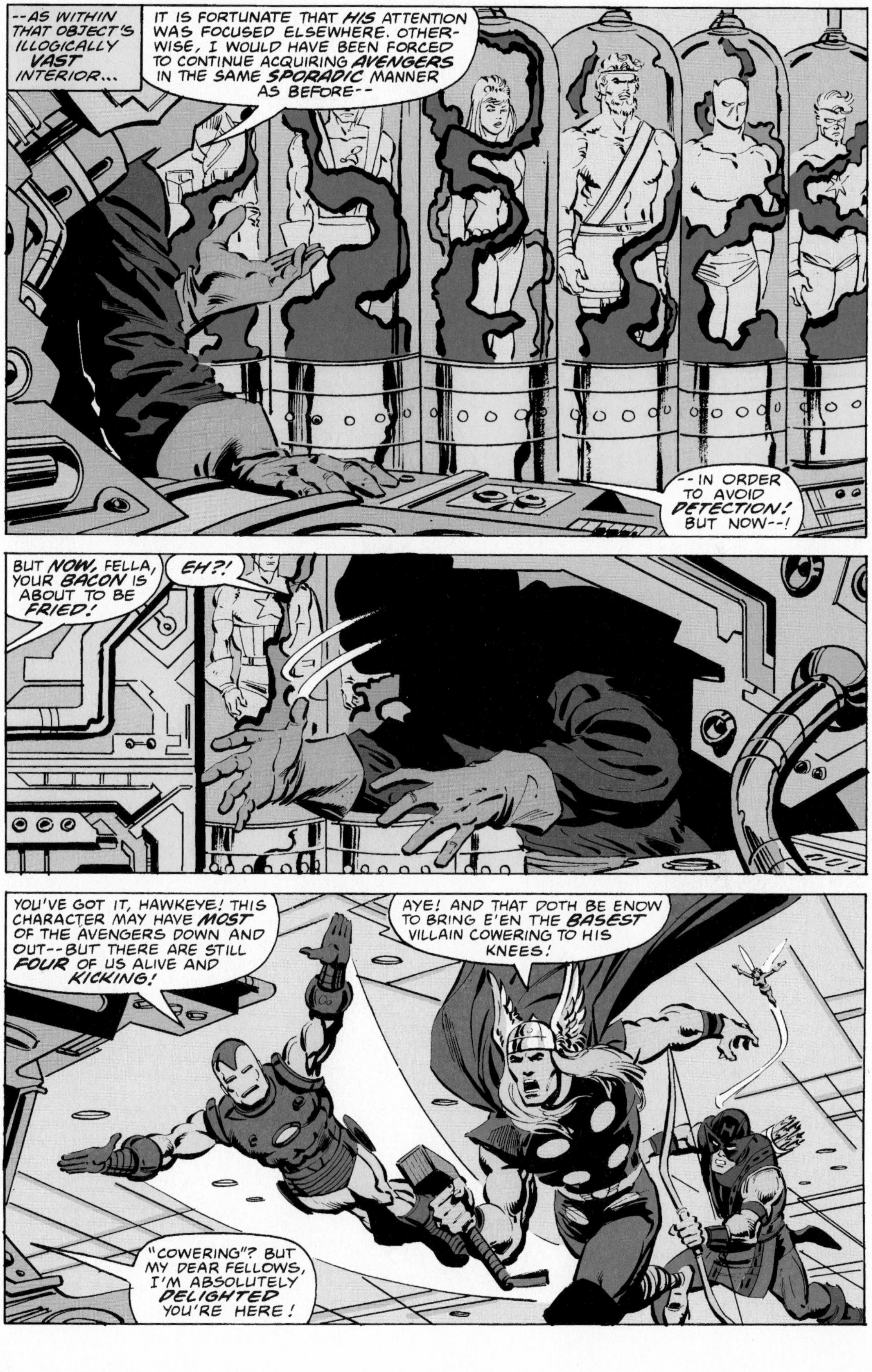
--AS WITHIN THAT OBJECT'S ILLOGICALLY VAST INTERIOR...
IT IS FORTUNATE THAT HIS ATTENTION WAS FOCUSED ELSEWHERE. OTHERWISE, I WOULD HAVE BEEN FORCED TO CONTINUE ACQUIRING AVENGERS IN THE SAME SPORADIC MANNER AS BEFORE--
--IN ORDER TO AVOID DETECTION! BUT NOW--!
BUT NOW, FELLA, YOUR BACON IS ABOUT TO BE FRIED!
EH?!
YOU'VE GOT IT, HAWKEYE! THIS CHARACTER MAY HAVE MOST OF THE AVENGERS DOWN AND OUT--BUT THERE ARE STILL FOUR OF US ALIVE AND KICKING!
AYE! AND THAT DOTH BE ENOW TO BRING E'EN THE BASEST VILLAIN COWERING TO HIS KNEES!
"COWERING"? BUT MY DEAR FELLOWS, I'M ABSOLUTELY DELIGHTED YOU'RE HERE!

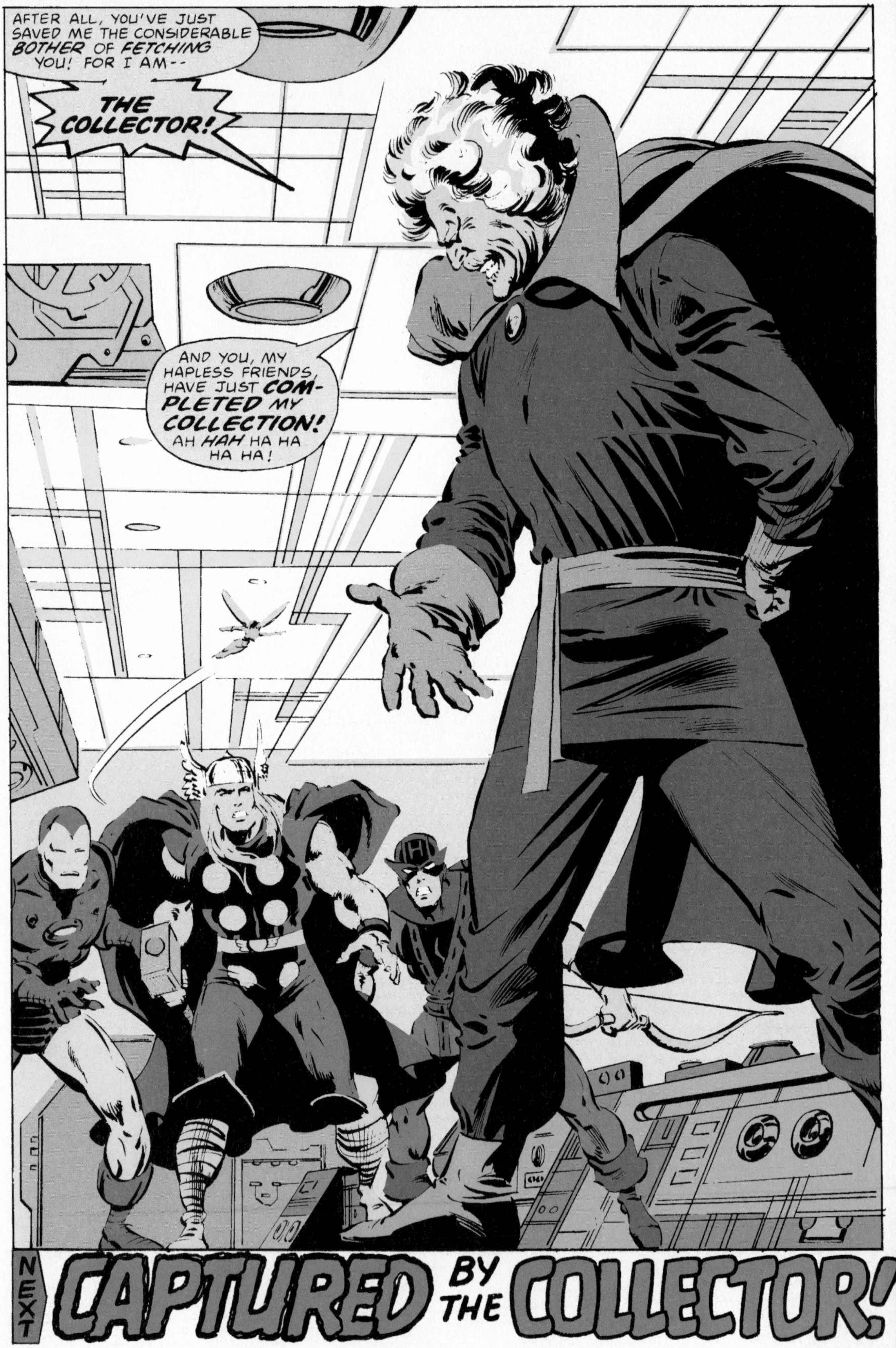
AFTER ALL, YOU'VE JUST SAVED ME THE CONSIDERABLE BOTHER OF FETCHING YOU! FOR I AM--
THE COLLECTOR!
AND YOU, MY HAPLESS FRIENDS, HAVE JUST COMPLETED MY COLLECTION! AH HAH HA HA HA HA!
NEXT CAPTURED BY THE COLLECTOR!

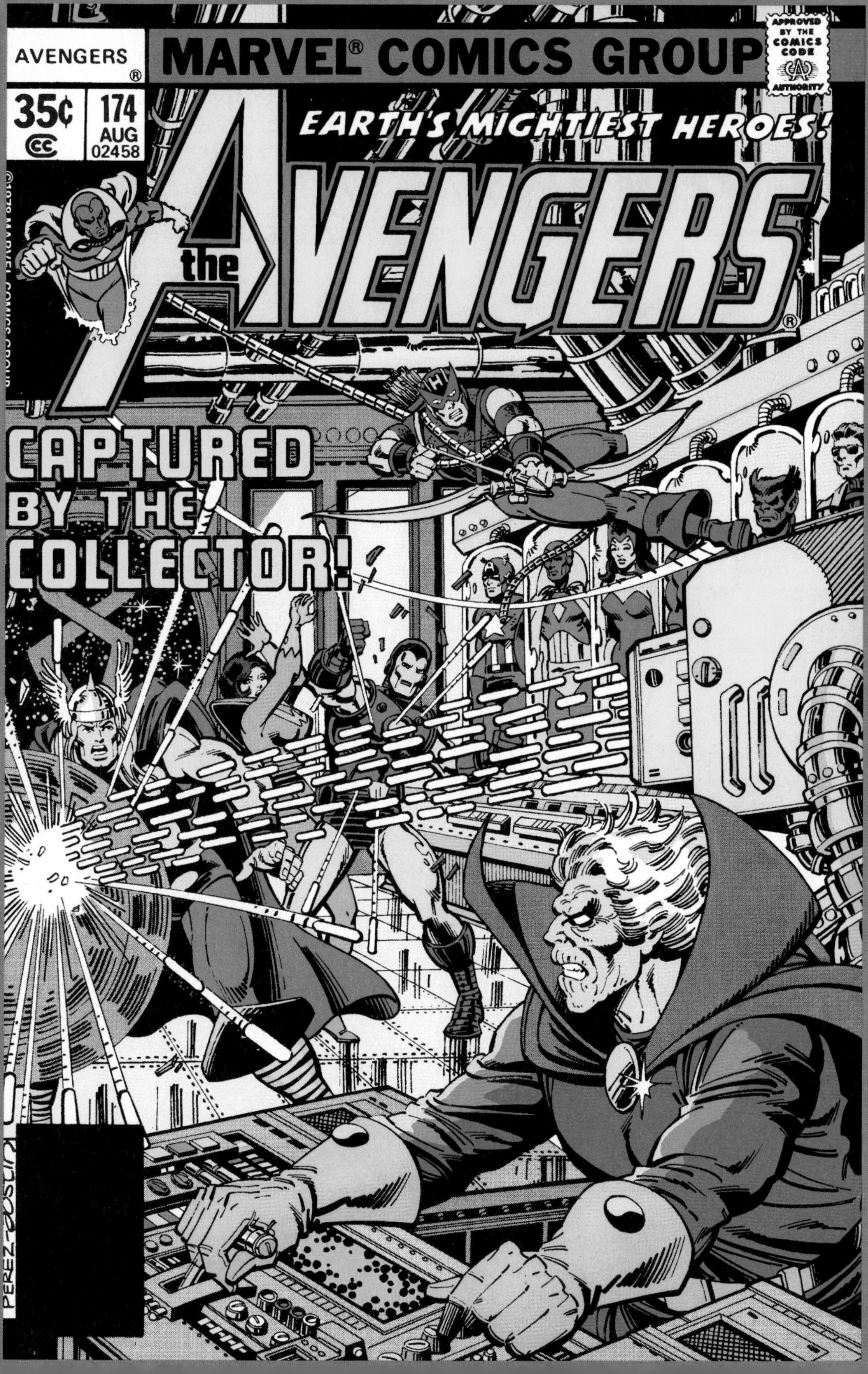
AVENGERS
MARVEL COMICS GROUP
APPROVED BY THE COMICS CODE AUTHORITY
35¢
174
AUG
02458
EARTH'S MIGHTIEST HEROES!
the AVENGERS
CAPTURED BY THE COLLECTOR!

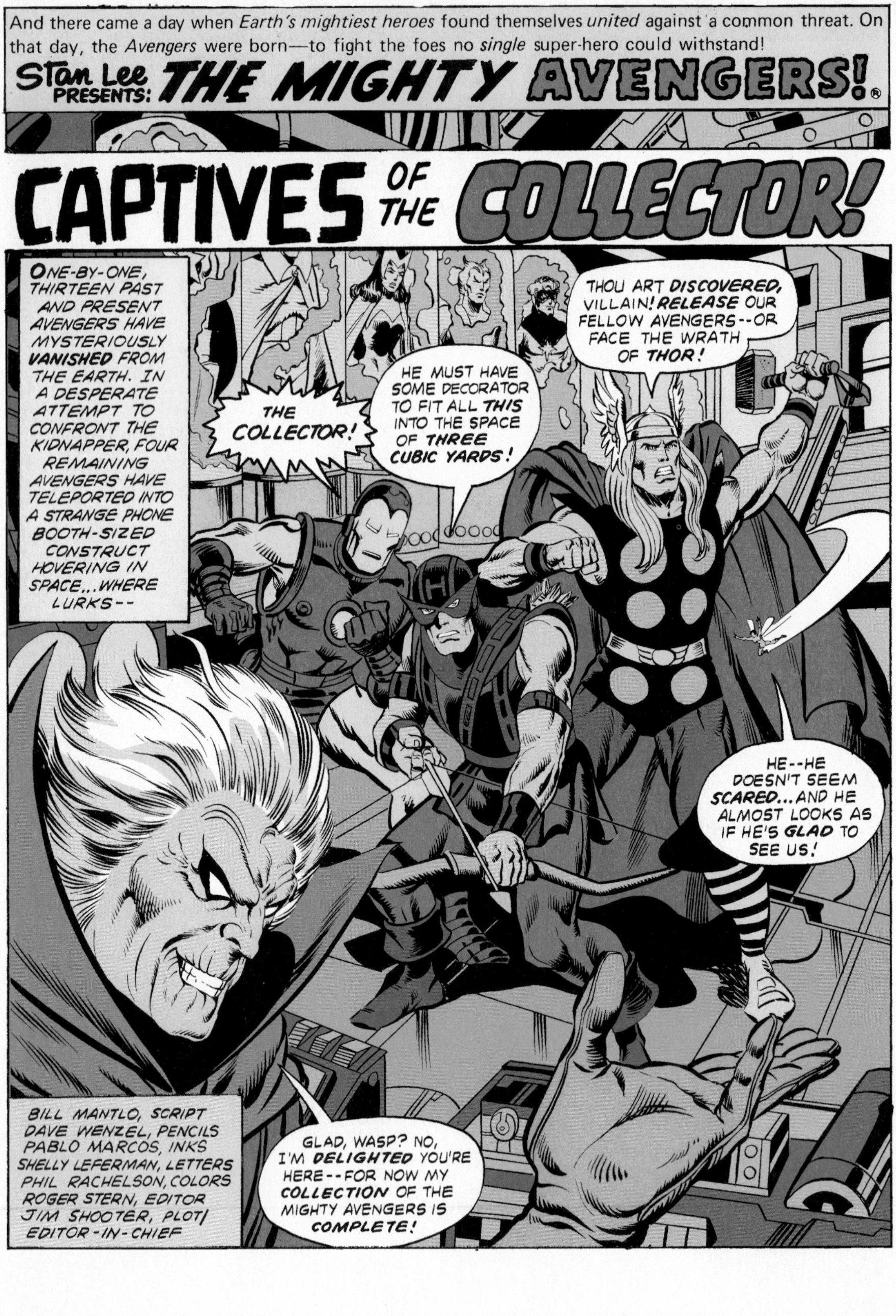
And there came a day when *Earth's mightiest heroes* found themselves *united* against a common threat. On that day, the *Avengers* were born—to fight the foes no *single* super-hero could withstand!
Stan Lee PRESENTS: THE MIGHTY AVENGERS!®
CAPTIVES OF THE COLLECTOR!
ONE-BY-ONE, THIRTEEN PAST AND PRESENT AVENGERS HAVE MYSTERIOUSLY **VANISHED** FROM THE EARTH. IN A DESPERATE ATTEMPT TO CONFRONT THE KIDNAPPER, FOUR REMAINING AVENGERS HAVE TELEPORTED INTO A STRANGE PHONE BOOTH-SIZED CONSTRUCT HOVERING IN SPACE... WHERE LURKS--
THE COLLECTOR!
HE MUST HAVE SOME DECORATOR TO FIT ALL **THIS** INTO THE SPACE OF **THREE CUBIC YARDS**!
THOU ART **DISCOVERED**, VILLAIN! **RELEASE** OUR FELLOW AVENGERS--OR FACE THE WRATH OF **THOR**!
HE--HE DOESN'T SEEM **SCARED**... AND HE ALMOST LOOKS AS IF HE'S **GLAD** TO SEE US!
BILL MANTLO, SCRIPT
DAVE WENZEL, PENCILS
PABLO MARCOS, INKS
SHELLY LEFERMAN, LETTERS
PHIL RACHELSON, COLORS
ROGER STERN, EDITOR
JIM SHOOTER, PLOT/ EDITOR-IN-CHIEF
GLAD, WASP? NO, I'M **DELIGHTED** YOU'RE HERE--FOR NOW MY **COLLECTION** OF THE MIGHTY AVENGERS IS **COMPLETE**!

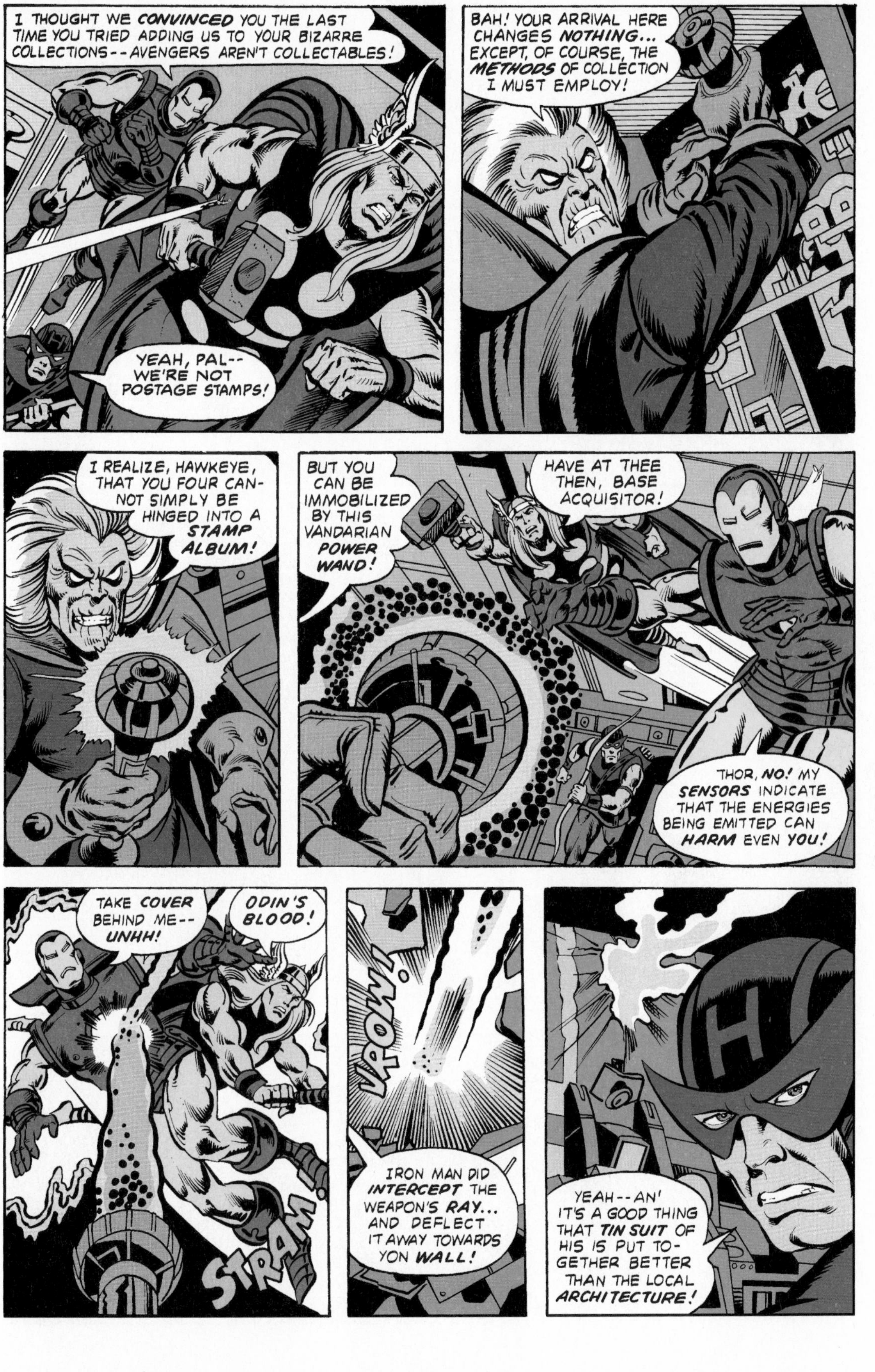
I THOUGHT WE CONVINCED YOU THE LAST TIME YOU TRIED ADDING US TO YOUR BIZARRE COLLECTIONS--AVENGERS AREN'T COLLECTABLES!
YEAH, PAL--WE'RE NOT POSTAGE STAMPS!
BAH! YOUR ARRIVAL HERE CHANGES NOTHING... EXCEPT, OF COURSE, THE METHODS OF COLLECTION I MUST EMPLOY!
I REALIZE, HAWKEYE, THAT YOU FOUR CAN-NOT SIMPLY BE HINGED INTO A STAMP ALBUM!
BUT YOU CAN BE IMMOBILIZED BY THIS VANDARIAN POWER WAND!
HAVE AT THEE THEN, BASE ACQUISITOR!
THOR, NO! MY SENSORS INDICATE THAT THE ENERGIES BEING EMITTED CAN HARM EVEN YOU!
TAKE COVER BEHIND ME--UNHH!
ODIN'S BLOOD!
STRAM
VROOM!
IRON MAN DID INTERCEPT THE WEAPON'S RAY... AND DEFLECT IT AWAY TOWARDS YON WALL!
YEAH--AN' IT'S A GOOD THING THAT TIN SUIT OF HIS IS PUT TO-GETHER BETTER THAN THE LOCAL ARCHITECTURE!

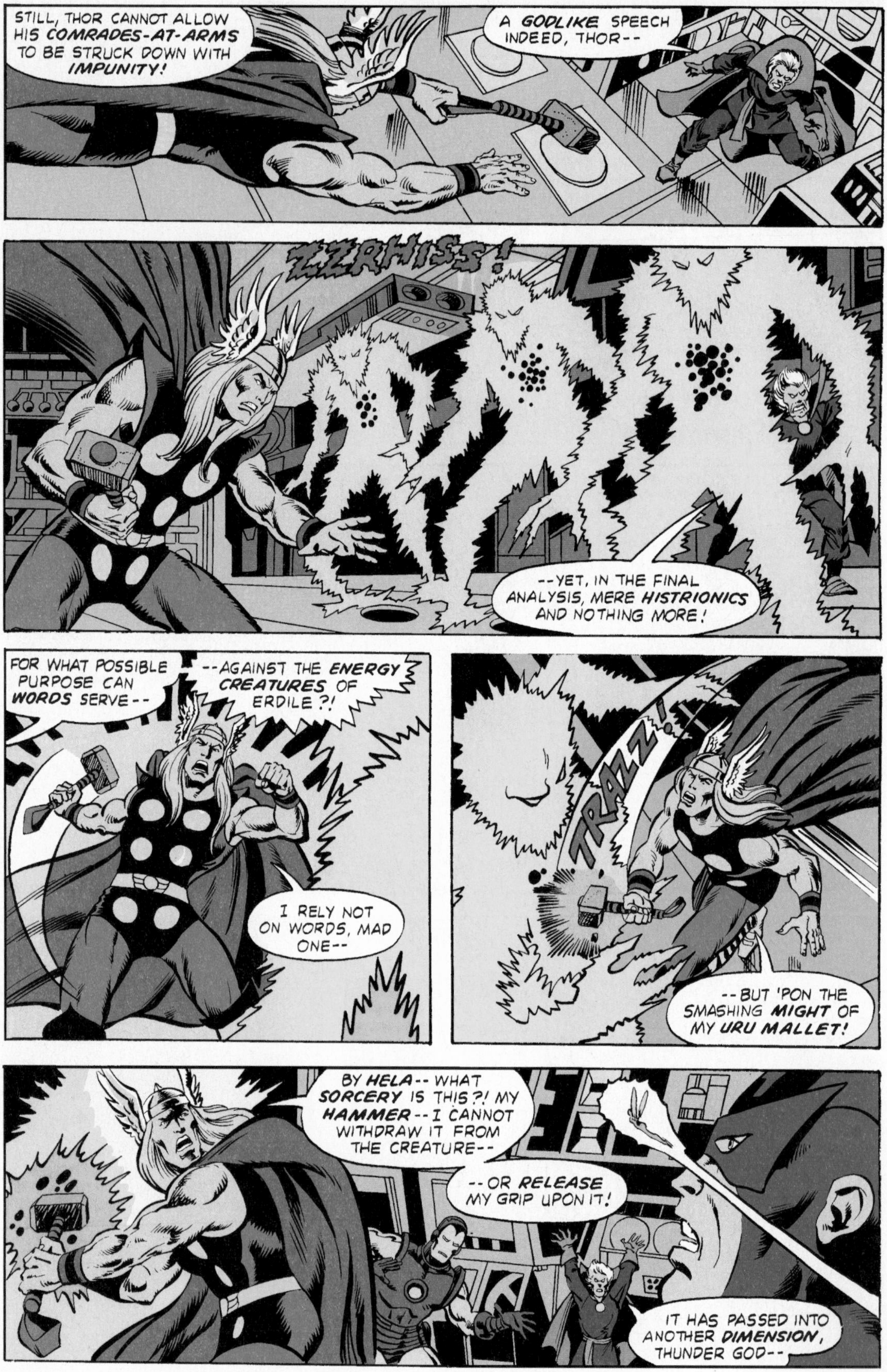
STILL, THOR CANNOT ALLOW HIS COMRADES-AT-ARMS TO BE STRUCK DOWN WITH IMPUNITY!
A GODLIKE SPEECH INDEED, THOR--
ZZRHISS!
--YET, IN THE FINAL ANALYSIS, MERE HISTRIONICS AND NOTHING MORE!
FOR WHAT POSSIBLE PURPOSE CAN WORDS SERVE--
--AGAINST THE ENERGY CREATURES OF ERDILE?!
I RELY NOT ON WORDS, MAD ONE--
TRAZZ!
--BUT 'PON THE SMASHING MIGHT OF MY URU MALLET!
BY HELA-- WHAT SORCERY IS THIS?! MY HAMMER--I CANNOT WITHDRAW IT FROM THE CREATURE--
--OR RELEASE MY GRIP UPON IT!
IT HAS PASSED INTO ANOTHER DIMENSION, THUNDER GOD--

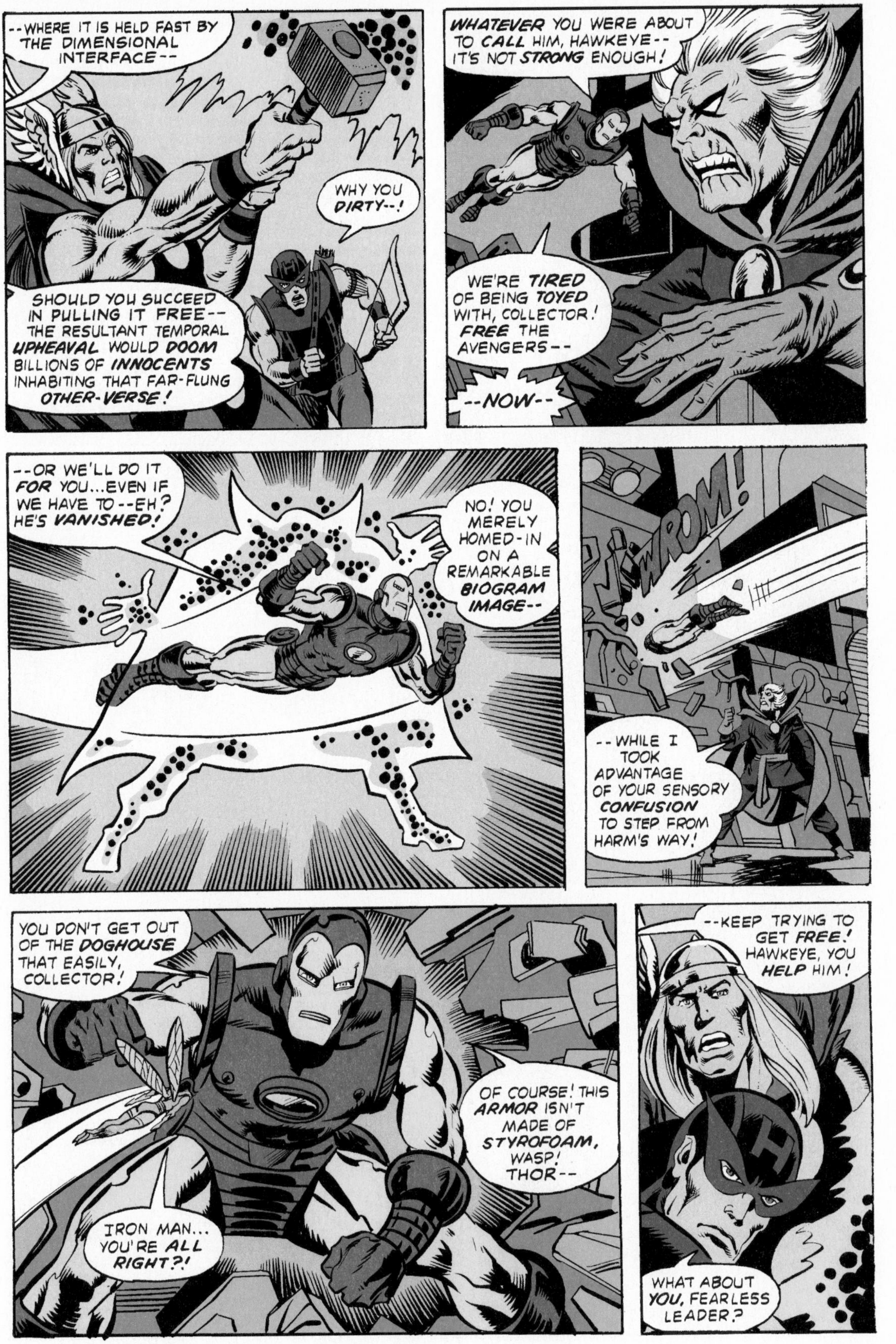
--WHERE IT IS HELD FAST BY THE DIMENSIONAL INTERFACE--
WHY YOU DIRTY--!
SHOULD YOU SUCCEED IN PULLING IT FREE-- THE RESULTANT TEMPORAL UPHEAVAL WOULD DOOM BILLIONS OF INNOCENTS INHABITING THAT FAR-FLUNG OTHER-VERSE!
WHATEVER YOU WERE ABOUT TO CALL HIM, HAWKEYE-- IT'S NOT STRONG ENOUGH!
WE'RE TIRED OF BEING TOYED WITH, COLLECTOR! FREE THE AVENGERS--
--NOW--
--OR WE'LL DO IT FOR YOU...EVEN IF WE HAVE TO--EH? HE'S VANISHED!
NO! YOU MERELY HOMED-IN ON A REMARKABLE BIOGRAM IMAGE--
WROM!
--WHILE I TOOK ADVANTAGE OF YOUR SENSORY CONFUSION TO STEP FROM HARM'S WAY!
YOU DON'T GET OUT OF THE DOGHOUSE THAT EASILY, COLLECTOR!
IRON MAN... YOU'RE ALL RIGHT?!
OF COURSE! THIS ARMOR ISN'T MADE OF STYROFOAM, WASP! THOR--
--KEEP TRYING TO GET FREE! HAWKEYE, YOU HELP HIM!
WHAT ABOUT YOU, FEARLESS LEADER?

I'M GOING TO TAKE ON OUR *ADDLED* HOST!

I'LL *CIRCLE* AND TRY TO *CONFUSE* HIM!

WELL, OKAY... BUT I DON'T *LIKE* IT!

THOR-- WHAT IF HE'S *LYING* ABOUT THOSE *BILLION* INNOCENT *WHATEVERS*?

DARE WE TAKE THE *CHANCE*, FRIEND ARCHER?

I ... GUESS *NOT*!

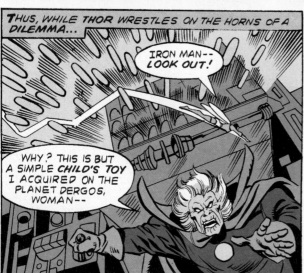

THUS, WHILE THOR WRESTLES ON THE HORNS OF A DILEMMA...

IRON MAN-- *LOOK OUT!*

WHY? THIS IS BUT A SIMPLE *CHILD'S TOY* I ACQUIRED ON THE PLANET DERGOS, WOMAN--

WASP! MANEUVER TO COVER! *I'LL* HANDLE THESE *MISSILES!*

--WHERE, ADMITTEDLY, THE *CHILDREN* MOVE *FASTER* THAN THOUGHT *ITSELF!*

PING PING PING!

PING PING!

EH? THEY'RE BURSTING *OPEN* ON CONTACT WITH MY ARMOR!

EMITTING SOME KIND OF *GAS!*

NO *PROBLEM* THERE! MY ARMOR'S AUTOMATICALLY *SEALED* ITSELF OFF!

PRECISELY WHAT I'D *ANTICIPATED* YOU'D DO, IRON MAN-- FOR THE GAS WAS *NOT* POISONOUS! ITS PURPOSE WAS TO *FREEZE* YOUR METAL JOINTS--

--THUS RENDERING YOU A *PRISONER* WITHIN YOUR OWN *ARMOR!*

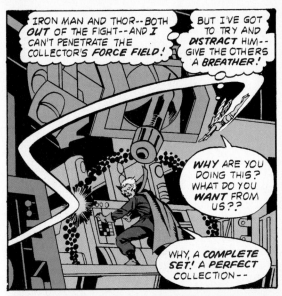

IRON MAN AND THOR--BOTH *OUT* OF THE FIGHT--AND *I* CAN'T PENETRATE THE COLLECTOR'S *FORCE FIELD!*

BUT I'VE GOT TO TRY AND *DISTRACT* HIM-- GIVE THE OTHERS A *BREATHER!*

WHY ARE YOU DOING THIS? WHAT DO YOU *WANT* FROM US??

WHY, A *COMPLETE SET!* A *PERFECT* COLLECTION--

--OF EARTH'S *MIGHTIEST HEROES!* THE *ONLY* SUCH COLLECTION OF ITS KIND--

--THAT WILL SURVIVE THE *TIME SOON TO COME!*

CRIPES! HE'S *FLAKEY*--TALKING IN *RIDDLES!*

RIDDLES? PERHAPS... BUT WHAT MATTER? IT IS NOT NECESSARY THAT YOU UNDERSTAND--ONLY THAT YOU *FALL*--TO MY *POSITRON CANNON!*

ZZRAM!

U-UNGHH!

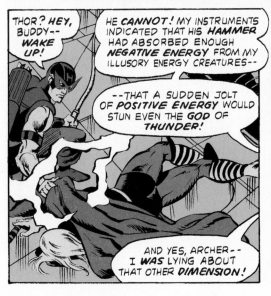

THOR? HEY, BUDDY-- *WAKE UP!*

HE *CANNOT!* MY INSTRUMENTS INDICATED THAT HIS *HAMMER* HAD ABSORBED ENOUGH *NEGATIVE ENERGY* FROM MY *ILLUSORY ENERGY CREATURES*--

--THAT A SUDDEN JOLT OF *POSITIVE ENERGY* WOULD STUN EVEN THE *GOD OF THUNDER!*

AND YES, ARCHER-- I *WAS* LYING ABOUT THAT OTHER *DIMENSION!*

WHY, YOU DESPICABLE OLD *FOSSIL!*

YOU MAY HAVE US *ALL* IN THE END--

--BUT, BEFORE WE'RE *DONE,* YOU'LL KNOW YOU'VE FOUGHT--

AVENGERS!

HEY... JAN??!

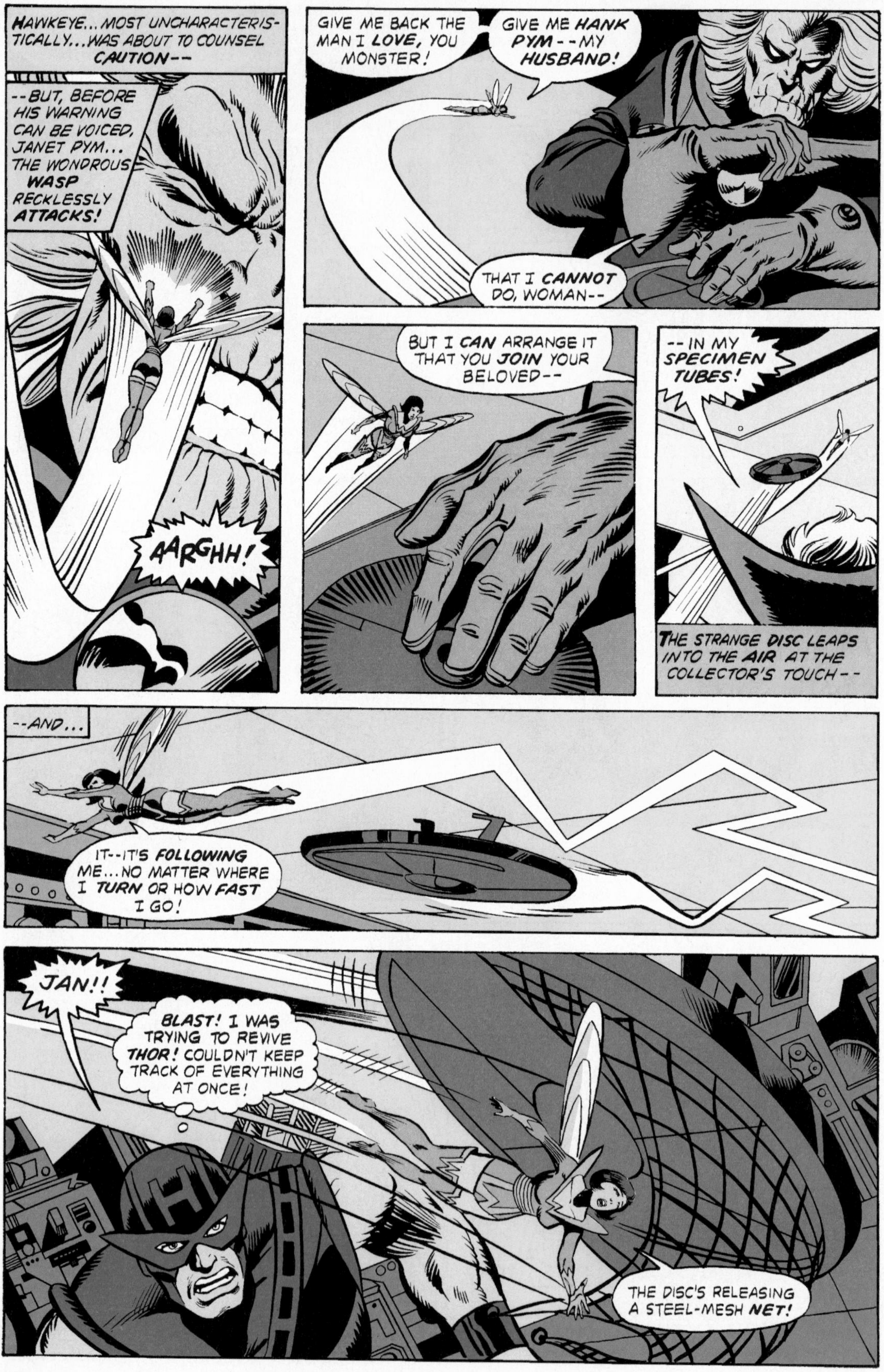
HAWKEYE... MOST UNCHARACTERISTICALLY... WAS ABOUT TO COUNSEL CAUTION--
--BUT, BEFORE HIS WARNING CAN BE VOICED, JANET PYM... THE WONDROUS WASP RECKLESSLY ATTACKS!
AARGHH!
GIVE ME BACK THE MAN I LOVE, YOU MONSTER!
GIVE ME HANK PYM--MY HUSBAND!
THAT I CANNOT DO, WOMAN--
BUT I CAN ARRANGE IT THAT YOU JOIN YOUR BELOVED--
--IN MY SPECIMEN TUBES!
THE STRANGE DISC LEAPS INTO THE AIR AT THE COLLECTOR'S TOUCH--
--AND...
IT--IT'S FOLLOWING ME... NO MATTER WHERE I TURN OR HOW FAST I GO!
JAN!!
BLAST! I WAS TRYING TO REVIVE THOR! COULDN'T KEEP TRACK OF EVERYTHING AT ONCE!
THE DISC'S RELEASING A STEEL-MESH NET!

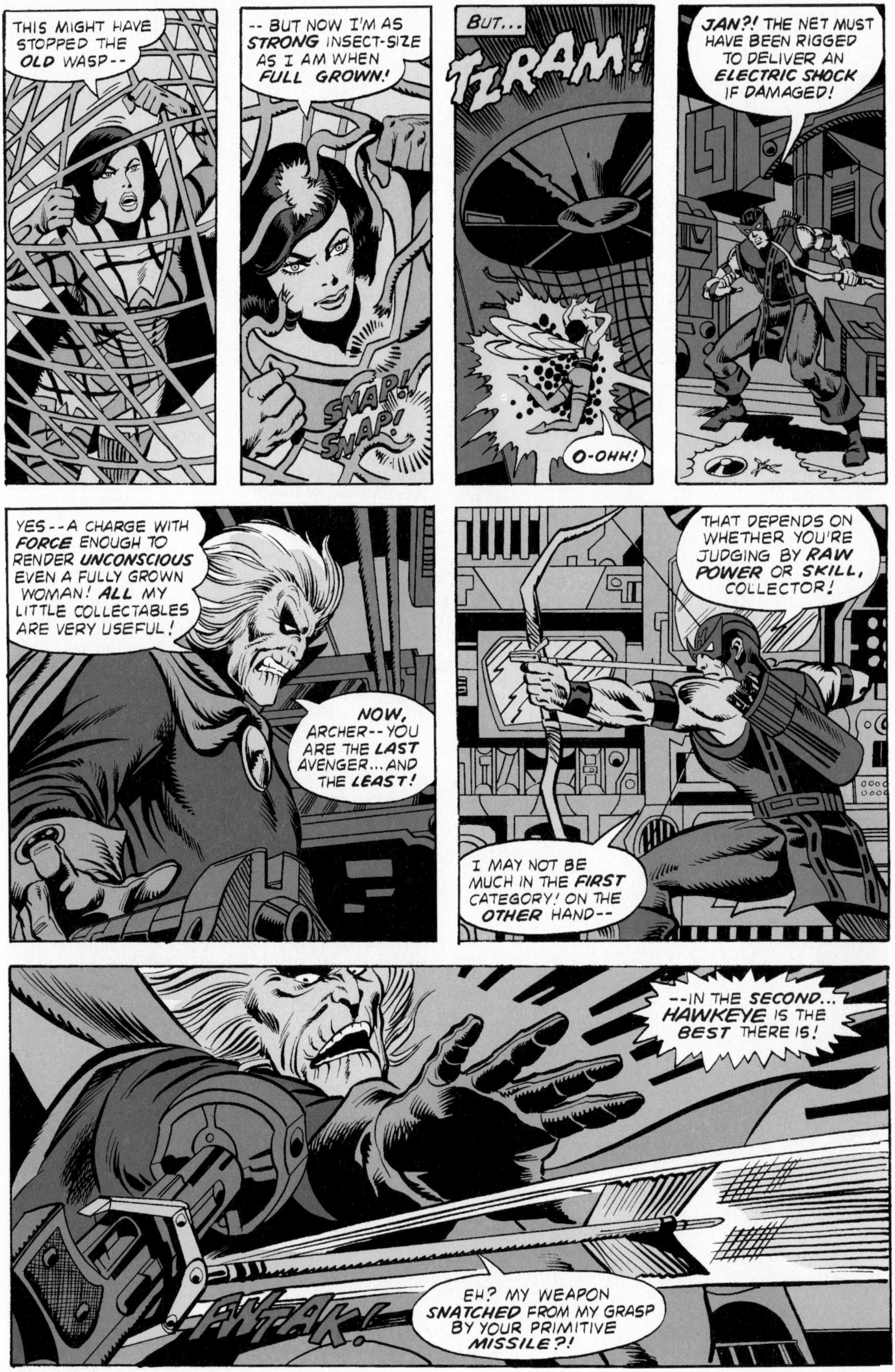
THIS MIGHT HAVE STOPPED THE OLD WASP--
-- BUT NOW I'M AS STRONG INSECT-SIZE AS I AM WHEN FULL GROWN!
SNAP! SNAP!
BUT...
TZRAM!
O-OHH!
JAN?! THE NET MUST HAVE BEEN RIGGED TO DELIVER AN ELECTRIC SHOCK IF DAMAGED!
YES--A CHARGE WITH FORCE ENOUGH TO RENDER UNCONSCIOUS EVEN A FULLY GROWN WOMAN! ALL MY LITTLE COLLECTABLES ARE VERY USEFUL!
NOW, ARCHER--YOU ARE THE LAST AVENGER...AND THE LEAST!
THAT DEPENDS ON WHETHER YOU'RE JUDGING BY RAW POWER OR SKILL, COLLECTOR!
I MAY NOT BE MUCH IN THE FIRST CATEGORY! ON THE OTHER HAND--
--IN THE SECOND... HAWKEYE IS THE BEST THERE IS!
FWAK!
EH? MY WEAPON SNATCHED FROM MY GRASP BY YOUR PRIMITIVE MISSILE?!

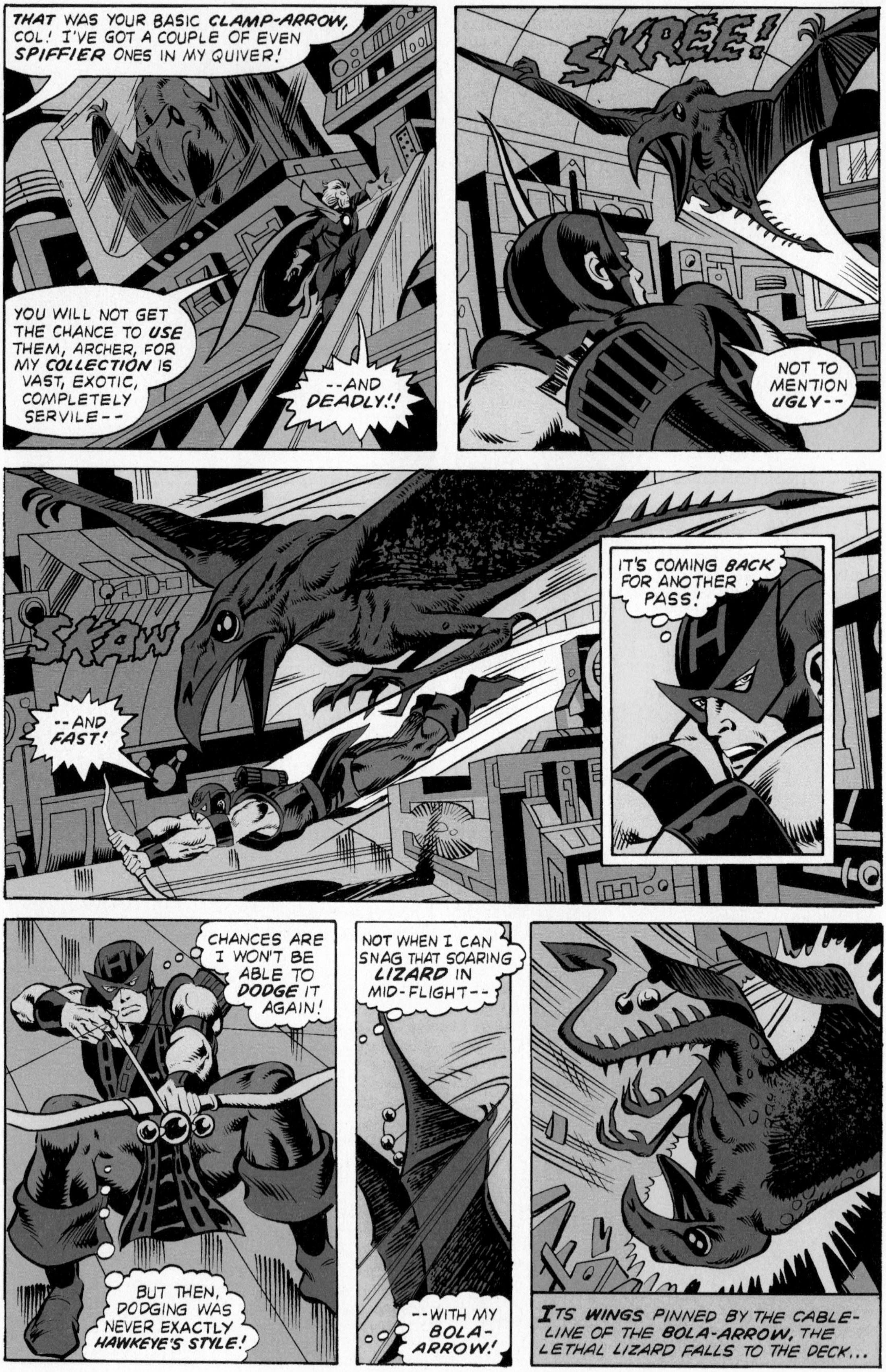
THAT WAS YOUR BASIC CLAMP-ARROW, COL! I'VE GOT A COUPLE OF EVEN SPIFFIER ONES IN MY QUIVER!
YOU WILL NOT GET THE CHANCE TO USE THEM, ARCHER, FOR MY COLLECTION IS VAST, EXOTIC, COMPLETELY SERVILE--
--AND DEADLY!!
SKREE!
NOT TO MENTION UGLY--
SKAW
--AND FAST!
IT'S COMING BACK FOR ANOTHER PASS!
CHANCES ARE I WON'T BE ABLE TO DODGE IT AGAIN!
BUT THEN, DODGING WAS NEVER EXACTLY HAWKEYE'S STYLE!
NOT WHEN I CAN SNAG THAT SOARING LIZARD IN MID-FLIGHT--
--WITH MY BOLA-ARROW!
ITS WINGS PINNED BY THE CABLE-LINE OF THE BOLA-ARROW, THE LETHAL LIZARD FALLS TO THE DECK...

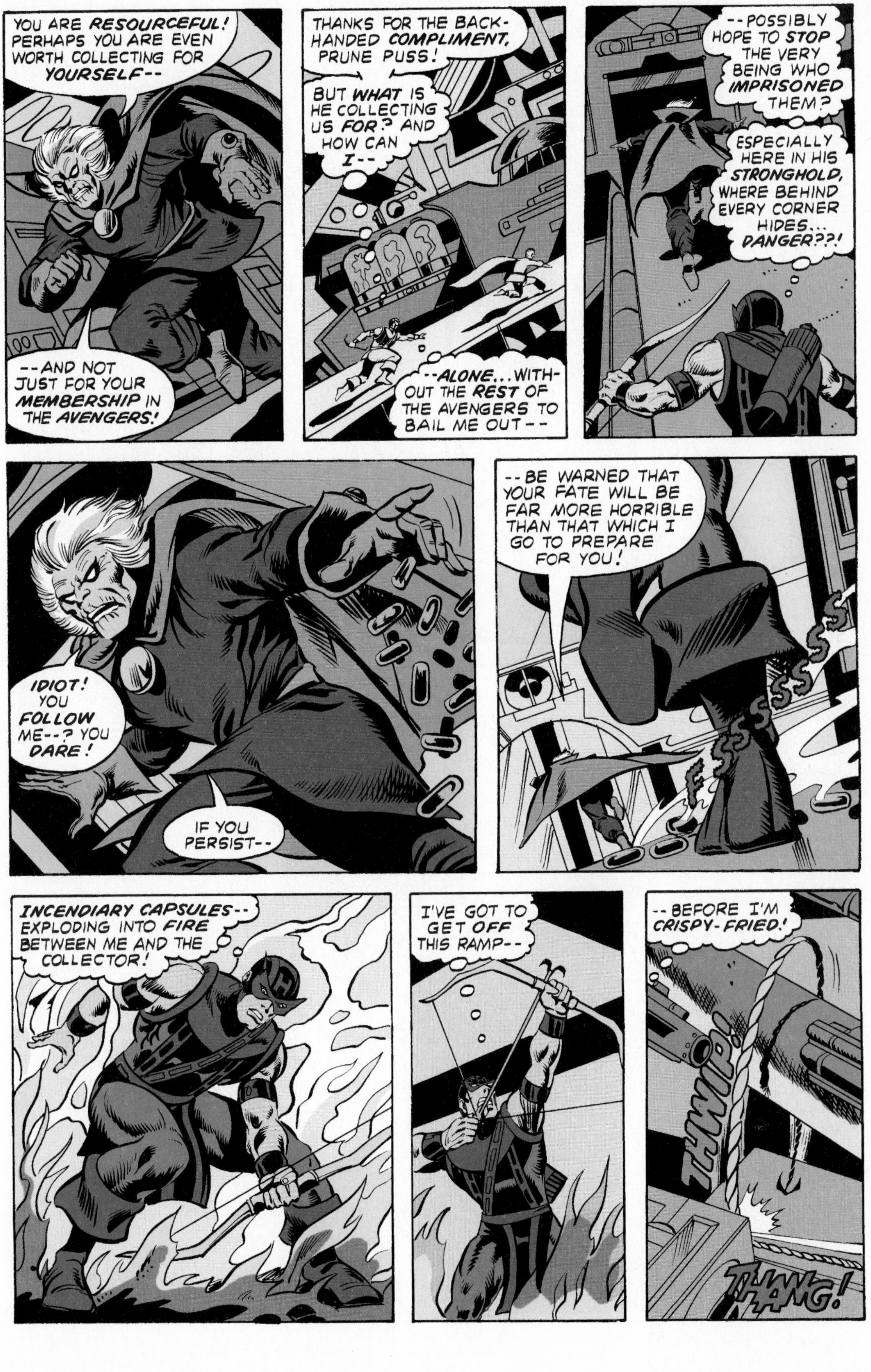
YOU ARE RESOURCEFUL! PERHAPS YOU ARE EVEN WORTH COLLECTING FOR YOURSELF--
--AND NOT JUST FOR YOUR MEMBERSHIP IN THE AVENGERS!
THANKS FOR THE BACK-HANDED COMPLIMENT, PRUNE PUSS!
BUT WHAT IS HE COLLECTING US FOR? AND HOW CAN I--
--ALONE...WITH-OUT THE REST OF THE AVENGERS TO BAIL ME OUT--
--POSSIBLY HOPE TO STOP THE VERY BEING WHO IMPRISONED THEM?
ESPECIALLY HERE IN HIS STRONGHOLD, WHERE BEHIND EVERY CORNER HIDES... DANGER??!
IDIOT! YOU FOLLOW ME--? YOU DARE!
IF YOU PERSIST--
--BE WARNED THAT YOUR FATE WILL BE FAR MORE HORRIBLE THAN THAT WHICH I GO TO PREPARE FOR YOU!
SSSSSS
INCENDIARY CAPSULES-- EXPLODING INTO FIRE BETWEEN ME AND THE COLLECTOR!
I'VE GOT TO GET OFF THIS RAMP--
--BEFORE I'M CRISPY-FRIED!
THWIP!
THANG!

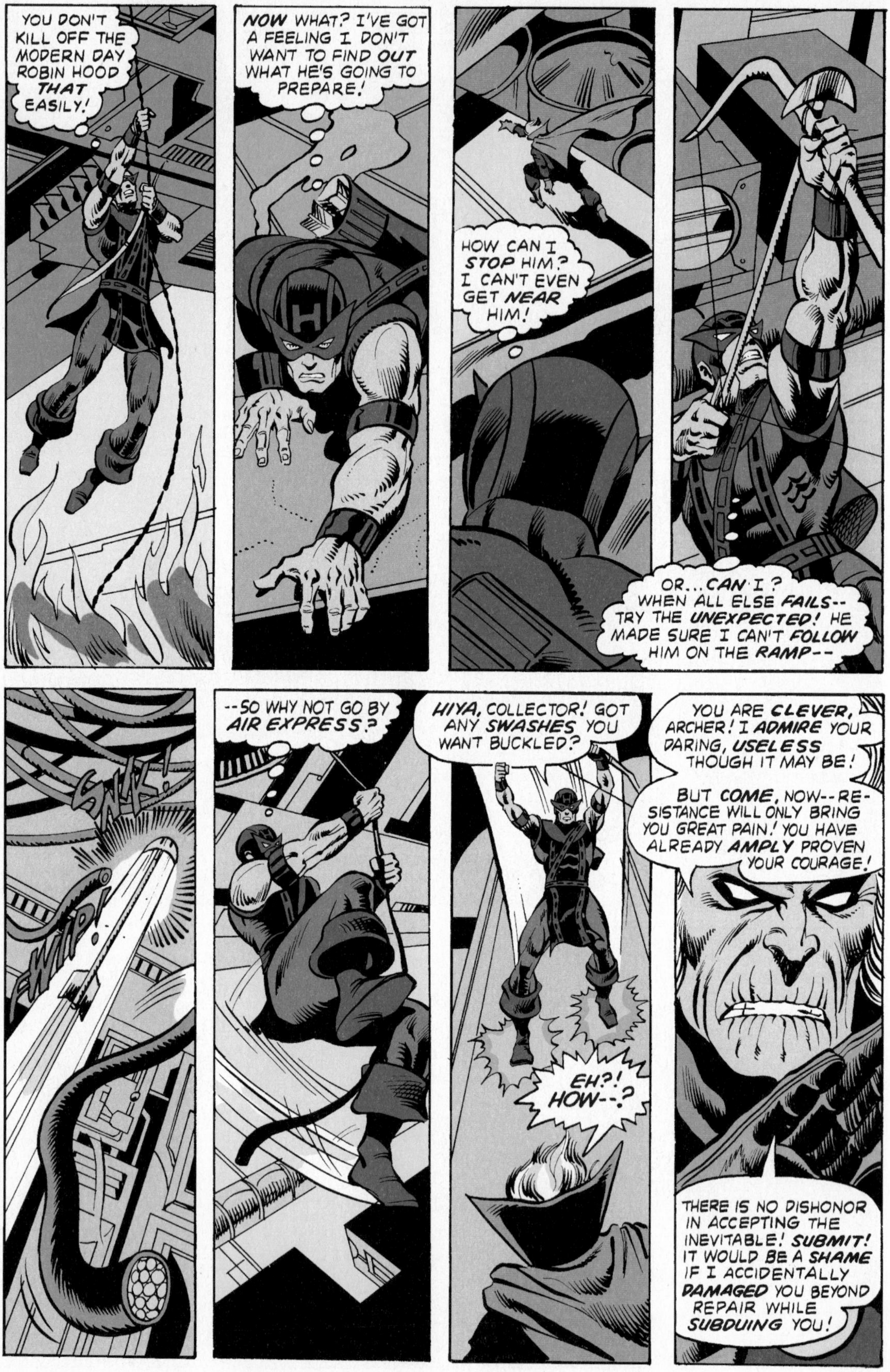
YOU DON'T KILL OFF THE MODERN DAY ROBIN HOOD THAT EASILY!
NOW WHAT? I'VE GOT A FEELING I DON'T WANT TO FIND OUT WHAT HE'S GOING TO PREPARE!
HOW CAN I STOP HIM? I CAN'T EVEN GET NEAR HIM!
OR...CAN I? WHEN ALL ELSE FAILS-- TRY THE UNEXPECTED! HE MADE SURE I CAN'T FOLLOW HIM ON THE RAMP--
SNK!
WHIP!
--SO WHY NOT GO BY AIR EXPRESS?
HIYA, COLLECTOR! GOT ANY SWASHES YOU WANT BUCKLED?
EH?! HOW--?
YOU ARE CLEVER, ARCHER! I ADMIRE YOUR DARING, USELESS THOUGH IT MAY BE!
BUT COME, NOW--RESISTANCE WILL ONLY BRING YOU GREAT PAIN! YOU HAVE ALREADY AMPLY PROVEN YOUR COURAGE!
THERE IS NO DISHONOR IN ACCEPTING THE INEVITABLE! SUBMIT! IT WOULD BE A SHAME IF I ACCIDENTALLY DAMAGED YOU BEYOND REPAIR WHILE SUBDUING YOU!

SORRY, PAL, I DON'T *BUY* IT! I FIGURE OUR SURPRISE ENTRANCE CAUGHT YOU MORE OFF-GUARD THAN YOU'LL ADMIT!

YOU *LUCKED OUT* AGAINST THE OTHERS, WITH GADGETS YOU HAD LYING AROUND...

...BUT IF YOU HAD ANYTHING TO THROW AT ME NOW, YOU WOULDN'T BE STANDING THERE FLAPPING YOUR LIPS!

BAH! ONE *NEEDS* NO GADGETRY--

--WHO COMMANDS *POWER COSMIC!*

I AM OLD BEYOND YOUR *KEN*, INSECT-- AND IT HAS BEEN *EONS* SINCE I WIELDED THE ENERGIES I POSSESS!

IT IS A *CHORE* AT MY AGE! I *RESENT* BEING FORCED INTO THIS!

HUH? HOW--?

YOU WOULD NOT SUFFER TO BE BOTHERED BY A *MOSQUITO!* YOU WOULD CARELESSLY DESTROY ANY IRRITATING LOWER LIFE-FORM--EVEN A SOME-WHAT INTERESTING SPECIMEN!

CAGED--! THE DECK ITSELF JUST WRAPPED AROUND ME AT HIS WHIM! IT'S GONNA *CRUSH* ME!

¿UHH¿ WHAT AN *IDIOT* I AM! WHY DIDN'T I TRY TO FREE THE *OTHERS?* WHY DID I TRY TO TAKE HIM *ALONE?* NOW WE'VE *ALL* HAD IT!

WHY DID *I* HAVE TO BE... THE *LAST?*

¿ARRHH¿ T-TIME... TO FIRE OFF... A *HOPE!* PLEASE...!

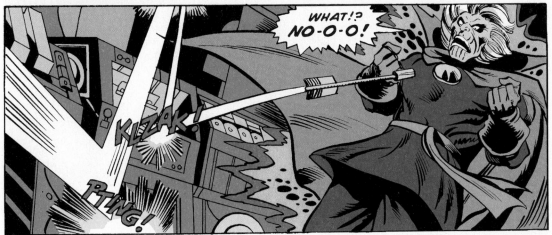

WHAT!? NO-O-O!

KIZZAK

PTING!

161

ARRGH!

THAK!

IMPACT! THE COLLECTOR STAGGERS--

--AND COLLAPSES IN *PAIN* AS THE *SOPHISTICATED* WARHEAD RELEASES A *STUNNING ELECTRICAL CHARGE!*

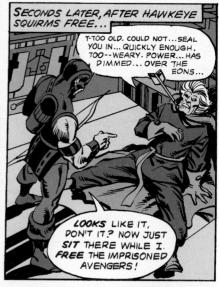

SECONDS LATER, AFTER HAWKEYE SQUIRMS FREE...

T-TOO OLD. COULD NOT...SEAL YOU IN... QUICKLY ENOUGH. TOO--WEARY. POWER... HAS DIMMED...OVER THE EONS...

LOOKS LIKE IT, DON'T IT? NOW JUST *SIT* THERE WHILE I. *FREE* THE IMPRISONED *AVENGERS!*

"--AND REVIVE THOSE YOU *KAYOED!*"

SPLASH!

BY *ASGARD!* WHAT--?!

SORRY FOR THE *UNDIGNIFIED* AWAKENING, THOR--

--BUT EVERYONE *ELSE* WAS UP AND *WAITING!*

AND THE *COLLECTOR* HAS GOT A LOT OF *EXPLAINING* TO DO!

I--? EXPLAIN TO SUCH AS *YOU?* ABSURD!

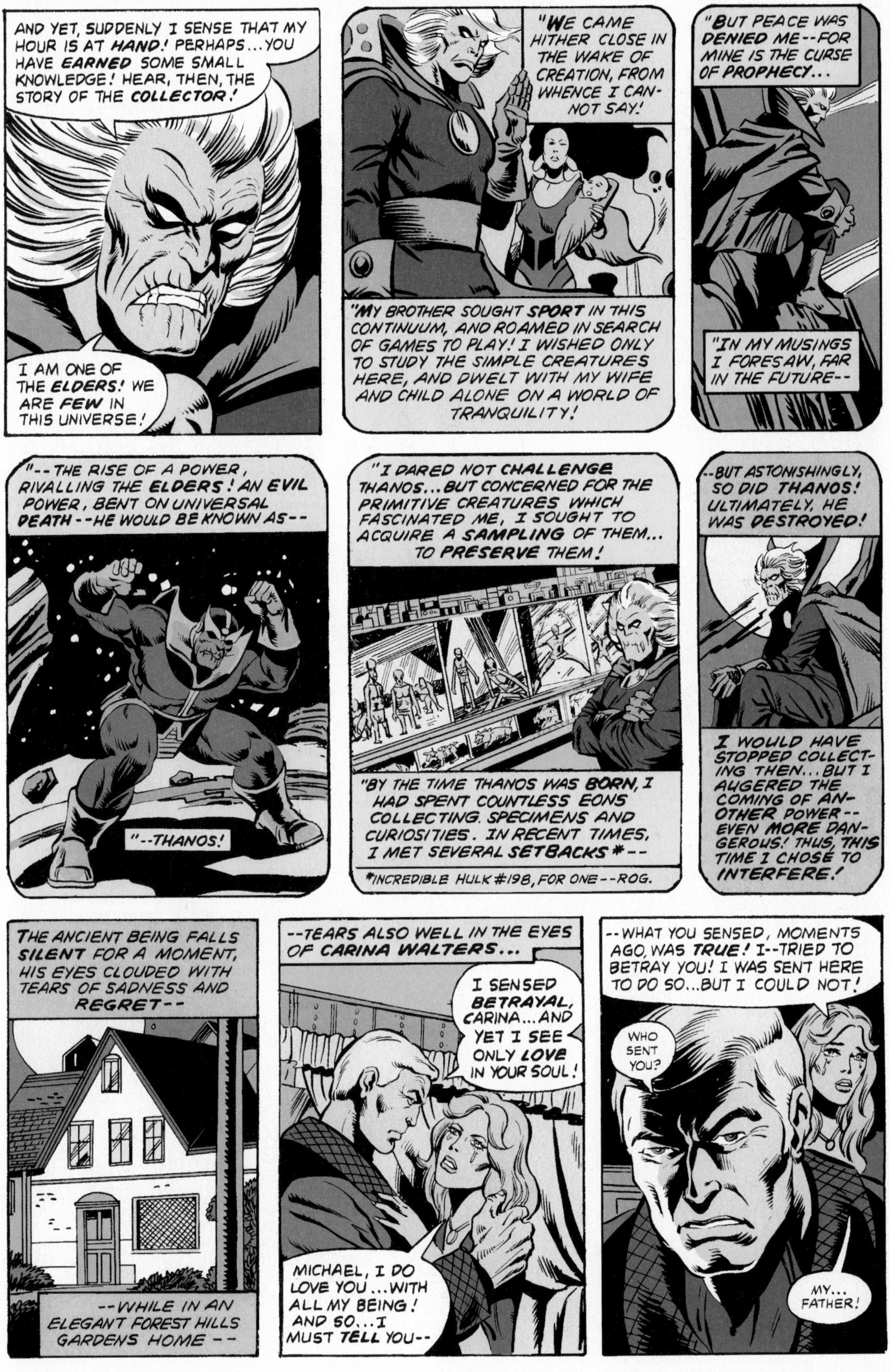
AND YET, SUDDENLY I SENSE THAT MY HOUR IS AT HAND! PERHAPS... YOU HAVE EARNED SOME SMALL KNOWLEDGE! HEAR, THEN, THE STORY OF THE COLLECTOR!
I AM ONE OF THE ELDERS! WE ARE FEW IN THIS UNIVERSE!
"WE CAME HITHER CLOSE IN THE WAKE OF CREATION, FROM WHENCE I CAN-NOT SAY!
"MY BROTHER SOUGHT SPORT IN THIS CONTINUUM, AND ROAMED IN SEARCH OF GAMES TO PLAY! I WISHED ONLY TO STUDY THE SIMPLE CREATURES HERE, AND DWELT WITH MY WIFE AND CHILD ALONE ON A WORLD OF TRANQUILITY!
"BUT PEACE WAS DENIED ME--FOR MINE IS THE CURSE OF PROPHECY...
"IN MY MUSINGS I FORESAW, FAR IN THE FUTURE--
"--THE RISE OF A POWER, RIVALLING THE ELDERS! AN EVIL POWER, BENT ON UNIVERSAL DEATH--HE WOULD BE KNOWN AS--
"--THANOS!
"I DARED NOT CHALLENGE THANOS...BUT CONCERNED FOR THE PRIMITIVE CREATURES WHICH FASCINATED ME, I SOUGHT TO ACQUIRE A SAMPLING OF THEM... TO PRESERVE THEM!
"BY THE TIME THANOS WAS BORN, I HAD SPENT COUNTLESS EONS COLLECTING SPECIMENS AND CURIOSITIES. IN RECENT TIMES, I MET SEVERAL SETBACKS*--
*INCREDIBLE HULK #198, FOR ONE--ROG.
--BUT ASTONISHINGLY, SO DID THANOS! ULTIMATELY, HE WAS DESTROYED!
I WOULD HAVE STOPPED COLLECT-ING THEN...BUT I AUGERED THE COMING OF AN-OTHER POWER--EVEN MORE DAN-GEROUS! THUS, THIS TIME I CHOSE TO INTERFERE!
THE ANCIENT BEING FALLS SILENT FOR A MOMENT, HIS EYES CLOUDED WITH TEARS OF SADNESS AND REGRET--
--WHILE IN AN ELEGANT FOREST HILLS GARDENS HOME--
--TEARS ALSO WELL IN THE EYES OF CARINA WALTERS...
I SENSED BETRAYAL, CARINA...AND YET I SEE ONLY LOVE IN YOUR SOUL!
MICHAEL, I DO LOVE YOU...WITH ALL MY BEING! AND SO...I MUST TELL YOU--
--WHAT YOU SENSED, MOMENTS AGO, WAS TRUE! I--TRIED TO BETRAY YOU! I WAS SENT HERE TO DO SO...BUT I COULD NOT!
WHO SENT YOU?
MY... FATHER!

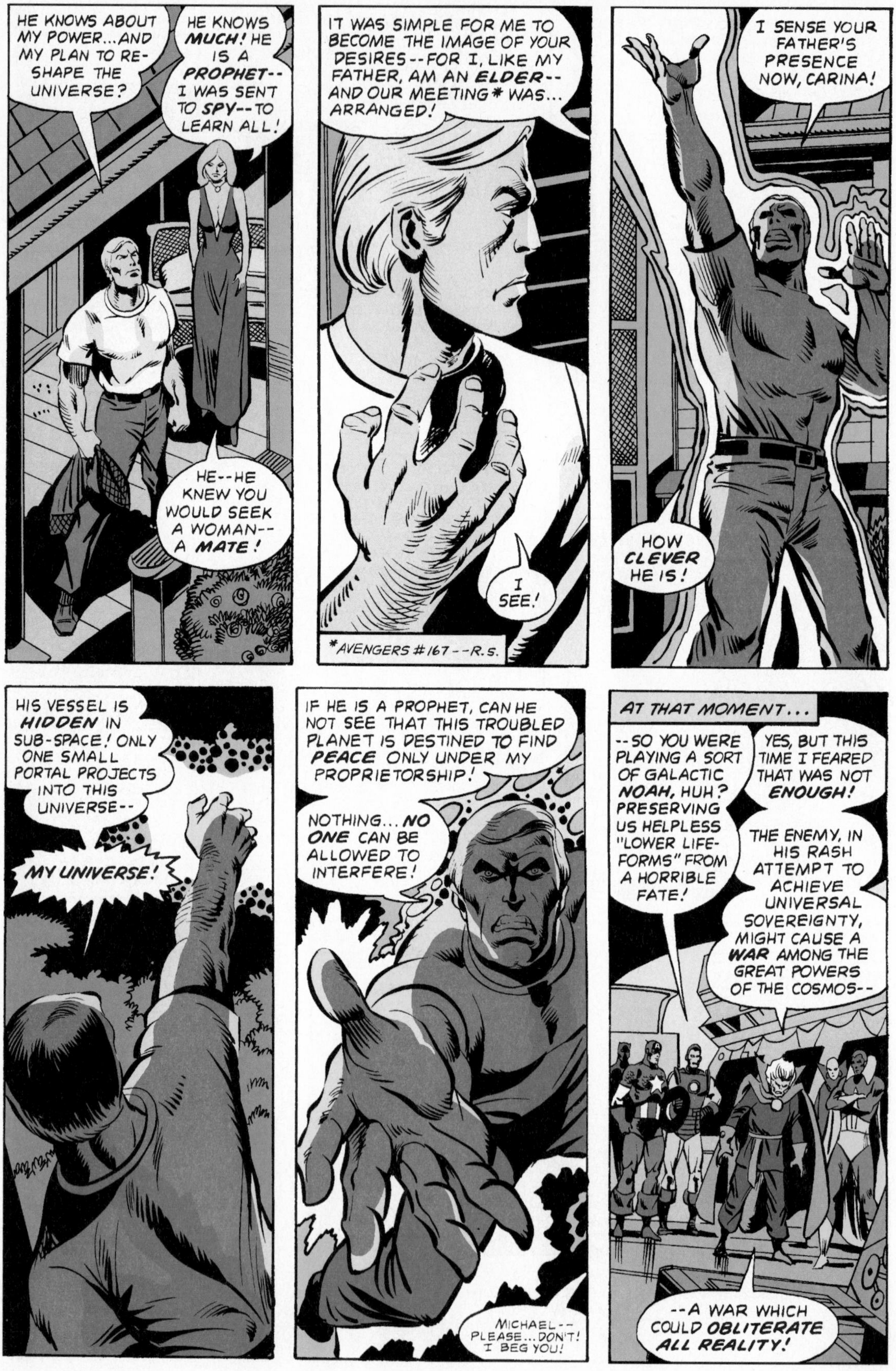
HE KNOWS ABOUT MY POWER...AND MY PLAN TO RE-SHAPE THE UNIVERSE?
HE KNOWS MUCH! HE IS A PROPHET-- I WAS SENT TO SPY--TO LEARN ALL!
HE--HE KNEW YOU WOULD SEEK A WOMAN-- A MATE!
IT WAS SIMPLE FOR ME TO BECOME THE IMAGE OF YOUR DESIRES--FOR I, LIKE MY FATHER, AM AN ELDER-- AND OUR MEETING* WAS... ARRANGED!
I SEE!
*AVENGERS #167--R.S.
I SENSE YOUR FATHER'S PRESENCE NOW, CARINA!
HOW CLEVER HE IS!
HIS VESSEL IS HIDDEN IN SUB-SPACE! ONLY ONE SMALL PORTAL PROJECTS INTO THIS UNIVERSE--
MY UNIVERSE!
IF HE IS A PROPHET, CAN HE NOT SEE THAT THIS TROUBLED PLANET IS DESTINED TO FIND PEACE ONLY UNDER MY PROPRIETORSHIP!
NOTHING... NO ONE CAN BE ALLOWED TO INTERFERE!
MICHAEL-- PLEASE...DON'T! I BEG YOU!
AT THAT MOMENT...
--SO YOU WERE PLAYING A SORT OF GALACTIC NOAH, HUH? PRESERVING US HELPLESS "LOWER LIFE-FORMS" FROM A HORRIBLE FATE!
YES, BUT THIS TIME I FEARED THAT WAS NOT ENOUGH!
THE ENEMY, IN HIS RASH ATTEMPT TO ACHIEVE UNIVERSAL SOVEREIGNTY, MIGHT CAUSE A WAR AMONG THE GREAT POWERS OF THE COSMOS--
--A WAR WHICH COULD OBLITERATE ALL REALITY!

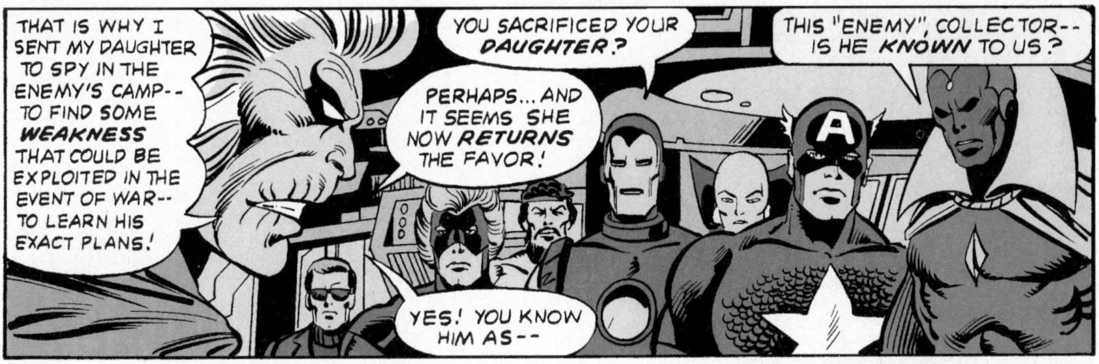
THAT IS WHY I SENT MY DAUGHTER TO SPY IN THE ENEMY'S CAMP-- TO FIND SOME WEAKNESS THAT COULD BE EXPLOITED IN THE EVENT OF WAR-- TO LEARN HIS EXACT PLANS!
YOU SACRIFICED YOUR DAUGHTER?
PERHAPS... AND IT SEEMS SHE NOW RETURNS THE FAVOR!
THIS "ENEMY", COLLECTOR-- IS HE KNOWN TO US?
YES! YOU KNOW HIM AS--

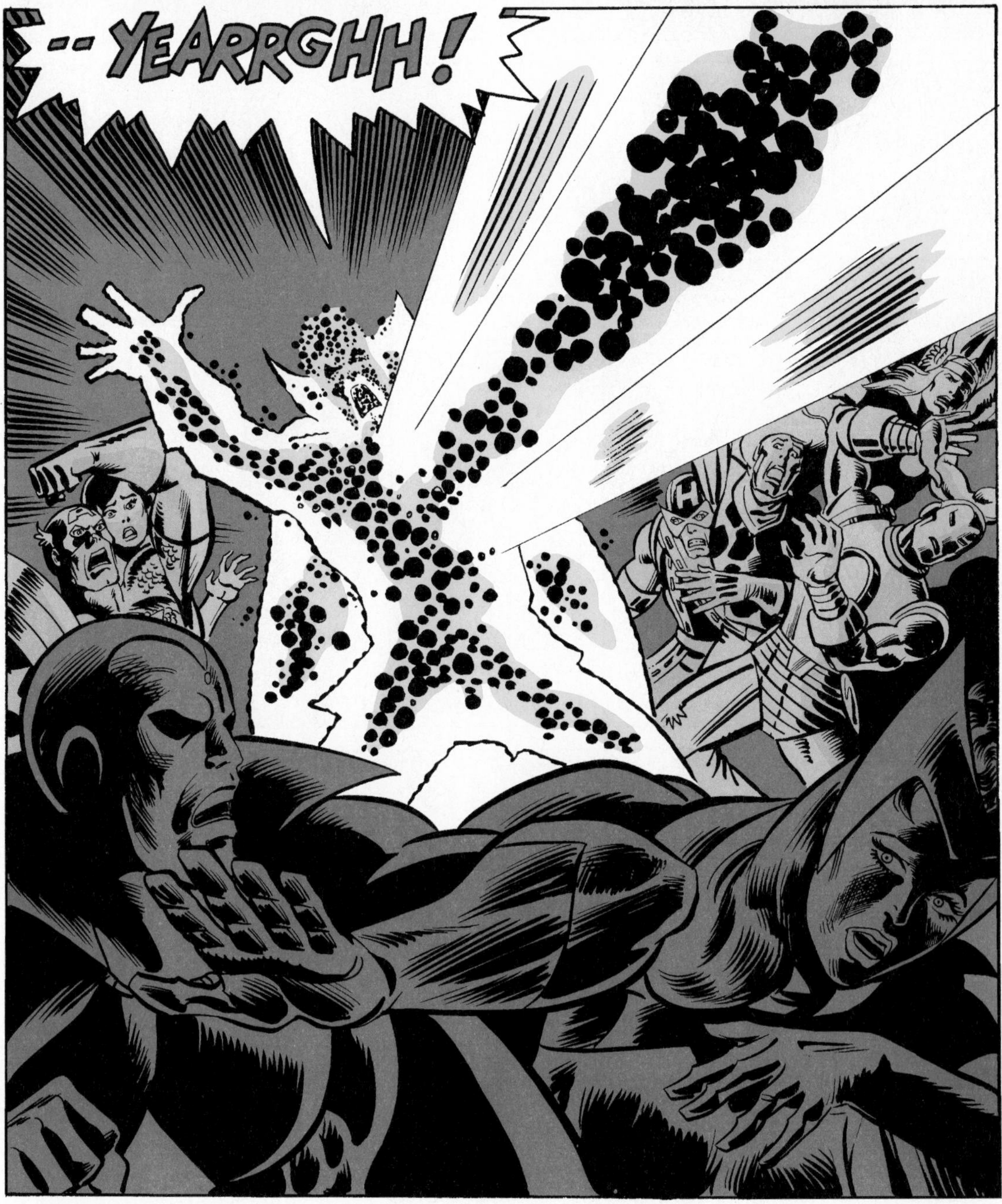
--YEARRGHH!

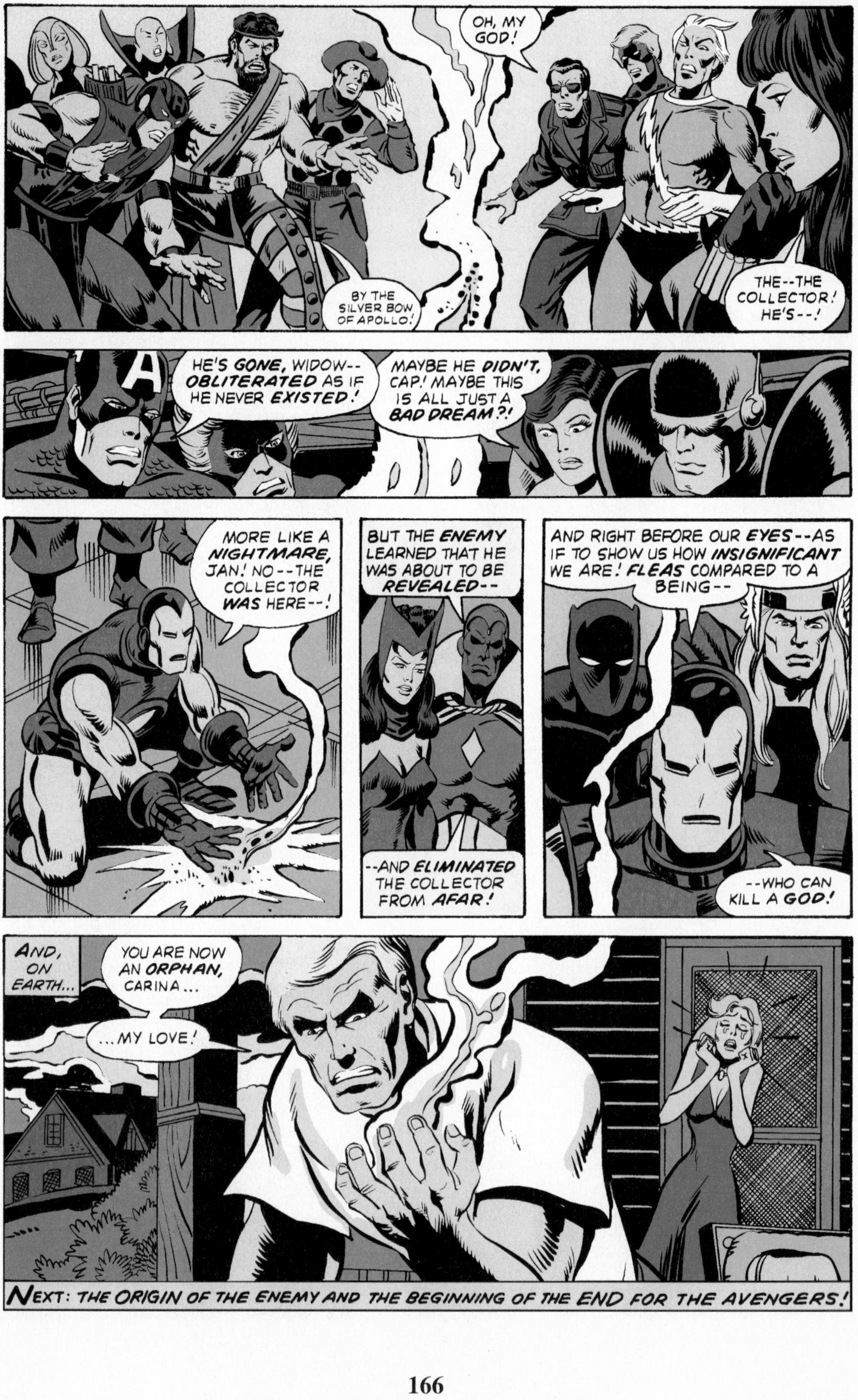
OH, MY GOD!
BY THE SILVER BOW OF APOLLO!
THE--THE COLLECTOR! HE'S--!
HE'S GONE, WIDOW--OBLITERATED AS IF HE NEVER EXISTED!
MAYBE HE DIDN'T, CAP! MAYBE THIS IS ALL JUST A BAD DREAM?!
MORE LIKE A NIGHTMARE, JAN! NO--THE COLLECTOR WAS HERE--!
BUT THE ENEMY LEARNED THAT HE WAS ABOUT TO BE REVEALED--
--AND ELIMINATED THE COLLECTOR FROM AFAR!
AND RIGHT BEFORE OUR EYES--AS IF TO SHOW US HOW INSIGNIFICANT WE ARE! FLEAS COMPARED TO A BEING--
--WHO CAN KILL A GOD!
AND, ON EARTH...
YOU ARE NOW AN ORPHAN, CARINA...
...MY LOVE!
NEXT: THE ORIGIN OF THE ENEMY AND THE BEGINNING OF THE END FOR THE AVENGERS!

AVENGERS
MARVEL® COMICS GROUP
APPROVED BY THE COMICS CODE AUTHORITY
35¢
175
SEPT
02458
EARTH'S MIGHTIEST HEROES!
the AVENGERS
FROM WHENCE CAME...THE ENEMY?
COCKRUM · austin

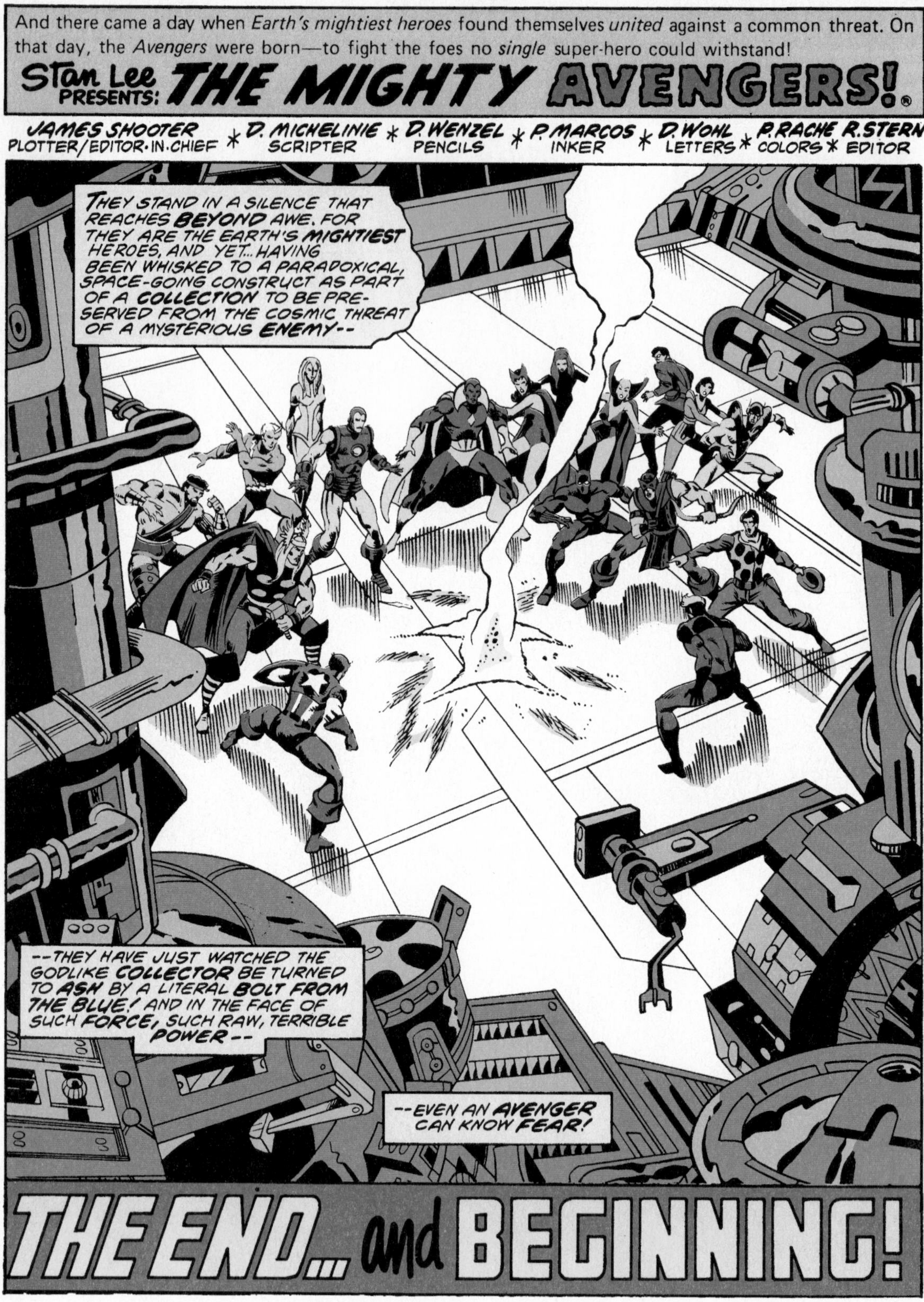

And there came a day when *Earth's mightiest heroes* found themselves *united* against a common threat. On that day, the *Avengers* were born—to fight the foes no *single* super-hero could withstand!
Stan Lee PRESENTS: THE MIGHTY AVENGERS!®
JAMES SHOOTER PLOTTER/EDITOR-IN-CHIEF * D. MICHELINIE SCRIPTER * D. WENZEL PENCILS * P. MARCOS INKER * D. WOHL LETTERS * P. RACHE COLORS * R. STERN EDITOR
THEY STAND IN A SILENCE THAT REACHES BEYOND AWE. FOR THEY ARE THE EARTH'S MIGHTIEST HEROES, AND YET... HAVING BEEN WHISKED TO A PARADOXICAL, SPACE-GOING CONSTRUCT AS PART OF A COLLECTION TO BE PRESERVED FROM THE COSMIC THREAT OF A MYSTERIOUS ENEMY--
--THEY HAVE JUST WATCHED THE GODLIKE COLLECTOR BE TURNED TO ASH BY A LITERAL BOLT FROM THE BLUE! AND IN THE FACE OF SUCH FORCE, SUCH RAW, TERRIBLE POWER--
--EVEN AN AVENGER CAN KNOW FEAR!
THE END... and BEGINNING!

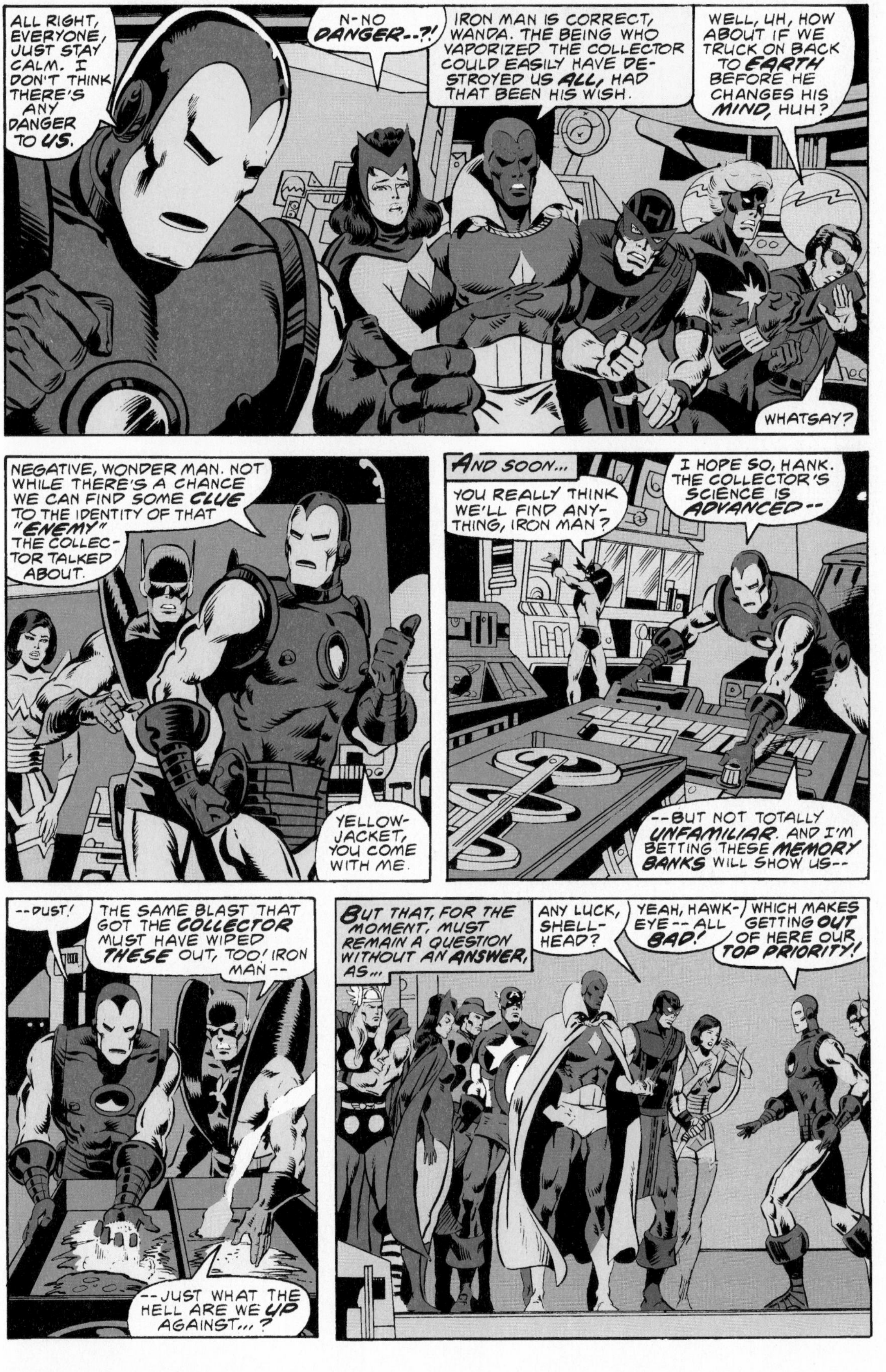

ALL RIGHT, EVERYONE, JUST STAY CALM. I DON'T THINK THERE'S ANY DANGER TO US.
N-NO DANGER--?!
IRON MAN IS CORRECT, WANDA. THE BEING WHO VAPORIZED THE COLLECTOR COULD EASILY HAVE DESTROYED US ALL, HAD THAT BEEN HIS WISH.
WELL, UH, HOW ABOUT IF WE TRUCK ON BACK TO EARTH BEFORE HE CHANGES HIS MIND, HUH?
WHATSAY?
NEGATIVE, WONDER MAN. NOT WHILE THERE'S A CHANCE WE CAN FIND SOME CLUE TO THE IDENTITY OF THAT "ENEMY" THE COLLECTOR TALKED ABOUT.
YELLOWJACKET, YOU COME WITH ME.
AND SOON...
YOU REALLY THINK WE'LL FIND ANYTHING, IRON MAN?
I HOPE SO, HANK. THE COLLECTOR'S SCIENCE IS ADVANCED--
--BUT NOT TOTALLY UNFAMILIAR. AND I'M BETTING THESE MEMORY BANKS WILL SHOW US--
--DUST!
THE SAME BLAST THAT GOT THE COLLECTOR MUST HAVE WIPED THESE OUT, TOO! IRON MAN--
--JUST WHAT THE HELL ARE WE UP AGAINST...?
BUT THAT, FOR THE MOMENT, MUST REMAIN A QUESTION WITHOUT AN ANSWER, AS...
ANY LUCK, SHELLHEAD?
YEAH, HAWKEYE--ALL BAD!
WHICH MAKES GETTING OUT OF HERE OUR TOP PRIORITY!

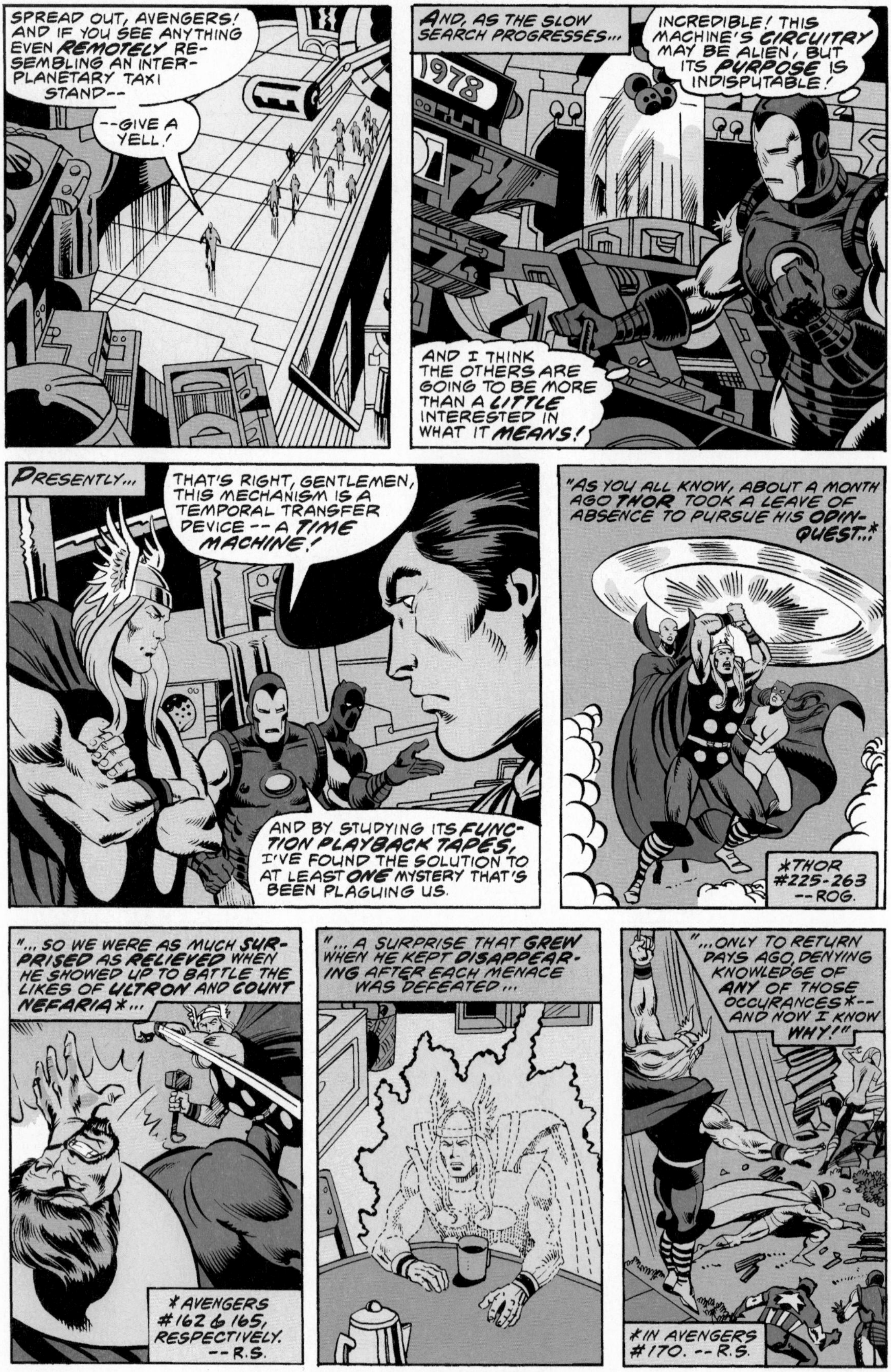
SPREAD OUT, AVENGERS! AND IF YOU SEE ANYTHING EVEN REMOTELY RESEMBLING AN INTER-PLANETARY TAXI STAND--
--GIVE A YELL!
AND, AS THE SLOW SEARCH PROGRESSES...
INCREDIBLE! THIS MACHINE'S CIRCUITRY MAY BE ALIEN, BUT ITS PURPOSE IS INDISPUTABLE!
1978
AND I THINK THE OTHERS ARE GOING TO BE MORE THAN A LITTLE INTERESTED IN WHAT IT MEANS!
PRESENTLY...
THAT'S RIGHT, GENTLEMEN, THIS MECHANISM IS A TEMPORAL TRANSFER DEVICE -- A TIME MACHINE!
AND BY STUDYING ITS FUNCTION PLAYBACK TAPES, I'VE FOUND THE SOLUTION TO AT LEAST ONE MYSTERY THAT'S BEEN PLAGUING US.
"AS YOU ALL KNOW, ABOUT A MONTH AGO THOR TOOK A LEAVE OF ABSENCE TO PURSUE HIS ODIN-QUEST...*
*THOR #225-263 --ROG.
"... SO WE WERE AS MUCH SURPRISED AS RELIEVED WHEN HE SHOWED UP TO BATTLE THE LIKES OF ULTRON AND COUNT NEFARIA*...
*AVENGERS #162 & 165, RESPECTIVELY. --R.S.
"... A SURPRISE THAT GREW WHEN HE KEPT DISAPPEARING AFTER EACH MENACE WAS DEFEATED...
"...ONLY TO RETURN DAYS AGO, DENYING KNOWLEDGE OF ANY OF THOSE OCCURANCES*-- AND NOW I KNOW WHY!"
*IN AVENGERS #170. --R.S.

ACCORDING TO THE *TAPES*, THE COLLECTOR WANTED THE AVENGERS *INTACT*, SO HE PLUCKED THOR OUT OF TIME AND SPACE TO *HELP* US--

--AND THEN SENT HIM *BACK* WITH ALL MEMORY OF SUCH INCIDENTS *ERASED!*

UH, SAY PARD, I HATE TO *INTERRUPT*, BUT I WAS WONDERIN' ABOUT THAT THERE *TIME* GIZMO. YA RECKON IT COULD WORK ON *"ME?*

WHA-- *TWO-GUN?!*

I'M SORRY, FELLAS, IT'S NOT THAT I DON'T *LIKE* THE 20TH CENTURY. I JUST FEEL SORTA ... OUT OF *PLACE.*

Y' UNDER-STAND?

YES, TWO-GUN ... I THINK WE DO.

AND SO...

HAVE A NICE TRIP, TWO-GUN. AND DON'T TAKE ANY *WOODEN PESOS*, HEAR?

I WON'T, WONDER MAN. SO LONG. I'LL MISS YA ALL!

THE FEELING'S *MUTUAL*, MATT --IT'S BEEN FUN.

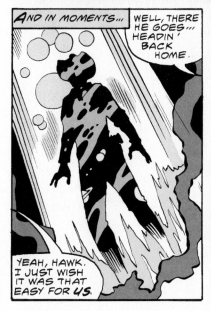

AND IN MOMENTS...

WELL, THERE HE GOES ... HEADIN' BACK HOME.

YEAH, HAWK. I JUST WISH IT WAS THAT EASY FOR *US.*

IT MAY *BE*, MY FRIENDS. WHILE YOU WERE OTHERWISE ENGAGED, I TOOK THE OPPORTUNITY TO *EXPLORE* THIS CONSTRUCT-- AND DISCOVERED THE SAME *TELEPORTATIONAL* DEVICE THAT BROUGHT US HERE!

IF YOU'LL JUST STEP THIS WAY...?

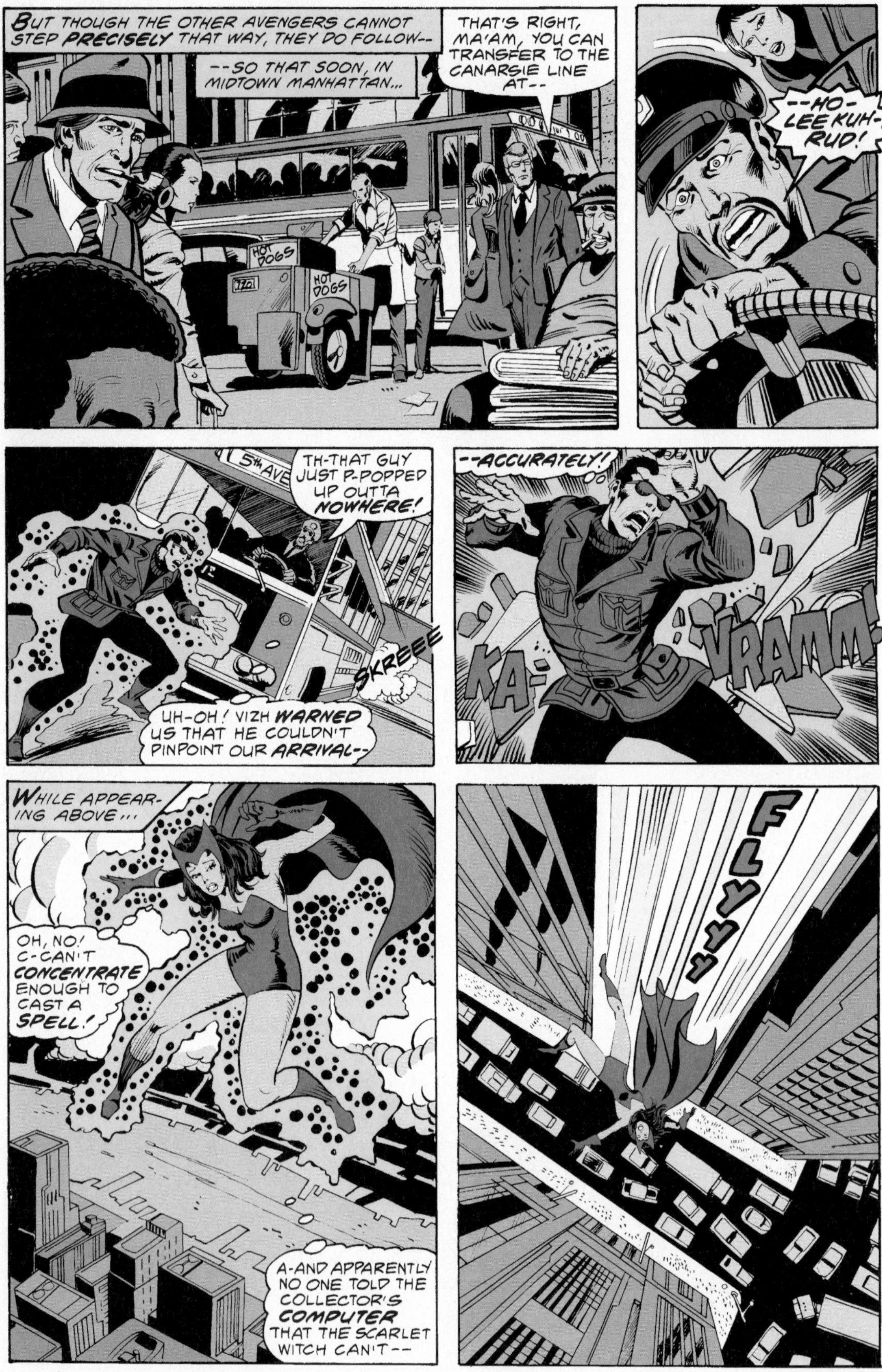
BUT THOUGH THE OTHER AVENGERS CANNOT STEP PRECISELY THAT WAY, THEY DO FOLLOW--
--SO THAT SOON, IN MIDTOWN MANHATTAN...
THAT'S RIGHT, MA'AM, YOU CAN TRANSFER TO THE CANARSIE LINE AT--
HOT DOGS
HOT DOGS
--HO-LEE KUH-RUD!
5th AVE
TH-THAT GUY JUST P-POPPED UP OUTTA NOWHERE!
SKREEE
UH-OH! VIZH WARNED US THAT HE COULDN'T PINPOINT OUR ARRIVAL--
--ACCURATELY!
KA-VRAMM!
WHILE APPEARING ABOVE...
OH, NO! C-CAN'T CONCENTRATE ENOUGH TO CAST A SPELL!
A-AND APPARENTLY NO ONE TOLD THE COLLECTOR'S COMPUTER THAT THE SCARLET WITCH CAN'T--
FLYYYY

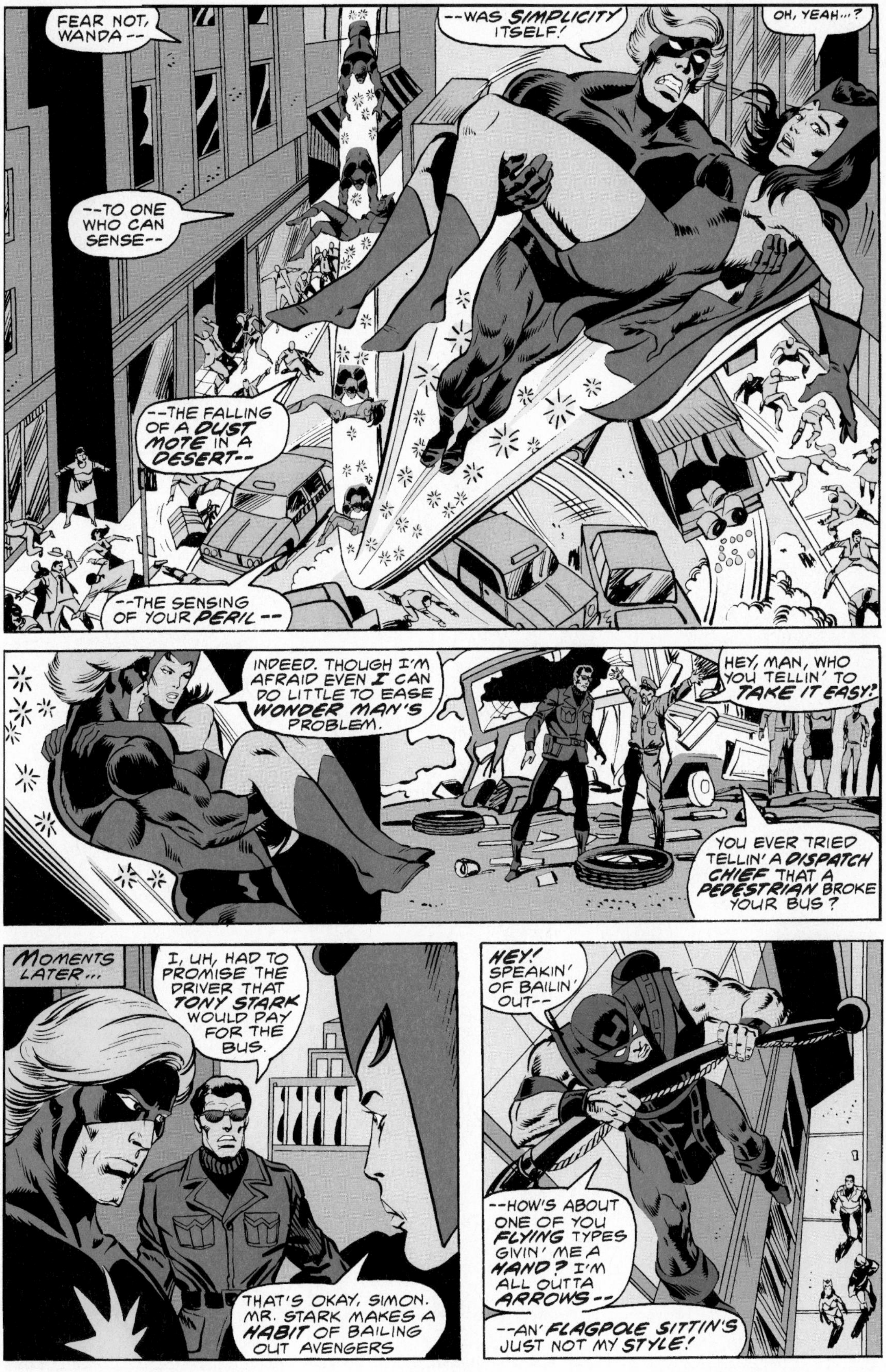
FEAR NOT, WANDA --
--WAS SIMPLICITY ITSELF!
OH, YEAH...?
--TO ONE WHO CAN SENSE--
--THE FALLING OF A DUST MOTE IN A DESERT--
--THE SENSING OF YOUR PERIL --
INDEED. THOUGH I'M AFRAID EVEN I CAN DO LITTLE TO EASE WONDER MAN'S PROBLEM.
HEY, MAN, WHO YOU TELLIN' TO TAKE IT EASY?
YOU EVER TRIED TELLIN' A DISPATCH CHIEF THAT A PEDESTRIAN BROKE YOUR BUS?
MOMENTS LATER...
I, UH, HAD TO PROMISE THE DRIVER THAT TONY STARK WOULD PAY FOR THE BUS.
THAT'S OKAY, SIMON. MR. STARK MAKES A HABIT OF BAILING OUT AVENGERS
HEY! SPEAKIN' OF BAILIN' OUT--
--HOW'S ABOUT ONE OF YOU FLYING TYPES GIVIN' ME A HAND? I'M ALL OUTTA ARROWS--
--AN' FLAGPOLE SITTIN'S JUST NOT MY STYLE!

MEANWHILE, AT AN INCREASINGLY-FAMILIAR HOME IN FOREST HILLS GARDENS --

--A MAN CALLED *MICHAEL* RISES FROM CHLORINED WATERS, SOMBERLY AWARE THAT HIS ATTEMPT AT *RELAXATION HAS FAILED*...

...FOR *CONFLICT* STILL GNAWS AT HIS MIND LIKE A PERSISTENT FLEA... CONFLICT THAT *MUST* BE RESOLVED.

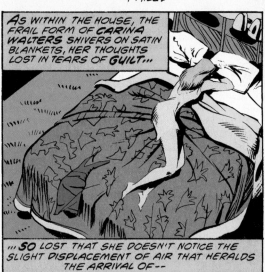

AS WITHIN THE HOUSE, THE FRAIL FORM OF *CARINA WALTERS* SHIVERS ON SATIN BLANKETS, HER THOUGHTS LOST IN TEARS OF *GUILT*...

...SO LOST THAT SHE DOESN'T NOTICE THE SLIGHT *DISPLACEMENT* OF AIR THAT HERALDS THE ARRIVAL OF --

--M-MICHAEL?!

I'VE COME TO FIND OUT, CARINA. TO FIND OUT... WHAT YOU *FEEL*.

I- I'M NOT SURE *WHAT* I FEEL, MICHAEL.

...I'D DO IT *AGAIN* IF I HAD TO, AND I DON'T EVEN KNOW WHY.

TO PROTECT YOUR DREAMS, I BE-TRAYED MY *FATHER* --AND LET YOU *KILL* HIM! I SHOULD *HATE* YOU, BUT...

BUT THE TALL, MUSCULAR MAN, LOOKING INTO EYES FILLED *ONLY* WITH LOVE, *DOES* KNOW...

174

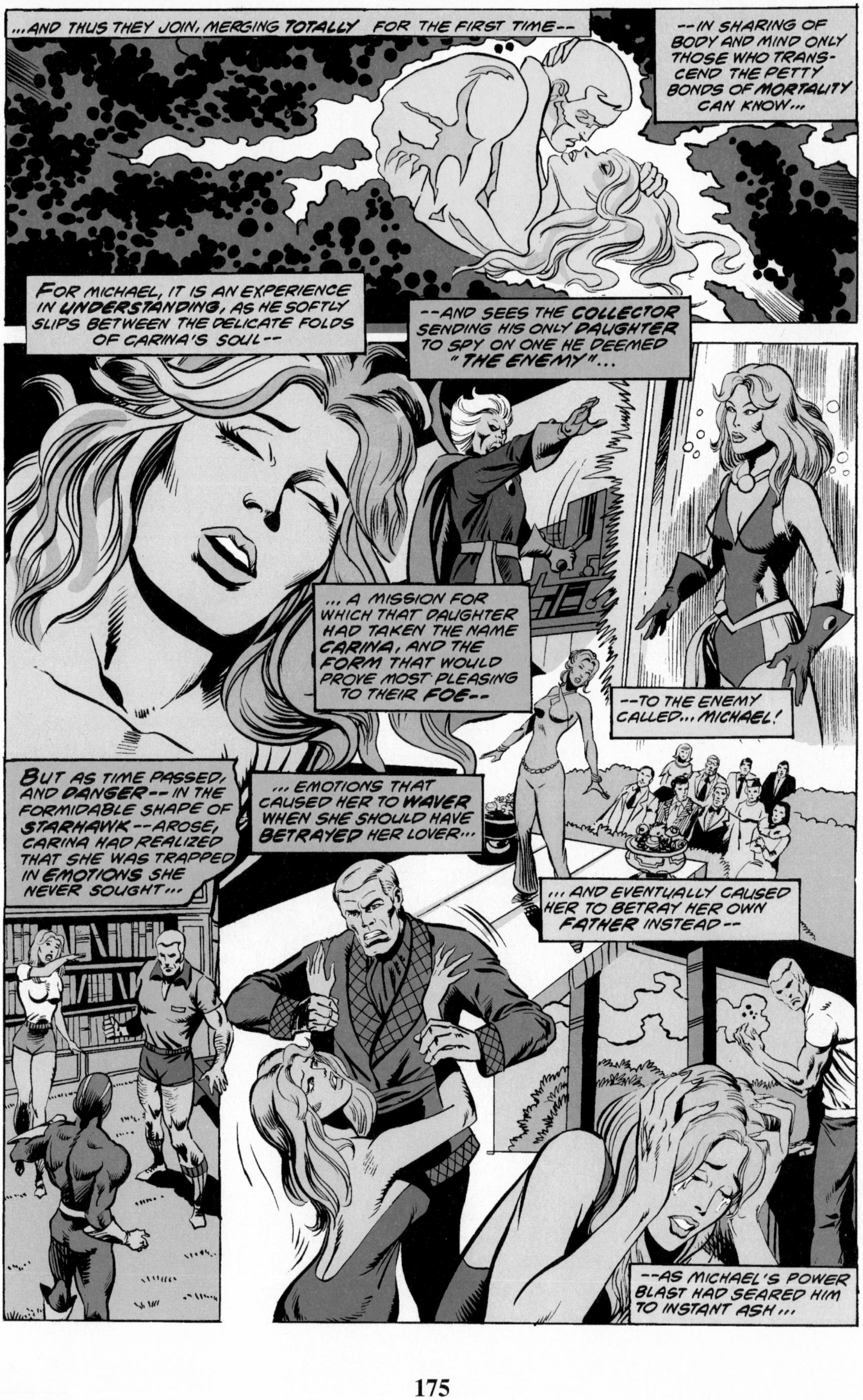
...AND THUS THEY JOIN, MERGING TOTALLY FOR THE FIRST TIME--
--IN SHARING OF BODY AND MIND ONLY THOSE WHO TRANSCEND THE PETTY BONDS OF MORTALITY CAN KNOW...
FOR MICHAEL, IT IS AN EXPERIENCE IN UNDERSTANDING, AS HE SOFTLY SLIPS BETWEEN THE DELICATE FOLDS OF CARINA'S SOUL--
--AND SEES THE COLLECTOR SENDING HIS ONLY DAUGHTER TO SPY ON ONE HE DEEMED "THE ENEMY"...
...A MISSION FOR WHICH THAT DAUGHTER HAD TAKEN THE NAME CARINA, AND THE FORM THAT WOULD PROVE MOST PLEASING TO THEIR FOE--
--TO THE ENEMY CALLED...MICHAEL!
BUT AS TIME PASSED, AND DANGER-- IN THE FORMIDABLE SHAPE OF STARHAWK --AROSE, CARINA HAD REALIZED THAT SHE WAS TRAPPED IN EMOTIONS SHE NEVER SOUGHT...
...EMOTIONS THAT CAUSED HER TO WAVER WHEN SHE SHOULD HAVE BETRAYED HER LOVER...
...AND EVENTUALLY CAUSED HER TO BETRAY HER OWN FATHER INSTEAD--
--AS MICHAEL'S POWER BLAST HAD SEARED HIM TO INSTANT ASH...

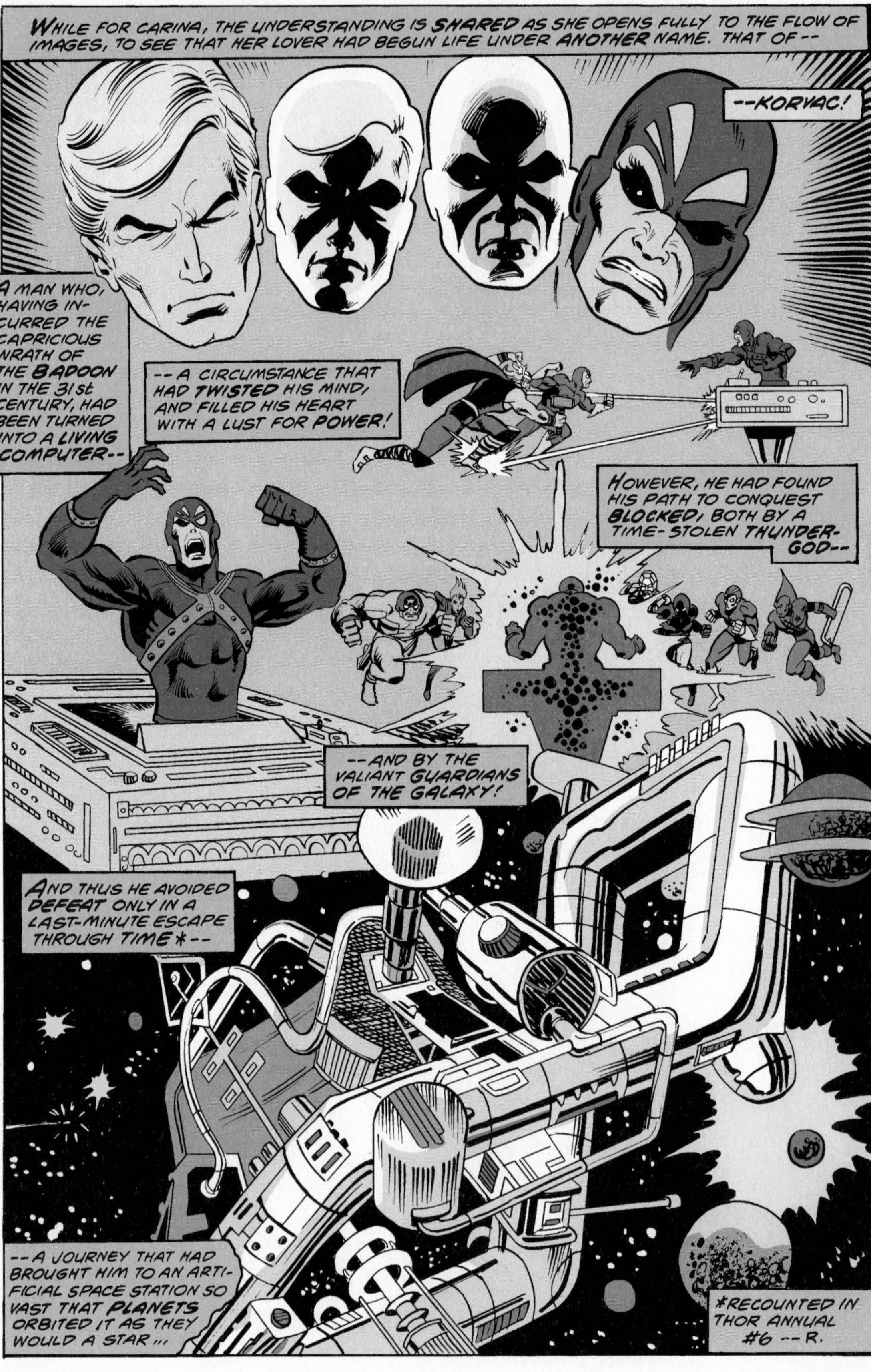
WHILE FOR CARINA, THE UNDERSTANDING IS SHARED AS SHE OPENS FULLY TO THE FLOW OF IMAGES, TO SEE THAT HER LOVER HAD BEGUN LIFE UNDER ANOTHER NAME. THAT OF --
--KORVAC!
A MAN WHO, HAVING INCURRED THE CAPRICIOUS WRATH OF THE BADOON IN THE 31st CENTURY, HAD BEEN TURNED INTO A LIVING COMPUTER--
-- A CIRCUMSTANCE THAT HAD TWISTED HIS MIND, AND FILLED HIS HEART WITH A LUST FOR POWER!
HOWEVER, HE HAD FOUND HIS PATH TO CONQUEST BLOCKED, BOTH BY A TIME-STOLEN THUNDER-GOD--
--AND BY THE VALIANT GUARDIANS OF THE GALAXY!
AND THUS HE AVOIDED DEFEAT ONLY IN A LAST-MINUTE ESCAPE THROUGH TIME*--
--A JOURNEY THAT HAD BROUGHT HIM TO AN ARTIFICIAL SPACE STATION SO VAST THAT PLANETS ORBITED IT AS THEY WOULD A STAR...
*RECOUNTED IN THOR ANNUAL #6 --R.

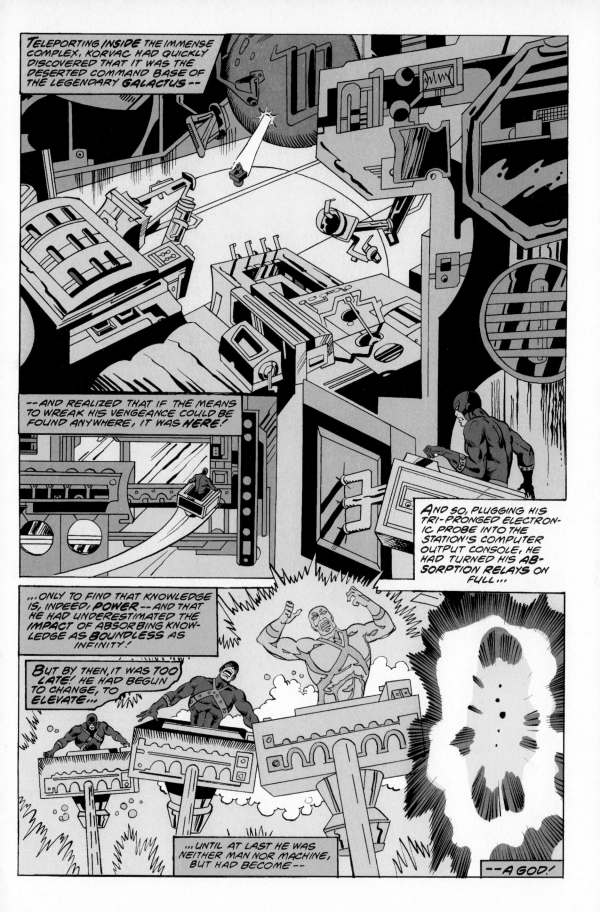

TELEPORTING INSIDE THE IMMENSE COMPLEX, KORVAC HAD QUICKLY DISCOVERED THAT IT WAS THE DESERTED COMMAND BASE OF THE LEGENDARY GALACTUS--

--AND REALIZED THAT IF THE MEANS TO WREAK HIS VENGEANCE COULD BE FOUND ANYWHERE, IT WAS HERE!

AND SO, PLUGGING HIS TRI-PRONGED ELECTRON-IC PROBE INTO THE STATION'S COMPUTER OUTPUT CONSOLE, HE HAD TURNED HIS AB-SORPTION RELAYS ON FULL...

...ONLY TO FIND THAT KNOWLEDGE IS, INDEED, POWER -- AND THAT HE HAD UNDERESTIMATED THE IMPACT OF ABSORBING KNOW-LEDGE AS BOUNDLESS AS INFINITY!

BUT BY THEN, IT WAS TOO LATE! HE HAD BEGUN TO CHANGE, TO ELEVATE...

...UNTIL AT LAST HE WAS NEITHER MAN NOR MACHINE, BUT HAD BECOME--

--A GOD!

177

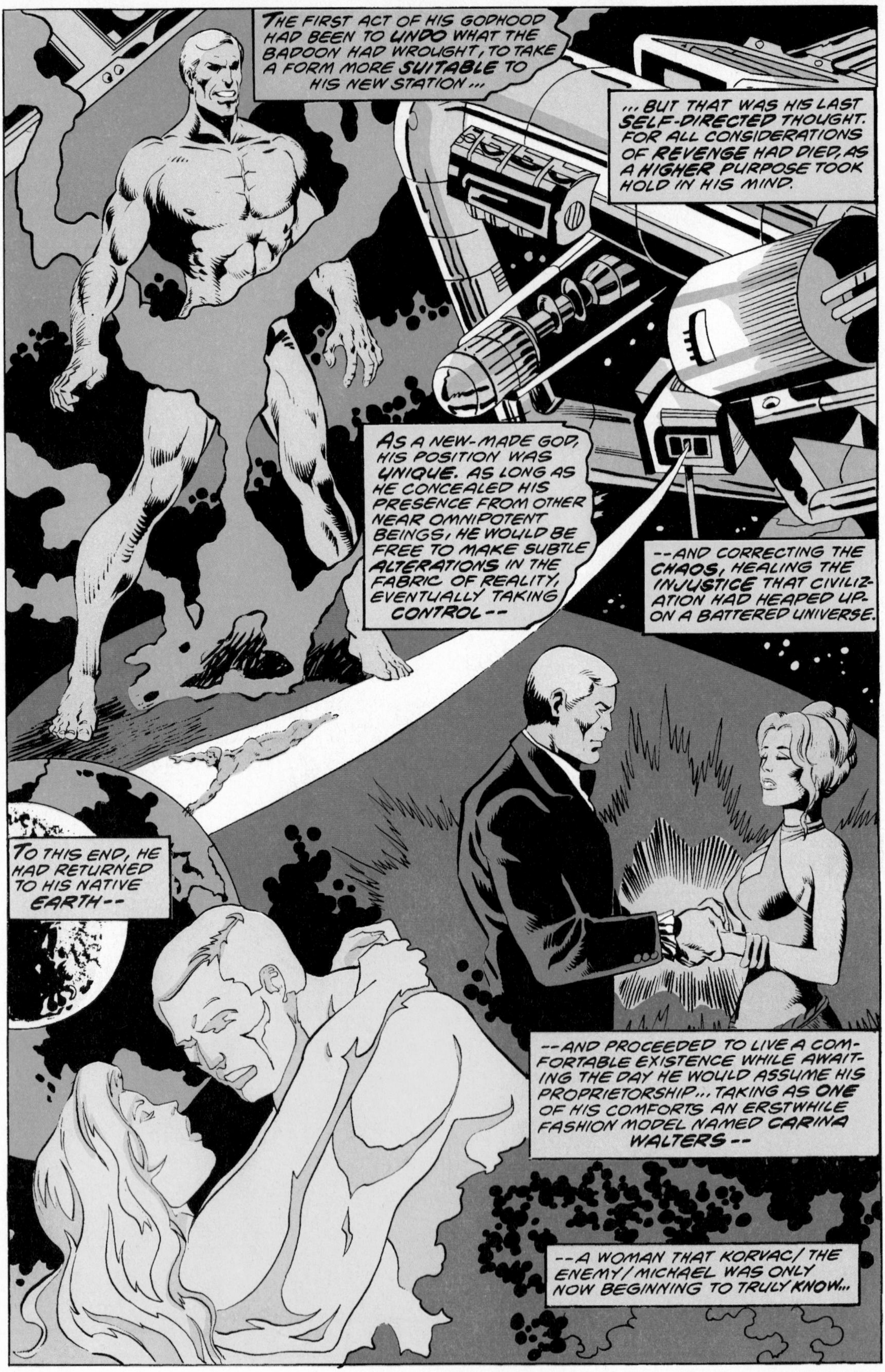
THE FIRST ACT OF HIS GODHOOD HAD BEEN TO UNDO WHAT THE BADOON HAD WROUGHT, TO TAKE A FORM MORE SUITABLE TO HIS NEW STATION...
...BUT THAT WAS HIS LAST SELF-DIRECTED THOUGHT. FOR ALL CONSIDERATIONS OF REVENGE HAD DIED, AS A HIGHER PURPOSE TOOK HOLD IN HIS MIND.
AS A NEW-MADE GOD, HIS POSITION WAS UNIQUE. AS LONG AS HE CONCEALED HIS PRESENCE FROM OTHER NEAR OMNIPOTENT BEINGS, HE WOULD BE FREE TO MAKE SUBTLE ALTERATIONS IN THE FABRIC OF REALITY, EVENTUALLY TAKING CONTROL--
--AND CORRECTING THE CHAOS, HEALING THE INJUSTICE THAT CIVILIZATION HAD HEAPED UPON A BATTERED UNIVERSE.
TO THIS END, HE HAD RETURNED TO HIS NATIVE EARTH--
--AND PROCEEDED TO LIVE A COMFORTABLE EXISTENCE WHILE AWAITING THE DAY HE WOULD ASSUME HIS PROPRIETORSHIP... TAKING AS ONE OF HIS COMFORTS AN ERSTWHILE FASHION MODEL NAMED CARINA WALTERS--
--A WOMAN THAT KORVAC/THE ENEMY/MICHAEL WAS ONLY NOW BEGINNING TO TRULY KNOW...

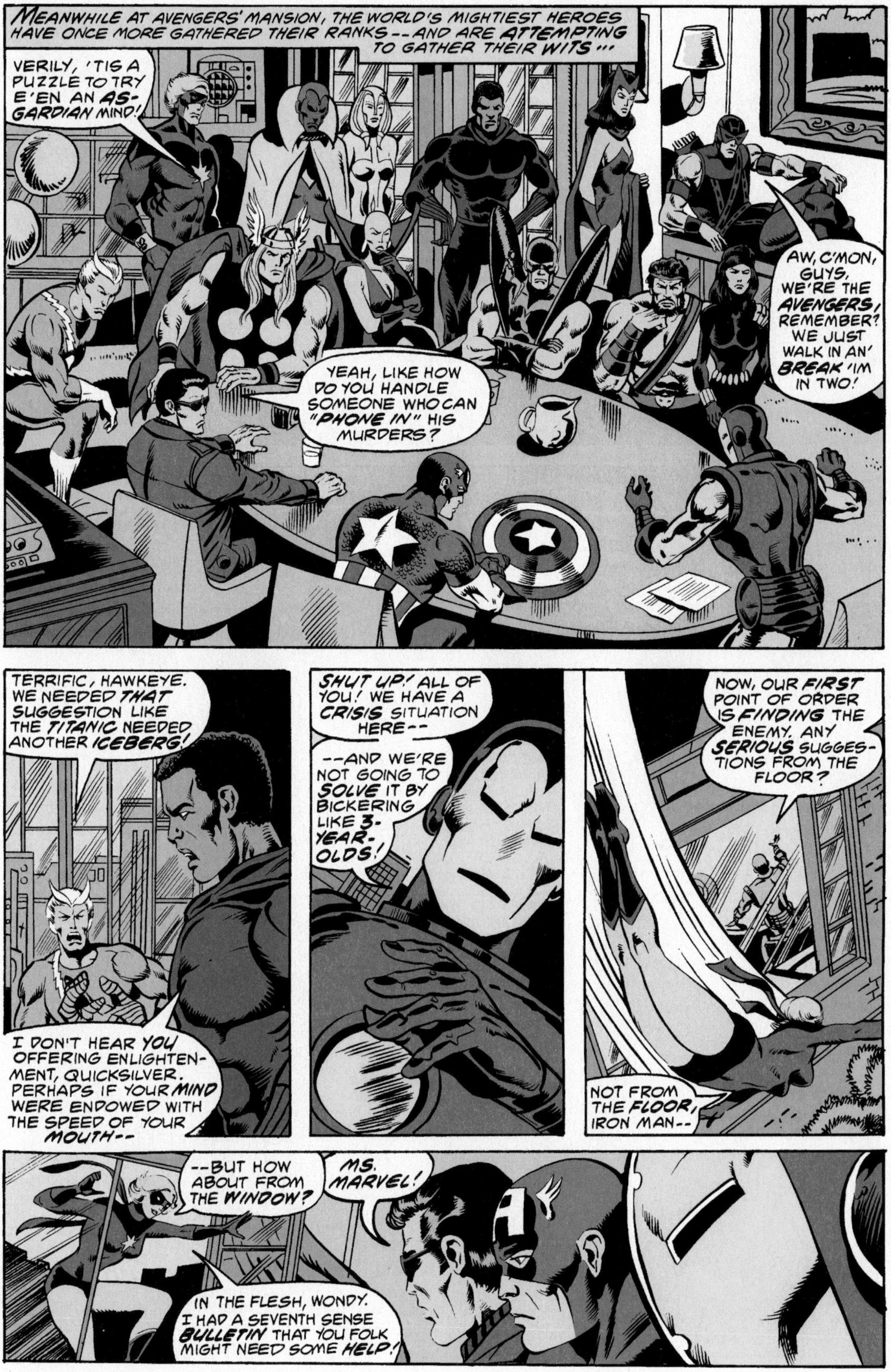
MEANWHILE AT AVENGERS' MANSION, THE WORLD'S MIGHTIEST HEROES HAVE ONCE MORE GATHERED THEIR RANKS -- AND ARE ATTEMPTING TO GATHER THEIR WITS ...
VERILY, 'TIS A PUZZLE TO TRY E'EN AN ASGARDIAN MIND!
YEAH, LIKE HOW DO YOU HANDLE SOMEONE WHO CAN "PHONE IN" HIS MURDERS?
AW, C'MON, GUYS, WE'RE THE AVENGERS, REMEMBER? WE JUST WALK IN AN' BREAK 'IM IN TWO!
TERRIFIC, HAWKEYE. WE NEEDED THAT SUGGESTION LIKE THE TITANIC NEEDED ANOTHER ICEBERG!
I DON'T HEAR YOU OFFERING ENLIGHTENMENT, QUICKSILVER. PERHAPS IF YOUR MIND WERE ENDOWED WITH THE SPEED OF YOUR MOUTH--
SHUT UP! ALL OF YOU! WE HAVE A CRISIS SITUATION HERE--
--AND WE'RE NOT GOING TO SOLVE IT BY BICKERING LIKE 3-YEAR-OLDS!
NOW, OUR FIRST POINT OF ORDER IS FINDING THE ENEMY. ANY SERIOUS SUGGESTIONS FROM THE FLOOR?
NOT FROM THE FLOOR, IRON MAN--
--BUT HOW ABOUT FROM THE WINDOW?
MS. MARVEL!
IN THE FLESH, WONDY. I HAD A SEVENTH SENSE BULLETIN THAT YOU FOLK MIGHT NEED SOME HELP!

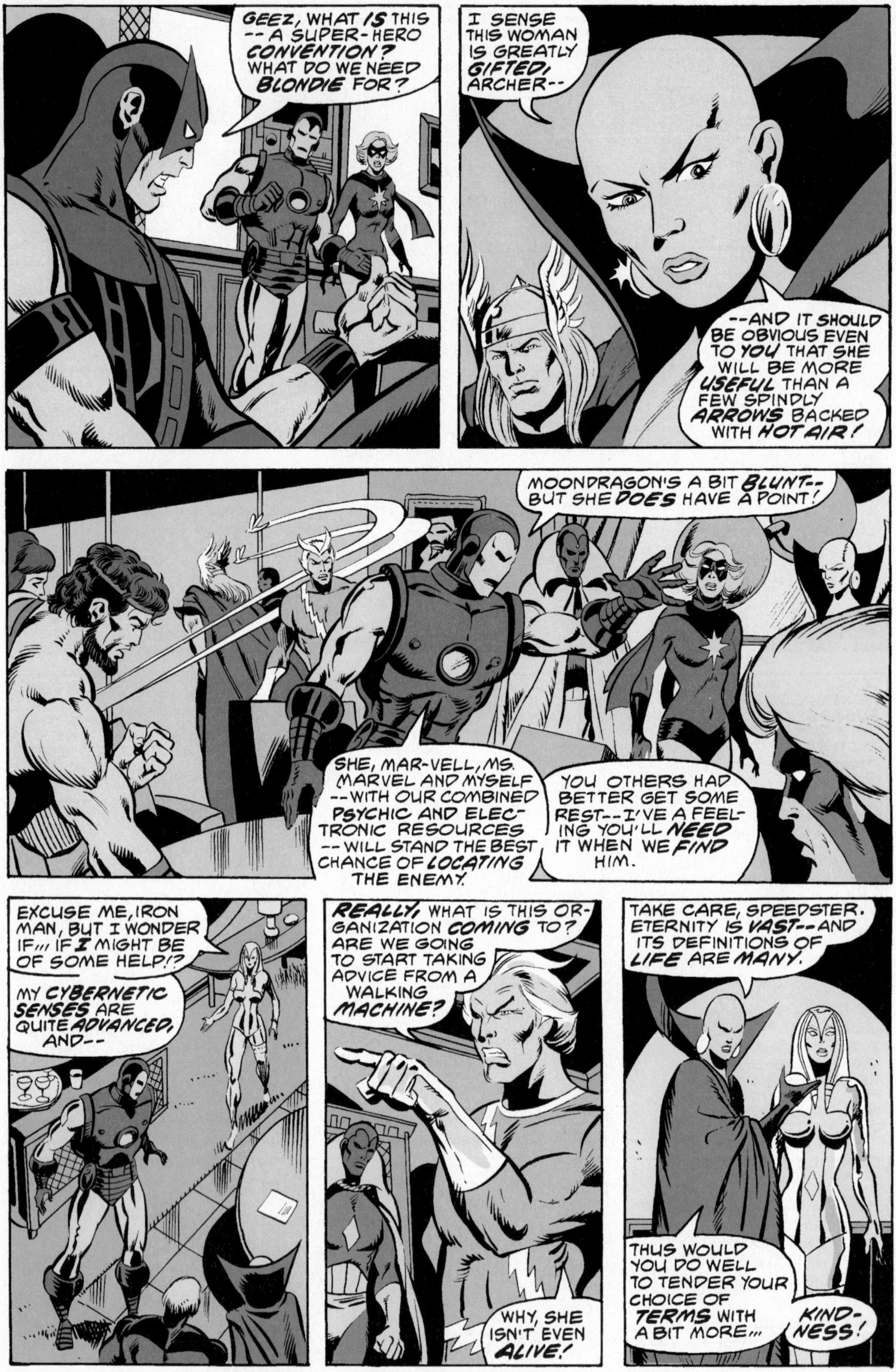

GEEZ, WHAT IS THIS -- A SUPER-HERO CONVENTION? WHAT DO WE NEED BLONDIE FOR?
I SENSE THIS WOMAN IS GREATLY GIFTED, ARCHER--
--AND IT SHOULD BE OBVIOUS EVEN TO YOU THAT SHE WILL BE MORE USEFUL THAN A FEW SPINDLY ARROWS BACKED WITH HOT AIR!
MOONDRAGON'S A BIT BLUNT-- BUT SHE DOES HAVE A POINT!
SHE, MAR-VELL, MS. MARVEL AND MYSELF --WITH OUR COMBINED PSYCHIC AND ELECTRONIC RESOURCES --WILL STAND THE BEST CHANCE OF LOCATING THE ENEMY.
YOU OTHERS HAD BETTER GET SOME REST--I'VE A FEELING YOU'LL NEED IT WHEN WE FIND HIM.
EXCUSE ME, IRON MAN, BUT I WONDER IF... IF I MIGHT BE OF SOME HELP!?
MY CYBERNETIC SENSES ARE QUITE ADVANCED, AND--
REALLY, WHAT IS THIS ORGANIZATION COMING TO? ARE WE GOING TO START TAKING ADVICE FROM A WALKING MACHINE?
WHY, SHE ISN'T EVEN ALIVE!
TAKE CARE, SPEEDSTER. ETERNITY IS VAST--AND ITS DEFINITIONS OF LIFE ARE MANY.
THUS WOULD YOU DO WELL TO TENDER YOUR CHOICE OF TERMS WITH A BIT MORE...
KINDNESS!

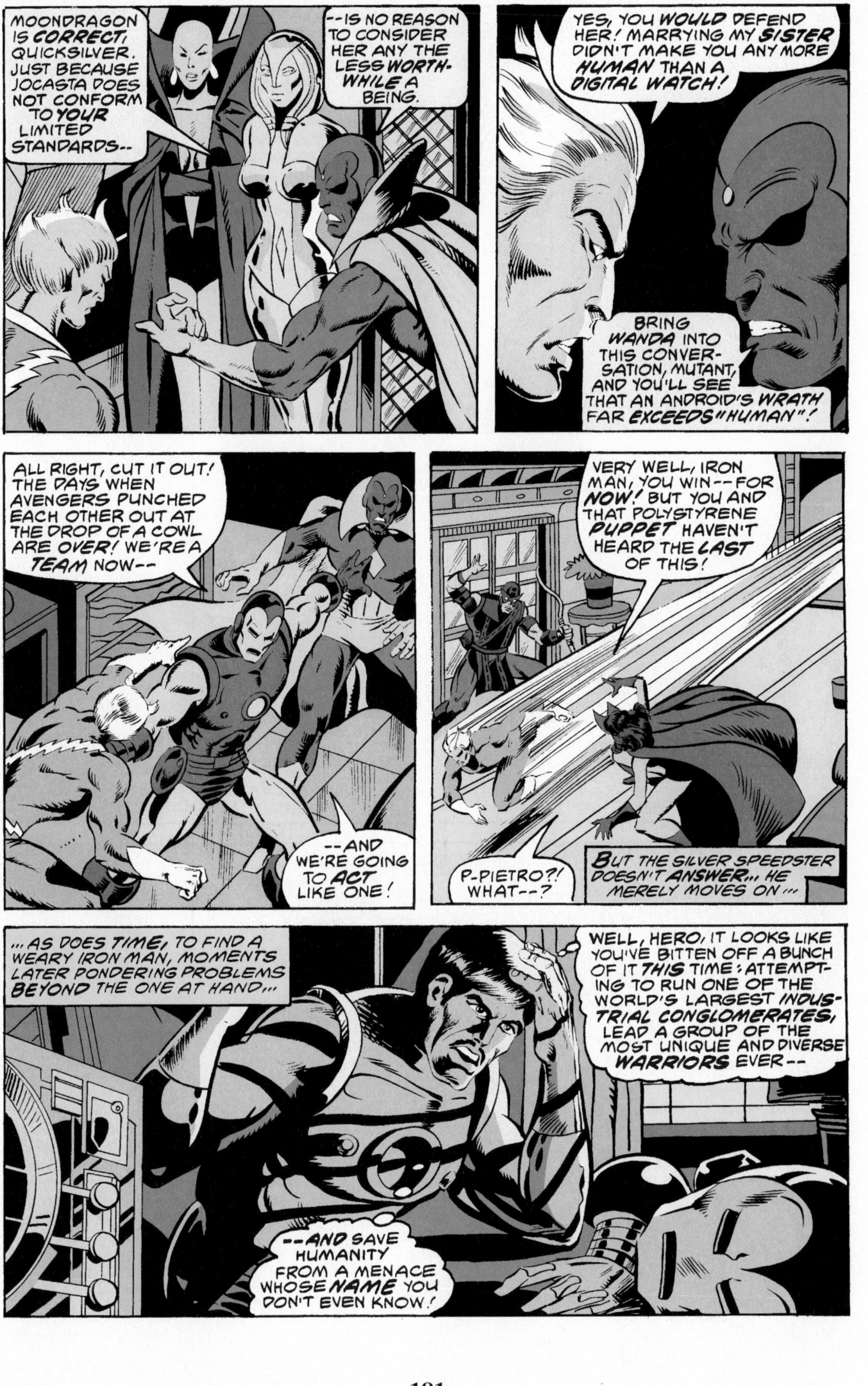
MOONDRAGON IS CORRECT, QUICKSILVER. JUST BECAUSE JOCASTA DOES NOT CONFORM TO YOUR LIMITED STANDARDS--
--IS NO REASON TO CONSIDER HER ANY THE LESS WORTH-WHILE A BEING.
YES, YOU WOULD DEFEND HER! MARRYING MY SISTER DIDN'T MAKE YOU ANY MORE HUMAN THAN A DIGITAL WATCH!
BRING WANDA INTO THIS CONVER-SATION, MUTANT, AND YOU'LL SEE THAT AN ANDROID'S WRATH FAR EXCEEDS "HUMAN"!
ALL RIGHT, CUT IT OUT! THE DAYS WHEN AVENGERS PUNCHED EACH OTHER OUT AT THE DROP OF A COWL ARE OVER! WE'RE A TEAM NOW--
--AND WE'RE GOING TO ACT LIKE ONE!
VERY WELL, IRON MAN, YOU WIN--FOR NOW! BUT YOU AND THAT POLYSTYRENE PUPPET HAVEN'T HEARD THE LAST OF THIS!
P-PIETRO?! WHAT--?
BUT THE SILVER SPEEDSTER DOESN'T ANSWER... HE MERELY MOVES ON...
...AS DOES TIME, TO FIND A WEARY IRON MAN, MOMENTS LATER PONDERING PROBLEMS BEYOND THE ONE AT HAND...
WELL, HERO, IT LOOKS LIKE YOU'VE BITTEN OFF A BUNCH OF IT THIS TIME: ATTEMPT-ING TO RUN ONE OF THE WORLD'S LARGEST INDUS-TRIAL CONGLOMERATES, LEAD A GROUP OF THE MOST UNIQUE AND DIVERSE WARRIORS EVER--
--AND SAVE HUMANITY FROM A MENACE WHOSE NAME YOU DON'T EVEN KNOW!

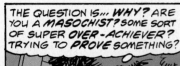

THE QUESTION IS... *WHY?* ARE YOU A *MASOCHIST?* SOME SORT OF SUPER *OVER-ACHIEVER?* TRYING TO *PROVE* SOMETHING?

OR ARE YOU JUST SLINKING AWAY FROM THE *MESS* YOU KEEP MAKING OF YOUR *PRIVATE LIFE?*

NO ANSWERS? SWELL. THAT'S JUST WHAT I NEED--

--A *TACITURN* CONSCIENCE. WELL, NO MATTER. YOU'RE STILL A *LEADER,* TONY STARK--SO *LEAD!*

AND THE FIRST *STEP* IN THAT LEADERSHIP IS CHECKING THE COMPU-TER BANKS.

MAYBE THEY CAN--

--EH?

AND THIS IS OUR *ELECTROCISER.* BEST THING IN THE WORLD FOR BUILD-ING MUSCLES.

WANT TO GIVE IT A GO?

WELL, WONDY, SINCE YOU'VE BEEN GOOD ENOUGH TO GIVE ME THE TEN-CENT *TOUR,* I GUESS I CAN TRY MY--

--H-HAND? I... I CAN HARDLY *BUDGE* IT!

YEAH, I KNOW. THOSE MAGNETIC *PLATES* ON THE FLOOR VARY THE 'CISER'S *WEIGHT.* AND RIGHT NOW--

--THEY'RE SET FOR *THOR!*

BUT IF YOU'LL JUST STEP ASIDE, I'LL SHOW YOU WHAT ≥HNPH≥ *WONDER MAN* CAN DO!

AND I THINK ≥UGH≥ THAT IN A VERY FEW *SEC-ONDS* ≥URK≥ Y-YOU'LL SEE THAT I... I-I'M...

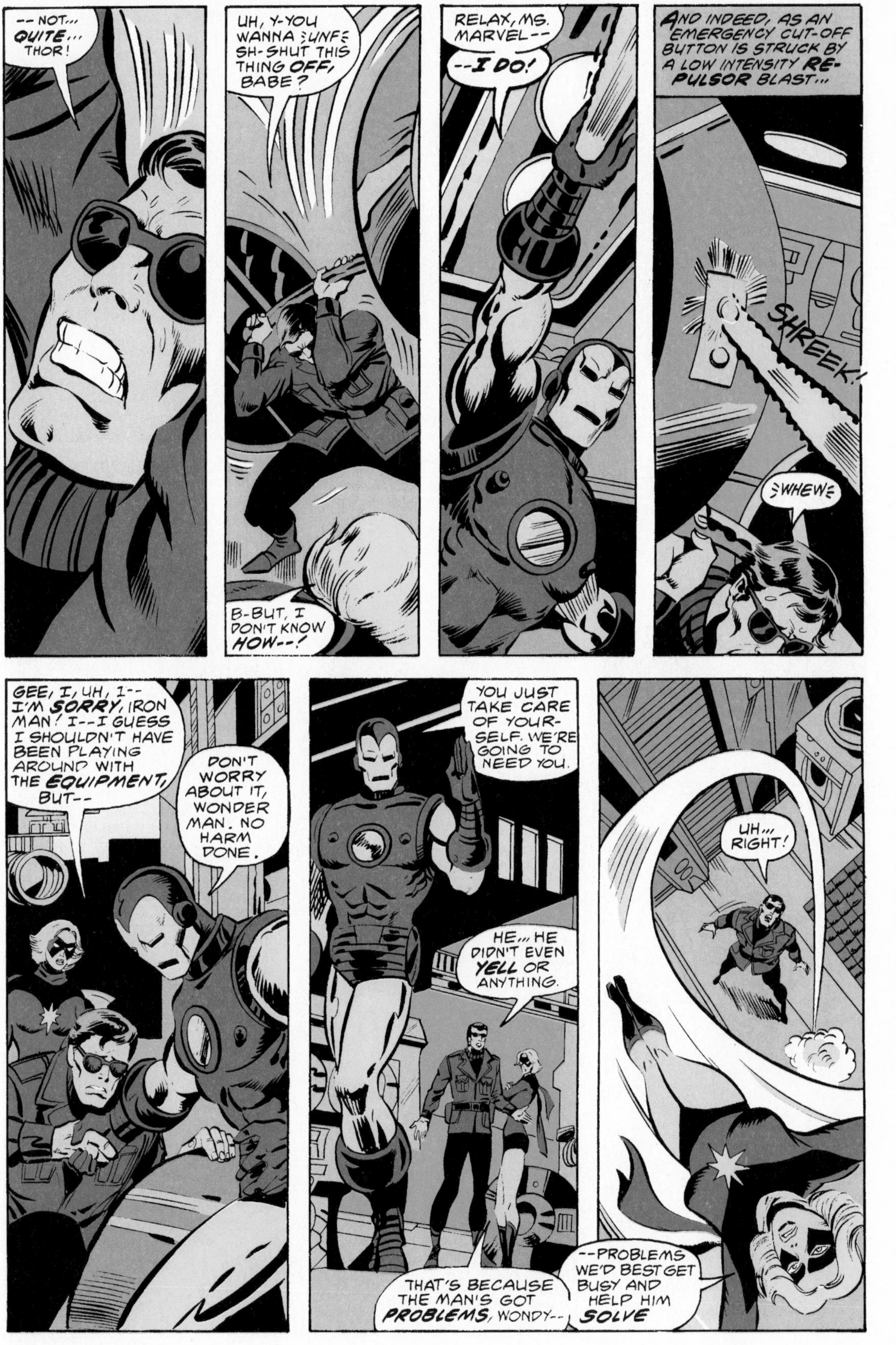
--NOT... QUITE... THOR!
UH, Y-YOU WANNA UNF SH-SHUT THIS THING OFF, BABE?
B-BUT, I DON'T KNOW HOW--!
RELAX, MS. MARVEL--
--I DO!
AND INDEED, AS AN EMERGENCY CUT-OFF BUTTON IS STRUCK BY A LOW INTENSITY REPULSOR BLAST...
SHREEK!
WHEW
GEE, I, UH, I-- I'M SORRY, IRON MAN! I--I GUESS I SHOULDN'T HAVE BEEN PLAYING AROUND WITH THE EQUIPMENT, BUT--
DON'T WORRY ABOUT IT, WONDER MAN. NO HARM DONE.
YOU JUST TAKE CARE OF YOURSELF. WE'RE GOING TO NEED YOU.
HE... HE DIDN'T EVEN YELL OR ANYTHING.
THAT'S BECAUSE THE MAN'S GOT PROBLEMS, WONDY--
UH... RIGHT!
--PROBLEMS WE'D BEST GET BUSY AND HELP HIM SOLVE

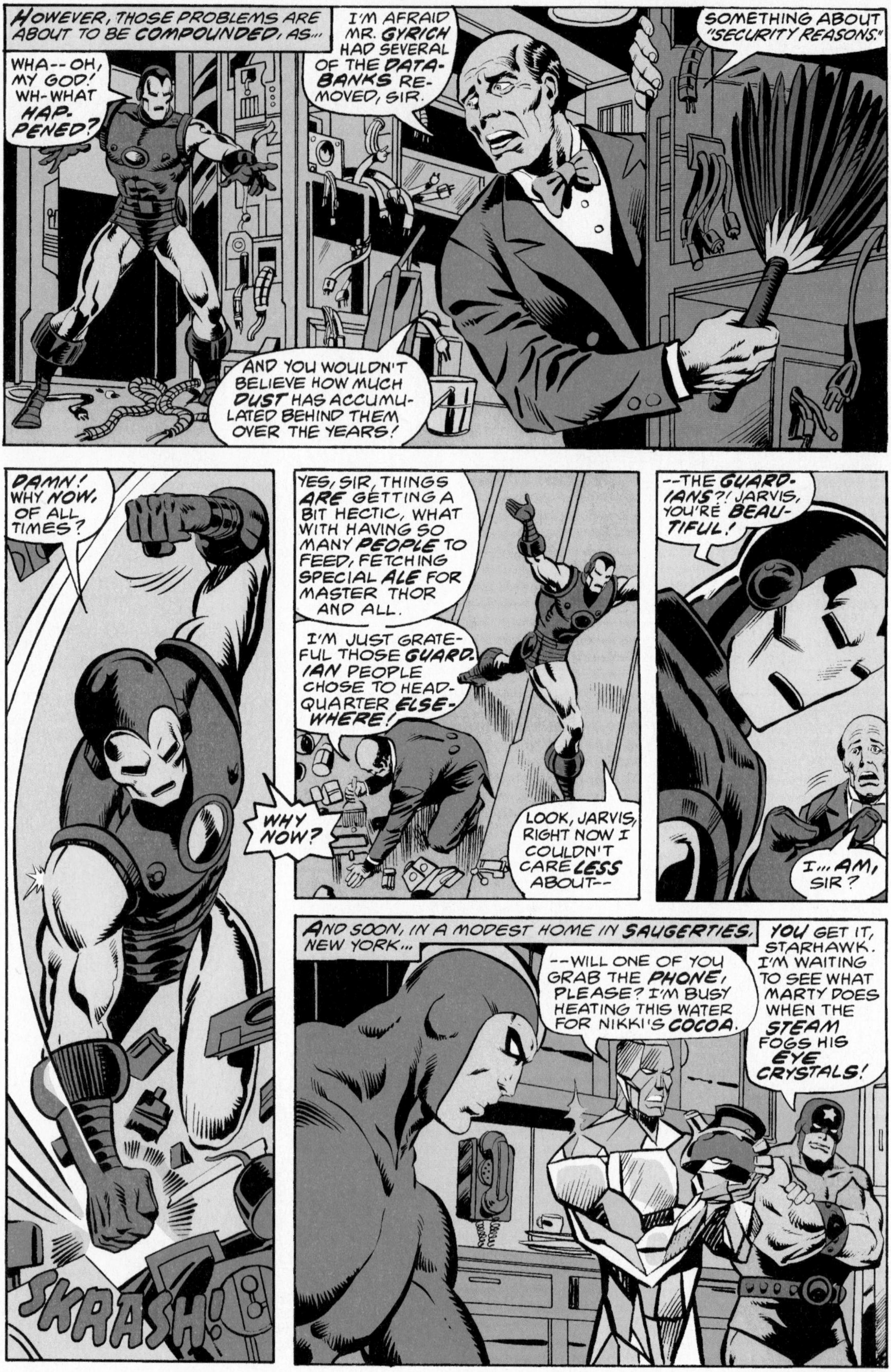
HOWEVER, THOSE PROBLEMS ARE ABOUT TO BE COMPOUNDED, AS...
WHA-- OH, MY GOD! WH-WHAT HAP-PENED?
I'M AFRAID MR. GYRICH HAD SEVERAL OF THE DATA-BANKS RE-MOVED, SIR.
SOMETHING ABOUT "SECURITY REASONS."
AND YOU WOULDN'T BELIEVE HOW MUCH DUST HAS ACCUMU-LATED BEHIND THEM OVER THE YEARS!
DAMN! WHY NOW, OF ALL TIMES?
SKRASH!
YES, SIR, THINGS ARE GETTING A BIT HECTIC, WHAT WITH HAVING SO MANY PEOPLE TO FEED, FETCHING SPECIAL ALE FOR MASTER THOR AND ALL.
I'M JUST GRATE-FUL THOSE GUARD-IAN PEOPLE CHOSE TO HEAD-QUARTER ELSE-WHERE!
WHY NOW?
LOOK, JARVIS, RIGHT NOW I COULDN'T CARE LESS ABOUT--
--THE GUARD-IANS?! JARVIS, YOU'RE BEAU-TIFUL!
I... AM, SIR?
AND SOON, IN A MODEST HOME IN SAUGERTIES, NEW YORK...
--WILL ONE OF YOU GRAB THE PHONE, PLEASE? I'M BUSY HEATING THIS WATER FOR NIKKI'S COCOA.
YOU GET IT, STARHAWK. I'M WAITING TO SEE WHAT MARTY DOES WHEN THE STEAM FOGS HIS EYE CRYSTALS!

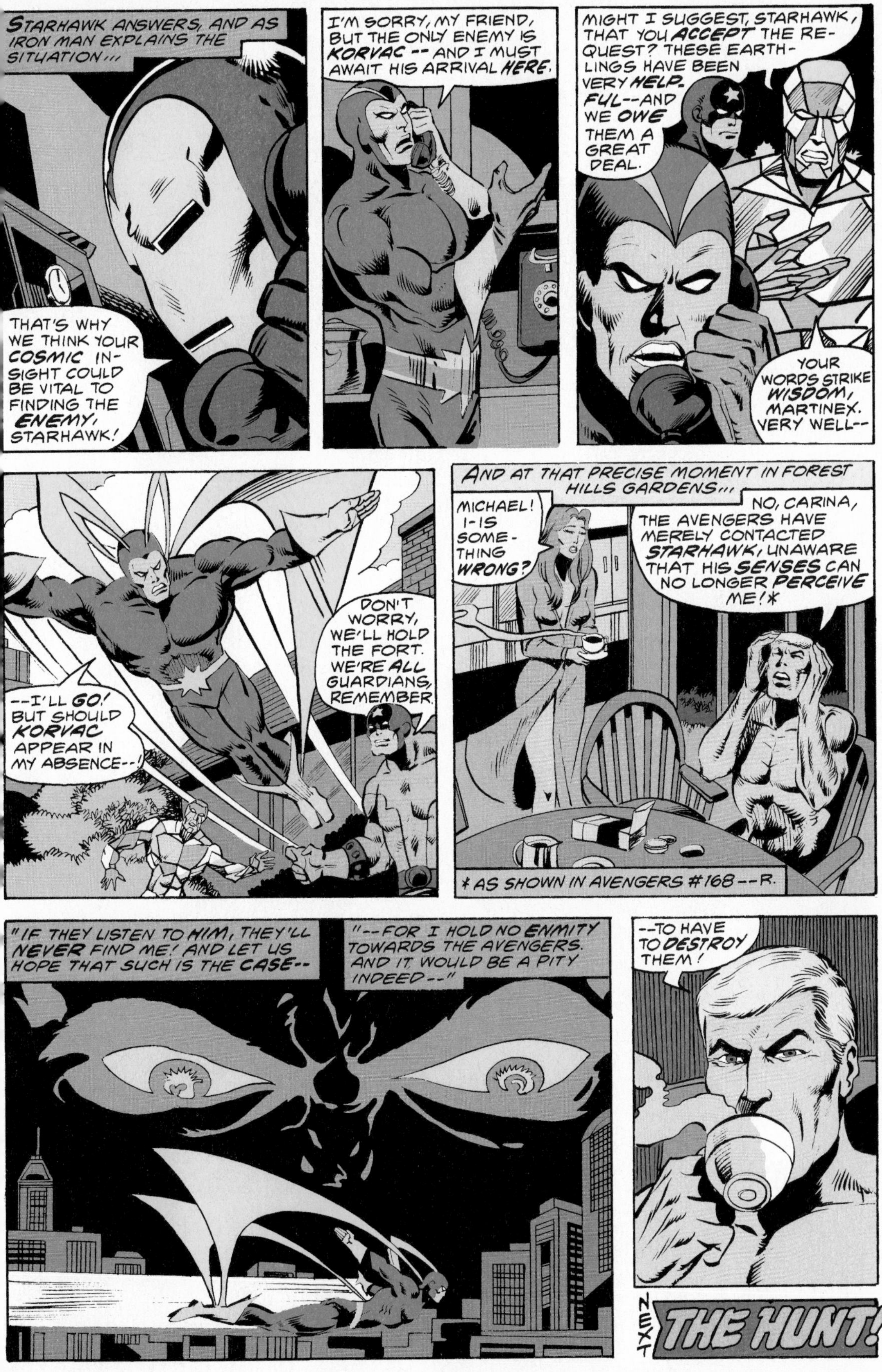
STARHAWK ANSWERS, AND AS IRON MAN EXPLAINS THE SITUATION...
THAT'S WHY WE THINK YOUR COSMIC IN-SIGHT COULD BE VITAL TO FINDING THE ENEMY, STARHAWK!
I'M SORRY, MY FRIEND, BUT THE ONLY ENEMY IS KORVAC -- AND I MUST AWAIT HIS ARRIVAL HERE.
MIGHT I SUGGEST, STARHAWK, THAT YOU ACCEPT THE RE-QUEST? THESE EARTH-LINGS HAVE BEEN VERY HELP-FUL--AND WE OWE THEM A GREAT DEAL.
YOUR WORDS STRIKE WISDOM, MARTINEX. VERY WELL--
--I'LL GO! BUT SHOULD KORVAC APPEAR IN MY ABSENCE--!
DON'T WORRY, WE'LL HOLD THE FORT. WE'RE ALL GUARDIANS, REMEMBER.
AND AT THAT PRECISE MOMENT IN FOREST HILLS GARDENS...
MICHAEL! I-IS SOME-THING WRONG?
NO, CARINA, THE AVENGERS HAVE MERELY CONTACTED STARHAWK, UNAWARE THAT HIS SENSES CAN NO LONGER PERCEIVE ME!*
* AS SHOWN IN AVENGERS #168 --R.
"IF THEY LISTEN TO HIM, THEY'LL NEVER FIND ME! AND LET US HOPE THAT SUCH IS THE CASE--
"--FOR I HOLD NO ENMITY TOWARDS THE AVENGERS. AND IT WOULD BE A PITY INDEED--"
--TO HAVE TO DESTROY THEM!
NEXT
THE HUNT!

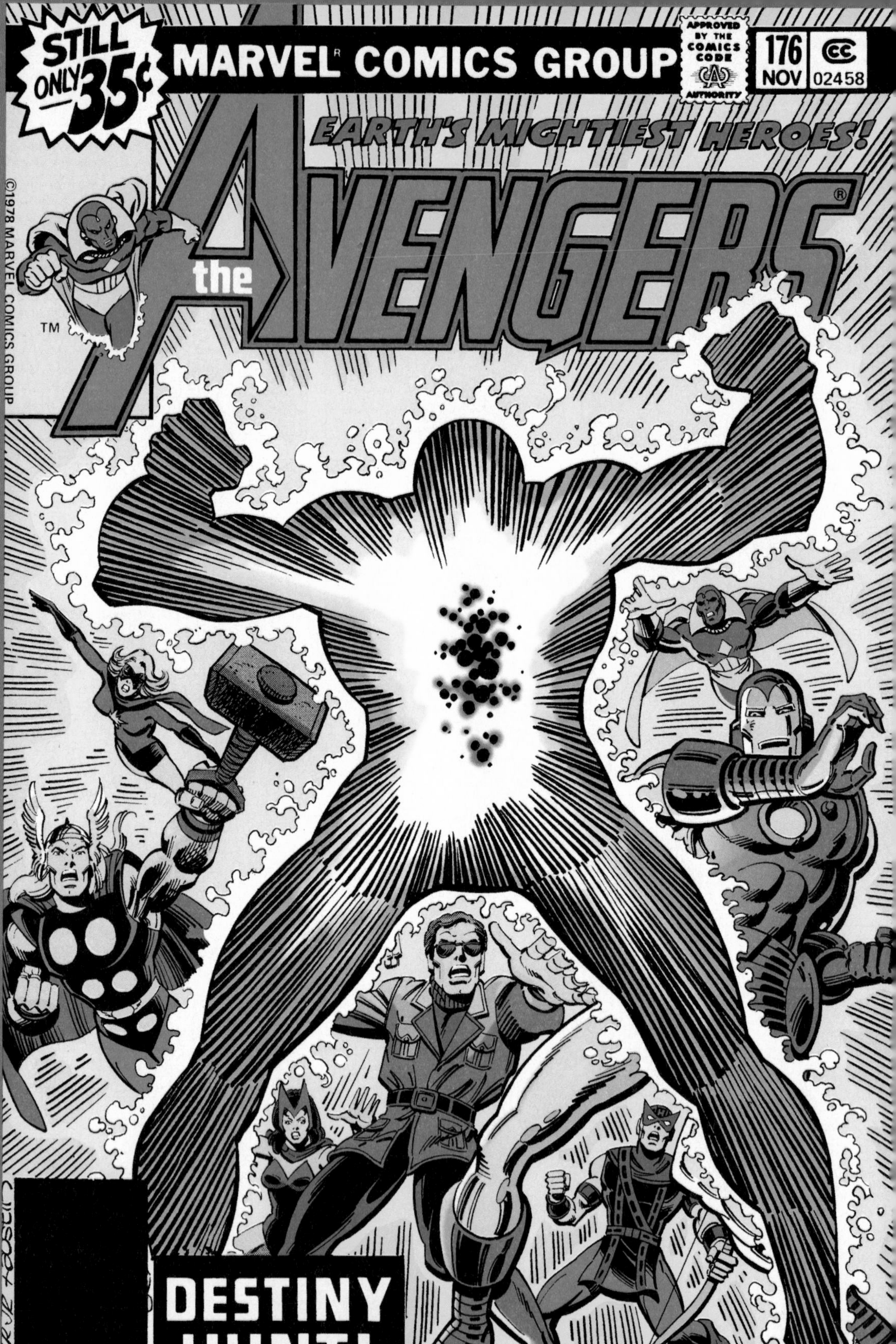
STILL ONLY 35¢
MARVEL COMICS GROUP
APPROVED BY THE COMICS CODE AUTHORITY
176
NOV
02458
EARTH'S MIGHTIEST HEROES!
the AVENGERS
©1978 MARVEL COMICS GROUP
DESTINY HUNT!

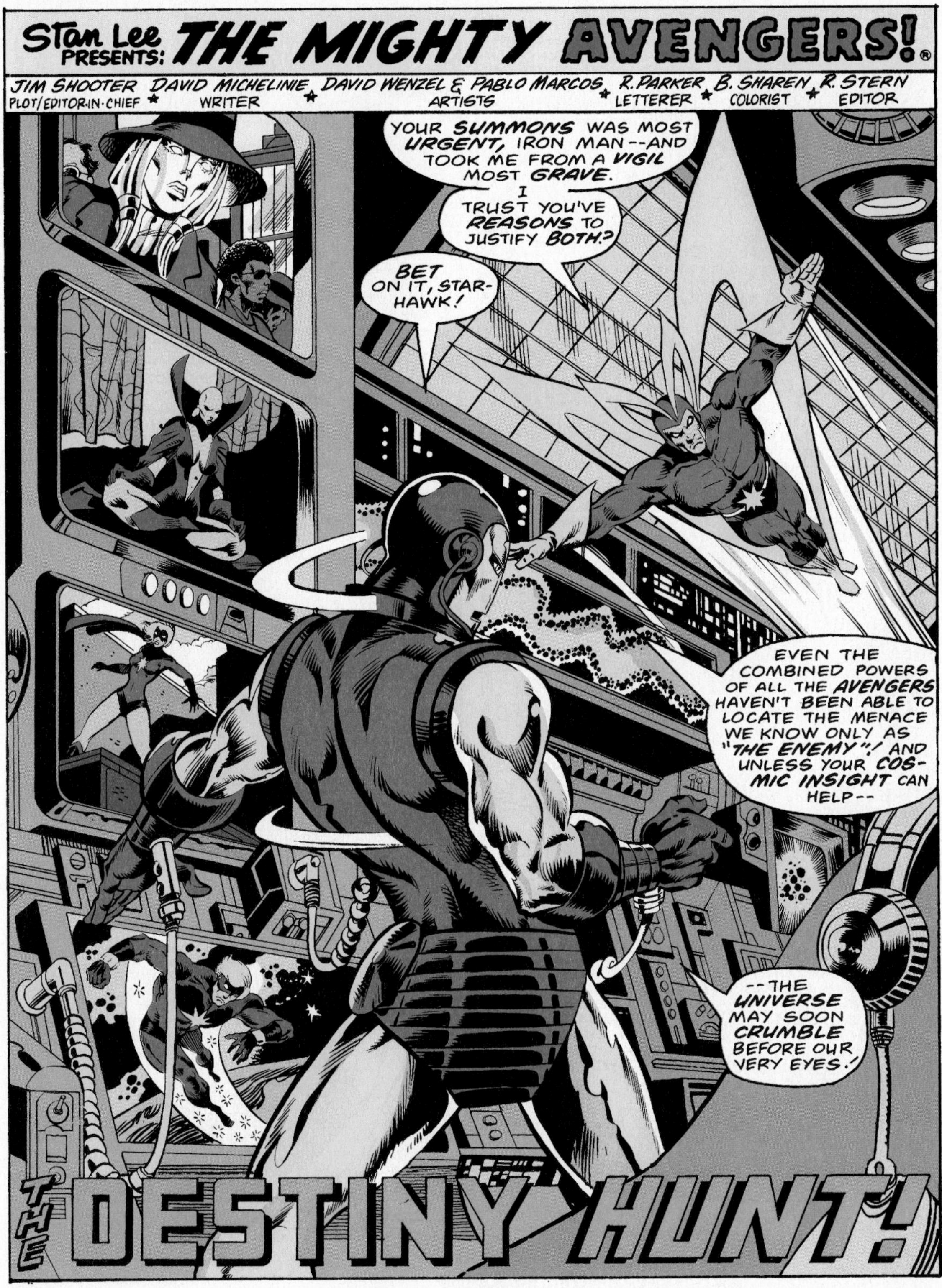
Stan Lee PRESENTS: THE MIGHTY AVENGERS!®
JIM SHOOTER PLOT/EDITOR-IN-CHIEF ★ DAVID MICHELINIE WRITER ★ DAVID WENZEL & PABLO MARCOS ARTISTS ★ R. PARKER LETTERER ★ B. SHAREN COLORIST ★ R. STERN EDITOR
YOUR SUMMONS WAS MOST URGENT, IRON MAN--AND TOOK ME FROM A VIGIL MOST GRAVE.
I TRUST YOU'VE REASONS TO JUSTIFY BOTH?
BET ON IT, STAR-HAWK!
EVEN THE COMBINED POWERS OF ALL THE AVENGERS HAVEN'T BEEN ABLE TO LOCATE THE MENACE WE KNOW ONLY AS "THE ENEMY"! AND UNLESS YOUR COSMIC INSIGHT CAN HELP--
--THE UNIVERSE MAY SOON CRUMBLE BEFORE OUR VERY EYES!
THE DESTINY HUNT!

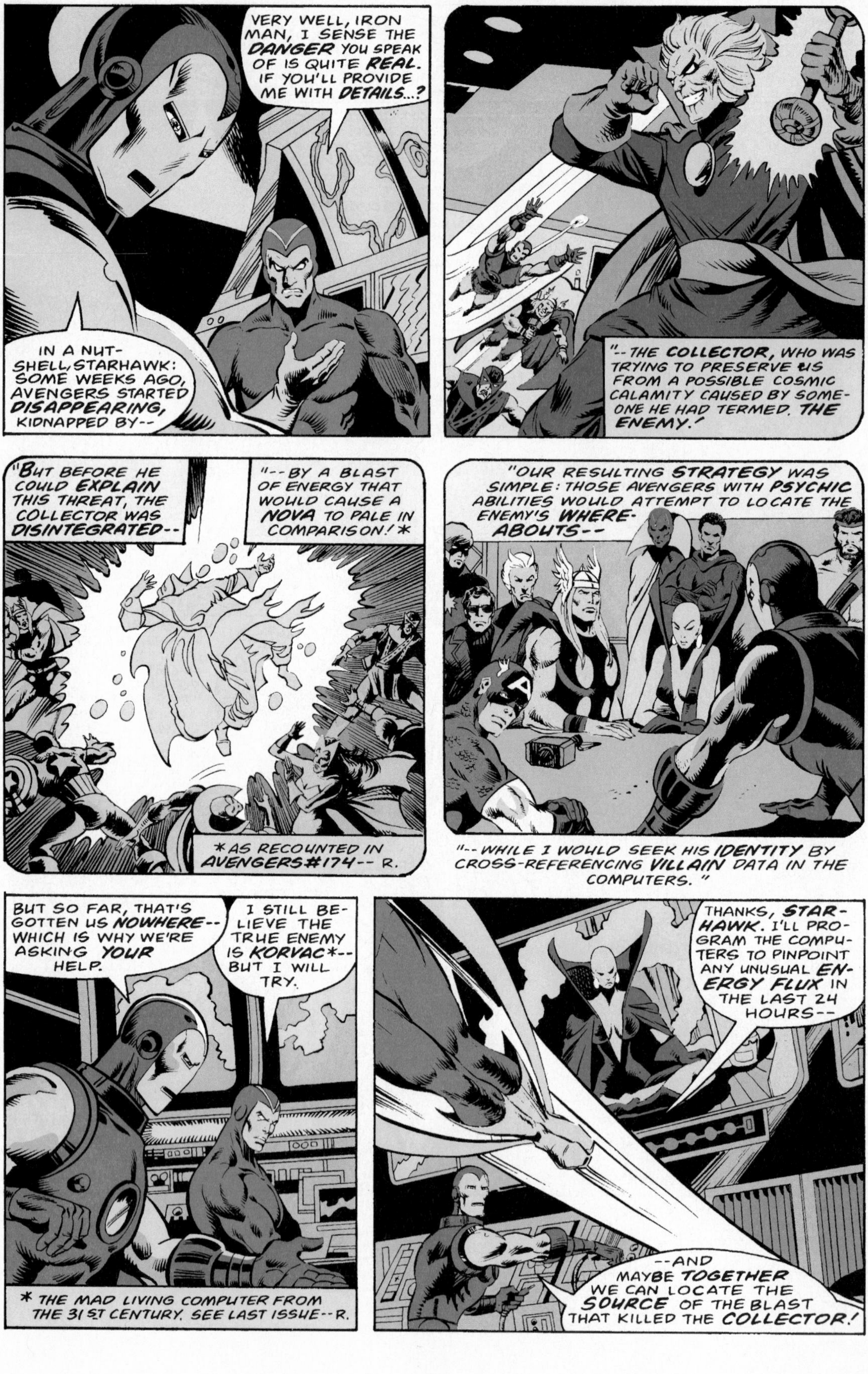
VERY WELL, IRON MAN, I SENSE THE DANGER YOU SPEAK OF IS QUITE REAL. IF YOU'LL PROVIDE ME WITH DETAILS...?
IN A NUT-SHELL, STARHAWK: SOME WEEKS AGO, AVENGERS STARTED DISAPPEARING, KIDNAPPED BY--
"--THE COLLECTOR, WHO WAS TRYING TO PRESERVE US FROM A POSSIBLE COSMIC CALAMITY CAUSED BY SOMEONE HE HAD TERMED THE ENEMY.'
"BUT BEFORE HE COULD EXPLAIN THIS THREAT, THE COLLECTOR WAS DISINTEGRATED--
"--BY A BLAST OF ENERGY THAT WOULD CAUSE A NOVA TO PALE IN COMPARISON! *
*AS RECOUNTED IN AVENGERS #174-- R.
"OUR RESULTING STRATEGY WAS SIMPLE: THOSE AVENGERS WITH PSYCHIC ABILITIES WOULD ATTEMPT TO LOCATE THE ENEMY'S WHERE-ABOUTS--
"--WHILE I WOULD SEEK HIS IDENTITY BY CROSS-REFERENCING VILLAIN DATA IN THE COMPUTERS."
BUT SO FAR, THAT'S GOTTEN US NOWHERE-- WHICH IS WHY WE'RE ASKING YOUR HELP.
I STILL BELIEVE THE TRUE ENEMY IS KORVAC*-- BUT I WILL TRY.
* THE MAD LIVING COMPUTER FROM THE 31ST CENTURY. SEE LAST ISSUE-- R.
THANKS, STARHAWK. I'LL PROGRAM THE COMPUTERS TO PINPOINT ANY UNUSUAL ENERGY FLUX IN THE LAST 24 HOURS--
--AND MAYBE TOGETHER WE CAN LOCATE THE SOURCE OF THE BLAST THAT KILLED THE COLLECTOR!

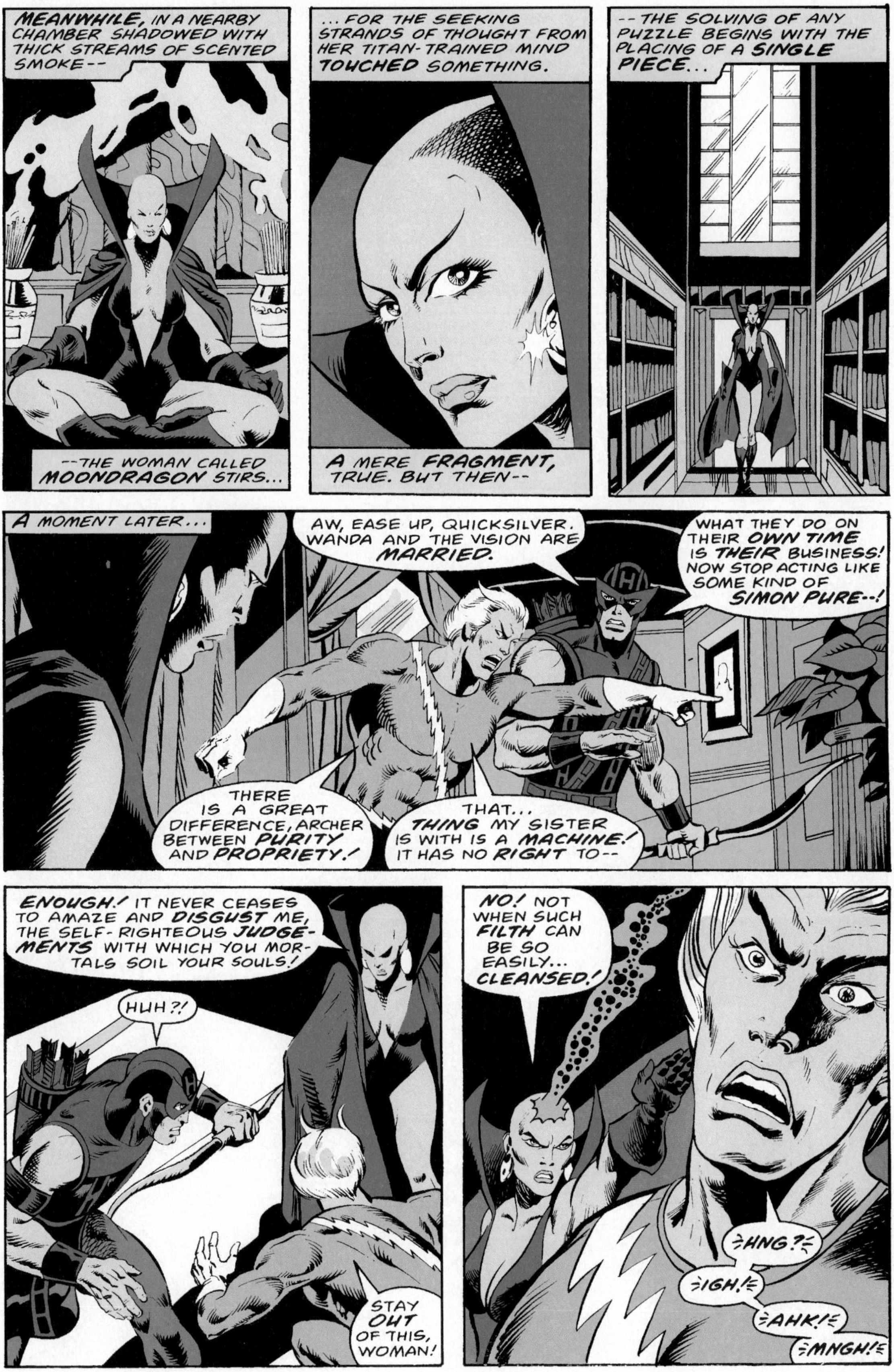
MEANWHILE, IN A NEARBY CHAMBER SHADOWED WITH THICK STREAMS OF SCENTED SMOKE--
--THE WOMAN CALLED MOONDRAGON STIRS...
...FOR THE SEEKING STRANDS OF THOUGHT FROM HER TITAN-TRAINED MIND TOUCHED SOMETHING.
A MERE FRAGMENT, TRUE. BUT THEN--
--THE SOLVING OF ANY PUZZLE BEGINS WITH THE PLACING OF A SINGLE PIECE...
A MOMENT LATER...
AW, EASE UP, QUICKSILVER. WANDA AND THE VISION ARE MARRIED.
WHAT THEY DO ON THEIR OWN TIME IS THEIR BUSINESS! NOW STOP ACTING LIKE SOME KIND OF SIMON PURE--!
THERE IS A GREAT DIFFERENCE, ARCHER BETWEEN PURITY AND PROPRIETY.!
THAT... THING MY SISTER IS WITH IS A MACHINE! IT HAS NO RIGHT TO--
ENOUGH! IT NEVER CEASES TO AMAZE AND DISGUST ME, THE SELF-RIGHTEOUS JUDGEMENTS WITH WHICH YOU MORTALS SOIL YOUR SOULS!
HUH?!
STAY OUT OF THIS, WOMAN!
NO! NOT WHEN SUCH FILTH CAN BE SO EASILY... CLEANSED!
HNG?
IGH!
AHK!
MNGH!

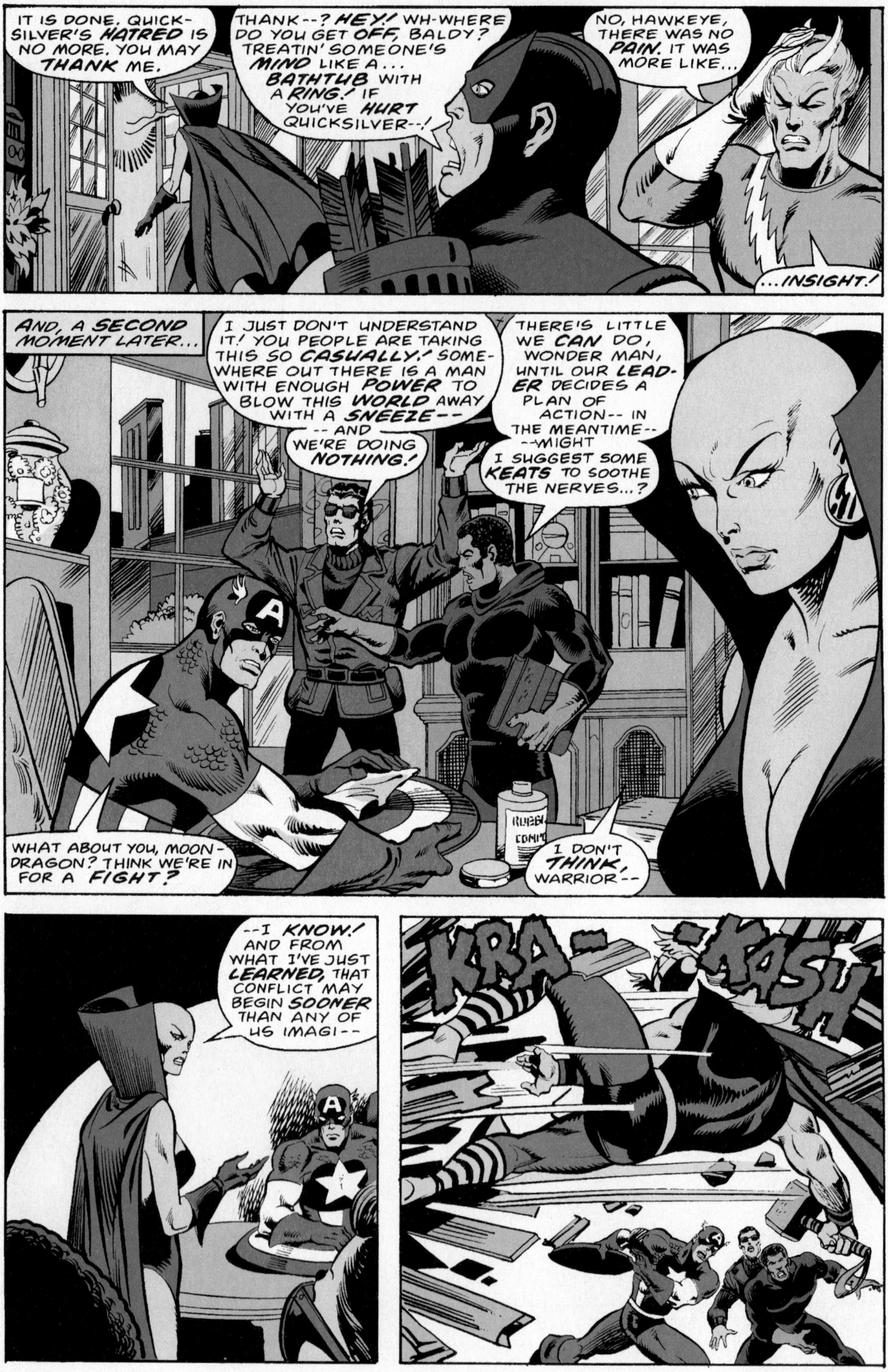
IT IS DONE. QUICKSILVER'S HATRED IS NO MORE. YOU MAY THANK ME.
THANK--? HEY! WH-WHERE DO YOU GET OFF, BALDY? TREATIN' SOMEONE'S MIND LIKE A... BATHTUB WITH A RING! IF YOU'VE HURT QUICKSILVER--!
NO, HAWKEYE, THERE WAS NO PAIN. IT WAS MORE LIKE...
...INSIGHT!
AND, A SECOND MOMENT LATER...
I JUST DON'T UNDERSTAND IT! YOU PEOPLE ARE TAKING THIS SO CASUALLY! SOMEWHERE OUT THERE IS A MAN WITH ENOUGH POWER TO BLOW THIS WORLD AWAY WITH A SNEEZE--
--AND WE'RE DOING NOTHING!
THERE'S LITTLE WE CAN DO, WONDER MAN, UNTIL OUR LEADER DECIDES A PLAN OF ACTION-- IN THE MEANTIME--
--MIGHT I SUGGEST SOME KEATS TO SOOTHE THE NERVES...?
WHAT ABOUT YOU, MOONDRAGON? THINK WE'RE IN FOR A FIGHT?
I DON'T THINK, WARRIOR--
--I KNOW! AND FROM WHAT I'VE JUST LEARNED, THAT CONFLICT MAY BEGIN SOONER THAN ANY OF US IMAGI--
KRA--KASH

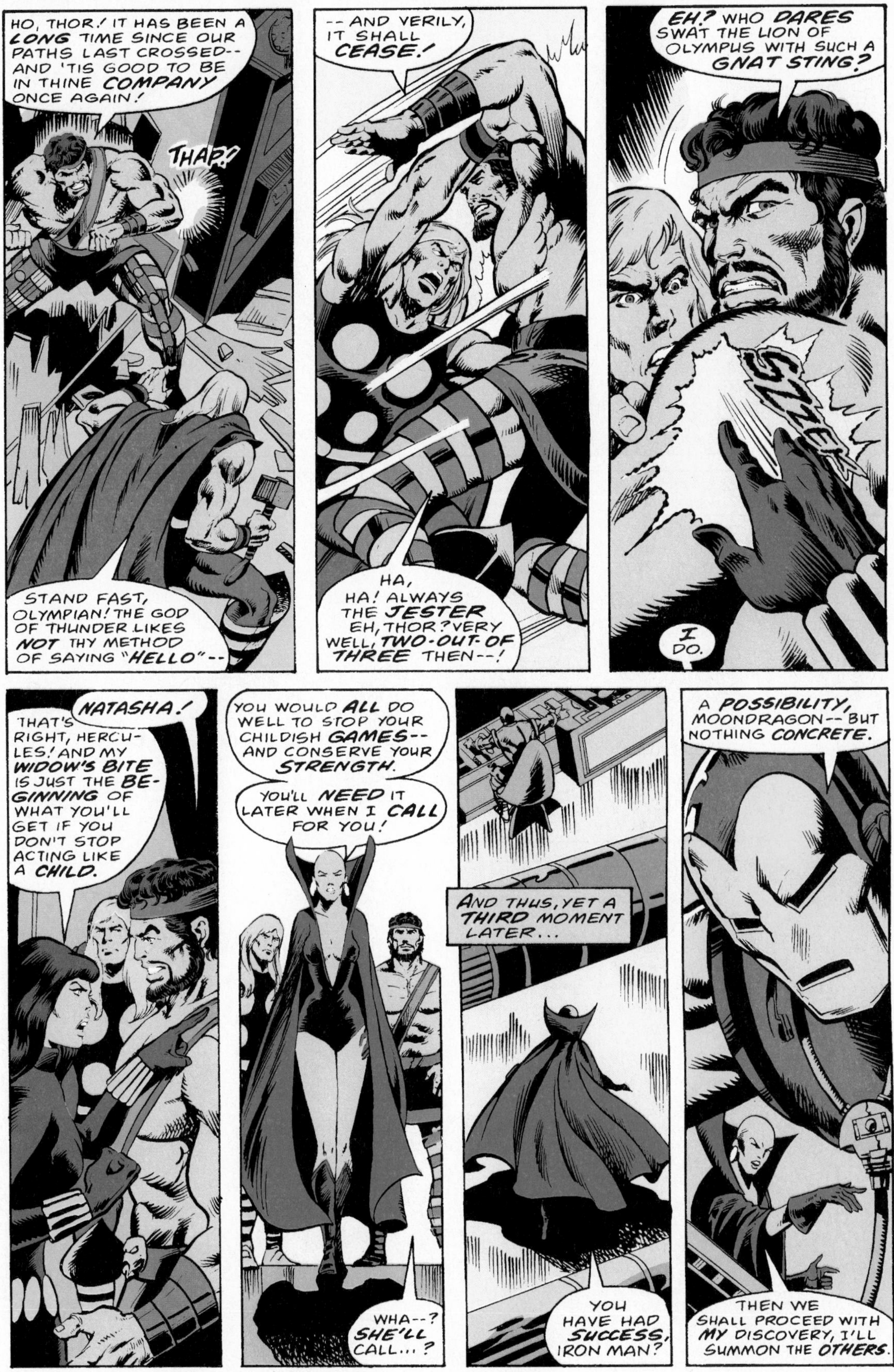
HO, THOR! IT HAS BEEN A LONG TIME SINCE OUR PATHS LAST CROSSED-- AND 'TIS GOOD TO BE IN THINE COMPANY ONCE AGAIN!
THAP!
STAND FAST, OLYMPIAN! THE GOD OF THUNDER LIKES NOT THY METHOD OF SAYING "HELLO"--
-- AND VERILY, IT SHALL CEASE!
HA, HA! ALWAYS THE JESTER EH, THOR? VERY WELL, TWO-OUT-OF THREE THEN--!
EH? WHO DARES SWAT THE LION OF OLYMPUS WITH SUCH A GNAT STING?
SZZK
I DO.
NATASHA!
THAT'S RIGHT, HERCULES! AND MY WIDOW'S BITE IS JUST THE BEGINNING OF WHAT YOU'LL GET IF YOU DON'T STOP ACTING LIKE A CHILD.
YOU WOULD ALL DO WELL TO STOP YOUR CHILDISH GAMES-- AND CONSERVE YOUR STRENGTH.
YOU'LL NEED IT LATER WHEN I CALL FOR YOU!
WHA--? SHE'LL CALL...?
AND THUS, YET A THIRD MOMENT LATER...
YOU HAVE HAD SUCCESS, IRON MAN?
A POSSIBILITY, MOONDRAGON-- BUT NOTHING CONCRETE.
THEN WE SHALL PROCEED WITH MY DISCOVERY. I'LL SUMMON THE OTHERS.

YOU?! NOW WAIT A MINUTE! I'M THE LEADER OF THIS TEAM! WHAT--

SILENCE! I MUST CONCENTRATE!

WHILE ON A ROOFTOP IN BENSONHURST...

DARN! IF ONLY I COULD CONTROL THESE POWERS OF MINE! I'VE BEEN TRYING TO PICK UP A SEVENTH SENSE COGNITION FOR HOURS, BUT--

--WAIT! I'M GETTING A MESSAGE! SOMETHING IMPORTANT'S GOING DOWN AT AVENGERS' MANSION!

AND ON A LITTERED CANARSIE SIDEWALK...

THIS COULD BE IT, HANK!

LET'S HOPE SO, JAN. ANTS HAVE DIFFERENT LEVELS OF PERCEPTION THAN HUMANS AND ACCORDING TO THESE--

--THE STORM THAT DESTROYED SO MANY OF THEIR COMMUNITIES IN FOREST HILLS LAST WEEK* WAS PSYCHIC IN NATURE! WHICH COULD MEAN--

*AVENGERS #168 -- R.

I KNOW, DARLING, I FEEL IT, TOO! SOME SORT OF MENTAL SIGNAL FROM AVENGERS' MANSION!

WE'D BETTER GET BACK THERE AND-- WASP! WHAT ARE YOU DOING?

YOU CAN'T FLY WHEN YOU'RE FULL-SIZED!

I KNOW--

--BUT THIS WAY IS JUST AS FAST, AND IT'S SO MUCH MORE... COZY, DON'T YOU THINK?

DA WIFE AIN'T GONNA BELIEVE DIS!

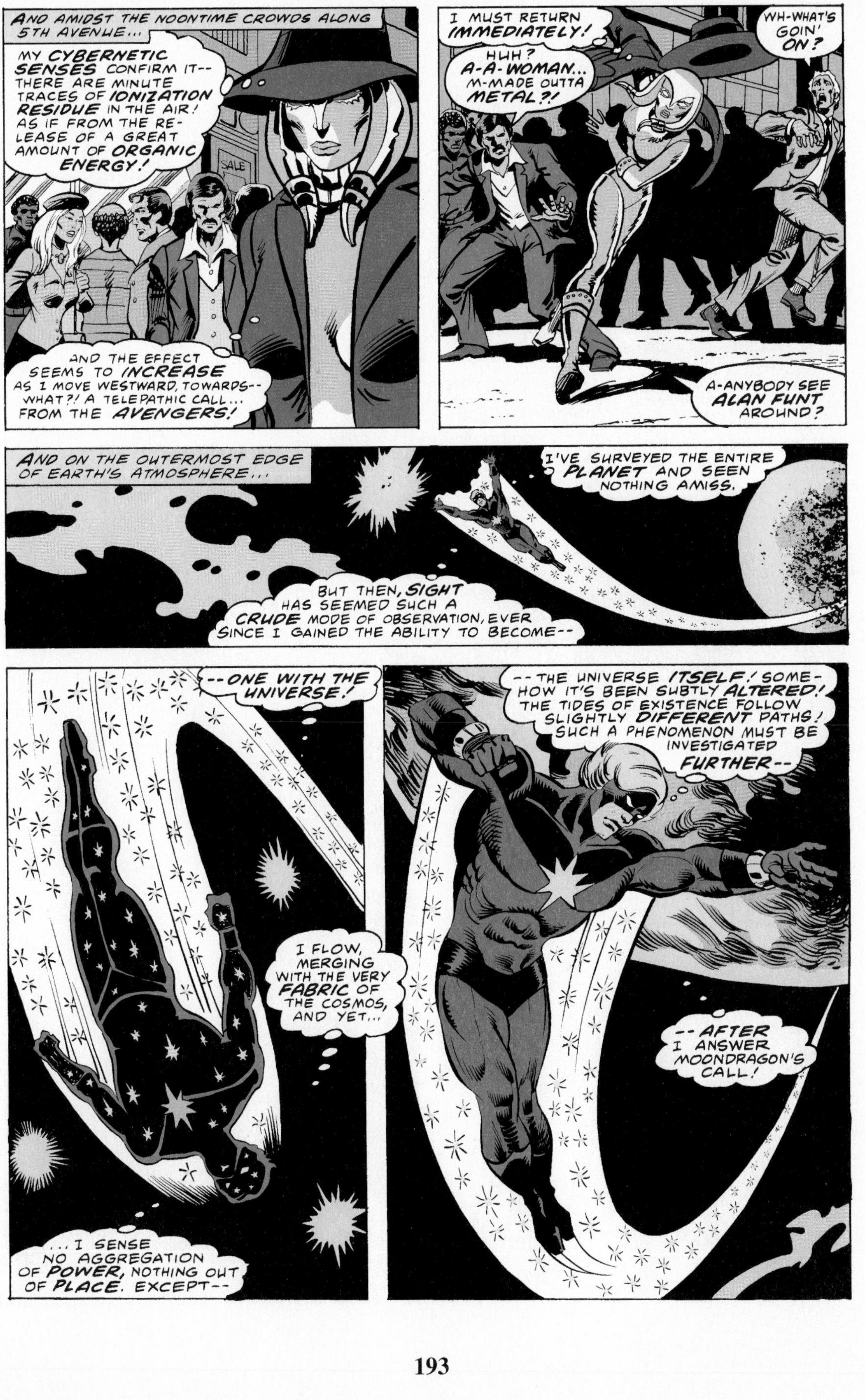
AND AMIDST THE NOONTIME CROWDS ALONG 5TH AVENUE...
MY CYBERNETIC SENSES CONFIRM IT-- THERE ARE MINUTE TRACES OF IONIZATION RESIDUE IN THE AIR! AS IF FROM THE RELEASE OF A GREAT AMOUNT OF ORGANIC ENERGY!
SALE
AND THE EFFECT SEEMS TO INCREASE AS I MOVE WESTWARD, TOWARDS-- WHAT?! A TELEPATHIC CALL... FROM THE AVENGERS!
I MUST RETURN IMMEDIATELY!
WH-WHAT'S GOIN' ON?
HUH? A-A-WOMAN... M-MADE OUTTA METAL?!
A-ANYBODY SEE ALAN FUNT AROUND?
AND ON THE OUTERMOST EDGE OF EARTH'S ATMOSPHERE...
I'VE SURVEYED THE ENTIRE PLANET AND SEEN NOTHING AMISS.
BUT THEN, SIGHT HAS SEEMED SUCH A CRUDE MODE OF OBSERVATION, EVER SINCE I GAINED THE ABILITY TO BECOME--
--ONE WITH THE UNIVERSE!
I FLOW, MERGING WITH THE VERY FABRIC OF THE COSMOS, AND YET...
...I SENSE NO AGGREGATION OF POWER, NOTHING OUT OF PLACE. EXCEPT--
--THE UNIVERSE ITSELF! SOMEHOW IT'S BEEN SUBTLY ALTERED! THE TIDES OF EXISTENCE FOLLOW SLIGHTLY DIFFERENT PATHS! SUCH A PHENOMENON MUST BE INVESTIGATED FURTHER--
--AFTER I ANSWER MOONDRAGON'S CALL!

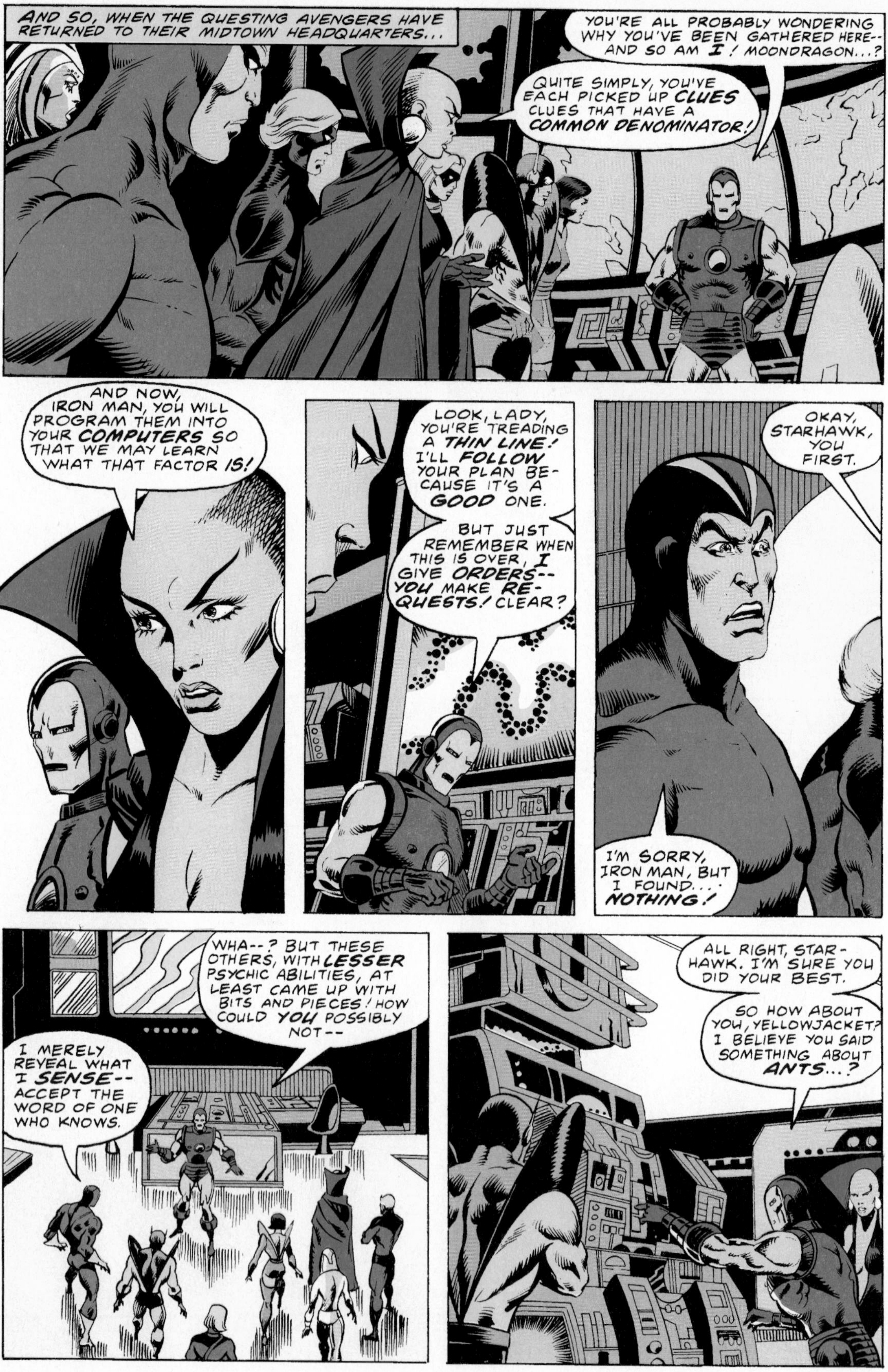
AND SO, WHEN THE QUESTING AVENGERS HAVE RETURNED TO THEIR MIDTOWN HEADQUARTERS...
YOU'RE ALL PROBABLY WONDERING WHY YOU'VE BEEN GATHERED HERE-- AND SO AM I! MOONDRAGON...?
QUITE SIMPLY, YOU'VE EACH PICKED UP CLUES CLUES THAT HAVE A COMMON DENOMINATOR!
AND NOW, IRON MAN, YOU WILL PROGRAM THEM INTO YOUR COMPUTERS SO THAT WE MAY LEARN WHAT THAT FACTOR IS!
LOOK, LADY, YOU'RE TREADING A THIN LINE! I'LL FOLLOW YOUR PLAN BE- CAUSE IT'S A GOOD ONE.
BUT JUST REMEMBER WHEN THIS IS OVER, I GIVE ORDERS-- YOU MAKE RE- QUESTS! CLEAR?
OKAY, STARHAWK, YOU FIRST.
I'M SORRY, IRON MAN, BUT I FOUND... NOTHING!
WHA--? BUT THESE OTHERS, WITH LESSER PSYCHIC ABILITIES, AT LEAST CAME UP WITH BITS AND PIECES! HOW COULD YOU POSSIBLY NOT--
I MERELY REVEAL WHAT I SENSE-- ACCEPT THE WORD OF ONE WHO KNOWS.
ALL RIGHT, STAR- HAWK. I'M SURE YOU DID YOUR BEST.
SO HOW ABOUT YOU, YELLOWJACKET? I BELIEVE YOU SAID SOMETHING ABOUT ANTS...?

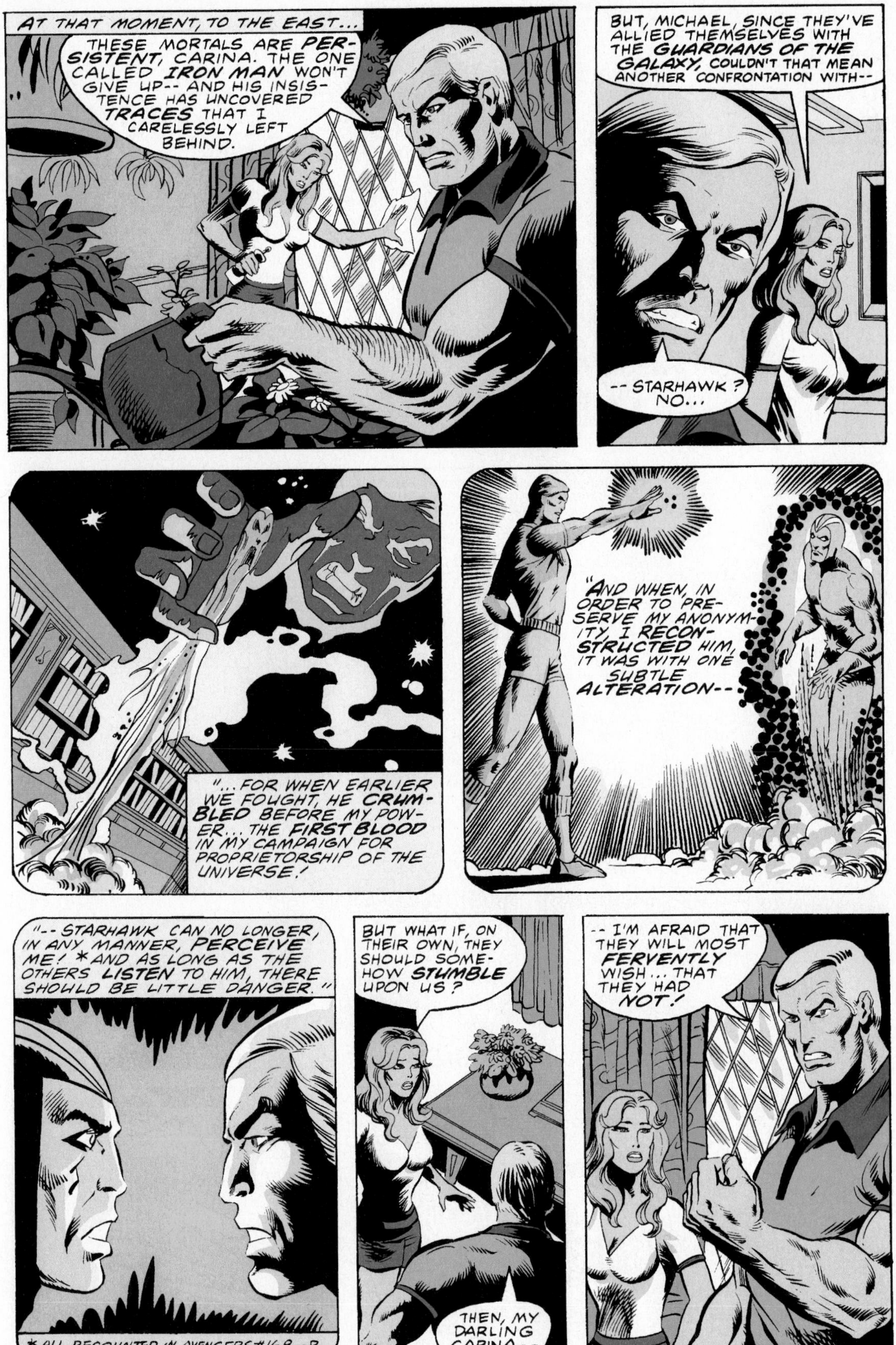
AT THAT MOMENT, TO THE EAST...
THESE MORTALS ARE PERSISTENT, CARINA. THE ONE CALLED IRON MAN WON'T GIVE UP-- AND HIS INSISTENCE HAS UNCOVERED TRACES THAT I CARELESSLY LEFT BEHIND.
BUT, MICHAEL, SINCE THEY'VE ALLIED THEMSELVES WITH THE GUARDIANS OF THE GALAXY, COULDN'T THAT MEAN ANOTHER CONFRONTATION WITH--
-- STARHAWK? NO...
"... FOR WHEN EARLIER WE FOUGHT, HE CRUMBLED BEFORE MY POWER... THE FIRST BLOOD IN MY CAMPAIGN FOR PROPRIETORSHIP OF THE UNIVERSE!
"AND WHEN, IN ORDER TO PRESERVE MY ANONYMITY, I RECONSTRUCTED HIM, IT WAS WITH ONE SUBTLE ALTERATION--
"-- STARHAWK CAN NO LONGER, IN ANY MANNER, PERCEIVE ME! *AND AS LONG AS THE OTHERS LISTEN TO HIM, THERE SHOULD BE LITTLE DANGER."
*ALL RECOUNTED IN AVENGERS #168 -- R.
BUT WHAT IF, ON THEIR OWN, THEY SHOULD SOMEHOW STUMBLE UPON US?
THEN, MY DARLING CARINA --
-- I'M AFRAID THAT THEY WILL MOST FERVENTLY WISH... THAT THEY HAD NOT!

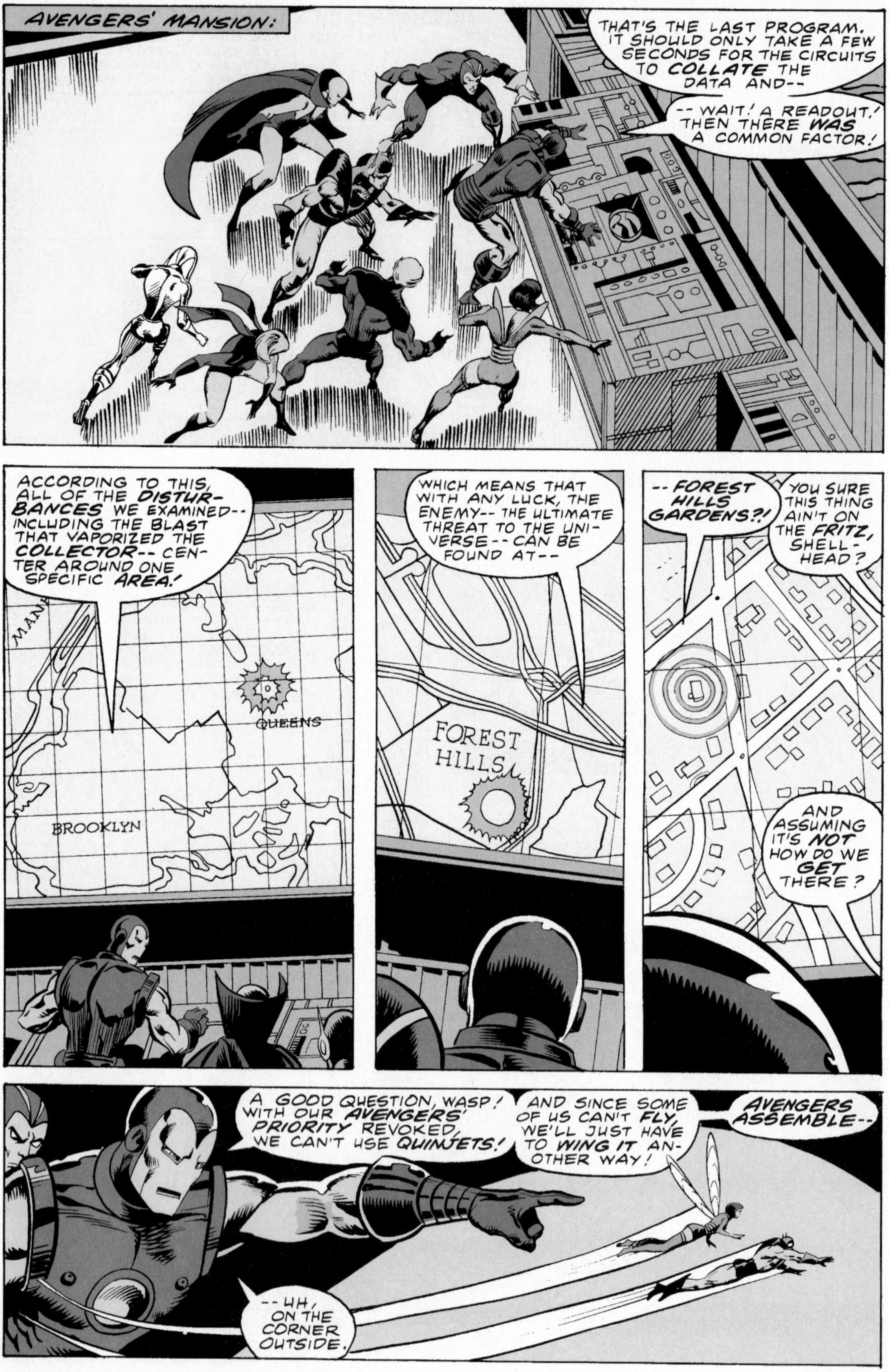
AVENGERS' MANSION:
THAT'S THE LAST PROGRAM. IT SHOULD ONLY TAKE A FEW SECONDS FOR THE CIRCUITS TO COLLATE THE DATA AND--
--WAIT! A READOUT! THEN THERE WAS A COMMON FACTOR!
ACCORDING TO THIS, ALL OF THE DISTURBANCES WE EXAMINED--INCLUDING THE BLAST THAT VAPORIZED THE COLLECTOR--CENTER AROUND ONE SPECIFIC AREA!
QUEENS
BROOKLYN
WHICH MEANS THAT WITH ANY LUCK, THE ENEMY--THE ULTIMATE THREAT TO THE UNIVERSE--CAN BE FOUND AT--
FOREST HILLS
--FOREST HILLS GARDENS?!
YOU SURE THIS THING AIN'T ON THE FRITZ, SHELL-HEAD?
AND ASSUMING IT'S NOT HOW DO WE GET THERE?
A GOOD QUESTION, WASP! WITH OUR AVENGERS' PRIORITY REVOKED, WE CAN'T USE QUINJETS!
AND SINCE SOME OF US CAN'T FLY, WE'LL JUST HAVE TO WING IT ANOTHER WAY!
AVENGERS ASSEMBLE--
--UH, ON THE CORNER OUTSIDE.

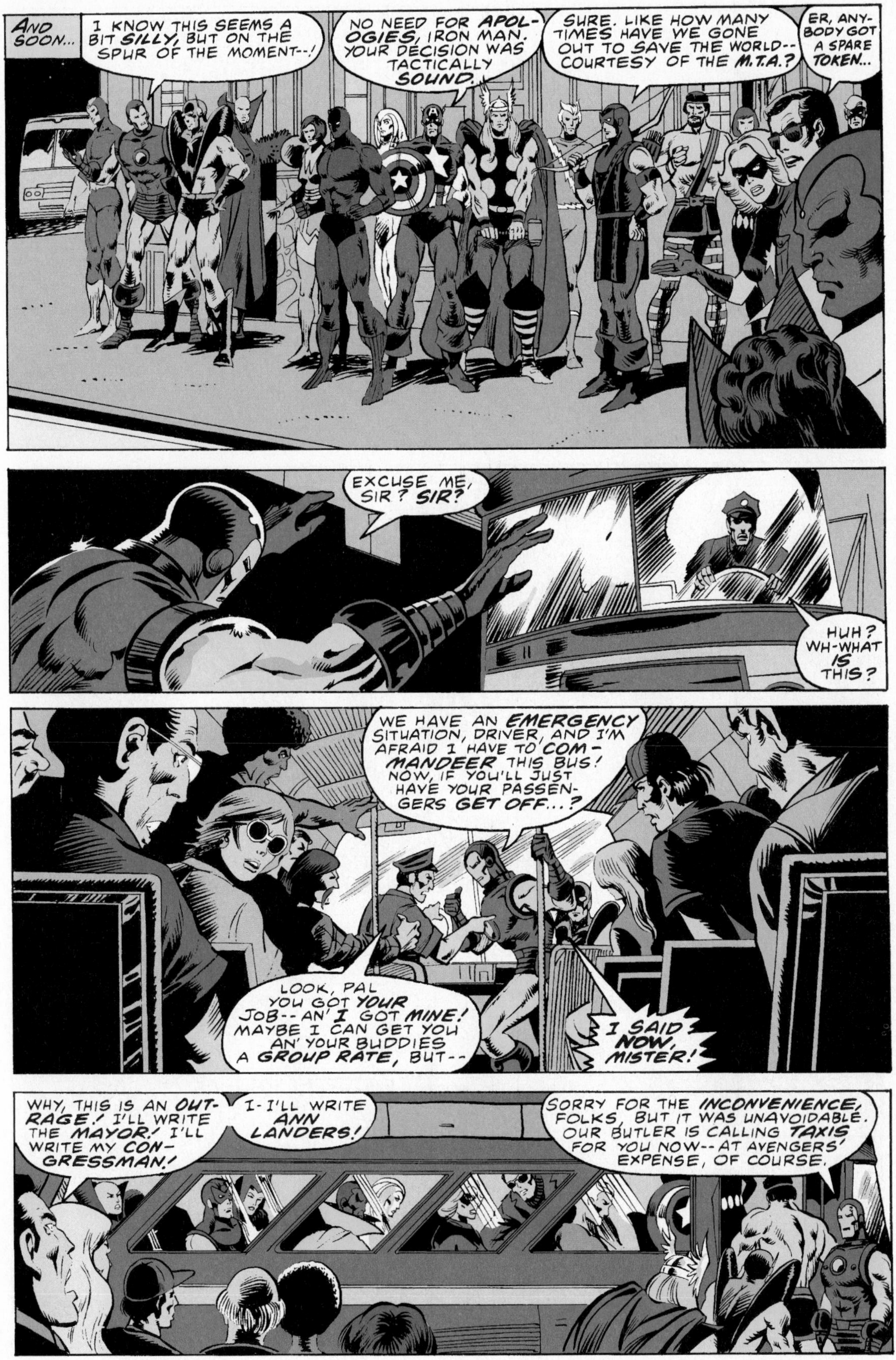

AND SOON...
I KNOW THIS SEEMS A BIT SILLY, BUT ON THE SPUR OF THE MOMENT--!
NO NEED FOR APOLOGIES, IRON MAN. YOUR DECISION WAS TACTICALLY SOUND.
SURE. LIKE HOW MANY TIMES HAVE WE GONE OUT TO SAVE THE WORLD--COURTESY OF THE M.T.A.?
ER, ANYBODY GOT A SPARE TOKEN...
EXCUSE ME, SIR? SIR?
HUH? WH-WHAT IS THIS?
WE HAVE AN EMERGENCY SITUATION, DRIVER, AND I'M AFRAID I HAVE TO COMMANDEER THIS BUS! NOW, IF YOU'LL JUST HAVE YOUR PASSENGERS GET OFF...?
LOOK, PAL YOU GOT YOUR JOB--AN' I GOT MINE! MAYBE I CAN GET YOU AN' YOUR BUDDIES A GROUP RATE, BUT--
I SAID NOW, MISTER!
WHY, THIS IS AN OUTRAGE! I'LL WRITE THE MAYOR! I'LL WRITE MY CONGRESSMAN!
I-I'LL WRITE ANN LANDERS!
SORRY FOR THE INCONVENIENCE, FOLKS, BUT IT WAS UNAVOIDABLE. OUR BUTLER IS CALLING TAXIS FOR YOU NOW--AT AVENGERS' EXPENSE, OF COURSE.

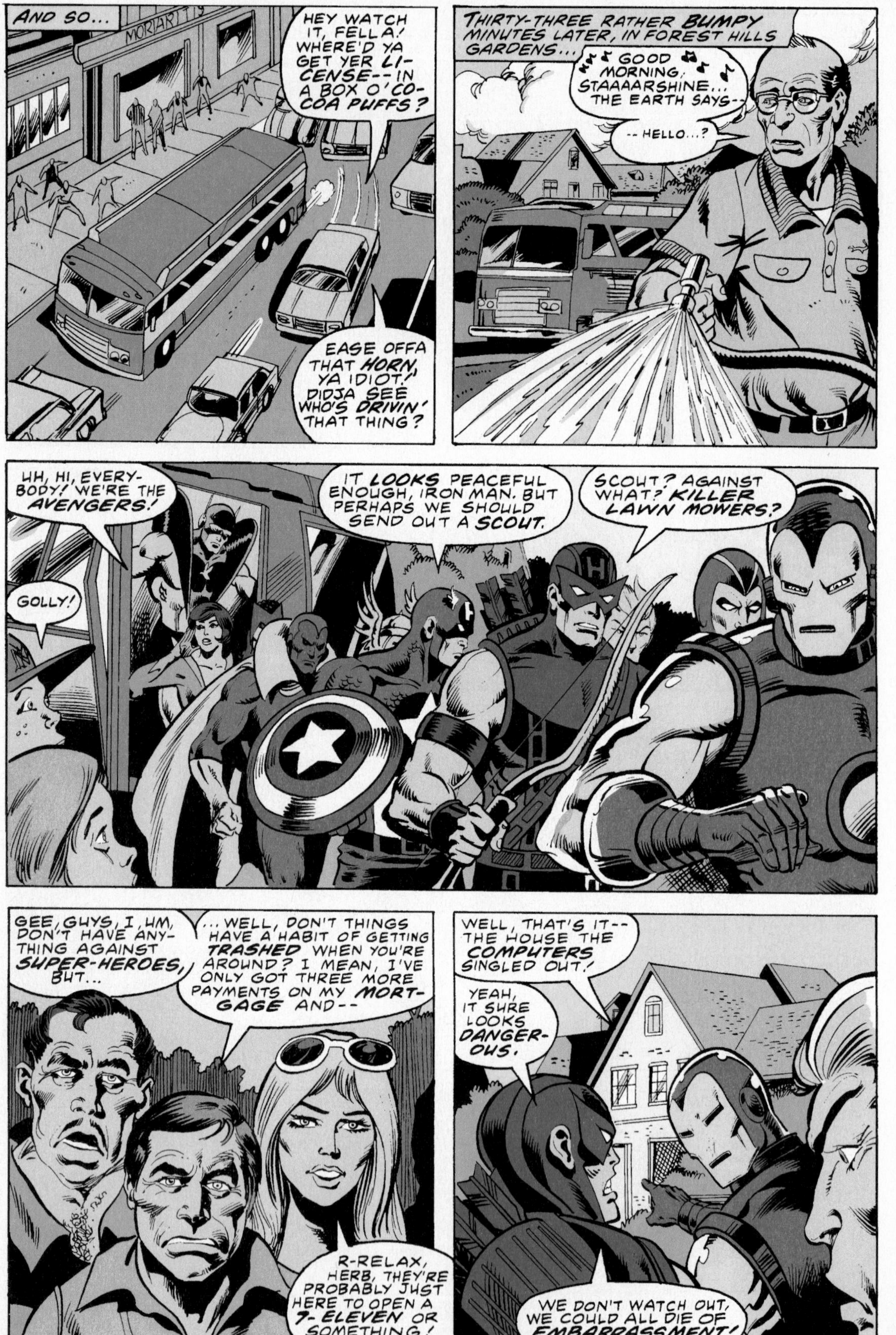

AND SO...
MORIARTY'S
HEY WATCH IT, FELLA! WHERE'D YA GET YER LI-CENSE--IN A BOX O' CO-COA PUFFS?
EASE OFFA THAT HORN, YA IDIOT! DIDJA SEE WHO'S DRIVIN' THAT THING?
THIRTY-THREE RATHER BUMPY MINUTES LATER, IN FOREST HILLS GARDENS...
GOOD MORNING, STAAAARSHINE... THE EARTH SAYS--
--HELLO...?
UH, HI, EVERY-BODY! WE'RE THE AVENGERS!
GOLLY!
IT LOOKS PEACEFUL ENOUGH, IRON MAN. BUT PERHAPS WE SHOULD SEND OUT A SCOUT.
SCOUT? AGAINST WHAT? KILLER LAWN MOWERS?
GEE, GUYS, I UM, DON'T HAVE ANY-THING AGAINST SUPER-HEROES, BUT...
...WELL, DON'T THINGS HAVE A HABIT OF GETTING TRASHED WHEN YOU'RE AROUND? I MEAN, I'VE ONLY GOT THREE MORE PAYMENTS ON MY MORT-GAGE AND--
R-RELAX, HERB, THEY'RE PROBABLY JUST HERE TO OPEN A 7-ELEVEN OR SOMETHING!
WELL, THAT'S IT--THE HOUSE THE COMPUTERS SINGLED OUT!
YEAH, IT SURE LOOKS DANGER-OUS.
WE DON'T WATCH OUT, WE COULD ALL DIE OF EMBARRASSMENT!

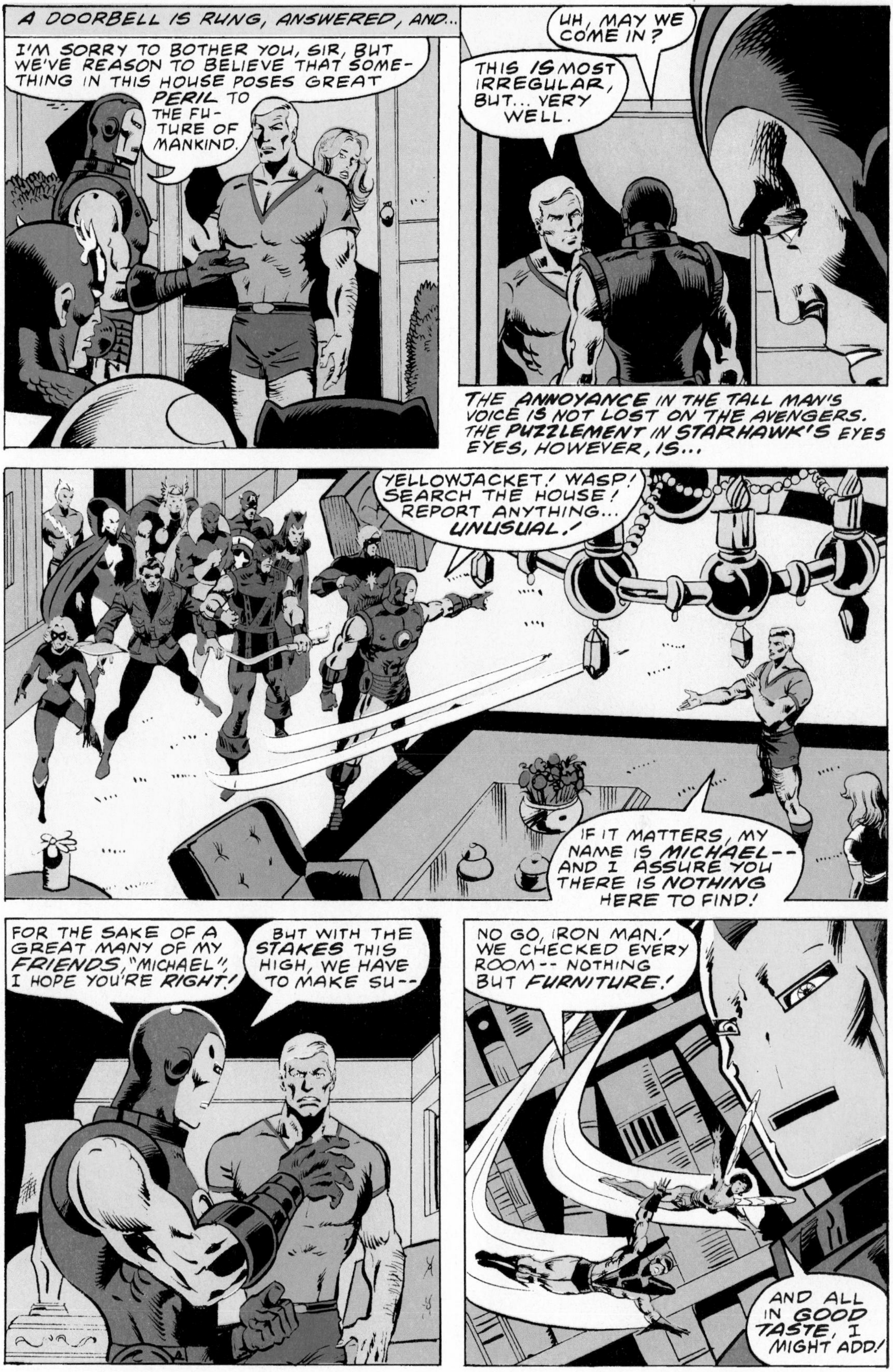

A DOORBELL IS RUNG, ANSWERED, AND...
I'M SORRY TO BOTHER YOU, SIR, BUT WE'VE REASON TO BELIEVE THAT SOMETHING IN THIS HOUSE POSES GREAT PERIL TO THE FUTURE OF MANKIND.
UH, MAY WE COME IN?
THIS IS MOST IRREGULAR, BUT... VERY WELL.
THE ANNOYANCE IN THE TALL MAN'S VOICE IS NOT LOST ON THE AVENGERS. THE PUZZLEMENT IN STARHAWK'S EYES EYES, HOWEVER, IS...
YELLOWJACKET! WASP! SEARCH THE HOUSE! REPORT ANYTHING... UNUSUAL!
IF IT MATTERS, MY NAME IS MICHAEL-- AND I ASSURE YOU THERE IS NOTHING HERE TO FIND!
FOR THE SAKE OF A GREAT MANY OF MY FRIENDS, "MICHAEL", I HOPE YOU'RE RIGHT!
BUT WITH THE STAKES THIS HIGH, WE HAVE TO MAKE SU--
NO GO, IRON MAN! WE CHECKED EVERY ROOM-- NOTHING BUT FURNITURE!
AND ALL IN GOOD TASTE, I MIGHT ADD!

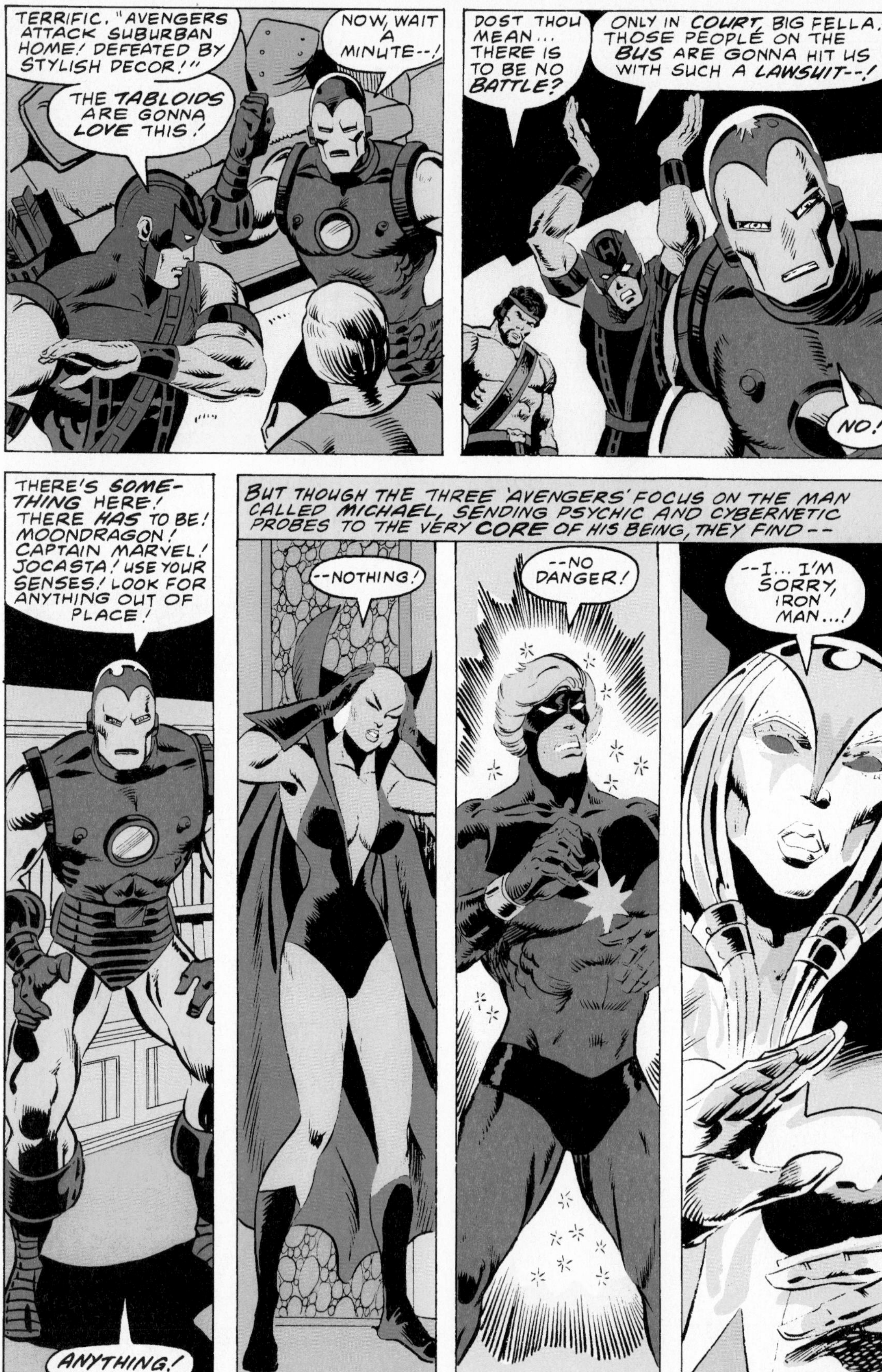

TERRIFIC. "AVENGERS ATTACK SUBURBAN HOME! DEFEATED BY STYLISH DECOR!"
THE TABLOIDS ARE GONNA LOVE THIS!
NOW, WAIT A MINUTE--!
DOST THOU MEAN... THERE IS TO BE NO BATTLE?
ONLY IN COURT, BIG FELLA! THOSE PEOPLE ON THE BUS ARE GONNA HIT US WITH SUCH A LAWSUIT--!
NO!
THERE'S SOMETHING HERE! THERE HAS TO BE! MOONDRAGON! CAPTAIN MARVEL! JOCASTA! USE YOUR SENSES! LOOK FOR ANYTHING OUT OF PLACE!
ANYTHING!
BUT THOUGH THE THREE 'AVENGERS' FOCUS ON THE MAN CALLED MICHAEL, SENDING PSYCHIC AND CYBERNETIC PROBES TO THE VERY CORE OF HIS BEING, THEY FIND--
--NOTHING!
--NO DANGER!
--I... I'M SORRY, IRON MAN...!

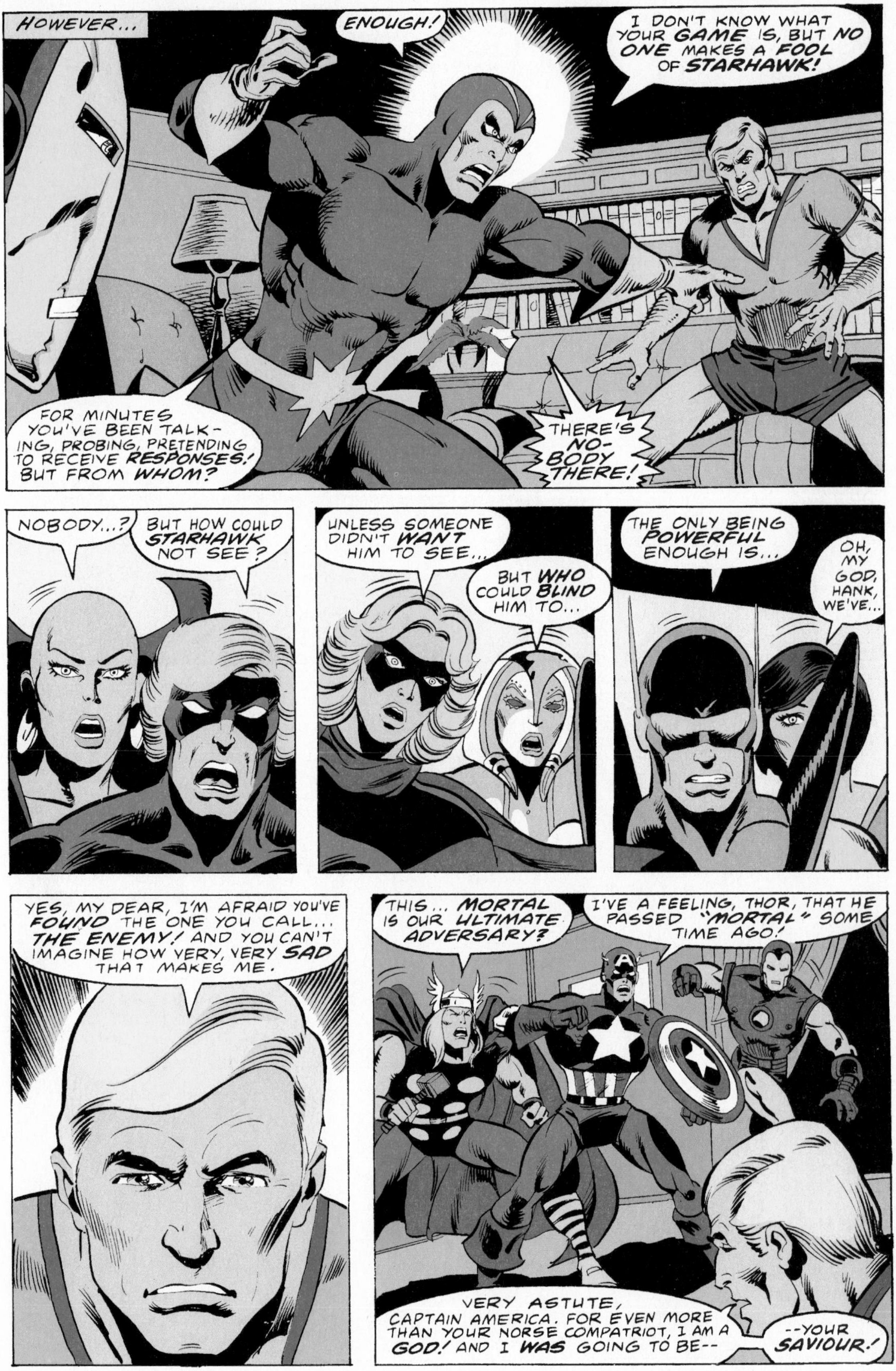
HOWEVER...
ENOUGH!
I DON'T KNOW WHAT YOUR GAME IS, BUT NO ONE MAKES A FOOL OF STARHAWK!
FOR MINUTES YOU'VE BEEN TALKING, PROBING, PRETENDING TO RECEIVE RESPONSES! BUT FROM WHOM?
THERE'S NO-BODY THERE!
NOBODY...?
BUT HOW COULD STARHAWK NOT SEE?
UNLESS SOMEONE DIDN'T WANT HIM TO SEE...
BUT WHO COULD BLIND HIM TO...
THE ONLY BEING POWERFUL ENOUGH IS...
OH, MY GOD, HANK, WE'VE...
YES, MY DEAR, I'M AFRAID YOU'VE FOUND THE ONE YOU CALL... THE ENEMY! AND YOU CAN'T IMAGINE HOW VERY, VERY SAD THAT MAKES ME.
THIS... MORTAL IS OUR ULTIMATE ADVERSARY?
I'VE A FEELING, THOR, THAT HE PASSED "MORTAL" SOME TIME AGO!
VERY ASTUTE, CAPTAIN AMERICA. FOR EVEN MORE THAN YOUR NORSE COMPATRIOT, I AM A GOD! AND I WAS GOING TO BE--
--YOUR SAVIOUR!

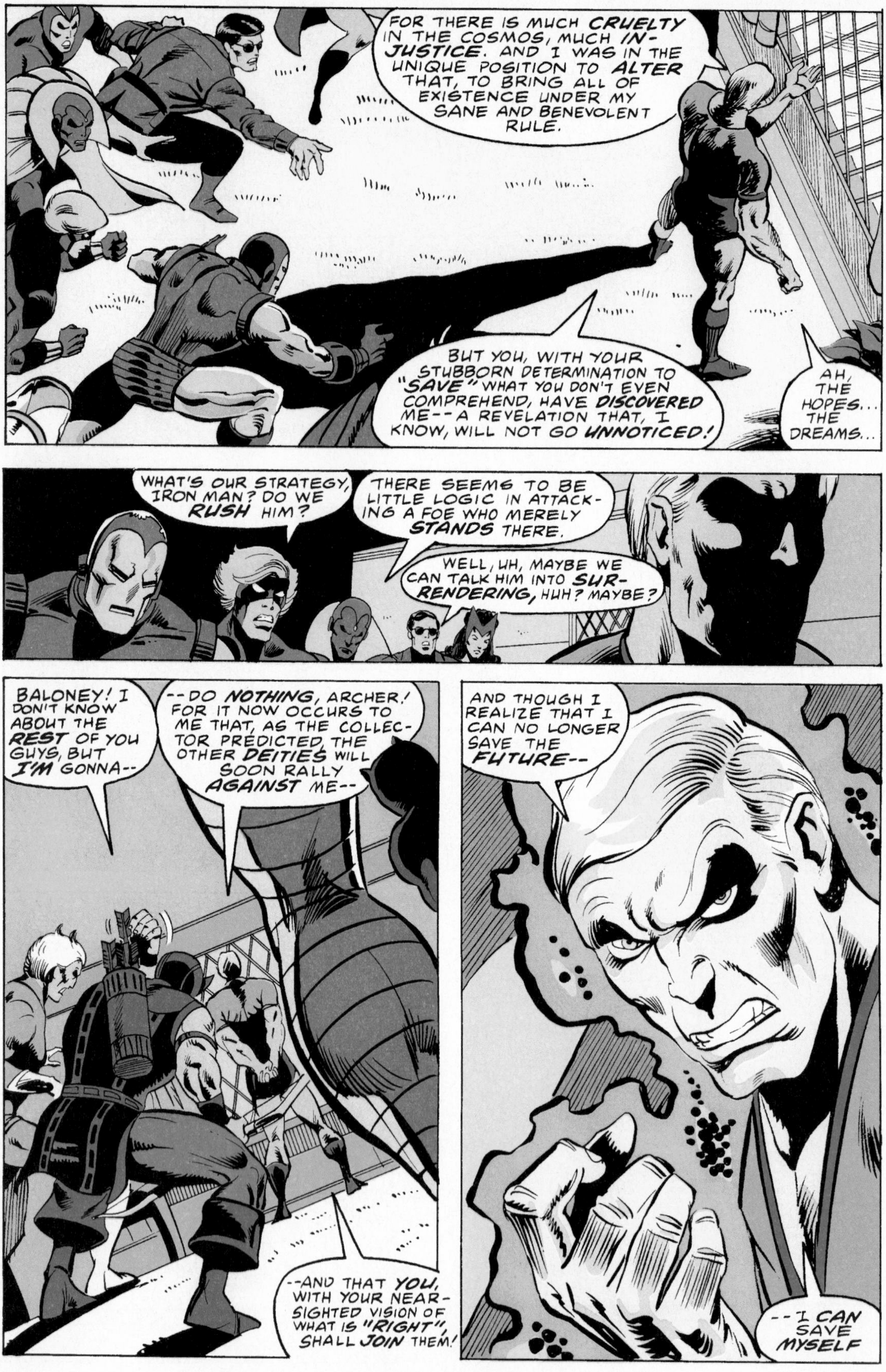

FOR THERE IS MUCH CRUELTY IN THE COSMOS, MUCH INJUSTICE. AND I WAS IN THE UNIQUE POSITION TO ALTER THAT, TO BRING ALL OF EXISTENCE UNDER MY SANE AND BENEVOLENT RULE.
BUT YOU, WITH YOUR STUBBORN DETERMINATION TO "SAVE" WHAT YOU DON'T EVEN COMPREHEND, HAVE DISCOVERED ME-- A REVELATION THAT, I KNOW, WILL NOT GO UNNOTICED!
AH, THE HOPES... THE DREAMS...
WHAT'S OUR STRATEGY, IRON MAN? DO WE RUSH HIM?
THERE SEEMS TO BE LITTLE LOGIC IN ATTACKING A FOE WHO MERELY STANDS THERE.
WELL, UH, MAYBE WE CAN TALK HIM INTO SURRENDERING, HUH? MAYBE?
BALONEY! I DON'T KNOW ABOUT THE REST OF YOU GUYS, BUT I'M GONNA--
--DO NOTHING, ARCHER! FOR IT NOW OCCURS TO ME THAT, AS THE COLLECTOR PREDICTED, THE OTHER DEITIES WILL SOON RALLY AGAINST ME--
--AND THAT YOU, WITH YOUR NEAR-SIGHTED VISION OF WHAT IS "RIGHT", SHALL JOIN THEM!
AND THOUGH I REALIZE THAT I CAN NO LONGER SAVE THE FUTURE--
--I CAN SAVE MYSELF

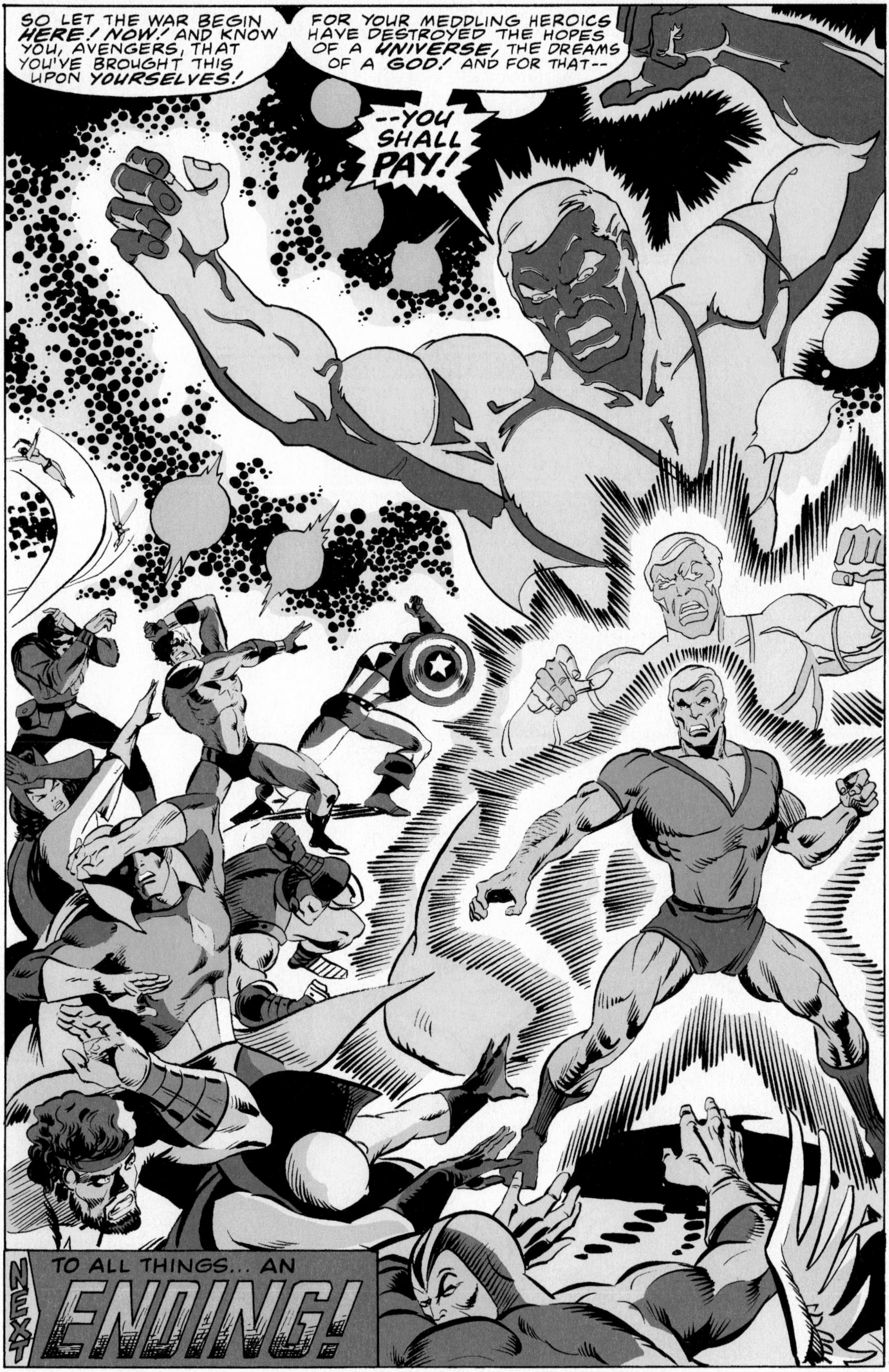
SO LET THE WAR BEGIN HERE! NOW! AND KNOW YOU, AVENGERS, THAT YOU'VE BROUGHT THIS UPON YOURSELVES!
FOR YOUR MEDDLING HEROICS HAVE DESTROYED THE HOPES OF A UNIVERSE, THE DREAMS OF A GOD! AND FOR THAT--
--YOU SHALL PAY!
NEXT TO ALL THINGS... AN ENDING!

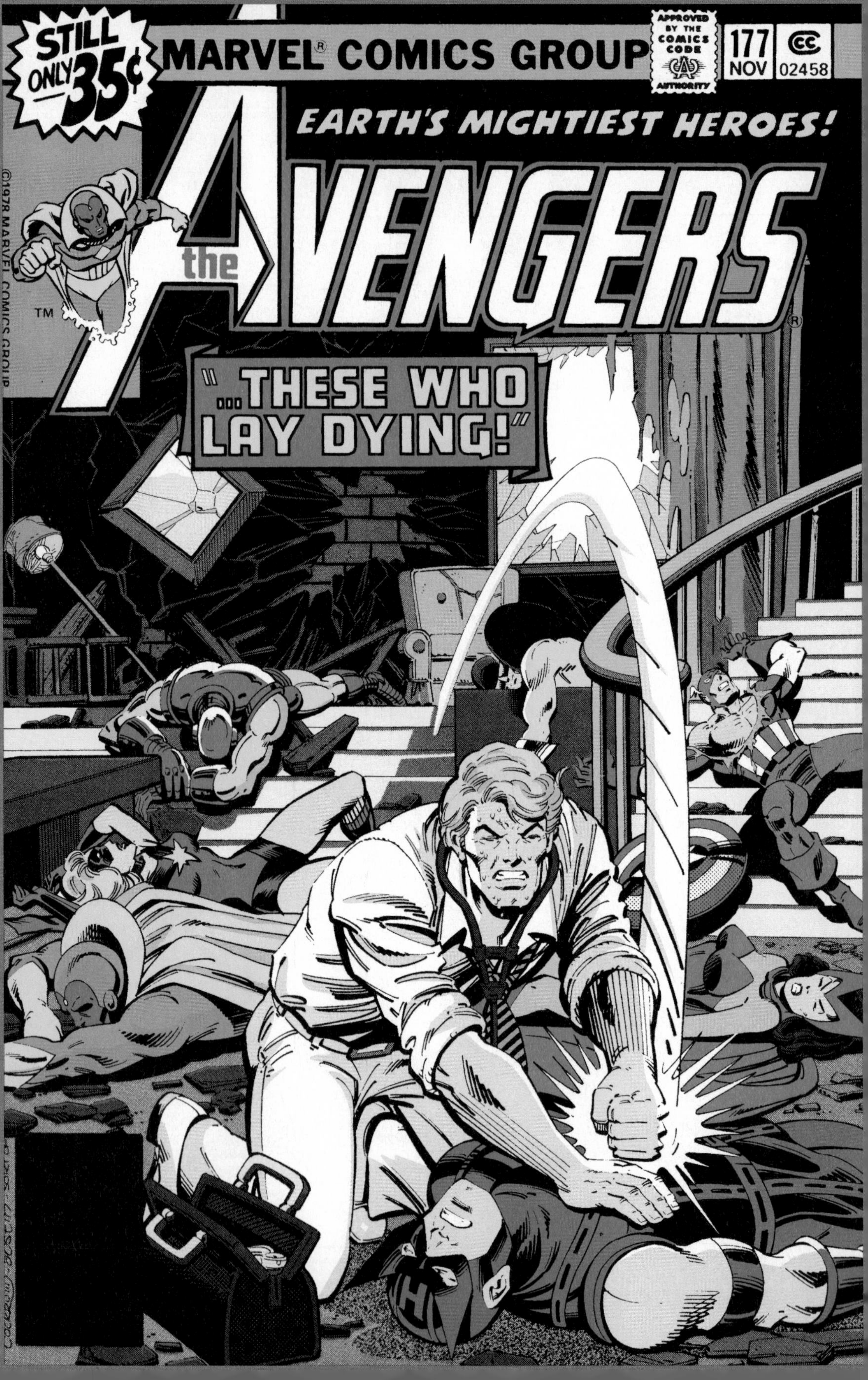
STILL ONLY 35¢
MARVEL® COMICS GROUP
APPROVED BY THE COMICS CODE AUTHORITY
177 NOV
CC 02458
EARTH'S MIGHTIEST HEROES!
the AVENGERS®
TM
©1978 MARVEL COMICS GROUP
"...THESE WHO LAY DYING!"

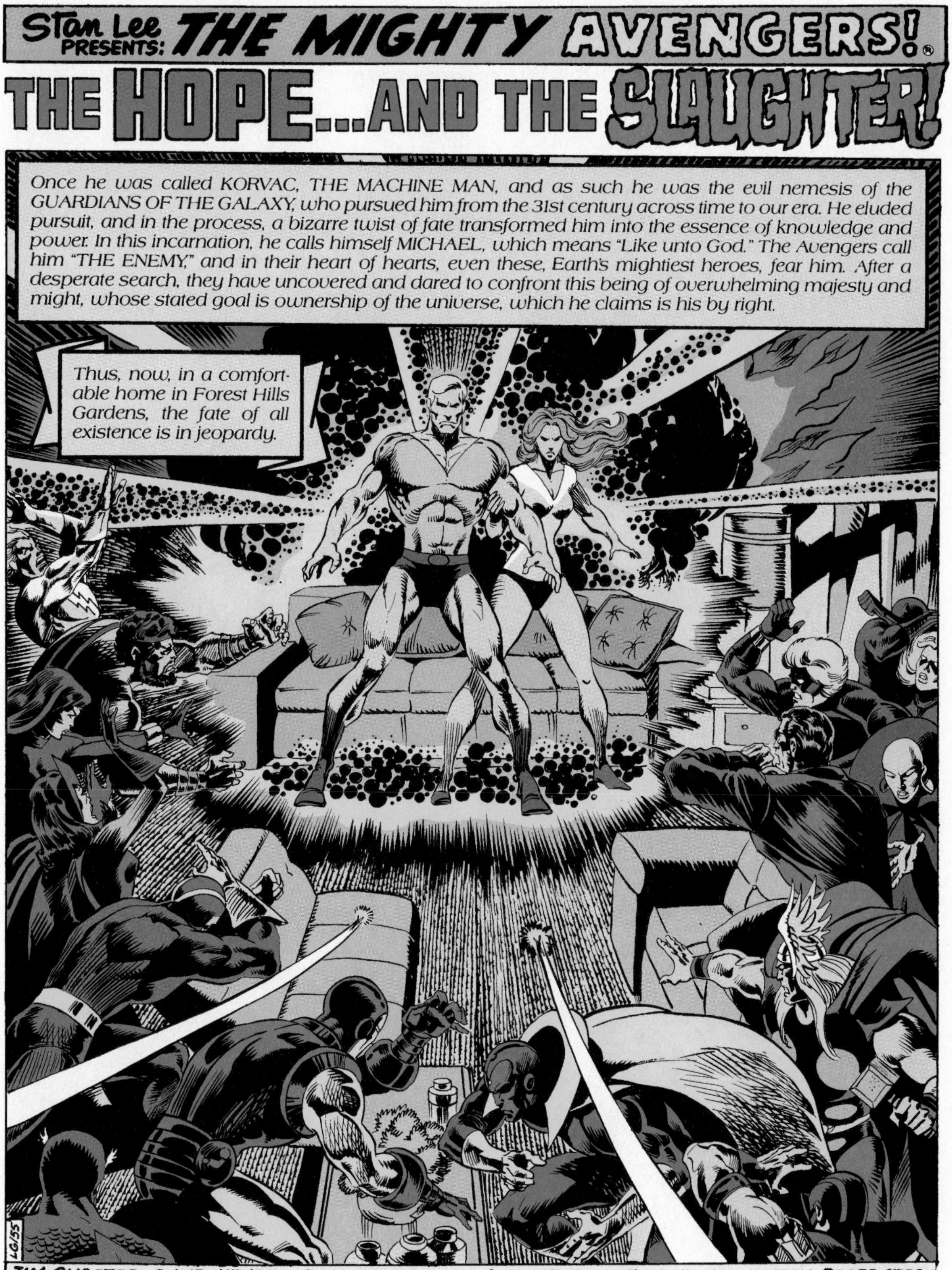
Stan Lee PRESENTS: THE MIGHTY AVENGERS!
THE HOPE...AND THE SLAUGHTER!
Once he was called KORVAC, THE MACHINE MAN, and as such he was the evil nemesis of the GUARDIANS OF THE GALAXY, who pursued him from the 31st century across time to our era. He eluded pursuit, and in the process, a bizarre twist of fate transformed him into the essence of knowledge and power. In this incarnation, he calls himself MICHAEL, which means "Like unto God." The Avengers call him "THE ENEMY," and in their heart of hearts, even these, Earth's mightiest heroes, fear him. After a desperate search, they have uncovered and dared to confront this being of overwhelming majesty and might, whose stated goal is ownership of the universe, which he claims is his by right.
Thus, now, in a comfortable home in Forest Hills Gardens, the fate of all existence is in jeopardy.
JIM SHOOTER, WRITER/ED. IN CHIEF • DAVE WENZEL, PENCILER • P. MARCOS & R. VILLAMONTE, INKERS • DENISE WOHL, LETTERER • NEL YOMTOV, COLORIST • ROGER STERN, EDITOR

YOU HAVE RUINED *EVERYTHING!* BEFORE YOU PIECED TOGETHER THE CLUES WHICH LED YOU HERE, I HAD *VEILED* MY EXISTENCE FROM, THE GREAT POWERS OF THE COSMOS--

--BUT AN ENCOUNTER THIS *SIGNIFICANT* SHALL NOT ESCAPE THEIR NOTICE!

"EVEN NOW, ON THE MYSTIC RAINBOW BRIDGE TO *ASGARD, HEIMDALL,* THE ALL-SEEING SENTINEL OF THE NORSE GODS, CASTS HIS GAZE HITHER.

"SOON, WORD WILL REACH THE EAR OF ALMIGHTY *ODIN!*

"AND ON EARTH'S *MOON,* THE LEGENDARY *WATCHER,* WHOSE SWORN DUTY IS TO *OBSERVE* AND RECORD ALL THAT TRANSPIRES IN THIS SECTOR OF THE UNIVERSE, IS *AWARE* OF THIS CONFRONTATION... AND MY *POWER!*

"HE IS BOUND BY *OATH* NEVER TO INTERFERE -- AND YET, I SENSE HIS FEAR OF MY AMBITION. HE MAY *FORSAKE* HIS WORD.

"WORSE, *ETERNITY* HIMSELF, THE COSMIC ENTITY WHOSE *BODY* IS THE VERY UNIVERSE, NOW HAS DETECTED ME.

LIKE A *VIRUS,* TO WHICH A HUMAN BODY MAY EVENTUALLY *SUCCUMB,* I WAS A MOTE UNKNOWN TO ETERNITY TO WHICH HE MIGHT FALL. NOW HE WILL RESIST!

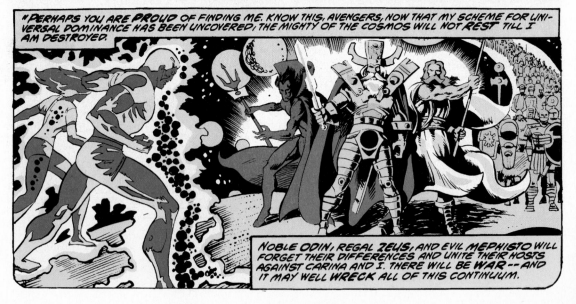

"PERHAPS YOU ARE *PROUD* OF FINDING ME. KNOW THIS, AVENGERS, NOW THAT MY SCHEME FOR UNIVERSAL DOMINANCE HAS BEEN UNCOVERED, THE MIGHTY OF THE COSMOS WILL NOT *REST* TILL I AM DESTROYED.

NOBLE *ODIN,* REGAL *ZEUS,* AND EVIL *MEPHISTO* WILL FORGET THEIR DIFFERENCES AND UNITE THEIR HOSTS AGAINST CARINA AND I. THERE WILL BE *WAR* -- AND IT MAY WELL *WRECK* ALL OF THIS CONTINUUM.

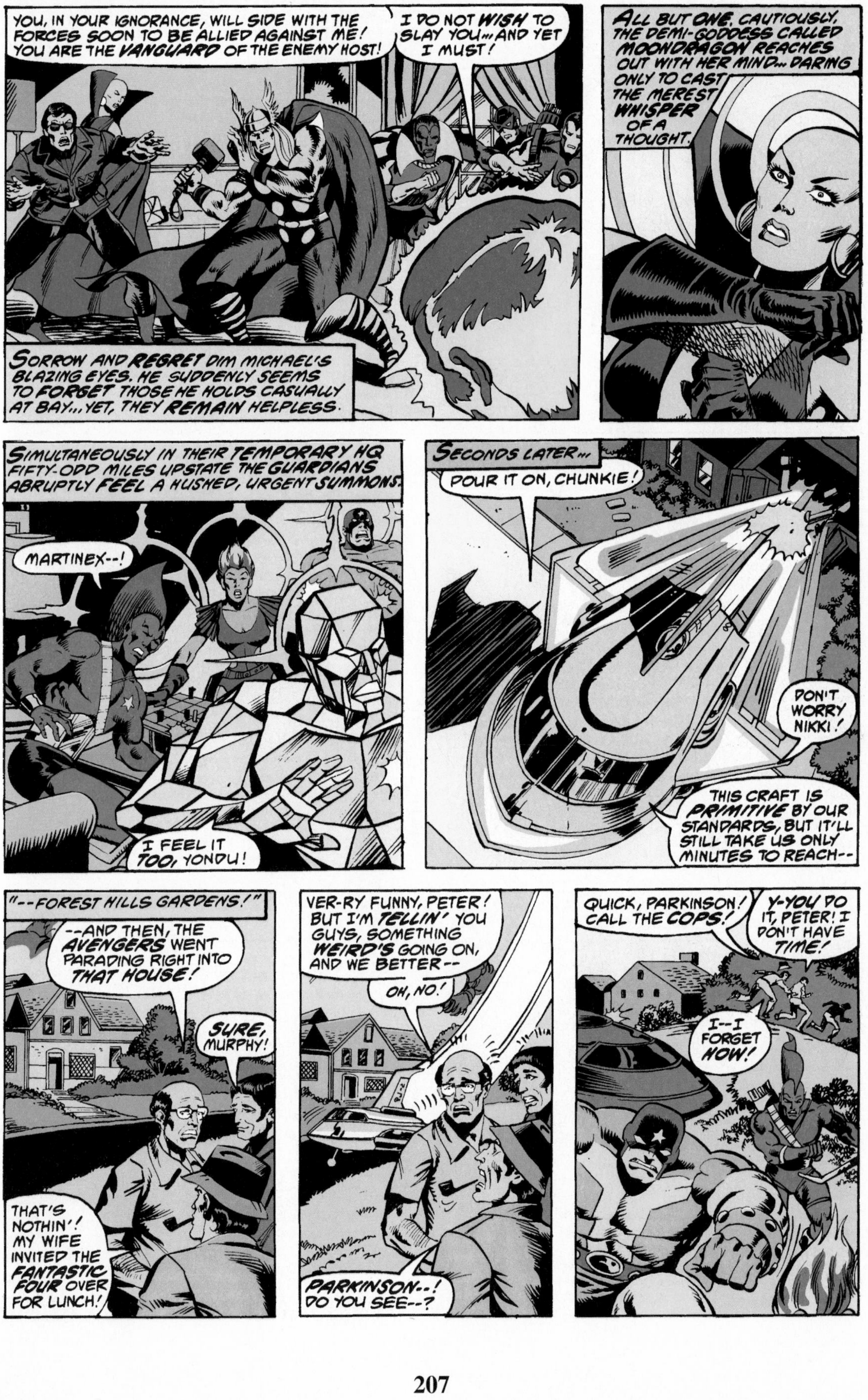
YOU, IN YOUR IGNORANCE, WILL SIDE WITH THE FORCES SOON TO BE ALLIED AGAINST ME! YOU ARE THE VANGUARD OF THE ENEMY HOST!
I DO NOT WISH TO SLAY YOU... AND YET I MUST!
SORROW AND REGRET DIM MICHAEL'S BLAZING EYES. HE SUDDENLY SEEMS TO FORGET THOSE HE HOLDS CASUALLY AT BAY... YET, THEY REMAIN HELPLESS.
ALL BUT ONE. CAUTIOUSLY, THE DEMI-GODDESS CALLED MOONDRAGON REACHES OUT WITH HER MIND... DARING ONLY TO CAST THE MEREST WHISPER OF A THOUGHT.
SIMULTANEOUSLY IN THEIR TEMPORARY HQ FIFTY-ODD MILES UPSTATE THE GUARDIANS ABRUPTLY FEEL A HUSHED, URGENT SUMMONS.
MARTINEX--!
I FEEL IT TOO, YONDU!
SECONDS LATER...
POUR IT ON, CHUNKIE!
DON'T WORRY NIKKI!
THIS CRAFT IS PRIMITIVE BY OUR STANDARDS, BUT IT'LL STILL TAKE US ONLY MINUTES TO REACH--
"--FOREST HILLS GARDENS!"
--AND THEN, THE AVENGERS WENT PARADING RIGHT INTO THAT HOUSE!
SURE, MURPHY!
THAT'S NOTHIN'! MY WIFE INVITED THE FANTASTIC FOUR OVER FOR LUNCH!
VER-RY FUNNY, PETER! BUT I'M TELLIN' YOU GUYS, SOMETHING WEIRD'S GOING ON, AND WE BETTER--
OH, NO!
PARKINSON--! DO YOU SEE--?
QUICK, PARKINSON! CALL THE COPS!
Y-YOU DO IT, PETER! I DON'T HAVE TIME!
I--I FORGET NOW!

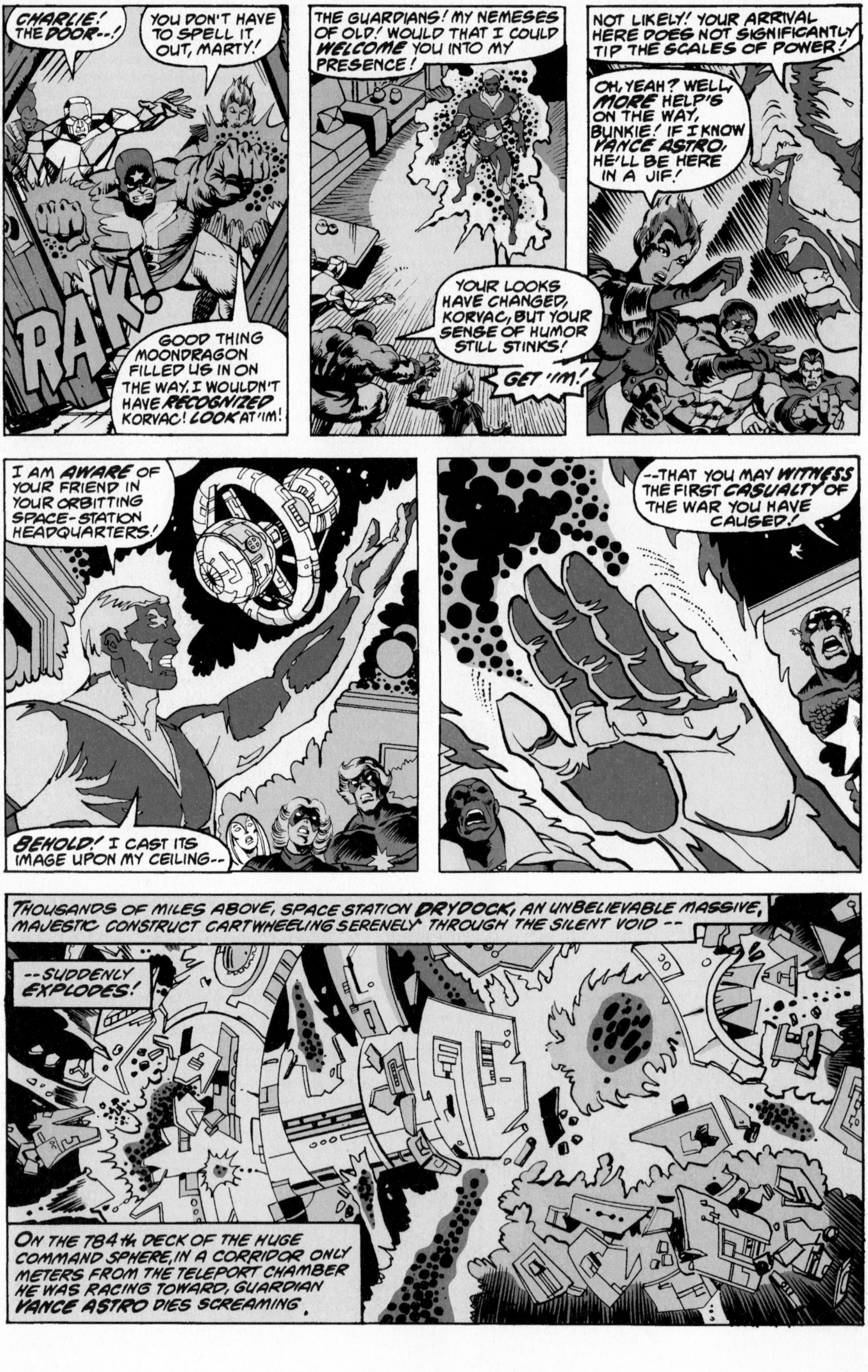
CHARLIE! THE DOOR--!
YOU DON'T HAVE TO SPELL IT OUT, MARTY!
RAK!
GOOD THING MOONDRAGON FILLED US IN ON THE WAY. I WOULDN'T HAVE RECOGNIZED KORVAC! LOOK AT 'IM!
THE GUARDIANS! MY NEMESES OF OLD! WOULD THAT I COULD WELCOME YOU INTO MY PRESENCE!
YOUR LOOKS HAVE CHANGED, KORVAC, BUT YOUR SENSE OF HUMOR STILL STINKS!
GET 'IM!
NOT LIKELY! YOUR ARRIVAL HERE DOES NOT SIGNIFICANTLY TIP THE SCALES OF POWER!
OH, YEAH? WELL, MORE HELP'S ON THE WAY, BUNKIE! IF I KNOW VANCE ASTRO, HE'LL BE HERE IN A JIF!
I AM AWARE OF YOUR FRIEND IN YOUR ORBITTING SPACE-STATION HEADQUARTERS!
BEHOLD! I CAST ITS IMAGE UPON MY CEILING--
--THAT YOU MAY WITNESS THE FIRST CASUALTY OF THE WAR YOU HAVE CAUSED!
THOUSANDS OF MILES ABOVE, SPACE STATION DRYDOCK, AN UNBELIEVABLE MASSIVE, MAJESTIC CONSTRUCT CARTWHEELING SERENELY THROUGH THE SILENT VOID --
--SUDDENLY EXPLODES!
ON THE 784th DECK OF THE HUGE COMMAND SPHERE, IN A CORRIDOR ONLY METERS FROM THE TELEPORT CHAMBER HE WAS RACING TOWARD, GUARDIAN VANCE ASTRO DIES SCREAMING.

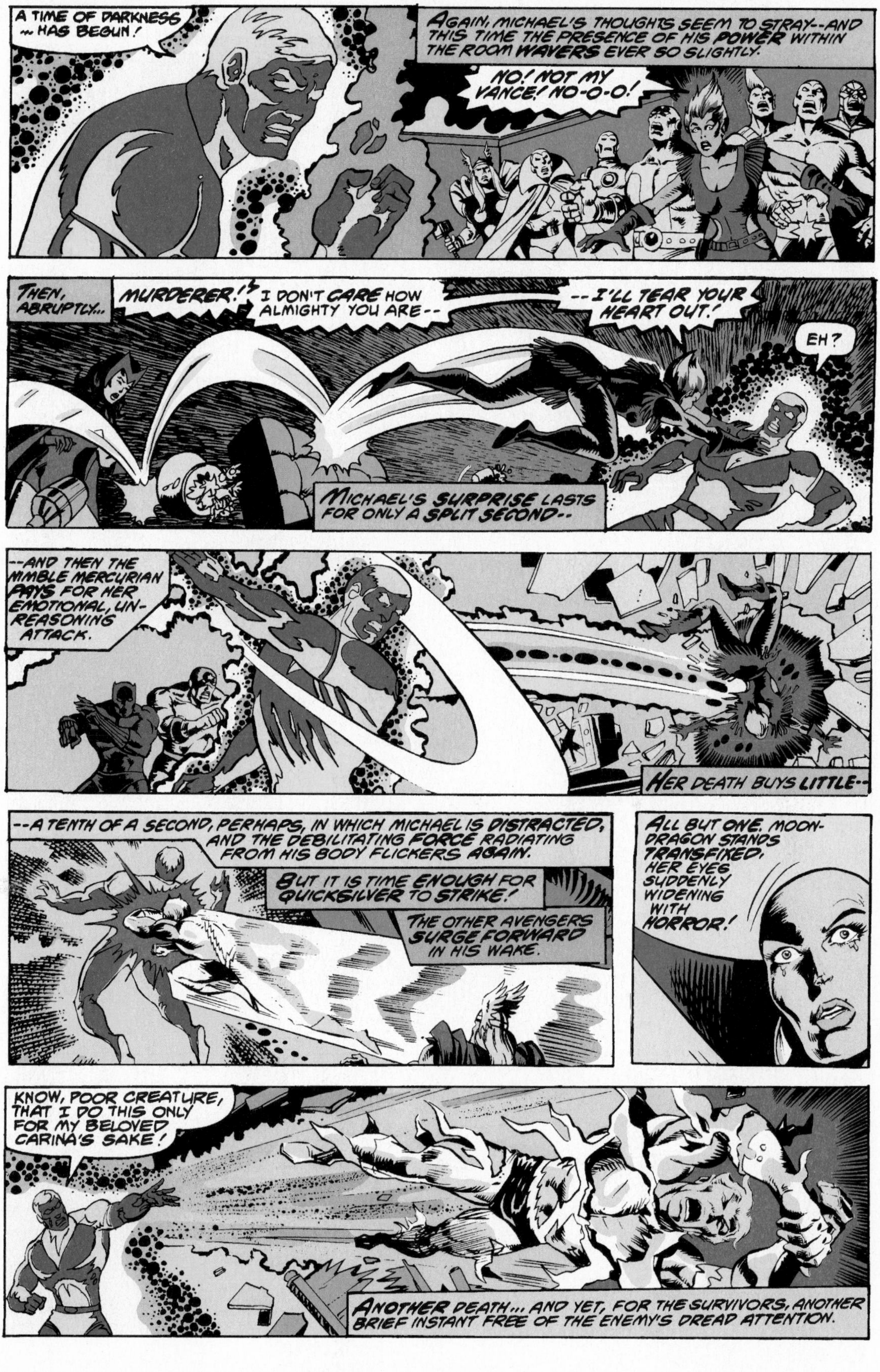

A TIME OF DARKNESS ... HAS BEGUN!
AGAIN, MICHAEL'S THOUGHTS SEEM TO STRAY--AND THIS TIME THE PRESENCE OF HIS POWER WITHIN THE ROOM WAVERS EVER SO SLIGHTLY.
NO! NOT MY VANCE! NO-O-O!
THEN, ABRUPTLY...
MURDERER! I DON'T CARE HOW ALMIGHTY YOU ARE--
--I'LL TEAR YOUR HEART OUT!
EH?
MICHAEL'S SURPRISE LASTS FOR ONLY A SPLIT SECOND--
--AND THEN THE NIMBLE MERCURIAN PAYS FOR HER EMOTIONAL, UNREASONING ATTACK.
HER DEATH BUYS LITTLE--
--A TENTH OF A SECOND, PERHAPS, IN WHICH MICHAEL IS DISTRACTED, AND THE DEBILITATING FORCE RADIATING FROM HIS BODY FLICKERS AGAIN.
BUT IT IS TIME ENOUGH FOR QUICKSILVER TO STRIKE!
THE OTHER AVENGERS SURGE FORWARD IN HIS WAKE.
ALL BUT ONE. MOONDRAGON STANDS TRANSFIXED, HER EYES SUDDENLY WIDENING WITH HORROR!
KNOW, POOR CREATURE, THAT I DO THIS ONLY FOR MY BELOVED CARINA'S SAKE!
ANOTHER DEATH... AND YET, FOR THE SURVIVORS, ANOTHER BRIEF INSTANT FREE OF THE ENEMY'S DREAD ATTENTION.

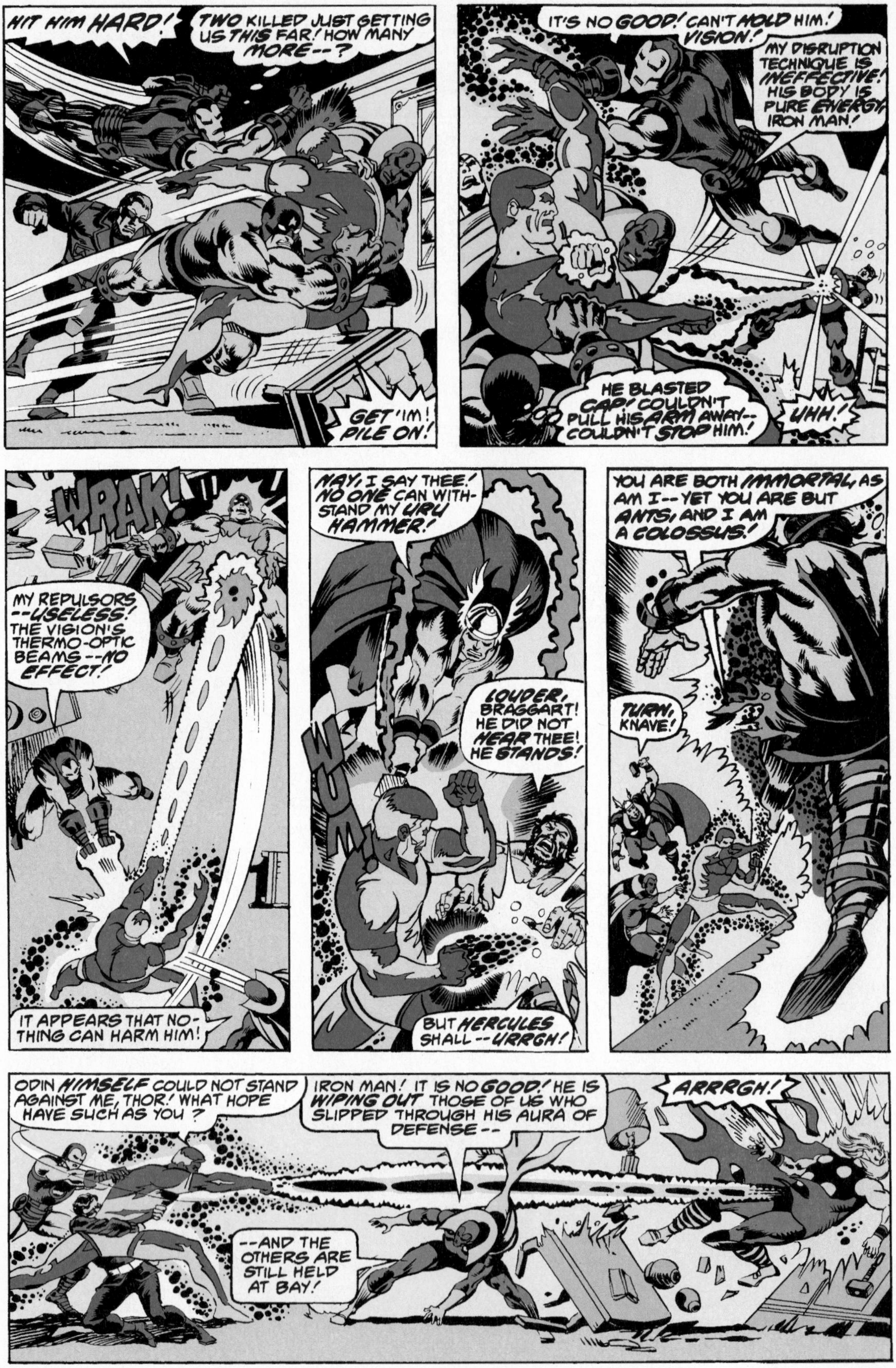

HIT HIM HARD!
TWO KILLED JUST GETTING US THIS FAR! HOW MANY MORE--?
GET 'IM! PILE ON!
IT'S NO GOOD! CAN'T HOLD HIM! VISION!
MY DISRUPTION TECHNIQUE IS INEFFECTIVE! HIS BODY IS PURE ENERGY, IRON MAN!
HE BLASTED CAP! COULDN'T PULL HIS ARM AWAY-- COULDN'T STOP HIM!
UHH!
WRAK!
MY REPULSORS --USELESS! THE VISION'S THERMO-OPTIC BEAMS--NO EFFECT!
IT APPEARS THAT NOTHING CAN HARM HIM!
NAY, I SAY THEE! NO ONE CAN WITHSTAND MY URU HAMMER!
LOUDER, BRAGGART! HE DID NOT HEAR THEE! HE STANDS!
BUT HERCULES SHALL--URRGH!
YOU ARE BOTH IMMORTAL, AS AM I--YET YOU ARE BUT ANTS, AND I AM A COLOSSUS!
TURN, KNAVE!
ODIN HIMSELF COULD NOT STAND AGAINST ME, THOR! WHAT HOPE HAVE SUCH AS YOU ?
IRON MAN! IT IS NO GOOD! HE IS WIPING OUT THOSE OF US WHO SLIPPED THROUGH HIS AURA OF DEFENSE--
--AND THE OTHERS ARE STILL HELD AT BAY!
ARRRGH!

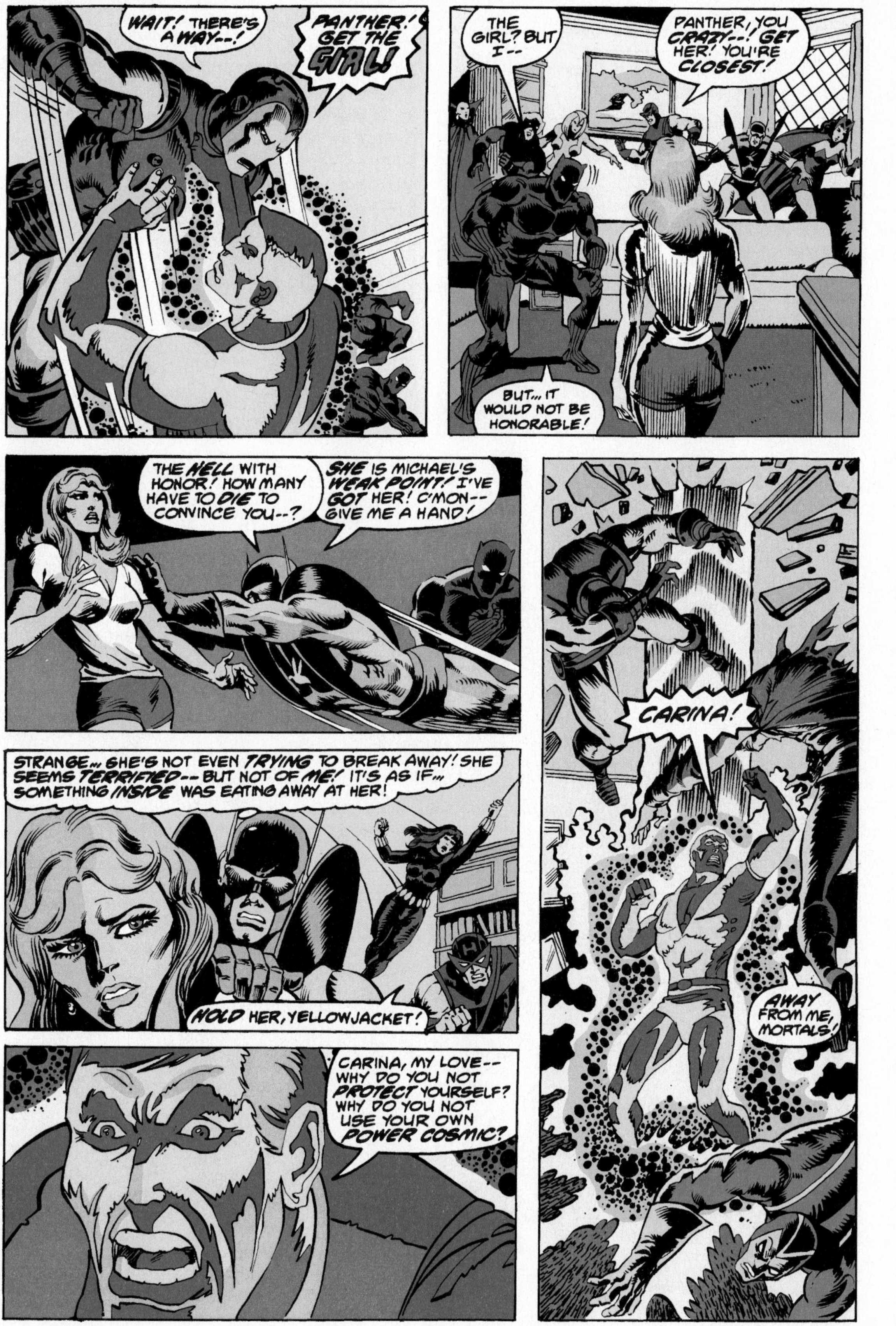
WAIT! THERE'S A WAY--!
PANTHER! GET THE GIRL!
THE GIRL? BUT I--
PANTHER, YOU CRAZY--! GET HER! YOU'RE CLOSEST!
BUT... IT WOULD NOT BE HONORABLE!
THE HELL WITH HONOR! HOW MANY HAVE TO DIE TO CONVINCE YOU--?
SHE IS MICHAEL'S WEAK POINT! I'VE GOT HER! C'MON--GIVE ME A HAND!
STRANGE... SHE'S NOT EVEN TRYING TO BREAK AWAY! SHE SEEMS TERRIFIED-- BUT NOT OF ME! IT'S AS IF... SOMETHING INSIDE WAS EATING AWAY AT HER!
HOLD HER, YELLOWJACKET!
CARINA, MY LOVE-- WHY DO YOU NOT PROTECT YOURSELF? WHY DO YOU NOT USE YOUR OWN POWER COSMIC?
CARINA!
AWAY FROM ME, MORTALS!

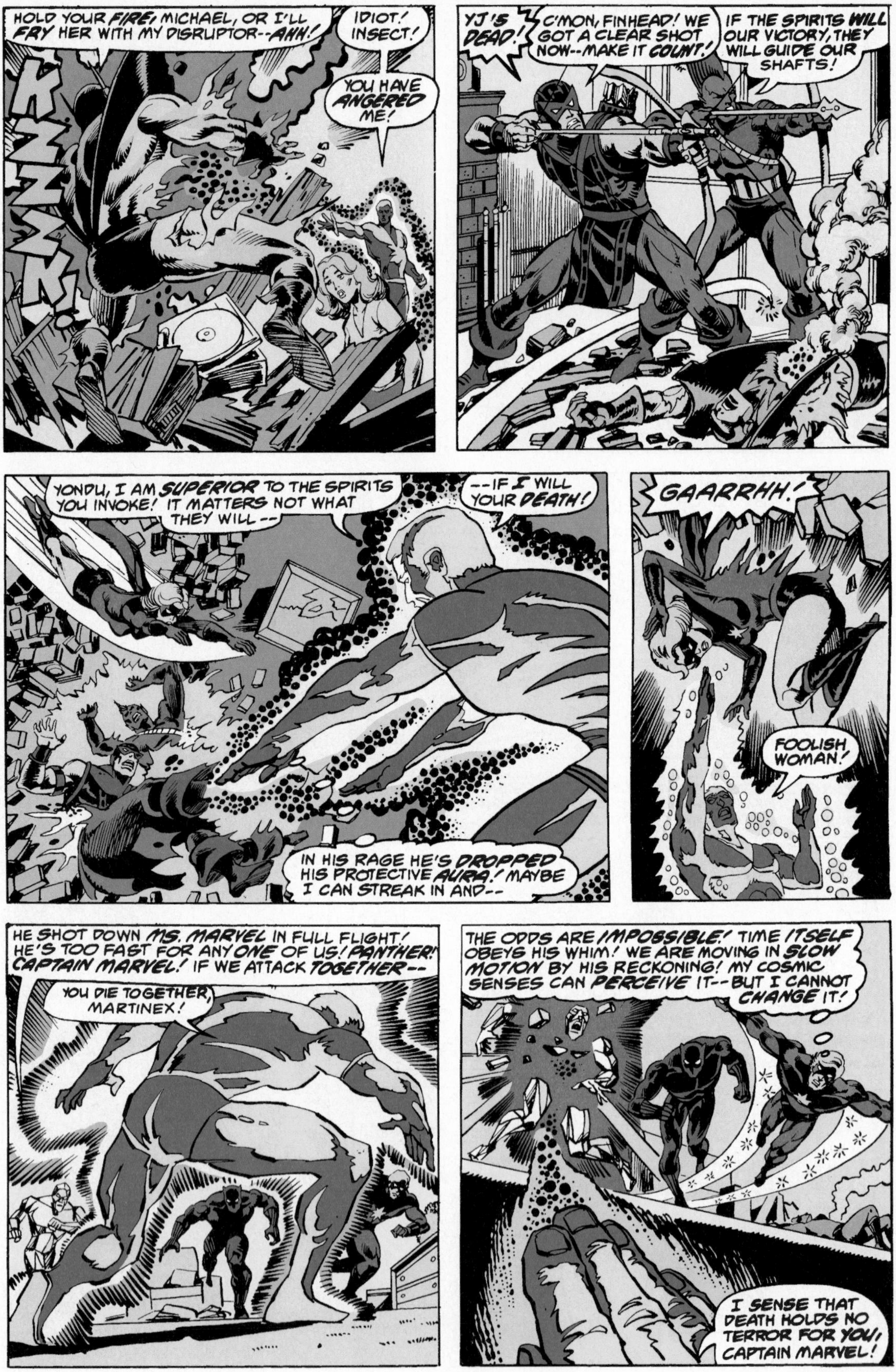
HOLD YOUR FIRE, MICHAEL, OR I'LL FRY HER WITH MY DISRUPTOR--AHH!
KNNNK!
IDIOT! INSECT!
YOU HAVE ANGERED ME!
YJ'S DEAD!
C'MON, FINHEAD! WE GOT A CLEAR SHOT NOW--MAKE IT COUNT!
IF THE SPIRITS WILL OUR VICTORY, THEY WILL GUIDE OUR SHAFTS!
YONDU, I AM SUPERIOR TO THE SPIRITS YOU INVOKE! IT MATTERS NOT WHAT THEY WILL--
--IF I WILL YOUR DEATH!
IN HIS RAGE HE'S DROPPED HIS PROTECTIVE AURA! MAYBE I CAN STREAK IN AND--
GAARRHH!
FOOLISH WOMAN!
HE SHOT DOWN MS. MARVEL IN FULL FLIGHT! HE'S TOO FAST FOR ANY ONE OF US! PANTHER! CAPTAIN MARVEL! IF WE ATTACK TOGETHER--
YOU DIE TOGETHER, MARTINEX!
THE ODDS ARE IMPOSSIBLE! TIME ITSELF OBEYS HIS WHIM! WE ARE MOVING IN SLOW MOTION BY HIS RECKONING! MY COSMIC SENSES CAN PERCEIVE IT--BUT I CANNOT CHANGE IT!
I SENSE THAT DEATH HOLDS NO TERROR FOR YOU, CAPTAIN MARVEL!

THAT IS *GOOD!* YOU ARE WISE BEYOND YOUR STATION!

YOU ARE ALL PARTICULARLY *ADMIRABLE* INSECTS!

AND NONE MORE THAN *YOU,* PANTHER!

KNOW THIS, AS HUMBLE AS YOU ARE, I WOULD RATHER ENTER INTO DEATH *MYSELF* THAN SLAY YOU--

--WERE IT NOT FOR *CARINA* AND WHAT I HAVE FOUND WITH HER!

THERE IS FAR MORE AT STAKE HERE THAN *MY* LIFE, MY *POWER* AND ALL THE GOOD THAT I *ALONE* MIGHT ACCOMPLISH!

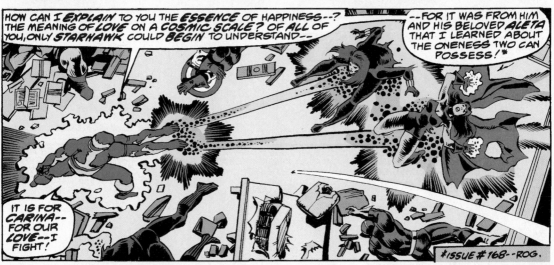

HOW CAN I *EXPLAIN* TO YOU THE *ESSENCE* OF HAPPINESS--? THE MEANING OF *LOVE* ON A *COSMIC* SCALE? OF ALL OF YOU, ONLY *STARHAWK* COULD *BEGIN* TO UNDERSTAND--

--FOR IT WAS FROM HIM AND HIS BELOVED *ALETA* THAT I LEARNED ABOUT THE ONENESS TWO CAN POSSESS!*

IT IS FOR *CARINA*-- FOR OUR *LOVE*--I FIGHT!

ISSUE #168--ROG.

OUR LOVE IS A *BEACON,* LIGHTING UP THE UNIVERSE ...YET NOW, OUT OF FEAR, MANY FORCES WILL GATHER TO *DESTROY* US!

YOU ARE FIRST AMONG THOSE!

OUR LOVE MUST GO ON AT *ANY* COST!

UHH.... MUST HAVE PASSED OUT! TOOK A BLAST... ON MY SHIELD... *STILL,* IT ALMOST KILLED ME!

YOU, JOCASTA, I PITY, FOR YOU WERE *CREATED* IN THE NAME OF LOVE!*

*BY ULTRON IN ISSUE #162, IN- TENDED TO BE HIS BRIDE--ROG.

YOU HAVE NO *STAKE* IN THIS CONFLICT! YOU ARE MERELY LOYAL TO THOSE YOU THINK ARE *FRIENDS!* I AM SORRY IT MUST BE THUS!

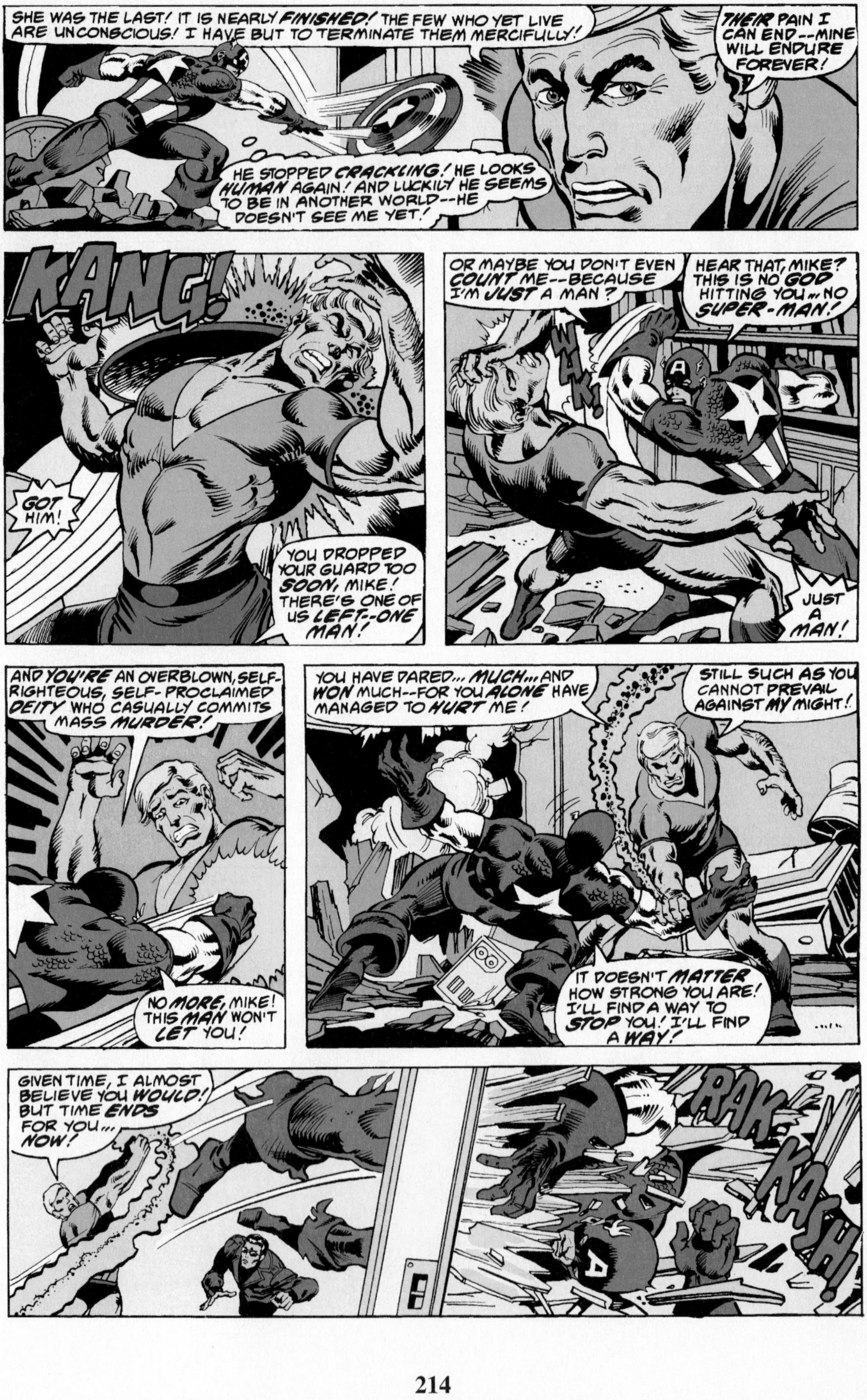
SHE WAS THE LAST! IT IS NEARLY FINISHED! THE FEW WHO YET LIVE ARE UNCONSCIOUS! I HAVE BUT TO TERMINATE THEM MERCIFULLY!
THEIR PAIN I CAN END--MINE WILL ENDURE FOREVER!
HE STOPPED CRACKLING! HE LOOKS HUMAN AGAIN! AND LUCKILY HE SEEMS TO BE IN ANOTHER WORLD--HE DOESN'T SEE ME YET!
KANG!
GOT HIM!
YOU DROPPED YOUR GUARD TOO SOON, MIKE! THERE'S ONE OF US LEFT--ONE MAN!
OR MAYBE YOU DON'T EVEN COUNT ME--BECAUSE I'M JUST A MAN?
HEAR THAT, MIKE? THIS IS NO GOD HITTING YOU... NO SUPER-MAN!
WAK!
JUST A MAN!
AND YOU'RE AN OVERBLOWN, SELF-RIGHTEOUS, SELF-PROCLAIMED DEITY WHO CASUALLY COMMITS MASS MURDER!
NO MORE, MIKE! THIS MAN WON'T LET YOU!
YOU HAVE DARED... MUCH... AND WON MUCH--FOR YOU ALONE HAVE MANAGED TO HURT ME!
STILL SUCH AS YOU CANNOT PREVAIL AGAINST MY MIGHT!
IT DOESN'T MATTER HOW STRONG YOU ARE! I'LL FIND A WAY TO STOP YOU! I'LL FIND A WAY!
GIVEN TIME, I ALMOST BELIEVE YOU WOULD! BUT TIME ENDS FOR YOU... NOW!
RAK
KASH!

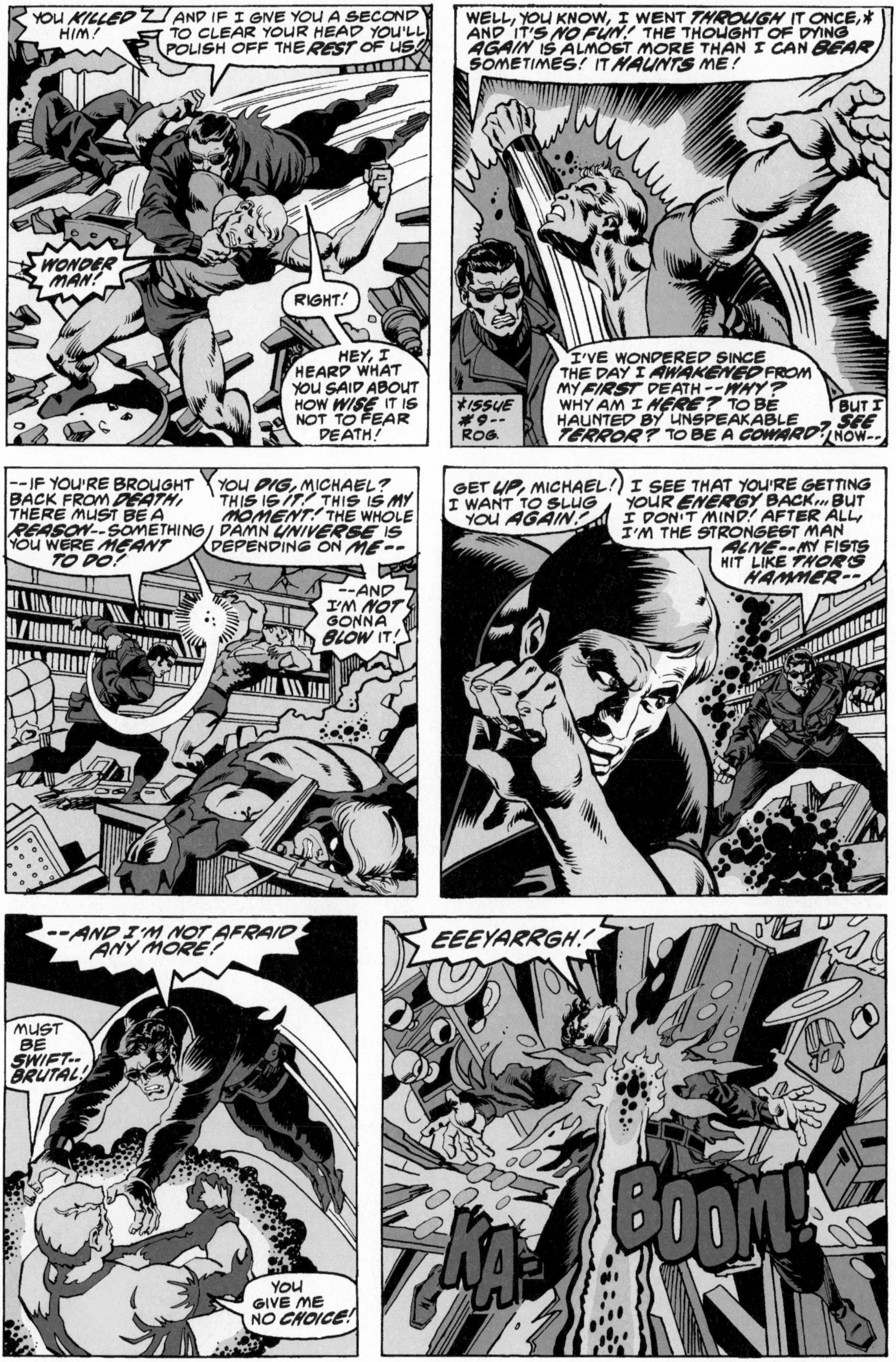
YOU KILLED HIM!
AND IF I GIVE YOU A SECOND TO CLEAR YOUR HEAD YOU'LL POLISH OFF THE REST OF US!
WONDER MAN!
RIGHT!
HEY, I HEARD WHAT YOU SAID ABOUT HOW WISE IT IS NOT TO FEAR DEATH!
WELL, YOU KNOW, I WENT THROUGH IT ONCE,* AND IT'S NO FUN! THE THOUGHT OF DYING AGAIN IS ALMOST MORE THAN I CAN BEAR SOMETIMES! IT HAUNTS ME!
I'VE WONDERED SINCE THE DAY I AWAKENED FROM MY FIRST DEATH--WHY? WHY AM I HERE? TO BE HAUNTED BY UNSPEAKABLE TERROR? TO BE A COWARD?
BUT I SEE NOW--
*ISSUE #9--ROG.
--IF YOU'RE BROUGHT BACK FROM DEATH, THERE MUST BE A REASON--SOMETHING YOU WERE MEANT TO DO!
YOU DIG, MICHAEL? THIS IS IT! THIS IS MY MOMENT! THE WHOLE DAMN UNIVERSE IS DEPENDING ON ME--
--AND I'M NOT GONNA BLOW IT!
GET UP, MICHAEL! I WANT TO SLUG YOU AGAIN!
I SEE THAT YOU'RE GETTING YOUR ENERGY BACK... BUT I DON'T MIND! AFTER ALL, I'M THE STRONGEST MAN ALIVE--MY FISTS HIT LIKE THOR'S HAMMER--
--AND I'M NOT AFRAID ANY MORE!
MUST BE SWIFT--BRUTAL!
YOU GIVE ME NO CHOICE!
EEEYARRGH!
KA-BOOM!

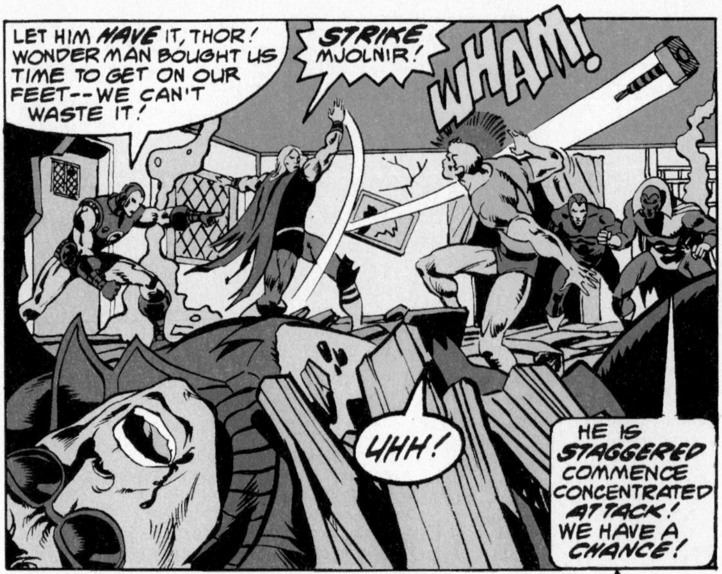
LET HIM HAVE IT, THOR! WONDER MAN BOUGHT US TIME TO GET ON OUR FEET--WE CAN'T WASTE IT!
STRIKE MJOLNIR!
WHAM!
UHH!
HE IS STAGGERED COMMENCE CONCENTRATED ATTACK! WE HAVE A CHANCE!

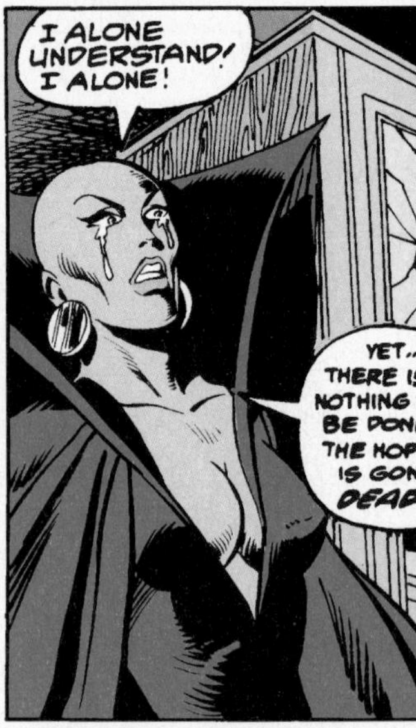
I ALONE UNDERSTAND! I ALONE!
YET... THERE IS NOTHING TO BE DONE! THE HOPE IS GONE... DEAD!

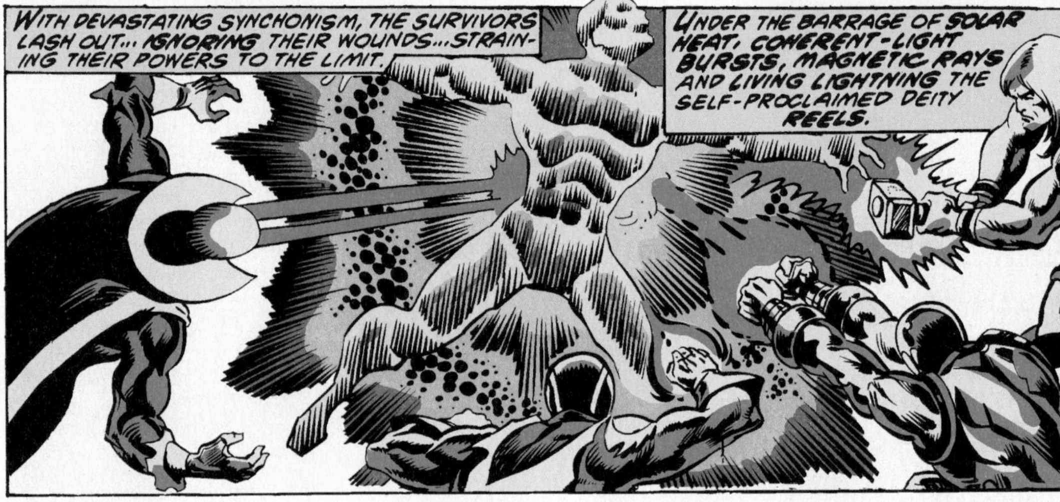
WITH DEVASTATING SYNCHONISM, THE SURVIVORS LASH OUT... IGNORING THEIR WOUNDS... STRAINING THEIR POWERS TO THE LIMIT.
UNDER THE BARRAGE OF SOLAR HEAT, COHERENT-LIGHT BURSTS, MAGNETIC RAYS AND LIVING LIGHTNING THE SELF-PROCLAIMED DEITY REELS.

IN HIS MOMENT OF TRIAL AND PAIN, MICHAEL CASTS HIS GAZE TOWARD CARINA, HIS BELOVED.

ONCE SHE WAS THE DAUGHTER OF THE COLLECTOR, WHO WAS, IN TRUTH, ONE OF THE ELDERS OF THE UNIVERSE. HE PERCEIVED MICHAEL'S EXISTENCE. THOUGH NO OTHER COULD. FEARING MICHAEL, HER FATHER SENT HER TO MICHAEL'S SIDE, THAT SHE MIGHT BETRAY HIM --

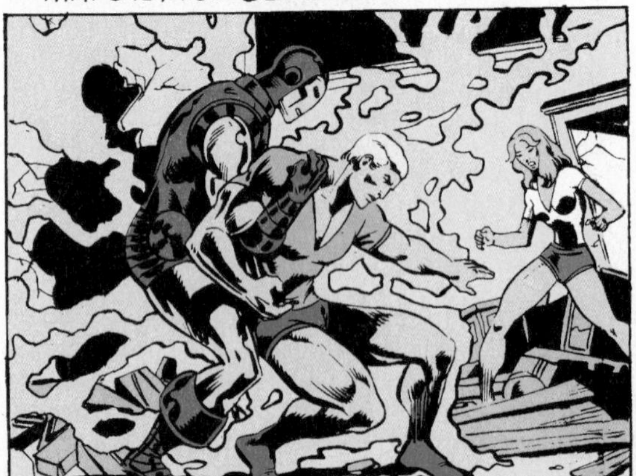

--BUT WHEN THE MOMENT CAME, SHE WAS TORN, FOR SHE HAD GROWN TO LOVE MICHAEL. AND SO, SHE HESITATED -- AND IN THAT MOMENT, CAUSED THE END OF HER FATHER'S LIFE!

NOW MICHAEL REACHES OUT TO HER... FOR LOVE... FOR RESPITE... FOR STRENGTH TO GO ON.

AND THOUGH SHE LOVES HIM BEYOND ALL EARTHLY KEN, THE PANORAMA OF BLOODSHED BEFORE HER AND THE DARK PROSPECT OF COSMIC WAR AHEAD HAVE WROUGHT TURMOIL IN HER SOUL. SHE IS TORN... AND SHE HESITATES --

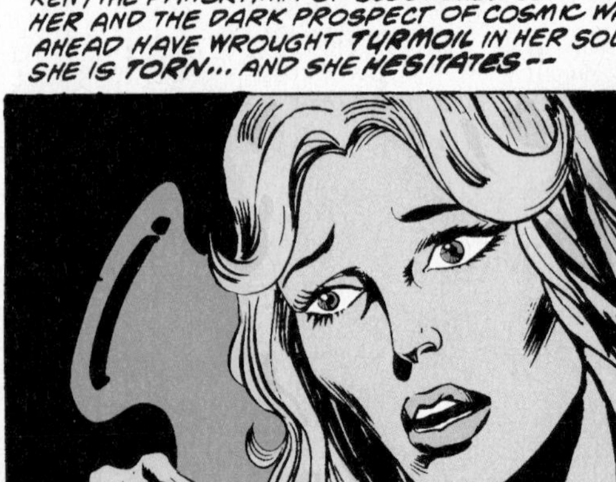

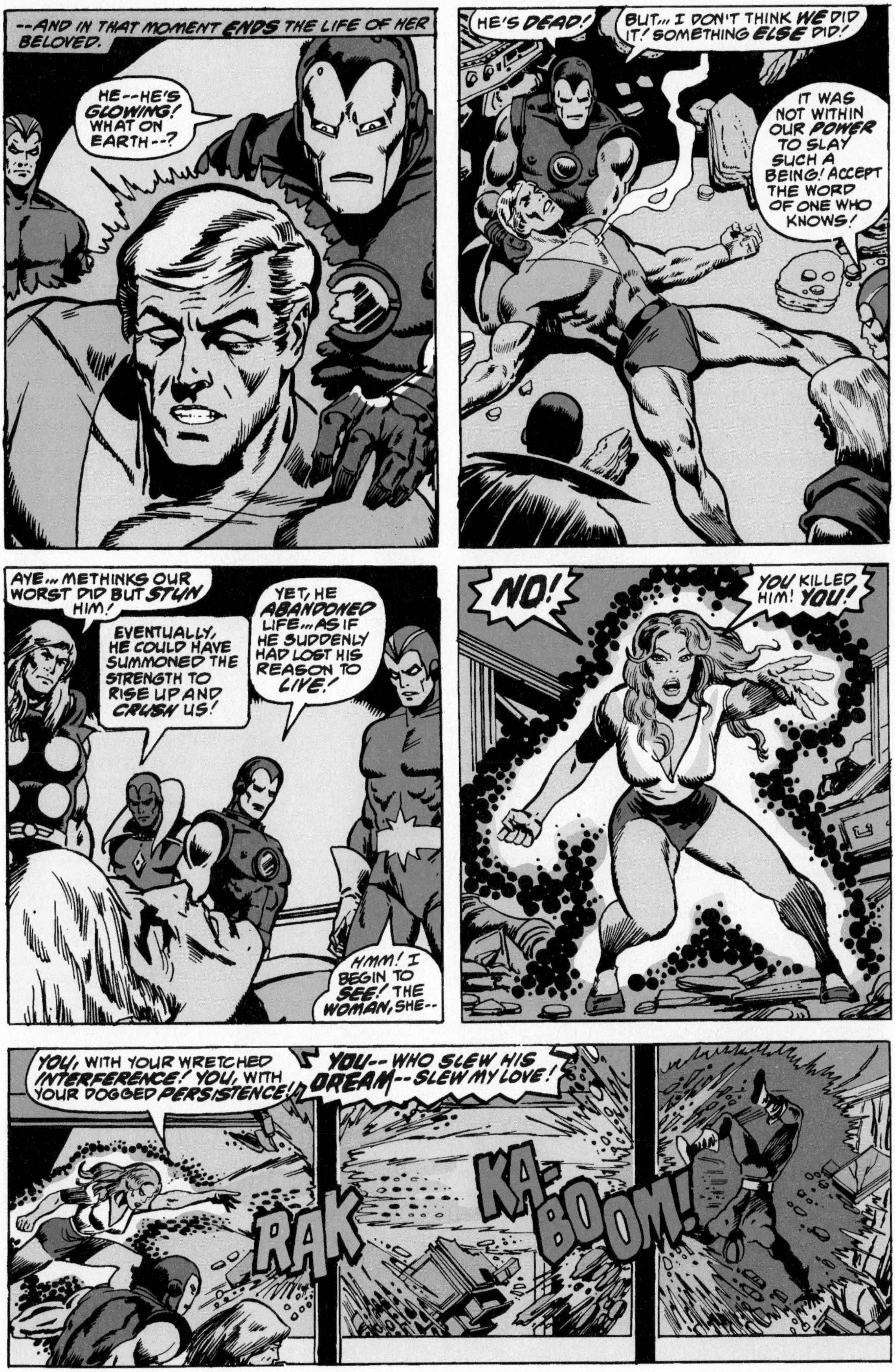
--AND IN THAT MOMENT ENDS THE LIFE OF HER BELOVED.
HE--HE'S GLOWING! WHAT ON EARTH--?
HE'S DEAD!
BUT... I DON'T THINK WE DID IT! SOMETHING ELSE DID!
IT WAS NOT WITHIN OUR POWER TO SLAY SUCH A BEING! ACCEPT THE WORD OF ONE WHO KNOWS!
AYE... METHINKS OUR WORST DID BUT STUN HIM!
EVENTUALLY, HE COULD HAVE SUMMONED THE STRENGTH TO RISE UP AND CRUSH US!
YET, HE ABANDONED LIFE... AS IF HE SUDDENLY HAD LOST HIS REASON TO LIVE!
HMM! I BEGIN TO SEE! THE WOMAN, SHE--
NO!
YOU KILLED HIM! YOU!
YOU, WITH YOUR WRETCHED INTERFERENCE! YOU, WITH YOUR DOGGED PERSISTENCE!
YOU-- WHO SLEW HIS DREAM-- SLEW MY LOVE!
RAK
KA-BOOM!

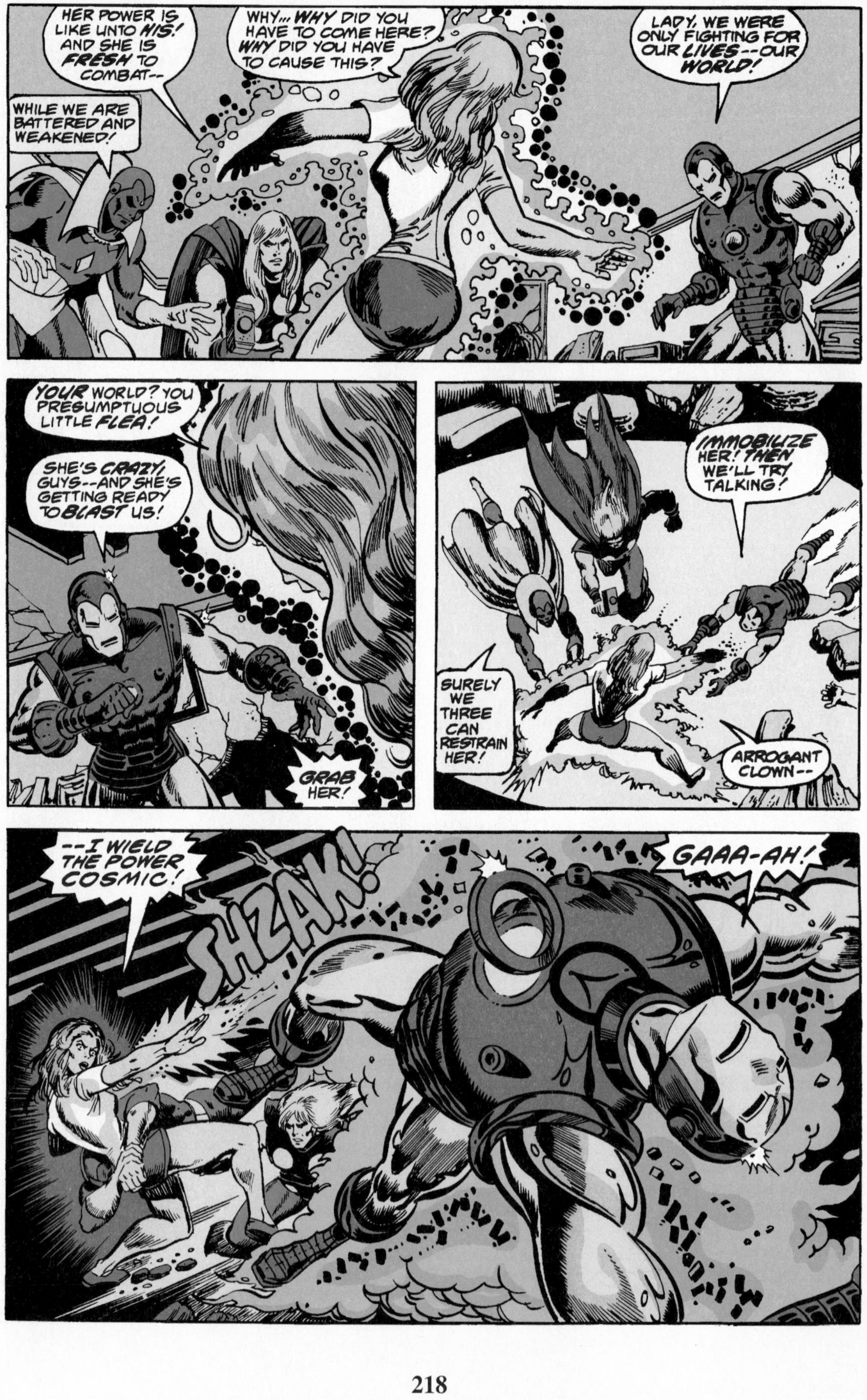
HER POWER IS LIKE UNTO HIS! AND SHE IS FRESH TO COMBAT--
WHILE WE ARE BATTERED AND WEAKENED!
WHY... WHY DID YOU HAVE TO COME HERE? WHY DID YOU HAVE TO CAUSE THIS?
LADY, WE WERE ONLY FIGHTING FOR OUR LIVES--OUR WORLD!
YOUR WORLD? YOU PRESUMPTUOUS LITTLE FLEA!
SHE'S CRAZY, GUYS--AND SHE'S GETTING READY TO BLAST US!
GRAB HER!
IMMOBILIZE HER! THEN WE'LL TRY TALKING!
SURELY WE THREE CAN RESTRAIN HER!
ARROGANT CLOWN--
--I WIELD THE POWER COSMIC!
SHZAK!
GAAA-AH!

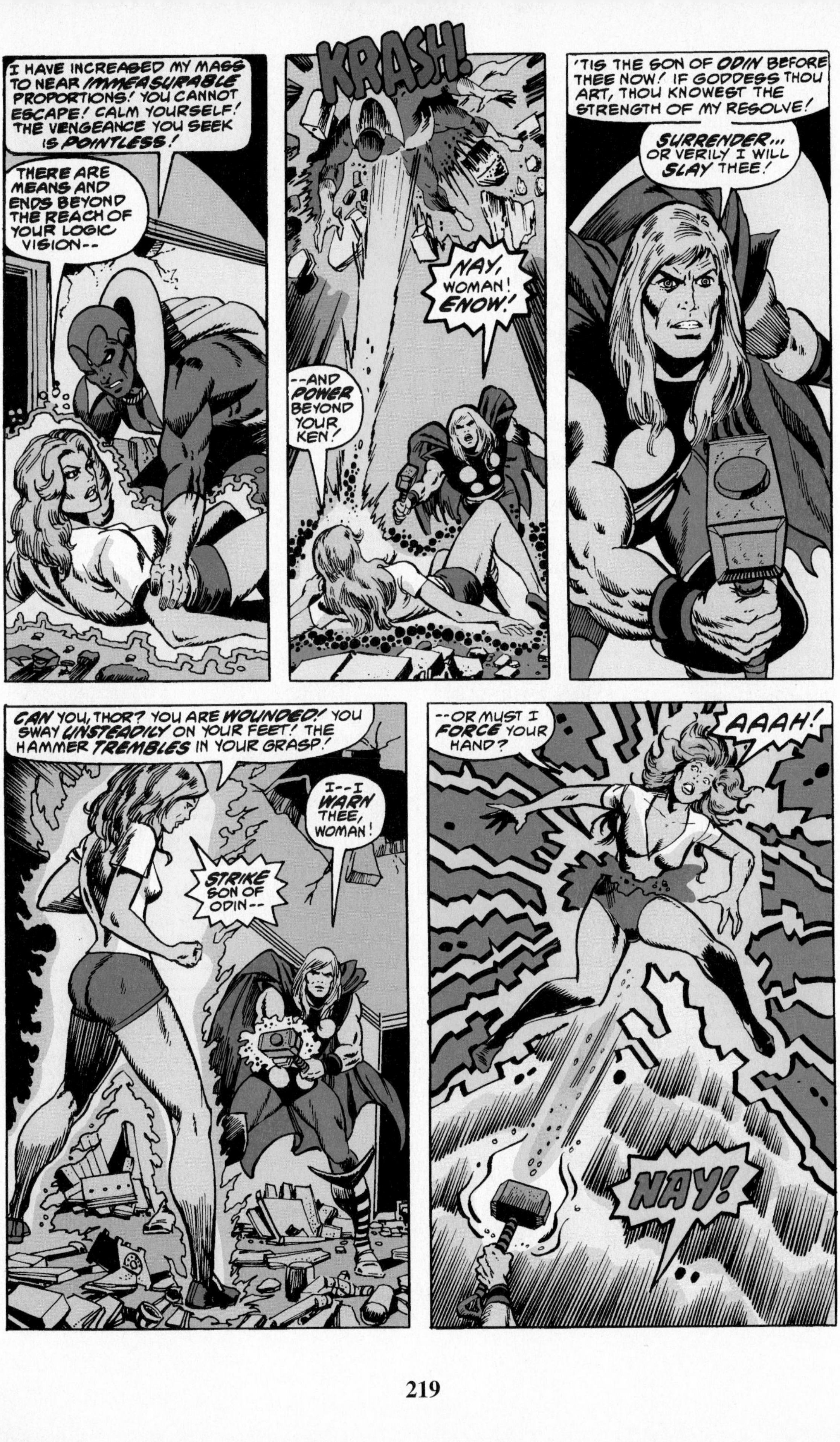

I HAVE INCREASED MY MASS TO NEAR IMMEASURABLE PROPORTIONS! YOU CANNOT ESCAPE! CALM YOURSELF! THE VENGEANCE YOU SEEK IS POINTLESS!
THERE ARE MEANS AND ENDS BEYOND THE REACH OF YOUR LOGIC VISION--
KRASH!
NAY, WOMAN! ENOW!
--AND POWER BEYOND YOUR KEN!
'TIS THE SON OF ODIN BEFORE THEE NOW! IF GODDESS THOU ART, THOU KNOWEST THE STRENGTH OF MY RESOLVE!
SURRENDER... OR VERILY I WILL SLAY THEE!
CAN YOU, THOR? YOU ARE WOUNDED! YOU SWAY UNSTEADILY ON YOUR FEET! THE HAMMER TREMBLES IN YOUR GRASP!
I--I WARN THEE, WOMAN!
STRIKE SON OF ODIN--
--OR MUST I FORCE YOUR HAND?
AAAH!
NAY!

ODIN'S BEARD--! MY HAMMER DID STRIKE 'GAINST MY *WILL!*

SHE LEFT HERSELF *UNDEFENDED!* THE BOLT STRUCK HER *FULL...* BUT--

I...COME TO YOU ...*MY LOVE!*

SHE IS...*DEAD!* BUT... EH? *MOONDRAGON!*

SON OF ODIN, CAN YOU NOT SEE? SHE *WISHED* ONLY TO DIE!

I OBSERVED ALL! IN THE HEAT OF THE BATTLE I DARED TO WALK THE PLANES OF MICHAEL'S MIND! I HAVE SEEN INSIDE HIS *HEART*... AND TOUCHED THE *SOULS* OF MICHAEL AND HIS BELOVED!

HE WAS *NOT* EVIL, THOR! HE SOUGHT NOT TO *RULE* US... NOR EVEN TO *INTERFERE* WITH OUR MADNESS! HE WISHED ONLY TO FREE US FROM THE CAPRICIOUS WHIMS OF *ETERNITY!*

WHAT *SAYEST* THOU, WOMAN? SHOULD WE HAVE DIED IN HIS *STEAD?*

NO. ONCE IT HAD BEGUN, THERE WAS NO WAY TO STOP FATE'S RELENTLESS ADVANCE! WHAT *COULD* HAVE HAPPENED... *DID!* NONETHELESS, *WE* ARE TO BLAME!

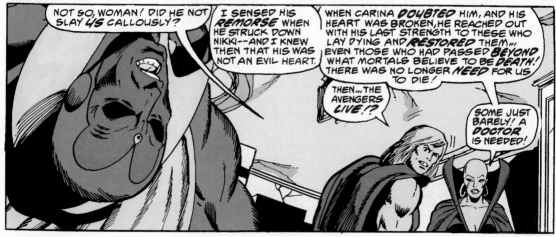

NOT SO, WOMAN! DID HE NOT SLAY *US* CALLOUSLY?

I SENSED HIS *REMORSE* WHEN HE STRUCK DOWN NIKKI--AND I KNEW THEN THAT HIS WAS NOT AN EVIL HEART.

WHEN CARINA *DOUBTED* HIM, AND HIS HEART WAS BROKEN, HE REACHED OUT WITH HIS LAST STRENGTH TO THESE WHO LAY DYING AND *RESTORED* THEM... EVEN THOSE WHO HAD PASSED *BEYOND* WHAT MORTALS BELIEVE TO BE *DEATH!* THERE WAS NO LONGER *NEED* FOR US TO DIE!

THEN...THE AVENGERS *LIVE!?*

SOME JUST BARELY! A *DOCTOR* IS NEEDED!

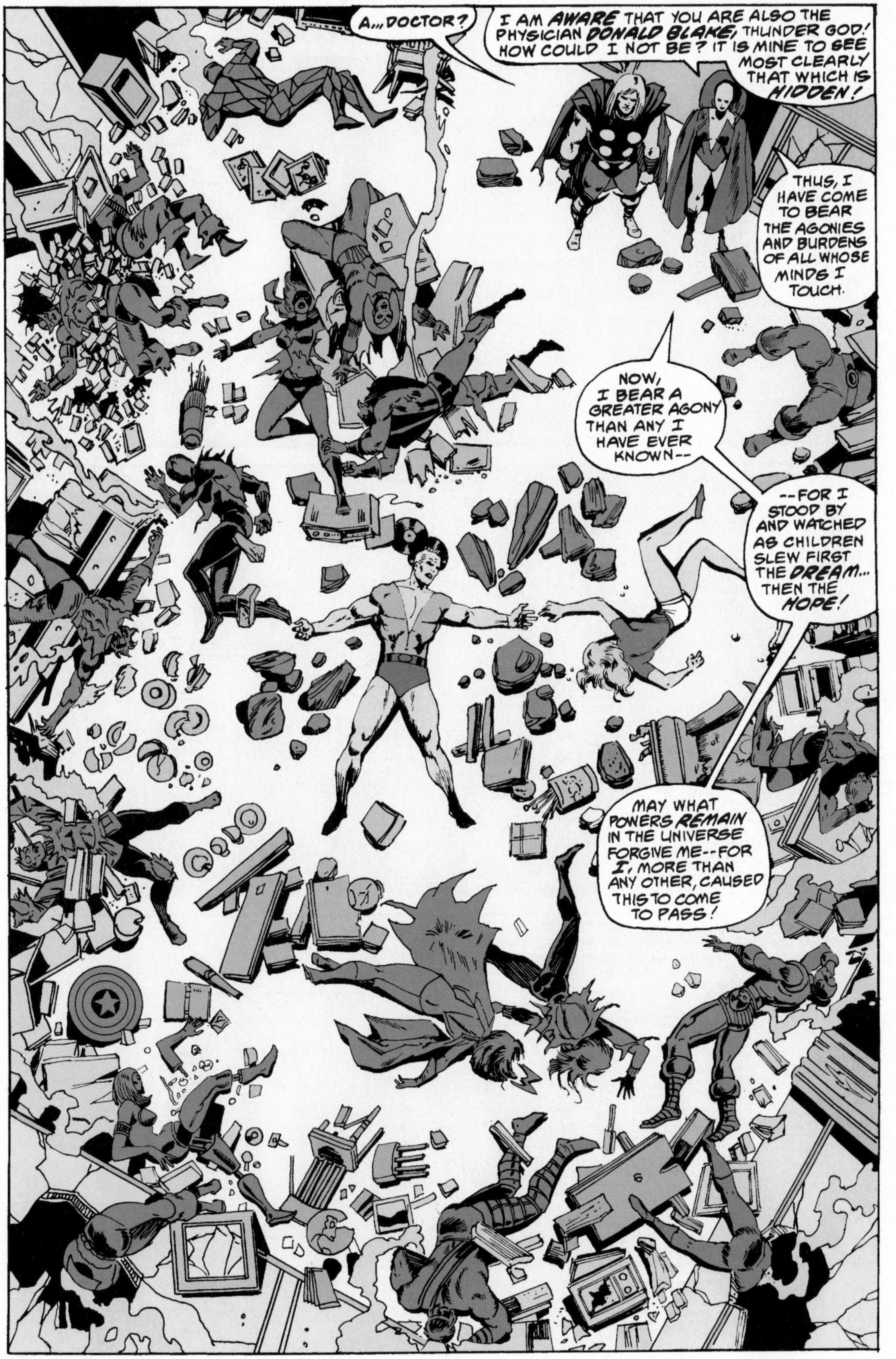
A... DOCTOR?
I AM AWARE THAT YOU ARE ALSO THE PHYSICIAN DONALD BLAKE, THUNDER GOD! HOW COULD I NOT BE? IT IS MINE TO SEE MOST CLEARLY THAT WHICH IS HIDDEN!
THUS, I HAVE COME TO BEAR THE AGONIES AND BURDENS OF ALL WHOSE MINDS I TOUCH.
NOW, I BEAR A GREATER AGONY THAN ANY I HAVE EVER KNOWN--
--FOR I STOOD BY AND WATCHED AS CHILDREN SLEW FIRST THE DREAM... THEN THE HOPE!
MAY WHAT POWERS REMAIN IN THE UNIVERSE FORGIVE ME--FOR I, MORE THAN ANY OTHER, CAUSED THIS TO COME TO PASS!

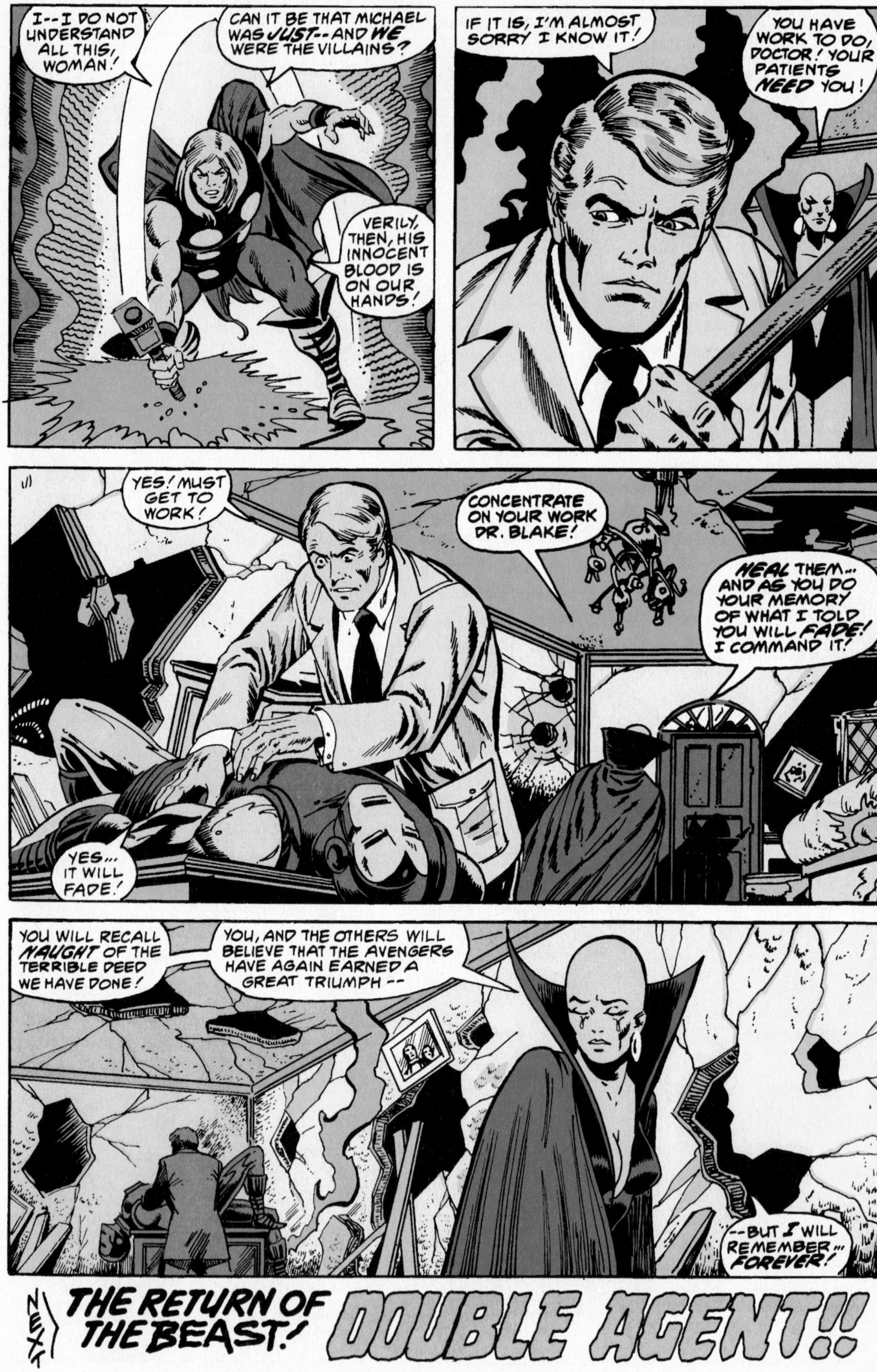
I--I DO NOT UNDERSTAND ALL THIS, WOMAN!
CAN IT BE THAT MICHAEL WAS JUST--AND WE WERE THE VILLAINS?
VERILY, THEN, HIS INNOCENT BLOOD IS ON OUR HANDS!
IF IT IS, I'M ALMOST SORRY I KNOW IT!
YOU HAVE WORK TO DO, DOCTOR! YOUR PATIENTS NEED YOU!
YES! MUST GET TO WORK!
CONCENTRATE ON YOUR WORK DR. BLAKE!
HEAL THEM... AND AS YOU DO YOUR MEMORY OF WHAT I TOLD YOU WILL FADE! I COMMAND IT!
YES... IT WILL FADE!
YOU WILL RECALL NAUGHT OF THE TERRIBLE DEED WE HAVE DONE!
YOU, AND THE OTHERS WILL BELIEVE THAT THE AVENGERS HAVE AGAIN EARNED A GREAT TRIUMPH --
--BUT I WILL REMEMBER... FOREVER!
NEXT
THE RETURN OF THE BEAST!
DOUBLE AGENT!!

Known as Korvac the Machine Man, he comes from an unimaginable era—the 31st century, the present-day Earth. Fleeing through the timestream from the pursuing team of futuristic defenders—The Guardians of the Galaxy, he has established a secret presence on Earth in the self-created persona of the mysterious Michael. Through such an unassuming guise, Korvac contemplates the elements of a universe he thirsts to command. Yet, despite the subtlety of Michael's machinations, the world's greatest super-team—The Mighty Avengers—catches wind of the cosmos-conquering scheme of the once-Korvac, thus drawing the two titanic forces into inevitable conflict.

All this awaits, plus an all-new epilogue to properly punctuate this multi-part masterpiece.

$12.95 U.S.
$15.75 Can.
£ 6.50 U.K.

ISBN #0-87135-760-7

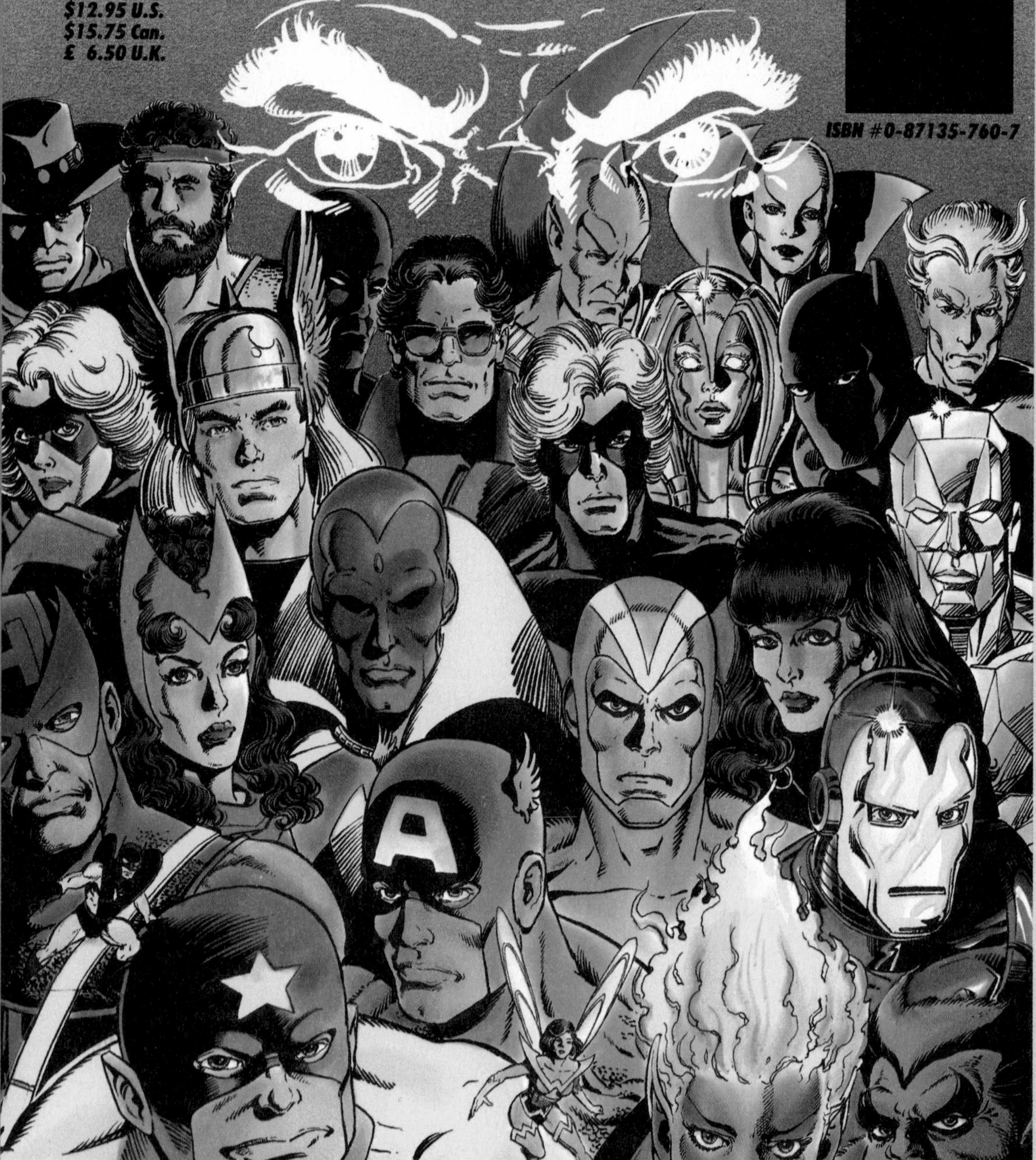
GEORGE PEREZ

YONDU

Real Name: Yondu Udonta
Occupation: Adventurer
Identity: Publicly known in own time-era
Legal status: Last surviving member of Zatoan tribe of Centauri IV in an alternate future of the 31st Century
Former aliases: None
Place of birth: Plysa Forest, Centauri IV, Beta Centauri system
Marital status: Single
Known relatives: None
Group affiliation: Guardians of the Galaxy
Base of operations: Starship *Freedom's Lady*, Milky Way Galaxy
First appearance: MARVEL SUPER HEROES #18

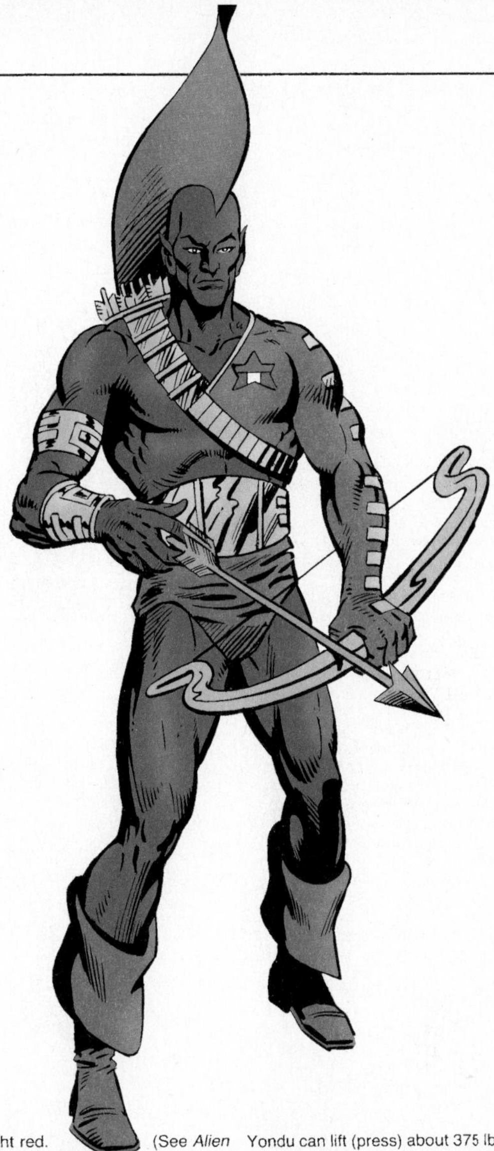

Origin: Yondu Udonta was a game hunter of the primitive Zatoan tribe of humanoid beings who were native to Centauri IV, the first planet to be colonized by Earth outside the solar system, some time in the early 29th Century. Intimidated by Earth's superior technology, most Centaurian tribes established peaceful relationships with the settlers. Yondu's tribe, the Zatoans, however, migrated from their ancestral forests to the less accessible plains to avoid contact with the outworlders. 200 years after the Centaurians' first contact with Earth, a ship bearing Major Vance Astro, launched in 1988, arrived on Centauri IV, using an antiquated mode of star travel (see *Vance Astro*). Finding that Earth had beat him to his destination centuries before, using advanced star-drive engines, Astro set about to perform his reconnaissance mission of the planet, despite the fact that it was now obsolete. While performing his geophysical survey, Astro came across Yondu who was in the midst of his ritual of manhood ordeal. Although Yondu tried to avoid contact with the outworlder, the planet-wide attack by the extraterrestrial Badoon (see *Alien Races: Badoon*) brought the two men together. The Badoon massacred the entire human settlement and began circling the planet trying to eradicate the scattered tribes of native Centaurians. With the first evidence of hostilities, Astro took Yondu aboard his survey ship and set out for the nearest known planet in the Centauri trinary star system.

Due to the antiquated nature of Astro's ship, however, the two were swiftly overtaken by the Badoon. Intrigued by the ancient vessel, the Badoon did not annihilate it upon sight, but instead captured it and took its passengers captive. The two were taken prisoner under Badoon escort to the Badoon's base of operations on Earth once Earth was secured by the alien invaders. On Earth, the two were taken before Drang, head of the Badoon militia, but managed to escape. They soon encountered two other fugitives of the Badoon invasion, Charlie-27 of the Jupiter colony, and Martinex of the Pluto colony. Banding together to battle Badoon oppression, the four founded the Guardians of the Galaxy. For the next few years, the four survivors attacked the Badoon's outposts in the solar system. Finally, with the aid of the time-travelling Defenders, they managed to repel all the Badoon from Earth's dominion. Having secured the freedom of their people, the Guardians remained together to safeguard the galaxy.

Height: 6'2" **Eyes:** Blue
Weight: 210 lbs. **Hair:** None

Unusual features: All Centaurians have bluish skin and brightly colored dorsal fins. Yondu's fin, like that of all the males of his tribe, is bright red. (See *Alien Races: Centaurians.*)

Powers: Yondu possesses no superhuman physical powers, but is a natural mystic, like his entire tribe. Yondu possesses an intuitive "sixth sense" that permits him limited empathic relationships with other lifeforms. The higher the lifeform the more limited is his empathic potential. Yondu possesses an intuitive almost mystical rapport with nature, particularly that of his own world, but also any world that still possesses natural wildlife. With this rapport, he can sense incongruous elements (foreign bodies or substances) or focus on specific elements within the whole (such as the location of a given plant). He is also sensitive to mystical beings and forces and is able to detect their presence and activities without effort. By going into a trance, Yondu is able to replenish his own inner strength by communing with natural forces.

Yondu is an above average physical specimen of his race. He has slightly more endurance than the average human male and is about 1.5 times as strong as human. Yondu can lift (press) about 375 lbs. An apprentice hunter, Yondu is proficient in the use of bow and arrow. His four-octave range ability to whistle aids him in his archery (see *Weapons*). The native Centuarian language is a system of grunts, clicks, and whistles, but Yondu has managed to master the English language, although it is painful for him to speak for too long without resting his throat.

Weapons: Yondu employs a 5-foot single curve bow and a quiver of arrows composed of *yaka*, a special sound-sensitive metal found only on Centauri IV. A *yaka* arrow can actually change its direction (but not speed) in response to certain high-octave whistle-sounds some Centaurians can produce. It is not yet known precisely what pitch causes a *yaka* arrow to move in what way. Yondu is so skillful at controlling his arrows, he can cause an arrow to return to his hand or weave its way in flight through a crowd of people without touching them. Yondu's arrows are 15 inches in length and are very flexible. He carries about 20 of them at one time.

VANCE ASTRO

Real Name: Vance Astrovik
Occupation: Former astronaut, now adventurer
Identity: Publicly known in 31st century
Legal status: Citizen of the United States, 20th Century, citizen of the United Federation of Planets, 31st Century
Former aliases: None
Place of birth: Saugerties, New York
Marital status: Single
Known relatives: Arnold Astrovik (father), Norma Astrovik (mother)
Group affiliation: Guardians of the Galaxy
Base of operations: Starship *Freedom's Lady*, Milky Way Galaxy, in an alternate future of the 31st century
First appearance: MARVEL SUPER HEROES #18
Origin: Vance Astrovik was the only son of a small-town butcher and his wife. Going into the U.S. Air Force at the age of 18, Astrovik (who changed his name to Astro when he was 21) became the youngest man to be accepted into the astronaut training program several years later. In 1988, Astro volunteered for the first manned interstellar mission ever conducted by the United States. (In this alternate future, Reed Richards never released his own experimental faster-than-light ship to the government, and they were unaware he even had such a capacity.) His ship, *Odysseus I*, was not equipped with the capability for faster-than-light speed; hence the journey to earth's nearest interstellar neighbor, a planet in the Alpha Centauri system, would take about 10 centuries. To protect him from aging, Astro was covered with a skin-preserving copper alloy bodysuit, and his blood was transfused with some kind of preservative fluid. Astro was launched into space from the Houston Spaceport in the fall of 1988. While on his way to Alpha Centauri, the ship automatically awoke him from his suspended animation in order for him to perform routine course adjustments. During the periods he was awake, sometimes for a year in duration, Astro eventually went insane with loneliness on several occasions, returning to a semblance of normality after the ship automatically put him under suspended animation again. During his long periods of sustained dream-state activities, Astro's latent psionic powers emerged. By the time he emerged on Centauri IV almost a thousand years later, he had full control over his psychokinetic abilities.

Upon arrival, Astro learned that Earth had beat him to Centauri IV by two hundred years, having developed a faster-than-light drive since the time he left. Although Earth was unable to intercept his flight, the Centaurian colony afforded him a hero's welcome. Disturbed by his reputation, Astro was determined to carry out the mission he was assigned a millennium ago even though it would be superfluous. While engaged in his geophysical survey, he encountered Yondu Udonta, one of the humanoid natives of the planet (see *Yondu*). When the alien Badoon launched an attack on Centauri IV, annihilating the human colony and methodically eradicating the natives, Astro and Yondu attempted to escape in Astro's ship. They were overtaken and transported to Earth. There they escaped and joined with two other survivors of the Badoon's massacre to form the Guardians of the Galaxy. After liberating Earth, the Guardians set out on a random course across the galaxy, in the hopes of safeguarding freedom everywhere.

Height: 6'1"
Weight: (with protective suit): 250 lbs.
Eyes: Hazel
Hair: Black
Powers: Vance Astro possesses the psionic ability of psychokinesis, the ability to affect matter with his mind. In some unknown manner, Astro's brain generates psionic energy which he is able to project as concussive force. Astro can focus the energy at will, creating anything from a narrow 2-inch diameter "beam" of force to a 360 degree expanding sphere of force. At maximum concentration, Astro's narrow focus is capable of penetrating a 1-inch steel plate, and his wide focus is capable of knocking seven 250-pound men standing 10 feet from him a distance of 5 feet. Astro does not yet have the mental discipline to use his psionic power delicately. Whenever he taps the power at all, it is accompanied by a minimum of ½ pound per square inch force. Astro cannot use his psionic energy powers for anything other than his "psyche-blasts;" not levitation, telepathy, nor precog-

nition. He can use his psionic energy at maximum exertion for about a half hour before his mind suffers from fatigue or headaches. This is not because he has depleted the psionic energy available to him. It is because he has exceeded his physical capacity to manipulate the energy without effort.

Astro is an above average athlete with a basic knowledge of unarmed combat learned while in the Air Force.

Note: While visiting the 20th Century, Vance sought out his former self, the teen-aged Vance Astrovik, to convince him not to enter the astronaut training program and thus not go through the experiences that would culminate in his becoming a Guardian. In this encounter, psychic feedback between the two identical brains occurred, unleashing the psionic power of Vance Astrovik centuries earlier than in his elder self. Hence the time-line of the Guardians of the Galaxy diverges from present-day reality by this point.

STARHAWK

Real Name: Stakar and Aleta
Occupation: Adventurer, protector
Identity: Secret
Legal status: Citizen of Arcturus IV, circa 31st Century A.D. in an alternate Earth future
Other current aliases: "One Who Knows," "Giver of Light"
Place of birth: Arcturus IV, Arcturus System, Milky Way
Marital status: Married
Known relatives: Ogord (adoptive father), Salaan (adoptive mother), Tara, Seta, John (children, deceased)
Group affiliation: Guardians of the Galaxy
Base of operations: Starship *Freedom's Lady*
First appearance: DEFENDERS #27
Unusual features: Starhawk can manifest itself in either his male or female forms.

Origin: The being known as Starhawk is actually a composite being made up of two separate humanoid entities, one a male mutant and one a normal female, who are natives of Arcturus IV. In the early 20th Century (Earth-designation), scientists on Arcturus IV had seized control of the propagation of the species and consigned it to the laboratory where specific benevolent traits could be implemented. The populace soon revolted and attacked the government birth installations. The battle ended with a planet-wide nuclear conflagration and the near-extermination of the race. The genetically-bred Arcturans had the capacity to mutate faster and so they survived in greater numbers than the normal Arcturans. Their forms, however, were diversely and inhumanly mutated. The surviving band of normal Arcturans struggled to wrest control over the planet from the dominant mutants. Bands of mutant-slaying non-mutants calling themselves Reavers roamed the world, destroying all the mutants they found. On one of the last of the Reavers' raids before they eliminated all of the mutants, a Reaver named Ogord came upon a mutant male infant who appeared to be unmutated. Sparing the infant's life, Ogord brought him to his commander who granted Ogord permission to keep the child and raise it as his own. Ogord went home and presented the child whom he named Stakar to his wife Salaan and daughter Aleta. As Stakar grew to adulthood, his pacifistic tendencies disappointed his family. He was adventurous, however, and one day set out to explore the forbidden radioactive ruins of the old civilization. There he discovered the Temple of the Hawk-God, a technological shrine to one of the Arcturans' deities. Followed by his step-sister Aleta, Stakar convinced her to stay with him rather than reveal his whereabouts. He then set about trying to master the knowledge of the past using his heightened cognitive powers. When Aleta impatiently wrested a learning helmet from his hands, she accidentally activated its energy-converting mechanism, and was projected into the 30-foot idol of the hawk-god. Disoriented by the occurrence, Aleta animated the statue and went on a rampage, destroying patrols of Reavers searching for them. Using the helmet, Stakar managed to achieve a telepathic link with Aleta, and in a manner not yet understood, merged his physical being with hers. Adopting the distinctive garb of Starhawk, the composite being left Arcturus to its own fate, in order to find peace and purpose among the stars.

Starhawk has roamed the Milky Way Galaxy since his/her creation in the 21st Century, his/her activities unknown. At certain times, Stakar and Aleta managed to manifest themselves in physical space simultaneously, enabling them to mate and issue three offspring. (These children were slain by Aleta's father Ogord in an attempt at revenge upon Starhawk for abandoning Arcturus.) Starhawk assisted the Guardians of the Galaxy in their liberation of the Earth's solar system from the Badoon (see *Alien Races: Badoon*), and has since accompanied them in an unofficial capacity in their mission to protect the Milky Way Galaxy. During a time trip to the 20th Century, Starhawk was killed and recreated by

the 31st Century human cyborg-turned-god Korvac. Presumably this new Starhawk is identical to his/her former self down to the atomic level.

Height: 6' 4"   **Weight:** 450 lbs
Eyes: White   **Hair:** Reddish blond
Powers: Starhawk possesses a number of superhumanoid physical and energy-manipulative powers. Like all Arcturans, Starhawk is long-lived (the average lifespan of an Arcturan is 1,820 Earth years). Starhawk, whose male self is the last known Arcturan mutant, shares his breed's immunity to most known diseases and radiation sickness. His/her strength exceeds human levels: Starhawk can lift (press) about 5 tons. Although he/she is stronger than human, he/she can be rendered unconscious by a sufficiently powerful force.

Starhawk's major power is the manipulation of light-energy. By as yet unknown means, Starhawk can tap light from any source and transform it for a variety of uses. He/she can project it as blasts of concussive force or heat. He/she can create temporary bridges of "solid light" by forcing large groups of photons into orbits around gravitons (sub-atomic particles that carry the force of gravitational attraction between particles) and psions (particles whose wavelengths are in the psionic portion of the electromagnetic spectrum). Starhawk can also employ his/her light-powers to enable him/her to penetrate certain types of energy fields by jamming its specific wavelengths upon contact.

Starhawk can fly by surrounding him/herself with a nimbus of photon/graviton clusters and by creat-

ing a careful imbalance in the construction of this field can generate an intense beam of gravitons. He/she is capable of attaining near-light speeds in the vacuum of interstellar space. Reaching such speeds near planetary objects could cause irreparable harm to them. In Earth's atmosphere, Starhawk can attain speeds of Mach 10 (10 times the speed of sound: 7,700 miles per hour) within seconds. His/her reflexes are enhanced in direct proportion to the speeds attained, enabling him/her to perform complicated aerial maneuvers with ease.

Starhawk has an extrasensory sensitivity to the patterns and flux of energies within a 100 million mile radius (in deep space; within a gravitational field and/or a radio flux-filled environment, this sensitivity diminishes by a factor of a million) of him/herself. Consequently, he/she can sense abnormal concentrations or expenditures of energy, or disruptions in the space/time continuum.

Paraphernalia: Starhawk employs a retracting transparent facemask and an oxygen-synthesizing life support system within his (but not her) uniform. Solar wind (highly charged particles ejected into outer space from the hot "atmosphere" of the sun) collector "wings" unfold from his/her back when in flight to aid in the gathering and generation of photons and associated gravitons necessary to sustain flight. Also in the vanes of the wings are numerous devices that accumulate energy from the solar wind and generate power for the various subsystems of the uniform.

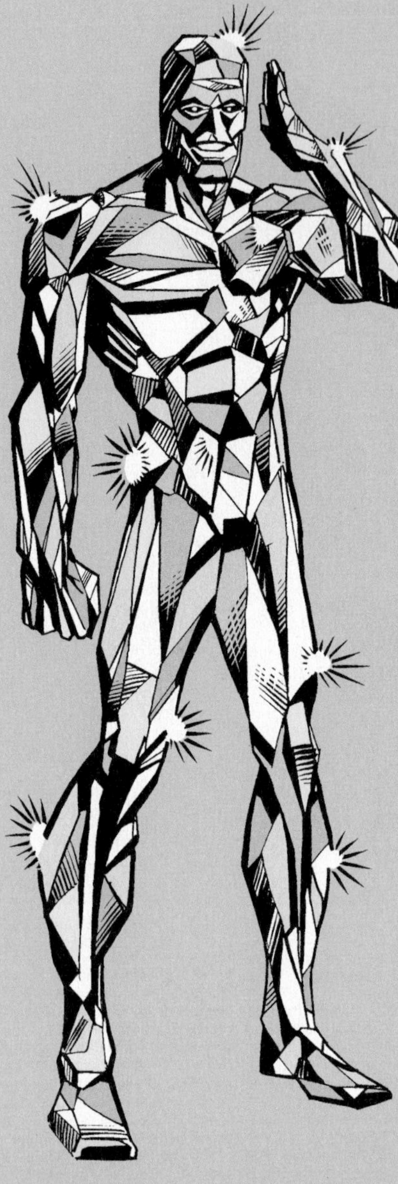

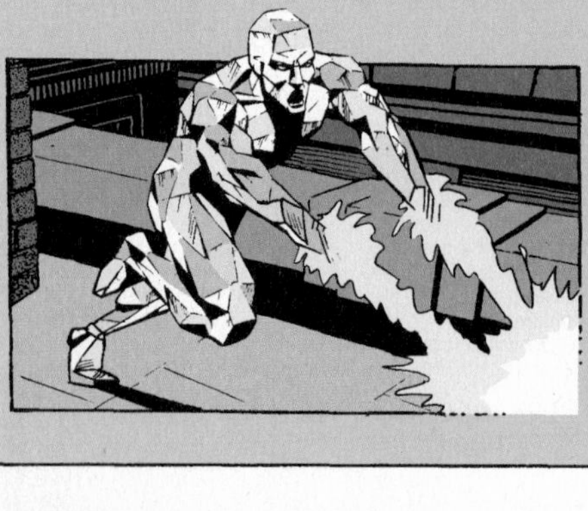

MARTINEX

Real Name: Martinex
Occupation: Ex-space technician, now adventurer
Identity: Publicly known
Legal status: Citizen of Earth colony on Pluto, last known survivor
Former aliases: None
Place of birth: Cerberus Center, Pluto
Marital status: Single
Known relatives: None
Group affiliation: Guardians of the Galaxy
Base of operations: Starship *Freedom's Lady,* latter half of the Thirtieth Century
First appearance: MARVEL SUPER HEROES #18
Origin: Martinex was born in 2986 A.D. to two professional technicians of the Earth colony on the planet Pluto. Like all those who volunteered to live on Pluto, Martinex's body tissues were biogenetically restructured entirely out of silicon so that he could withstand the extremes of cold and atmosphere of that planet. Martinex attended the Pluvian Technical Academy and trained for his father's line of work. When Pluto was evacuated during the Badoon Invasion of 3007, Martinex remained behind to destroy Pluto's advanced technological industrial complexes to keep them out of the hands of the enemy. Rescued by Charlie-27 of the Jupiter colony, Martinex joined with a handful of survivors of several Earth colonies to form the Guardians of the Galaxy. Martinex helped liberate Earth from the Badoon and went on to be a self-appointed champion of free space.
Height: 6' 1" **Weight:** 455 lbs
Eyes: Black **Hair:** None
Powers: Martinex possesses the ability to generate regions of intense heat and cold that he can project from his hands. Martinex's body is made of extremely complex, silicon-isotope organic compounds. The outer layers of the crystalline "skin" in his hands contain two artificial, complex impurities that cause a solid-state lasing action (from LASER: Light Amplification by Stimulated Emission of Radiation) which convert sources of bodily energy into beams of energy at two principal frequencies. One of these frequencies is in the infra-red portion of the electromagnetic spectrum and it stimulates heat in any object. The other, in the micro-wave portion of the spectrum, generates a frequency whose wavelength reduces overall thermal energies in an object by a stimulated re-radiation of energy. This occurs only in objects within a certain size range (.01 to .001 inches, the size of most water droplets).

Martinex can vary the power output of both effects with great precision of temperature. For example, he could warm a tub of water to precisely human skin temperature (92° F.) or cool off a hot room to freezing (32° F). He can also cut his way through stone (using a beam of 20,000° Fahrenheit) or precipitate carbon dioxide "snow" out of a small volume of Earth atmosphere (about −175° F.). Because energy from his body powers his energy beams, he can only generate his maximum output for a short period of time, on the order of a few minutes. At that point he risks reducing his body's total energy content below normal levels of functioning. The maximum distance at which he can employ his powers is about 28 feet.

Martinex employs his right hand for the generation of heat effects and his left for cold. It is not known whether this has any genetic basis, as right-versus left-handedness does in normal humans.

Martinex is relatively resistant to the effects of great heat or cold. His body's melting point is about 2,500° F. and he can function almost normally in the temperatures encountered on Pluto: about 3.2° above absolute zero (−459.7° F.). His silicon-based form possesses greater mass and strength than human. He can lift (press) about 1 ton.

KORVAC

Real Name: Michael Korvac
Occupation: Former computer technician, would-be master of the universe
Identity: His existence was not known to the general public of 20th Century Earth.
Legal status: Citizen of Earth, subject of the Badoon Empire
Former aliases: Michael, "The Enemy"
Place of birth: North America, Earth in an alternate future of the 31st Century
Place of death: Forest Hills Gardens, Queens, New York
Known survivors: None
Group affiliation: Former leader of a band of alien renegades
First appearance: GIANT-SIZE DEFENDERS #3
Final appearance: AVENGERS #178

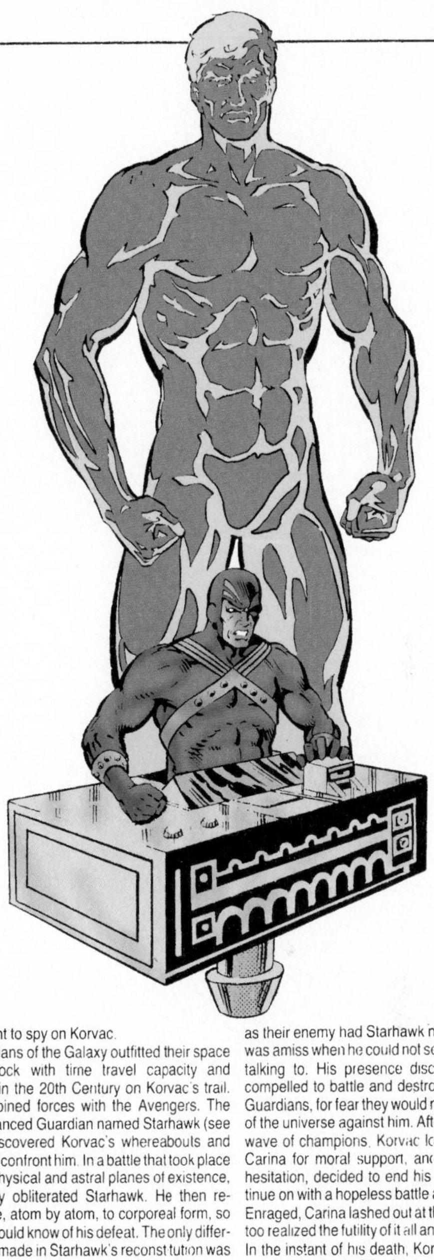

History: Michael Korvac was a highly-skilled computer technician of 31st Century Earth who offered his services freely to the Badoon (see *Alien Races: Badoon*) when they invaded the solar system in 3007. His superior abilities were recognized by the alien conquerors, and Korvac was soon given the task of overseeing the analytical computer system governing the Badoon Empire on their throneworld Moord. A zealous worker, Korvac collapsed one day while on the job. His supervisor decided to punish him by amputating the lower half of his body and grafting the remaining part to a mobile computer module, in effect, turning him into a cyborg (cybernetic organism). Awakening to discover the cruelty enacted upon him, Korvac used his cybernetic abilities to slay those who had performed the operation. Korvac soon realized the vast potential of his new form and, tapping into the Badoon's master computer system, he began to plot the takeover of the whole empire. Before he could carry out his plan, however, he was transported through time by the galactic gamesman called the Grandmaster (see *Grandmaster*) to be used as a pawn in one of the alien's games. Korvac allowed himself to be beaten so he could computer-scan the Grandmaster's power without his knowledge. Korvac's cybernetic console had the capacity to tap and synthesize virtually any type of energy. In such a manner, Korvac analyzed the Grandmaster's power and siphoned part of it. Returned to his own era, the 31st Century, Korvac used his expanded abilities to teleport himself to a desolate planetoid where he built himself a stronghold. Now able to travel through time like the Grandmaster, Korvac recruited an elite group of alien henchmen, and plotted the takeover of the galaxy.

One of Korvac's earliest known stratagems was to send a power siphon beam into the sun of his native solar system in order to cause it to go nova so he could siphon its energies. However, thanks to the intervention of the Guardians of the Galaxy and the Asgardian thunder god Thor (who had been accidentally teleported from the 20th Century by Korvac's time-probe), Korvac's scheme was foiled. Korvac himself teleported to safety, but the Guardians soon picked up his trail. In the 20th Century, Korvac's sensors detected an enormous power-source, which proved to be the worldship of the planet-eater Galactus. Plugging himself into the ship's central computer system, Korvac absorbed such knowledge and power that he became nearly omnipotent. Using this godlike power, he created for himself a perfect human body. With his expanded consciousness, his desire for revenge was supplanted by loftier ambitions: to become the benevolent proprietor of the entire universe. After assuming control, he planned to reshape the universe in order to eliminate all chaos and rectify all the injustices that the civilizations of the universe had wrought. Until such time as he could bring about his vision, he decided to return to Earth, his homeworld, there to live comfortably among humankind. On Earth, he went by the name "Michael" and took for a consort a model named Carina Walters, who was in reality the daughter of the Grandmaster's "brother", the Collector (see *Collector*) sent to spy on Korvac.

The Guardians of the Galaxy outfitted their space station Drydock with time travel capacity and materialized in the 20th Century on Korvac's trail. There they joined forces with the Avengers. The sensory-enhanced Guardian named Starhawk (see *Starhawk*) discovered Korvac's whereabouts and went alone to confront him. In a battle that took place on both the physical and astral planes of existence, Korvac totally obliterated Starhawk. He then restored his foe, atom by atom, to corporeal form, so that no one would know of his defeat. The only difference Korvac made in Starhawk's reconstitution was that Starhawk would no longer be able to perceive Korvac's existence in any way. Starhawk was sent away with no memory of what transpired, and Korvac returned to his meditations. The next time Korvac was forced to act was when the Collector began to capture the Avengers to save them from Korvac. The Collector foresaw that Korvac's attempt to attain universal sovereignty would cause great conflict among the powers of the cosmos which could ultimately destroy the universe. To prevent the Collector from revealing his premonitions to the Avengers, Korvac disintegrated him with a long-distance power-blast. By this time, Carina had switched allegiances from her father to Korvac.

When they pinpointed the source of the beam that killed the Collector, the Avengers and the Guardians traveled to Korvac's home in Forest Hills. The teams would not have recognized the unassuming Michael as their enemy had Starhawk not known something was amiss when he could not see the man they were talking to. His presence discovered, Korvac felt compelled to battle and destroy the Avengers and Guardians, for fear they would rally the great powers of the universe against him. After slaying wave after wave of champions, Korvac looked to his beloved Carina for moral support, and finding a flicker of hesitation, decided to end his life rather than continue on with a hopeless battle against the universe. Enraged, Carina lashed out at the survivors until she too realized the futility of it all and committed suicide. In the instant of his death, Korvac magnanimously restored to life all of the Avengers and Guardians he had slain. Moondragon, one of two survivors of the carnage, explained to fellow survivor Thor that she had telepathically been in rapport with Korvac and believed him not to be evil, by her definition.

Height: (in human form) 6' 3" **Eyes:** Blue
Weight: (in human form)230 lbs **Hair:** Blond
Powers: In his ultimate form, Michael Korvac possessed cosmic power on a vast scale making him a peer to such Earthly gods as Odin and Zeus, and such alien entities as Galactus, the Collector, and the Grandmaster. Among the multitude of ways in which he could manifest his power were the resuscitation of life force, time travel, astral projection, long-range energy bombardment, and telepathy. Capable of absorbing power from any source including the abilities of his foes, Korvac had the potential for infinite power.

COLLECTOR

Real Name: Taneleer Tivan
Occupation: Curator
Identity: Secret. His existence is not known to the general public of Earth
Legal status: Possesses no citizenship
Former aliases: None
Place of self-awareness: Cygnus X-1
Marital status: Widowed
Known relatives: Matani (wife, deceased), Carina (daughter, deceased)
Group affiliation: Elders of the Universe
Base of operations: The known universe
First appearance: AVENGERS #28
Origin: Like all the Elders of the Universe, the origin of the Collector is lost in antiquity. What is known is that he is one of the oldest living beings in the universe, having been a member of one of the first of the universe's races to become sentient in the wake of the Big Bang. Virtually immortal, the Collector spent the first millennia of his existence with his wife and daughter on the tranquil world he chose as his home base. When their daughter had grown to maturity and left them, the Collector's wife died of mysterious causes. The Collector was unprepared for her demise: he had thought her as immortal as he. In meditation, he realized that an important factor in an Elder's immortality is the will to live, and his wife had simply lost hers. Determined not to succumb to his wife's malady, the Collector meditated upon what he might do to give his life meaning. In a vision, he foresaw that beings of great power would arise one day determined to destroy all life in the universe. To prevent this from happening, he decided to devote his life to collecting living beings and artifacts from throughout the known universe, and placing them in safekeeping. If what he foresaw came to pass, he could repopulate the universe and bequeath to them the knowledge and culture of the past. Building himself a vast starship, the Collector set forth, stopping at every inhabited world he found to acquire a sample of their finest achievements as well as living representatives of the world's lifeforms. In a matter of millennia, his ship was completely filled, and the Collector was forced to suspend his mission in order to build expanded facilities for his permanent collection. With the aid of robo-mechanics acquired from the planet Cron, the Collector converted several extra-dimensional worlds into giant museums, and transferred his collection there. Every ten millennia or so, he would return to the museum-worlds to deposit his recent acquisitions. At present, the Collector has filled ten museum-worlds with artifacts from a hundred thousand planets. Over the eons, the Collector's monomania became more and more obsessive, making him lose sight of the original reason for which he began his collection. In recent years, the first being of great power he had foreseen as a threat to all life, Thanos of Titan, had been born and defeated. The second of these, Korvac of Earth, managed to kill the Collector when he perceived the Elder's opposition to his plans. A short time later, the Collector's kinsman, the Grandmaster, played a contest of champions with the spirit of Death itself, winning the power to resurrect the Collector at the cost of his own immortal life. Among the living once more, the Collector's current whereabouts are unknown.

Height: 6' 2" **Eyes:** White
Weight: 450 lbs **Hair:** White
Powers: As an Elder of the Universe, the

Collector possesses an immortal body, immune to the cellular deterioration of aging and impervious to conventional harm (disease, penetration wounds, etc.). Only the dispersion of a major portion of his bodily molecules could prevent his regenerative powers from functioning and cause death. Unlike some of the Elders (such as the Champion or the Contemplator) who have used their long lifetimes to develop vast powers of the body or mind, the Collector has not devoted any of his energies on self-perfection. Hence he has no special superhuman physical or mental abilities. The Collector is more interested in acquiring physical objects of power rather than developing his own potential.

Though he is capable of certain precognitive visions of the future, he must meditate for approximately fifty years (Earth-time) in order to reach the necessary state of consciousness to precognate. He has only devoted the time to do this four times in his eons-long life. Even when he has had a vi-

sion of the future, they have usually turned out to have been of events not realized in his own Reality but an alternate one, as in the case of his vision of Thanos destroying the universe.

Weapons: The Collector possesses the finest technology of a hundred thousand worlds, giving him a virtually limitless arsenal of weaponry. He is only limited by what he can lay his hands upon in a given situation. One of his most frequently used devices is his Temporal Assimilator, a handheld machine which enables him to time travel for short temporal distances and durations. He also has a large-scale time probe enabling him to fish for artifacts in other time periods of a given world's history than its present.

Transportation: The Collector's ship has warp drive, dimension-spanning capacity, as well as the means to permit him access to the ship through a small booth-shaped portal while docked in hyper-space.

CHARLIE-27

Real Name: Charlie-27
Occupation: Ex-space soldier, now adventurer
Legal status: Citizen of Earth colony on Jupiter, last known survivor
Identity: Publicly known
Place of birth: Galileo City, Jupiter
Marital status: Single
Known relatives: Charlie-26 (father, deceased), Mabel-15 (mother, deceased)
Group affiliation: Guardians of the Galaxy
Base of operations: Starship *Freedom's Lady,* latter half of the Thirtieth Century
First appearance: MARVEL SUPER HEROES #18
Origin: Charlie-27 was born in 2981 AD to two mine workers of the Earth colony on the planet Jupiter. Like all those who were to live on Jupiter, Charlie's body was bio-genetically engineered to withstand Jupiter's gravity (triple that of Earth). This process gave him a massive body and corresponding strength and endurance. Charlie-27 enlisted in the space militia when he was 16 and served the United Lands of Earth until the militia was decimated by the Badoon invasion of 3007 AD. Joining with a handful of survivors of other colonies to form the Guardians of the Galaxy, Charlie helped liberate Earth from the Badoon, and went on to be a self-appointed champion of free space.
Height: 6'
Weight (on Earth): 555 lbs
Eyes: Blue
Hair: Red
Powers: Like all Jovian settlers, Charlie-27 possesses a superhuman body bio-engineered for the rigors of life on Jupiter. Charlie's body is eleven times more massive than the average human body and about three times as wide. His bones are larger, denser, and more durable than a human's, enabling him to resist Jupiter's three times Earth gravity. His muscle tissue is also about three times as dense as that of the average human body, granting him normal human-level strength in Jupiter's gravity and superhuman strength on Earth. On Jupiter, Charlie can lift (press) about 500 pounds. On Earth, he can lift 1,500 pounds. Charlie has sufficient strength in his arms and hands to bend a six-inch diameter solid steel bar. He has sufficient strength in his legs and feet to dent, and eventually cause a six-inch thick steel plate to rupture, after repeated blows. Despite his weight and size, Charlie has slightly above average human-level reflexes and is capable of running at human-level speeds, approximately 22 miles per hour. His endurance is about four times that of an average human being due to his expanded cardiovascular and respiratory capacities and slower metabolism. Charlie's skin is also denser and more durable than human skin. He is impervious to penetration wounds up to and including the impact of a .45 caliber bullet.

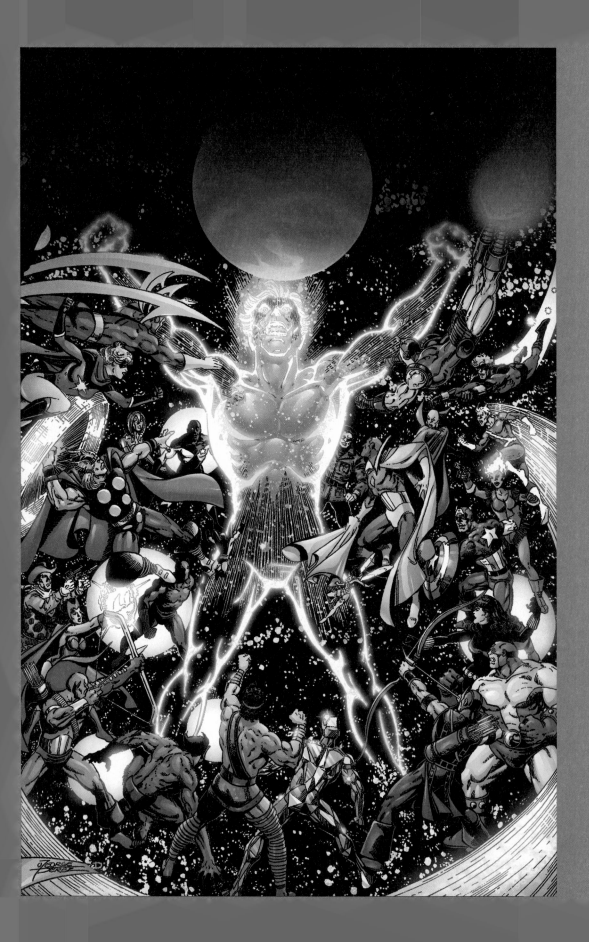

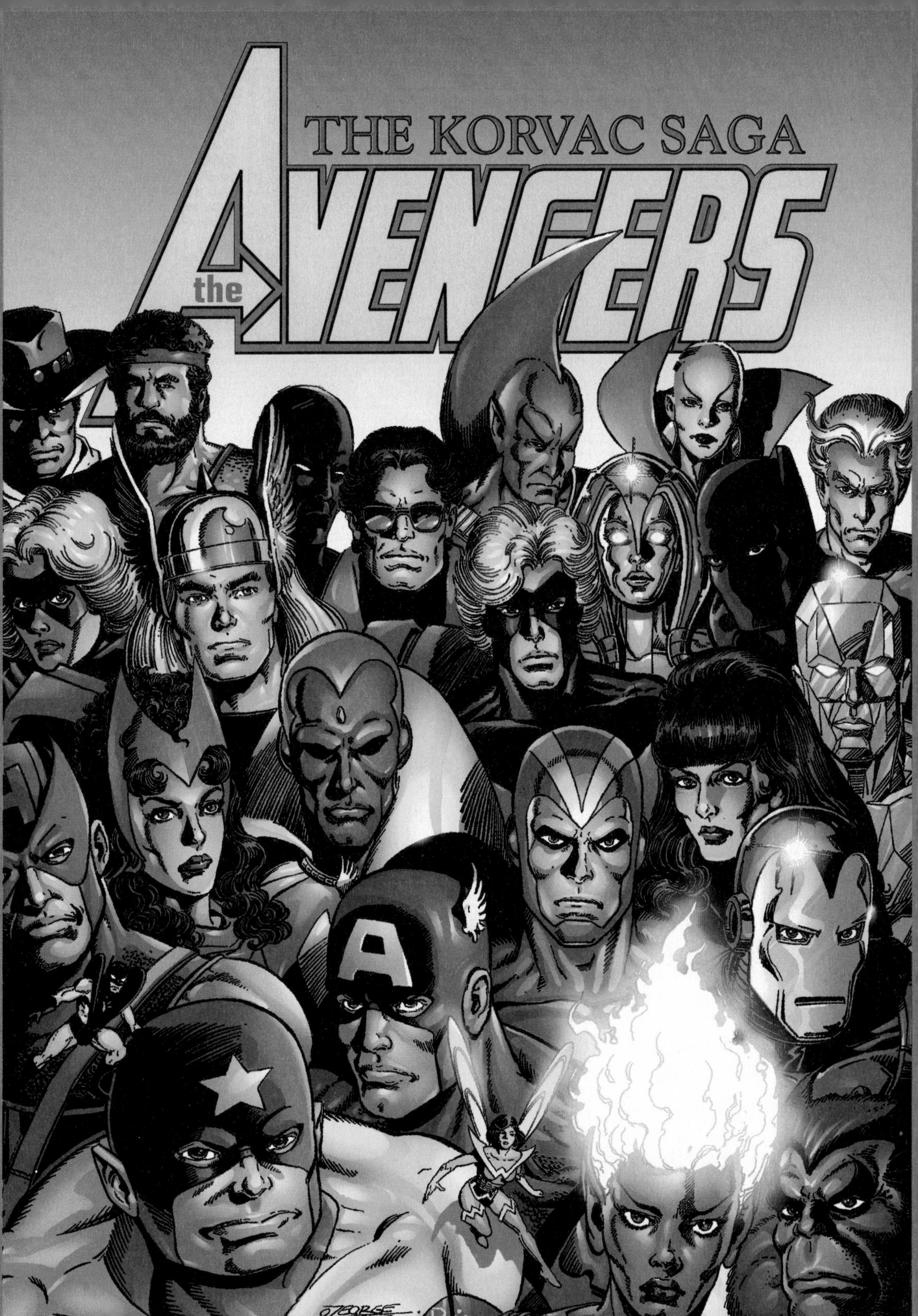
THE KORVAC SAGA
the AVENGERS
GEORGE PEREZ

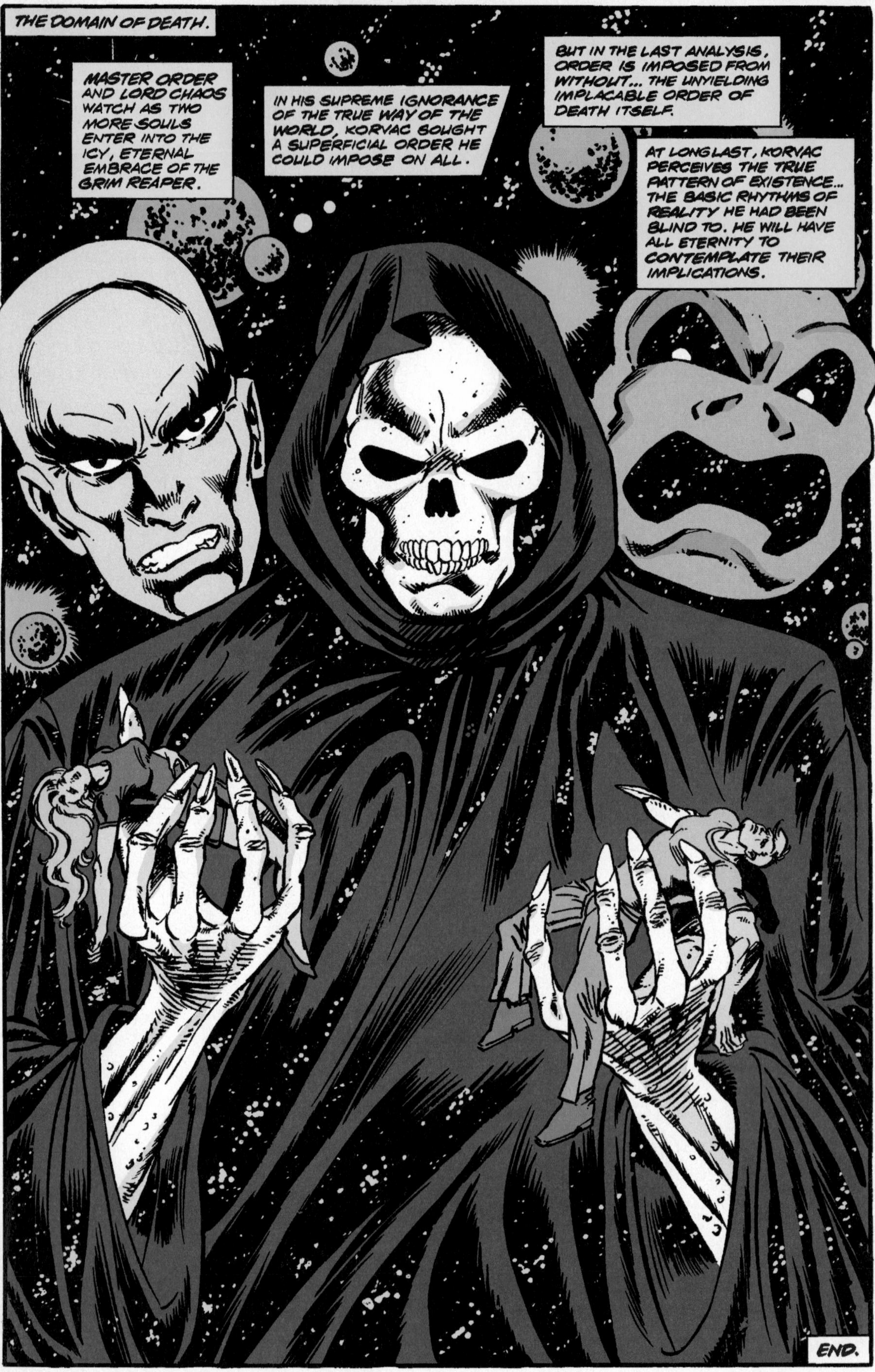
THE DOMAIN OF DEATH.
MASTER ORDER AND LORD CHAOS WATCH AS TWO MORE SOULS ENTER INTO THE ICY, ETERNAL EMBRACE OF THE GRIM REAPER.
IN HIS SUPREME IGNORANCE OF THE TRUE WAY OF THE WORLD, KORVAC SOUGHT A SUPERFICIAL ORDER HE COULD IMPOSE ON ALL.
BUT IN THE LAST ANALYSIS, ORDER IS IMPOSED FROM WITHOUT... THE UNYIELDING IMPLACABLE ORDER OF DEATH ITSELF.
AT LONG LAST, KORVAC PERCEIVES THE TRUE PATTERN OF EXISTENCE... THE BASIC RHYTHMS OF REALITY HE HAD BEEN BLIND TO. HE WILL HAVE ALL ETERNITY TO CONTEMPLATE THEIR IMPLICATIONS.
END.

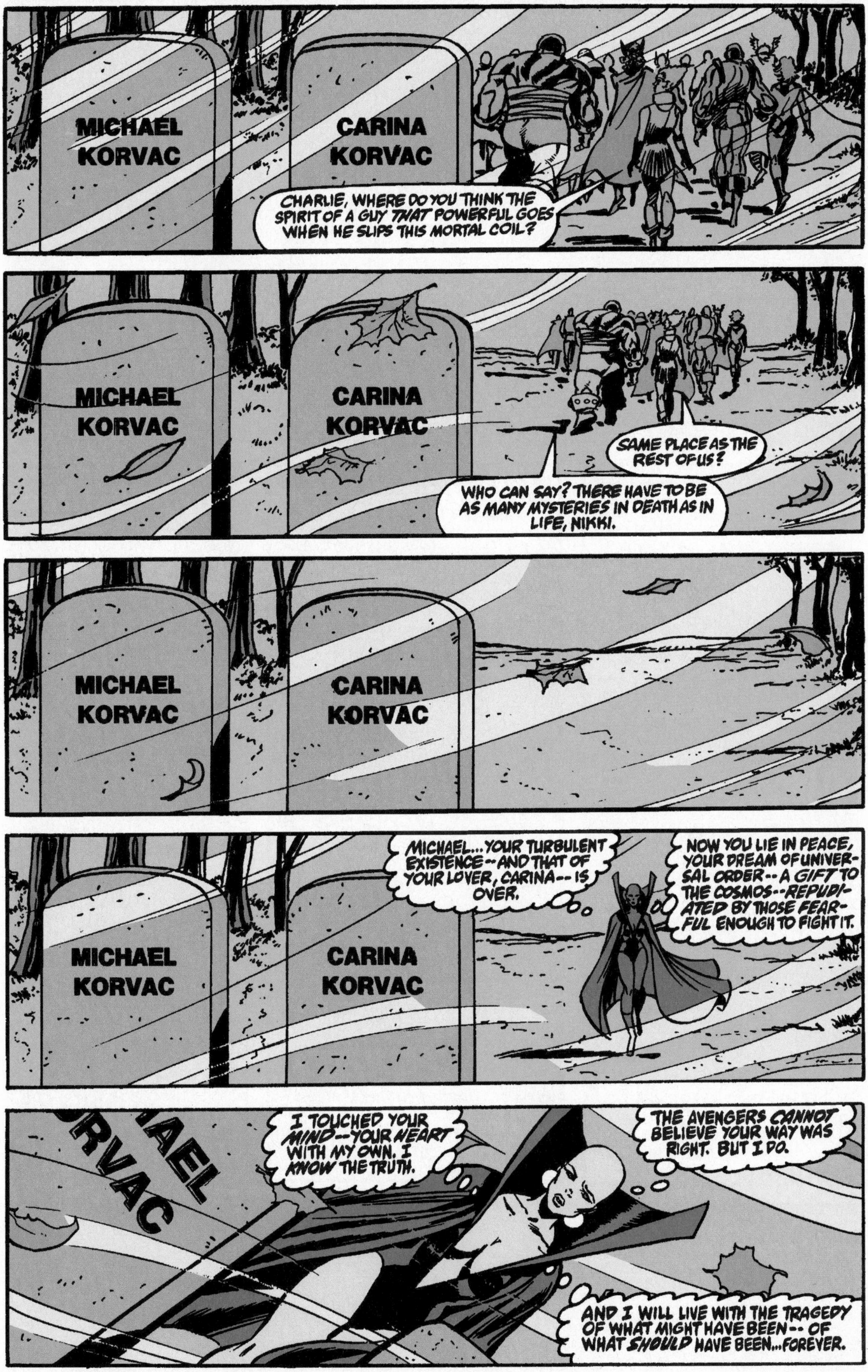
MICHAEL KORVAC
CARINA KORVAC
CHARLIE, WHERE DO YOU THINK THE SPIRIT OF A GUY *THAT* POWERFUL GOES WHEN HE SLIPS THIS MORTAL COIL?
MICHAEL KORVAC
CARINA KORVAC
SAME PLACE AS THE REST OF US?
WHO CAN SAY? THERE HAVE TO BE AS MANY *MYSTERIES* IN *DEATH* AS IN *LIFE,* NIKKI.
MICHAEL KORVAC
CARINA KORVAC
MICHAEL KORVAC
CARINA KORVAC
MICHAEL... YOUR TURBULENT EXISTENCE -- AND THAT OF YOUR LOVER, CARINA -- IS OVER.
NOW YOU LIE IN PEACE, YOUR DREAM OF UNIVERSAL ORDER -- A *GIFT* TO THE COSMOS -- *REPUDIATED* BY THOSE *FEARFUL* ENOUGH TO FIGHT IT.
I TOUCHED YOUR *MIND* -- YOUR *HEART* WITH MY OWN. I *KNOW* THE TRUTH.
THE AVENGERS *CANNOT* BELIEVE YOUR WAY WAS RIGHT. BUT I DO.
AND I WILL LIVE WITH THE TRAGEDY OF WHAT MIGHT HAVE BEEN -- OF WHAT *SHOULD* HAVE BEEN... FOREVER.

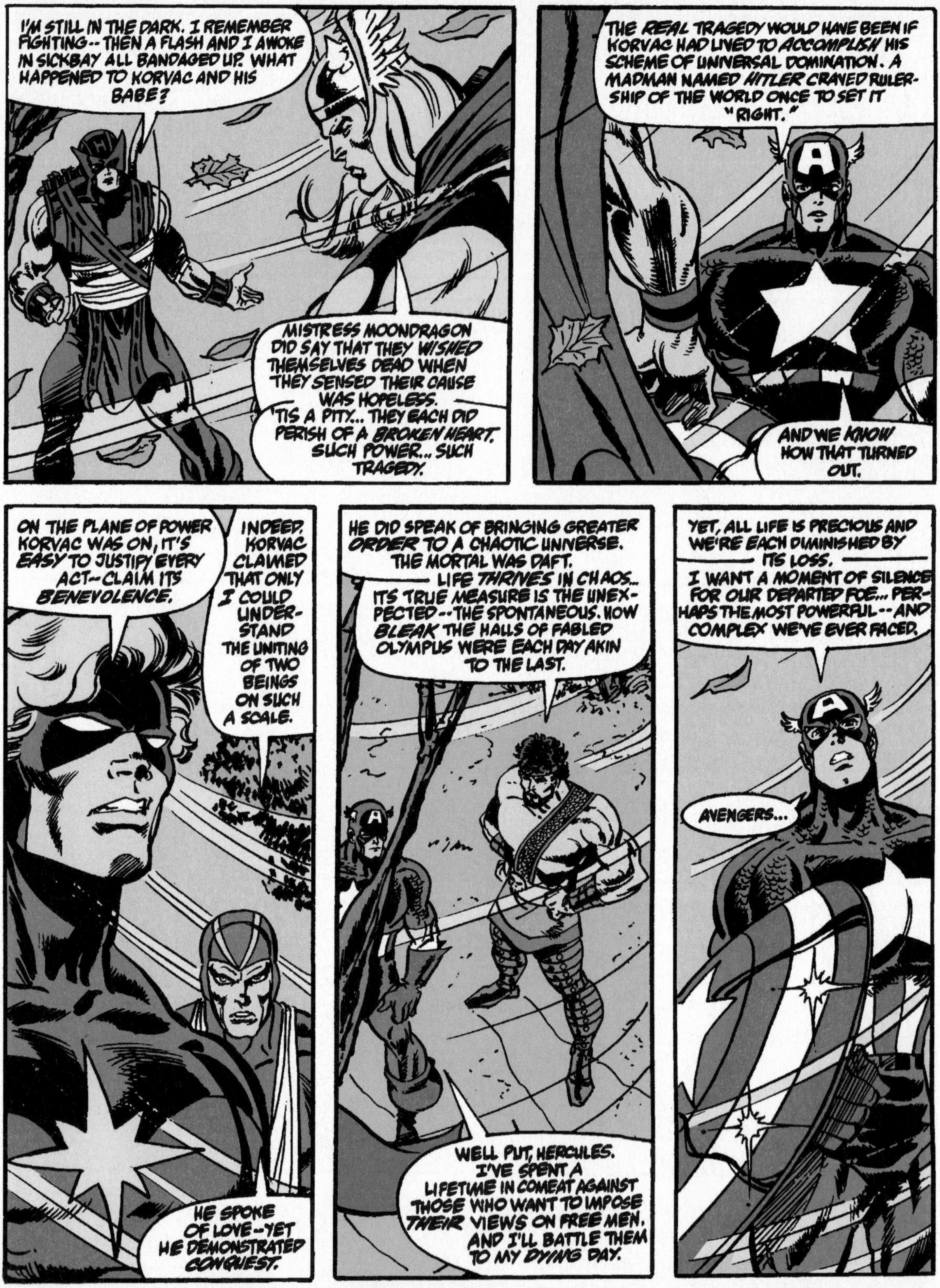
I'M STILL IN THE DARK. I REMEMBER FIGHTING-- THEN A FLASH AND I AWOKE IN SICKBAY ALL BANDAGED UP. WHAT HAPPENED TO KORVAC AND HIS BABE?
MISTRESS MOONDRAGON DID SAY THAT THEY WISHED THEMSELVES DEAD WHEN THEY SENSED THEIR CAUSE WAS HOPELESS.
'TIS A PITY... THEY EACH DID PERISH OF A BROKEN HEART. SUCH POWER... SUCH TRAGEDY.
THE REAL TRAGEDY WOULD HAVE BEEN IF KORVAC HAD LIVED TO ACCOMPLISH HIS SCHEME OF UNIVERSAL DOMINATION. A MADMAN NAMED HITLER CRAVED RULERSHIP OF THE WORLD ONCE TO SET IT "RIGHT."
AND WE KNOW HOW THAT TURNED OUT.
ON THE PLANE OF POWER KORVAC WAS ON, IT'S EASY TO JUSTIFY EVERY ACT-- CLAIM ITS BENEVOLENCE.
INDEED. KORVAC CLAIMED THAT ONLY I COULD UNDERSTAND THE UNITING OF TWO BEINGS ON SUCH A SCALE.
HE SPOKE OF LOVE--YET HE DEMONSTRATED CONQUEST.
HE DID SPEAK OF BRINGING GREATER ORDER TO A CHAOTIC UNIVERSE. THE MORTAL WAS DAFT.
LIFE THRIVES IN CHAOS... ITS TRUE MEASURE IS THE UNEXPECTED--THE SPONTANEOUS. HOW BLEAK THE HALLS OF FABLED OLYMPUS WERE EACH DAY AKIN TO THE LAST.
WELL PUT, HERCULES. I'VE SPENT A LIFETIME IN COMBAT AGAINST THOSE WHO WANT TO IMPOSE THEIR VIEWS ON FREE MEN. AND I'LL BATTLE THEM TO MY DYING DAY.
YET, ALL LIFE IS PRECIOUS AND WE'RE EACH DIMINISHED BY ITS LOSS.
I WANT A MOMENT OF SILENCE FOR OUR DEPARTED FOE... PERHAPS THE MOST POWERFUL--AND COMPLEX WE'VE EVER FACED.
AVENGERS...

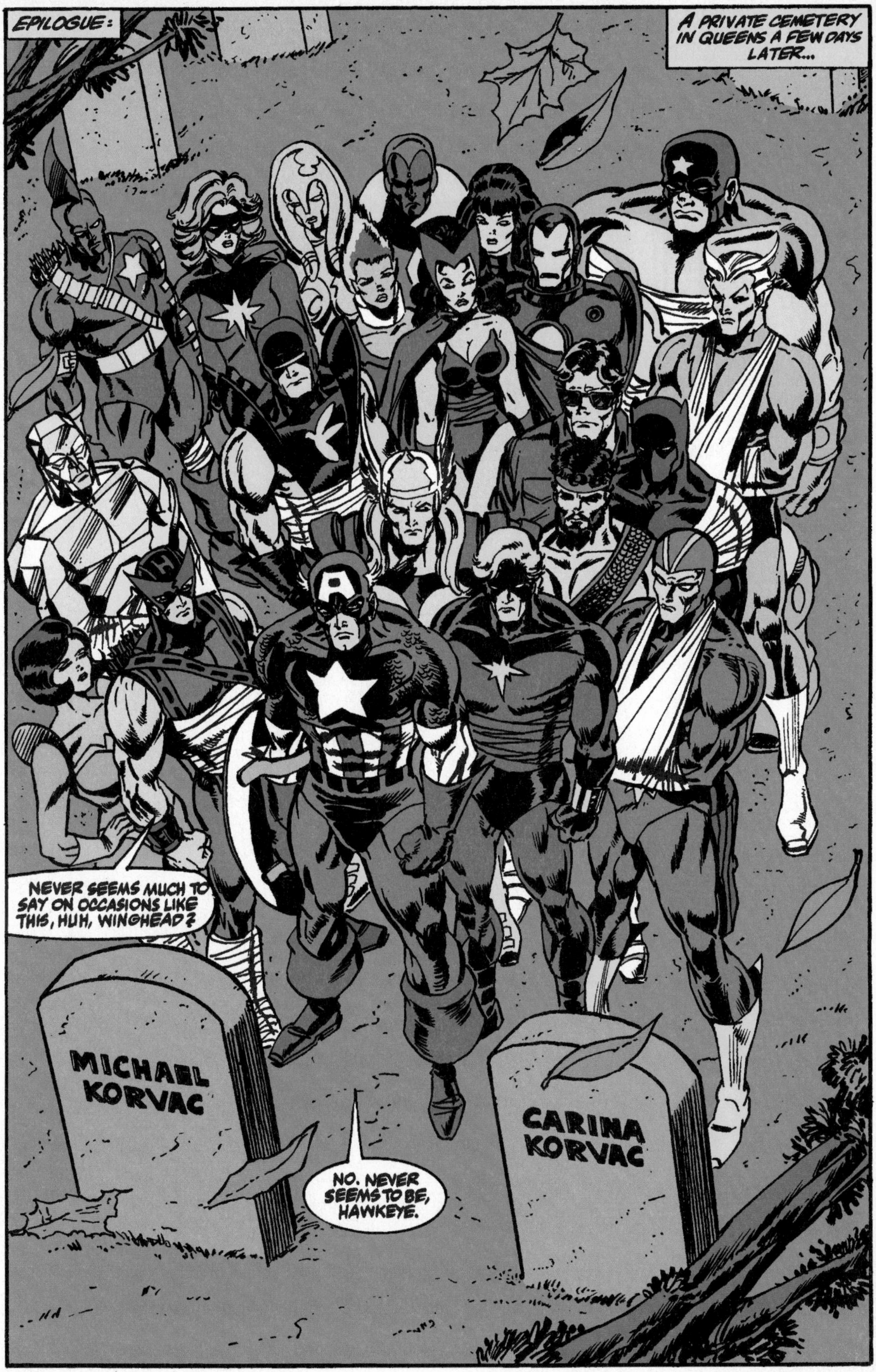
EPILOGUE:
A PRIVATE CEMETERY IN QUEENS A FEW DAYS LATER...
NEVER SEEMS MUCH TO SAY ON OCCASIONS LIKE THIS, HUH, WINGHEAD?
NO. NEVER SEEMS TO BE, HAWKEYE.
MICHAEL KORVAC
CARINA KORVAC

and artist Tom Morgan. It's presented on the following pages for the sake of completeness.

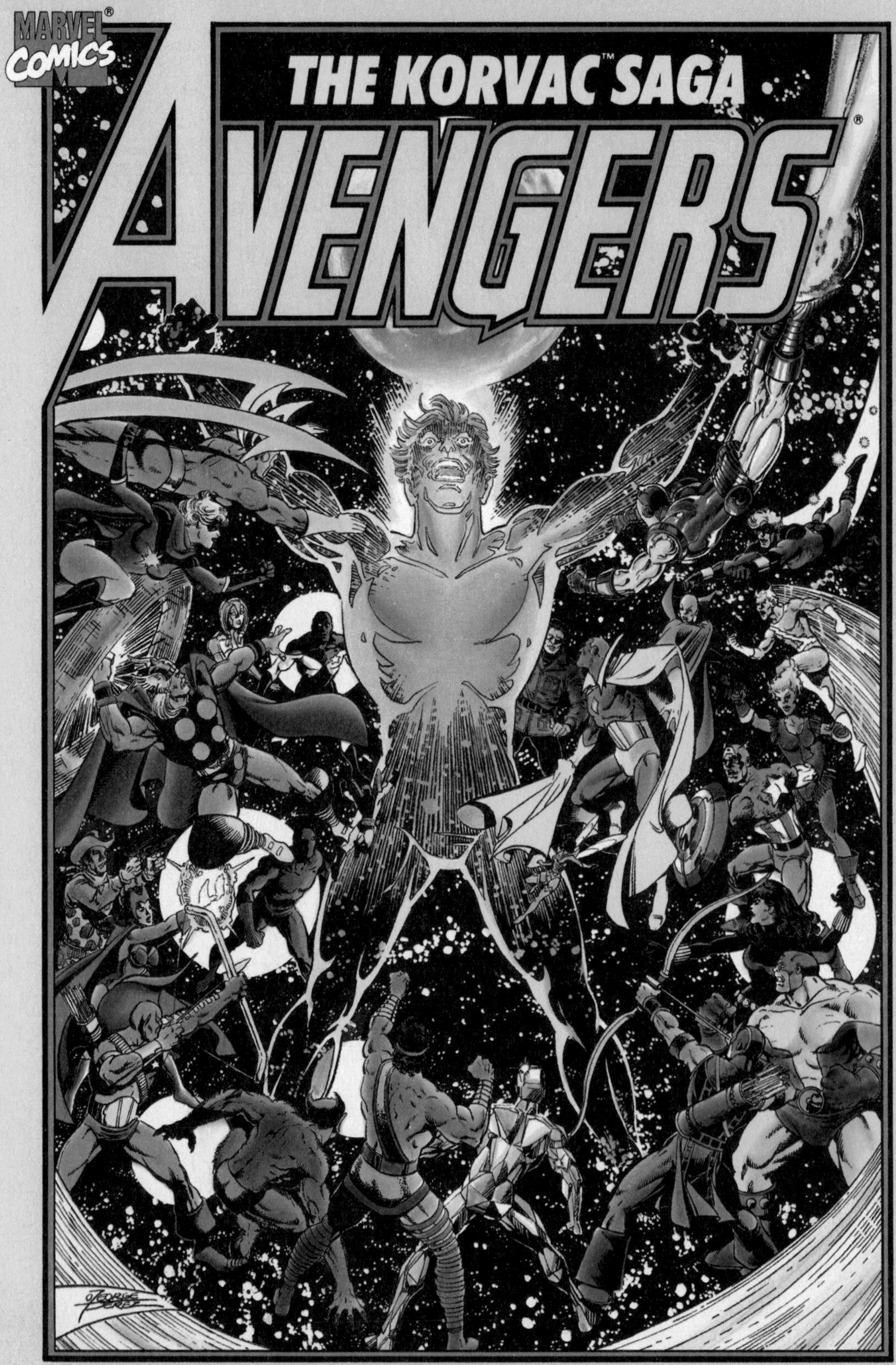
MARVEL COMICS
THE KORVAC SAGA
AVENGERS